THE DIARIES OF NANCY A. BROWN

AND

WILLIAM H. BROWN

OF

EDWARDS, NEW YORK

1877, 1878, 1879, 1880, 1881, 1883, 1884, 1885, 1886,
1887, 1888, 1889, 1892, 1894, and, 1898-9

HERITAGE BOOKS
2004

HERITAGE BOOKS

AN IMPRINT OF HERITAGE BOOKS, INC.

Books, CDs, and more – Worldwide

For our listing of thousands of titles see our website
at
www.HeritageBooks.com

COPYRIGHT © 2004
GERALD GARTH JOHNSON

Published 2004 by
HERITAGE BOOKS, INC.
Publishing Division
1540 Pointer Ridge Place
Bowie, Maryland 20716

International Standard Book Number: **0-7884-2511-0**

For the Families of

Nancy A. Johnson Brown

And

William H. Brown

The Editor

Gerald Garth Johnson, Ph.D. is a retired educator and State of Oregon education and social service program administrator who lives in Salem, Oregon. He is the author of several education, law, historical non-fiction books, and family genealogies as well as an editor of various newsletters and books. He holds Bachelors and Masters Degrees in Education from Willamette University and a Ph.D. in Public Administration from California Western University.

Also by Gerald Garth Johnson

Alan, Lord of Buckenhall

The Johnson Papers, Volumes I and II

The Biography and Genealogy of Captain John Johnson from Roxbury Massachusetts, (Heritage Books, Inc.)

The Ancestors and Descendants of Ira Johnson and Abigail Furbush Johnson (1984 edition)

The Oregon Book of Juveniles Issues (Portland State University Press)

Post-High School Planning (copyright transferred to Cascade High School, Turner, Oregon)

The Stage-Curtis Genealogy

Understanding the Alcoholism in Your Family and Its Effect on You (copyright transferred to NW Kaiser Permanente Health Organization)

A Family Portrait in Letters (now included in The Ancestors and Descendants of Ira Johnson and Abigail Furbush Johnson, (Heritage Books, Inc.) 2003

The Ticknor Family in America, Supplement

The Ancestors and Descendants of Ira Johnson and Abigail Furbush Johnson (Heritage Books, Inc.) with William A. Blandin, co-editor. Revised version, 2003

Textual Notes: In cases where passages from the diaries seemed ambiguous because of spelling and punctuation of the Nineteenth Century, the sentence structure has been changed as well as the punctuation. Further, in cases where the meaning or relationship is in need of clarification the meaning has been added within [brackets.]

It is possible that they never intended the diaries to be read by anyone else. What they wrote was important to them and probably provided an outlet for both of them in the times they lived whether the times were good or bad.

In comparing a previously transcribed 1879 diary of Nancy Johnson Brown, it was found that many words, phrases and whole date entries were omitted. We have restored the missing information to make the edition of the 1879 diary in this book complete.

The printed text, for the most part, has been left as they wrote it including what now would be considered inappropriate capitalization and spelling. Both Nancy and William Brown separated "to day" and "to night" instead of "today" and "tonight." In the diaries within this book, the words were combined. In addition, Nancy consistently capitalized lower case "a" to "A" throughout her diaries.

Listed in the glossary beginning on the next page are commonly misspelled words used by both Nancy A. Johnson Brown and William H. Brown who spelled words as they sounded to them.

GLOSSARY

Diary spelling	Present-day spelling
acounts	accounts
afful	awful
aful	awful
airs	heirs
anough	enough
ant	ain't
aple	apple
atend	attend
atending	attending
audence	audience
ax	axe
beried	buried
beries	berries
blesings	blessings
blosom	blossom
blow	below
blowes	blows
bord	board
borow	borrow
borowed	borrowed
bot/boght	bought
bough	bought
bountifly	bountifully
brite	bright
brot	brought
brout	brought
bufalow	buffalo
bugy	buggy
butiful	beautiful
buter	butter
cabage	cabbage

cald	called
cand	canned
carid	carried
caried	carried
carots	carrots
cary	carry
catle	cattle
cacus	caucus
cept	kept
cheries	cherries
chours	chores
chors	chores
churnd	churned
citty	city
clared	cleared
cleand	cleaned
cleard	cleared
cloths	clothes
clowdy	cloudy
cofin	coffin
coffen	coffin
colect	collect
comense	commence
couberd	cupboard
corse	course
cowes	cows
crakers	crackers
cubert	cupboard
cuting	cutting
daming	damning
diferent	different
diging	digging
diseased	deceased
dockeer	doctor
dosen	dozen
dresed	dressed

drest	dressed
durty	dirty
emtied	emptied
enclined	inclined
entied	emptied
eveing	evening
eveng	evening
envite	invite
envited	invited
evry	every
fens	fences
fenses	fences
feset	faucet
fet	feet
fether	feather
fifeen	fifteen
filed	filled
fild	filled
filld	filled
fiting	fighting
fixt	fixed
floore	floor
fogy	foggy
foote	foot
fourth	forth
fraim	frame
freesing	freezing
fritiful	frightful
ganes	gains
geathered	gathered
geting	getting
gingam	gingham
gon	gone
graps	grapes
haild	hailed
hear	here

hole	whole
hotell	hotel
interist	interest
ise	ice
kild	killed
liing	lying
litle	little
litning	lightning
lode	load
loged	logged
loosing	losing
lowery	lousy
maid	made
maile	mail
male	mail
maried	married
machein	machine
mashine	machine
match	much
medeson	medicine
medison	medicine
meting	meeting
Michagon	Michigan
midle	middle
milner	milliner
mitens	mittens
moping	mopping
moove	move
mooved	moved
most	almost
murcary	mercury
neace	niece
nocked	knocked
ocloc	o'clock
ocupied	occupied
of	off

ofice	office
pacage	oackage
peaces	pieces
prfct	perfect
pild	piled
pilling	piling
plase	place
prayr	prayer
preaced	preached
prety	pretty
prys	press
pye	pie
putting	putting
quire	choir
qute	quite
raind	rained
revew	review
rite	right
rhode	road
rods	roads
roling	rolling
rool	roll
round	around
Saboth	Sabbath
saushage	sausage
scain	skein
scarsely	scarcely
scater	scatter
scy	sky
seller	cellar
servis	service
setle	settle
setling	settling
shead	shed
shoe	show
shoed	showed

shoos	shows
sider	cider
sireped	syruped
sirup	syrup
sistern	cistern
shour	shower
shugar	sugar
siting	sitting
snowes	snows
soe	sew
soed	sewed
somewhare	somewhere
spliting	splitting
stare	stair
stayd	stayed
stid	stead
storys	stories
strawbery	strawberry
stichen	stitching
subpena	subpoena
sufering	suffering
sugur	sugar
suller	cellar
super	supper
sweete	sweet
swep	swept
taped	tapped
taping	tapping
teem	team
terible	terrible
thare	there
thundred	thundered
tobacko	tobacco
torents	torrents
treas	trees
turnd	turned

twise	twice
vail	veil
vesel	vessel
vilage	village
ware	we are
watter	water
wed	weeded
wether	weather
whare	where
wheete	wheat
whifeltres	whiffletree
whiped	whipped
whipings	whippings
wint	went
wit	wet
witnys	witness
writen	written
youse	use
yuse	use
zink	zinc

Except for the 1880 and 1881 diaries written exclusively by William H. Brown, those sentences or phrases that are his within the diaries of Nancy A. Johnson Brown, are identified as [WB] preceding the phrase or sentence.

TOWNS, STATES, COUNTRIES REPRESENTED WITHIN THIS DIARY BOOK

Bellville, NY	Linden, MI
Binghamton, NY	Little York, NY
Canada	Marshville, NY
Canada West	Melport, NY
Canton, NY	NY City, NY

Christian City, IL
Colorado
Cooperville, MI
Deer River, NY
DeKalb, NY
DeKalb Junction, NY
DePeyster, NY
Detroit, MI
Edwards, NY
Edwards Village, NY
Elmira, NY
Fine, NY
Fowler, NY
Fullerville, NY
Gouverneur, NY
Hailesborough, NY
Hailesburg, NY
Harrisville, NY
Heuvelton, NY
Hermon, NY
Hington City, NY
Ingersol, Canada
Jayville, NY

Ogdensburg, NY
Olean, NY
Oswego, NY
Pierrepont, NY
Pike County, IL
Pitcairn, NY
Pittsfield, IL
Pond Settlement
Portland, OR
Potsdam, NY
Richville, NY
Rochester, NY
Russell, NY
Salem, OR
Shawville, NY
So. Edwards, NY
St. Lawrence Co.
Syracuse, NY
Taylorville, NY
Tilsonburg, Can.
West Edwards
Willsboro, NY
York, NY

Kansas and Saginaw City, MI

Time Frames - The Brown Family

William H. Brown was born on October 10, 1824 in Edwards, St. Lawrence Co., NY and died March 3, 1914 in Edwards, St. Lawrence Co., New York.

Nancy A. Johnson (Brown) was born November 7, 1825 in Russell, St. Lawrence Co., New York and died March 23, 1909 in Edwards, St. Lawrence Co., New York.

Alvah Percival Brown was born September 16, 1846 in Pitcairn, St. Lawrence Co., New York and died March 3, 1906 in Edwards, St. Lawrence Co., New York.

Charles Hiram Brown was born November 30, 1848 in Edwards, St. Lawrence Co., New York and died March 31, 1929 in Edwards, St. Lawrence Co., New York.

Clara E. Brown was born July 22, 1859 in Edwards, St. Lawrence Co., New York and died November 17, 1868 in Edwards, St. Lawrence Co., New York.

William H. Brown

Nancy A. Johnson Brown

Alvah Percival Brown

Charles Hiram Brown

Clara E. Brown

THE DIARIES OF
NANCY A. JOHNSON BROWN
AND WILLIAM H. BROWN

years represented

1877, 1878, 1879, 1880 (2), 1881, 1883, 1884, 1885,
1886, 1887, 1888, 1889, 1890, 1892, 1894, 1898

CONTENTS

Textual Notes   vii

Glossary   viii

Towns, States, Counties Represented   xiv

Time Frames of the Brown Family   xvi

Pictures of the Browns   xvi-xvii

Acknowledgements   xxiii

Introduction   1

Map: Edwards, NY Township; location of
homes and farms of William H. Brown
and Nancy A. Johnson Brown   6-B

Map: Edwards Village, NY, circa 1890s   6-C

Picture: The Brodie Mansion purchased by
   William H. Brown   6-D

1877   7

1878   7

1879   7

1880 (William only)   101

1880 (Nancy only)   146

1881 (William only)   204

1883   264

1884   311

1885   326

1886   326

1887   326

1888   433

1889   434

1890   440

1892   443

1894   443

1898-9   444

Epilogue   544

Index   545

ACKNOWLEDGEMENTS

The Johnson and allied families are extremely grateful to Mary Buck Spadaro, Syracuse, NY and Richard D. Brown, Edwards, NY who so graciously and willingly provided the diaries of their direct ancestors, Nancy A. Johnson Brown and William H. Brown, for the future generations to enjoy.

Both William H. and Nancy A. Johnson Brown most likely wrote more diaries in years not represented in this book. It appears to have been their custom to write each year of their marriage. If they did write other diaries, they have not been located. However, the twenty-two year diary series contained in this book is representative of the lives of William H. and Nancy A. Johnson Brown as well as the extraordinary life in Northern New York near the Saint Lawrence River.

The Nineteenth Century handwriting in the 1879, 1883, 1880, 1881, 1884, and 1898-9 diaries that were in the possession of Carson and Martha Clark Buck was a challenge to decipher but with the expert assistance of Karlene Johnson Messer, Nancy Ticknor Johnson, and especially Mary Buck Spadaro who not only photocopied the original diaries for me but also willingly and patiently deciphered words and phrases as well as proof-read this Diary book, the diaries of Nancy A. Johnson Brown and William H. Brown are now available for all of us.

Portions of some of the diary years in the possession of Constance Brown McElwain, Potsdam, NY and Richard D. Brown, Edwards, NY were originally transcribed by Judith Fuller Perpente, Sarasota, Florida with excerpts by LaVerne H. Freeman, Edwards, NY. We acknowledge and appreciate their contributions to our understanding of the lives of Nancy A. Johnson Brown and William H. Brown.

I am especially indebted to cousins Dr. Joseph and Mary Spadaro and to Mr. Chris Waits for applying computer technology on the pictures of the Brown family so that the old pictures can have new clarity and new life for the readers. This book is greatly enhanced also by the map of homes of the Brown's and locations of their neighbors developed by Mary Buck Spadaro, Syracuse, NY and LaVerne Freeman, Edwards, NY Historian.

Grateful acknowledgement is due Mr. Daniel D. McNaughton, Paleograph Editing Services, Chicago, IL who willingly and expertly provided the technical aspects for the indexing of names and places. LeAnne M. Johnson Shaw deserves a huge expression of appreciation for her efforts in refining the expanded Index. Thank you, LeAnne. Also, Roxanne Carlson of Heritage Books, Inc., Bowie, MD "saved my life" with her helpful suggestions regarding format and page numbering for the publication of these diaries. Thanks, Roxanne. Further, Dot Miller at *Kinko's* was extraordinary in her assistance in experimenting with the pictures to get them to print as best as possible with pictures more than a hundred years old.

Finally, I want to express my sincere thanks to Todd Baker, Operations Manager and Senior Customer Consultant at the Salem, Oregon *Kinko's* for his cheerful, knowledgeable, and professional advice throughout the process of developing all aspects of this book. Thank you, Todd, for your patience with me!

Gerald Garth Johnson, Editor
Salem, Oregon, October, 2003

INTRODUCTION

Diaries! "How boring," one publisher said. "They are full of things like the weather."

If this particular publisher had lived in Edwards, NY near the St. Lawrence River in the 1800s, the three-foot snowfalls and the freezing weather were certainly factors to reckon with and surely influenced the history of William H. and Nancy A. Johnson Brown. In the 1880s, the weather in agrarian, rural communities like Edwards, NY, was always a factor in regard to planting, sugaring, and harvesting. The growing season was extremely short. Severe snow storms and extreme cold temperatures limited their travel to town and church, and their contact with friends and relatives outside of their own homes. It also limited their ability to purchase ready-made products, therefore, they had to become very self-sufficient and self-reliant.

In order to assist readers to know who Nancy A. Johnson Brown and William H. Brown are talking about in this book, the following short genealogy is offered:

BROWN:

Robert Brown and Agnes [also called Mother Brown, Mother] **Gowen** Brown, parents of William H. Brown.

Brothers and Sisters of William H. Brown and their children:

Joseph Brown [usually referred to as Jo] m. Adaline Whitford Brown.
Children: (1) Susan Brown m. William Clair
Children: Jane, Mabel Lucille, and Arthur

Robert Brown and wife, Elizabeth <u>Webb</u>
Children: (1) Agnes [Brown] and John <u>Hughes</u>
(2) Stillman E. Brown m. Laura <u>Johnson</u>
(3) Percival Brown
(4) Sidney (Sid) Brown m. Julia A. <u>Wight</u>
(5) William Brown m. Olive <u>Wells</u>
(6) Ira Brown m. Lilia M. <u>Allen</u>

John Brown m. Elizabeth _____

William H. Brown and Nancy A. <u>Johnson</u>
      Children: (1) Alvah Percival [A.P.] Brown m.
      (1) Manie <u>Cleland</u>; m. (2) Sarah <u>Grant</u>
      Children: Sherman [by Manie], by Sarah:
      Manie, Mary Rose, Harold, Clara Pearl
      (2) Charles [Charley,C.H.] Hiram Brown m. Martha
          <u>Noble:</u> Children: Clarence, Oswald Bower [Bower
          in this Book], and Mabel
      (3) Clara E. [also Clarah]

Isaac Brown m. Margaret _____
      Children: (1) William Brown, (2) Theresa Brown, (3)
      Vincent Brown

Margaret Brown m. Joseph <u>Brodie</u>
      Children: (1) Harriet Louisa Brodie m. Dr. G. <u>Reno</u>
      (2) Alexander Oswald Brodie m. Louise <u>Hanlon</u>
      (3) Robert B. Brodie, (4) Elizabeth [Lizzie] B. Brodie
      m. Wilber A. <u>Bignal</u>
          Children: Robby B., Clinton, and, Louise

David Brown m. Perlina Hall
      Children: (1) Edward J. Brown m. (1) Alice <u>Joiner</u>: m.
(2) Rose <u>Tetheron:</u> Children by Rose: Wirth, Dora, and Lulu

Harriet Brown

Harvey A. Brown m. Nancy <u>Allen</u>
    Children: (1) Lona [Leona] Brown m. <u>Hoffman</u>
    (2) Mary A. [Metta] Brown m. Wright <u>Robinson</u>
        Children: Frank Robinson, Lee Robinson

Percival [Perce] Brown m. Eliza Jane Hitchcock
    Children: (1) Robert B. Brown m. Martha Lena <u>Atkins,</u>
    (2) Ida Brown, (3) Purtha L. Brown, and (4) George O.
    Brown

JOHNSON:

Nancy A. Johnson's parents: Charles Alvah Johnson
and Rachel Pratt Viall Johnson [Rachel was previously
married to Samson Viall who died in 1813]

Nancy A. Johnson's brothers and sisters:

Viall (half-sisters):

Harriet Viall m. Porter Wesley <u>Harmon</u> [brother of
Ebenezer, also Eben in this book]
Susan Viall m. Dr. James <u>Foster</u>
Levitia/Louisa Viall m. Elijuh Phelps
Phila Viall m. Ebenezer <u>Harmon,</u> [bro. of Porter
Wesley Harmon]

Johnson brothers and sisters:

Charles V. Johnson m. Emily <u>Spann</u> [also C.V. in this
    book]
Hiram Alvah Johnson m. Elizabeth Jane <u>Whitley</u>

[also H. A. in this book]
Abel P. [also A.P. in this book] Johnson
  m. Lucy <u>Haile</u>
Eliza B. (died young)
William Warren Johnson [usually called
  Warren in this book] m. Moriah [also Hannah]
  <u>Merrill</u>
Emmorancy [called Emma, Em, Emmah in this book]
  Johnson m. Alfred B. <u>Hall</u> [called A.B. in this book
  at times]

There is a reference in the diary to a "Charley Johnson" [John Charles Johnson], called Charles or Charley, who was a son of Hiram A. and Elizabeth Whitley Johnson of Oregon, and who did visit relatives in Edwards, Hermon, and Russell, New York and other points of interest on his train trip across America in 1885. No other Oregon Johnsons except for Hiram and Elizabeth Johnson who traveled to St. Lawrence County, NY in 1876, are listed in the diaries as traveling to Northern New York by train to St. Lawrence County, New York.

Nancy A. Johnson was born November 7, 1825 in Russell, NY to Charles Alvah Johnson and Rachel Pratt Viall. Previously, Rachel Pratt had been married to Samson Viall. After his death in 1813, she married Charles Alvah Johnson.

On September 19, 1844, Nancy A. Johnson married William H. Brown in Edwards, NY and had three children by him: Alvah Percival, Charles Hiram, and Clara E. Clara died at almost ten. Nancy Johnson Brown lived in the areas of Russell, Pitcairn, and Edwards all of her life. While married to William H. Brown, she lived in: a shack, as she described, in Pitcairn, the overseer's house on the Brodie farm, the Max Lanphear [originally her father Charles Alvah Johnson's] place in the Creek Settlement of Edwards, a house in the village near the Island, the Brodie mansion that the Browns

4

bought, the home of William's mother during her illness, and lastly, a new home built on the foundation of the old overseer's house on the part of the Brodie farm that they retained after selling the Brodie mansion and land across the road. [*See map on page 6-B regarding location of the homes*]

It is clear from the diaries that they had significant household and farm responsibilities but found time to visit and receive friends and relatives and keep these informative diaries.

As we look beyond the "weather reports" in the diaries, we get more than a glimpse of the social and personal life in Edwards, NY and the relationships Nancy Johnson Brown and William Brown had with their family and friends. More importantly, we receive a strong sense of their character and energy. She definitely comes across as a well-educated, independent thinker. She expressed, for example, her dissatisfaction about the lack of help from her husband in the care of his elderly mother yet she also showed great compassion for her children, relations, and friends. William Brown was an extremely energetic, hard working man, who was astute in business as well as money management and who loaned interest-bearing money to various St. Lawrence County residents and relatives. Brown was skilled in building chimneys, laying flooring, building walls, painting, papering walls, building stone footings for buildings, sugaring, and all aspects of farming including milking cows and butchering his hogs. Later in life, he spent a great deal of time assisting both of his sons on their farms. Even after grandson Clarence Brown and his wife, Carrie Cleland Brown, lived with Nancy and William Brown, William continued to help his sons with their chores.

Some entries in Nancy Johnson Brown's own diaries are obviously those made by William Brown himself [identified as WB]. But most are Nancy Johnson Brown's reflections on life in St. Lawrence County, New York. She kept track of births, deaths, and marriages in her extended families and even those outside of the family. Her recordings are a genealogical goldmine! William H. Brown diaries that he wrote by himself are those of years 1880 and 1881. Typically, Brown entered information about the farm, price of products, visits, deaths, marriages, births, and sized up the weather on a daily basis. The 1870 US Census for Edwards, New York was used as a reference to identify many of the spellings of those people who are mentioned in the *Diaries of Nancy Johnson Brown and William H. Brown.* LaVerne Freeman of Edwards, New York provided additional documentation regarding many of the families who were cited in Nancy Brown's Diaries. However, not all of the surnames or even the given names, are guaranteed to be absolutely accurate. They have been typed as we interpreted the spelling.

Nancy Brown also was prolific in letter writing and kept up a nearly sixty year correspondence with all of her brothers, sister, and her four Viall half-sisters. In the two diaries written solely by William Brown, and in comments by Nancy Brown in her diaries, it is evidenced that William wrote and sent letters to various relatives. Unfortunately, we could not locate any of his letters nor any that he had received.

To read the diaries of both Nancy Johnson Brown and of William H. Brown and Nancy Brown's numerous letters [included in the *Ancestors and Descendants of Ira Johnson and Abigail Furbush Johnson* published by Heritage Books, Inc., Bowie, MD, 2003] is to know, admire, respect, love, honor, and even to laugh with them.

The complete genealogy of William H. Brown and Nancy A. Johnson Brown is in the *Ancestors and Descendants of Ira Johnson and Abigail Furbush Johnson*, 2003, Heritage Books, Inc., Bowie, MD.

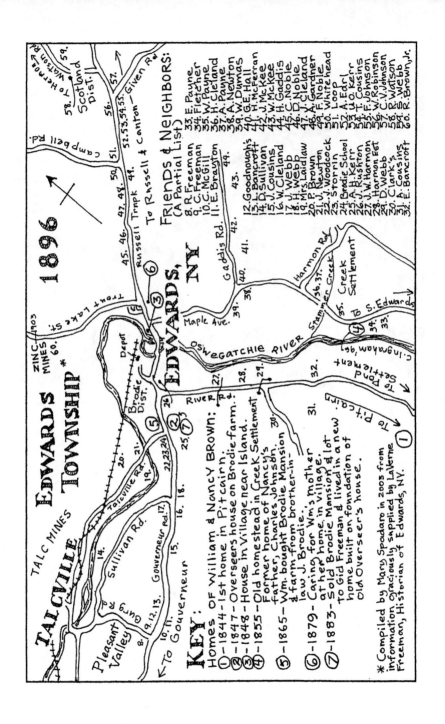

THE BRODIE MANSION *

William and Nancy Brown lived in the Brodie Mansion, as it is called, from 1865 to 1883. The wood frame house is located about ½ mile south of the Village of Edwards, NY, on the old Gouverneur Road. It was built about 1847 for Joseph Brodie, a wealthy Scottish immigrant and his bride, Margaret Brown (William Brown's sister). After the house was remodeled in 1856, it had 22 rooms and stood three stories high with a ballroom on the third floor. There is a long central hallway on both the first and second floors with a banister extending from the first floor to the third. In August of 1883, William Brown sold the Brodie Mansion and farmland to Gideon Freeman. It has remained in the Freeman family to this writing.

*Photo and information courtesy of LaVerne Freeman, Town and Village Historian of Edwards, NY. September, 2003.

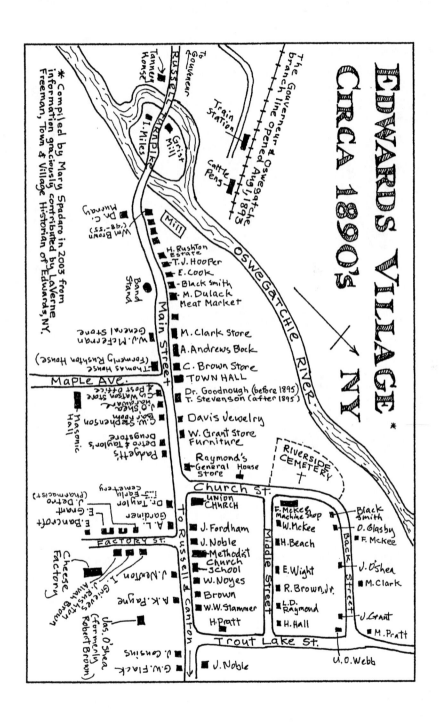

EDWARDS VILLAGE
CIRCA 1890's * NY

* Compiled by Mary Spadaro in 2003 from information graciously contributed by LaVerne Freeman, Town & Village Historian of Edwards, NY.

The Gouverneur & Oswegatchie branch line opened Aug 1, 1893

Train Station

Cattle Pens

To Gouverneur

Tannery House

I. Miles

Grist Mill

RUSSELL TURNPIKE

OSWEGATCHIE RIVER

Mill St

Dr. C. Murray

Wm Brown ('48 - '55)

H. Rushton Estate
T. J. Hooper
E. COOK
Black smith
M. Dulack Meat Market

Band Stand

Main Street

W.J. McFerman General Store

M. Clark Store

A. Andrews Bock

C. Brown Store

TOWN HALL

Dr. Goodnough (before 1895)
T. Stevenson (after 1895)

Thomas House (formerly Rushton House)

MAPLE AVE.

Post Office

Davis Jewelry

W. Grant Store Furniture

C.W. Watson Store
Dr. Shea Drug Room
C.W. Stephenson Drugstore

Masonic Hall

Padgett's

Dr. Taylor & Taylor's Drugstore

Raymond's General Store

House

RIVERSIDE CEMETERY

Church St.

E. Grant

E. Bancroft

A. L. Gardiner

Dr. Detro
Dr. Earll Cemetery

J. Detro (Pharmacist)

UNION CHURCH

F. McKee Machine Shop
W. McKee

Black smith
O. Glasby
F. McKee

J. Fordham

H. Beach

FACTORY ST.

Cheese Factory

J. Newton

J. Grieves
Alva Brown

A. K. Payne

Robert Brown

Jas. O'Shea (formerly Robert Brown)

J. Cousins

G.W. Flack

J. Noble

Methodist Church

School

W. Noyes

Brown

W.W. Stammer

H. Pratt

To Russell & Canton

Middle Street

E. Wight

R. Brown, Jr.

L.D. Raymond

H. Hall

TROUT LAKE ST.

Back Street

J. O'Shea

M. Clark

J. Grant

M. Pratt

U. O. Webb

THE DIARIES

[Note: It was a common practice of diary writers in the 1800s to use every possible blank page. Many times the entries were for another year. Nancy Johnson Brown used the front and back overleaf pages to record, not necessarily in date order, the births, deaths, marriages, and other facts that she wanted to keep for remembrance. Not every entry was a completely composed sentence as we understand sentence structure today.] GGJ

1877

Memoranda Page

October 17   paid $130 for part of interest on Brown bond

November 15   paid $335 balance of interest for year 1877

1878

Memoranda Page

December 11   Henry Tom[p]son of Edwards was sent to State
                        Prison for two years for stealing a horse.

1879

[Note: Both Nancy and William Brown made entries in the 1879 Diary but most entries are by Nancy Brown; his identified by [WB] within brackets]

Wednesday, January 1 [WB] Anne Grant told Mrs. Alfred Hall [Nancy A. Brown's sister, Emmorancy Johnson Hall] that James Grant came in to ask her to let him have the mony that's up in the patry [perhaps, pantry] That he wanted it to pay to James Noble. She went and got the money for him. Said she did not count it. Said thare was a little roll of it. James said he payed it to James Noble to pay to Mr. Brown to aply on Mortgage. Of corse we done know whether he payed it to Mr. Brown or not. Pleasant, quite warm.

Little Mabel Brown was three years old yesterday morning.

Thursday, [Nancy]   January 2   It is snowing and blowing today. One foote last night and today. [WB] A. B. Hull says that James Grant said he expcted to have some trouble with Brown. Grant said that thare was not so match endorsed on the mortgage as he had a recept [receipt] for. Grant said thare was only $133,35 endorsed on the Mortgage and he had a recept for $1233,35. Grant said he went over to pay Mr. Brown but Brown told him that he was not dealing with him. Then Grant said he gave James Noble the money to pay Mr. Brown but did not know whether he payed. Snowed & blew fearfully.

Friday, January 3   Then Grant said he gave James Noble the money to pay Mr. Brown but did not know whether he payed him the money or not. Snowed and blew fearfully. Grant said that he let him have that amount. Grant told Hall that he got all the money from his deary and it took it all. He, Grant, got between four and five hundred from his deary and had to pay all his help out of that. ["deary" is not a term used in the 1880s and is not in any dictionary of the time. It is possible that "deary" was misread by the original transcriber.]

Sat, Jan 4   [WB]   Sent forty dollar to Joseph Brown to subpena A. P. Johnson, Sid [Sidney] Whitford, Adaline Brown, and Joseph P. Brown as witness in a suit in the Suprem Cort between Wm Brown Executor James Noble.

January 13   [WB] paid Sarah McFerans $2.50 for her subpoena fees. [Nancy] Robby B. Biglel [Bignel] was three years old last November 1878. Clinton Bignel was one year

8

old this January 1879. Born January 1878. [WB] Broadie & Oswald & Lizzie and her children was here in July & part of August 1878. Soon after they went home. Broadie and Oswald went to Kansas and bought a lot of land and cattle.

Monday, January 6

Charles Johnson born in Brookfield, Mass. Feb. the 26th 1785. Died April the 20th 1847.

Rachel Johnson born in Wilsbourough NY May 15th 1787 Died June the 20th 1860

Samson Vial[l] died Feb the 4th 1813. Age 36 first husband of Rachel Pratt, late wife of Charles Johnson in Russell, NY

Births of children of Charles & Rachel Johnson
    [correct birthdates in brackets]

Tuesday, January 7, 1879

Charles V. Johnson, born May the 11th 1815
Hiram A. Johnson, born Feb 22, 1817 [1819]
Abel P. Johnson, born June the 7th 1827 [1821]
Eliza B. Johnson, Feb. ---, 1819 [1817] Died May 22.
Wm. W [arren] Johnson, born Dec the 1st, 1823
Nancy A. Johnson, born November the 7, 1825
Emmy [Emmorancy] Johnson, May the 27, 1827

Charles and Rachel Johnson married December the 16th 1813 Russell [NY]

Weddings of children [of above]

Charles and Emily Johnson married in Pike [Co] Ill July the first 1837

9

Hiram A Johnson married to Elizabeth Whitney [Whitley] July 25 1841 Pike Co [IL]

Nancy A. Johnson married Sep the 19th 1844 [Wm. Brown]

Emmy Johnson married [Alfred B. Hall] January first 1845 Edwards NY

Abel P Johnson married to Lucy Haile Sept the 15th 1846

Warren W [actually William Warren] Johnson married Sept the 15th 1846 to Mariah [Moriah] Meril [Merrill] of Russell NY

Friday, January 10   Oct 17 th 1877   Paid $130.00 part of interest on Brown's Bond. Nov. 15 1877. Paid $335 cents taken of interest for year 1877.

Saturday, January 11   Have made a suit of clothes for Sherman Brown [grandson]   Made a new flannel shirt for Sherman [grandson] & one for Bower [Oswald Bower] Brown. Bought the flannel myself . Paid for it in sugar. William bought the fullcloth for Clarence's coat. I furnished the cloth for Sherman's cloths.

Sunday, January 12   William went to Gouverneur [NY] today to see Judge Neary & to send for Jo & Ad [Brown] & A. P. Johnson & J. B. Whitford for witnys in the suit between Wm Brown & James Noble

Tuesday, January 14   Eliza Payn[e] died today. She has been sick a long time with consumption. Leaves two boys, one ten & the other five years old. Beried a little girl one year ago last October. Agnes Brown is boarding with us four days a week while she is taking music lessons. She takes a term & a half.

Wednesday, January 15 [WB] George Ivers burnt his house. His House was burnt this evening. He drew his wife to her father's on a hand sled & in less than one hour the house was

10

all in flames so they could not save one article. Insurance three hundred dollars. He took his money & left for Colorado.

Thursday, January 16   Eliza Payn[e] is beried today. It is an awful stormy day.   I went to the funeral with Charley & Martha [Brown]. William stayed with his mother.

Lowisa Ivers was working for George at the time the house was Burnt. She had all her clothing burnt & lots of pictures. The people in this village got up a subscription & made her a present of 25 dollars.

Friday, January 17   This is a pleasant day but quite cold.   I was cald over to Jim Rushton's this evening to help take care of Ida Ivers.   She was very sick until two o'clock in the morning when Dr. Murry [Murray] presented her with a little girl.   She had not a dud to put on it. Evry article of clothing was all burnt with the house two nights before but its granma found some old cloths so that we drest it & the next day the neighbors brot in lots of cloths for the baby.

Saturday, January 18   I am kniting a pair of socks for Clarence Brown. I just finished a pair for Sherman Brown and finished one for Bower Brown. [grandsons]

Sunday, January 19   William has writen for Jo & Adaline [Joseph and Adaline Brown] & Abel Johnson her brother] & Jo Whitford all to be here next Friday to be on hand to atend the suit that comes of[f] next week between Wm & James Noble & Grant.

Wednesday, January 22 Mrs. Alex Kerr had a baby today. It did not live but a little while. Bad luck for her. It was her first one.

Friday, January 24   Joseph & Adaline Brown & Jo Whitford

& Abel P. Johnson came here this evening from Pine Valley [NY] Perce & Charley brout them from Gouverneur [NY] went after them today. Adaline has been very sick. Her health is very poor now. She has got a fearful cough.

Saturday, January 25 We are all having a visit with Jo's folks. Abel has gone up to Warren's [his brother, William Warren Johnson] to visit them. I am having a good time now days doing the work for a house full of company.

Sunday, January 26 Jo[seph Brown] & Adaline & Sid & Abel & Mrs. Gorden & Libcorb & I don't know many are here today. Bill Noys was here while we was at breakfast. This evening the house is full. John McFerin [Throughout this book, Nancy Brown spelled McFerran in various ways, but McFerran is the way it is spelled now by most] & Alex Kerr [Nancy spelled it Alax Keer many times], Cyrus Clealand,[the surname is spelled Cleland but Nancy Brown continually spelled it "Clealand."] Jo[seph] & Ad & Jo Whitford & Alfred Hall, A.P. Johnson, Mrs. Gorden & I can't tell near all are here tonight.

Monday, January 27 This morning they all went to Canton [NY] a sleigh load of them. Mr. White, AP Johnson & Jo Brown, William Brown & Adaline & Jo Whitford & Cyrus Clealand & Mrs. Gordan with Alvah's teem [team] to attend the lawsuit between Wm & Jim Noble & Grant. I have had a time picking up & slicking up the house & doing a large washing.

Tuesday, January 28 Charley Brown [her son] went to Canton today & Jason Woodcock. William & John Allen came from Canton this morning at three o'clock. Started back at five [o'clock]. They was after a little book of Father Brown's. We had a great hunt for it last evening but could not find it. Dr. Goodnough came over & helped search the house over. He was going in the morning to Canton & wanted to carry it to William. We could not find it but Wm. Soon found it when he came.

Wednesday, January 29   Suit put over to the 27 of May. All came home this evening from Canton.   I had the supper waiting for more than one hour.   Agnes & Stilman Brown stayed with me while they was gone to Canton.   Stillman is teaching school up by Charley Brown's but he came here to stay nights while Wm was gone to Canton.

Thursday, January 30   Abel [Johnson] has gone up to see Phila [Phila Viall Harmon, his half-sister] today. Jo & Ad & William & I went up to Charley's today. Agnes stayed with Mother. [William's mother]   I am home before dark.   Wm stayed in the evening.   Jate [sic] brought me home.   Agnes was afraid to stay here after dark with Graney so I had to come home. Jo folks stayed to Charley's all night.

Friday, January 31   Today they all went to Alvah's for a visit. Jo & Charley went up to Robert's a little while today. They all came back here tonight.

Saturday, February 1   Jo & Ad has gone over to Bill Noyses [spelled Noys in the 1870 Census] today to stay a little while. They are here tonight.

Sunday, February 2   This is a very cold day.   Jo Brown's folks & A P Johnson are here today. Write [Wright] Robinson was presented with a little boy this afternoon.   Write & May [Mettie] E. Brown was married in September 1878 at the Canton fair time.   Joe's folks intend to start for home tomorrow.

Monday, February 3   Today, Charley Brown carried Jo & Ad & Sid & Abel P Johnson to Gouverneur to take the train for

Pine Valley [NY]. They took the evening train. They got home the next morning. We got a letter from them the same week.

Tuesday, February 4   Johnsons: these are the names of my brother Charley's family: Charles Victor Johnson and wife, Emily Spann of Pittsfield, IL   girls & their husbands. The oldest is Mary, her husband's name is John Nicholson. They live in Missouri, Greenwood, Jarson Co.   They next one is Rebecca married Mr. Samuel Miller. They live in Pike Co. Illinois, Pittsfield, I.   Phila Johnson maried a Mr. Richard Thornton Pa Nebo Pike Co, Illinois.

Wednesday, February 5   Emma Johnson married a Mr. Monral [Monroe] D. Ransom, Pittsfield, Pike Co, Illinois. [He was called "Roe."]

Thursday, February 6   My Brother Hiram Johnson has six boys & one girl, all maried. Their names are Charles & George & Warren & Alvah. Thurstin & Frank Johnson & the girls name is Rachel Earl. I do not know the names of the boys wives. My brother Hiram & family [Hiram Alvah Johnson and Elizabeth Jane Whitley] all reside in Salem, Oregon & in the Wilmetta [Willamette] Valley, 50 miles from the city of Portland. Has been there 30 years & then he and his wife came home & made us all a visit in the year of 1876.

Saturday, February 8   In the year of 1885, his oldest son Charley [John Charles] made us a visit. He came in August. Got back to Oregon in October. He visited NY City & Washington & Philadelphia & Chicago and lots of large places in the United States. He was worth 30 thousand dollars at the time he was here.

Sunday, February 9   My brother Abel P[ratt] Johnson & family reside in Pine Valley, Chemung County, NY. Mooved there with his family from Edwards NY in the spring of 1869. He is 10 miles from the City of Elmira. He has four girls & 2 boys.

Monday, February 10   Their names are Elgin & John & Adelia & Stellah & Dora & Jessie Johnson. 2 oldest girls married. Adelia Pery and Stellah Ward of Binghamton, NY.

Tuesday, February 11   Town meeting today. Carter [was] Supervisor. It is raining today. Thaws considerable today. Bot 3 lbs tea at one dollar for 3 pounds and one quire of paper. Charley Harmon & Charley H. Brown took dinner with us today. Alvah & Sarah & Sherman was here this evening.

Wednesday, February 12 [WB] It is cold and snowing, blowing most fearful today. [Nancy]Wm Went up to Alvah's to do the chores for him today. I have been knitting a pair of stockings for little Mabel Brown.

Thursday, February 13 [WB] It is cold today. Murcary down to eight above sifer [perhaps silver] all day. Kingsbury filling the ise house today.

Friday, February 14   [WB] It is clear and cold today but pleasent. Alvah finished drawing wood today. C. H. Brown helped draw wood today.

Saturday, February 15 [WB] It is cold today. Went up [and] done Alvah's chores for him to go out to Grants'.

Sunday, February 16   [WB] It is a little warmer today but blowes and snows some. Nancy went to meeting today. Left me with Mother.

Monday, February 17 [WB] Clear and pleasent. Wind blowes hard this afternoon. Had two bushels of wheet ground today.

88 lbs of flour.

Tuesday, February 18   [WB] It is very cold today. Wind blows from the Northeast and very cold.

Wednesday, February 19   [WB] Pleasent but very cold. Mercury 8 below zero. Sold Storen 50 lbs flour, 13 lbs pork. Paid Storen one dollar in cash for stakes   bot   500 hundred cedar stakes of Storen for six dollars 25 cents.

Thursday, February 20   [WB] Went up to Charles'. Set up the machine to saw wood. It is quite cold today. Charley Whitford's little Willey died today. We got a letter from A. P. Johnson today. [A.P. Johnson was the brother of Nancy Johnson Brown]

Friday, February 21 [WB]   It is cold today. The murcary is eight above zero today. Sarah Brown [wife of Alvah Percival Brown] was here today.

Saturday, February 22 [WB] The murcary is 20 below zero this morning. It is clear and cold.

Sunday, February 23 [WB] Warmer today but snowed about four inches this afternoon.

Monday, February 24   [WB]   Helping Charles [Brown]   to saw wood.

Tuesday, February 25   [WB]   Helping Charles to saw wood today. It is some warmer. Al Wiles' folks have got one more girl.

Wednesday, February 26   [WB] It is thawing very fast today. It rains some.   Turned into snow this afternoon.

Thursday, February 27 [WB] It is awful cold today. Mother [William Brown's mother] is taken sick today. She is quite crazy. Doctor came to see her tonight. We was up most of the night with her.

Friday, February 28 [WB] The mercuary is down to 28 degrees below the sifer this morning and it is very cold. Mother is a little better today. She cept in bed most all day. Sat up awhile in the evening.

Saturday, March 1 [WB] The mercury is 24 degrees above zero and snowd a little. The wind [from the] south. Old Mrs. James McKee died today about twelve.

Sunday, March 2 [WB] Pleasant this morning. Mercury 8 above zero. Carter went to Canton today to see Russell about David Noble giving the airs [heirs] of Robert Brown a Deed for the old farm.

Monday, March 3 [WB] Pleasent and clear this morning. Wind south west. Murcary 8 below zero this morning. [Nancy] Jane McKee & Helen Cleland caled here today to borow my black dress & vail & gloves for Ann to wear the next day to her mother's funeral.

Tuesday, March 4 [WB] Pleasent this morning. Wind south, mucary 29 above zero. Mrs. McKee is buried at one o'clock today. It is thawing considerable today. [Nancy] This is little Bower Brown's birthday. He is five years old today.

Wednesday, March 5 [WB] It is colder this morning. The murcary is 12 above zero & snowd a little. Wind, North East. Got a letter from A.P. Johnson and Sid [ney] Whitford for Joe's folks.

Thursday, March 6 [WB] It is warmer today. It snowes &

17

blowes very hard all day. Murcary is 30 above zero today. We heard tonight that Wm. Green's grandchild is to be buried tomorrow. It was Libbie Green's child. Frank Green made us a call tonight. Libby Green's little boy is beried tomorrow.

Friday, March 7   [WB]   It ant [ain't] very cold today. Mercury is 26 above zero. I have been sick all day with sick headache.

Saturday, March 8   It has been very pleasant today. Murcuary was above zero this morning. It is thundering and litning tonight.   Mercury is 30 above zero this evening. [Nancy] Charley and Martha & the children are here tonight. They just got home before the shower.

Sunday, March 9   [WB] This is a butiful day.   Murcury ranged from 34 to 58 today. Alvah went out to Grant's today. Left Sherman with us. Elder Dicke [Dyke] did not come to preach today.

Monday, March 10 [WB] The mercury stands at 48 in the shade today. It is thawing fast. [Nancy] Wm is up home to help Charley build his sugar arch. The sun shines & it is a beautiful day.

Tuesday, March 11   [WB] The mercury stands at 44 above zero this morning. It is cloudy and it looks like rain. It thundered very heavy at three o'clock this morning. [Nancy] It is now 10 o'clock. The mercury stands at 52. The South wind blows very strong. The sky is clear as a bell. It is a most beautiful day. William is away up to Charley's to finish the arch & I am here alone as usual [with] only his mother. She [is] asleep in her bed. We found a little calf in the barn this morning.

Wednesday, March 12 [WB]   It is colder this morning.

18

Murcuary 26 above zero. It has been a butiful day today. Got a letter from Joseph Whitford & Susa Brown this evening. Adaline is very sick.

Thursday, March 13 [WB] It is snowing a little this morning. Murcery 26 above. Finished building C. H. Brown's sugar arch this afternoon. Charles drawed down two loads of wood for me today. Alvah gone after his hired girl. Pet Hunt, today to Hermon. [NY]

Friday, March 14   [WB] It is snowing a little this morning. Murcery 26. It is pleasant today. I helped Alvah today tap a part of his sugar trees. The sap ran well. Mr. John Kingsbury & wife came here this evening from DeKalb [NY] staid [stayed] with us overnight. C.H. Brown taped part of his shugar bush today. A. P. Brown taped part of his bush today. Kiled [Killed] the little calf tonight. Let Kingsbury have the rennet.

Saturday, March 15   It is froze quite hard this morning. It is snowing & blowing at a fearful rate until past ten o'clock then the sun shone & was very pleasant until little past 12. Now it is all cloudy & the wind is howling.

Sunday, March 16   It is pleasant today but cold. Professor Lee preach [ed] his last sermon here today.

Tuesday, March 17 [WB]   It is cold & snowing this morning. Wind is north. Mercury 20 degrees above zero. Snowed all day. Philip Woocok [Woodcock] was married to the widow Sprague today. She is his third wife. He is her third husband.

Tuesday, March 18   [WB] It is a butiful [beautiful] day but quite cold. The murcary was 4 above zero this morning. Albert Wight left the Wilson farm today. Went in over Jim Brown's old store.

19

Wednesday, March 19   [WB] It is pleasent this morning. Mercury 4 above zero. Sun shing and clear as a bell. Paid A.[Abram] Dumas forty cents for mending boots. Bot [bought] 64 lbs Brand for .70 cents cash. Paid Miles. Mother Brown is sick this morning.

Thursday, March 20 [WB]   It is pleasant this morning. Mercury 20 above zero. Nancy went up to Alvah's today for the first time since the midle of January. Found Sarah with a very sore foot. Mother is feeling better today. [Nancy] Mrs. Corrine [sic] had an addition to her family today. It was a little girl.

Friday, March 21   It is snowing this morning but very mild. Thaws a little in the shade. Frank Loops' litle baby is beried this afternoon. Bill Noise [Noyes, Noys] has gone out thare just now with the little casket in his cutter. James Noble has gone to carry Mr. Padget's family to the funeral. It has cleard of [up] pleasant this afternoon. It is perfectly beautiful. The mourners have just returned from laying their little darling boy in the cold and silent grave.

Saturday, March 22   Cold and cloudy this morning. It is snowing fearfuly this afternoon.   Wm has got the sick headache terible today. Cousin Mariah Bunel came to James Rushton's this afternoon.   Jurane [Juraine] Noble died this morning. Been sick since the first of January. Frank Loops little boy was buried the 21 of March 1879.

Sunday, March 23 [WB] It is a butiful morning. Has been a butiful [beautiful] day. Mercury 30 above zero.

Monday, March 24 [WB]   It is cloudy this morning but not very cold. Mercury 28 above zero. Jurane [Juraine] Noble is buried this afternoon. George Phelps made a call today & the

Agent brought Clara's [Nancy Brown's daughter] picture for which I gave him two dollars.

Tuesday, March 25   It is cloudy this morning. Snowes a very little.   Mercuary is 28 above zero this morning.   John Laidlaw's wife maid us a visit today. [Nancy] Sister Harriet [Viall Harmon] gave us a call this morning. Cousin Mariah Bunnell [Bunnell not in 1870 Census] went to visit sister Phila today. She has been staying with Cornelia four days. James Noble started for the west before daylight this morning & Rod Smith went with him. James Noble ran away. Gone of west. It is hopeful he will never come back. Mag & Jim Grant had a row the next morning.

Wednesday, March 26   [WB] It is pleasant and clear this morning but cold. Mercuary at zero. [Nancy] Mother is not very well today. Wm has gone up home to doctor a sick cow for Alvah.   Nicolas Cole whiped his boy most beastley & nocked down his wife twise.   John McFerin [McFeran in 1870 Edwards NY Census] & wife went to Coles & parted them from quariling. Cole has the name of being a hard cud.

Thursday, March 27   It is a nice day thaw some. Wm has gone up to Alvah's to tap trees. The sap run quite well. Mrs. McCargin [Actual spelling: McCargen] made us a call this forenoon.   She has been living all alone for three weeks. Edward Brown ate dinner with us today. Nicolas Cole went away today. Nobody knows whare. Jim Grant gave Mag Noble a terible jawing today.

Friday, March 28   This is a beautiful day. The mercury stands at 50 in the shade today noon. William is away to finish taping [tapping] the sugar trees. Willy Brown made us a call today & took dinner with Mother and me.

Saturday, March 29   It is raining this morning. It has rained all day but quite warm. The sap did not run much. We have got some new maple syrup today. The first we have had this spring. Jim Grant got back this afternoon with his horse that Jim Noble & Rod Smith ran away with Monday night. It has raind all day.

Sunday, March 30   It is snowing this morning. The wind North but not very cold. Wm is away up home. I am here alone again as usual. Mother is grunting fearfully. She has lain in bed until six o'clock. Bell Clealand gave us a call & took supper with us. It has snowed most all day. Mrs. Gorgon made us a call this evening.

Monday, March 31   It is clear & pleasant this morning but quite cold. It froze hard last night. Mercury stands at 20 at nine o'clock. The weather continued cold all day. The sap did not run any. Mr. Kingsbury made us a call this afternoon. Seven years today Henry Webb died. Seven years today Bertie Harmon, son of Charles V. Harmon, was beried [buried].

Tuesday, April 1   Cold & cloudy all day. Wm cherned [churned] and sugared of twice for Alvah. I commenced to make some new clothes for our little boys, Clarence & Sherman & [Oswald] Bower Brown. I love to work for them. They are three good boys. The sap run some this afternoon. We received a letter from Uncle George Johnson [George John Johnson] today from Canada & one from Jo Whitford, Pine Valley & one from Mrs. Finney Witney.

Wednesday, April 2   Cold & wind blows hard from the West. Sawing wood for Alvah. Emma Hall made us a visit today. Dave Noble signed the Deed of the old farm to the heirs of Robert Brown today. Carter took supper with us this evening. A part of Jim Noble's cows was sold today. Jim Grant is just rairing [raring] mad. He has given Mag two or three good blowings. Came very near slaping her in the face. Horace Buck steped [stepped] between them & bade Grant stand back. No sap today, too cold.

Thursday, April 3   It is cold & cloudy & the wind blows hard. It snows a little. William Buck took a large load of hay from Jim Noble's barn this noon. Got 2 bushels of wheat ground. It made 80 lbs of flour for the family of Robert Brown deceased.

Friday, April 4   [WB] It is very cold today. It snowed some last night. Mercury stands at 22 at noon above. Mother [Brown] was crazy all night. [Nancy] I got a letter from Brother Hiram A. Johnson. [of Oregon] It was writen March the 25.

Saturday, April 5   The weather continues cold. No sap today. Mother has been very bad all day. She gave me her gold rings today. She put one on my finger herself. Bade me keep it & wear it. Made me promise to stay with her while she lives & let no one take her away.   Sarah Brown [wife of Alvah Percival Brown] made us a visit this afternoon. I have made 20 lbs of butter. Have had milk 21 days.

Sunday, April 6   It is very pleasant today. Some prospects of a thaw. William has gone up home with Sherman & I am here alone with Mother as usual. She is better this morning. She has slept very good all night & is sleeping yet at noon. She slept all day & all night until 7 o'clock Monday morn.

Monday, April 7   This has been a cold day for the season. Thawed some whare the sun shone.   Froze in the shade. William has been up home all day. Done of some sugar in the woods. Al sent a tub of butter to Gouverneur [NY] by rayin [wagon] & the stage. Carter went with Lev to setle the Noble & Grant lawsuit. Grant has sold the farm to Mr. Woolever.

23

He will pay the mortgage & the cost. We got a letter from Adaline tonite.

Tuesday, April 8   This has been a beautiful day. The sleighing is done, the wagons are running. Lev went with his sleighs today. I think it will be the last time this spring. We got a letter from Jo Brown tonight & one from Judge Neary. William stayed with his mother this afternoon and I went out making calls. Called at J. Rushton's [James and Cornelia] & at Albert Wites & then to John Cousins store & bought me a calico dress & cloth for a bonnet. The sap runs well today. William wrote a letter this evening to send to Jo Brown. [John Brown]

Wednesday, April 9   William is away up to help Alvah today. It is a very nice day. It thaws fast. Mercury at fifty. Sarah McFerran made us a call today. She is home on a visit from Gouverneur. She has been thare eight months. Returns tomorrow. Had a call from Mr. Carter & Mr. Woolever today to settle with William the Noble & Grant buisness. Did not find Wm at home. Got a letter from Brother Edward Brown & Sarah from Canada. Matilda has another girl. Alvah boiled 7 pails of syrup today.

Thursday, April 10   It is quite cold this morning. Mercury at 40. Is clowdy & a cold wind. William is away up to Alvah's to do the chours and sugur off. I have churnd 5 lbs of butter this morning this makes 25 lbs in all. We are having quite a snowstorm this afternoon. Thare was ninety lbs of sugar today up to Alvah's. I am making my new dress.

Friday, April 11   This is [a] very stormy morning but not so very cold. Mercury stands at 30 but it snows & the wind blows at a fearful rate. Mr. Woolever just caled to see Wm about setling with him but did not find him at home. It snowed all day. Sugared of [f] one hundred pounds of sugar.

The stage went to Gouverneur with a sleigh.

Saturday, April 12 [WB] It was very cold this morning but it has been butiful and clear all day. Nancy went up to Alvah's today. Took dinner at Alvah's. Carter & Woolever came & settled up James Noble's cost of his lawsuit. The sap run well today. Nancy came home on the stage this afternoon from Alvah's. Charley's family all came here this evening. Clarence stayed with us all night.

Sunday, April 13 It is quite cold this morning. Thermometer sets 32. The sky is clear and it is a beautiful morning. William is away up to Alvah's to do the choors & sugar of [f]. Clarence [grandson] is staying with me today. It is snowing some tonight. Cilva White & family came to James Rushton's today. Sugared of[f] 50 lbs of sugar today up to Alvah's.

Monday, April 14 This is a beautiful morning. Mercury at 33 in the shade. William is away up to Alvah's to do chores and shugar of [f] twice. Clarence went home with him. I am doing a large washing. Mag Noble is doing the barn chours this morning. She is reaping the fruits of her own bad deeds. One hundred pounds of sugar today up to Alvah's. Fourteen years today, President Lincoln was assassinated.

Tuesday, April 15 It is quite pleasant this forenoon. William is away up to Alvah's as usual. Mrs. Goodnough [Jane] made me a visit today. It is snowing this afternoon. We received a letter from Adaline Brown tonight. One hundred lbs of sugar today.

Wednesday, April 16   It froze a little in the night. It is clowdy this morning but not very cold. Aunt Liza Whitehead came to see Mother this forenoon. The sap did not run but a little while this morning. One hundred lbs of sugar today. We wrote a letter to send to Jo Brown this evening.

Thursday, April 17   It is a nice pleasant morning. It froze some last night. The mercury is at 39 at 8 o'clock. William is away home to boil sap today. I have churnd this morning five lbs of buter. This is 30 lbs in all I have made.

Friday, April 18   It is cloudy this morning. Looks like storm. Froze a little. William went over to the old farm to fix the fences. Robert came here to see about buying the farm. I went to Alfred Hall's [brother-in-law] in the afternoon. Found Sylvia & family thare. Flora & Cora came home with me & and stayed all night. Wm bought 3 lbs of tea this afternoon. Ten cents worth of tobacko for Mother.

Saturday, April 19   It is very windy & cool this morning. Froze some last night. William has gone to work for Alvah today.   Sylvia White came here today from her sister Cornelia's to do her washing as it is very necessary that she must be ready to start for Kansas & her sister would not let her wash in her house, not in her back shead. A very hard sister. Mr. Todd's house roof took fire today from the chimney burning out. They put it out before much damage was done.

Sunday, April 20   This is a beautiful day. William has put up a new eavespout this morning. Sylvia has gone to Albert White's this afternoon. A little stranger made it appearance to Hiram Hall's [son of Emmorancy Johnson Hall and Alfred B. Hall] last night. Left 10 lbs. It was a daughter. Hiram Hall's folks has one more girl.

Monday, April 21   This morning is clear & pleasant & it froze some last night. William has gone up to Alvah's to work. Adah White has come here to do her ierning [ironing]. Their little Jenny is sick over to Albert Wite's [White's]. I have my washing done at nine o'clock this morning.

Tuesday, April 22   It is a beautiful morning. Froze quite hard last night. Wm has gone to Alvah's to sugar off. Sherman has come to stay with me today while Alvah & Sarah has gone out to Grant's for a visit. I have got my ironing all done at nine o'clock & I have churned six lbs of butter. This is 36 lbs in all. It is twelve & the mercury is up to 70 in the sun & 60 in the shade.

Wednesday, April 23   We have had a beautiful shower this morning. William has gone up to Alvah's to do the chours [chores]. Sylvia White & the two little girls took dinner with us today. The girls are staying all night. Mrs. McCargin made us a call this afternoon. We received a letter from J.P. Brown tonight. Wm wrote one to them this evening. Ira Fordham & Maybee is having a lawsuit this afternoon & evening. Wm has gone over to hear them.

Thursday, April 24   This is a beautiful morning. William has gone up to Alvah's to sugar off & do chours. Sylvia White & her two little girls & Agnes Brown took dinner with us today. It is cloudy & looks like rain this afternoon. Sylvia stays to Dumas's tonight. Is geting Mrs. Dumas to do some work for her. Adah & the children stays with me tonight.

Friday, April 25   It is cloudy & windy this morning. No rain yet. William is away up to Alvah's as usual. Adah has gone to Mrs. Dumas's to take care of her little sister. Cora & Flora are staying with me today. Mrs. McFerran made us a visit today & took dinner with us & Mrs. Alfred [Emmorancy Johnson] Hall took supper with us this afternoon. They commenced to wash the sap buckets up to Alvah's this afternoon. We are having a splendid shower this evening. Thare is a sugar party at the hotel.

Saturday, April 26   This is a Beautiful morning. This is the warmest day thare has been this spring. The grass looks green today for the first time. Cora & Flora White are staying with me yet. Wm is away up to Alvah's to help wash sap buckets. Mother got up at 8 o'clock this morning. We got a letter from A. P. [Abel Pratt] Johnson tonight.

Sunday, April 27   it is a nice mild morning. Some cloudy. Sylvia & Adah White came here this morning before breakfast. Stayed all day. Adah has gone to Alfred Hall's tonight. Sylvia & I took a walk to the graveyard & then to All Wites & Sylvia called at the hotell. This is eight nights the girls has stayed here with me, five of them stays with me tonight.

Monday, April 28   It is cloudy & looks like rain. Wm and Charles has gone to fix the fence & took the colts over to the farm. Sylvia & her family are all here today as usual. We are doing a large washing today. They are all with me tonight but Fred. It has raind some today. Mr. Kingsbury started his factory today.

Tuesday, April 29   This is a beautiful day. I have churnd this morning five lbs of butter. This is forty one lbs in all. Sylvia is doing her ironing this morning. Adah is playing on the piano & taking care of the baby. Wm has gone to hear a lawsuit between Jim Grant & Ed Noble. Mariah Bunnel made me a call this morning. She has gone to Sister Em [Emmorancy Johnson] Hall's. We got a letter from Jo Whitford to night. Sylvia & family stays with me tonight. A young girl came to Henry Dumases today.

Wednesday, April 30   This is a beautiful & lovely morning. William has gone to Gouverneur today to settle with lawyer Nery. [Neary] Sister Em [Emmorancy Johnson Hall] caled on me this morning. I am so homesick I don't no what to do. Sylvia & her family all but the boy has gone away this afternoon. I think they have gone to Jap [Jasper] Ward's. The band is playing tonight. It is most 9 o'clock & Mr. Brown has

28

not come yet from Gouverneur. Alvah milked our cow tonight. Stellah Barns & Emmy Hall [sister of Nancy Brown] gave me a call this afternoon.

Thursday, May 1 [WB] It is cold and wet this morning with some flakes of snow. Paid E. H. Neary one hundred & eight dollars & fifty cents yesterday cald on the suit between Executors & James Noble, James Grant. [Nancy] William is away up to Brother Robert's. I went over to Rob Alens [Allen's] this afternoon to see their little girl baby that came to town at 3 o'clock this morning. It snowed from 8 this morning until 3 in the afternoon.

Friday, May 2 It is cold & cloudy this morning. William has gone over to the farm with the colts. Alvah & Hugh Prat is here with the teem to draw out the manure & plow the corn ground. Sherman stays with me today. Sylvia & family went to Charley's today. Robby B. Brown is eight years old today.

Saturday, May 3 This is a pleasant day but rather cool. William is making the soap today. Alvah is plowing the garden. Mother is sick today. Emma Hall and Mariah Bunnel made me a visit this afternoon. Sylvia & Jap Ward went to Canton today. Charley & Martha & the children & Ella Hughs & Cora & Flora & Freddie White came here this evening. Put eggs under a hen to hatch today. She sat three weeks & died. Then he sat another & something destroyed her eggs then in a few days the black hen came with two chicks so we have had great luck in the chicken line.

Sunday, May 4 This is a beautiful day. Wm has gone over to the farm to look after the colts. Elder Dyke preached today. Mariah Bunnell stayed with me today. Sylvia & Jap Ward came from Canton this evening. Mr. Whiple spoke to the people in the church this evening. Ed Brown made us a call this afternoon. William caried in the soap. He has got two barrels full of good soap.

Monday, May 5   This has been rather a showery day. I have done a large washing today.   Mother is not much better. William & Charles has gone over to the farm to make fence. Mariah [Bunnell] is with me today. Alvah brot down a fifty weight tub two thirds full of sugar. It is very nice. About forty lbs of sugar.

Tuesday, May 6   It is raining this morning. William is away up to Alvah's to make the leach & start the making soap. Mariah Bunnell is with me today. I churned this morning five lbs of butter. This is forty six lbs in all.

Wednesday, May 7   It is pleasant this morning but rather cool. Wm is away up to Alvah's to make the soap. He has got two large kettles full of good soap. Mariah Bunnell is with me today. Mrs. Albert White made me a call this afternoon. Jim Rushton plowed his garden today.

Thursday, May 8   This is a beautiful morning, warm and sunshine. Mariah Bunnell has gone home with Wade Rice on the milk wagon this morning.   William has gone up to Charley's to make their soap.   Ed Noble came here this morning to tell Wm to make his fence.   The Methodist Minister moved in town today & the teems came from Colton after Mr. Kenyon's goods.   They started at five PM.   Jim Rushton is making his garden today. Mariah Bunnell stayed with me 5 days.

Friday, May 9   Thare was a frost this morning. It is clear & pleasant & quite warm. Little Sherman came to see me this morning. Mrs. Kingsbury and Ruby cald on me last evening. Mr. Woolever paid William some money last evening.   Wm went up to Alvah's this morning. He sowed wheat for Charley in the forenoon & in the afternoon, split rails down on the old farm. Agnes Brown made me a visit today. They make fourteen cheeses a day at the factory here.

Saturday, May 10   This is a beautiful morning. The birds are singing so sweetely. One little bird came into the house & stayed with me a long time & and then I took it in my hands & let it fly away. William & Mr. Gorden & Frank Raymond with his horse have gone down to the old farm to make fence today. A. B. Hall gave me a call this forenoon. He has been plowing Rob Allen's garden. Mrs. McCargins & Mr. Gardener's. Sarah J. Brown spent this evening with me & Sherman stayed with me all night.

Sunday, May 11   It is very pleasant & very dry & dusty. The warmest day this spring. William has stayed with his Mother all day & had a bad time with the sick headache. I went to church & then over to Alfred Hall's. Sylvia White & family left Jap Ward's today & went to Alvah Brown's. Mariah Bunnell started for home today with Lilly Rice. Emmy Hall made us a call this evening. I made a call on Jenny Hall this evening.

Monday, May 12   This is a pleasant morning, no rain yet. It is very dry. Alvah came this morning & harowed in our wheat. William & Mr. Gorden has planted [our potatoes & corn today & we have planted] the beets & onions. Charley drove some cattle down on the farm today to pasture.

Tuesday, May 13   A beautiful May morning. Hot, no rain yet. A brisk south wind. Wm is away up to Alvah's to work & Charley has gone to carry Sylvia White & family & goods to DeKalb [NY] [as] she starts for Kansas. Mother Brown went over to Gorden's' this afternoon. Stayed one hour. They are making 17 cheeses a day at our factory. The cornet band played in the village this evening. Wm [and] John McFerran commenced work on Burdock's house today. I have churnd 5

31

lbs of butter today. This is 51 lbs in all.

Wednesday, May 14   It continues pleasant but no rain. The Plum trees are in full blosom this morning. William & Robert & Stillman Brown have gone down to the old farm to make fence.

Thursday, May 15   It looks some like rain this morning. William stays at home with his Mother today. I have been up to Charley's & Alvah's all day cleaning house. Jenny Hall & Stella Barns [Barnes] come here while I was gone. I came back with Celia Cleland. Wm put ashes on his potatoes & planted the cucumbers today.

Friday, May 16   It is raining a little this morning. Wm is planting carots today when it don't rain & when it does he is away over in the village. It is quite cool today. We took down our stove this afternoon & put it in the back kitchen.

Saturday, May 17   This is a lovely morning. The grass & trees all look so beautiful & green. Wm is away up to Alvah's to work. Clarence & Bower are here with me today. Robert Brown drove some cattle down on to the old farm to pasture. Sid came in to let us know of it this morning.   The Band played this evening in the street. I took my bonnet to Miss Grifon to get new ties for it & Martha & Mable came home with me.

Sunday, May 18   It is a beautiful morning. The sun is shining brite [bright] & it is very warm. Sherman has come to stay with me today while Alvah goes out to Tom Grant's to get a horse. One of his has a sore neck [and] he is not fit to use. I went to church today. Heard Reverend Mr. Whiple for the first time. I cald [called] over to the factory in the evening. They are making 24 cheeses a day. Mrs. Gear cald on us today looking for Charley to praise [appraise] damage on a dead sheep [that] dogs had kild. Our wheat is up nice this morning.

Monday, May 19   Very pleasant but very dry & warm. William is away down on the old farm to work today. Took his dinner. I am washing. I have got an awful sore throat today. Emmy Hall & Josephine White caled on us this evening. Charley Brown came & got a bushel of potatoes to plant. William paid Em Hall one dollar for medicine. Charley Brown went with his teem [team] to work on the old farm today. Is twoloads of cheese sold from this factory at 7 & one eighth of a cent a lb caried to the junction today. [probably DeKalb Junction, NY]

Tuesday, May 20   One more beautiful morning but no rain yet. Charley & William is away over on the old farm geting in a peace [piece] of oats. I have churnd this morning 5 lbs of butter, 56 lbs in all. I have gave Mother Brown's back piasa a thorough cleaning today. It was nasty enough for anything. I walked out after to the village after supper. Caled at Mrs. McCargin's & Janet McKee's & H. Gardner's & Mrs. Gorden's & George Padget's. Saw Mrs. Hosferd from Russell [NY]. Alvah brout [brought] down some wheat flour yesterday for us.

Wednesday, May 21   It is cloudy & cool this morning. Has been a little shower in the night. Wm has gone to work down on the old farm today to pick of stones from the meadow. Mr. Jourden [Jordon] came here today to get a peace [piece] of pork to pay for a stick of timber that Wm got of him. I gave him the pork. Mrs. Padget & Mrs. Hosford, her mother, caled to see us this evening. Ellie Hughs [Hughes] came here from Charley's & brout [brought] me a pail of beer.

Thursday, May 22   This is a beautiful morning but very cool. Some frost this morning. William began to hoe his corn last night & this morning. Wm & Alvah & Charley & Hugh Prat with their teems [teams] have gone down on the old farm to work today. They are making 28 cheeses a day at the factory. Mr. Woolever paid eleven hundred dollars to William this evening to be endorsed on the Jim Noble mortgague. I have whitewashed Mother's kitchen overhead today & washed all of the ceilings ready for painting & papering.

Friday, May 23   This is a very cold morning. A hard frost. The sun is shining very brite [bright]. William has brot [brought] me 5 lbs of white lead & 4 quarts of oil to paint the woodwork in Mother's kitchen & paper to paper the walls of the same room. I have papered the room today. Wm went over to the old farm to sow oats for Charley this afternoon. They are making 30 cheeses at our factory a day. Yesterday was sister Emma Hall's birthday.

Saturday, May 24   This is a beautiful day. Another hard frost this morning. William & Alvah & Charley & Hugh have gone over to the old farm to plant corn today. Sherman stayed with me today. Sarah came down and stayed with us this evening & Sherman stayed all night. Mr. George Freeman came here today & hired fifty dollars of William. James & Henry Brown signed the note. The band played in the street this evening. Dave Loap [Loop] came after Pet Hunt & caried her to Hermon this evening from Alvah's.

Sunday, May 25   A nice pleasant morning but no rain. It is awful dry. I went to church today. Wm went with Sid Brown to drive some cattle back to the old farm to the pasture. Lileon [Lillian] Gorden stayed with Mother. Little Mabel & Charley Brown & Ellie Hughs & Emmy Hall came home with me from church. Charley brout [brought] us A nice peace [piece] of veal this morning. Edward Brown gave us a call this afternoon. We got a letter from Adaline & Susa Brown last night.

Monday, May 26   This is a very cold morning. The wind blows from the north. Thare was a hard frost this morning. The sun is shining brite & a man needs on an overcoat to ride out. William & two of Robert's boys have gone over to the old farm to make fence. It is ten o'clock & I have got my washing all done. Mother is asleep in bed yet she is not feeling very well. Alvah Brown & Hugh Pratt are down here with the team working on the rhode [road]. They come here for their dinners workingthe tax for the heirs of Robert Brown, deceased.

Tuesday, May 27   Another frost this morning. It is looking some like rain. 2 o'clock no rain yet. William & Alvah & Hugh are working on the rhode in the village beat with two teems. They was here to dinner. Sherman is with me today. I have washed six windows this forenoon. Took them out & put them back in. At six o'clock it is raining. We are glad to see it come. Mother is feeling bad tonight. She is crazy again. I have churnd five lbs of butter today.

Wednesday, May 28   This is a nice morning after the little shower of last night. Mother Brown put in a bad night & has been crazy all day. She is some better tonight. William & Alvah & Hugh worked on the rhode today with two teems. Was here to dinner. The boiler burst in the factory today. They had a bad time scalding the curd but they made 30 cheeses. I have tried to paint some today but Mother has took on so [that] I could not do anything scarsely. Mrs. James McKee made me a call this evening.

Thursday, May 29   This is a beautiful morning. Lovely & the sun shining bright but how dry. William is away to work on the road. I am here alone with Mother. She has slept good all night, is sleeping yet. Alvah & Charley begins to work on the rhode in their beet [beat] today. I have painted the woodwork in the kitchen & sulerway [? Cellar way] & pantry today & went to the store after my paint. It is most four o'clock. Mother is sleeping yet. Has not been up but once.

Friday, May 30   It looks like rain today.   Mother is better. She ate a good meal this morning but she did not dress & does not feel able to sit up much today.   William is working on the rhode [road] over Trout Lake way.   Mrs. Gorden came over this morning & got some butter to pay Gorden for planting corn.   It did not rain one drop here today.   Maggy went A visiting up to Sandy's tonight.   Mrs. Mc gave me a call today.

Saturday, May 31   This is a warm & pleasant morning but no rain.   William is away working on the rhode.   I have been cleaning house this forenoon.   Clarence & Bower come here this afternoon.   Charley & Martha & Ellie came in the evening. Thare was a nice thunder shower at half past ten.   We got a letter from Adaline Brown tonight.   She is no better.   Em [Emmorancy Johnson Hall] got a letter from Uncle George Johnson's daughter.

Sunday, June 1   A most lovely morning after the rain. Jap Ward gave us a call & Stillman Brown stayed here while Perce went to salt the cattle on the old farm.   It has raind some today.   A little cooler tonight.   I went to church today & sister Emmy came home with me.   Sherman stayed with us today. Edward Brown gave us a call this afternoon.   Dave Noble sold the cheese today at 7 & one eighth [cents per pound].   Wm is over helping to box the cheese tonight.   Mother is crazy tonight, I have got her away to her bed.

Monday, June 2   This morning is misty & cloudy.   The cheese has gone today.   Alvah went with a load.   I have done my washing today.   Got done at 10 o'clock.   Cleaned in the suller [cellar] this afternoon.   Miss Amelia Gardner cald here this morning.   William is working on the rhode [road] today.

Mother is sleeping all day. It is raining some today. The grass & grain & everything looksbeautiful. Cyrus Cleland came here tonight & payed the interest on a five hundred dollar note. Clarence C. Brown is seven years old today.

Tuesday, June 3   It is clowdy & cool this morning. William is hoing [hoeing] in the garden this morning. I sent a letter to Adaline Brown today. William went over to the farm this afternoon to fix fence. We have had a terible shower at seven o'clock. The rain came down in torents. I have painted the woodwork in the dining room today. Willy Raymond cald [called] here tonight to get leave to put his horse in the pasture over on the farm.

Wednesday, June 4   This is a beautiful morning after the rain of last night. William is away working on the rhode over to Trout Lake. Took his dinner with him. Mother is up at ten o'clock & is feeling quite well. It raind some today. Alvah cald [called] here tonight when he came with the milk. The band teacher was in town tonight & the band played this evening.

Thursday, June 5   It has been raining in the night. Is quite showery this forenoon. William is away on the rhode. Took his dinner. Alfred Hall came here this morning & got a bushel of potatoes. We got a letter from Canada from Sarah Brown & Hannah last evening. It is very pleasant this afternoon. I have got my ironing all done & my baking & have just wrote a letter to brother Ed & Sarah Brown. Mother is eating her dinner. I made a few calls this evening at the PO & Browns store & John Cozens [Cousins] & Dr. Murey's & Mrs. McCargins & J. Gordens.

Friday, June 6   It was clear & beautiful this morning but it has clowded over & looks like rain & is very cool. William is hoeing in the garden today. He put a hen setting this morning.

Mother went over to Gorden's last night alone, After I went away. William went after her. She stayed one hour. Was awful tired when she got home.

Saturday, June 7   Clear & pleasant this morning but very cool a little frost. Aunt Liza Whitehead made us a visit today. Stayed to dinner. William & Alvah with the teem worked on the rhode today. It finished the rhode work here. Lidia Bennet, daughter of Henry & Lidia Web[b] died this morning. Sherman has stayed with me today. Alvah & Sarah Brown & Thomas & Julia & Cora Grant & Celia Laidlaw & Celia Cleland gave us a call this evening. The brass band played in the street tonight. Mother is geting daft again.

Sunday, June 8   This is a lovely morning. Thare was some frost. William brot [brought] home one pound of tea last night. I churnd four lbs of better yesterday. I have atended the funeral of Lyda Bennet this afternoon at the church here in Edwards [NY].   William Green from Hermon attended as undertaker. Was out with his new horse. It is a splendid rig. Funeral services by the Methodist Preacher from Hermon. The church was fild with people. Sarah & Sherman stayed here while I was gone.

Monday, June 9   It has raind some today. William hoed in the garden in the forenoon & in the afternoon he wrote letters to his brother & to Osweld [Oswald], Brodie & Lizzie Bignel. Mr. Austin sawed wood for us this afternoon at the door. Daniel Glasby got two bushels of potatoes. Pays for them at Brown's store.

Tuesday, June 10   This is a beautiful & lovely morning. I was up at 3 o'clock & took a ride up to Alvah's. At six o'clock thare was a little stranger made its apearance. It was a little girl & so they kept it for the present. Sherman was well pleased with a little sister. I came home at ten o'clock. Found

Mother quite poorly. Mr. Austin is sawing wood today at the door. Wm finished hoeing his garden this afternoon. Austin finished the wood this afternoon. Mother has not yet set up only long enough to have her bed made. Mrs. Grant [Sarah Brown's mother] has come to stay with Sarah a week or two.

Wednesday, June 11 This is a warm, clowdy morning after a heavy thunder shower in the night. William has gone to Gouverneur today to express the money to the boys. Alexander Watson caled here this morning to get a colt pastured. I have oiled over the woodwork in the parlor today. Sister hall cald [called] on us this evening. Ruby came here & heat over her lard & put it in one of Mother's jars & put it in our seller. William got home at seven tonight. Brot [brought] me a pair of kid gloves & himself a coat & hat & two pairs of boots.

Thursday, June 12 This is a very warm morning. Looks some like rain. William is weeding his carots. I have churnd four lbs of butter this morning. The bugs are plenty on the potatoes. William brot a new drum for Oswald B. Brown & a pair of shoes for Clarence last night from Gouverneur. Alvah bought a new pair for Sherman yesterday. Mrs. Grieves gave us a cake yesterday afternoon. We have had a nice thunder shower this afternoon. I sent a letter to Brother Ed & Sarah Brown yesterday. On lend 38 dollars.

Friday, June 13   It is very cool this morning but clear & pleasant. Wm is hoing his corn. It is most [almost] ten o'clock. I have got my baking & ironing done. It is most four o'clock & Mother has not got up to dress yet. She ate her dinner in bed. Charley Brown took dinner with us today. Young George Freeman was here today trying to sell Wm a bugy. After he went away, Wm went away up to Alvah's & back home before supper. After supper I took a walk over to sister Emma's [Emmorancy Johnson Hall], caled at

Goodnough's. Milo & Stillman ran away tonight.

Saturday, June 14   This is a beautiful, pleasant morning. Wm finished hoing his corn & helped me set up a bed. He has the sick headache today but he wed [weeded] his carots this afternoon. I got Mother up at dinner time then I had a good time cleaning her bedroom & putting clean cloths on her & the bed for three times in the last week. I called on Millia McKee & Jenny Hall & Corudia Rushton this afternoon. Woodcock's folks are in fear of trouble with Milo & Ellie Hughs just now. I made a call at Dr. Goodnough's & at Jim Brown's store tonight.   Bought four lbs of rice, a fine came calico for Mother's apron, [and] a paper of tobacco.

Sunday, June 15   It is raining this morning. William is away over to Gorden's. I did intend to go up to Alvah's this morning but am disapointed. The Methodists have their quarterly meting at Pitcairn today. No meeting here today until evening. Brother Robert & Agnes [Brown] came here today. Wm is writing a letter to Matilda Stanton. I went to church this evening. The Presiding Elder spoke to the people. Thare was not but a few in attendance. It was a dark night. It raind all day.

Monday, June 16   It does not rain this morning but it is cool & clowdy. I have done a large & dirty washing this forenoon. It is three o'clock & Mother has not got up yet. She ate her dinner in bed. My baking is just done. William has gone up to Alvah's to fix their sistern. It broke loose yesterday & let the watter of[f]. Brother Robert has gone after Stillman. Mother is not feeling very well today.

Tuesday, June 17   This is a cold morning but no frost. I went up to Alvah's and Charley's on the milk wagon this morning. Charley carried Ellie Hughs [Hughes] home today. Away up in Fine 20 miles from here. It is raining this noon so Alvah came home with me with the horse & bugy. Wm has gone over to the old farm to take cattle out of the meadow. Mother is feeling pretty well today.

Wednesday, June 18   This is a very nice morning but quite cool. Charley came over here this morning to bring my basket of things & got a bushel of corn for himself. William has gone up to Alvah's to fix his sistern [cistern]. I churnd this morning. Took one hour & a half & then it did not come good at all. I have washed the windows in the parlor & put up my white curtains today & washed the windows in the kitchen. Took up one end of the carpet & made it tight & fasend it down again.

Thursday, June 19   It is a beautiful morning. Warmer than it has been for quite a few days. William has gone up to Alvah's to fix the cistern. Sarah's Mother went home today. I got a letter from Mariah Bunnell tonight. Wm got a letter from Brother Edward Brown today. Sidney Brown [nephew of William Brown] cald [called] here this morning to let us know they had heard from Stillman. I had company this afternoon. It was Mrs. Maltby & Sister Phila Harmon [Nancy's half-sister] and Maryelle Harmon & a call from sister Hall & C. V. Harmon and Alice Harmon.   Wm brot me four lbs of crackers today. Ed Noble is married.

Friday, June 20   One more beautiful sunshiny morning but not very warm. Mr. Woolever cald here and left the deed from Dave Noble of the old farm. William has gone up to the Pond Settlement. I have just got my ironing & baking done this forenoon. Mr. Todd cald here this forenoon to see Wm about paying the interest on A note. Martha & the children stayed here this evening while Charley played in the band. Baker was with them tonight. I caried Phila [Harmon] from Woolever's over to Alfred Hall's tonight. Mr. Todd came over this evening & payed [paid] the interest on a note.

Saturday, June 21   A very pleasant morning. I don't know whare Wm is today. He came home at noon. He had been up to Alvah's & brought down a load of wood to George Padget & drove the teem back to Alvah's.   This afternoon he is making a tub to put in the new well. It is most [almost] three o'clock & Mother has just got up & drest since Thursday night. We got a letter from Susa Brown. Jo sent back the receipt of the money that Wm sent him. Susa wrotes that her Mother was not any better.

Sunday, June 22   This morning it is raining some. Mrs. Woodcock made us a call this morning. She is feeling very bad about Milo. Mother got up at 8 o'clock this morning. I went to church today. This afternoon it is clear & pleasant. Dave sold the cheese last night for six cents. I found they are boxing them today. Mother is geting daft again tonight. She is rgging [raging] all over the house into evry thing that she can get into. We had new letuce for breakfast for the first time this year. Mother makes awful work with her pipe today.

Monday, June 23   It is a beautiful morning. The cheese goes to DeKalb today.   Charley Brown is away with a load. William went up to Charley's to do his milking early this morning. Came back on the milk wagon. Has finished his tub & got all ready to go diging the well in the morning. This afternoon, he is picking bugs. I have done my washing this forenoon & this afternoon am baking. Agnes Brown made us a visit today. It is 3 o'clock & Mother is not up yet. She has not been up to be drest today. Thare is a tent show tonight. The tent is set up by the Rushton's dry house.

Tuesday, June 24   A beautiful & lovely morning. Nemiah Wiley & Al Wite & William are diging the well today. I have churnd four lbs of butter this morning. It is nine & Mother is not up yet. We got a letter from Isaac Brown last night. This

42

has been the hotest day we have had yet this spring. The men have got the well done. Wm paid Wiley one dollar & fifty cents in money & a bushel of potatoes. Wm got a letter tonight from Watertown & would not let me see it but I saw more than he thinks I did. I saw J Rushton go by.

Wednesday, June 25   This is a very warm morning. No rain for a week past. William is over to Mrs. McCargin's helping Wiley to clean out her well & fix the pump. Albert Wite came here this morning & got a bushel of potatoes to help pay for his work at the well yesterday. I just heard that the lawyers went to Fine [NY] yesterday to see Ellie Hughs and she took her oath that Milo came to her bed four times & the fourth time he got in bed with her & and she could not hinder him. I have been over to Gorden's this afternoon to stitch Sherman a coat. Alvah caled here while I was gone. He has been hoing [hoeing] his corn over on the old Brown farm. Wm hoed potatoes this afternoon. It is warmer today.

Thursday, June 26   It is cloudy & a little cooler. It raind a very little last night. A very heavy shower of south thundered & lightned. Wm is hoing his potatoes in the garden today. He has finished them in the garden & hoed five rows in front of the house. I made a call over to A [Alfred] Hall's today. George Padget brot [brought] me a spring bed this afternoon. We are to pay him four dollars for it. Alvah brot a grist of wheat to mill today. It has not raind any today. Yesterday was the hotest day thare has been yet. The Mercury run at 95 in the shade more than one hundred in the sun.

Friday, June 27 Wm got two lbs of tea. It is clowdy & looks like rain this morning. Wm is hoeing his potatoes. The Masons from the Edwards Lodge have gone to Hermon to attend a Masonic funeral today. Alvah & Charley has gone with their teems to cary some of the Brother Masons. Wm finished hoeing his potatoes today & wed the carots [carrots].

Mother did not get up until 6 o'clock. After supper I made a few calls. I bought 25 cents worth of goods of Mrs. Gardner at her five cent stand. Caled on Mrs. McCargin. Got home at ten o'clock. We had no rain today.

Saturday, June 28 Corn totaled taseled today. It is very warm this morning. Cloudy & looks very much like rain. William is hoeing his corn today. I must go to my mopping & do my Saturday's work. I am tired of cleaning after Mother. It is mop & wash every two hours in the day. My life is just one round of care & toil. Charley's family made us a call this evening. Sherman stays all night. The band played tonight. We got a letter from Ed & Sarah Brown to night. Stillman Brown is thare in Canada. Milo has gone to Michigan on a visit to his uncles. Wilber & Theodore Stevenson had a fight tonight. Wm & Couine [Conyne] put in the new pump in the well today.

Sunday, June 29 It is raining this morning a litle. Has been quite a shower in the night. I have been to church today. Martha & Charley & the children came here after meeting [meeting]. Stayed until after supper then Charley went to John Cleland's after Emmy Noble to go there to work for them. Pet Webb has a boy last night. Perce & Agnes Brown came here this afternoon & little Ira Brown. At one or two o'clock we had a splendid shower. The rain fell beautifully. Everything looks beautiful. They have sold the cheese. Are boxing it today.   Graham Watson & Betsy came last night from Michigan to H. Rushton's.

Monday, June 30 Em Noble began working to Charley's. This is a beautiful morning. Rather cool. William has gone over to the old farm with Robert Webb to let him cut the hay around the house & some in the pasture whare thare has been no cattle. He has put Parish green on his potatoes this afternoon. Conine came & fixt the pump this noon & Wm has got the platform fixt & all rite now ready for pumping water. Nermiah Wiley came this afternoon & got his bushel of potatoes. I have churned & washed & baked this forenoon. Alvah brot [brought] down forty lbs of cake sugar last Saturday night. Wm got a letter from A. V. Brodie tonight with the receipt.

Tuesday, July 1 Alvah brot us a bag of flour. This is a lovely morning, clear & sunshine. Wm finished puting Parish green on his potatoes this morning for this time. George Padget came here this morning & got three & a half lbs of butter. One shilling a lb. Mother has not sat up any since Sunday. Alvah cald here this morning & Wm went home with him to grind a cythe. Mr. Sam Padget came here this morning to borrow a rake & a hay fork. He took them. George Padget brot me a wider spring bed & took back the other. Martha & the children all came here this evening. Stayed while the band marched round the square & played til ten o'clock. Clarence stayed all night.

Wednesday, July 2 One more beautiful & lovely morning. The birds are singing so sweetly although I am obliged to stay here in the house with our invalid Mother. I try to be happy in the thoughts that I am doing some good. I can get a moment now & then [to] go to the door & listen to the songs of the birds & to the pratling of the children as they are skiping along to school & the ringing of the school bell or the clatter of the milk wagon as they are rushing for the factory & lots of other music to numerous to mention. William is away to little York today to get his new wagon. Ida Ivers made me a call today. Wm went to the Pond Settlement with his new wagon to get it ironed at Luke Van Ornum's.

Thursday, July 3 This is a very warm morning. Looks some like rain. The People of this village is very buisey today geting ready for the fourth. Charley Brown is away to

Gouverneur to bring a load of groceries for the band. They intend to have a stand to sell to the People. Alvah is down helping to make the shanty for the grocery. He took dinner with me today noon. I have been baking, mopping & ironing. Wm is over in the village helping. Mr. Baker cald [called] here today. I went to the grave yard tonight. Mrs. Mc Cargin's. Potatoes are in blossom. Billy Webb & Sind [Lucinda] Stevenson was married today.

Friday, July 4   The wind blows hard & it looks very much like rain. It is five o'clock & the cannons are going of every few minutes. The People are geting together for the Celabration. The band is in the streete in front of Raymond's sounding their horns & beating the Drums & making ready for the march to the grove. Their speaker is from Potsdam [NY]. I have a few of my friends here to dinner. I have had to stay in all day with Mother. I went out at ten in the evening to see the balloon Ascension. Stayed about twenty minets [minutes]. Clarence & Oswel came home with me & stayed all night. It has not raind any today. It is awful dusty. Mother has not been up any today. A dance in the evening at the hotell.

Saturday, July 5   It is very cool this morning. No rain yet. The sky is as clear as a bell. William is away up to help Alvah do the milking. His man & girl is at the dance. They dance all night til daylight & forget to go home in the morning. Wm is lolling around today. I have done lots of moping & other work & now must churn. We got a card from Mariah Bunnell last night. I have churned today. I have had company this afternoon. Mrs. Noble & Martha Brown & little Mabel made us a visit. Charley & the boys came after them in the evening. Sherman stayed all night. Neary Hall made me a call this afternoon. Our potatoes is in blosom. One kind the [perhaps meant "has"] dark green tops.

Sunday, July 6   This is a nice cool morning. Hugh Pratt has gone to carry Pet Hunt home today three miles beyond Hermon. She cald at Dr. Murray's to get medicine. She says she is sick & not able to work. I went to church this morning. Professor Lee spoke to the People. He preached in the grove at Trout Lake at 2 o'clock this afternoon. Wm is away to get some strawberies for supper. He stayed with his mother this forenoon. We have had a strawbery shortcake for supper. The first one this summer. Wm is over to the factory boxing cheese. Have sold today. Wm has to go up to Alvah's & help milk tonight.

Monday, July 7   It is raining hard this forenoon. Wm has gone to Luke Van Ornum's today to help iron his new wagon. Alvah has got to look for a girl to work for them. Sherman stayed with me last night. Gone home today. Charley milked our cow last night & he brought me a bowl of strawberies [strawberries] from Benny Noble. Mother has not been up much for the last week, only enough to have her bed made. Mother has got up & drest [dressed] this afternoon at five. Brother Pearce came in to see her today. Stayed about half an hour. She did not know him at first until he told her who he was. It has rained most all day. George Padget came & got some butter today. 2 lbs & three quarters.

Tuesday, July 8   It is cloudy & misty this morning. A nice growing time. Alvah brot me five quarts of tame strawberies last night. I have got them cand this morning. Fanny Henderson commenced work for Alvah yesterday. Wm & Alvah went to the wood and got sticks to make a hay rack. They was here to dinner. Wm has gone up to Alvah's this afternoon. I have just commended to knit a pair of cotton socks for Clarence. Have a pair of woolen socks just done for Sherman. Have knit him one pair of cotton striped stockings. Pet Hunt came back to Alvah's Sunday.

Wednesday, July 9   This is a lovely morning. I have got my

47

work all done for this morning at eight o'clock. Wm is mowing around the border of his front meadow with a hand sythe to be ready for the mashine. Alvah has come with the mashine at nine o'clock. He is all done cuting the grass at eleven o'clock & has gone home to dinner. Wm has gone up to Charley's this afternoon to make a hay rack. It is clow[d]ing up & looks like rain. Quincy Madison of Hermon died this morning. Jim Brown got a dispatch at four o'clock. Alvah & Wm came down in the afternoon & raked the hay & put it up. Was here to supper.

Thursday, July 10 It is a beautiful morning. Thsre was a nice shower in the night but it is clear as a bell this morning. Wm is away up to Charley's to finish his hay rack. It is three weeks last Tuesday since I have been up home. I am so sick of staying here in the house so close. Sometimes I am more than half enclined to dig out entirely. I have not anything to encourage me to stay here & clean up after Wm's Mother. No not even love nor money. Thare is no one here that cares for me, only for my work. Sister Hall made me a visit today & Mrs. A. White made me a call this afternoon. Hugh Pratt & John Allen & Wm took in our hay this afternoon. Was caut [caught] in the shower.

Friday, July 11 It is a nice warm morning but it looks some like rain. William is away up to Alvah's to help them with the haying. I have done a large ironing. Done lots of starched caps & things for Mother & a linen coat for Sherman. Done at ten AM. I have just been cleaning Mother's bedroom & her old stinking chair stool. Mr. Madison of Hermon was beried yesterday. Byron Allen's wife of Russell is berried today. She leaves a little baby two weeks old for its grandma to take care of. Charley & Martha went to Gouverneur this afternoon & carried John McFerran [McFeran] & Uncle Sam to the Orange celebration [perhaps Grange].

Saturday, July 12   This is a beautiful & lovely morning. Wm hoed his corn this forenoon & went up to Alvah's to rake up some hay in the afternoon. Alvah & Hugh hoed a part of their corn over on the old farm. Sarah came down here with her baby for the first time. She stay all day & Ida came over in the afternoon. Mother got up to supper. Sherman went home with his uncle Cyrus this morning. Stayed all day. Charley's folks got home tonight from Gouverneur. We got a card from Sid Whitford last night. Adaline is no better. Mother got up at 2 o'clock.

Sunday, July 13   A beautiful Sunday morning. William went away as soon as after breakfast. I don't know whare. I hope he will get back in time for me to go to meting [meeting]. I went to church this forenoon. Clarence stayed with us all day. Has gone home tonight. Robert & Lizia [Elizabeth] Brown made us a call this afternoon. They had just got a letter from Stilman & Matilda Stanton. Josephine Wite made me a call this afternoon with her two little girls. Mother got up at three this afternoon. Pet Hunt stayed all the week to Alvah's & went home today. I think she will stay at home this time.

Monday, July 14   A pleasant morning. A splendid hay day. William is away up to Alvah's to help with the hay. I have done a large washing & moped [mopped] the dining room & kitchen. Did not get done until [al]most noon. Six loads of cheese went to the station this morning from our factory. Sold for six cents a pound. We have had a delightfulvshower this afternoon at 4 o'clock. I think the hay raker was glad to get under shelter. It thundered & lightned quite hard. James McKee called here Awhile this evening. Mother got up at five this afternoon.

Tuesday, July 15   This is the hotest morning thare has been here this summer but at ten the wind begins to blow a cooler breeze which is a great relief. It was so still and mugy [muggy]. I have churnd this morning. The butter is nice for such a warm time. Wm is away up home to work at the haying. John Allen comenced to help them yesterday. He works for one dollar a day. Mother got up at four this afternoon. I wrote a letter to Adaline Brown today. Sherman caried [carried] it to the PO. He stayed with me all night. Thare was a shower at five this afternoon.

Wednesday, July 16   It has been a very warm night. It is a little cooler this morning. It is clowdy & looks like rain. William is away up to Alvah's to work at the haying. He put Parish green on his potatoes this morning. Berney is puting Parish green on his potatoes this morning. He is putting it on with water. Padget has just finished shingling Wm Gardner's house on this side. John Bancroft & his wife are in town from NY city visiting their friends in Edwards and Hermon.   A shower at eleven before noon. The sun is shining. George Padget come & got some butter. Wm went to Shawville this afternoon. Did not get home until dark. I had the cow to milk the first time this summer.

Thursday, July 17   It is a pleasant morning but it is rather cool. William is away up to Alvah's to work in the hay field. Vanila Ward & Vanera Hall made me a visit today & little Lena Ward. They went home at half past four. I have done my ironing & baking today. Mother has got up at four o'clock. Wm did not get home until dark. I had the cow to milk. Mr. Pasco Whitford cald here tonight & Wm payed him ten dollars in money for puting the irons on his new wagon. There was a shower up home today but thare was not a drop of rain here.

Friday, July 18   This is a cool & pleasant morning. William is up to Charley's helping with the hay. Charley cald here this morning & left some yarn for me to knit for Clarence. Thare was a very little rain here today. Mrs. Gorden & Laura & Lil & Ida Ivers cald on us today. William brot me four lbs of cheese & two lbs of crackers last night from J. Brown's. Mrs. Goodfellow started for Kansas the 7 of July with three children. Left three about here somewhare taking care of themselves. Her husband went last fall. Wm did not get home until dark.

Saturday, July 19   It is very cool this morning. The wind is north but it is a little warmer than it has been for two days. It bids fair for a good hay day. William has gone up home to help with the hay. He took a little pail of cream to Martha. Sherman went up to his grandpa Cleland's this morning on the milk wagon. They do not make but 25 cheeses a day now at our factory. The Millers wife is very sick. Has been for two weeks. Ed Noble's wife is sick with the lung fever. Alice Earl is sick with the bleeding of the lungs. She has quit her school & come home. They are quite alarmed about her. We hope she will get better soon.

Sunday, July 20   This is a nice pleasant morning. Warmer than it has been for three days. Wm got up at half past four, was up to Charley's before they was up & took breakfast at Alvah's. Then went to Fine after Alvah's hired girl. Got back here at six at night. Alfred & Emmy Hall came over & stayed with me awhile in the middle of the day. Sherman went home with Elen [Ellen] Cleland today noon. He came back here tonight & stayed with me all night. William Cleland's twin boys was one year old the 18 of July 1879.

Monday, July 21   One more pleasant morning. William is away up home to help with the haying. Charley was down with the milk at half past five this morning. I have done a large washing this forenoon. Had two bed quilts in the wash today. I have washed eight bed quilts this spring. Wm got home just before dark tonight in time to give me one of his blesings before bedtime. Of corse, I deserve such treatment for staying here one hole year & cleaning up & washing after

51

his nasty old Mother.   It is now nineteen days since I have sat down in a neighbor's house.   It is five weeks today since I have been up home.

Tuesday, July 22   it is cloudy & looks like rain. William has gone to Alvah's to work.   They finished Charley's hay yesterday. Have more yet to do to Alvah's. I have churned this morning. Had good butter. It is raining some at half past ten. Now it is raining some at noon. Wm got home at five. They did not work at the hay this afternoon. It is raining stedy & nicely this evening. Mother has not got up until since dark. She has only sat up a litle while & she sleeps in her chair while she is up. She ate a good hearty supper but she is very stupid. Emmy Allen commenced work for Alvah Monday the 21 of July.

Wednesday, July 23   This is a clowdy & misty morning & looks very much like rain. It has rained considerable in the night. It will be no hay day this. William is away up home. Thinks he will find something to do. I did think he would stay at home today & let me get out once more at the end of five weeks but I see my chance is slim for the present. I may as well be reconcild to my fate. I live on anticipation the rest of this summer. It is an old saying that it is a long rhode that never turns. I think thare will be a crack in the lane before many months. Wm did find something to do. He & Alvah went over to the old farm & fixt the barn for the hayfork. Ate dinner with me.   Thare was an awful thunder shower this afternoon.

Thursday, July 24   It is pleasant this morning but it is quite cool. It bids fair for a good hay day. William is away up to Alvah's to work in the hayfield. Mother did not set up any yesterday.   H. Gardner & family & Nin & Charley Hails [Haile?] family are here spending a couple of weeks over to Trout Lake. Since I wrote the above, I have got news that

Martha Gardner is brought from the lake this afternoon on a bed by six men. She was taken very sick. They started to bring her home [but] sent for the Dr & he met them beyond Ed Noble's. He said she could not live but a short time. She died in five minutes after they got her in the house. I went over to see her. They have got her laid out at three o'clock. I cald at the Doctor's a moment.

Friday, July 25   It is a nice cool morning. William is away up to Alvah's. He thinks they will finish the haying today. He took two bags full of corn from here to the mill this morning. Mother is eating her breakfast in bed at eight. She did not set up any yesterday. Sister Em Hall cald here last evening. Lill stayed here with mother while I was out yesterday. Hiram Hall has quit working for Burlingame. Watson Hitchcock's family started for Colorado yesterday. He went last winter with Harriet Pratt, his sister. Laura Allen made me a call this afternoon. Brot her baby. Prety soon Lill came with Willie. Mother has not been up today.

Saturday, July 26   It is clowdy & looks like rain. Wm has gone to Alvah's to try & get in the hay. It raind yesterday so they could not finish. Brother Rob has been haying over on the old farm yesterday. Martha Gardner was beried [buried] this afternoon. Mr. Whipple Preaced the funeral sermon. I attended the funeral.   Lill Gorden stayed with Mother. Martha came home with me. Charley & the children came in the evening. Sherman stayed with me all night. William & the boys finished their haying up home today. Agnes Brown came home with me & stayed all night. Mrs. Graham Watson & Mrs. Albert White made me a call today.

Sunday, July 27   It is warm & cloudy & a little misty this morning.   Agnes Brown & I went to church today. Wm stayed with his Mother. Elder Dyke Preaced today. Martha & the children came here after meting. Charley went to the Lake today. Emah [Emma] Noble & Josephine cald here this afternoon. Mother has been up all day. It has all cleared of[f] this afternoon. Has not raind any to speak of. It is very hot this afternoon. Sherman is away up to his Grandpa Cleland's today. Alvah & Sarah went up to Cyrus Cleland's today & Sherman went home with them.

Monday, July 28   This is a beautiful morning. Wm & Alvah & Charley & Hugh Pratt & John Allen went down on the old Brown farm to commence haying today. I sent their dinner to them & they came here for their supper at dark. Emmah [Emmorancy Johnson Hall] Hall has come to help me this week while the men are haying. Thare is shows at the hotell tonight. The Edwards band played for them this evening. I bought six lbs of beries today. Paid seven cents a pound. Mother did not sit up any today. She sat up most all day yesterday. Sister Phila Harmon is very sick today. Emmah [Emmorancy] Hall went up thare today.

Tuesday, July 29   One more clear & pleasant morning. Wm & the men are all away down on the old farm haying. Wm comes home & caries their dinner to them. They eat supper here with me. It has been a beautiful hay day. Thare is shows over in town tonight. The Band is playing for them. I have finished Clarence's stocking & a pair for Sherman today. I have started a pair for Bower Brown. Mother has been up most all day. I have give her room a thorough cleaning today & caried her beds out & gave them a good airing. I got a card from Mariah Bunnell tonight.

Wednesday, July 30   This is a pleasant morning. William & the men are away over on the old farm haying today. Wm came home for their dinner at eleven. Emmy Hall went over home a little while this afternoon. We churned this morning. I sent Emmah Hall for three lbs of crakers. I sent the money to Pay for them. She got them to H. Gardner's.

Thursday, July 31   It is a beautiful morning. William & the men are all away down on the old farm haying. Brother Rob finished his haying down thare [there] last night. Today, Billy Rice has gone thare to do a job of haying. Mrs. Scot [t] from Fine brot me six lbs of beries today. I paid 50 cents. Amelia McKee & Emma Hall cald on us this afternoon. I went out to the end of the lane with Em. Em Allen left Alvah's today & went home in the stage. Laura McGill went to Alvah's tonight to work for them. This makes five diferent girls they have had to work for them this summer.

Friday, August 1   One more pleasant morning. It is getting very dry. We would be glad of a shower. It would do good. Preacher Hitchcock has sold his house & lot for 500 hundred dollars to Mr. Cole. Ann Noble & Ellen Cleland is away up to Charley Brown's today for a visit. Sherman was six years old yesterday. Six years ago today David Laidlaw was beried. We are having very hot wether every day this last week, cool nights. Wm & the boys have finished haying today. Put in fifty two large loads of hay in the barn over on the old farm in five days.

Saturday, August 2   This is a pleasant morning. William is stay at home today & Emmy Hall is hear to do the work. I went to Brother Warren Johnson's today for the first time in fourteen months. Went up on the milk wagons. Warren brot me home in the Buggy. I found Josephine Wite & Nera Hall here with Emmy. The Band played this evening. Mother sat up most all day. She was quite daft tonight. It looks some like rain. We hope it will rain all night. The ground is very dry. Robert Brown put in thirty loads of hay in the Barn down on the old farm. Billy, ten loads of hay.

Sunday, August 3   No rain last night. Very drying wind today. I started to go to Sister Hall's but heard she was not at home so I cald at Mrs. McCargin's a few moments then I came home. Now Wm has gone with Rob Allen to drive a cow to the pasture down on the old farm. Alvah & Sarah has gone out to Tom Grant's today. Sherman stayed with me last night. He has gone up to his grandpa Cleland's today on the milk wagon.

Monday, August 4   One more warm dry morning. No rain yet. William & Alvah has gone to take some shingles over to the old farm on the milk wagon to patch the roofs of the barn. I have done my washing this forenoon. I sent a letter to Mariah Bunnell today. Mr. Woolever has begun his harvesting today. I saw the new reaper go up the lane this morning. The wind is blowing hard & dry this afternoon & the air is full of smoke. We have had new cucumbers for three days. We had new Potatoes for the first time last night for supper. Wm worked until dark tonight. Wm boght 2 lbs of tea today.

Tuesday, August 5   This is a nice cool morning but no rain yet. William is away over to the old farm at work on the barn. Alvah & Sherman & Bower Brown cald here this morning. I let Alvah have a plate full of buter.   Aunt Liza Whitehead gave us a call this morning. Brother Robert sent me a little pail of beries [berries] this morning. Wm got a letter from Hannah Brown this morning. Mary has got a little boy, two weeks old. Graham Watson & family started for home today. Harry Winslow caried them to Gouverneur to take the cars for Coopersville.

Wednesday, August 6   One more dry & dusty morning. The people all wishing for rain but no rain for two weeks today. William is staying at home with his Mother today. I have been up home all day at Charley's in the forenoon & Alvah's in the afternoon. Charley had gone to Ogdensburg & Emmy Noble had gone to Gouverneur with her father. I rode home in the stage as far as the Bridge. They had up some planks. Mag

Noble & I came home on foot the rest of the way.

Thursday, August 7   This is a nice cool, dry morning. No rain yet. William has gone with Alvah to get some blackberies. Mother has got up before noon today. Mrs. McCargin made us a call this forenoon. I have done my ironing this forenoon. I had string beans for dinner. Wm came home at six this afternoon with five quarts of black beries. [He] went away beyond Fullerville [NY].   I have just emptied a bag of flour that Alvah brot down the other day.

Friday, August 8   It looks like rain this morning. Thare is a picnic party at Trout Lake today. The Edwards Brass Band is to be in Attendance. The People was all on the start at nine o'clock. It commenced to thunder & rain. Some went & some turnd & came back. Others waited until the shower was over & then went & they say they had a good time. Had a dance at the hotell at the Lake. Sarah came here & stayed with me. This is the last day of the school up to Charley's. Wm has had the headache all day but he went up & helped Alvah milk.

Saturday, August 9   A beautiful morning after the little bit of a shower Friday. Alvah & William & all of Charley's folks has gone after hucle berries today. Clarence stayed with me all day & night. Wm got home at six, got seven quarts of beries. It has been a very cool day. I had some new corn for supper for the first of this summer. It was plenty large enough to boil. While I was picking the corn, in the farther corner of the garden, Clarence thought he would get a handful of cheries but Corneel came out & drove him away. Would not let him have one. She showed herself a perfect hog. Thare is a circus show today at Gouverneur. Lots have gone from here.

Sunday, August 10   This is a nice cool morning but very dry. I have been to church this forenoon. Mr. Whipple spoke to the

People. Edward Brown made us a call this afternoon. Took supper with us. He came from Gouverneur last night. He says his Mother was maried to a Mr. Cole last May. Alvah has gone to Hermon today after Pet Hunt to come & work for them. Sarah & Sherman is up to Cy [rus] Cleland's today. Wm is away to Alvah's to help milk tonight. Pet did not come with Alvah. She was not well enough to work.

Monday, August 11   One more dry day & cool morning. Everything is sufering for the want of rain. A sale of cheese went to the Junction [DeKalb Junction, NY] for shiping [shipping] today from our factory.   Alvah & Charley & George Davis went after blackberies [blackberries] today out on Russell turnpike near Tom Grant's. Got home at five. Wm has been drawing stove wood today from Alvah's and put it in our woodhouse here at Mother's. Since supper, he has gone over to the old farm house to get Mr. Austin to come & cradle his wheat. I have done my washing this forenoon & baking this afternoon. Mother got up at noon today.

Tuesday, August 12   A nice cool morning. No rain yet. Wm is away up to Alvah's to help get the reaper ready for reaping the oats. Hugh Pratt come here this morning at eight to cradle our wheat. He got it done at ten o'clock & has gone back up to Alvah's. Wm found the cattle has been in the grain last night down on the old farm. He had the fence to fix so he did not get home until long after dark. Laura McGill is working at Alvah's this week.

Wednesday, August 13   A very dry & dusty morning. No rain yet. Wm is away up to Alvah's to help with the oats. He Bound in the forenoon & set up oats in the afternoon over 1500 bundles. As soon as after supper he went down to the old farm & fixt fence until after dark. John Allen came tonight after his pay for working in haying. Wm paid him all up. It looks like a awful shower just after dark tonight but

58

thare is lots of wind not much rain. I have churned this morning. The buter was nice & hard.

Thursday, August 14   This morning it is clowdy, looks like rain. Thare was a little rain in the night & a little dash this morning. Wm is away up to Alvah's to help with the harvesting. Sherman is here with me today. Stayed all night. Had quite a shower at four this afternoon & a cold night after the rain. Mariah [Merrill] Johnson came down on their milk wagon this morning to make Mrs. McCargin a visit. She stayed with Mrs. Mc all night. Rob Allen will get a cow of John McKee tomorrow.

Friday, August 15   This is a cool & pleasant morning. We are glad to have a fire this forenoon. Brother Warren [Johnson] cald here this morning to see if Mariah was here but she was not & she had not been here so he had to go home without her. William is away up to Alvah's to help with the harvesting. Sherman has gone home with his uncle Cyrus this morning. Mother has not been up much for two days. She got up at four this afternoon. Sat up until nine o'clock. I went over to Mrs. Mc's at dark tonight. Stayed one hour. It was very dark when I came home. We got a letter from Susa Brown tonight.

Saturday, August 16   It is clowdy & looks like rain & very cool. Wm has gone up to Alvah's to bind & set up oats. At half past nine it began to rain. Susa wrote that her Mother is no better, not able to be up long enough to have her bed made. Sherman stayed with me last night & he has gone home with his uncle Cyrus [Cleland] this morning. Cora Noble is quite sick, has been for two days. Lill Gorden has gone to help Mag take care of her. Mag was intending to start for Kansas in a week. It is now five at night & it has been raining hard all of the time since half past nine this morning. This is the last day of this school. It is just out now at five o'clock.

Sunday, August 17   It is raining this morning & has raind all night. It has rained all day today. It is now six o'clock. It is just coming rite down. I have been over to Alfred Hall's today. Took dinner with them. Came home with Charley Johnson. He was at Alfred's to try & get some money of Alfred. William has stayed at home all day today. He has got the headache. Mother has not been up much today. She eats her meals good as ever but she eats liing in bed. The teacher of our school in this village has gone home today. Her brother came after her today. I wrote a letter to Susan M. Brown yesterday.

Monday, August 18   It is clowdy & cool this morning. William thinks he will find something to do up home so he has gone up on the milk wagon. It has not been a very good harvest day. Has not raind any today. I have done my washing this forenoon & churned this afternoon & cand some Blackberies [blackberries]. Mrs. Scot sold me three quarts today. Wm has just got home. He has not been harvesting today. He has been after the Hop Press up to the Pond Settlement with Charley. Mother has been up all the afternoon. I sent a letter to Susa Brown today.

Tuesday, August 19   It has cleard of [off] quite nice this forenoon. William has gone over [to] the old farm to notify Mr. Austin to leave the house but he did not find him at home so he had to go to Jack Noble's. He found him thare so then he came home to dinner & has gone up to Alvah's to band grain. He got a line from Fred Haile last night saying he would take the hops at five cents. I sent a line to Sarah today. Sherman stayed with me last night. He has gone up to his Grandpa Cleland's today. Wm brot me a panful of crab aples from Charley's last night.

Wednesday, August 20   This is a beautiful & lovely morning. The sky is clear as a bell. Bids fair for a good harvest day.

William and Mr. Gorden has gone up to help Alvah bind grain. Gorden ate his breakfast with us. Alvah sent me 25 lbs of sugar by Charley this morning. Thare was five little cakes. Mother has got up at nine this morning. Early for her. I cald over to Gorden's about a half hour last night. Left Mother in bed. When I got back, she had got up & pild her bedclothes all on the floor & was standing on them. She was rather daft & is today. Padget is puting a new roof on Gardner's house today.

Thursday, August 21   It is clowdy this morning. Looks some like rain. Wm is away up to help Alvah with the harvesting. He thinks they will get it all bound today. They have got eight thousand Bundles of oats & fifteen hundred of wheat & we have got 180 bundles of wheat here to take up thare. We put in a hard night last night. Mother was crazy all night. Did not sleep any until five this morning. She got up two diferent times & took everything of her bed, even the fether bed & piled the cloths up & set on them. I made her bed twice in the night & got her into it. The last time, she went to sleep. It is awful the way she takes on. Crazy all day yesterday. Sister Hall [Emmorancy] cald here a while last night. Took tea with me.

Friday, August 22   It has rained through the night but it is pleasant today. Wm & Alvah got the grain all bound & sat up & took the load of wheat from here yesterday up home & put it in Alvah's barn. Wm is away to help Charley today. Charley went to Canton yesterday. [she crossed out several lines concerning the birth of a baby, and said, "The Above is all a mistake, what I have marked out."] Mother is up early this morning. Up all the afternoon yesterday. Mrs. Gorden got 3 lbs of butter of me 21.

Saturday, August 23   It has been a rough windy night. Thundered & lightned some but no rain here & it has cleared of today & has been a good harvest day. Wm is away up to help Alvah draw in grain. Charley is harvesting down on the old Brown farm. We put in one more bad night with Mother. She did not sleep any, was just tareing [tearing] at her bed all night. She took her pillows & started for down cellar. Wm got hold of her & brot her back to her bed. She has fell down six times today & we have had to lift her up. She would not help herself one bit. Mrs. Raymond made us a call this afternoon. She helped me lift Graney [Granny] of the floor once & Lill helped me three times & I got her up alone twice. I Churned today.

Sunday, August 24   This is a nice pleasant morning. No rain today. William has gone over to the old farm to look after things & drive the sheep out of the corn. I had to stay at home with Mother. Could not go to meting. Agnes Brown came down on the milk wagon this morning & went to church. Then came here & stayed till night. Isaac Brown came here to see his mother. Has been gone fourteen years in Michigan. He went home with Agnes to night. Wm cald in the Dr to see Mother today & he came again tonight. Perce & Robby came to see Mother tonight & Charley & Martha & the children came here this evening.

Monday, August 25   This is a beautiful & cool morning. Wm is away up to help Alvah to draw in grain. They drew in nine load[s] last Saturday. Wm has let the cow into the front meadow today. Mother is not able to sit up much today. She has got up this afternoon. Has stayed up until nine. She has fell on the floor twice this afternoon. Isaac Brown came back here today noon. Stayed the afternoon & all night. Wm got home at dark. He took a letter to the office for [on behalf of] Isaac to be sent to his children at Mich [igan]. I have done my washing this forenoon & got dinner & then done some baking this afternoon. Mrs. Tom Noble made us a call this afternoon. Padget is shingling Nin Gardner's house.

Tuesday, August 26   This is a lovely morning but quite cool. William has gone up to help Alvah to draw in grain. Isaac went with him.   Sherman went with his uncle Cyrus this morning. It is most three & Mother has not got up yet. She falls down every times she tries to walk. I have been mopping four rooms this forenoon & have been baking this afternoon. Charley Noble was made acquainted with a 12 lb boy last Saturday. They say it looks like Charley. Perhaps they will call it young Charley Noble. The Minister's son is shingling Nin Gardner's barn. Willie Brown called here today & brot a cake of sugar for Isaac to take home [to Michigan] with him.

Wednesday, August 27   One more pleasant morning. William has gone up to Alvah's. Isaac stayed here last night & Agnes Brown came here today. Hattie Padget commenced work for Alvah Monday the 25. She is a good girl & I hope they will like her. One more sale of cheese. It was carried away on Monday of the week 25th. I have washed ten quilts this spring & summer.   Emmy Hughs was maried last Saturday the 23. The Dr thinks Mother has had a slight shock of Palsy last Saturday. He was here to see her on Sunday. Isaac stayed here tonight & Agnes Brown.   I went to the Gardner's last night. Bought two lbs of crackers, 2 balls of cotton, one dosen of cookes [cookies] for which I paid 40 cents.

Thursday, August 28   This is a nice morning. Isaac & Agnes Brown is here with us & Clarence stayed with me all night. Charley & Martha & the children & Mrs. Kingsbury & Emma Hall was here last evening to make us a call. Mr. Absalem & his wife & Alvah & Sarah & Isaac Brown was here today to make us a visit. Took dinner with us. Jim Grant came here today & payed a note of hired   [meaning, loaned] money. Mother is crazy all of the time. Wm is up to Charley's to help Press the Hops. I cald [called] at Dr. Goodnough's & Charley

Haile's yesterday.

Friday, August 29   It rained in the night but it is pleasant today, & warm. William is up to Charley's to help Press the Hops. Mother has slep [slept] this forenoon. She has ate a hearty dinner. She wet the bed. I have had every dud to put on clean on her & the bed. I have done my Ironing & cand some Plums today. I have eight quarts of cand Plums. Mrs. Hariet [probably Harriet] McKee & her little girl made me a visit this afternoon. Wm got home at dark. He finished the hops. They intend to go to Gouverneur tomorrow with the Hops. They have sold them to Fred Haile for five cents a pound.   Graney [Granny] stayed in bed until five this afternoon. Em [Emmorancy Hall] sent me two lbs of roots today.

Saturday, August 30   This is a beautiful but cool morning. A very heavy dew. Wm was up at four & started for Gouverneur with Charley to cary the Hops. Alvah & Sarah went out to Tom Grant's yesterday for a visit. Sherman stays with me every night & goes up to Cyrus Cleland's most every day. Granny has got up at four this afternoon. She has not been able to walk any without help for one week today. We got a letter from Susa Brown last night. Ad is not any better. I have churnd today. Ed Noble is taking away Mag's stuff.   She breaks up today, intends to start next week for Kansas. Goes to Sandy's tonight.

Sunday, August 31   One more beautiful morning. I have been up to Alvah's & Charley's this morn. Came home when Charley's folks came to meting. Brot down a lot of old sugar. Robert & Isaac & Agnes [Brown] came here this afternoon. Took dinner with us. Charley's folks cald here after meting. I made a call on John McFerran's folks. Just night a little while. Mrs. McFerran is sick. Mother is crazy tonight. [note: Nancy Brown crossed the following four sentences out: She is as crazy as the very devil. She wants Wm to sleep with her. Is awful mad because he won't do it. She tore her bed all to peaces but got to sleep after a long time.]

Monday, September 1   This is a nice morning. Isaac [Brown] stayed with us last night. He stayed to dinner [and] then he went up to Robert's. Then he and Agnes Brown went down to Perce's tonight to start for home in the morning. Agnes is going with him to Canada to make a visit. Mrs. McCargin made us a visit this afternoon. Mag Noble started for Kansas today. Good by to Mag. Wm has made fence around the Potatoes today to keep the cow out of them. Clarence has stayed with me all day. Will stay all night. Looks like rain. Is very warm.

Tuesday, September 2   No rain yet. It is very dry. A little cooler this morning. Wm is making a tub to put in the well to make the well deeper. The water is nearly gone out. Mother is up early this morning. She was not so bad last night but I have had brot all her cloths to put on clean & all the cloths on her bed & so I did the same yesterday noon. Isaac & Agnes has started today for Michigan. Mother has been crazy all this afternoon. She has been up all day. Alvah and Wm has been working at the well all this afternoon.

Wednesday, September 3   It is very warm this morning. No rain yet. Alvah stayed awhile this morning when he came with the milk & helped his father finish cleaning out the well & then Wm went home with him to help burn a peace of brush. I have churnd this morning. Charley & Martha & Mable has started for Michigan this morning. George Davis & Mariah Noble has gone with them to Gouverneur to the fair today. Mrs. McCargin cald on us today. Wm came home tonight back as a Negro after loging [logging] up to Alvah's.

Thursday, September 4   It is raining some today. It raind in the night. The wind blows hard & has all night. Wm is away up to Alvah's to work at something, most anything to get away from here & make me stay alone with his crazy old Mother. I am as mad as my skin can hold. I have been melting old sugar this morning making pickles. William Noys cald here today noon to let us know that he had served a supreme writ on Perce Brown last night. Hugh Pratt & Emmy Noble is away to the fair today. Alvah & Sarah is up to Cy Cleland's for a visit.

Friday, September 5   It is cold & clowdy today. William has put the Pump in the well this morning. Mr. Payn came here and payed the interest on a four hundred Dollar note today. Mother has not been up much for two days. I cald on Mrs. Kingsbury last evening. Wm is cuting [cutting] his corn this afternoon. This is the last day of the Gouverneur fair. It was put over on account of the rain yesterday.   Wm has gone over on the old farm to see to the colts & cary them salt. Did not get back until dark.   He went away at four o'clock this afternoon.

Saturday, September 6   This is a nice cool morning. No frost as was expected last night.   William is spliting wood at the door this forenoon & this afternoon he is filling it in the woodhouse.   I have been ironing & mopping & baking & washing some things for Mother. I have washed nine shirts & nine night dresses & ten sheets & three bed quilts this week for Mother Brown besides all the other washing & ironing. William got a letter from his neace Theresa Brown the other day. She wrote the letter last Monday. They sent a basket of grapes, started them that day.

Sunday, September 7   This is a pleasant morning but rather cool. I did not go to church today. The Quarterly meting is at Fine today so I went over to Alfred Hall's & stayed to dinner. Then Emmy came home with me & we both went to the evening meting. The Presiding Elder Preached. It was terible dark when I cam home at half past nine. Found Sherman crying with the toothache. I soon got him quiet. Mother sat up all afternoon.

Monday, September 8   It looks like rain today. William went to York this forenoon. He drew wood this afternoon from Alvah's & put it in the woodhouse here. The Basket of grapes came tonight that Isaac sent from Michigan. They are splendid. I sent some up to Alvah's & Charley's children. George got a letter from Charley tonight. They was safe in Michigan. We got a letter from Agnes Brown tonight to let us know that she & Isaac had got home all safe & found them all well. I have done a large washing today & spun a scain of yarn ten nots. [knots]

Tuesday, September 9   It is clowdy & rains some this morning. It raind hard last evening. William is drawing stove wood from Alvah's today with Charley's teem. Mother did not sit up any yesterday. The Ogdensburg fair begins today. Mrs. Jim Rushton went yesterday. She will be sure to be on hand early this morning. Jim Rushton boards at the hotell this week while his wife is gone to the fair & Noris goes to Russell for a visit this week.

Wednesday, September 10   This is a beautiful day but rather cool. Thare has been a Sunday School Picnic today. They met at the church & marched after the Band up to Tommy Tods grove thare. Had dinner & a good time for the children. I went over with them but did not stay long. I had to come home & let Wm go to the fair at Ogdensburg. He started this afternoon. There is a theatrical performance here at the hotell tonight. Ruby Hepenstoll made me a call this evening. Mother has set up all of the afternoon. She tried to get out of doors but fell down in the doorway. George Padget cam along & he helped me get her up.

Thursday, September 11   This is a cold, pleasant morning. Some frost. Sister Hall stayed with me last night. Went home soon after breakfast. Jean & Emmy Herington cald here last night to leave a letter for me from Wm. They was going to the theater. Sixteen loads of cheese went to the [station] today from our factory. Sold for six & a quarter cents a pound. I sent a basket of eatibles to Mariah Bunnell by Wm yesterday when he went to the fair. I have done a large ironing today.

Friday, September 12   One more very pleasant but cool morning. No frost. William got home last night from the fair at eleven o'clock. The theater performance continued last evening. The Edwards Band played for them both evenings. William has been drawing of Percival's acount to send it to Judge Neary. He got a card from Neary this morning. Wm is trying to settle with Perce on the book acount between Perce & his father that has been running for the last thirteen years. I cald on Mrs. Gorden & Millie McKee this afternoon. Gone from home two hours. Wm is out in the village to night making calls.

Saturday, September 13   This is a most lovely morning, cool & pleasant. I have worked very hard today. Have done a large washing this forenoon. Churnd & baked aple Pies & cake & biscuit for supper. Had company to dinner & supper. Eugene Herington & Emmy & her little girl & George Johnson & William Green was here today to make us a visit. Thare is a caucus over in town this afternoon. A great gathering of townsmen. They say it is more like a town meting. William has been out in the village all day, only come home to his meals. I have got such a lame back tonight I can scarsely [scarcely] walk.

Sunday, September 14   It is raining this morning & quite cool. It has raind all day, is raining tonight. I have wrote a letter to send to Brother Joe's folks. Wm has been writing most all day. He has got his acount all wrote out & caried it over to Henry Rushton for him to take it to Judge Neary tomorrow. I cald over to the factory this morning. Stayed one hour with Ruby. We got a letter from Charley & Martha last night. They was well & having a good time. Sarah McFerran cald on us today. Mother has not been up much since Wednesday.

Monday, September 15   It is clear & pleasant today. William is drawing stove wood from Alvah's today. Hiram Hall is spliting wood at the door & pilling wood in the woodhouse. Clarence & Bower is here today. I have done my washing this forenoon & baking this afternoon. I have done quite a large ironing this evening. The cloths that I washed on Saturday. Wm gave me a terible daming to night for loosing his pen. Corneel gave Norris two whipings today. She pounded him fearful the last time. It was most night but it is no uncommon event.

Tuesday, September 16   This morning is quite windy. Looks some like rain today. Wm is away up after more wood & he caried up Alvah's window blinds & hung them this morning. I have been making jell this afternoon. Wm brought me a pailful of crab aples from Charley's yesterday & he brought me one pailful last week one day. I have had a general time of sweeping all over in every room in the house. I cald in to Mrs. Gorden's a litle while this evening.

Wednesday, September 17   It is pleasant this morning. For one hour thare was a hard shower last night just before dark & a thunder shower a litle before daylight this morning. The wind blows hard. A hard shower between seven & eight this morning. William has gone up to Alvah's to work on the rhode. Mother is crazy again today. I have done a large ironing & some baking between running at Mother's calls. She has took on terible all day. Wm went down to the old

69

farm tonight to see if the catle is in the meadow & Mrs. Gorden came & stayed with me.

Thursday, September 18   It is clowdy & rains a little. William has gone to mend a gate down by Ed Noble's. Caried a load of boards on his shoulders. Mr. Erwin, the mason, came here this morning & borowed some trowels.   He is Plastering Mr. Burdick's house. Mother had a very bad night last night until three o'clock this morning then she went to sleep & is sleeping yet. It is now after nine. This is the last day of the Canton [NY] fair. I sent a letter to Charley this morning to Coopersville, Michigan. Sister Phila [Harmon] is very sick.

Friday, September 19   Mother is crazy again today.   It commenced on her before daylight. She is taking on [fearfully] all day.   It is a beautiful morning.   It was a rainy day [yesterday]. William bought me a pound of tea & and a can of kerosene oil last evening. Wm is up to Alvah's to get things ready to moove the dry house. [probably the hop house]

Saturday, September 20   A pleasant morning. William is up to Alvah's to work. They are mooving the hop house over to make a woodhouse for Alvah. Mother is some better today. Wm got a letter from Lona Brown last night. She was maried [married] the 3 of July to a Mr. Huffman [Hoffman] of Kansas. Lona went to Kansas one year ago last April with Birt's family. We have had quite a shower this afternoon at five o'clock. Alvah & Sarah has gone to Russell today to Davenports for a visit. Don't intend to come home until Sunday night.

Sunday, September 21   This is a beautiful morning. Quite a hard frost. This is Elder Dyke's day to preach. I went to go to Church today but the elder did not come. He was cald away to Fine to Preach a funeral sermon. So I cald at Albert Wite's a little while then I went over to Sister Hall's and stayed to dinner. Jenny Dumas & Emma J Hall cald here this afternoon after I came home. Mother has got up & is siting [sitting] up awhile & looking in her Bible for the first time in ten days. Wm dug out as soon as he got his dinner.

Monday, September 22   One more clear & pleasant morning. Some frost. William is away up home helping Alvah. He went last night over [to] the old farm to tell Austin that he must get his family out of the house this week. I have done a large washing this forenoon. Am baking cake & pies & buiskit [biscuit] this afternoon. Sarah McFerran made us a call last night. Hiram Hall commended work for Peck of Gouverneur today. His father caried him out thare yesterday. He gets 12 dollars a month. Mother wants to eat & drink all of the time today & something else.

Tuesday, September 23   It is clowdy & looks like rain. Alvah came over & drew in the corn this morning on the milk wagon. Now William has gone up home to help Alvah moove the Hop house. We have just got word that Lidia Ward died this morning at five o'clock. Sister Hall came here this afternoon. Took tea with me. She had been up to Mr. Ward's all night & she was thare when Mrs. Ward died. Emma D. Hall cald here a little while today. Wm & Sherman came home at dark tonight. Mother has been up all of the afternoon till bed time.

Wednesday, September 24   It is raining hard this morning until half past ten. William has just gone home with Alvah to help again on the house. Taking down the chimney today. Aunt Lizzie Whitehead came here to see Mother yesterday. She is an old Pest. I wish she would stay to home. I have attended Mrs. Ward's funeral this afternoon. Mr. Whiple Preached the sermon. The church was well fild with People. The midle seats was all ocupied with relatives of the diseased. I went to H. Gardner's & done some trading after the funeral. I paid five dollars for what I traded. Lillian Gorden stayed with Mother.

Thursday, September 25   This is a pleasant but cool & frosty morning. William is away up to help Alvah today. Alvah drove over here this morning. Brought us a bag of salt & some candles & I let him have some butter. Young Albert White & wife & children came to visit their father here in Edwards last Monday the 22 from Michigan. They all went to Fine last night to visit Frank Burdick & family. I have done my Ironing this forenoon & some baking. I bought a new gingam dress for myself yesterday. Mr. Carter took super [supper] with us tonight.

Friday, September 26   Thare is a hard frost this morning. It is quite cold all day but pleasant. William has gone up to help Alvah moove the building. Sarah McFerran made us a visit yesterday afternoon. Stayed to supper & then went to the Prayr meeting. Carter has gone to Canton today. I have to wash everyday for Mother. She makes fearful work with herself & bed & I has had to have clean cloths everyday for four weeks. I have churnd today. George Davis got a letter from Charley Brown last night from Mich. We got a letter from Susa Brown last night & Sid Whitford.

Saturday, September 27   It is pleasant this morning. No frost. William is away up to help Alvah as usual & I am diging away here alone. I have just got Mother's room cleaned out once more. I have cleaned four rooms today. Hers was the nastyest [nastiest] one of all. I am baking bread & Pies this afternoon. We got a letter from Margaret Phinney last night. She is in Ill [inois] with her daughter. This is Hattie's last day to Alvah's. They have got to look for another girl. They have had six diferent girls this summer. Alvah got some more butter from C.V. Harmon's tonight. This is the third time this summer.

Sunday, September 28   It is clowdy. Looks like rain this

morning. William is staying with his Mother today. I have been to church this forenoon. Mr. Frasure [Frasier] spoke to the People today & also this evening. Alvah & Sarah came here this afternoon to make us a call. They stayed to supper. Dave has sold the cheese for seven cents a pound. It goes to the station Tuesday if it don't rain. Sister Phila [Harmon, Nancy Brown's half sister] is some better. Emma Hall [Nancy's sister] went to see her today. She can sit up some today. I would like to go & see her. It is 17 months since I have been to her house.

Monday, September 29   It looks like rain today. Did not rain but a little yesterday. Wm is away up to help Alvah. I have done a large washing this forenoon. Mother makes me lots of work today. Bill Noyes came here a minute today. He said he had been up to Gades & served the papers on him that Wm put in to his hands last Saturday. Lilian Gorden is going to Alvah's tomorrow morning to work for them. Mother is crazy this afternoon & evening. Mrs. McCargin made us a call tonight.

Tuesday, September 30   It is clowdy & windy & looks like rain. William has gone up to help Alvah with the mooving of the hop house. Sherman stays here every night & goes home every day. George Davis got a card from Charley last night. They are yet in Coopersville, Mich. Mother is a litle better this morning. George Davis brought me two Pumpkins & two squashes from Charley's last night. Sister Hall made me a visit this afternoon. Stayed until evening. I went as far as Jim McKee's. We both cald thare awhile. Milly McKee cald here a while in the afternoon & Mrs. Grieves made us call.

Wednesday, October 1   It has raind a very little this forenoon. It is pleasant this afternoon. William has gone up to help Alvah to finish setting the building to its place. They have been nine days mooving the house. Mother was crazy all day yesterday & all night last night. She sat up all day until ten last evening. I have churnd today four lbs of butter. Chauncy Gibbons drove in here tonight with a load of apples. I bought a half bushel. Wm had just bought one bushel of Rob Webb. Frank Beech came & got the winless[?] and tub for cleaning out wells.

Thursday, October 2   This is a pleasant & warm morning. The Wether [weather] has been very warm all this week. William has gone up to Alvah's today as usual to work. Brother Robert Brown cald here this morning to see his Mother. He had not seen her for more than four weeks. She is failing every day. She can't sit up any for two days past. Hattie Padget & Josephine Noble cald here last evening. Mrs. Kingsbury was here this noon & she invited me to go over & eat dinner with her. So I shut up the house & went. They had a good dinner. Mother was asleep. Mila came in just as I came home after milk.

Friday, October 3   This is a soneshiny [sunshiny] day but terible windy day & it is warm weather. We got a letter from Charley & Martha last night from Coopersville. I sent a letter to Mary McKinney in Canada today. Wm got a letter from Juge [Judge] Neary last night. The Doctor came over to see Mother this morning. Little Mabel Cousins came with him. Mrs. John McFerran was sick last night. She had a little girl & it died & is beried today. Mr. Cole & his wife had a supreme rit [writ] served on them the 1 of October.

Saturday, October 4   A Pleasant day this. Wm is up to help Alvah. I have done a large washing & took care of Mother as usual. Received a few callers. Mrs. Henry Brown & Mrs. Hiram Hall & Mrs. Albert White cald here this afternoon & Mrs. Eri Knox came here this afternoon & stayed all night & Mrs. Noble & Mariah & the litle boys & George Davis came in the evening. Mrs. Gorden & Laury cald in the afternoon. I cleaned the wood up in the Parlor & the Piassa. I done a large days work.

Sunday, October 5 It is clowdy. Rained a little this morning. I got up t four & put the cloths on Mother & on her bed. Mrs. Knox & I went to church today. We cald at Jim Rushton's then Mrs. Knox went home with John Newton's folks to stay all night. Mrs. Charley Beech and Lillian Gorden & Laura Allen cald here awhile today. William is away over to the old farm to show young Austin whare he can chop some wood. Mr. Whiple Preached today. He let the audience know that he believed thare is a Devil going about like a roaring lion & here in Edwards to in this Pious Place.

Monday, October 6 This is a very foggy morning. The sone [sun] did not shine until [al]most eleven. Alvah & Sherman is here today helping Wm dig the potatoes. I am not washing today. I am baking & have lots of other work to do. Mother is quite bad today. She has not been up any since last Wednesday. Only long enough to have clean cloths put on & her bed made & that is twice a day. She does everything in bed. She will not tell us when she should get out & yuse the vesel. It is wash & clean every day but we do not think she will be with us many days. We shall be glad that we have done all that we can for her & we hope she will be happy when she meets dear father on the other shore.

Tuesday, October 7 It is a very warm day. William is away up to Alvah's to fix for the thrashing. He came home to dinner & got the tyers [tires] set on the mashine wagon. Mother is failing very fast today. I have been baking this forenoon & washing this afternoon. Mrs. Gorden stayed in with Mother. Mrs. Mc & Kate Griffin cald here awhile. Kate went for the Dr. He said Mother could not live through the night. William took down our bed & caried it upstairs. Sister Hall came over in the evening & Mrs. Gorden then stayed all night. Sat up with Mother.

Wednesday, October 8   This is a nice cool morning. Mother died at three o'clock this morning. William has been going about the Place over to Bill Noys & to the store & different Places. Mrs. White & Mrs. Conine & Mrs. Gorden & Mrs J. H. Rushton & Mrs. James Brown & Ellen Cleland & Mrs. Kingsbury has cald here today. Mrs. Bill McKee & Ann Noble. Sister Hall stayed with us till after dinner then went home. Sister Hall & Mrs. Gorden laid Mother out at three o'clock after she died. She was laid out splendid so Bill Noys said.

Thursday, October 9   This is a very warm day. We are very busy geting ready for Mother's funeral that will take place tomorrow. Emmy D. Hall is here helping me today. We are baking cake & cookies & pies & bread. William Grant & his wife stayed with us last night. We got a Dispatch from Brother Ed Brown that he can't come to the funeral of his Mother. Mrs. Albert White cald here today & Ruby Hepenstall cald on us & Sister Hall stayed with us till in the evening. Brother John Brown & Sister Elizabeth came here at eight this evening from Deer River.

Friday, October 10   This is William's birthday. He is 55 years old. This is a very hot day. Just like a summer day. This is the day for the funeral of our Mother. Noys came over at ten & put her remains in the casket. She has cept splendid. Has not turned a Particle. The friends met here at the house at one o'clock. Had singing by the quire & Prayr by the Reverend Mr. Whiple of this place. Walked over to the cemetery. Beried [buried] her before servis [service] at 2 o'clock. Thare was quite a large congregation. The text was in Lamentations, The Lord is my Portion. Mrs. Gorden & Lilian stayed here at the house. Had dinner ready when we got home. Alvah & Sarah stayed until night.

Saturday, October 11   It is not quite so hot today as it was yesterday. Wm is diging his potatoes today. John & Lizie stayed with us last night. They have gone down to Perce's today. Mrs. Gorden came here this forenoon & got six lbs of pork. James Noble & Ruby Hepenstall & Ann Noble stayed with us Thursday night. William & I went over to the grave yard this afternoon & caried the footstone for Mother's grave & set it. The grave is all finished of very good. Bob Allen done the work. John & Lizzie Brown cald here after they came from P. H. Brown's.[William's brother] Have gone to Robert's tonight.

Sunday, October 12   It is clowdy & looks some like rain. It is quite warm. I went to church this forenoon. Went home with Charley Harmon. It had been 16 months since I had been in Sister Phila's house. I stayed until [al]most night.   Came home with George Davis & Mariah & Clarence & Bower. They had been up to Ben Noble's. They left Gramma Noble at her house.   Bob Allen's mother came to Gorden's last Friday night from Canada.

Monday, October 13   It is quite cool this morning. The wind is north. It has been cold all day. William & Alvah has commenced to thrash today. Mrs. Gorden & I have done a large washing this forenoon. She went home after dinner. Then I took out & washed eight windows & put all back in then. Washed the dining room floor & kitchen. Mrs. Gorden & Bob Allen's Mother took dinner with me today. She came last Friday from Canada for a visit. We have got a letter from Lona Brown tonight from Kansas.

Tuesday, October 14   It is a Beautiful & sunshiny morning but rather cool. A hard frost this morning. William is up to help Alvah with the thrashing. I have been Ironing this forenoon & have plenty of cloths to keep me Ironing all day & have got churning to do. It is five o'clock & my Ironing and churning is done & all taken care of & have been out in the garden & got cabage & onions & beets & turnips. Have them washed & ready to cook for dinner tomorrow. Thare has not been any one but Mrs. Kingsbury in here today. Wm don't get home any night until dark. We got another letter from Leona Hoffman tonight from Kansas.

Wednesday, October 15 One more lovely day. William is up to Alvah's to help with the thrashing. I baked this forenoon & had an old fashion boiled dinner. Pork, cabage, beets, turnips, & potatoes. This afternoon I went out calling. First on Mrs. John McFerran, then over to the beringing [burying] ground, then to Albert Wites,[White's] then to Mrs. Gardner's store, then to Jenny Hall's then to Mrs. Gorden's. Then came home & milked my cow & fed the Pigs. Then ate my super & now it is after dark & Wm has not come yet. Thare is to be a republican lecture this evening at the hotell from a Mr. Swift.

Thursday, October 16   It is clowdy & smoky this morning. Very dry. It is twenty-one days since thare has been any rain of any account. Wm is up to Alvah's. They will finish the thrashing today. We went to the lecture last evening. Thare was a large crowd. Thare is to be a lecture in the church this evening by a Mr. Clark. I have colored some yarn red for Sherman some stockings. We got a letter from Susa M. Brown last night from Pine Valley. The Brass Band Played last evening in the hall.

Friday, October 17 It is very warm & smoky. Thare is fires in the woods in every direction. Payns [Payne's] Shugar [Sugar] tools, Buckets & Pan is all Burnt. The fire was set by some men that was hunting bees. I went home today on the milk wagon. Stayed to Alvah's in the forenoon & to Charley's in the afternoon.   Came down with Leo Rayment [Leverett Raymond] in the stage. It had been forty-four days since I had been up home. William & I went over to Mrs. McCargen's

[McCargin] this evening. Wm fixt [fixed] her clock. The Wind has blown fearful all day. Wm has finished husking his corn today.

Saturday, October 18   It is windy & clowdy & has raind a little this morning. Wm is diging [digging] his Potatoes today. Intends to finish them. It has raind most of the day but Wm finished diging his Potatoes this afternoon. Then he helped Alvah load up his cheese. It goes to Gouverneur next Monday. Mrs. Gorden & Angelia & all their little ones cald here awhile this afternoon. Had Gardner & Dave Noble set their wives gravestones yesterday afternoon.

Sunday, October 19   It is pleasant today but quite cold. The wind blows harde from the north. William went over to the old farm to salt the colts. I have been to church this forenoon. Elder Dyke Preached today.

Monday, October 20   It is a cool morning. Some frost, fogy all the forenoon. It has been very pleasant this afternoon. I have done a large washing this forenoon. This afternoon I have took up the carpet in the parlor & washed all the windows & the woodwork & the floor & the Piasa & baked Bread. William has been lolling round in the village all day. Alvah has gone with a load of cheese to Gouverneur today. Mrs. McCargin made me a call this afternoon. Alvah & Sherman came here tonight. Sherman will stay all night. The Band is Playing in the street tonight. Wm is over in the village tonight.

Tuesday, October 21   This is a lovely morning. The sky is clear & the great fountain of light is Pouring fourth it's beautiful rays on the Inhabitants of this Beautiful Earth. Sherman stayed with me last night. He has gone with his grandpa up home this morning. They have a Sugar Arch to build this week. I have done lots of work this afternoon. I went over to Gorden's & stitched a bedtick & a pair of Pillow ticks. Emtied two feather beds. Fild the feather ticks. Got them all soed up ready for use. William went up to call on Mrs. Eveline Grant yesterday afternoon to get some money on her note & Bond. Could get none nor no promise of Any. I churned today.

Wednesday, October 22   It is cool & clowdy. Looks like rain today. William has gone up to help Alvah Build his Arch. I am washing bedticks. Wm went to the Republican lecture last evening. I had to stay here with Sherman. I was much disapointed. The Band Played & thare was a Great turnout. Mr. Curtis of Odgensburg gave the lecture. Reuby [Ruby] Hapenstall made me a call this morning. Sherman has caried the milk straner [strainer] over to the tin shop to get a new strainer Put in. A letter came from Charley last night saying they would be home next Friday. We got a letter from Susan Brown tonight.

Thursday, October 23   It is awful windy & looks very much like a storm this morning. William has got a sick headache today. It is nine o'clock & he has not got up yet. Sherman has gone up home to let Alvah know that Wm can't go & help with the Arch today. I made a visit to sister Hall's yesterday afternoon. I done my Ironing & wash [ed] some bedticks yesterday forenoon. It did not rain any yesterday. Old Mr. Gardener Died today noon. He has been sick a long time. It is five o'clock. Wm is better. He is out, has gone over in the village. I have emtied one more feather Bed today & swep & moped [mopped] the Chambers.

Friday, October 24   It is snowing this morning. Before daylight we got up at half past four & William got ready & started for Gouverneur at six. He had to wrap up like he would in a cold winter day. He has gone after Charley's folks. They are getting home from thier visit from Michigan. It haild some last night. The ground is white with snow today. It is freezing quite hard. Ruby Hepenstall [Heptonstall] made me a call this forenoon. Stayed to dinner. She has gone to Berlingame's to. A rag sewing bee this afternoon. William got home at dark. Brought me some nice large Aples that was sent from the West by Charley.

Saturday, October 25   It is Pleasant but very cold this morning. It froze hard. Wm has gone up to help Alvah with the Arch. I am Baking Pumkins [Pumpkin] Pies this forenoon & cleaning upstairs & down, after William's seting up a stove in the dining room.   Thare was a little boy just cald here to leave a notice of a Printing Ofice just opened in this place next door to the Boot & Shoe Shop. Mr. Gardner is to be beried at one o'clock today. I have attended the funeral of Mr. Gardner this afternoon.   Sister Hall came home with me. Stayed in the evening.

Sunday, October 26   This is a cold morning but it is pleasant & sunny. This is Mr. Lee's day to Preach. Wm is away up to Wiley's today. Sherman & I am staying here today. I am [al]most sick with a cold. Mr. Whiple Preached the funeral Sermon of Mr. Gardner yesterday. Wm has wrote a letter to Wilber Allen. It starts tomorow. Emmy D. Hall & Ruby Hepenstall & Mrs. Gorden & Laura & Lilian & Angelia Gorden has cald here today. It has been a Lovely day & it is a beautiful evening. The moon is shining lovely & bright.

Monday, October 27   It is a pleasant day, not as cold as it was last week. William has gone up to help Alvah with his Arch. I have done my washing this forenoon & cleand a bedstead & done my mopping & have got to Bake Bread this afternoon. Sherman has gone up to his grandpa Cleland's today.   His uncle Alax [Alex] came down home with him tonight. Wm did not get home until after dark. Mrs. Kingsbury & Ruby made us a call this evening.

Tuesday, October 28   It is clowdy. Looks some like rain. This morning the ground is very dry. William is away up to help Alvah with the Arch. Mrs. Gorden made me a call this morning. George Ivers came to town last night. He has been gone to Ledville [Leadville] Colorado since last March. Ida came to her father's from Harisville [Harrisville] last week. She has been gone up thare [al] most three months. They are both stoping [stopping] at James Rushton's at Present. Melia McKee made me a call this morning. Forest McKee cald here this forenoon to say that he was going to take home John McKee's cattle from the Pasture down on the farm.

Wednesday, October 29   This is a lovely morning. Warm & pleasant for the season. Had a litle rain last night. Thare was a Democrat Lecture in the Hall last evening. The Band Played. Was a large atendance. The Speaker made lots of fun for the fun loving part of the audence but it was no sound lecture. Just a mess of funny storyes. William is away up to Alvah's to work on the Arch. Charley's folks was all here last evening before the entertainment. Mrs. Kingsbury & Ruby made me a call yesterday afternoon. I ate dinner with them yesterday.

Thursday, October 30   It has been a rather rough day. The wind has blown very hard all day & has raind some. William went up to finish his Arch & Sarah & I went out to Tom Grant's. Drove our own horse. Mrs. Grant is very sick. Has been since Monday. Dr. Murray is attending her. He was thare to see her today. We got home at dark. We cald at the store. Sarah got some calico for her Mother. James McKee & Milla was here this evening to make us a call. Wm has dug the Beets this afternoon.

Friday, October 31   It is a sunshiny today but it is terible cold. The wind blows hard & cold all day. William has dug his carots & beets & cabage & took them up home this afternoon. We kild the old rooster today & a Pot pye for dinner. Celia

Cleland is sick today. Sarah is up thare all day & Mrs. Padget. I have been doing some sewing for Sarah's Mother this afternoon & evening. It is after ten. I will go to bed. Wm & Sherman has gone to bed long ago. Warren Glasby is very sick.

Saturday, November 1   This has been a beautiful sunshiny day but cold & A strong wind. It has froze hard all day. It is a lovely evening. The wind has gone down. William has been up to help Alvah make a rhode [road] to the woods. I have done lots of work today. Am very tired tonight. We have had company this evening. Mr. Cole & family. It is eleven o'clock. We must go to bed.

Sunday, November 2   It has been A clowdy cold day. It is snowing now at five in the afternoon. William & I have been up to Charley's today. Charley & Martha & all the children came home with us with the horses & buggy. Alvah & Sarah went up to Cy[rus] Cleland's. Clarence & Sherman came with us to stay all night. Warren Glasby is some better. He has been very sick for four days.

Monday, November 3   The ground is all covered with snow this morning. It looks quite like winter. Wm has gone away some Place. I don't know whare he is today. Clarence & Sherman has gone home this afternoon. It is now four o'clock & it has snowed some all day. It is snowing & the wind is blowing quite hard now. It has thawed some. The water ran of [off] the house three pails full in the barrel but it is freezing now. Thare is a family moving in to the house whare Mag Noble moved out of the first of September. Celia Cleland was sick today. She had a Babe & it died. She has been sick a Week.

Tuesday, November 4   It froze hard last night. The snow is quite deep this morning. Robert's folks came down with a sled to election today. Rob & Stilman & Agnes & Willie Brown & Mr. Carter & Charley Brown was here to dinner. And Sherman & Wm & myself. Robert took his catle home today from the Pasture on the old farm. Old Mr. Carnel cald here for Mr. Carter this noon. It has been a beautiful day, clear & pleasant. The Brass Band Played A number of Peases [pieces] today noon at the hotell in the street.

Wednesday, November 5 It has been A very good day. Froze some all day in the shade. No snow nor rain. It is freezing quite hard this evening. William has been up to help Alvah all day. He wrote a letter to Mr. Huffman of Kansas & caried it to the PO to night. I have been fixing A Black Dress today & making a flanel shirt for Sherman this evening. It is after ten o'clock & I must go to Bed. Wm & Sherman has gone long ago. Mrs. Gorden & Angelia made me a call this Afternoon & litle Willie Allen. Wm made litle Maine [Manie] A Present of A silver dollar today to wear on her neck.

Thursday, November 6 It has been clowdy all day but no snow or rain. Has not thawed any. It snowed a litle in the night, some time before daylight. William brought home a Pair of Boots for a Present for Sherman last night & a little Box & a lot of Postage Stamps for me. William went up to help Alvah today. Gorden was here this morning to hire [rent] this house. Has not got the Promise of it yet. Angelia was here this afternoon. Alvah was here this forenoon with the teem [team] so Sherman went home with him but he came back here with his grandpa tonight. I have not been out to make a call since last Sunday.

Friday, November 7 It has been warmer today. It has thawed some & the snow is going of[f]. It was very Pleasant most of the day but it is blowing tonight & the wind is strong in the South & looks like rain. Wm has been up to help Alvah with his sugar house, did not get home till after dark. I cald over to

84

Mr. Kingsberies [Kingsbury] a few moments today. Ruby cald here A litle while this afternoon. This is my birthday. I am 54 years old.

Saturday, November 8   This has been a nice warm day. The snow is all gone. No rain yet. Wm has been up to help Alvah build a sugar shanty. Clarence & Bower has been down here all day. They have a good time here with Sherman. Sherman went home with them at four & came back here at dark. Granma [Grandma] Cleland made us a visit this afternoon. L. M. Gardener [Gardner] has sold his house & lot here in Edwards village to Henry King.

Sunday, November 9   It has been a nice warm day. It raind just a very litle. I went to church today. Wm stayd here. He had the sick headache this morning. Sherman has gone up to his grandpa Cleland's today. Mr. Whiple Preached today. It is clowdy & looks like rain tonight. At eight o'clock now the rain is pouring down right smartely [smartly]. Wm has just got in from a call at Wm Noyes.

Monday, November 10   It has been a nice warm day. William has been up helping Alvah get some logs cut & put in to the river. Wm came down the river on the logs tonight. I have done my washing today & have picked up Mother Brown's Bedcloths & other cloths & divided them as best I could.

Tuesday, November 11   It was clear & pleasant this morning. This afternoon it is raining. It looks like being a rainy night. William has been working in the saw mill today helping Jim saw some hemlock lumber for to cover the sugar shanty. I have done my Baking today & got my Dress most done. Sherman went home today but he came back about dark tonight. Mrs. Gorden & Leanra was here this afternoon. The rain has just poured right down this evening since dark.

Wednesday, November 12 It has been a nice warm day but about five tonight it began to rain. It has raind hard this evening. Elix Cleland came home with Sherman tonight. They got here just as the rain was coming rite down & the wind was blowing a nice gale. William has been up to work on his sugar house. Got home at dark. Robert Brown & Agnes was here today & took home some of Mother Brown's clothing & a set of chairs and a lounge & a stand. Laura Allen brought home a pair of mitens for Sherman that she had just knit for him.

Thursday, November 13 It has been clowdy all day but no rain. Wm has been up to work for Alvah all day. Ruby Hepenstall has been working for me today fixing my overskirt to my black Dress. Clarence has been down here to Play with Sherman. They both went up home at 3 o'clock. Alvah & Charley sold their buter today to John Cousins for 30 cents a Pound.

Friday, November 14 It was clear & Pleasant early this morning but at half past seven it has clowded up & raining a little. William has gone up to the Pond Setlement [Settlement] to Preys Hops for James Brown on the Thompson Place. Had Gardner was maried last evening in his own house to Miss Casady. Ruby has been here most of the day to finish of the work that she commenced yesterday. Mrs. Kingsbury made a call this afternoon. Wm got home [al]most 8 o'clock tonight.

Saturday, November 15 It was raining hard this morning. It held up about 2 hours in the forenoon & was quite pleasant. A litle afternoon it raind hard & at three it just come down in torents. It has raind most of the time until after dark. At ten the stars are shining. Alvah has just been here & got his horse & gone home. The Band has been Playing tonight. Wm has been up to work for Alvah today. Alvah & Sarah went up to Cy Cleland's this afternoon. Sherman came & stayed with me

[and] is staying all night. I have been at work on his coat all the evening. It is [al]most 11 o'clock.

Sunday, November 16   It was clear & Pleasant this morning but thare has been two or three short showers at diferent times to day. One litle hail storm. Did not last but a few moments. I went to church today. It was Dikes [Dyke's] day to Preach but he did not come so thare was no Preaching. After Sunday School, Charley & Martha & the children came over here & stayed untill after dinner. They have all gone home now. William has gone over to the old farm to salt the colts. Mrs. Gorden & Sister Hall made me a call tonight.

Monday, November 17   This has been a nice day. William is away up to the Pond Settlement to Prys Hops. He did not get home untill ten in the evening. I have done a large washing, took down a Bedstead & cleaned it & swep[t] the chambers & moped [mopped] them all & the kitchen. Ruby cald at noon & in the afternoon Mrs. Kingsbery [Kingsbury] came & stayed until four & then a call from Mrs. McCargin. So I did not get my work done until after dark. At ten o'clock it looks like a storm. The village school commenced today.

Tuesday, November 18   This morning the ground is all covered with snow. It has froze some & it is snowing quite fast now at eight. William has gone up home to get a large kettle to heat water in. He and Mr. Kingsbery intends to kill their Pork today if it does not storm to hard. The school up at Charley Brown's commenced yesterday. Miss Ada Fellows is the teacher. She boards at Charley's. Wm borowed a Pan of flour of Kingsbery today.

Wednesday, November 19   I is a very good day today. It was a stormy day yesterday & quite cold. Wm & Kingsbery kild their Hogs yesterday. James Rushton & Alvah Brown helped them. Wm has cut up his Pork today. Alvah & Sarah was here to dinner today. I have Baked Bread & tried out my lard today & lots of other work.

Thursday, November 20   This has been a very stormy day. It has snowed & Blowed fearful all day. The Wind north & is very cold. Wm has stayed in the house most of the day. He went to the store tonight & Bought a half bushel of large Aples for me to make my mince Pies. Alvah drew some hay for Dr. Goodnough today. Was here to dinner & took home a load of stalks from here. I have done my Ironing & mopping & lots of mending. Wm bought a half bushel of nice Apples for mince Pies.

Friday, November 21   This has been a very cold day. A stiff breeze from the North all day. The scy [sky] has been clear all day. William has been up to help the Boys kill their hogs today. Alvah Brought one of his down & sold it to John Cousins. Wm did not get home until dark. Stilman Brown cald here tonight on his way home from his school & took super with me. The minister & his wife made us a call this evening for the first time. They stayed until of most 10 o'clock. We had a good visit with them.

Saturday, November 22   This has been quite a cold day but not as cold as Friday. Wm went up to cut up & salt Alvah's pork. Charley brought down half of his & sold it today noon. Clarence & Bower came here with Charley & stayed with me until [al]most dark. Ruby Hepenstell came over & done some stitchen on the machine today. I made my Mince meat today & made a Pan of fried Cakes.

Sunday, November 23   When we got up this morning it was snowing, blowing fearfully. At 10 it was Pleasant. The sone shining then About noon it was snowing hard again. Now at one it is Pleasant. This is Mr. Lee's day to Preach. I am staying at home today. I made a call to Mr. Gorden's this evening. Thare was a terible wind & snow Just at dusk. Now at seven it is nice & pleasant. A Beautiful moonlight night.

Monday, November 24   This is a mild nice morning. We are up before daylight geting ready to move up home. It is now six in the evening & I am here all alone yet. Wm is away up home with a load of Potatoes. This has been a very buisy [busy] day for me. I have been Picking up & Packing things all day & doing some Baking. I am very tired tonight & yet thare is lots to do yet to be all ready to go in the morning. The Boys has took two loads of goods & one of wood & one of Potatoes & thare will be two loads more for tomorrow & then lots of wood & some corn & hay. It has been a Beautiful day. It is a lovely evening.

Tuesday, November 25   It snowed very hard for a while this morning. We are geting ready to go with the last load. William got a letter from Wilber Allen last night from Nebraska. I am all ready to start & am waiting for the Boys to come with the teem. It is 10 o'clock. At one we was ready to start, now at 2 we are at home, our old home on the farm. I have said goodbye to Father Brown's old home whare we have stayed one year & four months & I am glad to get home.

Wednesday, November 26   This is a beautiful morning. The sleighing is done for this time but it is splendid wheeling. This morning finds us in our own old home but evrything in our Part of the house in a mess & I am so tired I don't feel Able to fix up much but I shall have it all to do with a little of William's help. Wm went to the vilage last night & the boys spent the evening. I went in & stayed with Martha & the girls & the children. They all stay with me this evening.

Thursday, November 27   This is Thanksgiving Day. It is not as pleasant today. The wind blows hard all day. Cold in the morning but warmer at noon. Raind a little just night. It is thawing this evening. Wind strong in the south. Wm has gone to bed at seven tonight. Charles & family all went up to Benny Noble's for a Thanksgiving visit today. I have worked hard all day. Have not got things halfput right yet but I don't get much help.

Friday, November 28   It is warm & a very nice morning. Alvah & Charley are Plowing. Wm is doing the chors [chores] for Alvah. He dug a ditch in the afternoon. [Al]most night it began to rain. It raind terible in the evening. Charley finished his Plowing. I have worked hard all day trying to get things Put to their Place.

Saturday, November 29   It is colder today. The thaw is freezing up. It is snowing tonight right smart. Alvah has Plowed all day but did not finish. William done the choors [chores]. I worked hard all day. It is freezing hard this evening.

Sunday, November 30   This is a very cold morning. It froze hard last night. The sky has been clear all day but freezing cold. Charley & Martha & the children & I all went to church today. Mr. Whiple Preached. We stayed to the Saboth School. They decided to have a Christmass tree & gave notice for a donation for Mr. Whiple on Wednesday evening of this week at the hotell.   Alvah & Sarah took dinner with us this afternoon. Martha & the teacher cald on us this afternoon.

Monday, December 1   This has been a very windy day. It was cold in the forenoon but it thawed some this afternoon. Is clowdy this evening & looks like a storm. William went to Fine today up as far as Welches. Got home at seven this evening. Charley & Martha has been up to John McKee's all day today.   I have done a large washing today. Sherman stayes with me every night but one since we mooved back home.

Tuesday, December 2   This has been a nice mild day. It has raind a litle & snowed a very litle this afternoon. Alvah & Sarah went out to Tom Grant's today. Wm & Charley kild a pig & I made a visit to Alfred Hall's today. I have made a call in Charley's room this evening. Wm has done the choors for Alvah today.

Wednesday, December 3   This morning the ground was all covered with snow & it has snowed a litle all day & this evening. It is raining & freezing on so it is making sleighing. Thare is a donation Party at the Hotell tonight for Mr. Whiple. Alvah & family & Charley & his family have gone to the donation this evening. Wm & Sherman & I are staying at home this evenight. I have cut out a suit of cloths for Sherman today & made my saushage this afternoon. It is now 'most ten o'clock & it is raining hard.

Thursday, December 4   It has been a nice mild day & snowed a litle this morning. It has been clowdy all day. It raind most all night last night & froze on & made a hard ice crust on the snow. So it is quite good sleighing. Alvah drew us one load of wood from the village tonight. Wm has been sick all day with a sick headache. Has not sat up only while I was making his bed. I have made a pair of Pants today for Sherman. It is now ten & I must go to bed.

Friday, December 5 This is a lovely morning. The trees are all laden with ice & as the sun shines on them they look like crystall. The sleighing is splendid this forenoon. At noon the ice is falling from the trees. It has commenced to thaw but it has been a beautiful day. Wm & Alvah drew wood from the village today. Three loads. Charley went to Hermon with a horse & cutter after their show bills. Stilman Brown came here this evening from his school. Took super with us. Sarah & Pet came over this evening.

Saturday, December 6   It looks pleasant this morning but the wind has been blowing hard since midnight. It is thawing fast, the wind is just howling this evening & it is raining. The streets are all mud tonight. The Boys are down to the village preparing for their Entertainment that is to be next Thursday evening at the Hotell. John Laidlaw & Altha has been here today to make us a visit. Stilman stayed with us all night. Took breakfast with us. He has bought the old farm.

Sunday, December 7   It has been a windy day & it raind some this afternoon. I went to church today with Charley's family. Mr. Whiple Preached. I cald in to Mr. Gorden's a litle while. They has just got a letter from Joe's [Joseph Brown] folks. Ad is no better. I too dinner with Charley's folks today. Wm has been gone all day I don't know whar. I made a call at Alvah's tonight. It raind hard all last evening. The rhodes are very muddy today.

Monday, December 8   This has been a very nice day. Quite cool near night. Wm went with Wm Beech down on the old farm & got a load of hay. I have made a vest for Sherman today & cut out a red coat & helped Martha to make it for Charley. I did not go to bed untill after twelve. The sky is clear this evening & it is freezing quite hard.

Tuesday, December 9   This has been a lovely day. Not very cold. The sun has shone all day. I have commenced to make a coat for Sherman today. I have helped Sarah to make a red coat for Alvah to wear to their exhibition. William & Alvah has been skidding logs & doing the chours. Charley has been to the village a part of the day.

Wednesday, December 10   It has raind all day. Has been a very windy & stormy day. The wind has just howld. The mud is quite deep tonight. The boys has gone to the village to Practice for their entertainment for tomorrow evening. They will have a dark & muddy time. Sarah & Martha & I have been making red coats for the boys & I am making a suit of cloths for Sherman. It is a very buisy time with all of us.

Thursday, December 11   It is a litle colder this morning. The storm is over for the Present at all events. We all hope it is. It is clowdy most of the day. It is freezing a litle tonight. We are all getting ready to go to the entertainment tonight. It is dark as the old black man himself.

Friday, December 12   This has been a lovely day, rather cool but Pleasant. The ground has froze quite hard. We all went to the shoos [shows] last night. We had a good time. The entertainment was a success. They done it up brown. We caried a lantern to light us on the way down & we had a full load & a good time. Got home at 12. Thare was a full house in attendance. The Band took in 63 dollars. They had a dance after the exhibition. There is a new moon this morning. It is very pleasant tonight. Stilman Brown is staying with us tonight.

Saturday, December 13   This has been a cold day but Pleasant most of the time. A few litle squalls of snow. William went to the village with Stilman Brown this morning to get a contract drawn for the sale of the old farm. They came home to dinner then. Wm went home with Stilman to make a finishing up of the trade. It is now nine o'clock & he is not got home yet. Alvah's folks & Charley's have all been up to Cy Cleland's for a visit today. Alvah sent me a crock of butter today. 25 lbs.

Sunday, December 14   It is clowdy & looks like snow. I went to church today.   Dyke Preached. Charley's family went to Write Robinson's for a visit today. Alvah & Sarah went to John McKee's today. Wm got home from Brother Robert's [Brown] this afternoon. I cald at Sister Hall's after meting. It is snowing fast tonight. It has not been very cold today.

Monday, December 15   It has snowed most all day & it is snowing & the wind is blowing quite hard this evening. William & Alvah went to the woods & drew wood for the sugar arch this forenoon. This afternoon Wm plastered over the new door.   Robert Webb & his Boys came here this evening & payed the Interest on a couple notes that Wm holds against Webb.   Charley & Em Noble are away to the village tonight. Martha made a call over to Jim Harmon's today.

Tuesday, December 16   This has been a stormy day but not very cold. I have had company today. Mrs. Payn & Laureta Allen & Sister Hall. We had a good visit. Wm & Charley went to the village this afternoon to listen to a lawsuit but it was ajournd [adjourned].

Wednesday, December 17   It has been a nice day. It has been Pleasant most of the time. It is rather cool tonight, quite frosty & nice moon. Charley went to Gouverneur today with a load of Potatoes. He sold them for forty cents a Bushel. Got home at half past ten tonight. It is past 12 o'clock. Wm has just gone to bed. He has been writing a letter to Brother Jo [Joseph Brown] and I have just finished it. Alvah & Sarah has been out to Wm Grant's today for a visit. Wm has done all the choors for Alvah & Charley today. I had better go to bed.

Thursday, December 18   This has been the coldest day this winter & it is very cold tonight. Wm & the Boys have been doing their choors & churning & drawing stove wood from the village to our door. Sarah & Pet Hunt went to Had Gardner's for a visit this afternoon. Alvah took supper with us tonight. Sherman has stayed with me evry night but one since we came home. I have made a vest for Bower Brown today. It has snowed a litle today.

94

Friday, December 19   This has been a nice day. The sun has shone nicely. The Water ran of the house at noon quite fast & did until 3 o'clock. William & Charley drew 2 loads of hay from Father Brown's barn. Drew it here & put it in our Barn & Alvah finished drawing the stove wood. I have done my Ironing and mopping & cleaning up & Baking. Sarah came over this afternoon & done some stitching.

Saturday, December 20   This has been a stormy day. Snowed all day. Charley & Martha went up to the Pond Settlement. Charley took the cutter to Luke's [Van Ornum] & got new shoos [shoes] put on it. I went with them as far as Charley Harmon's.

Sunday, December 21   This was a very cold morning. The coldest of the season yet the sun is shining & looks very pleasant but it is fearful cold. Charley's folks stayed all night up to Ben Noble's & I stayed with Sister Phila [Viall Harmon]. We all got home at eleven today. This is Professor Lee's day to Preach. It is too cold to go to church today. The thermometer indicated 30 degrees below zero. Rob Wilson came here today to ask Em to go to a New Year dance.

Monday, December 22   This morning it was snowing & blowing at a fearful rate. The wind & storm has cept up all day but it turned a litle warmer in the afternoon. This evening it is nice & pleasant. William & the Boys kild & dresed a beef cow this afternoon. I made a call over to Alvah's this evening.

Tuesday, December 23   It was mild & a very nice morning. It has been a nice day all day. No storm of any kind. Wm & I went to John Laidlaw's today & made a good visit. Got home at ten in the evening. Charley went to Hermon this afternoon. Martha & Emmah went to John Cozen's [Cousin's] for a visit.

Wednesday, December 24   It has raind most all day today. It is snowing this evening at ten o'clock. Wm brought home flannel for Sherman two shirts & a Watch chain for a Preasant & a chain for Clarence & Bower & a nice earthen Box for Mable. Tomorrow is Christmass. Dan Noble beried one of their children today.

Thursday, December 25   This has been a cold day but no storm of any sort. This is Christmas day. Martha has got company today. Alvah & Sarah has gone up to Cy Cleland's for a visit. I am at home today. Stilman Brown & Pet Hunt took dinner with us today. I intend to go to the Christmass entertainment tonight.

Friday, December 26   This has been a very cold morning. We don't wish to have any colder wether this winter. John Absalan & his wife & Fanny came to Alvah's today for a visit. Wm & I was invited over to dinner. John & Family came to Charley's this afternoon & evening. Wm & I was invited in to take supper & visit with them. We all went to the Christmas last night. Had a good time but the air was fearful cold. Alma Pratt came home with Charley's folks to work for them.

Saturday, December 27   This has been a very cold day. A high cold wind all day & late in the evening. William has gone to Canton today. He caried Pet Hunt home from Alvah's. She has got through working thare for this term. Charley drew wood for the Preacher today Mr. Whiple.

Sunday, December 28   This is a very nice mild day. Great change in the weather since yesterday. Charley's family has just got home from church. Mr. Whiple Preached today. I have stayed at home today. William got home from Canton this afternoon. He stayed at Dave Hunt's in Hermon last night. Charley's folks had company this evening or the girls did. It was Rob Wilson & Forest McKee.

Monday, December 29   This has been a warm day. It has thawed fast all day. It has raind most of the day. I went over to Alvah's & stayed untill most 3 o'clock.   William has been away to the village this afternoon & evening. He has not got home yet.   The teacher & Emma Noble has cald on me this evening.

Tuesday, December 30   This has been a very cold day & it is very cold this evening. I have done my washing today. The teacher sent John McGill home from school this forenoon for ill behaviou in school. Wm went to the village tonight. Mr. Homes & Charley has been geting wood today over to P. H. Brown's. Alma Pratt made me a call this evening. Thare is an old man Pedler staying at Charley's tonight.

Wednesday, December 31   Thursday the 11 of December the Band held their entertainment at the Rushton House in Edwards. Received 53 dollars. December the 13th William brought me the crock of Butter from Alvah's 25 lbs. It was very cold this morning at noon it began to snow & blow. Now at four it is storming fearfuly. This is the last day of this year. It is going out with a storm. George Beech came here today & took away his colt. Payed 5 dollars on the Board bill which is nine dollars. Gave his note for four dollars.

[On the end overleaf pages, Nancy Johnson Brown, added these notes]:

June the 8 Lidie Bennet was berid today
May the 24th Wm lent George Freeman 50 dollars
September the 17 William lent Mr. John Ellis one hundred & forty dollars
Lillian Gorden went to Alvah's to work the 30 of September
February 17 88 lbs of flour from 2 bushels of wheat
November the 13   The Boys sold their Butter today for 30 cents a pound

June the 27 2 lbs of tea

June 17 Ed Noble was maried

June the 13 Milo & Stilman ran away to Canada

June the 7 one lb of tea

September the 24 2 lbs of crackers, 2 lbs of raisins, 2 lbs of
  rise [rice]

3 lbs of tea the 11 of February 1879

November 13 one can of lamp oil

September the 18 one pound of tea. One can of oil. Four
  quarts

September 19 one bag of flour

August the fourth 2 lbs of tea

August the 7 one bag of flour

July the 1 one bag of flour

Oct the 9th one can of oil

Hattie Padget commenced work for Alvah the 25th of August

Hattie Padget quit work at Alvah's the 27th of September

March the 20 Mrs. Conine had a little girl

July 26 Martha Gardner beried today

August 29 A letter from Susa. Sulivan Paid me 5 dollars of
  borowed money today he got it of William

October the 9 one can of oil

November the 3 Mrs. Cyrus Cleland had a Babe. It died, A
  Girl

Mrs. Hiram Hall had a girl the 20 of April 1879

Mrs. Rob Allen had a girl the first day of May 1879

Mrs. Dr. Murray had a girl the 18 of June 1879

Mrs. Mettia Robertson had a boy the 2 day of February 1879

Mrs. Albert Wite had a girl February the 13 1879

Mrs. Frank Burdick a Boy

May the 13th McFerran commenced work on Burdick's house

Mrs. Alvah Brown had a girl June the10 1879

Mrs. L. M. Gardner had a girl August the 27

Betsy Gleason had a little girl born August the 25 1879

Mrs. Charles Noble had a boy August the23. Weight 12 lbs
  1879

Mrs. Steven Ward had a Boy September the 17 1879 it is her first child. She is forty years old. They call his name Guard Lions Ward after a hunter in NY City. He has got a Present of a Beautiful Silver Cup with A gold linen [lining]Presented by Mr. Lions of NY

Mrs. Steven Ward died this morning at five o'clock September the 23

Mrs. Steven Ward was beried the 24 Sept 1879

Jurane Noble died this morning March the 22 1879

Frank Loops litle boy beried March the 21 1879

James Noble & Rod Smith ran away March the 25. Mag went the l of September

Mother [Agnes Brown] died the eighth of October, was beried the tenth. She was 85 years old September 10

Mother has gone & left us. She is waiting on the other shore. We went with her to the river & saw her pass for evermore. We hope she is hapy & has met dear father on the shining shore. Whare bright angels will greet them & they will meete loved ones that has gone on before. I hope they will meete my darling Clara that has gone & left me in sorrow to mourn. Yes, Clara has gone & left us & our hearts was nigh to breaking when we saw her go. But the Savior cald her from this world of grief & woe.

November the 17 it is eleven years today since Clara died. It was on Tuesday of the week but it comes on Monday this year.

Our school commended Monday, November the 17

The teacher boards at Charley Brown's

First big snow & wind storm November the 20

We moved back up home November the 25

Pet Hunt commenced work again for Alvah November the 26

Pet Hunt went home from Alvah's December the 27

Ama Newton died February the 19 1880

Wm Rice & Ellen Burdick was maried the last day of

November 1879

March the 14th 1879 commenced to tap the sugar trees

For making Sausage: to 25 lbs of meat

> Twenty spoonfuls of Sage
> 25 spoonfuls of salt
> 10 of pepper
> four of summer savory
> Keep in a cool place

December the 5th Charley went to Hermon

Dec the 6th Stilman Brown agreed to buy the old farm

November the 8 Mr. Ben Cross of Hailsburg paid eighty
dollars in cash to me to Aply on a note that William
Brown held against him. He came with Wm Cleland this
afternoon. Wm Brown was gone from home so he left
the money with me. Nancy A. Brown

October the 27 George Ivers got back from Colorado. He ran
away last March

October the 29 Agnes Barford [Barraford] had a boy. It did
not live long.
They sent for Dr. Drury of Gouverneur

Had Gardner was married November the 13 1879 at 8 o'clock
in the evening to Malice Casada

March the 4th 1880 commenced to tap the sugar trees

Nin Gardner moved today in to her shop November the 14.
She has bought the McMilon shoeshop. 1879

October   John McKee took his cattle out of the Pasture
down on the Brown farm

December the 17 1879 Mrs. James Harmon had a litle boy
baby. They have now four children

Mrs. Margaret Phinney Taylorville Christian City Illinois

Charley's folks was gone away on their visit fifty two days

Agnes Brown was gone on her visit west 53 days to Mich &

Canada

Wm bought 3 lbs of tea for one dollar October the 11

Oct the 23 1879 Old Mr. Gardner died today

Oct 25 Mr. Gardner beried today

John McKee paid the Interest on his note tonight Oct the 30 by
the hand of James McKee his brother

James Noble, Twon of Jacson, Co of Osberne, Kansas

Laura McGill went to Alvah's the 31 of July to work

Lona Brown was maried to a Mr. Law Huffman of Kansas
July the 3 1879

Mettie Brown was maried to Write Robertson September 1878

September 29 Bill Noys served a supreme writ on Henry
Gadas today

September 29 Frank Austin Payed William three dollars for
house rent

Lona L. Huffman Vienna Kansas

James Noble, Plantive [Plaintiff] called lives in Edwards.
Knows the mare in question and nowes [knows] the horse.
He will be ten years old in May and knoes the mare
backed once. See her whipped once.

Recalled I have owned the mare and I call this team a good
true team. I now [know] the horse is a good one & the team
is worth three hundred dollars. 177 dollars the 5th of Sept in
the trunk.

1880
[Written by William H. Brown]

[Printed materials on the front overleaf pages included:
Astronomical Calculations, Calendar for 1880, Monthly
Range of the Gold Premium for 17 years, Table of Wages by
the week, Domestic Postage, Foreign Postage, Principal Cities
and population, and, Presidents of the United States from
George Washington to Rutherford B. Hayes.] GGJ

101

Thursday, January 1   This is a butiful Day. Hugh Prat[t] had Charley's horse and new cutter to go to Little York to New Years.

Friday, January 2   It is thawing today. The wind blowes very hard.

Saturday, January 3   It frose [froze] tart night. It is a butiful day today. The Cornet Band went to Fine today. Took dinner thare & advertised for a exhibition on the Sixteenth.   It commenced to raning [raining] this evening. Got a card from Joseph Brown stating he got the pacage [package] of money.

Sunday, January 4   It is raining this morning. Frose tonight.

Monday, January 5   Pleasent today. Went up to Wm Cleland to get sticks [of timber] for timber. Went to mill today with wheat and oats.

Tuesday, January 6   It is raining today and thawing fast. Went after another stick [of timber] today. James Harmon paid me forty five Dollars fifty cents interest on Band. It is still raining.

Wednesday, January 7   This has been a butiful day. Alvah & I was cuting timber to day. Got a letter from L. W. Russell & Poste to night. Got a letter from C. V. Johnson [likely Charles Victor Johnson from Pittsfield, IL] to night.

Thursday, January 8   This is a butiful day. Alvah & I was hewing timber.

Friday, January 9   This is a butiful day. I went into the woods to cut logs alone to day.

Saturday, January 10   It frose a very little this morning.   We went up to Robert's today.

Sunday, January 11 The wind blows like fury. Peter Homes Died this morning. It thawes fast today.

Monday, January 12   It snowed a very little today. Turn very cold. Mr. Homes beried this afternoon. Bouht 8 ½ yards of flanel of James Brown. Received $12 Dollars of Cary.

Tuesday, January 13   It is Still butiful weather. Hewed timber by the road.

Wednesday, January 14   It is a butiful Day. Received a dispatch from Joseph Brown to nigh that Adaline was Dead.

Thursday, January 15   It is a little colder today. Hewing timber in the sugar bush.

Friday, January 16 It is a butiful day. The Cornet Band had a exhibition in Fine to night. Joe's wife was buried today.

Saturday, January 17   It is a butiful morning. It has thawed today. It rained this afternoon. Carter was here tonight. I went after Mrs. Phiney.

Sunday, January 18   It is fogy today.   Gon to take two hundred & five Dollars forty seven cents.

Monday, January 19   Warm but snowes a little. Went to Canton on Gaddis Wuit. Mrs. Gordon, Phiney, Webb & Brown commenced Bord tonight at Cleveland's.

Tuesday, January 20 Frose up last night. Cold as blixson today. James Harmon commensed Bord Tuesday noon.

Wednesday, January 21   It is plesent today.   We are all at Canton yet.

Thursday, January 22   It is Raining this after noon.   Tried the Gadis Suit today.

Friday, January 23   Paid Carter five Dollars.   Started for home today from Canton.   Paid Mr. Cleveland Seventeen Dollars for Bord for self & witness in the Gadis Suit.

Saturday, January 24   It is a butiful day.   Cared [meaning carried] Margaret Phiney up to Pitcairn.

Sunday, January 25   It is a butiful day.   Robert Dunn Died today.

Monday, January 26   It is a butiful day.   Alvah & Charles drew two loads of Bark to Fine for John McKee.

Tuesday, January 27   It Rains today.   Went up to Robert Brown for two sticks of timber.   Went to the vilage today. Paid A. B. Goodnough & Rushton twelve shillings balance of there subpoena.

Wednesday, January 28   Pleasent weather.   It thawed some today.

Thursday, January 29   Frose up last night.   The Cornet Band went to Harisvill to hold a exhibition.   Rather poor luck. Barly paid their expensis [expenses].

Friday, January 30   Pleasent but aful windy.   The Cornett Band went to Little York to hold a exhibition.   They cleared about Six Dollars.   It comensed to rain about dark.   Rained most of the night.

Saturday, January 31   The wind blowes a perfic huracane today. It is thawing some today. I went to the vilage this afternoon. Grahm Stevenson little girl February 1th, 1880 Died. [recorded in the January 31 box]

Sunday, February 1 This is a fearful morning. It snowes & blowes a perfic storm. Cleared off this afternoon. Alvah & Sarah came home from Grant's tonight. It is quite cold tonight. I done all the Chores for Alvah today.

Monday, February 2   Cold but pleasent. Pafro ["Paphro," nickname for Epaphroditus] Buck & Brown & Brothers had a lawsuit. Charles was on the jury. Made writings today with Robert Allen for to rent the Brown Resident for one year for $70.00 per year. Take two Double harness for the rent.

Tuesday, February 3   Snowed all day. Fell about 1 foot. Brown & Brothers beat Buck in his lawsuit. No cause of action. Wm Noys [Noyes] went with the hears [hearse] to bury one Rhodes in Fowler.

Wednesday, February 4   Pleasent today. Alvah & I are drawing timber.

Thursday, February 5   Pleasent today. We are still drawing timber.

Friday, February 6   Pleasent today. Colder towards night. Quite cold. Finished drawing timber from Wm Cleland's today.

Saturday, February 7   Quite cold but pleasent. Went up to Robert's for two sticks of timber today. Republicans held a cockis tonight to choos town officers.

Sunday, February 8   It is pleasent this morning but the wind

105

has risen and blowes a perfic gale. Stilman stayed at Charles last night. Stayed here all day. Robert Wilson stays with Emma Noble tonight.

Monday, February 9   A fearful cold Day. Sarah Brown was sick. Took pump out of well.

Tuesday, February 10   A little warmer this morning. Town meeting today. Five tickets running today. Snowed all afternoon.

Wednesday, February 11   This is a butiful day. We went up to Charles Harmon's today to see Philey [Phila Viall Harmon]. She is very sick. Murry [Dr. Murray] came up to see Philey today.

Thursday, February 12   It rains this morning. The wind blowes a perfic gale. It thawed the snow al away. Gott a letter from Joseph Brown today.

Friday, February 13   It is a warm day. Went to get some lumber planed. Could not get it planed.

Saturday, February 14   It snowed about six inches last night. Nancy Stayed over to Mr. Newton last night.

Sunday, February 15   It is a butiful day. Nancy went over to Newton's. The sun shone all day.

Monday, February 16   It is a butiful day. The sun shone all day and thawed some in road. Alvah drawing logs for William Cleland. Curtis Gorden worked for me this afternoon.

Tuesday, February 17   It is a butiful day. It is thawing very fast. Alvah drawed logs for Wm Cleland this forenoon.

Sleighing all gon [gone].

Wednesday, February 18   This is a butiful morning. It rained some last night. It rained all day most. Libie Gordin came up today.

Thursday, February 19   It is afful cold.   Cold west wind. Amos Newton Died today about four o'clock. Went down to Jason Woodcock. Went to the viledge today.

Friday, February 20   It is pleasent but cold.   Alvah went to mill today 2 bushels for me, 2 bushels for himself.

Saturday, February 21   It is cold and stormy. Snowed a little all day. Amos Newton was buried today. We all went to the funeral. Bought three pounds of tea, fifty cents per pound.

Sunday, February 22   It is pleasent but rather cold.   Wind blowes from West. Quarterly meeting today. Went down to H. Pratt's today.

Monday, February 23   It is snowing some this morning. Snowed about 2 inches last night.   It snowed most all day. Drawed one load of hay from the old Brown farm.

Tuesday, February 24   It is a butiful day but cold. Alvah and I drawed two loads of hay from the old Brown farm.

Wednesday, February 25   It is a butiful day.   Good sleighing but very thin.   Alvah & I drew two loads of hay from the old Brown farm.   The snow is all gon today at noon.   Write Robison baby Died today.

Thursday, February 26   This is a butiful day.   Warm as summer.   Rods [roads] getting very muddy. Went down to the Old Brown farm for a feset [faucet] to put in the gathering tub.

Baker and his wife came to Charles today to atend the exhibition tonight. Our schol closed today.

Friday, February 27   This is a butiful day. The sap Runs well today. I was sick all day. Baker & Wife went to Fine [NY]. The mud is getting very deep. Write Robison baby was buried today.

Saturday, February 28   This is a butiful morning. Clouds up rains before ten o'clock but very warm. Rained a little every litle while all day. Wind blowed hard all day. Let Robert Webb take a note that I had against Hiram Hall dated January 5, 1880 for $21.59 cents.

Sunday, February 29   This is a butiful morning. It rained last night. Cleared off this morning. Turning colder. Wind blowes a perfec gale this morning. Growes very cold. Freesing very fast.

Monday, March 1   It snowed a very little & it is very cold. Went to the vilage. Got the sap pan home tonight.

Tuesday, March 2   It has been a very pleasent day. Not very cold. Charles & I begun to cut his wood today. Nick Glasby was here to day. Tried to sell some Gloves. Nancy was gon to the vilage all day.

Wednesday, March 3   It has been nice warm day. Comensed to tap sugar bush today. Went to vilage tonight.

Thursday, March 4   It is warm this morning. The sap runs well today. Thomas Grant help to scatter the tubs. Nancy is over to Jap Ward's tonight. Nile [Nellie] sick. Got a letter from Russell.

Friday, March 5   It is warm. Rains this morning, rains this

afternoon. Turns into snow. Boiled sap from four o'clock till night. Boiled enough to make one hundred weight of sugar.
Saturday, March 6   It is colder today. It snowed about two inches last night. Boiled sap all day. Went to viledge tonight.

Sunday, March 7   It is quite cold. Thawes some about noon. Snowes before five o'clock. Snowed about half inch. Made two hundred 225 weight of sugar.

Monday, March 8   It is very cold today. Help C. H. Brown saw wood today. Been very cold all day. Lawrence Scene comensed work for Alvah today.

Tuesday, March 9   It is cold this morning. Help C. H. Brown saw wood today. Mr. Whipple & Wife made Charles' folks a visit today. It thawed a little about noon. Clouds up, looks like snow. Wind begins to blow this evening.

Wednesday, March 10   It is quite cold this morning. It snowed a very little last night. It is cloudy this morning, pleasant but quite cold all day.

Thursday, March 11   It is quite cold this morning. Cloudy and wind North East. Alvah went got his hierd Girl today. Nancy has gon over to Jap Ward's. Jap[Jasper] came after her. It has been very cold all day.

Friday, March 12   It is pleasant but cold. Alvah & I drew hay from the old Brown farm. Nancy went down to Agnes' [Hughs] when we went for a load of hay.

Saturday, March 13   It is cold but pleasant. Drew one load of hay. Geathered the sap this afternoon. Nancy went up to see Aunt Philes [Phila] Harmon. George Freeman's wife died today.

Sunday, March 14   It is cloudy & wind south. Snowed a very little last night. Murcuary two degrees below freesing.

Monday, March 15   It is cold but pleasent. Alvah went out to Grants'. Mrs. Grant is very sick. I was sick all day with sick headache. George Freeman's Wife was buried today.

Tuesday, March 16   It was cloudy and begins to snow. Snowed a little all day. Snowed quite fast about noon. Snowed about three inches. I went down to Stillman Brown's to weigh hay for C. H.   Went shoed [showed] Stillman the line of his land between Noble's and him.

Wednesday, March 17   This is a butiful day but quite cold. Cuting and drawing hemlock sawlogs to the River. Baker is up tonight to play with the Band. Lawrence Scene hurt his leg today.

Thursday, March 18   It is pleasent but no sap yet. Alvah & I tap some treas [trees] this afternoon. Nancy & Sarah went out to Grant's. Drove there own horse.

Friday, March 19   It is pleasent today. Rather Warmer. The sap runs a little today. Alvah & I finished taping sugar bush today. They have a nicktye [necktie] party this Evening.

Saturday, March 20   It is a butiful morning. Clouds up & snowed a very litle. Made a sap spout for C. H. Brown. CHB Boiled some sap today. Henry Grant came out & told Sarah that her Mother was worse.

Sunday, March 21   It snowed a very little last night. Snowes a little this morning. Cleared of[f] about noon & very pleasent. McGill's folks had three shep [sheep] tore by dogs last night. One of them killed. Alvah & Sarah gon out to Grants'.

110

Monday, March 22   It is snowing this morning and very cold this morning.   Geathered sap this afternoon.   Cleared off pleasent about noon.   About 3 o'clock began to snow and blow. Cleared off & pleasent again.

Tuesday, March 23   Pleasent this morning. Clouds up about 10 o'clock & looks like rain but begins to snow at 12 o'clock. Snowes all afternoon. Melts about as fast as it falls. Robert Allen worked for Alvah today.

Wednesday, March 24   It is very cold this morning. Snowes & Blowes most fearful. Snowed about five inches. It is cold tonight. Alvah & I sugared off seventy pound of sugar. We have twelve cowes to milk now.

Thursday, March 25   It is clear & butiful today but afful cold. Alvah Sold five Deacons skins for a dollar apeas. Alvah & Sarah gon out to Grant's with Cuter.   Thare is a leap year Dance at the Rushton house to Night.

Friday, March 26   This has been a butiful day.   The Sun Shone brite all day. Not a cloud to be seen. Quite cold in the morning but got warm before noon. The sap run a little whare the sun shone. Let C. H. Brown two loads of hay & A. P. two lode hay.

Saturday, March 27   It is a butiful morning. Clouds up & rather colder. Sap runs a very little. Geathered [gathered] up what sap thare was in the bush. Alvah went to mill with oats for the cowes. Old White cow came in. She makes the 13 teenth that has come in.

Sunday, March 28   It is snowing & blowing this morning & quite cold.   Charles folks are gon to meeting & Nancy & Sherman. Fixed C. H. Brown's clock.

111

Monday, March 29   Pleasent but cold. Boiled some sap &
geathered some sap.

Tuesday, March 30   This is a butiful day but quite cold. I
went up to John McGee's.   Saw Carter & was getting
testimony on the Gaddis suite. [suit]

Wednesday, March 31   This is a butiful day. Boiled sap
today & went to vilage at night to see Carter. Went up to John
McGee's to take his testimony about Gaddis.

Thursday, April 1   This is a butiful day. Boiled sap today.
Lawrence came back to go to work again.

Friday, April 2   This was a butiful day. I went to Canton with
Carter to see Judge Russell.   Got to Canton about noon.
Carter went up to John Cleland to see what he new [knew]
about Gaddis. It is cloudy. Looks like rain.

Saturday, April 3   I stayed at Canton all night. It rained some
this morning. I cam home from Canton today. Boiled sap this
afternoon. It is raining quite hard this Evening. We got ten
pailes full of surip today.

Sunday, April 4   This has been a very warm day. Rained a
little this afternoon. Boiled sap today. Got it all gathered up
and boiled. The roads are fearful mudy. Sugared off 160
pound sugar. Conyne cam to the sugar bush today.

Monday, April 5   It rained most of last night. I shugared of[f]
twise this forenoon. Churned once. Went to sugarbush.
Entied the watter out of the buckets. It rained some this
afternoon. Turned quite cold. C Conyne got the lite wagon
today.

Tuesday, April 6   This is a pleasent day. Alvah & I fixed a

112

place for the cowes in forenoon. Went to the vilage this afternoon. Got my boots mended. Saw Westely McBrier.

Wednesday, April 7   It is pleasent but afful cold wind blowes hard from the north. Alvah went out to Grant's & I did the chores. Went to sugar bush. Helped Lawrence to saw wood. Charles has a party to eat Shugar tonight.

Thursday, April 8   It is pleasent but afful cold. Wind North West. I boiled sap this afternoon. Robert Dunn was here this Evening to get contract.

Friday, April 9   It is cloudy. Wind South West. We sireped [syruped] down what sap that was in the bush. Westley McBrier was up to the Sugarbush today. Made me a call to.

Saturday, April 10   It is warmer this morning. The sap run well last night. The buckets are most all full. Boiled sap all day. Boiled anough [enough] for 125 lbs sugar.

Sunday, April 11   It is cold and snowing this morning & the wind blowes like Blicsom. [Blixson] Cleared off about noon & pleasent but cold. Mrs. Thomas Grant died this evening about Nine o'clock.

Monday, April 12   It has been very cold all day. The wind has blown very hard from the North West. The snow has blown like Winter. I been sick all day.

Tuesday, April 13   It is quite cold this morning. Wind south West. Growing warmer. Sap runs this afternoon. Boiled sap this afternoon. Mrs. Tomas Grant was burried this afternoon. Wm Cousins had a sheep killed by dogs last night. R. Wilson had his sap farm burned Saturday night.

Wednesday, April 14   It has been a butiful day. Rained a

little in the morning. It thundred about noon for the first time this Spring. Sap run well last night. Boiled sap all day. Everything is full of sap tonight.

Thursday, April 15   It was a butiful warm day. Boiled sap all day. Lawrence got a postral card to let him know that Carter had left his place. Ruby Hepenstall was here today.

Friday, April 16   It was a plesent morning. Commensed to rain about three o'clock. Boiled sap today. Lawrence left today. Carter was here today. Gaddis has been denied a new trial.

Saturday, April 17   It rains this morning. Wind is very cold. It snowed & rained all day. I sugared off and done the chores for Alvah to let him & Sarah go out to Grant's. Pernel went past here Drunk as a full [fool]. They arested Casada & then Cole for fiting. [fighting].

Sunday, April 18   This is a butiful day. Charles & family gon to Meeting. Nancy has gon with them to meeting. Left me sick abed with sick headach.

Monday, April 19   This has been a afful Windy day. It has blowed & thundred and rained today. I went down to the vilage this afternoon to here Brown's lawsuit but it was setteled. Gave hieseell [hiself] Mr. Cleland's mortgage to colect.

Tuesday, April 20   This has been a butiful day but cold. West wind. We washed all the sap buckets today. Wm Grant & John McFarlen started for Rockaway Beach. Charles worked on bridge.

Wednesday, April 21   Pleasent but quite cold. Wind West. Alvah & I went to the Sugarbush. Put store tubs away. Brot home the Vapporator put the buckets all away.

Thursday, April 22   Looks like rain this morning but did not rain till afternoon. I went up to Thomas Grant's to try and settle with Eveline. Paid Carter Ionas [loan] money that Father Gave her $50.

Friday, April 23   It is pleasent but quite cold. Wind North. Frose quite hard last night. Alvah & I drew hay from the old Brown place. Nancy Went up to ant [aunt] Herriet's [Harriet Viall Harmon] with Martha. Sarah went up to Cleland.   Hat Earl sicked Sherm Dulette Friday night.

Saturday, April 24   It was pleasent but quite cold. Frose last night. Wind North East. Alvah & I drew hay from the old Brown farm. Nancy went to the vilage this afternoon.

Sunday, April 25   Pleasent & quite Warm. Wind West. Rained a very little this afternoon. Went down to Stilman Brown's. Called on Robert Allen & Jame Rushton's. Alvah & Sarah went up to Harvey Winslow's & hired the Watson boy to work for him.

Monday, April 26   It looks like rain. Rain some about ten o'clock. Cleared off. Pleasent afternoon. I went to Little York to see about getting milk wagon. Alvah tok [took] his milk to the factery. Bought a electrick batery.

Tuesday, April 27   Pleasent but quite cold. Robert Allen is to work here today helping to hew timber. George W. Freeman paid me fifty, his fifty dollar Note. Got me pme & a half bushels grass seed.

Wednesday, April 28   It is pleasent but quite cold. It rained some this afternoon. William Watson is helping to score timber. Robert Allen is helping to score today.

115

Thursday, April 29   It looks like rain. Wind blowes a perfect Huracane. It rains tonight. William Watson & Robert Allen scored today. Hued five sticks of timber. Robert Dunn made me call. Alvah is drawing out manure.

Friday, April 30   It is quite Cold. Wind West. It rained about noon. Snowed this afternoon about two inches. S. Rise [Rice] paid & took up his Note of one hundred Dollars and interest. I hued timber part of the day With Watson & Allen.

Saturday, May 1   This has been quite pleasent this forenoon. Wind blowes strong from the West & cold. It snowed & rained a little this afternoon. Raining quite hard tonight. Watson & Robert Allen scored today & I hewed.

Sunday, May 2   It has been a pleasent Day. Some warmer then it has been. Old Mr. Sturd Died yesterday at 9 o'clock. The School marm came to Charles tonight. Charles' family all went to meeting and N,A,B,. I staid to home. They have all gon to meeting tonight.

Monday, May 3   It has been quite Warm. Wind blowed from south West. William Watson & Robert Allen Worked for me today scoring. Old Mr. Sturt was buried today. I hued timber today.

Tuesday, May 4   It has been a butiful day. The Wind North. I drew out manure for Alvah for Alvah was sick today. Charter Went out to Odgensburg yesterday, came back today.
Wednesday, May 5   It has been a butiful Day. Wind South West. Drew dung for Alvah. Charles let one cow lay in a mud hole all last Night.

Thursday, May 6   This was a pleasent day but quite cold. Rained a little last night. I planted some potatoes in Alvah &

116

our garden.

Friday, May 7   It is a pleasent morning. It frose some last night & rained a few drops this evening. I drove horses to cutti-ate [cultivate] for wheat. Got a letter from F. W. Russell about the Cleland Mortgage.

Saturday, May 8   This has been a very Warm Day. I went up to see Mrs. Eveline Grant to try and Settle With her on the mortgage. Nancy & Sherman Went up to Cleland's.

Sunday, May 9   This has been a butiful Warm day. Wind South West. I was down to Woodcock's this forenoon. Took five yearlings & two cowes up to Robert Brown's to pasture tonight.

Monday, May 10   It has been a very warm day. It has thundred very hard but has not rained a great deal. The plum trees are in ful bloom. A.P. & I went up to Wm Cleland's. Cleaned wheat. Sowed C. Brown's wheat.   Sowed part of Alvah Wheat.

Tuesday, May 11   It is some colder this morning. Rained some last night. Been pleasent all day. Wind West and quite cold. Percival [his brother] had a lam killed last night. Sowed Charles oats by the road. Got Jason Woodcock roler.

Wednesday, May 12   It is quite cool this morning but clear & pleasant. Alma Pratt came to soe for Charles' folks last night. The Wind blowes hard from the West & very cold.
Thursday, May 13   It is raining this morning & very cold but did not frieze. I finished sowing Alvah's oats today. Went down and plastered for Albert White this forenoon.

Friday, May 14   Thare was a little frost last night. Been afful cold all day. I went to Little York today to get lite Waggon

117

but did not get it. Cyras Cleland paid me 102.92 cents. C. Brown sowed his oats at Perce's.

Saturday, May 15 It frose hard last night. Been quite cold all day. Planted potatoes for Alvah. Harvy Cleland was here to see about settling about Mortgage that I hold against James Cleland Estate.

Sunday, May 16 It is pleasent but cloudy this morning. Alvah & Sarah went out to Thomas Grant.

Monday, May 17 It has been very pleasent but quite cool. Wind north West. Quite strong Wind. Finished planting potatoes today. Alvah went With a load of Chees to DeKalb. Sold for twelve & one sixteenth [per pound].

Tuesday, May 18 It is quite Warm. Looks rain. Commensed to rain about eight o'clock. Rained all forenoon. I went to Canton today to see Russell. Came back to Hermon.

Wednesday, May 19 It thundred & rained this morning. Cleared off pleasent all day but very warm. Came home from Hermon, planted beets & cucumbers, peas & cabges. Sarah & Cela went to Marshville to get boots.

Thursday, May 20 It has been a very hot day. I planted corn on the side hill today. Alvah fixed fens. Charles Johnson was here this morning peding. Charles fixed his corn ground.
Friday, May 21 It rained last night. Been pleasent but cloudy. It is raining tonight. Wind North East. I helped Charles to plant his corn today.

Saturday, May 22 It has been quite Warm and aful Windy. I went up to Harvy Cleland's to see him about Setting the Mortgage. Nancy Went up to W. W. Johnson. They have gon from home. Alvah had a cow come in today.

Sunday, May 23   Henry Watson came back tonight. It has been a butiful day. Got our new milk wagon ready fore the firste time tonight. Wilson's Brother preached today. He is from Canada. Charles & family went to meeting. Nancy went with them.

Monday, May 24   It has been a warm and pleasent day. I took some lumber down to plain for a cubert [cupboard] worked at the cuberts [cupboards]. Charles filed the leach to make soap.

Tuesday, May 25   It has been a warm butiful day. I finished making Nancy's cubert. Charles made soap today. I went to the vilage tonight. Alvah & Sarah papered their kitchin.

Wednesday, May 26   It has been a very warm day. I was helping Alvah & Honey to draw dirt. John & Altha called here tonight. I sint twenty dollars by Milo Woodcock to Goodnough to pay for the lite Waggon.

Thursday, May 27   It has been a very Warm day. Wind South West. Blowed very hard. Looks like rain tonight. I was blasting with Alvah. Found some oar [ore]. I saw Harvy Cleland. He has agreed to settle Mortgage.

Friday, May 28   It has been pleasent but quite cold. Wind South West. Blowes hard. I has blasting a place for the Barn. Nancy gone to the vilage to get her new hat.

Saturday, May 29   It has been a butiful day. A very little frost this morning. The Cornett Band is playing tonight. We are Still Blasting.

Sunday, May 30   It has been a nice rain. Rained quite hard all forenoon. I went down to Henry Johnson's this afternoon.

Robert Wilson & Forest McKee are here to see the girls at Charles'.

Monday, May 31   It has been a nice day after a night's rain. Alvah & I down to the vilage back of the dam.   I sent letters away to all of the Boys today & one to L. W. Russell.

Tuesday, June 1   It was pleasent after the rain.   It was quite cold all day.   Looks like frost.   Charles is away sesing [assessing].

Wednesday, June 2   It has been a pleasent day after the frost last night.   Notified to go and work on the road tomorrow. Cyrus Cleland paid interest on their note today.

Thursday, June 3   This has been a butiful day.   We all been working on the road eleven days.   2/3 of a day Alvah, 1 day 22 days Father's estate.

Friday, June 4   It frose a very little last night.   It has been a butiful day.   Not very warm.   I was working on the road. James Harmon's bull jumped over into our pasture.   It looks like Rain.

Saturday, June 5   It was a good heavy rain this morning and it is raining some this evening.   We worked on the road today. James Harmon was over tonight.   Charles Hulbert died today.

Sunday, June 6   It has been a butiful day after the rain this morning.   It rained hard till about nine o'clock.   Nancy & I went down to Sillman [Stillman] Brown's.

Monday, June 7   It has been a fine day but quite cold.   It feels like frost tonight.   We finished working our road taxes today. Charles Hulbert got killed by the cares runing over him.

Tuesday, June 8   It has been a fine day. We was Blasting today. Alvah bought a soing [sewing] machine of George Freeman for thirty five [dollars].

Wednesday, June 9   This has been a butiful day. Quite Warm. Henry & I was Blasting. The assesors called to asses today. Asesed Alvah side 2880.00. Vilage tot[al] 100,0.00. Personal property of Brown est 1900.

Thursday, June 10   It has been a warm day. I was blasting today. Alvah & Sarah went out to William Grant's.

Friday, June 11   This has been a very warm day. A hevy thunder shour this evening. I was Blasting today. Alvah was sick today. Pet Webb was up to Alvah all day.

Saturday, June 12   This was a plesant morning after the rain. It rained most all afternoon. Nancy & I went out to Alalon's today. The roads ware very bad. Sold chees for 8 10 7/8.

Sunday, June 13   It is quite warm.   Looks like rain. Comensed to rain about 8 o'clock. Cloudy all day. A hevy thunder shour this afternoon. We came home from John Abaslom. Stoped at Hiram Bencraft through the rain.

Monday, June 14   It was a butiful day. Alvah & I was Blasting.

Tuesday, June 15   It has been a butiful day. Sprinkeled a little rain. Sarah & Clara went to the Store. Clarah bought her a new dress. We was Blasting.

Wednesday, June 16   This has been a butiful day. Alvah, Sarah, Nancy, & I went down to Nelson Freeman's to see the talc works. Carter was here and took the Sensus today.

Thursday, June 17   This has been a butiful day. Quite warm. I went to the vilage. Got Mrs. Grieves' lot surveyed. James McKee surveyed it.

Friday, June 18   This has been a butiful day. I was diging stone with Alvah today. Robert Webb paid me Sixty two Dollars 27 cents. Elder Dike paid me thirty Dollars on his Note.

Saturday, June 19   It has been a butiful day. Very warm. No rain for 8 days. It rained a week ago today. I went to up H. Cleland's. Alvah & Sarah went out to John Abaslon.

Sunday, June 20   It rained a very little about ten o'clock. Clared off pleasant. Henry Watson went away yesterday & today. Alvah & Sarah come home. Kelsy was out to see Clara.

Monday, June 21   This has been a butiful day but Rather cool. I was down too the vilage Surveying   Henry Watson quit Working last Friday.

Tuesday, June 22   This has been a butiful day. Alvah & I pulled thisels out of the wheat. I went to the vilage. Wind North and some cold.

Wednesday, June 23   It has been very warm. I mad[e] a wagon tong today. A. P. Johnson & Stelly came tonight.

Thursday, June 24   This has been very Warm. A heavy thunder shour tonight. I was hoing potatoes. Got a letter from V. P. Abbot.

Friday, June 25   This has been a very warm day. A. P. Johnson & I went down to the talc works. It rained some tonight.

Saturday, June 26   It is very warm today. Rained some this morning. Alvah going to Draw lumber from the mill. I made a pair of Whifeltres today.

Sunday, June 27   It has been a very warm day. I went up to Carter's. Called on Wm Noys, C. H. Raymond & Mury about V. P. Abbot. Charges against Robert Brown Estate.

Monday, June 28   It has been a warm day. Showers in the afternoon. Alvah & I was drawing lumber from the mill. The Band was playing & marching this afternoon. Lent George Pagget 3 ¼ lbs of pouder, 5 fet [feet] fuse.

Tuesday, June 29   It is rather colder today but pleasent. I drew one load of lumber today. Hoed potatoes this afternoon.

Wednesday, June 30   It has been a butiful day. Quite cool for the season. Wind blew hard from the West. Finished hoing potatoes.

Thursday, July 1   It has been a pleasent day. I was drawing lumber from the Mill. Some signs of rain. Kettie Rushton came home from Michagan.

Friday, July 2   It has been a pleasent day. I went to Hermon to get a rope for hay fork. Thare is a dance at the vilage tonight. Thare was a funeral at Hermon this afternoon.

Saturday, July 3   It has been a pleasent day. It fell a few drops of rain tonight. I made a fraim [frame] to the grindin stone today. They all went up to Shawville to a picknic.

Sunday, July 4   It has been a butiful day. We went out to Jene Hermyton with A. P. Johnson. Henry Earl was haying.

Monday, July 5   This has been a butiful day. I drew lumber

123

from the Mill. Alvah was sick today. Charles went with a load of chees today.

Tuesday, July 6   It has been a butiful day. Finished drawing lumber from the mill.   I went down to Sillman [Stillman] Brown for a load of hay. Helped him to put up his hay fork.

Wednesday, July 7   This has been a butiful day. Drew one load of hay from Stillman brown's.   Put Paris Green on the potatoes. Nancy & Martha went up to the Pond Settlement.

Thursday, July 8   This has been a warm day. I went out to Glasby's to get the Waggon tiers sat. Charles took the double buggy out to get the tiers sat on it.

Friday, July 9   This was a pleasent day. Alvah commensed haying today.   Drew in 3 loads.   Charles helped in the afternoon.

Saturday, July 10   This has been pleasent day. Been haying. Charles helped this afternoon. Looks like rain tonight. Robert Dunn paid me one hundred Dollars on the lot by L. Rushton on the 12th of July.

Sunday, July 11   It has been a very warm day. Nancy & Charles' family are all gon to Sarah McFarlen's funeral. Alvah's folks left the baby with Sherman and me.

Monday, July 12   It was a warm forenoon. Commensed to Rain about two o'clock. Rained a little all afternoon. Rains very hard to night. Alvah & Charles & all the Cornet Band have gon to Heuvelton [NY] to the orang man walk.

Tuesday, July 13   It has been a very warm day. Cleared off pleasent after the rain. The Band came home this morning. Playing for the orangmon. Forest McKee commensed to work

124

for Alvah this afternoon.

Wednesday, July 14   It was a butiful day. We drew in 9 loads of hay. Charles Commensed to mow his hay today.

Thursday,   July 15   This has been a warm dry day.   We finished Drawing in our hay about two o'clock Drew in hay for Charles this afternoon. Took in five load.

Friday, July 16   It looked very much like rain this morning but clared of [f] without any. Rained a few drops about three o'clock. Wind blowed very hard. Drew in hay for Charles today.

Saturday, July 17   Cloudy and quite cold. Rather poor hay day. The boys mowed Charles' side of the road this forenoon. Drew in hay this afternoon. They are all gon to the vilage.

Sunday, July 18   This has been a pleasent day.   Alvah & Sarah has gon out to Grant's. Charles' family all went to the meeting. Nancy with them. I stayed to home all alone.

Monday, July 19   This was a warm pleasent day but looks like rain. Comensed to rain about Six o'clock. Drew in 10 loads of hay for Charles, 1 for Alvah.

Tuesday, July 20   It has rained good part of the day.   A tremendious [rain?] the afternoon.   Fix Waggon ract.[rack] Laid flour [floor] in hop house.

Wednesday, July 21   Cleared of[f] this morning. Hay most of the day. Rained a little about three o'clock. Drew in four loads of hay.

Thursday, July 22   This has been a rather poor hay day. Cloudy most of the day. Drew in Seven loads of hay. The agent for the Republican paper.

Friday, July 23   It has Been a rather poor hay day. Took in seven loads of hay. Rained a little about five o'clock.

Saturday, July 24   Rather poor hay day. Rained about nine o'clock. Quite a heavy Shour. Cleared of[f] in the afternoon. Took in two loads of hay.

Sunday, July 25   This have been very warm today. Charles' family all went to meeting. Nancy went with them. Robert Wilson is here tonight to see Emma Noble.

Monday, July 26   This has been a poor hay day. We drew in 4 loads. Alvah went with a load of chees to the Juncktion [meaning DeKalb Junction].

Tuesday, July 27   This was a cloudy forenoon. Cleared off about noon. Drew in 6 loads of hay.

Wednesday, July 28   This has been a poor hay day. Rained about two o'clock. Drew in 4 loads of hay.
Thursday, July 29   It has been rather beter [better] hay day today. Took in 6 loads of hay. Finished haying today.

Friday, July 30   This was a very pleasent day. Alvah & I cut the grasssed today. Went to the vilage after we got done.

Saturday, July 31   This has been a warm pleasent day. Nancy & I went up to John Laidlaw today. He was haying. O Soll was quite lame. The Cornett Band went to Gouverneur to play for a Republican Meeting.

Sunday, August 1   This has been a warm pleasent day. We staid to home all day. Alvah went and caried Agness down home.

Monday, August 2   One of M Wiles babes died. It has been showery all day. We drew one load of lumber home from the mill. I fixed the reaper. Had a affull hunt for Old Casey cow.

Tuesday, August 3   This has been a cool pleasent day. I was fixing door to hop house. A. P. Brown & Charles went Black berien. Lent G. W. Freeman fifty Dollars tonight.

Wednesday, August 4   This has been a very witt day. Maryett Harmon was here this afternoon. I found my sledge hammer of over to Mr. Payns. S. Brown Paid me one hundred Dollar on his contract.

Thursday, August 5   It has been a butiful day. Not very Warm. Alvah went to Odgensburg with a load of Chees. I comensed to cut oats.

Friday, August 6   This has ben a butiful day. Alvah got home from Ogdensburg. I was cuting & binding oats. Mrs. James Harmon was here today to make a visit. Nila Beech and Rodie Ward.

Saturday, August 7   This has been a nice Warm day. It looks some like rain tonight. Alvah & I bound ten hundred bundles of oats today. Charley cut his oats by the road today.

Sunday, August 8   This has been a warm day.

Monday, August 9   It has been warm and dry but looked like rain this evening but did not rain. Finished cuting oats. Cut some for James Harmon. James Harmon bound oats for Alvah this afternoon.

Tuesday, August 10   It is still very dry and warm. Finished binding oats today. Clary Kelsey left Alvah today. Sarah got mad at her.

Wednesday, August 11   This has been a butiful harvest day. Not very warm but very drying. We drew in five loads of oats.

Thursday, August 12   This has been a warm day. We finished drawing in our oats today.   Old Mrs. Raymond was up to Charles' visiting with Herriett Manchester. They stayed all day.

Friday, August 13   This has been a nice pleasent day. It has rained a little tonight. Alvah and I was drawing timber today. One of Charles Cowes got hoked [hooked] tonight.

Saturday, August 14   It cleared of[f] pleasent after the rain last night. We cut our Wheat today. Charles Harmon helped Bind.   Horis [Horace] Beech, Moris [Morris] Pratt & James Hermon all helped to bind.

Sunday, August 15   This has been a cool pleasent day. Alvah Went out to Grant's. Nancy & I went up to William Cleland this evening.

Monday, August 16   This has been a fritiful day.   It frose quite hard last night. Finished drawing timber today. Charles Cut his Wheat today.

Tuesday, August 17   This has been a butiful day. A very little frost this morning. Alvah & I drew in wheat all day. This was the sessors [assessors] Revew day. Charles was gon all day.

Wednesday, August 18   This has been nice day but looked like rain all day. But has not rained any yet. The wind has blowed very hard all day. Danual [Daniel] Cleland and his Wife was here today from the West.

Thursday, August 19   The sawmill was burned at Shawvil[le] last night. It has been a lowery day after the thunder Shower last night. The lighting Struck and burned Henry Johnson's barn and all his hay and grain. The lighting killed five cowes for Noah Shaw last night.

Friday, August 20   It has been a pleasant day. Alvah went to the picknic today. I fixed the road fence and yard fence & dug stone the rest of the time.

Saturday, August 21   This has been a pleasent day but quite warm. Alvah 7 I was laying the foundation for the barn.

Sunday, August 22   This has been a warm pleasent day. I went out to Dan Darts. Nancy went out to Clark's Cheese factery.

Monday, August 23   This has been a warm pleasent day. Dan Dart comensed to fraim the basement for the barn. Got here at ten o'clock. Daggot is to work for Dart.

Tuesday, August 24   This has been a very warm day. We have been framing today. Dart & Daggot Worked today. Baker came up to Alvah today.

Wednesday, August 25   It has been quite cool today after the rain last night. Wind blowed quite hard from North East. Dart & Daggot worked on the fraim today. Alvah & Charles' folks went out to the lake today.

Thursday, August 26   It has been a pleasent day. Dart & Daggot Worked on the fraim. Alvah & I worked on the fraim. Alvah Sold the Bull today for $14.50.

Friday, August 27   It has been a pleasent day. Rained some thiss forenoon. We are still framing.

Saturday, August 28   This has been a very Warm pleasent day. Finished framing barn. Paid Danual Dart fifteen Dollars for his work. Alvah got the horses Shod today.

Sunday, August 29   It rained a little all day and quite Warm. Old Mr. James McKee died Saturday morning and buried today. I made some Sider today.

Monday, August 30   This has been a pleasent day but quite warm. I went to Richville for a load of lime. Paid five Dollars and five cents. Stoped at Cambells' to supper.

Tuesday, August 31   This has been a pleasent day. Looks like rain tonight. Alvah man comensed to Work yesterday for twelve Dollars per month. We was building the wall for the barn.

Wednesday, September 1   This has been a pleasent day but very Dry. No rain. Mr. Erwin is to Work building the wall for the barn. I am helping him. Alvah drawing Stone. Payn paid the interest on his note today.

Thursday, September 2   It has been a warm pleasent day. Afful dry. We are all working at the wall yet Erwin is to work today. Charles & Martha went to the fair at Gouverneur today. They took Alvah bugy.

Friday, September 3   Pleasent Day till most night then it rained some. The Cornett Band Went to Harisville to play for Fine Lodge. Erwin worked today.

Saturday, September 4   This has been a pleasent day. Not quite so warm. Erwin worked till after three o'clock then he went home. Spaldins [Spaldings] & Wife is here yet & Mrs. Clark.

Sunday, September 5   Pleasant Warm day. I went up to Harvy Harvey] Cleland. Went up to Shawville.

Monday, September 6   This has been a nice pleasant cool day. We raised the Basement to the Barn. S. Rise [Rice] paid me $13.84 Cash on his Note. Sent the pay to Horis [Horace] Beech & Moris [Morris] Pratt by Hew [Hugh] Pratt for Binding.

Tuesday, September 7   This has been a pleasent day. Quite cool. We are all to Work at the Wall yet Irwin [Erwin] is helping. Got a Dispatch from Will Brown that his Father was worse.

Wednesday, September 8   This has been a cool pleasant day. Some frost this morning. Ware to work at the Wall yet With Erwen. Charles & Martha went up to Pitcairn & then to Fine with Spaldings & Wife.

Thursday, September 9   This has been a cold pleasant day. We are to Work ate the Stone Wall. Erwin is helping. Comber helped today. I went up to Robert Brown's tonight.

Friday, September 10   This has been a warm pleasant day. We are to Work at the wall. Erwin & Cumber is helping. Corbin took the bull away today. A Republican Lecture night.

Saturday, September 11   This has been a pleasent Warm day. But very dry. We are all at work at the wall. Erwen and Cumber helping. A Republican lecture last night.

Sunday, September 12   This has been a pleasent day. I Staid at home. The rest all went to meeting. Warren & Maria [Moriah Johnson] came home with Nancy after Meeting.

131

Monday, September 13   this has been a wit day. We finished building the Wall. Erwin Worked today. Charles went to Fine for lime today. Old Mr. McColum Died last night.

Tuesday, September 14   This has been a butiful day. I started for Canada With Leveret this morning.

Wednesday, September 15   It has been a pleasent day. I got to Edward's [Edward Brown] this morning at sunrise. Found Edward some better than he had been. Went over to Thomas McKiney's this afternoon.

Thursday, September 16   This has been a pleasent day. Will is plowing for Wheat. Sarah and I went over to Furgason's [Furguson] this afternoon. Had a good time. Thare is three Corps in Tilsonburg today.

Friday, September 17   This has been a warm pleasent day. Will & I went down to Furgason's. Cleaned up some Wheat for seed. I comensed to paint Edward's house over today.

Saturday, September 18   It has bee a pleasent Warm day. Will finished Sowing his Winter Wheat. Will & I went to Filsonburg this Eavening [evening]. Edward is some better today. I helped the girls pare appels [apples] this afternoon.

Sunday, September 19   The dockeer [doctor] was here today. It looks like rain. Eanis & Matilda came to Edward's today. Thomas & Mara came over today. Enis [Enos] and Matilda Staid all night. It rained quite hard tonight.

Monday, September 20   It is pleasent today. I painted today. Will finished [up sowing] his Wheat. Eanis [Enos] & I went up to the grapery. Got all the graps that we could eat.

Tuesday, September 21   It has been a pleasent day. I painted all day. It has been very Windy today. Very cold Wind West. Edward is feeling some better today.

Wednesday, September 22   It has been pleasent but cold. Wind West. Quite Strong. Hanny & I went to Tilsonburg. I went to the Sugar House then went to the grapery.

Thursday, September 23   It has been a butiful day. I painted all day. Will Went to the Fair at Hamilton with Miss Furgason. Edward ant [ain't] quite so well this evening. The Dockeer was here today.

Friday, September 24   This was a butiful day. I painted all day. Will went to a husking bee this afternoon. Edward ganes [gains] very slow.

Saturday, September 25   This is a butiful day. Will & I went to Tilsonburg.   Went to the Sugar works.   Bouh [bought] overcoat & hat $11. Paid for fixing Watch. Finished painting this afternoon. Will finished cuting corn.

Sunday, September 26   It is Raining this morning. Cleared of[f] after awhile. I was taken with the Disentary this morning. Was bad all day. Went over to Thomas' this afternoon. Staid thare all night. Taken worse in the night. It is raining very hard this Evening.

Monday, September 27   It was quite pleasent and Warm this morning after the Night rain. I felt a little better this morning. Road [rode] out with Thomas then came back to Edward [Brown's]. Felt quite well this Evening.

Tuesday, September 28   It rained hard all night & raining this morning. I was taking worse in the night and was very sick all day. Dockter Jay came to see Edward and he gave me some medison. He said it was a bilous atact.

Wednesday, September 29   The Wind is north and quite cold. Will has gon to Tilsonburg to see the Docter & see if thare was any mail. I have not got any papers yet. I am a good deal better today. Edward is feel quite bad today.

Thursday, September 30   This has been quite cold. Wind North. I helped Will husk Corn at night. I & Hany went over to Thomas to be ready to go to Eanis. Edward is quite well today.

Friday, October 1   This has been rather a dull day. It drisled rain most all day. I went out to Eanis today with Thomas & Mary Edward is worse today.

Saturday, October 2   This has been a butiful day after the rain. I helped Enos to pick up ears of corn. We took in two hundre & twenty one bushels. Did not get it all picked up then. Enos will have 6 or 7 hundred bushels of corn.

Sunday, October 3   A heavy thunder shour last night. Wind south. It has been shoury all day. The sun shines by spells. Quite Warm. I sent all over Enos' plase with him. Comensed to rain hard this evening.

Monday, October 4   This is a wet morning. Rained all night. Wind north this morning and cold. Rained all forenoon. Went squirl hunting this afternoon. Killed nine.

Tuesday, October 5   It has been a cold day. Cleared off pleasent. Hanny & I went up to Mr. Servins to see Mrs. Wilson. We had a splendid visit. Got home about three. Helped Enos a little on his corn crib.

Wednesday, October 6   Some Showers in the afternoon. Started at 4 fifeen to go to station to go to London [Canada] fair. It is a cold morning but pleasant. Wint round the citty a little with Enos then Wint to the fair ground. Thare was a splendid shoe of machinery & grain & vegetels [vegetables] & the largest cattle I ever saw. 1 stear 4 years old weighed 2800.

Thursday, October 7 This has been a pleasent day but some cold in the morning. Helped Eanos to build a corn house. I at Eanos, yet. Going to stay untill Sonday.

Friday, October 8 This has been a pleasent day. Cool in the morning but quite warm through the day. Helped Eanos to finish his corn crib. He was well pleased to have me help him.

Saturday, October 9 This is a butiful morning. Enos went to Ingersol this morning to get a hog. Came home. I went down this afternoon with him. Went to cheese factery. Went through Ingersol. Bough a gold watch for Nancy for forty Dollars.

Sunday, October 10 This is a butiful morning. Hanny & I are going back to Edward's today. Enos & the Girls are going With us. We got to Edward's at noon.

Monday, October 11 This has been a warm pleasent day. I have been breaking Will's colt. I harnesed him up. Put him in the buggy [and] drove round to Thomas & back. He went nice. Will finished diging his potatoes.

Tuesday, October 12 This is a butiful morning but rather cold. Will is going to Tilsonburg this morning. Been pleasant all day. I hitched up the colt this afternoon and drove it in the bugy.

Wednesday, October 13 This is a butiful morning but quite a frost. Clear and pleasant all day. Edward & I going to

Tilsonburg this afternoon.

Thursday, October 14   This is a butiful morning.   Will is going to kill a hog. I dresed up and helped him. We got it done before noon. We cut the hog up this evening. It is raining some this evening. Edward is feeling qute [quite] smart.

Friday, October 15   This is a butiful morning after the rain. Will and I went to Tilsonburg this morning. Got Stove pipe & zink. I made a bord to put under two stoves. Hitched up the colt and took a ride.

Saturday, October 16   It rained all forenoon. Cleared of[f] in the afternoon. Will and I over with the carpet Bags. Matilda came this Evening to stay all night.

Sunday, October 17   This is a very cold morning. Rained last night part of the night. Rained this morning. It snowed a very little today.   Mary & Thomas McKinney came over this afternoon.

Monday, October 18   This is a clear pleasent morning but very cold. I start for home this morning. Got to Bufalow [Buffalo] at two o'clock. The ground covered with snow. Cars [perhaps tires] got stuck in snow before got to Batava [Batavia, NY] Snow one foot deep.

Tuesday, October 19   Got to Gouverneur about one o'clock this morning. Staid at Gouverneur till one o'clock. Came up in the Stage. It snowed and rained all day. Thare is a big Republican Raly at Ogdensburg today. 15000 people present.

Wednesday, October 20   Got home last night. Fond the folks all Well. Went up to Cleland's with Sarah. Took Nancy & Martha to the vilage. Helped Alvah to milk.

136

Thursday, October 21   It has been some warmer today. Wind South West. Alvah and I put the plates on the barn. Martha & Moriah gon to Gouverneur this afternoon.   Thare is a Democrat meeting this evening.

Friday, October 22   It has been raining all afternoon. I was fixing barn.   Phila & James Harmon was here visiting & Emma Hall today.   [Phila Viall Harmon was a half sister of Nancy Brown and Emma Johnson Hall was Nancy's sister]

Saturday, October 23   This has been a Wet day. Raining this evening quite hard. Alvah churned today. I finished the wall. A republican lecture this evening. Charles and family are gon down to the lecture.

Sunday, October 24   It snowed about three inches last night. Snowed some this morning.   Bee Cloudy all day.   Charles went up to Benjaman Noble's for Spague's wife.

Monday, October 25   It has been quite cold. Thawed a little in the road. I went down to the vilage this afternoon. Bough pair of boots. Paid $2.50.

Tuesday, October 26   It has been a wet day.   It has been thawing all day. Sold the Cheese last Saturday for 13 cents. Gowes [Goes] away the 27, Goes to Madrid. I went to the vilage. Went to James Rushton's.

Wednesday, October 27   This has been a rainy day.   The snow is most all gon.   I was fixing wheelborow.   The Republicans had a big turnout at the vilage tonight.

Thursday, October 28   This has been a pleasent day but quite cold. I finished Wheelborow today.

Friday, October 29   It has been quite pleasant today but quite cold this morning. Hardes [t] frost last night of the Season. I went back to the woods to look for Sleepers.   Called at Harmon's. Took diner with them.

Saturday, October 30   This has bee cloudy and Wet all day. It is raining hard tonight. I was diging stone today. Alvah Churned today. Filed one tub Thursday.

Sunday, October 31   This is a nasty wet morning. Raining and Snowing both togather. Cleared of[f] in the afternoon. I staid to home and wrote a leter to Edward Brown.

Monday, November 1   This has been a nasty day. Rained and snowed most of the day. Warm some of the time then turn cold and wind blow a prfct gale. Charles Harmon Wife had a dead baby.

Tuesday, November 2   This has been a pleasent day for Election. They turned out well tho Republicans carid the State. I was down to the vilage. Took diner at J. Gorden's.

Wednesday, November 3   This has been a butiful day after the hard frost last night. The sun Shone brite all day. I was blasting all day. Alvah was gon all day hunting for a Girl.

Thursday, November 4   This has been a butiful day. Nancy & I Went down to S[t]illman Brown's. Blasted in the forenoon.

Friday, November 5   This has been a butiful day. Warm and pleasent. I worked for C. V. Harmon building sugar arch.

Saturday, November 6   This has been a butiful day. Warm and pleasent. I finished C. V. Harmon's Sugar arch tonight. It began to rain this evening and the Wind blowes hard.

Sunday, November 7   This has been a cold Windy day.   It rained all last night.   The Wind blew a perfict huracane.   It blowes and snowes a little today.   Wind blowed our fenses down last night.

Monday, November 8   It has been quite pleasent but rather colder than Saturday Was.   I was making a platform the for Well and plastering the school house and fixing the floore.

Tuesday, November 9   It has been a butiful forenoon but rains most of the afternoon.   Charles Harmon's wife was buried this afternoon.   Nancy & I went to the funeral.   Alvah & I drew stone in the forenoon.

Wednesday, November 10   This has been a butiful day. Grahm[Graham] Stevenson put a new pump in the Well today for me and Charles.   I was helping Alvah to draw Stone and blast Some.   marting [Martin]   went out to Clark's Chees Factory Dance.

Thursday, November 11   This has been a nasty wet day.   It rained hard all last night and been showery all day but not very cold.   I went to the vilage for some glass & to get the drill sharpened.

Friday, November 12   It has been a nasty wet snowy day. Cold North West Wind blowed hard all day.   Rained all last night.   I built Charles Shugar Arch today.   Mr. Newton called. John Noble died at twelve o'clock today.   Buried tomorrow.

Saturday, November 13   Been quite cold today.   Snowed a very little.   Cold North Wind.   Plastered a little for Newton today and done Alvah's Chores.

Sunday, November 14   This was a butiful morning but stormed before noon.   Snowed most of the afternoon.   John

139

Noble was buried today. The house was crouded full. Holly preached.

Monday, November 15   This has been a pleasent day. It was cloudy in the morning. Cleared off nice and warm before noon. Charles killed his hog today. I helped him. Alvah & I went after the young cattle today.

Tuesday, November 16   This has been a butiful day. Thawed a little. The wind blowing quite hard from the West tonight. I helped Charles to put two Sleepers [beams] in the horse barn. Alvah and Martin was chopping wood today.

Wednesday, November 17   It has been Rather warmer today. It thawed in the forenoon. Snowed a litle in the afternoon and turned some colder. Alvah & I went down to Sillman's [Stillman Brown] and bought a bull for eight dollars.

Thursday, November 18   It Stormed all forenoon. I was doing Charles' Chores while Charles and Spague [Sprague] went to Russell visiting.

Friday, November 19   This has been quite pleasent. Alvah went to Gouverneur with his butter. He got twenty five cents for his butter. Alvah bought a bufalow skin. I done the chores for him.

Saturday, November 20   It snowed and blowed a little all day but not very cold. Martin went to DeKalb today. Alvah done his own chores. I drew some wood round on [the] piasa. Alexander Kerr paid some money on his bond & note.

Sunday, November 21   This has been a cold Windy day. Wind blowed a perfict gale. The snow is piled up in grate drifts. Charles went up to Benies [Benjamin Noble] with Sprague & Wife. Martha and chilren went with him.

Monday, November 22   This has been a clear cold day. I been sick most all day.

Tuesday, November 23   This has been a clear pleasant day. I made three ax helves today.   Charles and Martha went to Mariah Noble wedding today.

Wednesday, November 24   This has been a clear cold day. It is snowing a little tonight. I have bee Working on a door for Alvah.   Martin has been drawing Manure from A. B. Goodnough.

Thursday, November 25 This has been a pleasant day. I have ben working on a door for Alvah. Was here to Charles' to dinner today. A dance at Little York to night. Allen Wight going out with a load.

Friday, November 26   This has been a clear pleasant day but quite cold. Alvah & marting [Martin] was drawing hay to W. A. McFeren. I finished making the door today. Charles went up to Benjaman Noble today. Has not got back yet, nine o'clock.

Saturday, November 27   It has been a pleasant day. Some squalls of snow. Caried Nancy down to Robert Brown's. Alvah churned today. I worked at the stare [stair] railing today.

Sunday, November 28   Been cloudy all day but not very cold. Charles went to Russell with Clara Kelsy today. I have been sick today. Bengman Noble came down after Oren Sprague.

Monday, November 29   It has been quite warm but quite Windy. Growes colder in the afternoon. I finished Alvah's stairs railing & hung the door. Neary Hall has [married] last

Saurday to Moris Pratt. Alvah went to Mill for me.

Tuesday, November 30   It has been quite pleasent. Quite cold last night but some warmer today. Wind South West tonight. Alvah has been gon all day after a Girl. Hadent got back at dark. I done the chores & piled wood to home.

Wednesday, December 1   This has been a Stormy day. It has snowed all day. Fell about six inches of snow. I fixed the stares to go down Seller today. Alvah has been gon two days looking for a Girl. Can't find any.

Thursday, December 2   This has been a pleasent day but not very cold. We killed the hogs. Emma Hall came up to Alvah this afternoon. Martin's brother was here today. Alvah went up to Robert's after a load of hay.

Friday, December 3   This has been a pleasent day. Not very cold. Alvah comensed to draw this firewood. I went to the vilage to get met [not legible] Robert Webb & their wifes [not legible].

Saturday, December 4   This has been a butiful day. Pleasent as could wish for. I cut up Alvah hog for him. Finished churning for him. So he went to drawing Wood.

Sunday, December 5   This has been a stormy windy day. It has rained a little all day and thawed quite fast. The Wind blowes quite hard from the West tonight. It is some colder. Emma Hall came to Alvah to work tonight.

Monday, December 6   This has been a cold raw wind. Frose up last night. Alvah & Martin was cuting joists on R. Webb's. I done the chores and cut saucage meat. Charles and Sprague have gon a visiting.

Tuesday, December 7   This has been a cold Windy day.   It Snowed about three inches this morning.   Alvah broke the Sled with a load of manure.   Jason Woodcock and Wife was here this evning.

Wednesday, December 8   This has been Rather a cold raw day.   I was fixing the Sled today & done the chores.   Alvah drawing Wood.   Write Robinson and his Wife was here after the money Father gave her.

Thursday, December 9   This has been a aful Stormy day.   It has snowed and blowed all day and quite cold.   I finished the Sled today.   Ellen Cleland was here a visiting today.

Friday, December 10   This has been a clear cold day.   The coldest day we have had this Winter.   Alvah is drawing his Wood.   I am doing the chores.   Charles and Martha went up to Benjaman Noble's to see Mrs. Mabel.

Saturday, December 11   It has Snowed and blowed a little all day.   It was quite cold this morning.   I took Nancy and Sherman up to Mr. Cleland's today.   Alvah went down to the vilage this afternoon.

Sunday, December 12   It has not been very cold today.   Looks like a thaw.   Charle is going to Canton as a Juryman.   I send two of Father's deeds by him to get Recorded.

Monday, December 13   It has been quite warm.   Thawed a little all day.   Snowes a little in the evening.   Alvah drawing Wood & I done the chores.   Nancy & I went down to Jason Woodcock's this evening.   Charles Brown has gon to Canton today.

Tuesday, December 14   This has been a butiful day.   It snowed a little this afternoon. I fixed the sled this forenoon.

Went to the Blacksmith Shop with the Sled. Did not get home till night.

Wednesday, December 15   This has been a nasty Stormy day. It snowed and thawed all day. Turned colder about night. Emma Hall was here visiting today. Donation tonight for Elder Holly.

Thursday, December 16   This has been a pleasent day but rather colder. Alvah has been drawing Wood for me today. Martin Went to the vilage last nigh[t], got drunk. Did not get home till six o'clock this morning. Martin did not work today. I done the chores. Was sick.

Friday, December 17   This has been quite a cold day. Alvah was drawing Wood for me today. I went to the vilage today to get my boots mended. I done all the chores. The murcury all day at ten above zero.

Saturday, December 18   This has been a cold day. I went to the vilage to pay my taxes. They 3337.   & done the chores for Alvah. Drew Wood.

Sunday, December 19   This has been rather cold day. Been kind [of] misty. I have been sick most all day. Clara Kelsy came back to Charles' today. Charles and Sprague, Martha, Emaline went up to Benjaman Noble's.

Monday, December 20   This has been quite a pleasent day. But it has been cloudy all day & white frost on the trees. Alvah was drawing Wood for me. I done the chores. Grace Day called here today. Nancy went down to Woodcock's.

Tuesday, December 21   This has been quite pleasent but a chilly East Wind. Been cloudy all day. Murcuary stood at 18 above Zero. Nancy and I went up to Charles Harmon's.

Found Phila [Viall Harmon] quite sick.

Wednesday, December 22   This has been a pleasent day but cloudy and not very cold. I went down to the vilage with Martha. Brought home Nancy. She was down to Halls.

Thursday, December 23   It has been a pleasent day but not very cold. Been cloudy all day. I done the chores and drew Wood in the forenoon and drew Joists in the afternoon.

Friday, December 24   This has been a pleasent day. Not very cold but cloudy all day. I went to the vilage. Two Dreses, one for Nancy, one for Emma. The cornett Band is holding a exhibition tonight.

Saturday, December 25   This has been quite a pleasent day for Christmas. Not very cold but cloudy all day. Good sleighing for so little snow. Nancy & I went down to Robert Webb's for Christmas visit. The boys had quit[e] a Drunk.

Sunday, December 26   It has been quite pleasent today. Thawed a very little. Alvah & Sarah went up to Cleland's today. Martin & Emma just got back from the ball of Friday night.

Monday, December 27   This has ben a pleasent day. Not very cold. I went to the post ofes to a mail letter and card. Charles killed a pig and cow today. The frost has stayed on the trees for over a week. Just butiful.

Tuesday, December 28   This has ben quite a cold day. Wind West. Tried to snow a little. Alvah & Martin was cuting saw logs this forenoon. Was drawing this afternoon. I done the chores. Stillman Brown was here. The Murcery just stands at zero.

Wednesday, December 29   This has been a cold day. Mercury Stood at Zero all day. Stands thare this eveng. I done the chores. Alvah was drawing law logs. Frank Beech was here this evning to borow a croscut saw.

Thursday, December 30   This has been a cold windy day. It has snowed all day. Murcuary Stands 2 degrees below Zero. It is 10 degres this evning. William Raymond was Maried today. He Maried Miss Mina Hutchins.

Friday, December 31   This has been quite a cold day. Murcuary two degrees below Zero this morning. Snowed a very little today. Snow is about six inches deep in the woods. They are holding New Year's Ball at the Rushton House this evening. Emma Hall has gone to the dance with Martin.

[The remaining pages contained in the William Brown 1880 Diary contained memoranda of cheese sales, cash accounts of William and Alvah Brown, monthly cash accounts of receipts and expenditures by William Brown, and hours worked by Alvah Brown on the William H. Brown farm.]GGJ

1880
[Written by Nancy A. Johnson Brown]

Wednesday, December 31 actually written in [1879]   This has been a nice day. It is good sleighing today. Thare is a dance to Little York [NY] & one here at Wm. Burlingame's.

Thursday, January 1   It has commenced to thaw today. The sleighing is melting away fast. The ball chaps are huseling [hustling] home. They are having a tall time at the hotell today.

Friday, January 2   The sleighing is finished for this time.

Saturday, January 3   It froze last night. It is a pleasant day. The Band men & their wives went to Fine [NY] today. Took dinner & had a good time in general.

Sunday, January 4   It is raining this morning.

Monday, January 5   Pleasant today & thawing fast. William & Alvah went after a stick of timber today. James Harmon's came here to pay Wm. Some money.

Tuesday, January 6   This is a beautiful day.

Wednesday, January 7   Wm got a letter from brother Charles Johnson [Charles Victor Johnson of Pittsfield, IL] tonight.

Thursday, January 8   This has been a beautiful day. Wm & Alvah has been hewing timber today.

Friday, January 9   It is a Pleasant day. I went to the village & stayed all day. The Band went to Fine [NY] to have an exhibition. Charly caried a load & broke the Buggy.

Saturday, January 10 [or possibly Sunday the 11th]   Peter Holms died this morning. Mr. Whiple's little boy is very sick today.

Sunday, January 11   Mr. Whiple's little boy is better today.

Monday, January 12 [nothing entered]

Wednesday, January 14   It has been a Pleasant day but quite cold. This evening the wind is just howling. Sarah came over & stayed here this evening. The boys got home at eleven.

Friday, January 16th   Adaline Brown Died today. Received a dispatch tonight from Jo [Joseph Brown].

Thursday, January 15 [Nancy Brown was using a 1879 Diary book and attempted to change the dates to be correct for 1880. Sometimes the dates are not correct. She did not enter anything for "Thursday, January 15."]

Friday, January 16   Adaline Brown Beried today in Pine Valley, Chemung County, NY. Wife of Joseph P. Brown.

Saturday, January 17   William went to Pitcairn this afternoon after Mrs. Finney. They got here soon after dark. Carter was here waiting for them. It was raining quite hard.

Sunday, January 18   Mrs. Finney is here with me today. It has thawed tonight & all day today. The mud is geting quite deep.

Monday, January 19   William has gone to Canton today to atend a lawsuit with Gadas.[Gaddis]   Mrs. Finney & Mrs. Gorden & a number of others have gone as witneys for him.

Tuesday, January 20   I have cut & made a pair of Pants today for William. Sherman has got a very hard cold. He has not been out today. It has froze all day & been snowing all day.

Wednesday, January 21   I got a line & one dollar in money from A. Rilbown of Fine today by the hand of Alvah P. Brown. It has been very cold today. A foot of snow this morning.

Thursday, January 22   A nice day this. I got a dispatch from William. John Allen brout it to me today.

Friday, January 23   A very stormy day. William came home from Canton today from the law suit. Beat Gadas.[Gaddis]

Saturday, January 24   Wm caried Mrs. Phinney to Pitcairn today. She is staying with Mrs. John Graham this winter.

Sunday, January 25   We went to church today. Mr. Whiple preached. It has been a nice day. Warren & Mariah Johnson [William Warren & Moriah Johnson] was here this afternoon.

Monday, January 26   This is a Pleasant day but thawing all day. The Gadis [Gaddis] clan is howling fearfully because they have got beet [beat] on the suit.

Tuesday, January 27   Thawing all day. Raind hard this afternoon.

Wednesday, January 28   It has thawed all day.

Thursday, January 29   This has been a cold day. The thaw has froze up tight. The Band Boys have gone to Harrisville to hold an exhibition. I went to the village. Stayed all day.

Friday, January 30   Mrs. Adelle Grant had a Boy today. 8 pounds.

Saturday, January 31   The boys goes from Harrisville to York today. Hold an entertainment in the evening. It raind hard.

Sunday, February 1 [two lines crossed out by Nancy Brown] It snowed hard today. The above [two lines that were crossed out] is a mistake.

Monday, February 2   It is fearful cold today. Graham Stevenson folks beried their litle girl today.

Tuesday, February 3   It has snowed hard all day. A funeral today. Mrs. Amos Newton's Brother Rhodes of Fowler,

Wednesday, February 4   It is some stormy today. Alvah & Wm drew logs today from Wm. Clealands. I helped Sarah in the forenoon & quilted for Martha in the afternoon.

Thursday, February 5   Alvah & Wm is drawing logs today from William Clealand. The wind is blowing. The snow up in to piles today. Martha & Em has gone to Perce Brown's. I got a letter from Em Hall today.

Friday, February 6   It snowed in the night. It is quite cold today. Wm & Alvah has finished drawing their logs from Wm Clealand's. Charley & Martha has gone up to Benny Noble's to attend a Donation. I have quilted for Martha all day.

Saturday, February 7   It has been a stormy day. Wm & Alvah drew their last stick of timber from Roberts. Men all went to the Cawcous [caucus] in the evening. I stayed with Sarah.

Sunday, February 8   This has been a sunshiny day but the south wind is howlling fearfully. I went to Church today. Dyke Preached. Rob Wilson is staying here with Em Noble tonight.

Monday, February 9   This has been a pleasant day but very cold. Have done a large washing this forenoon & worked for Sarah all the afternoon. She & the babe is sick with hard cold.

Tuesday, February 10   This has been town meting day. It was very cold this forenoon & this afternoon it has snowed hard untill night. I have washed for Sarah today. Litle Mania [Manie] is 8 months old today. Sarah & the babe is better today.

Wednesday, February 11   This has been a very nice day. Wm & I have been up to visit sister Phila today. She is very sick. The south wind is blowing hard tonight.

Thursday, February 12   The thaw began in the night. It rained hard & the wind has blew a perfect gale all day.   Hit this evening. It is in the northwest. It is a little colder. We got a letter from Susa tonight.

Friday, February 13   Amos C. Newton is very sick with the Brain fever. One half of him is Parilized this morning. Dr. Drury is atending him. The thaw is froze up. It is snowing tonight.

Saturday, February 14   Thare is a nice lot of snow this morning. I stayed all night to Mr. Newton's. The whole family was up most of the night with Ama [Amos]. The did not think he would live till morning.

Sunday, February 15   It is snowing some today. I stayed to Mr. Newton's most of the day. Thare was 20 diferent persons cald [called]thare to day. The boy is yet Alive. Is failing fast. He has spasms evry 10 minutes.

Monday, February 16   This is a lovely day.   Warm & sunshiny. I have done my washing. Am baking this afternoon. Martha has gone to stay with Ama Newton. He was alive this morning. Gorden is helping Wm make a sap tub today.

Tuesday, February 17   It has thawed all day. The sleighing is done. Ama Newton is Alive this forenoon but no beter. Mary McGill was here today to sell Charley a farm, the old homestead. He did not buy it.

Wednesday, February 18   This has been a rainy day. Ed Brown stayed with us last night & all day today.   Lileon [Libby] Gorden is visiting here today & all night.   Ama Newton is no better.

Thursday, February 19   The thaw is ferse up tight today. The wind is blowing hard & cold. Amos C. Newton Died at four oclock this afternoon, February the 19th 1880.

Friday, February 20   This has been a pleasant day but cold. Charley went to Pitcairn today to let the friends learn of Ama Newton's funeral.

Saturday, February 21   This has been a Cold stormy day for a funeral. Ama C. Newton was beried today. Mr. Whiple Preached the funeral sermon.

Sunday, February 22   This has been A lovely day. We have atended the quartily meting today at the Church. The house was well filed. Mr. Wood the presiding Elder spoke to the people.

Monday, February 23   It has snowed most all day. Pleasant this evening but a cold wind. I have washed & done lots of cleaning upstairs & down today. Wm & Alvah drew hay from the old farm this forenoon.

Tuesday, February 24   This has been a beautiful day. Quite cold in the morning. Wm & Alvah drew hay. Charley drew Ice for Kingsbery. I made a visit to A.R. Payns today.

Wednesday, February 25   It was raining this morning. Has thawed fast all day. Wm & Alvah has drawn hay. Charley drew ice today. Mr. Baker & wife & girl came to Charley's tonight to stay until after the entertainments.

Thursday, February 26   This has been a lovely day. It has thawed fearfully. We all went to the Band entertainment tonight. The mud was terible deep. Thare was not a very full house.

Friday, February 27   It froze this morning but today noon it is thawing fast. Wm has got the sick headache today. He can't be up out of bed much. Yesterday was the last day of our school. Idda Fellows teachs.

Saturday, February 28   This has been a stormy day. High wind & rain. It has thawed fearfully all day. The Band held an exhibition last night & dance after. They had a full house.

Sunday, February 29   The wind blows fearfully today. We have been to Church & Sunday school. Mr. Whiple Preached today. I made a call at Dr. Goodnough a few moments.

Monday, March 1   The thaw is froze up this morning. I have done a large washing this forenoon. Elen Clealand made me a visit this afternoon. Ann Noble made me a call & a visit to Charley's. I sent a letter to A. P. today & Susa Brown.

Tuesday, March 2   This has been a lovely day. I have been to the village making calls all day. Wm & Charley has been sawing wood today.

Wednesday, March 3   It has been a nice day. Rather high wind all day. Raining in the evening. The men has taped [tapped] a part of the sugar trees. Tom Grant & wife made a visit to Alvah's today.

Thursday, March 4   It has been a good sap day. Our boys finished taping & commenced to boil. The wind has blowen hard all day. It raind this evening. I went over to Jap [Jasper] Ward's tonight. Nily is sick.

Friday, March 5   It has raind most all day. Charley siruped down or they sugared off today noon. Now at 3 o'clock it is snowing. Wm has been in the sugar woods all say since four this morning. I stayed all night to Japs [Jasper Ward].

153

Saturday, March 6   It snowed some last night. It has not thawed much today. Wm & Alvah has worked in the sugar bush all day. I went to Alvah's & done off the sugar. Was 100 lbs of sugar, the first.

Sunday, March 7   It frose hard this morning. It is pleasant. Alvah sugared off 125 lbs of sugar today. I went to Church with Charley's family. Elder Dyke's day.

Monday, March 8   It thawed some yesterday. The sap run a litle but this morning it is froze very hard. Cold North wind all day. No sap. Wm & Charley is sawing wood all day. I have done a large washing for Sarah & myself.

Tuesday, March 9   It has been a very cold day. Thawed A litle but no sap. Mr. Whiple & his wife came to Charley's for a visit. Wm & I took tea in Charley's room then they all came in my room in the evening to eat new sugar.

Wednesday, March 10   This has been a cold day. Stilman & Agness Brown moved on to their farm today. Wm & Alvah drew a load of hay from the old Brown farm. Finished sawing wood last night.

Thursday, March 11   It has been a cold day. No sap. Wm done Alvah's chours today. Alvah went to Russell [NY] after Cara Kelsay to begin work for them.

Friday, March 12   This has been a nice pleasant day. I was envited over to Jap Ward's last night. Stayed untill four this morning. This afternoon I went over to Stilman Brown's.

Saturday, March 13   This has been a cold day. Charley's family all went to Benny Noble's & I went with them far as Charley Harmon's. Wm & A.P. drew hay.

Sunday, March 14   It is storming all day. The wind is howling. I am at home today with Sherman & Mable. It is Lee's day to preach. Wm & Alvah is in the sugar Woods. Charley's folks are away to Church.

Monday, March 15   This has been a lovely day. No sap. Wm has had the sick headache very bad all day. Alvah & Sarah has been out to her father's all day. Her Mother is very sick. Mrs. George Freman was beried today.

Tuesday, March 16   This has been a stormy day. Snowed all the afternoon. Thare was a auction sale on the Ager Cole Property. A lot of cows. Mrs. Grant is no better. I am making my calico dress.

Wednesday, March 17   It has snowed some today but clear & cold this afternoon & evening. Maker came to Charley's tonight to give the band a term of lesons [lessons]. I am working till most eleven o'clock tonight on my dress.

Thursday, March 18   This has been a pleasant day but no sap yet. Sarah & I went out to Tom Grant's today. Julia is very sick yet. They think a litle better. Mrs. John Dygart died yesterday.

Friday, March 19   It has been a nice day. Wm & Alvah & Charley finished tapping their sap trees. The sap did not run very well. Litle mable has been sick all day. The Lady's Aid had a necktie party tonight at the Hotell.

Saturday, March 20   This has been a stormy day. It is snowing & blowing hard tonight. I have finished my dress today. Mariah Noble is here on a visit to Charley's. They all went to the party last night.

Sunday, March 21   This has been A clear & cold day. No sap.

Alvah & Sarah went out to Grant's today. I went to Church with Charley's folks. Rob Wilson is at Charley's tonight to visit with Emma Noble.

Monday, March 22   This has been a stormy day. The sap has run some. Martha & Emma went to Tom Noble's today to a quilting. Mrs. Tom Grant is no better. They have sent for Dr. Semore to day & discarded Dr. Murry [Murray].

Tuesday, March 23   This is a beautiful morning. Wm is away to the woods to boil sap. Took his dinner. Rob Allen is working for Alvah today. This afternoon is very stormy. They brought home the sirup at 5 o'clock & it was snowing terible.

Wednesday, March 24   It has been cold all day. No sap. They sugared off at A.P. & at Charley's 75 lbs of sugar each. Mrs. Grant is no better. Today it has snowed enough to make sleighing.

Thursday, March 25   This is a very cold day but very clear & Pleasant. No sap. To cold. Alvah & Sarah has gone out to Grants with the cutter. Wm is doing the chours at both barns. We got a letter from Ed Brown's in Canada last night.

Friday, March 26   This is a beautiful morning. Not a cloud in the sky. Charley & Martha went to the Dance last night. Got home at three this morning. Sister E [Emmorancy Johnson] Hall stayed at the dance untill near morning.   3 O'clock. Good example.

Saturday, March 27   It is rather cold this morning. No sap today. Full moon yesterday. C. H. went to Russell last night to a Band entertainment. Caried a load of village drunkards from Edwards. Got home this morning at 4 tight.

156

Sunday, March 28   It snowed in the night quite a lot & it is cold & stormy this morning. This afternoon it is very Pleasant. We all went to Church eight of us in the buggy. A.P. & Sarah went out to Grant's.

Monday, March 29   This has been a nice pleasant day. The sap has run this afternoon. Wm has boild sap all day that run last week. I am making my new Gingam dress.

Tuesday, March 30   This has been a Pleasant day but cool wind in North. The boys sugared off 75 lbs each. Sister Hall made me a visit today. Wm has been gone all day. I got a letter from Susa Brown [from Canada] tonight.

Wednesday, March 31   This has been a lovely day. The sap has run quite well. Wm has been working in the sugar woods all day. Went to the village tonight.

Thursday, April 1   It has been a very nice day. The sap run well. Wm has been in the sugar woods all day till after dark. John Cousin & his wife has been to C.H. Brown for a visit today & Mable to eat warm sugar.

Friday, April 2   This has been a good sap day. I have been over to Alvah's for all day. Wm has gone to Canton today. A 115 lbs of sugar today at A.P. [Alvah Percival Brown].

Saturday, April 3   Wm came home from Canton today noon. I helped sugar over to A.P.'s today all day. It is very warm. The frogs are out signing [singing] tonight.

Sunday, April 4   This has been a nice warm day. Raind a litle. Wm & Lawrence has been in the woods boiling sap all day. Alvah & Sarah went out to Grant's. Cary & I worked all day. A. C. Allen beried his babe today.

Monday, April 5　It has raind some today. I have done my washing & Wm has worked over to A.P.'s today. They boys has finished up all the sap. Not much signs of Any more. The weather continues warm.

Tuesday, April 6　This has been A good day. The sap has run well. Wm has been to the village to get the Papers made out between him & Rob Dunn for the selling the houses lot in the lane.

Wednesday, April 7　This has been A cold day. The ground was all covered with snow this morning. The wind North all day. Alvah & Sarah went out to Grant's today. Wm & I stayed to A.P.'s & done the chours & took care of the babe.

Thursday, April 8　It has been a cold day. The sap run a litle. Rob Dun[n] came here this evening to get the contract & is going to Harisville tomorrow. Charley's folks had company from the village last night.

Friday, April 9　It has been cold all day. Hard wind. Some sap. Mrs. Gorden made me a visit today. Wesley McBrier made us a Call today & a visit to Alvah's.

Saturday, April 10　It was raining this morning. The sap run all night. Tubs all full today. This afternoon is warm, no rain. Sixteen years today we mooved from the Creek Setlement down here on the Broadie Farm.

Sunday, April 11　It is snowing & blowing fearfully this morning. Wm started for the woods to boil sap at three o'clock this morning. None of going to Church today. All working at the sugar but me. I am writing.

Monday, April 12　It is Pleasant today but quite cold. Wind high, not much sap. Wm is sick with the headache. Just got

158

word that Julia Grant [mother of Sarah Grant Brown] died last night at nine O'clock. Funeral tomorrow at the Union Church, Edwards.

Tuesday, April 13   This has been a god [good] sap day. We all but Wm went to Mrs. Grant's funeral. Mr. Lent Preached the funeral sermon. McBrier & Jane leave town tomorrow.

Wednesday, April 14   This has been a nice day. The sap run well. Wm has been in the woods all day boiling sap. I have sugared of [f] 80 lbs of sugar. I had a call from Ruby Hepenstall & Mrs. Leveret Raymond today.

Thursday, April 15   This has been a pleasant day. Sap run a litle. Wm started for the woods at one this morning. Boyld [boiled] all day. Agness Brown made me a visit today. A call from Alma Pratt & Jane Laidlaw & Nettie Whiple.

Friday, April 16   This morning was beautiful. Clear & pleasant. In the afternoon it raind. Mr. Carter Drove in here this afternoon. Brought us good news from Canton.

Saturday, April 17   This has been a rainy day. Alvah & Sarah went out to Grant's. Mary Grant leaves home tomorrow for Michigan to live with her Aunt Jane. A gang of Drunken men went Past here tonight. One fell down. Some of them is trying to get him up.

Sunday, April 18   This has been a very Pleasant day. I went to Church with Charley's folks. Mr. Hitchcock Preached today. Our folks are all done making sugar for this Spring.

Monday, April 19   The wind is blowing hard. A thunder shower at 7 this morning. Charley is away to work on the Bridge by the sawmill. This is the day for Eliza Scott's lawsuit with Vanes Brown. The suit is setled.

Tuesday, April 20   This has been a terible windy day but no storm.   We washed six hundred tin buckets over to Alvah today.   33 years today since my father died.   He was 62 years old.

Wednesday, April 21   This has been a lovely day.   I commenced to clean house today in my kitchen & Bedroom. Wm & Alvah caried all the tin buckets up in the dry house chamber.

Thursday, April 22   It has raind some today.

Friday, April 23   This has been a very pleasant day.   Wind coal. [cool]   I drove the horses to Benny Noble's today. Martha & the children, Sherman & all went with me.   I went to Porter's.

Saturday, April 24   One more nice day.   Wm & Alvah drew hay from the old farm today.   I rode with them to the village.   I cald on Mrs. White & took tea at Mr. Kingsbery's.   Walked home at dark.

Sunday, April 25   It has been a very Pleasant day untill four this afternoon.   It is raining.   We have been to Church today. The new Methodist Preacher spoke to the people for the first time.

Monday, April 26   It raind today.   I did not wash today.   Wm went to York today with the Colts before the Buggy.   They made the first cheeses today at the factory.   Made five.

Tuesday, April 27   This has been a Pleasant but cold day. Rob Allen worked for Wm today.   They hewed timber for Alvah's barn.   I have to cook for the men.

Wednesday, April 28   It snowed a litle this morning then the

sone shone quite pleasant.   At five in the afternoon it raind.
Wm Watson & Rob Allen worked for us today.

Thursday, April 29   The wind has blown a perfict gale all day.
At four in the afternoon it began to rain. It is now nine & the
wind is howling & the rain is coming down fearfuly. .

Friday, April 30   It has been a stormy day.   Quite a snow
storm. Wm & Mr. Watson & Rob Allen went to the Woods to
hew timber. Took their dinner with them.

Saturday, May 1   It has been pleasant most of the day. Benny
Noble & Jenny & Mariah came down for a visit today. Wm &
the men has all been in the wood to work today. Took their
dinner.

Sunday, May 2   This has been a nice day.   I went with
Charley folks to church. Dyke Preached today. Bill Grant's
folks made a visit to A. P. Brown's today.

Monday, May 3   It has been a lovely day.   I went with
Charley's folks to atend Mr. Stuart's funeral today.   Took
dinner at Benny Noble's.

Tuesday, May 4 This has been a warm day. Wm has worked
for Alvah today.   Alvah has been sick all day.   Charley
Plowed the orched today. Our school commenced yesterday.
Adah Fellow teacher.

Wednesday, May 5 It has been a very nice day. The warmest
day this spring. Wm has worked for A. today. I have cleaned
my front room upstairs today. The children all go to school.
litle Mable also.

Thursday, May 6   It raind in the night & it is colder today.
Wm has been Planting Potatoes in Alvah's & Charley's

garden & some onions & letuse. Martha is cleaning house this week.

Friday, May 7   This has been a pleasant day. Rather cool. I made a call to Alvah's today. Jane Brown was visiting to Charley's today.

Saturday, May 8   This has been a warm day. Wm went up to see Evaline Grant today & Sherman & I went up to Mr. Clealand's for a visit. Came home at four this afternoon.

Sunday, May 9   It has been the warmest day of this spring. I went to Church with Charley's family. Profesor Lee spoke to the People this forenoon & in the evening. Wm & A.P. drove some catle up to pasture to Roberts Brown's.

Monday, May 10   A thunder shower this morn. Two this afternoon. Some very hard thunder today. Wm has been sowing wheat for the Boys today between the showers. The Plum trees are all in blosom today.

Tuesday, May 11   This has been a lovely day. Raind harde in the night. The grass & trees look beautiful. I have cleand my Parlor today. Am very tired tonight. Wm has been sowing grain all day.

Wednesday, May 12   It is quite cool this morn. The sky is clear & it is a beautiful day. I have cleaned my Parlor Bedroom today. The wind is Blowing hard tonight. It is cold. Some fears of a frost.

Thursday, May 13   A pleasant day. Alma Pratt is working for Martha making her silk dress.

Friday, May 14   A frost this morning. I went to the village. Done some trading at Jim Brown's. Have sold 43 lbs of sugar this Spring to J. Brown. Took it in goods.

Saturday, May 15   This has been a beautiful day. A hard frost this morning. Wm & Alvah has Planted their Potatoes today. They sold the cheese today for 12 cents & a 16th of a cent.

Sunday, May 16   It was cloudy & cold this morn. Raind a litle at noon but this afternoon it is warm & very Pleasant. Charley's folks all went to church this forenoon. Have all gone down to the talc Bed this afternoon. Rob Wilson & Em Noble rhod out today.

Monday, May 17   This has been a very Pleasant day. I have done my washing & Baking. Wm took a walk down to Ed Wite's talc mine yesterday.

Tuesday, May 18   It was raining this morning. Raind all the forenoon. Wm went to Canton today. Drove John Allen's Horse. The grain is up & look fine.

Wednesday, May 19   This has been a nice day after the hard thunder shower in the night. I stayed over to A.P.'s all day & took care of the Babe while Sarah went to Hermon to get her a new Hat.

Thursday, May 20   This has been the warmest day of this spring. Pleasant untill most dark. Now we have just had a thunder shower & hard wind. Did not last long. Wm has planted the garden.

Friday, May 21   Wm & Charly planted their corn today. Been pleasant all day. A litle cooler weather & looks like rain tonight. The Aple trees are in full Blosom. They look so beautiful. Evry thing is lovely.

Saturday, May 22   It raind splendid through the night but

Pleasant today untill five o'clock. We have a nice shower. Half past 6, the sun is shining beautiful. I have been up to Brother Waren's [William Warren Johnson] today & they was gone. I came back to town. Made some calls.

Sunday, May 23   This has been a nice day. We have all been to church. A Brother Wilson from Canada Preached today. It was Rev. Mr. Hawley's day. Charley's folks went up to see John McKee. He is better.

Monday, May 24   It has raind in the night but a lovely day this. Wm is making me a couberd for my dishes. We sent a letter to A. O. Broadia [Brodie]today. We all rode to the milner shop tonight.

Tuesday, May 25   This is a beautiful day. Martha & Emma Mable & I went down town last night to buy Bonnets, Hats & other articles. Got home at half Past nine. Wm is working at my cubbord today.

Wednesday, May 26   This has been a very warm day. I have been making a coat for Sherman today. John & Altha cald here to super as they was coming home from Gouverneur.

Thursday, May 27   This has been a very warm day. No rain since Monday morning. Wm & A.P. Brown is diging dirt & rocks making ready to moove the Barn. They are finding iron ore.

Friday, May 28   This is a lovely morning. It has raind some in the night. I have been Painting my New Couberd. Charley is Painting their Pantry & kitchen floor. I made a visit to J. Woodcock's today.

Saturday, May 29   Almost a frost this morning but a beautiful day. I went to town last evening. Got my new bonnet. Made a call to Dr. Goodnough's in the evening while waiting for Charley.

Sunday, May 30   it is raining nicely today.   We are all at home.   No going to Church today.   Wm has got the sick headache & I have a very bad headache today but would go to church if I could get a ride.

Monday, May 31   It is rainy this morning.   Emma Noble & I have done out a large washing.   Charley's folks have been painting.   They can't get to the sink to get water so they wash with me.

Tuesday, June 1   This is a cool day.   Wm finished my couboed yesterday.   Hung the door today.   I have been painting it today.   Charley is away cessing [assessing] this week.   He stayes away all night.

Wednesday, June 2   This is Clarence's birthday 8 years.   A litle frost this morn.   It has been a cool Pleasant day.   I have Irond my white curtains & Put them up in the Parlor today. Martha & Emma went to Mrs. Laidlaw's for a visit today.

Thursday, June 3   This has been a cool & pleasant day.   Thare is shows in town tonight.   Charley's family has all gone.   The first day of June Wm sent away letters to his brothers & one to J. Foster [not legible].

Friday, June 4   Some frost this morn.   The men all worked on the rhode today.   I set my new coubered today & got my dishes all put in nicely.   I am fixing my silk basik.

Saturday, June 5   It raind this morning hard.   A few showers through the day.   It a fine growing time.   Sarah has gone to the village.   Left the babe with Cora & Henry.

Sunday, June 6   It was raining nicely this morning before 10 it faird off. Charley's folks all went to church. Wm & Idrove over to Stilman's. Stayed the most of the day. Forest stayed with the teacher tonight.

Monday, June 7   This has been a pleasant day. The men are working on the rhode. I have done my washing this forenoon. Mr. Hulbert of Gouverneur was run over by the cars last week. Is not expected to live but a short time.

Tuesday, June 8   This has been a nice day. I have worked very hard. Been Painting my floor & front steps & Baked & irond. I took super with Charley's folks & Wm with Alvah. Sarah bought a new sewing mashine today of G. Freeman.

Wednesday, June 9   This has been a warm day. I have painted the front Piasa floor today. Wm got a letter from A. O. Broadia last night. Alvah & Sarah has gone out to Wm. Grant's today.

Thursday, June 10   A very warm day. Looks like rain tonight. We got a letter from Jo[seph] Brown & one from Mrs. Lizia Bignell this morn. Martha & I have made a visit to Charley Harmon's.

Friday, June 11   It has been a very warm day. A hard thunder shower near night. Wm is away with the milk. The rain is just pouring down. A.P. has been sick all day. I have done with my painting.

Saturday, June 12   Wm & I went out to John Absalom's today. We took Sherman with us. It raind hard last night but very muddy today.   No rain until noon today.   Showery all afternoon.

Sunday, June 13   A shower this morning. We stayed all night

& until 3 in the Afternoon to John's. Got home at 6. Cald at H. Bencrafts through a hard shower. My paint is nearly dry.

Monday, June 14   This has been a Pleasant day. I have varnished my wood work in my kitchen today. I am Boarding with Charley's folks for a week while my paint is drying.

Tuesday, June 15   I have commenced living in my own room today. My Paint is partely dry. A lovely day this. I have been Baking most of the time this afternoon. We are looking for Brother Abel's folks this week.

Wednesday, June 16   A nice cool morning this. Alvah & Sarah & Wm & I took a ride down to Nelson Freeman's and made a good visit. I took a look in to the talc mines.

Thursday, June 17   Very pleasant but cool this morning. Very warm in the afternoon. Wm has been gone to the village all day. Been surveying Rosa Vialson's lot that she bought of Wm Brown.

Friday, June 18   This has been a warm day. No rain since Sunday night. I commenced to make a Bed quilt today. I have been varnishing my two Beaurows [bureaus] & table & stand yesterday.

Saturday, June 19   It is very warm & dry today. Wm is away up to Harvy Clealand's & Sherman went up to his grandpa Clealand's on the milk wagon. Alvah & Sarah has gone to John Absalam for a visit. I am Baking.

Sunday, June 20   A shower this morn at 10 but we went to Church. Pleasant in the afternoon. Alvah & Sarah came home at five. Henry Watson did not come last night nor this morning.

167

Monday, June 21   This is a beautiful day. I have done my washing this morning.   A Pedler cald this morning with trunkes caring in his hands.   I bought some lace & some hamburg & two towels. I am to pay 75 cents for the towels.

Tuesday, June 22   This has been a Pleasant day. Looks some like rain tonight. Wm Brown & Cara has gone to the village. I bought 7 quartes of strawberies of Jenny Noble tonight.

Wednesday, June 23   This has been a very warm day. Geting quite dry. Brother A.P. Johnson & his daughter Stellah came here tonight on the stage to make us a visit from Pine Valley.

Thursday, June 24   Very hot today. Abel has gone down town this morn. A hard thunder storm this afternoon at five o'clock. A splendid shower. Stellah went to A. Hall's today.

Friday, June 25   A very warm day. Stellah Johnson went home with Nera [Venera] Hall tonight. Nera was here for a visit this afternoon. A nice shower at 5 tonight. Wm & Abel went to the talc bed today.

Saturday, June 26   It was raining this morning. A hard thunder storm last night at dark.   Sister Phila & Emmy Hall, Abel & Stella & Alvah & Sarah was here for a visit yesterday afternoon.

Sunday, June 27   This has been a very hot day. Wm went to Shawville [NY] today. I went with Charly's folks to church. Clark Maltby Preached to a full house. A needle Pedler stayed to Charley's over Sunday

Monday, June 28   It has been quite showery & some thunder today.   High wind tonight.   Brother Abel is visiting at Warren's. Baker is here tonight to Play in the band with the boys.

Tuesday, June 29   This has been a nice day. A litle cooler.
Wm drew lumber this forenoon & hoed Potatoes this
afternoon. Mrs. Conine sent me 3 quarts of strawberies this
afternoon.

Wednesday, June 30   A shower this morning early. Very
Pleasant this afternoon. Our men are all hoing Potatoes. John
Haile & Stellah Johnson drove up here this afternoon. The
Pedler Aldoes cald here today. He is 87 years old.

Thursday, July 1   This has been a nice day. The men all went
to the convention this afternoon.

Friday, July 2   Charley's folks went to Russell to a
celebration today. A. P. came here this afternoon. Took
supper with us. Wm went to Hermon to day to get a rope for
the fork.

Saturday, July 3   A Picnic to Shawville today. The Band
Played for them. Most of us went to the Party. A.P. came
home with me. Will stay with us tonight. Stellah went to
Porter's tonight.

Sunday, July 4   This has been a warm dry day. No rain. Wm
& Abel & I took a buggy ride out to Jene Herington's today.
The rhodes are very dusty. Hen. & Earl was drawing in hay
most of the day.

Monday, July 5   A nice day this. I have done a large washing.
Alvah is sick today. Wm is drawing lumber from the sawmill.
Abel and Stellah started for Pine Valley today.

Tuesday, July 6   This has been a very warm day. Wm went
over to Stilman's & help put up his hay fork & drew home a
load of hay. We had a call from Mr. Hawley tonight, the ME

(Methodist Episcopal) Preacher.

Wednesday, July 7   It has been warm & dry today. The rhodes are very dusty. Martha went up to Benny's today & I went with her as far as Charley Harmon's. Evah Rushton came home with us.

Thursday, July 8   A very dry & warm day. Mr. Wm Green & his wife came here today from Hermon to visit us.   Wm Brown & Charley has been gone all day out to Scotland, [NY] getting tires set on their wagons.

Friday, July 9   Some rain this morning. Green & Wm Brown took a ride down to the talc mines this morning. Green & his litle Willie went home today. Sarah & Martha & Mrs. Green & I all went up to Mr. Clealand's.

Saturday, July 10   no rain today. We have had a good visit with Mrs. Green. We took dinner with Charley's folks today. Mrs. Green has gone up to Mr. Clealand's tonight.

Sunday, July 11   Hot & dry today. We all went to Sarah McFerin's funeral today. The Church was full. Mr. Hawley Preached the funeral sermon. Mrs. Green has gone home today.

Monday, July 12   It looks like rain today. Our boys has gone with the Brass band to Heuvelton to play for the Orenge men. It has begun to rain at two o'clock this afternoon. It is raining hard at ten in the evening.

Tuesday, July 13   It was clowdy & misty this morning but pleasant this Afternoon.   The band Boys came home this morning. Forest McKee came to Alvah's to work in haying.

Wednesday, July 14   A lovely day.   The men are all at the haying. Charley is cuting his grass this afternoon on this side of the rhode & Wm & Alvah is drawing in hay on the other side of the rhoud. [road]

Thursday, July 15   This has been a very warm day. Wm & Sherman & I took dinner to Alvah's today. Had green Peas for dinner. The men all hayed for Charley in the afternoon. Drew in 5 load. Wm did the raking.

Friday, July 16   It looks very much like rain this morning. They took in one load of hay at 7 o'clock. The men had a good hay day. No rain. Showers all went around.

Saturday, July 17   A cool day. No rain. I made a visit to brother Warren's today. We got a letter from A.P. Johnson & one from James Foster. [half-sister Susan Viall's husband].

Sunday, July 18   This has been a nice cool day. We went to church with Charley's folks. Alvah & Sarah went out to Tom Grant's today.

Monday, July 19   Looks like rain. A.P. cut grass for himself part of this forenoon then took in hay for Charley. Finished up Charley's haying this afternoon & drew in one load for Alvah. Then a nice shower at dark.

Tuesday, July 20   A splendid shower this morning. All pleasant at ten o'clock. I have my baking & ironing done at 10 this morning. Sarah was sick all day yesterday. I stayed thare in the afternoon.

Wednesday, July 21   A Pleasant forenoon. A shower at 5 o'clock. The men are all haying for Alvah. We all had green Peas today. It raind fearfully yesterday afternoon.

Thursday, July 22   This has been a good hay day. No rain. I took a walk down town today. Made some calls & two visits. Five years today since Manie Brown [Alvah P. Brown's first wife] died.

Friday, July 23   Quite a good hay day but a shower came at six. Charley brought me a Pail full of Beries today. I have put them in cans. The men are haying for Alvah this week. Wm & Forest & Alvah & Charley.

Saturday, July 24   Not a very good hay day. Some rain in the forenoon. Sherman has been sick all day. John McFerren & Bill Grant came home last night from Rocaway Beech.

Sunday, July 25   This has been a warm & Pleasant day. We all went to Church but Wm he stayed at home. He & A.P. went to the factory to night & loaded their cheese.

Monday, July 26   Pleasant this morning but raind before noon. The men only took in four load of hay. Alvah went with a load of cheese. Brought a new commode for Charley from Green's in Hermon.

Tuesday, July 27   Lowery & misty all the morning but Pleasant in the afternoon. The men drew in six load of hay. Martha went out to Wilson's for a visit. I have been quilting for 2 days.

Wednesday, July 28   Pleasant most of the day. A shower at 5 just to wet the hay. I finished my quilt at five o'clock. Sherman has been sick all day with cold & the teeth ache.

Thursday, July 29   This has been a good hay day. Our folks has finished their haying. I Put on one more quilt today onto the frames. I took supper at A.P. Brown's. Sherman & I.

Friday, July 30   A nice day this. Charley & Matie has gone up to Benny Noble's. Wm & A.P. has cut the grass seed today. I have been quilting all day.

Saturday, July 31   A beautiful day.   Thare is a Picnic at Bellville today.   Allise Earl's School.   The Cornet Band has gone to Gouverneur today.   The rebublicans & democrats hoist their Pools [poles] and banners.

Sunday, August 1   This is a lovely day.   Wm & I went up to John Laidlaw's for a visit yesterday.   Mr. Storkels Johnson of Pitcairn Died Friday is Beried today near John Laidlaw's.

Monday,   August 2   Pleasant in the morning but a shower before nine o'clock.   Showery all day.   I done a large Washing & done some baking.   Very tired at night.

Tuesday, August 3   A lovely morning this.   Wm & the boys have gone after Black Beries. I have washed my kitchen windows & made a general slicking up.

Wednesday, August 4   It is raining this forenoon.   Pleasant this afternoon.   Mrs. Charley Harmon & Erwin made me a visit this afternoon.   Charley Brown & Martha made a visit to Wm. Clealand's.

Thursday, August 5   A pleasant day.   Alvah has gone to Odgensburgh with a load of cheese. Wm is reaping oats today. I am quilting.   I finished my second quilt today & put on one more.

Friday, August 6   This has been a very nice day.   I have had company all day.   Nily Ward & Rhoda Beech & Mrs. James Harmon.   This is the last day of our school.

Saturday, August 7   One more beautiful day.   Wm & A.P. is binding oats.   Charley cut his in the front meadow today.   I have Baked pies & done my Ironing. Sarah is sick today.

Sunday, August 8   This has been a very warm day. Charley's folks are all away up to Ben Noble's. They caried Mrs. Clark with them. She came from Russell last night. I had a call from Emmy Hall today.

Monday, August 9   This has been a warm day. The men have all been Cuting & Binding & drawing in oats. Perce has been helping Charley. I helped Martha milk tonight for the first time.

Tuesday, August 10   No rain last night or today. Been a good Harvest day. Charley has gone over to P. H. Brown's to cut oats with the reaper. Carie & Sarah had a row today so Carie left & came to Charley's to work.

Wednesday, August 11   A warm day. The men are all working in the harvest. I have cut & made a Pair of Pants for Sherman. Martha & Carie made a visit to Mr. Payn's today.

Thursday, August 12   One more good harvest day. We had company all day. Mrs. Hariet Manchester & Mrs. Ray next. Pa & Sherman & I took supper with Charley's folks & with the company.

Friday, August 13   This has been a good Harvest day but a thunder shower at dark. One of our cows got Hooked tonight. They will have to kill her. Benny is helping Charley take in grain.

Saturday, August 14   This has been a good day. Wm & Alvah & J. Harmon & Charley Harmon & Maud Pratt & Horise [Horace] Beech has cut & bound & set up their Wheat today. They are all done With the hay & grain.

Sunday, August 15   This has been a cool day but Pleasant. Charley's folks all went to church. Wm & I stayed at home. Alvah & Sarah went out to Grant's for a visit today.

Monday, August 16   A frost this morning. A Pleasant day. Charley cut his wheete today. I have done a large washing today. Wm & I made a call to Wm. Clealand last night.

Tuesday, August 17   No rain yet. It is very dry. Wm & Alvah Drew in their wheete today. Sherman & I made a visit today up to Silas Rises [Rice's] & to Abner Rises [Rice's]. I have my own horse.

Wednesday, August 18   It has looked like rain all day. Sprinkled a litle. Daniel Clealand & Mary visited us all day today. They are here from Mich[igan] making their friends a visit. They go home next week.

Thursday, August 19   A terible thunder storm this morning at four. The lightning struck Henry Johnson's Barn. Burnt it with all his grain & Hay & kild one cow. Kild five cows for Noah Shaw.

Friday, August 20   This has been a lovely day. We have all been to the Picnic today in Mr. Todd's grove. We had a splendid time. Took dinner in the grove. The Cornet Band Played for the Party.

Saturday, August 21   This is a lovely morning. Wm & A.P. are drawing stone for the Barn. Sherman has not gone up to his uncle Wm Clealand's. He backed out would not go.

Sunday, August 22   This has been a nice day. Wm & Sherman & I rhode out today as far as Miron [Myron] Clarkes. Charley's folks went to Church. Rev. Mr. Dyke Preached.

175

Monday, August 23   This has been a very hot day. The men are framing the timber for the Barn today.   Dan Dart of Hermon is the Boys workman. I have washed & Baked today.

Tuesday, August 24   Very hot today. It looks like rain tonight. Wm & A.P. & Mr. Dart are working on the Barn frame. Mariah Noble came to Charley's today. They are all up to Mr. Clealand's for a visit.

Wednesday, August 25   It raind very hard in the night & is raining some this morning. Thare is a Party at Trout Lake today. The Band has gone to Play for them. A.P. & family & Charley folks all gone.

Thursday, August 26   This has been a nice cool day. I have been tacking my quilt. Mrs. Wm Robertson & Mettie has been here & to Charley's today for a visit. Litle Mabel has very sick all day yesterday & all night & is today.

Friday, August 27   It raind a litle this morning. Alex Keer & wife & Nelson Freman & Eliza made a visit to Charley's today. They all made me a call. A dance at the Hotell tonight.

Saturday, August 28   This has been a very warm windy day. A thunder shower at dark.   Wm got a letter from A. O. Broadie today. Sherman is sick tonight. Carie McGill made us a call today.

Sunday, August 29   It has been a rainy day. We all attended Mr. McKee's funeral this afternoon. Mr. Hitchcock read the sermon. Charley & Martha caried Mariah up to Benny's at night.

Monday, August 30   This is a lovely morning. Wm has gone to Richville to get a load of lime. He got home at nine in the evening. A.P.s [Alvah Percival] hired man begun work today for 12 dollars a month. Martha began making a carpet today.

Tuesday, August 31   A litle cooller today. Sherman is sick today. I have been Baking Bread & Pies & Cake & mopping three rooms. I have a terible headache today. Am very tired.

Wednesday, September 1   Looked like rain this morning. Mrs. Cole & Bessie made me a visit today. Mariah made a visit to Charley today. She was thare most of the week. Last week Mr. Erwin commenced work to Al's.

Thursday, September 2   It has been a dry windy day. Charley's folks has gone to the Gouverneur fair. Horis Beech & Ann Noble was maried today. They have gone to the fair.

Friday, September 3   This has been a very Hot day. It began to rain at four. Have had a splendid shower. The Band Boys are all away to Harisville [Harrisville] to play for a dance.

Saturday, September 4   A very litle cooler today. I had company to dinner today. Mr. & Mrs. Spalding. Mrs. Clark from Russell & Mrs. Noble & Charley's folks. The Band Boys came home today from Harisville [Harrisville].

Sunday, September 5   A terible hot day. No meting here today. Quartily meting at Pitcairn. Charley's folks all went up to Benny's [Noble] today. Took their company all with them. A.P.'s folks all away visiting. Wm out riding up around Shawville. I at home all day. Sherman & I all alone.

Monday, September 6   A nice cool day. I have done a large washing today. Wm has had his new stable frame put up today. I sent a letter to Brother Abel [Johnson] today. S. P. Rise [Rice] took supper with us tonight.

Tuesday, September 7   Quite cool but Pleasant all day.

Robert Brown is very sick. Agness was here today to let us know about him. Charley cut his corn today. Wm sent a letter to E. Brown of Canada today.

Wednesday, September 8   Cool all day. A litle frost this morning. We got a telagram from Canada last night. Brother E. Brown is very sick. Wm sent a telagram to Tilsonbury [in Canada] today. Charley's folks have gone to Fine, NY today.

Thursday, September 9   No rain this week. Ground very dry. Wm is away to call on his Brother Rob tonight. A Gentleman is stoping over night with us. It is Mr. Cumber. He is working for Alvah.

Friday, September 10   A Pleasant day. A republican ralley [rally] this evening. The Cornet Band joind [joined] the Entertainment. A full house at the Rushton Hall. We all went down in the new Band Wagon.

Saturday, September 11   This has been a nice Pleasant day. I have done my house work & made a new flanel [flannel] shirt for Wm. I do my sewing by hand. Jap [Jasper] Ward lost his wallet & 50 dollars last Sunday.

Sunday, September 12   We all went to church today. Mr. Hawley Preached. Brother Warren & his wife came home with me. Stayed untill night. Wm brought me a new Pair of gaters last night.

Monday, September 13   It has raind nicely today. Wm & Mr. Erwin has finished their stone wall under the Barn tonight. Wm intends to start for Canada tomorow. He has gone down town tonight. C. H.[Charles Hiram Brown] is away for lime.

Tuesday, September 14   It is cold & clowdy this morning. Wm has gone with the stage this morning to take the train at noon for Tilsonbury, Canada.

Wednesday, September 15   A cold morning.   Some frost. Very pleasant all day.   Mr. Erwin & Hugh Pratt is working for Charley yesterday & today, building the ash house.   I got a letter from A. P. Johnson last night.   Jo & Susa talk of coming in two weeks.

Thursday, September 16   A beautiful day.   I have been to town all day.   Made six calls.   Took tea with Sister Hall. Bought 3 lbs of crackers & 1 lb of soda of James Brown.   Got home at dark.

Friday, September 17   No rain today.   Geting terible dry.   Mr. Erwin finished the ash house today noon & went home.   A. P. & his man is diging Potatoes this week.   Mattie is spinning her stocking yarn.

Saturday, September 18   A thunder shower this morning at 3 o'clock.   Been pleasant since nine this forenoon.   A lovely evening.   The boys all gone to town to a Band meting.   Wm been gone all the week.

Sunday, September 19   It has been a very warm day. Charley's folks all went to church.   I stayed at home.   Alvah's folks went for a visit some Place.   I got a letter from Wm last night from Canada.   He was well.

Monday, September 20   It has been a rainy day & quite warm. I have Peaced [pieced] a quilt & put it on to the frames so it is all ready to begin to quilt.   It is in stripes.

Tuesday, September 21   It has been a terible windy day & quite cool.   A. P. brought over some Potatoes tonight & put them in our cellar.   I have been very buisy today tacking a quilt.

179

Wednesday, September 22 It has been a cold day this. I got a letter from Wm tonight from Canada. I made a visit to Stilman Brown's today. Robert Brown sold his farm yesterday for 34 hundred dollars to Miron [Myron] Clark.

Thursday, September 23 It has been a Pleasant day but quite cold. Charley commenced his threshing today. Thare was six men at the work today with the mashine. He had six bushels of wheete of four bushels sowing.

Friday, September 24 This has been a lovely day. Charley finished his threshing tonight. Sarah made me a call this afternoon. I washed my windows today.

Saturday, September 25 A very warm day. I made a visit to Jap Warde's today. Sherman & Mabel went with me.

Sunday, September 26 It has been a warm day. The wind blows hard tonight & it has raind some just dark. Charley's folks went to Church. Mr. Lee Preached today. Mr. Woolever is very sick.

Monday, September 27 It raind quite hard this morning. Has been pleasant since ten o'clock. I done my washing & some Baking today & finished my quilt & cleand the chamber whare I done my quilting. I got a letter from William tonight.

Tuesday, September 28 This has been a rainy day & quite cold. Alvah went with a load of cheese to DeKalb today. The cheese was sold for 13 cents a pound. Charley went to Gouverneur today after Agnes Green.

Wednesday, September 29 Been a rainy day. Pleasant a litle while at a time. Charley came home from Gouverneur this morning. Agness Green & Harvey Osmore came with him. They all went to Benny's this afternoon.

Thursday, September 30   One more rainy day.   Charley Built a corn crib between the showers.   He has husked 30 Baskets of corn.   Sarah had company yesterday.   Nelson Freman & his wife.   I sent a letter to Wm today.

Friday, October 1   This has been a Pleasant day.   Charley finished diging his Potatoes.   Henry Tompson took 20 Bushels this afternoon.   Payed 30 cents a Bushel.   Thare is a Republican meting tonight.

Saturday, October 2   One more pleasant day.   Alvah finished diging his Potatoes today.   C. H. filed [filled] his Barn with corn today.   Hugh & Carie has gone to York [Little York] for a visit to Addia Webb's.   Sister Hall came here tonight.   Sent a Paper to Wm today.

Sunday, October 3   This is a nice morning.   Quite a high wind.   Warm & Pleasant.   Sister Hall stayed all night with me.   Charley caried her home when he & the Boys went to Benny Noble's.   They have gone after Martha.   She has been up thare since Wednesday.

Monday, October 4   It has raind hard all of this afternoon.   Charley's folks all went to Tom Noble for a visit.   Mrs. Noble & Mariah & Agness came home with Martha last night.   I got a letter from Wm tonight.

Tuesday, October 5   It has been a Pleasant day but the wind Blows hard tonight.   A. P. went to Russell after Apples today.   I went over & helped milk tonight.   Charley folks all went to Mrs. Laidlaw's today.

Wednesday, October 6   A visit from Mrs. Thomas Watson today.   Some showers & some sunshine today.   Martha & her mother & Agnes & Mariah have gone to John Newton's for a

181

visit this afternoon.

Thursday, October 7 Warren & Edward Streeter are in town visiting friends. Quite a number from Michigan that came on the Excertion [Excursion] train here & in Pitcairn & Hermon visiting friends. They intend to return next week. I sent a letter to Wm Tuesday the 5th to Canada.

Friday, October 8 This has been a very Pleasant day. Charley's folks all came home from Russell today noon & drove down to the talc mines in the afternoon. They went to Russell Thursday. I am staying at home as usual. A hard frost this morning.

Saturday, October 9 This is a lovely morning. One year yesterday since Mother Brown died the 8th of October 1879. James Harmon came in town Wednesday 6th to visit his friends. Is from Rochester, NY.

Sunday, October 10 This has been a warm day. Charley's folks went to Church today. Carie went up to Alen Payn's today. Em Hall made me a call tonight. I stayed at home all day today.

Monday, October 11 This has been a warm day. Alvah commenced his thrashing today. Had 52 Bushels of wheat. I worked for Sarah all day. Come home at eight in the evening. Sherman & I.

Tuesday, October 12 It was raining hard this morning until 9 o'clock. I worked for Alvah's folks today. They did not get through thrashing today. Benny Noble has gone to Gouverneur after Orin & Emeline Sprague.

Wednesday, October 13 This has been a pleasant day but quite cool. I done a large washing today. Orin Sprague &

Emeline came here today from Michigan on a visit to their friends.

Thursday, October 14   A nice warm day this. I got a letter from Wm this morning.   He is coming home next week. Agness Brown made a visit to Alvah's today & a call on me.

Friday, October 15   This has been a lovely day. I made a visit to Sister Hall's today.   Phila & James Harmon & Charley & Maryette was thare on a visit.   We had a good visit.   Alma Pratt is very sick with a fever.

Saturday, October 16   This has been a rainy day.   The wind is howling tonight & it rains hard.   The Band boys are all away to Russell to Play for a Democrat meting.   I have Been to work over to A. P. Brown's all day.

Sunday, October 17   It raind this morning.   Has been clowdy all day but very cold.   The Band boys got home from Russell at 3 o'clock this morning.   Had a wet time.   Charley went up to Ben Noble's to day.   Martha came home to night.   Been gone since Tuesday.

Monday, October 18   This has been a stormy Monday.   The wind Blew terible all the forenoon & at eleven o'clock the snow Began to come down at a fearful rate untill most three.

Tuesday, October 19   This has been a stormy day.   It has snowd fearfully today.   William got home tonight.   Been gone five weeks today.   He found the snow over one foot deep this side of Buffalo.

Wednesday, October 20   This has been quite a good day. Plenty of wind But no storm.   Wm Brought me a nice gold watch & chain for a Presant.   He bought it in Ingersol, Canada. Payed 47 dollars.

Thursday, October 21   It has not stormed today. Martha went to Gouverneur today. We sent our sewing mashine Back to Gouverneur. It would not run good. A call from the Preacher & wife today.

Friday, October 22   Pleasant this forenoon & raind all of the afternoon. I had company today.   Sister Phila & James Harmon & Sister Hall, Mr. Baker & Charley's folks. Martha & Moriah got home tonight.

Saturday, October 23   A lowry forenoon. It has raind all of the afternoon. A republican lecture tonight. I have done my washing today & washed four windows & cleand all the woodwork & cupboard.

Sunday, October 24   This morning it was snowing & was snowing at 10 the night before. A cold stormy day. The snow is quite deep tonight. Charley took Mariah home & brought Back Sprague & Emeline.

Monday, October 25   It has been quite a nice day after the storm. The Libra Agent cald here today. We payed him 90 cents to become a member of the reading club.

Tuesday, October 26   This has been a rainy day. The snow is most all gone. Charley's folks & Orin Sprague & Emeline went to Nelson Freman's today for a visit & see the talc mines.

Wednesday, October 27   This has been a cold day but no storm.   Raind hard last night.   Our folks are all to the republican letcture tonight. Sherman & I are here alone. It is fearfuly dark out tonight.

Thursday, October 28   This has been a Pleasant day But quite cool. It frose in the shade. Mrs. John Newton visited at Charley's all day. Wm took Dinner at James Harmon's today.

I sent a letter to Wm E. Brown & one to A. P. Johnson.

Friday, October 29   It has not stormed any today but it has been clowdy most all day. It frose hard last night. Wm took 2 Bushels of wheat to mill today. I commended to make a vest for Wm today.

Saturday, October 30   This has been a rainy day. It is raining hard tonight. I have been making a vest for William today. Wm has been Blasting rocks.

Sunday, October 31   A stormy day. No meting at our church today. The church was Plastered Saturday & was all in a mess. Alvah & Sarah came over hear to dinner.

Monday, November 1   Raind part of the time today. I have been over to Harmon's all day. They had a Party. Charley's wife had a little girl Baby. It Died. I dressed it to be Beried.

Tuesday, November 2   This has been a nice day. [T]his has been Election day. I have been to the village today. Cald at Sister Hall's & Albert Wites & George Ivers & at Jim Brown's store.

Wednesday, November 3   This has been a lovely day. I have been at home all day. Lillia Gorden made me a call & Martha stayed with me most of the afternoon.

Thursday, November 4   Not so Pleasant today. Clowdy & looked like rain. Did rain a litle. Wm & Sherman & I went over to Stilman Brown's this afternoon for a visit. We cald at the Doctor's in the evening a litle while.

Friday, November 5   Looked like rain this morning. Pleasant in the afternoon. Charley and Orin Sprague took Dinner with me today. William has gone to Charley Harmon's to Build a

185

sugar Arch. Martha has gone to Ben Noble's. Caria gone to help clean the church.

Saturday, November 6   This has been a warm day. Charley went up to Benny's after Martha. Sherman & I went with him as far as Charley Harmon's.

Sunday, November 7   It has been a terible cold windy day. It raind all night & snowed a litle today. Wm & I came home this morning. He finished Charley's [Harmon] Arch last night. Took 2 days.

Monday, November 8   This is a cold day. It frose some this morning. Martha has got a Dressmaker here from Gouverneur to make her new Dress & Mariah to Help.

Tuesday, November 9   A rainy afternoon. Pleasant in the forenoon. We attended the funeral of Alice Harmon this afternoon. She died last night. Mr. Wheeler Preached the funeral sermon at the house.

Wednesday, November 10   This is a lovely day. Warm & Pleasant. Martha has gone to cary Mariah home today. Graham Stevenson Brought us a new chain Pump. They have Put it in the well today.

Thursday, November 11   It has been a rainy day. Wm has been puting in glass in to the windows & in the clock. I have done my Ironing & finished Sherman's Pants & Baked Bread.

Friday, November 12   One more stormy day. Wm & Charley finished their sugar Arch. Martha finished her new dress. John Noble Died today, noon.

Saturday, November 13   This has been quite a good day. I have made Pies. Done my Saturday work. Done lots of mending.   Went over & stayed with Sarah in the evening. Alvah went to the village.

Sunday, November 14   This has been a terible stormy day. We have all that was Able to go.   Been to John Noble's funeral & the snow came down at a fearful rate.   Sprague & Emeline is at Charley's tonight.

Monday, November 15   This has been a very Pleasant day after the snow storm of last night.   I have done Sarah's washing & mine today.   Charley & Pa kild their Hog today.

Tuesday, November 16   One more Pleasant day but the wind is Blowing quite hard this evening.   It has snowed a litle.   The boys played Euchar [Euchre, card game] in Charley's tonight. Martha & Emeline & Carie stayed with me.

Wednesday, November 17   It was Pleasant this morning.   It snowed a litle in the night & a litle this afternoon.   Charley & Martha & Sprague & Emeline & Benny's folks all went to Russell today.   Intend to come home tomorrow.

Thursday, November 18   It has snowed 2 inches in the night & is snowing fast this morning.   William went down to Robert's [Brown] yesterday.   They have mooved down on to the old farm with Stilman.   Sold their farm up home.

Friday, November 19   This has been quite a cold day. Charley's folks got home from Russell today noon.   Alvah went to Gouverneur today.   Took his fall Butter.   3 tubs 60 lbs. Tubs got 25 cents a pound.

Saturday, November 20   It has been a stormy day.   Snowed a litle.   Is snowing tonight at 10 o'clock.   Sarah has been here this Evening while Alvah has gone to town.   Martin has gone to DeKalb [NY] today for a visit.

Sunday, November 21   This has [been] an awful day for November. The wind has Blown fearfuly all day. The snow has just come up in Piles. Charley's folks all went up to Ben Noble's today. Caria went up to Warren Payn's today.

Monday, November 22   This has been a cold Pleasant day. I have done my washing & done some stitching on my sewing mashine for the first time since last May when Em Noble broke it.

Tuesday, November 23   This has been a nice day. Charley's folks went up to Benny Noble's to attend the Weding of Mariah & Mr. Kirkbride. Caria came home today from Payn's.

Wednesday, November 24   This has been a rain cold day. The wind is blowing hard tonight. Wiley Newton is sick with the quinsa [inflammation of the tonsils of the throat.] Has been for a week. Cara went to see him today.

Thursday, November 25   This has been a Pleasant day. This is thanksgiven day.   Charley's folks made a Party.   Had roasted turkey & envited all of her folks to dinner. None of Charley's folks envited as usual.

Friday, November 26   This has been a Pleasant but quite cold. I made a call at A. P. Brown's today. Mrs. Soper is working for them this Week. Charley is away up to Ben Noble's all day. Martha & Cara have the choors all to do.

Saturday, November 27   This has been quite a good day. Snowed some. Sherman & I have been to Brother Robert's [Brown] today for a visit. Came home since dark. Charley went to Gouverneur today to cary Mariah's goods.

Sunday, November 28   This has been a good day. A trifle milder. Rob Wilson & Emma Noble is calling at Charley's tonight. Charley caried Caria Kelsa [Carie Kelsay] home today to stay 3 weeks.

Monday, November 29   This has been quite a good day. Snowed some in the night & a litle today. I have done a large washing today. My own & Sarah's. I done Sarah's washing two weeks ago today. Mrs. Soper left Alvah's yesterday to go to Tom Grant's.

Tuesday, November 30   Commenced yuseing [using] the flour of a bag of wheat today. This has been a nice day. Alvah has been gone all day looking for a girl. I have done my house work & cut & made a vest & one apron & done some Baking.

Wednesday, December 1   This has been a stormy day. Has snowed all day. Alvah has been looking two days after a girl to work. Hant [Haven't] found any yet. Wm made a Pair of stairs & Put them in the cellar from the hall.

Thursday, December 2   This has been a cold Pleasant day. Wm & Alvah done their killing Hogs today. I went over & helped in the house this afternoon. Emma Hall made us a call.

Friday, December 3   This has been a Pleasant day. Very Cold tonight. Rob Webb & wife & young Rob & his wife made us a visit this evening. Stayed until twelve o'clock.

Saturday, December 4   This has been a pleasant day. I have tried out the leaf lard today. Wm cut up the Pork at Alvah's & salted it & churnd. They fild a crock for me. Charley's folks went up to Noble's, Oren & Emeline came home with them.

Sunday, December 5   The thaw commenced in the night. This morning it was raining. Has thawed all day. The sleighing is most done. The wind is howling fearfuly tonight.

Monday, December 6   This has been a cold windy day but no storm. The sleighing gone. I have worked hard all day. It is most 10 o'clock. Made my sausage & Head cheese & mince meat & done my Baking. Lots of other choors.

Tuesday, December 7   It snowed all this forenoon. The sleighs are running a litle. We had company tonight. Mr. Woodcock & wife & Orin Sprague & Martin Bevins & C. H. Brown. The men had a game of Eucher. Had a call from Martha & Emaline today. A letter from J. Foster today.

Wednesday, December 8   This has been a bleak cold day. Snowed a litle. Rrite & Mettie Robinson cald on us today. Wm Payed her 50 dollars.

Thursday, December 9   A fearful stormy day. Sprague & Emaline went to Fullerville [NY] Charley went after them in the afternoon to go up to Benny's. Mrs. Noble is very sick. They all came back at dark.

Friday, December 10   This has been the coldest day this winter. The sone has shone all day but very cold. Charley & Martha went up to Benny Noble's to see her mother but she is better.

Saturday, December 11   Not quite as cold today. Wm & Sherman & I went to granpa Clealand's today. Alax has been home one week. Charley Johnson & Celia commenced housekeeping the last of November. They was maried the first of November.

Sunday, December 12   This has been a nice day. Alvah & Sarah went to Grant's today. Sprague & Emeline came down to Charley's today.

Monday, December 13   A mild thawing day. Charley went to

190

Canton today to sit on the Jury. I went to Rob Webb's this afternoon. Stayed one hour then went [to] J. Woodcock's in the evening. Wm came. We took super thare.

Tuesday, December 14   It has snowed some today but is thawing tonight. I made a call to Alvah's today. Sprague & wife & Martha made a visit to Sandy Noble's today.

Wednesday, December 15   A stormy day turning colder. A visit from Sister Hall today. A Donation at the Rushton hall for Brother Hawley. There was to be music by the Band.

Thursday, December 18   The weather quite cold today. Good sleighing. Emeline & Martha made a visit to James Harmon's today. Alvah's man Martin came home Drunk this morning.

Friday, December 19   This has been a cold day. Alvah has been drawing Wood for Wm two days. Wm went down town this afternoon. He does the chours for Alvah. Sprague & Emeline made a visit to Wm Barford's today.

Saturday, December 20   Charley is at Canton all this week. Sprague does his choors while he is gone. Mrs. Pratt made me a call today & a visit to Charley's. Mr. Hawley got 80 dollars for his donation on Wednesday evening, the 15th.

Sunday, December 20   Not very cold today. Snowed a litle. Charley's folks Went up to Ben Noble's today. Carie Kelsa came back to Charley's tonight. Been gone home 3 weeks. Charley came home from Canton last night.

Monday, December 21   Sister Phila is very sick. Has been nearly 2 weeks. This has been a nice day. I done my washing this forenoon then went to Woodcock's to dinner. Sherman & I. Wm took Diner to Alvah's.

Tuesday, December 22   This has been a nice day. Wm & I went to Charley Harmon's this afternoon to see sister Phila. She is very sick. I am knitting a Pair of double mittings for Wm.

Wednesday, December 23   One more beautiful winter day. Good sleighing. Not much snow. I made a visit to Sister Hall's today. Wm came after me with the colt & cutter at three. It is colder tonight.

Thursday, December 24   This has been a pleasant day. The trees are looking beautiful. They are covered with frost. Have been for three days. No wind this week so far.   We had a letter from Canada the 20 [th].

Friday, December 25   This has been a nice day. I went to the Band show with Charley's folks. Wm & Sherman stayed at home. The Hall was well filed [filled]. They took in 80 dollars & had a dance after the showes.

Saturday, December 26   November the 9th 1880 William Laidlaw died. He was formally of Edwards [NY]. He went to Indiana a few years, since he was 56 years old. Never maried.

Sunday, December 27   Maria Noble was maried November the 23, 1880. November the 10th 1880 Charles Johnson & Celia Laidlaw was maried in Pitcairn, NY.

Monday, December 28   November the 27, 1880 Moris [Morris] Pratt & Vanera Hall was maried In Russell [NY] of Edwards. Ellie Hughs Maried the last week in September 1880.

Tuesday, December 29   November the 12, 1880, Mrs. John Noble the 1 died at noon today. The effects of a sore hand from the poison of a sick cow.

Wednesday, December 30   Oct the 9 Mrs. Alfred Moors of Russell hung herself with towel.

Thursday, December 31   Mr. Starkes Johnson of Pitcairn died after a severe illness of eight days.   Beried the first day of August.

Memoranda portion of the diary:

Clealand Noble's house burnt March the 11, 1878.

John McFerin's house burnt November the 8 1877.

Janet Wilson died October the 6, 1873. Edwards NY.

Anna Beach died July the 24. Age four years & one month. 1881.

James Wilson died September the 5th, 1874, Edwards.

Thomas Clealand died April the 9th, 1878, Edwards, NY.

Robert McCargin died April the 23, 1877, Edwards.

Guy Earl died May the 14, 1877, Edwards, NY

John McFerin died March the 23, 1877 in Canada.   The old man

Aunt Susan Bunnell died November the 21, 1877 at Rensselear Falls, NY, aged 88 years.

Jessie Bunnell, uncle, died February 1876, age 90 years. Canton, NY

Otis Earl of Hermon formily [formerly] of Edwards, died Feb the 5th, 1877. Aged 50 years

Robert B. Brodie died January the 7th 1874. Aged 21 years & 3 months in Jacson, Florida.

Robert Brown, senior, died July 19, 1878. Age 86, Edwards, NY

Agness Brown died October the 8, 1879, age 85, Edwards, NY.

Jurane Noble died March the 23, 1879.

Lidia Ward died September the 23, 1879 at 5 O'clock in the morn. Lydia's buried the 24, 1879. Clinton, Iowa.

Margaret Brodie died July the 17, 1878. Age 50 years.

Hariet [Harriet] Brown died August 14, 1853, age 22 with consumption. Edwards, NY.

David Brown died February the 15, 1863, Edwards, NY

Harvy A. Brown died at the Batle [Battle] of Coal Harbour, June 2, 1864, from Edwards. Town of Mount Gilead, Marion County.

James Brown died July the 12th, 1851 in Ohio.

Abel Pratt died April 14, 1860, age 36 years.

Charles Johnson of Edwards died April the 20, 1847, age 62. Father. Oh weep no more for father. His troubles now are ore. He is free from storms & trials. His Bark has reachet the shore.

Rachel Johnson died June the 20, 1862. Age 74. Mother. Of

that celestial city whose inmates never die & if we love the saviour, we shall meet them by & by.

Eben Harmon died May, 1878. Age 70 years. Dear brother thou has gone & left us waiting on the other shore. We went with you to the river & saw you pass forever more. Edwards, NY.

Cash Accounts –Summary [in Diary book]

March the 11th, 1880 3 lbs of crackers
March the 24. A letter from Canada
March the 25 3 lbs of butter from A. P. Brown

April the 8th, 2 lbs of butter from C. H. Brown & Bower 10 c

May 14. Took some sugar down to Jim Brown's. 30 lbs.

October the 3rd   Mrs. Truman Thompson died in Edwards, NY.

May the 22 4 yds of lace bought of J. Brown. Four lbs of sugar, 3 lbs of Rice,1 lb of tea. 2 lbs of coffee.

May 28 goods of J. Brown: one yd of lace; one dozen coat butons [buttons] for Sherman. 2 spools of thread.

May 29 Sent ninety lbs of sugar to James Brown by Charley on the milk wagon.

June 15 3 lbs of crackers from J. Brown's

July 22 bought of H. & J. Brown one dollar & 25 cents of goods.
June 10 Payed 21 shilings to Charley for oil cloth carpet.

June 14 Payed 43 cents for varnish & carpet tacks.

June 22 Payed 70 cents for strawberies. 5 cents to Sherman.

August 3 Sent 56 lbs of sugar to James Brown.

August 18 Two lbs of crackers of James Brown

August 20 give Sherman 5 cents.

August 6 give Clarance 10 cents

August 6 gave Bower 10 cents

August the 18   Dan Clealand & Mary made us a good visit today. Took dinner & supper in Charley's. Wm & Sherman & I was envited in to visit & take dinner with them.

They came in my room part of the time. We had a good visit. Long to be remembered. They are here from Coopersville, Michigan visiting friends.

September 24 I bought 2 lbs of roales of H. Gardiner. I payed him 3 dollars & 25 cents for roals & gaters & envelopes & paper & postage stamps by Charley Brown.

Oct the 9 28 lbs of sugar to James Brown.

October the 20   Bought of James Brown   10 dollars & 43 cents in goods, 1880.

November 2 Bought of James Brown 12 yds of veil cloth, 5 shilings a yard.

September the 10 Bought of James Brown, 4 yards of flanel for Wm a shirt, 45 cents a yard; one scain of yarn, 18 cents, one box of colars 25 cents. September 10, 1880

September 16 Bought of James Brown, 3 lbs of crackers. 1 paper of saleratus.

March the 14 1881 sold James Brown one hundred lbs of sugar.

March 17 bought of J. Brown, 67 cents of goods

August the 10 Carie Kelsey left Alvah's & came to Charley's to work.

December the 11th, 1880, Payed Helen Clealand seven shillings for a hood.

November the 10th 1880 Charles Johnson & Celia Laidlaw was maried.

A daughter born to them the first of August 1881.

May 29 Payed Lizie Grifin three dollars for my new bonnet.

June 25 sold four bushels of potatoes for 50 cents a bushel. I have the money.

August 26 Payed a pedler 75 cents for goods.

September 10 Payed Willie Brown 30 cents to send for cardes.

August 9 Emmah Nobel [Noble] went home from Charley's. Got through work. Been thare over one year.

July 24 Payed 50 cts to Mr. Brayton for rasberies.

Payed 25 cents for package of Needles

June 21 payed one dollar for goods to a pedler

July 3 payed 25 cents to the Band up to the Shawville Picnic

June the 10 I bought 16 lbs of butter of Charley Harmon. Paid 20 cents a pound. Payed Charley Harmon 80 cents for building fires & taking care of church. Payed Silas Rice one dollar for Elder Dyke as missionary in our state.

June 21 Paid one dollar & 25 cents for goods of a pedler & 25 cents for soap.

April the 9th Wesley McBrier made us a call today & a visit to Alvah's. He is in town from Michigan calling on friends. Jane is staying with her sister Julia Grant. She is not expected to live but a few days.

May the 12 Alma Pratt came to Charley's to make a silk dress for Martha.

Died in Edwards, November the 17th 1878 of brain fever. Clara E. Brown in her tenth year.

Dear Clara thou hast gone and left us. Waiting on the other shore. We went with you to the river and saw you pass forever more. Our hearts with grief were breaking. When we saw you go but the Saviour cald you from this wourld [world] of sin and wo [woe]. Mother.

Died in Pine Valley, Chemung Co., NY Adaline Brown, third wife of J. P. Brown formaly from Edwards, NY. February the fourteenth 1880.

Died in Edwards July the 9th of consumption. Sarah McFerin. Oldest daughter of Samuel & Mrs. McFerin.
Edwards, July the 9[th] 1880.

In Edwards of consumption, July the 22, 1875. Mania Brown, wife of A. P. Brown. We were living in undisturbed pleasure. Not thinking but what it would last. When a messenger came in to our household and ore us a dark shadow cast, it was the angel of death and he summon[e]d dear Manie away unheeding our tears and our pleading, that with us our loved one mite stay. Mother

Died in Edwards, March the 13th 1880

Mrs. George Freeman, wife of the son of Thomas Freeman.

Mrs. John Dygart died yesterday, March the 17, 1880, Hermon.

Died in Russell [NY] April the 11, 1880 Julia Rushton, wife of Thomas Grant, age 45 years.

Died in Edwards [NY] Alice, wife of Charles L. Harmon, November the 8th. Beried the 9th. Her litle infant was beried with her in the same coffin.

November the 23. Mariah Noble was maried today to a Mr. Kirkbride formally of Pitcairn, NY but lately from Michigan.

October the 6th. James Harmon came from Rochester [NY] to visit his friends in Edwards & Russell & Pitcairn.

Oct the 19   Wm came home from Canada. He brought me a gold watch & chair. Cost forty seven Dollars. Bought for himself a good overcoat & hat & boots. A new dress for Mabel & one for Manie Brown.

May the 3   Miss Adia Felows [Fellows] commenced teaching our school Monday, May the 3. She hires her board to Charley's Brown's.

August 26   Gave Mettie Robertson a glass pitcher, 1 glass spoon holder, 1 glass butter dish that was her grandmother Brown's. & cups & sausers [saucers] & soap dish. 2 quilts. Flanel sheets.

Uncle Aaron Pratt died 1833, age 39.   He was a Baptist Minister of Edwards, NY. My Mother's brother.

Died in Edwards, May the 1 1880   Russell Stuart, aged 88 years.
1880 August 28 James McKee died age 84.

April the 19th. The 2 thunder shower.

December the 5, 1840   Grandfather Abel Pratt died, age 84. He was a pensioner of the Revalution [Revolution] War.

Grandmother Pratt died September the 15, 1842, age 84. Rachel Payn[e] was her maiden name.

March the 27, 1880   Wesley McBrier & Jane came from Michigan.   Arrived at Tom Grant's Saturday night.   Julia is very sick. Is not expected to live but a few days. Her sister Jane has come to visit her once more perhaps for the last time. April the 11, 1880 Julia Grant died tonight at nine o'clock.

April the 14   Miss Ann Noble & Miss Ruby Hefenstall, & Mrs. Jenney Raymond made a visit to Charley's & a call in my room.

Sept the 2   Alvah brought me 1 lbs of tea on the sugar that he took to Kingsbery.

October the 20 2 lbs of tea from Jim Brown.

December the 26   2 lbs of tea 1880

Ms. Jap Warde had a daughter born March the 12th, 1880.

April the 10th, 1880   Sixteen years today Wm Brown & family mooved on to the Brodie farm in 1865.

September the 14, 1880   Mr. McColume was beried today. He remains caried to Hermon.   The funeral service is at his house in Edwards near Charley Harmon's.

Alvah has four new milk cows before the 10 of March, March the 10, 1880.

Robert Brown & Stilman drove 25 cows down on to the old Brown farm today & mooved down to commence work on their new bought farm. Agness, Stilman & Perce Brown, March the 10, 1880.

March the 7, 1880. Wm brought me 45 lbs of new sugar from Alvah's.

March the 10th   Alvah brought me 55 lbs of sugar today.

April the 6, 1880   We got a letter from A. P. Johnson.   Wm sold the house & lot in the lane today.   April the 6, 1880

Died   In Edwards, Feb 19th, 1880 of brain fever.   Amos Newton in his thirteenth year of his age.

O weep no more for Amy [Amos]. His sorrows now are o'er. He's free from storms and trials. His bark [boat] has reached the shore. Of that celestial city Whose inmates never die, And if you love his saviour, You'll meet him by & by.   A friend.

April 6, 1880   Charley's folks envited a party of litle girls from the village to eat sugar.

April the 7 A sugar party to Charleys' in the evening.

A.P. Johnson & Stellah his daughter came here to make us a visit the 23 of June. They started for home the 5th of July to Pine Valley, NY.

Charles Johnson died April 20th 1847 age 62. Rachel Johnson died June the 20th, 1859, age 72. Father & Mother.
Clara E. Brown died November the 17th 1868 in her tenth year.
Brother E. Harmon died May the [ ] 1878, age 70 years.

February the 25, 1880   Write Robertson's litle boy died today age one year & 23 days. Born the 2 of Feb. 1879.

Franky Robertson beried today. Febuary the 27, 1880.

> We miss our darling baby
> Whose spirits bright has flown
> To ralms [realms] of life eternal
> And left us sad & lone.
> His litle spirit saved upon the shining shore.
> His litle heart is cold.
> His pulses beet no more.

Edwards. [NY]   John Dain hung himself, March the 25, 1875.

Wilber Dumas sent to Canton Jail October 16, 1877.

Wm & Warren & Mariah & I started for Pine Valley, October 8, 1877. Oct the 12, Warren & Mariah started for home & Wm & I started for Canada. Arrived at Brother Ed Brown's the same night. Started for home November the 7. Got home the 8 of November.

Lizie Brodie was maried Jan the 6, 1875 to Mr. A. Bignell. Went to Clinton, Iowa.

Loise H Brodie died June the 2, 1874.

Amelia Kerr died June the 16, 1874.

Manie Brown died July the 22, 1875.
Amos S. Newton died Febuary the 19, 1880 in his thirteenth year.

Feb the 25th A cake of sugar today. Commenced on two lbs of tea today. Feb 25th

Commenced to yuse of the flour of two bushels of wheat, February the 26. The flour of 2 bushels of wheat April the 5th.

One quarter of beef, 25th of December 1879. Cooked the last, 25th th of Febuary, 1880.

Commenced on our Pork, Febuary 27th, 1880

August 27, Carie Kelsey went to the Harvest dance with Albert Cousins.   .

July the 19, 1880 Alvah bought a new bugy of David Noble. Payed 68 dollars.

The last week in September a man by the name of McKiney was kild by the running away of his teem. The wheel ran over the man's head & kild him instantly. It hapened near Fullerville.

September the 4th. Received a letter from William Brown of Canada bringing the news that his father is very sick & wishes that Wm would come & visit him very soon.

September the 6, 1880 Mrs. George Smith started for Mich[igan] this morning.

William arived at Tilsonburg [Canada] widnes at sunrise Sept the 15.

76 Dollars

[on overleaf]

Nancy A. Brown   Book   Edwards NY 1880

6 lbs cakes of sugar to J. Brown, Oct 9, 1880

1881
[All Written by William H. Brown]

Overleaf: A listing of Presidents of the United States from George Washington to Rutherford B. Hayes

Saturday, January 1   This has been a pleasant day. Not very cold. The Murcary at two degres blow [below] zero. Stood at eight above zero this evening. Thare was one hundred and forty couple[s] at the ball last night at the Rushton house. They say they had a splnded time. We took diner [dinner] over to Alvah ['s] today.

Sunday, January 2   This has been a pleasent day. Murcuary at two degres below zero this morning and at Seventeen above this evening. It has been some cloudy today. Syras [Cyrus] Cleland and his wife was down to Alvah today. We stayed to home all day.

Monday, January 3   This has been a stormy day. Snowed a little all day.   Murcary stood at seventeen above zero this morning. It stands at eight this evening. The Boys fild the ice house today with ice. It snowed about three inches today.

Tuesday, January 4   This has been a pleasent day but cloudy most of the day. Murcuary stud at fifteen degres blow [below] zero this morning. Stands at fifteen above zero this evening. Alvah went for a load of wood for the Minister this afternoon. Emma Hall called this after noon. Mr. Powers called this afternoon.

Wednesday, January 5   This has been a pleasant day. Not very cold. Cloudy most of the day. Snowed last night a bout one inch of snow. Mercuary stood at thirty eight above zero this morning. I went out to James Storan's this afternoon. Nancy Went over helped Sarah tack a quilt. Agness Brown came to stay all night but her mother sent for her this evening [not legible].

Thursday, January 6   This has been a stormy day. Has snowed a little all day. It thawed a litle today. Snowed about three inches last night. James W. Harmon paid interest on his bond. Laura Gorden had a baby boy last [this sentence had been crossed out]. Mrs. Robert Allen had a baby last Tuesday morning.

Friday, January 7   This has been stormy day. It snowed and blowed all day. Murcury stood at twenty five above zero this morning and this evening it stands twenty eight degrees above zero.   Alvah was drawing logs to the mill and I done the chores and filed a crosscut saw for Charley.

Saturday, January 8   This has been a pleasant day but quite cold. Murcuary at zero in the morning and fifteen above in the afternoon. The cornet Band plaid this evening. Nancy [and] I went to the vilage. Been cloudy most of the day.

Sunday, January 9   It has been pleasant today. Not very cold. Mercury at ten above zero this morning, rose to thirty this afternoon. Alvah and Sarah went up to Cyras Cleland to day. Emma Hall and Martin Bevin took supper with us this afternoon.

Monday, January 10   This has been a stormy day. Snowed most all day. It snowed about eight inches last night and today Murcuary stud at twenty degrees above zero this morning. I went to the vilage this afternoon to mail a letter for Nancy to go to James Foster [husband of half-sister of Nancy, Susan Viall Foster].

Tuesday, January 11   This has been a pleasent day but quite cold. Murcuary stood at zero this morning. Stands at ten blow [below] zero this evening. I done the chores as usual. Alvah drew two loads of hay. Wind West what thare was but it did not blow any.

Wednesday, January 12   This has been a pleasent day but quite cold. Mercurary stood at ten below zero this morning. Rose to fifteen above zero this afternoon. The sun shone bright all day. We ware drawing hay today. Celia Cleland was down to Alvah ['s] today. Wind was West this afternoon.

Thursday, January 13   This has been a pleasent day. Mercury ten above zero and Mercury stands at forty above this evening. Thawing quite fast. It rains a very little this evening. Nancy and I went down to Nicleous Coles this Evening. We drew hay this forenoon.

Friday, January 14   This has been quite a cold day. Murcuary ten above zero this morning and it is fifteen blow this evening. Wind North West. Alvah went for a load of sleepers over to Bakers. I went to the vilage. Paid Gardner twenty five cents.

Saturday, January 15   This has been a cold day. Murcury stood at thirty below & zero this morning. Stands at five below this evening. The sun shone brite all day. The boys ware [were] drawing sleepers today. I went to the vilage this evening to pay up for the Dumas Contract and get a deed of the land.

Sunday, January 16   This has been a pleasent day but quite cold.   Murcuary stood ten degrees below zero this morning. Stud [stood] ten above this evening.   Nancy went up to Charles Harmon's today to see Phila. I went over to Mr. Pains [Payne's] to have him take a Deed to Canton [NY] for me. Thomas Grant was out to Alvah today.

Monday, January 17   This has been a butiful day. The sun shone bright all day.   Quite Warm.   The Murcury stood at twelve below zero this morning. Stood at fifteen above this evening. We went up to Westly [Wesley] Harmon's funeral this afternoon.

Tuesday, January 18   This has been another Butiful day. Mercuary stood at twelve below zero this morning. The sun shone bright all day. I went up to Fine [NY] to day. Went up to Erwin. Staid all night.

Wednesday, January 19   This has been another pleasent day. Quit[e] warm. I came home from Fine today. The sun shone bright all day. I went to Thomas Houlan today.

Thursday, January 20   This has been a butiful day. Mercuary at two below zero this morning. The wind South West but not much. Alvah was drawing logs today. Martin's brother was here today. Waren [Warren] W. Johnson and Mariah was here today visiting. Sent a letter to A. P. Johnson today.

Friday, January 21   This has been a cold raw day. Cold North east wind. Mercuary stood at twenty above zero this morning. Stood the same this evening.   It is snowing and blowing fearful this evening.   I took two bushels of Wheat to Mill today.

Saturday, January 22   This has been rather a cold day. Murcuary Stood at fifteen this morning above zero and it stood fifteen above this evening. It snowed about one foot last night. The wind was North East today. Alvah broke his sled today. Broke on of the nees.

Sunday, January 23   This has been rather cold today. Cloudy most of the day. A little snow flying. Murcuary stood at twelve above zero this morning.   Stands ten above this evening. Stillman Brown and Agness Brown was here today. Alvah [&] Sarah was over. Martin had a drunk last night and slept all day.

Monday, January 24   This has been a cold day. Mercuary was twenty below zero this morning and it is ten above this evening. Sprag[u]e came back to Chas today. Charles has gone to the vilage tonight. Alvah was drawing logs today. I done the Chores as usual. Powers was here to get the Dumas house to live in. I did not let him have it.

Tuesday, January 25   It has been quit[e] cold today. The Wind has been West and quite cold. It snowed some this afternoon.   The Murcuary stood at ten above Zero this morning. Stands at fifteen above this evening. Alvah drew logs this forenoon and went to the vilage twice this afternoon. I went to the vilage this afternoon to get a sled beem.

Wednesday, January 26   This has been a stormy day. It has snowed all day and quite cold. Murcury ten above Zero this morning. Fifteen above this evening. I was fixing Alvah['s] sled today. Charles went to the Mill with a grist today.

Thursday, January 27   This has been a cold day. The Murcury stud at zero this morning. Stands at zero this evening. The Wind blowed conciderable hard from the West today. Alvah took the sled to the shop today to have the tee [a short piece of connective pipe shaped like a "T"] put on. They drew straw this afternoon. I made a little chare [chair] for Mania Brown this afternoon.

Friday, January 28   This has been a cold pleasent day. Wind south West. Murcuary stood at fifteen below zero this morning. Stands at ten below zero this evening. I went to Gouverneur [NY] to see Docterr. Liston and Judge E. H. Nery. Went with Kit. Alvah & Martin drew hay. Martin gon [e] to Hermon to a ball with Emma Hall.

Saturday, January 29   This has been a cold day. Wind West but not much. Murcary stood at thirty four below zero this morning. Stands eleven below this evening. Martin & Emma Went to Hermon last night to a dance. Have not got home yet. The Republican Party had a corcas [caucus] this evening. Alvah & I done the chores.

Sunday, January 30   This has been a cold stormy day. It snowed all day. Fell about six inches. Murcuary Stood two degres below zero this Morning. Stands six above this Evening. Wind North East all day. We all staid to home all day. Cyras Cleland was down to Alvah and his wife.

Monday, January 31   This has been a cold day. Wind North West in the morning. North East in the Evening. Mercuary stood eleven blow zero this morning. Stands at zero this evening. Alvah and Martin drew hay today and I done the chores as usual. Wrote a letter to send to Edward last night.

Tuesday, February 1   This has been a cold day. The coldest day that has been this winter. The Murcuary stood at fifteen below zero this morning. Stands ten below this evening. Has not got above zero today. Alvah Went to Hearmon [Hermon], [NY] today. Bought a bed stid [bedstead] and a little rocking chair for Manie Brown. I went to the Vilage this afternoon with a letter to send to Edward Brown.

Wednesday, February 2   This has been a cold day.   The coldest day we had this winter.   Murcury stood at forty two this morning below zero. Stood ten below all day. The sun shone bright all day. Mercurary Stands at twelve below zero this evening. I done the chores as usual.

Thursday, February 3   This has been a cold day.   The Wind has been blowing in all directions today.   Mercuary Stands fifteen below Zero this Morning.   Stands five this evening blow zero. I has hewing sleepers [railroad ties] with Martin today. Alvah caried Sarah up to Cyras Cleland this morning. Went up after her this afternoon.

Friday, February 4   This has been a cold day. Cloudy Most of the day.   Murcuary stood at zero this morning.   Stands at twenty below zero this Evening.   It is clear as a bell.   I have been sick all day. Got the medison [medicine] from Doct[or] Liston today.   Henry Johnson is visit at C. H. Brown's this afternoon and evening a Demacrat corcus [caucus].

Saturday, February 5   This has been a butiful day. Sun shone bright all day. Murcuary twenty-two below zero this Morning and ten below this evening at Nine O clock. I done the chores as usual. Alvah up to Ervin today for a load of Shingles. C.H. Brown went up to B.F. Noble's with Sprague and his wife.

Sunday, February 6   This has been a butiful day.   The sun shone bright all day. Murcuary stood at thirty two blow zero this Morning at eight O clock. Stands at zero this Evening at half past eight. Nancy and I went down to Robert Brown's this afternoon. Benganan [Benjamin] Noble & Mrs. Noble & Oren Sprague & wife are here at C. H. Brown's tonight. Going to start for Gouverneur tomorow morning.

Monday, February 7   This has been a butiful day. Sun shone brite all day. No wind. Murcuary fifteen below zero this Morning. At dark this Evening it was twenty above zero. C.H. Brown went to Gouverneur today with Oren Sprague and his wife & Mrs. Noble. Going to start for Michagon [Michigan] tomorrow at noon. Martin & I was hewing sleepers [railroad ties] today.

Tuesday, February 8   This has been pleasent day but cloudy all day & thawing. Murcury at thirty five above zero this morning and it is forty above zero this evening. I went to town Meeting. Henry Webb Was elected Supervisor.

Wednesday, February 9   This has been a warm day. It rained a little and thawed all day. Murcuary at forty above zero this morning and forty five above this Evening. Wind blowes from the South. Martin and I was hewing sleepers today. Alvah went to the Blacksmith Shop to get the horses shoes sat for sawing Wood.

Thursday, February 10   This has been quite a warm day. It has thawed fast all day. It rained some and the sun shone some. Wind blew quite hard from the South. Murcuary was forty five above zero this morning. It is forty above this Evening. Martin & I was hewing Sleepers what time we could for the rain. Alvah Went to the Mill.

Friday, February 11   It has been cloudy all day. Not very cold. Wind West. Murcuary at thirty above zero this morning and it [is] thirty above this Evening. The Funeral of Mrs. John Cleland and baby. The baby was put in the cofin [coffin] with its Mother. Mr. Holly preached the funeral sermon. I was hewing joists today. The rest went to funeral.

Saturday, February 12   This has been a nasty wet day. Been showery all day. Murcury Stood thirty above zero this

Morning. Stands at forty this evening. Alvah & Charles was drawing Sawdust for the ice house. Mrs. Wear died today at Gouverneur [NY].

Sunday, February 13   This has been a Stormy day. Snowed and blowed most all day. Blowed hard all day. Murcuary stood at twenty five above zero this Morning. It about the same this Evnng [evening]. Thare was not any meeting at the church today.

Monday, February 14   This has been a butiful day but quite cold. Sun shone bright all day. The Murcuary was six below zero this Morning. It stands two above zero this Evening. Wind blowed from West. We comensed to saw Wood today. Mrs. Wear was buried here today. The bord of Excise met today. They did not grant Dewlitle [Doolittle] lisence.

Tuesday, February 15   This has been a butiful day. Been clear all day. Thawed a very little. Murcuary was two above zero this Morning & it is fourteen above Zero this Evening. Martin & I was sawing Wood today. Alvah & Charles went for two loads of sawdust. Ten loads of grain came from Gouverneur today for Miles & Butler.

Wednesday, February 16   It has snowed a little all day & thawed a very little. Murcury Stood at twenty two above zero this morning & it stands at twenty two above this evening. I was sick this forenoon. We sawed wood this afternoon. Edward Brown is staying here tonight.

Thursday, February 17   This has been a cold pleasent day. Wind blew quite hard from the West. Mercuary Sixteen above Zero this Morning and stands twenty five above this Evening. Alvah would of finished cuting his Wood today if the machine had not broke. Mrs. Charles Beech and Miss Lily Gorden was here visiting today.

Friday, February 18   This has been a stormy day. Snowed a little all day till about three inches today. Murcury Stood at 16 above zero this morning. Stands at thirty above this Evening. Fixed the Machine and finished Alvah's wood. Mooved the machine over to My Wood. It snowed so hard we did not set Machine up.

Saturday, February 19   This has been a butiful day. Wind West. Murcuary eighteen degrees above Zero this morning. It is twenty above Zero this Evening. Martin & I helped Charles to saw his Wood today.

Sunday, February 20   This has been butiful day. The Sun Shone bright all day. Murcuary was eight degrees above zero this morning and it is twenty five above this evening. Nancy & Charles folks went to meeting. It was quarterly Meeting today. I stayed to home keep house.

Monday, February 21   This has been quit[e] stormy this forenoon. It snowed and thawed as it fell. Murcuary stood at twenty six this Morning. It Stands at twenty five this Evening. Comensed to cut my wood this afternoon. Charles is helping me. Mr. Dolen brot the nives [knives] he took to plate. Made a poor job of them.

Tuesday, February 22   This has been a Butiful day. Thawed a little at noon. Murcuary Stood at Zero this morning. Stands at twenty eight above this evening. The Wind blowes hard from the South West. I got a letter from L.W. Burell last night stating that he had got   G.W. Rusel Dission [Decision] reversed in the Gaddy [Gaddis] Suit. Charles has gon[e] to Fine [NY] with Cornet Band to play in Fine.

Wednesday, February 23   This has been a stormy day. Snowcd and blowed hard. Wind North Murcuary at twenty six above zero this Morning.   Ten below this Evening.

Snowed about 4 inches. I went to the Vilage today. Alvah went out to Thomas Grant's after Mrs. Saper. Martin Went to the vilage today. He did not work today.

Thursday, February 24   This has been a cold day. Wind North West. Mercuary was thirty four blow zero this morning. It rose to ten below zero at noon. It is Eighteen below this evening. It was so cold we did not saw much Wood. I went to the Mill bougt a sack of flower, [flour] one of meal [as in ground grain.]

Friday, February 25   This has been a pleasent day but quite cold. Murcuary stood at four below Zero this morning. Stands at twelve below this evening. The Wind has been in all directions today. Charles was helping me to saw Wood today. Alvah took Mrs. Sapper home & brot Nora Grant home with him. Mr. & Mrs. John Laidlaw are here tonight.

Saturday, February 26   This has been a butiful day, clear and pleasent all day. Murcuary Stood at Seventeen below Zero this Morning. It stands at ten above Zero this evening. Finished sawing my Wood today. Mr. & Mrs. Alfred Hall was here visiting this afternoon and evening.

Sunday, February 27   This has been a butiful Warm day. It has thawed all day. Wind blows from the South and Warm. Murcury thirty two above Zero this Morning. It is forty five this evening. Sherman & I went out to Trout Lake today. Went down to Mr. Webb's this evening.

Monday, February 28   This has been a warm rainy day. It snowed a few minits this afternoon. Murcuary Stood at forty above zero this morning. It stands at thirty above zero this evening. I made three ax helves today. Alvah Wife is not quite so well today. Charles Went to Mill today.

Tuesday, March 1   This has been a stormy day. Snowed a little all day. Fell about four inches of snow. Murcuary Stood at Sixteen derees [degrees] above Zero this Morning. It stands 10 above this evening. Wind North West today. Charles went up to Sairsburg for a load of logs for John McFarlen. I split a little Wood today.

Wednesday, March 2   This has been pleasent but cloudy all day. Wind North West. Mercuary Was two above zero this Morning. It is fifteen above this evening. Alvah took a load of straw down to Docter Goodnough this afternoon. I went to the vilage this afternoon.   Commissioner Cole held exemanation [examination] at [the] Vilag this after noon.

Thursday, March 3   This has been a pleasent day. It thawed some today. Murcuary stood at ten above Zero this Morning. Is thirty above Zero this evening.   Alvah & I was cuting timber to move the barn on. Martin is still spliting wood yet. Sarah is geting some better.

Friday, March 4   It has been quite stormy. It snowed very hard this morning. It fell about three inches. It thawed a little about noon. Murcuary was thirty above zero this morning. It is thirty above this evening. Nancy & I went to Mrs. Downs' funeral today. We called over to Robert Allen's after funeral.

Saturday, March 5   This has been a stormy day. It snowed a little all day but thawed about as fast as it fell. Mercuary was 30 above zero this Morning. It is twenty degrees faxer above this evening. Alvah & I went for a load of sticks for timber this forenoon. I went to the vilage this after with Mr. Nelson & James McKee.

Sunday, March 6   This has been a Butiful day. All most warm enough for sap to run. Mercuary 30 above zero this Morning. 34 above this evening. I have been sick all day.

Mrs. Hitchcock Maried Mr. Storen to the Widow of McGill.

Monday, March 7   This has been a butiful day.   The sun shone brite all day. Murcuary was 20 above zero this Morning. It is 28 above zero this Evening.   Clear and Butiful.   Stars shining bright.   Alvah & I comensed to tap the Shugarbush this afternoon.   Martin was spliting Wood for me today. Nancy helped Alvah folks today.   Done the work let Emma wash.

Tuesday, March 8   It has been a pleasent day.   The sun shone bright all day. Murcuary was sixteen above Zero this Morning. It is twenty eight above Zero this evening. We finished taping the Sugar bush all but twenty two trees.   Charles taped the most of his trees. Mrs. & Mr. Baker are at Charles' tonight.

Wednesday, March 9   It has bee[n] pleasent today.   Been cloudy all day. Not very Warm. Murcuary 32 above Zero this Morning. 32 above this evening. We boiled sap today. Five pailfull syrup.   Emma Noble was buried today.   William Green furnished the coffen and tended funeral servis. Alvah & Charles gon down to play on the band.

Thursday, March 10   This has been a cloudy dull day.   Sap did not run any today.   Comensed to snow a little this afternoon.   Wind blowes quite cold from the North today. Murcury at 30 above Zero this and 25 above this evening. Sugared of 14 ½ cakes of sugar. Finished boiling all the sap. Charles sugared of 7 cakes of sugar. The first, the first that we have made.

Friday, March 11   This has been quite cold. Cloudy & Wind North. Murcuary ten above zero this Morning & stayed at ten all day.   I went to the vilage this afternoon & got my boots mended & bought a new pare of boots. Alvah sugared of 165 lbs of sugar today. I went over to Mr. John Newton's this

216

evening.

Saturday, March 12   This has been quite cold. Cloudy day. Murcuary stood at ten above Zero this morning. It was thirty this evening. I was piling up Wood this forenoon. Helped Alvah to fix place for the cowes to water. Three cowes came in last night. Martin was spliting Wood for me today.

Sunday, March 13   This has been a stormy day. It has snowed all day and thawed a very little. Murcuary stood at thirty two all day. It has made out to gain about four inches of snow. Sap run a very little today. Thare was one cow came in this morning. Martin & Emma has gon to the vilage this afternoon and evening.

Monday, March 14   This has been a cloudy day. Not very cold. Sap run some. Cleared of[f] at Sundown. Murcuary at thirty above Zero this Morning. It is thirty this Evening. I took 101 pounds of sugar down to Brown & Brothers. Gave one each to Mrs. A.B. Goodnough. Went to the Sugarbush this afternoon. Gathered one tub of sap.

Tuesday, March 15   This has been a butiful day. The sap run good today. We boiled this afternoon. Got four pailfulls. The Murcuary was fifteen above Zero this Morning. It is thirty two this evening. Charles boiled enough sap to get four pailsfull of syrup today.

Wednesday, March 16   It has been cloudy all day. It froze a very little last night. Sap did not [run] much today. Murcuary was at twenty eight this morning. It is thirty two this evening. I started for the sugarbush at three o'clock this morning. Boiled sap all day. Got the Milk can most full of syrup. Sugared of 11 caks [cakes] today.

Thursday, March 17   It has been cloudy all day. Comensed to

217

rain about three o'clock this afternoon.   Rain toll night. Sap did not run much today.   Mercury 25 above Zero this morning. It is thirty above this evening. I boiled sap all day. Got a can full of syrup. Alvah sugared of 125 lbs today. Old Mrs. Whitehead was buried today by Wm. Green.

Friday, March 18   This has bee a cloudy day. Rained a little this afternoon.   Murcuary was thirty two above zero this Morning. It is thirty above this evening. I finished Alvah Milk rack this forenoon. I went to the vilage this afternoon. Alvah sugared of[f] today.

Saturday, March 19   It has been a cloudy day. It has rained hard this evening. Wind North east. Murcury thirty four above Zero this Morning. It is thirty four this evening. It was forty above at noon today. Thare was a factery Meetin this evening.   Mrs. Dolittle was buried today. Wm Green furnished coffin.

Sunday, March 20   This has been a cloudy day. It rained hard last night & it has rained a little all day. It is raining this evening. Murcuary Stood at 45 above Zero this Morning. It is 45 above Zero this evening. Nancy Wrote a letter to Sarah Brown & I wrot one to Edward Brown tonight.

Monday, March 21   This has been a nasty stormy day. Snowed some all day. Melted as fast as it fell. Murcury 30 above Zero this Morning. It is thirty above Zero this evening. I boiled sap today. Had six pailful of syrup. Sent a letter to Edward Brown today.

Tuesday, March 22   This has been rather colder today. Snowed a little by spells. Wind blowed considerable hard from the West. Murcuary was twenty five above Zero this morning. It is twenty above Zero this evening. Freezing quite hard tonight.   Alvah went to the mill with oats for the cowes.

I split wood this afternoon.

Wednesday, March 23   This has been a stormy day. It has snowed in squalls all day. No sap today. Murcuary 25 above Zero this Morning. 29 above this evening. Finished spliting our wood this forenoon. Alvah & Martin went back to the wood to cut wood this afternoon. Jason Woodcock & his wife & Mary was here this evening.

Thursday, March 24   This has been pleasent but quite cold. Wind blew quite hard from the West. The sap run a little this afternoon. Murcuary was 28 above Zero this morning. It is 25 this evening. Martin & I was hewing timber this afternoon. Alvah gathered three tubs of sap. Mrs. George Pagget [Padget] & Miss Hatty Pagget visited at Charles Brown's today.

Friday, March 25   It has been a cold day. Cold North Wind blowed quite hard. Frose all day whare the sun did not shine. Murcuary 15 above Zero this morning. It is 28 above Zero this evening. Martin & I was hewing timber today. Alvah was boiling & geatherin sap today. He brought home about four pails full of syrup.

Saturday, March 26   This has been a cold raw Windy day. Wind North West. It frose all day. Murcury ten above Zero this morning. It is twenty above Zero this Evening. I went to the vilage this forenoon. Got a bunce [bunch] of cotin [cotton] yarn. I tried to hew sticks this afternoon. Charles boiled sap today. Charles Hall has not got over the Measels yet.

Sunday, March 27   This was a blustery Morning. Snowed and blowed like fury. Snowed about four inches. Been a cold North West Wind all day. Murcuary 16 above Zero this morning. 15 above this evening. I sent away three hundred and thirteen Dollars to A. O. Brodie by Leveret Raymond to Gouverneur to get a Draft to send to Kansas to him.

Monday, March 28   This has been pleasent but afful cold West Wind. It frose all day in the shade. Murcuary Was 18 above Zero this morning. 28 this evening. I done the chores & Alvah & Martin went to the sugarbush. Boiled some sap. The sap run a little today. Charles went to the Mill today. Overs hired man borowed the Drill.

Tuesday, March 29   It has been pleasent but rather cold. Frose all day in the shade. Wind changed round from one place to another. Murcury 10 above Zero this Morning. 28 above this evening. Alvah sugared of 55 lbs sugar today. I was hewing today. Sap did not run much today. Sid Brown was here this afternoon.

Wednesday, March 30   This has been a cloudy day all day. Cold Northeast wind. It is snowing quite hard this evening. Murcuary stood at 25 this morning. It stood at thirty this evening. The sap did not run much today. I was hewing today. Charles and Martha went up to Charles Harmon's today.

Thursday, March 31   This has bee a cloudy day after the heavy fall of snow last night it fell ten inches deep last night of heavy Wet snow. Murcuary stood at thirty this Morning. Stands at thirty two this evening. I been sick all day. Alvah went down to Robert Brown's after a load of stakes. Charles boiled sap today.

Friday, April 1   This has been quite pleasent day but quite cold. North Wind. The wind blowes quite hard from the North this evening. Murcuary Stood at 20 this morning. Stands at 25 this evening. Went to the Sugar bush. Found bukets full of sap. Boiled sap all day. Martin broke the Nickyoke today.

Saturday, April 2   This has been a cold pleasent day. A very cold hard West Wind. It frose hard all day in the shade. Murcuary Stood at fifteen above Zero this morning. It stood ten above this evening. I started for the Sugarbush at four o'clock this morning. Boiled sap enough for two hundred and fifty pounds of sugar today.

Sunday, April 3   This has been a cold pleasent day. The sun shone bright all day but a aful cold West wind. Murcuary at fifteen this Morning above zero. It stands at twenty above Zero this evening. I helped Alvah to do the chores and sugar off.

Monday, April 4   This has been a cold pleasent day. Sun Shone bright all day. A very cold West Wind all day. Murcuary Stood at four above Zero this Morning. Stands at Sixteen this evening. Alvah and Martin drew hay today. I done the chores & sugared off & went to the sugarbush & cleaned the pan.

Tuesday, April 5   This has been a cold stormy day. Snowed and blowed all day. Wind North West. Murcury ten above Zero this Morning. It is twelve above this evening. I was sick this forenoon. Went to the vilage this afternoon. Alvah went to the vilage this afternoon to get horses shod. Emma Hall & Ida Brown gon to the vilage this evening.

Wednesday, April 6   This has been a pleasent day but afful cold. West Wind. It frose all day. Murcuary at four above Zero this morning. At fifteen above zero this evening. I went down to the vilage this forenoon. Alvah was drawing manure. Martin Bevins quit working for Alvah yesterday morning.

Thursday, April 7   It has been rather Warmer today. The sap run a little. It snowed a little by spells today. Murcuary 20 above Zero this morning. At 32 this evening. It stood at 40 above Zero at noon today. I went up to Harvy Cleland today. Charles H. Brown went to Gouverneur [NY] today. Martin came up to A.P. Brown. They had quite a blowup.

Friday, April 8   This has been a pleasent day. Cleared off this afternoon. The sap run this afternoon. Murcuary Stood at twenty above Zero this morning.   It stands at thirty this evening. I went to the Sugarbush this afternoon. Mr. & Mrs. Paget [Padget] & Mr. & Mrs. McFarlen was up to Charles Brown this evening.

Saturday, April 9   This has been a butiful day. Sun shone bright all day. The sap run well today. Murcury was fifteen above Zero this morning.   It is breesing [breezing] some tonight. I boiled sap today. Alvah geathered the sap today.

Sunday, April 10   This has been a butiful day. The sun shone bright all day. The sap run splendid today. I boild sap all day. Got the milk can full of syrup. Murcuary was fifteen above Zero this morning. It is twenty five this evening.

Monday, April 11   It snowed a little this morning. Cleared off[f] at Nine O'clock. The wind was quite cold. Wind West. Sap did not run much today. Murcuary 25 above Zero this morning. 28 this evening. Alvah hird [hired] man comensed to work today. Nancy went over to Alvah and sugared off.

Tuesday, April 12   This has been a cloudy day. Sap run some. Wind quite cold. Sugared off in the Woods today. Murcuary 20 above Zero this morning. About 30 this evening.

Wednesday, April 13   This has been a cloudy day. The sun has not been seen today. The sap run all night. The buckets was full. Murcury 28 this morning. 35 above zero this evening. I boiled sap and sugared off in the woods today. It snowed and rained a little this forenoon. Had a cow get in the mud today. Charles drew her out by the head.

Thursday, April 14 This has been a butiful day. Sun shone all day. Sap did not run today. We finished up boiling sap today. Sugared of[f] 170 pound of sugar today in the Woods. Charls has gon to Gouverneur tonight. Alvah gon to the vilage [Edwards] tonight.

Friday, April 15   This has been a cloudy day. Frose quite hard last night. Sap run quite well today. I sugared off in the Woods today. Mrs. Gordin is helping Nancy today to twist carpet yarn. Alvah sent two tubs of butter by Charles to Gouverneur today. Sold for twenty two cents per pound.

Saturday, April 16   This has bee a pleasent day but the Wind blew quite hard from the North West. I boiled sap all day. Charles went and got his harowes yesterday. Came home last night with his harrows. Miss Agness Brown was here today. Mrs. Emmy Hall was here today.

Sunday, April 17   This has been a pleasent day. Wind North West. Murcuary twenty eight above Zero this morning. Sugared off in the sugarbush today all alone. Charles Johnson & Selah Johnson was here today.

Monday, April 18   This has been a pleasent day but quite cold. Frose quite hard last night. Wind North West. I was working at the Sleeper and brought over sugar. Alvah gon to the vilage tonight. His hird [hired] man quit work tonight.

Tuesday, April 19   This has been a pleasent day. Frose quite hard last night. Wind North West. I gathered and boiled sap all day alone. Done the milking alone this morning. Alvah been sick today. The two James Harmons came over to the sugar bush today.

Wednesday, April 20   This has been a butiful day. Sun shone bright all day. Finished boiling sap today. Charles gathered his buckets today. Murcuary 28 above Zero this morning.

Thursday, April 21   This has been a butiful day. Sun Shone bright all day. Murcuary 27 above Zero this Morning. We washed the sap buckets today. Nancy and Netta McGill & Marsha McGill helped to wash the buckets.

Friday, April 22   This has been a pleasent [day].   Looked some like rain.   Finished drawing up the buckets and pans today.   Thare is a dance at the Rushton House this evening. Charles famely are all gon to the vilage this evening.

Saturday, April 23   This has been a butiful day. Quite Warm. The Wind blew quite hard. Murcuary thirty above Zero this morning. I was framing Sleepers and fixing slates for Alvah's sugar.

Sunday, April 24   This has been a butiful day. Wind blew quite hard from the West. Murcuary fifty above Zero this forenoon. I went out to Don Darts. Went up to Manard Maybee's sawmill. Saped [sapped] at Sillmon [Stillman] Brown.

Monday, April 25   This was a warm pleasent day. Geting very dry. Alvah comensed to scater the manure in the lot. Commensed to take the milk to the factory. Payne's cattle was over in our lot today. The school comensed today. The teacher bords at Charles Brown.

Tuesday, April 26   This has been a wet day. Been showery all day. Thare was quite a thunder shower this afternoon. The first thunder that has been this spring. Murcuary stands at 58 above zero this evening. Hanry Bloss worked for Alvah today.

Wednesday, April 27   This has been a pleasent day after the rain. Murcuary thirty two degrees above Zero this morning. I went to the Mill with load of provender. Alvah & Bloss was drawing Manure. Nancy went down to Halls with her carpet to get Mr. Hall to weave it for her.

Thursday, April 28 This has been a pleasent day. Murcuary at forty eight above Zero this morning. I was doing the chores and trying to cleen some wheat for seed but made slow work at it. Mrs. Harriett Harmon was here today. Robert Brown was here today. The River was at its hight [height] yesterday.

Friday, April 29 This has been rather stormy day. Rained some. Turned quite cold. Wind blew a perfict gale all day. I went to Keneville today of seed wheat. Got eleven bushels and a half. Stoped [stopped] and stayed at John Abaslon's all night. Wind blew from the west.

Saturday, April 30 This has been a cold raw day. Wind North West. Blowed quite hard. I came home with my wheat this forenoon. Been sick all day. Let Robert Brown have four bushels & a half of seed wheat for one dollar & seventy five cents per bushel. Paid me six dollars of it. I've two Dollars of it yet.

Sunday, May 1 This has been a cold raw day. Wind West. Murcuary at twenty two above Zero this morning. Wind blowes hard this evening. Nancy & I stayed over to Alvah all day. Took care of the baby so Sarah and Alvah could go out to Grants. Alvah went to Russell [NY] to get a hire girl.

Monday, May 2 This has been a pleasent day but quite cold. And it rained quite hard last night. I took the yearlings and two year olds down to John Sulivan's today. Four red yearlings, two grisley ones, one white one, one red & white beled [bellied] two year old, one Brown & white soted [spotted], one red & whit spoted two year old.

Tuesday, May 3 This has been a pleasent day. Murcuary 22 above Zero this morning. I was fixing fenses today. Alvah was drawing Manure. Thare Was 273 lbs of milk today.

Wednesday, May 4   This has been a pleasent day. Murcuary 20 degres above Zero this morning. It has been some warmer today. Forest McKee worked for Alvah today. Dora Beech washed for Sarah today. I commensed to cultivate today. Elin Cleland was here today. Jane McKee was here today. Thare was 292 lbs Milk today.

Thursday, May 5   This has been a very pleasant day. Not very warm. Murcuary 25 above zero this morning. Quit[e] a frost this morning. I got the colt shod this morning at Fordham's for one dolar [dollar]. We have not got the ground ready to sow the wheat tomorrow.

Friday, May 6   It rained a little this morning. Been cloudy all day. I sowed wheat today. W. H. Noys paid his note $105.35 & paid up Nelson's Contract of $212.00. The Cole Boy that lived with Wilson died last night. Ida Ivers died today at noon.

Saturday, May 7   This has been a pleasent day. Not very warm and not very cold. Murcuary at 35 above zero this morning. We finished sowing the wheat today. Thare was 356 lbs of milk today. Forest McKee work for Alvah today.

Sunday, May 8   This is a butiful day. Alvah has gon to Russell after his hired girl and Nancy & Charles family has gone to I. Ivers funeral at ten o'clock today. Coles Boys funeral is at twelve o'clock today. Thare was 375 lbs of milk today.

Monday, May 9   This has been a warm day. It rained a little this forenoon. It looks like rain this evening. I sowed Charles oats for him today. Charles Harmon worked for Alvah today. I sowe 19 bushels of oats for Charles & ½ bushel of grass seed. 368 lbs of milk. Alvah hird girl commensed to work

today.

Tuesday, May 10   This has been a Warm day. It was a nice shour [shower] last night. I sowed oats this forenoon. Helped Silas Rice to graft apple trees this afternoon. Alvah sowed oats this afternoon & grass seed. Charles rol[l]ed his oats this afternoon. Thare was a nice thunder shower this evening.

Wednesday, May 11   This has been a warm day after the rain last night.   We finished sowing today.   Alvah & Charles famley are gon to the vilage. The Wind blew hard from the West.

Thursday, May 12   This has been a hot day. Wind blowes quite hard from the West today. It has been thundering quite hard of [off] to the North of us. Mercuary 78 above zero this evening. Alvah & Charles Harmon has been planting potatoes today. I have been roling all day on the grain.

Friday, May 13   This has been a pleasent day but rather colder. Alvah & Charles Harmon planted potatoes today. I was laid up with a lame back. The school teacher   has gon home. Her father came after her. Mr. John H. Maybee's wife died this forenoon.

Saturday, May 14   This has been a pleasent day. It sprinkled a little rain two or three times. Next very warm. I was framing Sleepers today.   Alvah finished planting potatoes today and drawing dirt from the barn. Alven Gardner raised the basement of his barn this afternoon.

Sunday, May 15   This has been a pleasent day after the heavy rain last night. It is raining this evening again.   Charles & famley went up to B.F. Noble's today. Nancy went up to C.V. Harmon's with them. I stayed to home all day alone. James Harmon came over after me tonight. Mrs. Maybee was beried

today.

Monday, May 16   This has been a wet day. It has rained most all day. It is raining hard this evening. Wind North East and very cold. I was planting potatoes on the side hill. Alvah was trying to paper the bedroom today. Put down the carpet in the hall this forenoon.

Tuesday, May 17   This has been a wet nasty day. It is raining quite hard this evening. I was drawing lumber home from the mill. Alvah was papering his bedroom. Thare was a man killed down to the Tealck [Talc] Works. He was from Canada. Been to work about two weeks.

Wednesday, May 18   It has been rather warmer today. Wind North East. We have been framing Sleepers today. The boys are gone to the vilage tonight. Charles has been making soap today.

Thursday, May 19   It has been quite warm today. Murcuary was 55 degrees above Zero this morning. We lolled [perhaps, rolled] our saw logs in to the river today. Alvah hird man commensed work today. James Scaval was killed the 17 of May by a tree falling on him. He was out near Sandy Crick[Creek].

Friday, May 20   This has been a warm day. It rained a very little. It thundred a quite hard at five o'clock. Alvah sowed his onions today. I washed the sap pan today. Phila has come to s[t]ay all night.

Saturday, May 21   This has been Warm this forenoon. Turned colder this afternoon. Wind turned to Northeast. Alvah planting his garden. I was framing Sleepers. The Band played at the vilage this evening.

Sunday, May 22   Thare was a nice rain last night. Been cloudy all day. Not very warm. Got a letter from Edward with the receipt for three hundred & seventy five dollars.

Monday, May 23   This has been a butiful day. Sun shone bright all day. Just warmanought [warm enough] to be pleasent. Was sick all day. Alvah drew one load of lumber from the Mill.

Tuesday, May 24   This has been a aful Warm day. Murcuary 84 in the shade at five o'clock today. I was framing Sleepers today. Alvah was cleening out his drean [drain] and he went down to see the shoes come in to the vilage today. They are showing this evening.

Wednesday, May 25   This has been a warm day. Murcuary 92 in the shade and 106 in the sun at noon today. It thundred tords [toward] the South this afternoon. Alvah got ten bushels of ashes of A.B. Goodanough and ten of Elder Hitchcock. I sent a card off to Mrs. Bignel this morning. Thare was 474 lbs of milk today.

Thursday, May 26   Another nice day. Geting quite dry. We was putting the Sleepers in the stable today. Albert Cousens maried Nettie Payn [Payne] last night. Charles soed [sowed] his corn today.

Friday, May 27   This has been a warm day. It rained a very little this evening. We had a spcial chool   [special school] meeting this evening to see about building a new school house. A. Gardner raised a larg[e] cow barn this afternoon.

Saturday, May 28   This has been a cloudy day. It has looked like rain all day. It sprinkled a little this evening. Nancy went to the vilag this afternoon. Traded eight dollars. Alvah & I have been lay[ing] flour [floor] in the new stable. I bought me

229

a new palm lief [leaf] hat tonight.

Sunday, May 29   This has been a wet day.   It rained at forenoon. I went out to Danual Dart's for his roters to move my barn.

Monday, May 30   This has been a pleasent day.   Alvah Went to Gouverneur [NY] with a load of cheese. Lent James Webb fifty five dollars. I made a botom to the milk waggon.

Tuesday, May 31   This has been a pleasent day.   We was working on the road today.   Miss Onele [O'Neil] worked for Nancy today on her new dress.

Wednesday, June 1   This has been a cool pleasent day. We have been working on the road today. Miss O'Neal worked for Nancy today on her dress.   Miss Ober was here this evening.

Thursday, June 2.   This has been a nice pleasent cool day. Thare was a lite frost last night.   It did not freese anything. We was working on the road today.   They have took up the bridge at thevtanery [tannery] today. They are building a new bridge. Mrs. Phiney was here all day. I caried her down to Eastman's.

Friday, June 3   It rained a little this morning. Been cloudy all day. A little Warmer today. We all worked on the road today. Pitcairn cow came in today.   William Grant built a flat bridge across the river above the Bridge at the tanery for fifty dollars.

Saturday, June 4   This has been a pleasent day. It came a few drops of rain this afternoon. We all worked on the road today. There was four hundred ninty [ninety] eight pounds of milk today.

Sunday, June 5   This has been a cold wet day. Rained most

all day. I went out to see Dan Dart then went over to John Gardner's. Stoped at Mr. Cambells. Thare was a boy out in Russell hung himself a week a go last Friday.

Monday, June 6   This has been a pleasent cold day. It frose hard last night. It frose corn & potatoes all to the ground. Alvah went to Pierrepoint today after a hired Girl. Sold all lazy cow today for Nineteen Dollars.

Tuesday, June 7   This has been a pleasant cool day. It frese quite hard last night. We was clearing out the middle of the barn fixing for moveing [moving] it. Baker has been at Charley's all this week so far.

Wednesday, June 8   It looks like rain this Morning. Been coud all forenoon. Look like rain this evening. Robert Webb was helping me on the barn. The assessors was here today. Valuations real Estate $2800. Personal 300.

Thursday, June 9   This has been a pleasent cool day. Wind North east. We got the flour [floor] all laid in the Stable. Robert Webb worked for me today. J. Carr Was sick this afternoon.

Friday, June 10   This has been a pleasent day. It is geting some warmer. We are still to work on the barn. I got fifty feet of elem [Elm] plank of George Paget. 75. Mrs. Lowery came to William Cleland from New Jersey this afternoon with her daughter Bell.

Saturday, June 11 This has been a pleasent day. It has been quite warm today. Robert Webb was helping me on the barn today. Thare was a special school meeting at the school house this afternoon. Cyras Cleland came home from New York today.

231

Sunday, June 12   This has been a warm day. Geting quite dry. Noe rain since last Sunday. I went out to Porter Hill for a Jackscrue [jack screw] to[day]. Stoped and took dinner with Mr. Ellis. Sold the cheese yesterday for 8 ½ cents. They held quarterly Meeting yesterday & today.

Monday, June 13   It has been a pleesent day. Wind blows from the south. Robert Webb helping me on the barn. It looks a little like rain.

Tuesday, June 14   This has been a pleesent day after the thunder shour last night. The wind blew hard from the south West. Robert Webb is helping me on the barn today. A.P. Johnson came here tonight from Pine Valley. Wind blew a perfict gale about six o'clock this afternoon with a little rain.

Wednesday, June 15   This has been a pleesent day but quite cold. It looks like frost to night. Robert Webb was helping me on the Barn today & Jason Woodcock help on the Barn. James Webb helped on the barn. Thare was a man here this evening that is looking for talk [talc].

Thursday, June 16   This has been a pleesent day. A very little frost. We moved the barn to day. Robert Webb worked for me today, & Jason Woodcock & James Webb & Charles Brown this afternoon. Wind blowed hard from the North West.

Friday, June 17   This has been a pleasant day. A little warmer. It looks like rain this evening. Robert Webb worked for me today. Thare has a man here today selling windowes holders. Our last cow came in today.

Saturday, June 18   This has been a lowery [meaning gloomy] day. It rained a little this morning & looked like rain all day. We made a bridge to get into the barn & laid the barn floor today. Took the Milk round by Roberts to the factery today. The advents [Adventists] have put up a tent at the vilage and are holding meetings in it.

Sunday, June 19   This has been a lowery day. Quite a shour last night. Rained a little this morning. Not very Warm. Wind blowed quite hard from the West. A heavy Thunder shower this afternoon about five O'clock. Gordin & I went down to see them run the logs of[f] of the rapets [rapids] by Edwen Wites.

Monday, June 20   This has been a wet day. A very heavy thunder shour this morning. One this afternoon & one last night. Robert Webb worked for me today on the Barn. Paid Webb Nine Dollars. A. P. Johnson left here for home this afternoon. He went by the way of Hermon [NY].

Tuesday, June 21   This has been a cool pleasent day. Rained a little this afternoon. Got the Money for the chees[e] in sail [sale] Nomber 5. Thomas Todd paid me the interest on his Note. Nine Dollars & five cents. Nancy gon over to stay at Alvah this evening.

Wednesday, June 22   This has been a pleasent cool day. Wind North West. I am still to work on the Barn. Ja [Jo] hoed my potatoes on the side hill today. Alvah hired Girl. Left to night. Jo has gon home with her this evening. Cyrus Cleland borrowed Gardner's jack scrue today.

Thursday, June 23   This has been a pleasent cool day. Wind North West. Jo got back from carrying Alvah hired girl home this morning about eight o'clock. Ja [Jo] has gone to Fine [NY] today. Has not got back this evening yet. Thomas Grant & Leveret Calister was at Alvah to day to dinner. I am still to work on the barn yet.

Friday, June 24   This has been a pleasent cool day. Wind South West.   Alvah bought his waggon Wheels home yesterday. I am still to work on the Barn.   I went to the vilage this forenoon.

Saturday, June 25   This has been another cool pleasent day. Wind West.   Thare was another schol meting to let the job of building a new school house but did not let the job.   Alvah went to Gouverneur [NY] today to get his waggon tier.   The band is playing tonight.

Sunday, June 26   It has been quite warm.   Murcuary 78 in the shade.   I went down to John Sullivan's to see the young cattle. Went to the talk [talc] mines.   The advents [Adventists] are still holding Meetings here yet.

Monday, June 27   It has been pleasent but thare has been a strong south wind all day.. It comensed to rain about five O'clock and it is raining this evening. I am still to work on the barn.   Sold the cheese last Saturday.   Murcuary was 68 in the shade this afternoon at 6 O'clock.

Tuesday, June 28   This has been a warm windy day.   Wind blowed hard from the south.   Another good thunder shower at Six O'clock.   Rained hard all the time that we ware [were] milking.   Martha Was down to Percival Brown's all day & Charles was at the vilage all day.   Gon to the vilage again this evening.

Wednesday, June 29   This has [been] pleasent part of the day & rained this afternoon.   Quite a heavy thunder shour.   Nancy and I went over to Trout Lake and took dinner at the hotell. Thare was a picknic from Hermon [NY] at the lake today.

Thursday, June 30   This has been a cool cloudy day.   Been showery all day.   I went and cut a log.   Took it to the Mill.

Had it sawed for to make a track for horse fork. Alvah & Sarah went away out to Grant's. Gon all day to sundown. Got a shoe set on Nelly. Milked 13 cowes.

Friday, July 1   This has been a warm pleasent day. Wind North West. Put up the track for the horse fork today.

Saturday, July 2   This has been a warm pleasent day. Wind West. Alvah has been sick today. I had the headache the same today. I got the colt shoed today. 3 shoes. I went for a load of shingles this afternoon. The President Garfield was killed today. He was shot. [Note: The President was shot July 2, 1881 but did not die of his wound until September 19, 1881. William notes this later.]

Sunday, July 3   Been a Warm pleasent day. Thare was a nice thunder shour this afternoon.

Monday, July 4   It looked like rain this morning but cleared of[f]. Pleasent all day. It was hot all day. Thare was a big Selabration [Celebration] here today. We all went down to the Selibration. Mr. Keeler delivered the Oration today.

Tuesday, July 5   This has been a hot day. The sun was scalding hot. I sot the boxes in the wagon wheels today. Went to the vilage for a load of shingles. Charles Went to DeCalb [DeKalb] this forenoon. His horses got fritened at the cars, tiped [tipped] him over in the ditch. Tore his pants most all of[f] of him but he held them.

Wednesday, July 6   This has been a Warm day No rain today. I was patching up the roof of the Barn & sprinkling potatoes with Paris Green. [Paris Green is an insecticide]   Joseph Anderson was here today to get me to give one half interest in all minerils on the Dumas place in Fine.

Thursday, July 7   This has been Warm and cloudy today. I went to Canton to settle with Russell for the Gaddis suit & get Eight hundred Dollars of Harvey Cleland for the estate of Robert Brown Deceased.

Friday, July 8   This has been a Warm day. I put two posts in the barn this forenoon. Drew a load of hay from Roberts this afternoon. Alvah Went to Hermon to get a hird girl but could not get one.

Saturday, July 9   This has been a hot day. I had the headache today. Alvah & Jay drew hay from Robert's today. I went to the vilage this afternoon & evening.

Sunday, July 10   This has been the hotest day of the season. The Murcary rose to one hundred and four in the shade this afternoon. I went to the vilage to send six hundred & twenty five Dolars by Leveret Raymond to express to at Gouverneur [NY] to Isaac Brown in Linden, Michagan.

Monday, July 11   This has been a pleasent cool day. No rain yet. Comensed haying today. Drew one load from Roberts. Elizabeth Brodie husband called here today but did not stop.

Tuesday, July 12   It was quite cool this morning. It was cloudy all forenoon. I went to DeKalb Junction [NY] today with cheese and got home about three o'clock. The Boys was haying. Drew in seven loads of hay today.

Wednesday, July 13   This has been a warm day. The wind blew hard from the West. Drew in six loads of hay today.

Thursday, July 14   This has been a cool & nise hay day. We drew in eight loads of hay today.

Friday, July 15   It has been rather warmer today. Murcury at

Eighty above Zero this afternoon in the shade. We drew in nine loads of hay today.

Saturday, July 16   Took in 2 loads of hay today. This has been looking like rain this forenoon but did not rain till five this afternoon and it came a very heavy thunder shower. The thunder was terific. The Wind blew very hard from the South all day and just as the rain was coming it wheaeeld in to the North. Blowed a firce gale. Blew the roof off at Braytons barn.

Sunday, July 17   This has been a cool pleasent day after the rain. Charles and family all went to meeting. Nancy went with them. The advents are holding Meeting in their tent yet.

Monday, July 18   This has been a wet day. Rained most of the day and has been quite cold. Wind blew from the North all day. I fixed the bugy seet for Charles today. Alvah drew some lumber home from the hill.

Tuesday, July 19   This has been quite pleasant. Not a very good hay day. Drew in three loads of hay. I mowed all day for Charles.

Wednesday, July 20   This was cloudy and dull all forenoon. Cleared of[f] a little before noon. We drew in five loads of hay for Charls this afternoon. Charles went to Ogdensburg today. Nancy Bencraft was buried today.

Thursday, July 21   This has been a poor hay day. Been cloudy all day. It was quite a shour last night. Alvah put Paris Green [insecticide] on his potatoes today.

Friday, July 22   This has been dull hay day. Been cloudy all [day] looking very much like rain but did not rain till evening. Drew in two loads of hay for Charles today.

237

Saturday, July 23   This has been another dull hay day.   Been cloudy all day.   Done nothing in the hay feld [field] today. Charles & famly have gone to the vilag to the Burmman licter [lecture] tonight.   Nancy has gone with them.

Sunday, July 24   This has been a butiful day.   First good hay day for a week.   Drew in five loads for Charles.   Little Amy Beech died this morning.   Charles Beech[s] little girl.

Monday, July 25   This has not been a very good hay day.   It has looked like rain all day and a heavy shour wen[t] to the South of us.   It looks like rain tonight.   We took in Nine loads of hay for Charles today.   Little Amy Beech was buried today.

Tuesday, July 26   This has been a cloudy wet day.   Cleared off a little in the afternoon.   I piled up wood today & done no haying today.   Charles went to DeKalb Junction with Burdik folks and Albert White.

Wednesday, July 27   This has ben another cloudy day. Rained a little this forenoon.   The Agent for the St. Lawrence Republican paper was here today.   Paid him three dollars.   I maid two neckyokes and on[e] Whfeltree [whiffletree].

Thursday, July 28   This has been a rather poor hay day.   A heavy shour this afternoon.   Drew in three loads of hay for Charles & two for Alvah before the rain finished.   Charles haying today.

Friday, July 29   This has been a good hay day till about five o'clock then it began to rain.   We drew in Eight loads of hay for Alvah.

Saturday, July 30   This has been quite a good hay day. Looked like rain all day but did not.   Drew in five loads of hay for Alvah today.   Laura Johnson had a school picknick in

238

Brown's grove close by the house. The scolers [scholars] all had pices to speek and sing. They all done first rate. Could not ask any better of them.

Sunday, July 31   This has been a Warm day. Been cloudy all day. Quite a shour this afternoon. Nancy, Sherman & I went up to Joseph Gouldston. Picked some buries and bought some of Charles Broytons.

Monday, August 1   This has been a loury day. Got no hay up to day. I was fixing screnes [screen] frames for the windows and doore.

Tuesday, August 2   This has been a poor hay day. Rained a little at noon. Clered of[f] hot in the afternoon. Finish cuting the hay today. Racked & cocked up all we cut today.

Wednesday, August 3   This has been a warm day. First rate hay day. We took in Eight loads of hay for Alvah today. We finished all our haying today.

Thursday, August 4   This has been a very warm day. Wind West. We all went up to Joseph Golston[s] a berying [berrying]. It was so hot we did not get many. Thare Was a thunder shour North of here at five o'clock. Sprinkled a little here.

Friday, August 5   This has been another hot day. Murcuary stood all day at one hundred degrees above zero. Quite warm. Alvah comensed to cut his oats. Charles cut round his oats. Got them ready for the machene.

Saturday, August 6   This has been a hot day. It has bee hot and clear all forenoon. Began to thunder about noon and a heavy thunder shour got along between four and five O'clock. George Baraford died today.   Been sick only a few days.

239

Sunday, August 7   This has been a cloudy. It has been a kin[d] of a fogy rain all day.   George Baraford was buried today. Charles and family & Nancy Went to his funeral.   And I stayed to home. Alvah Went out to Grant's.

Monday, August 8   This has been quite a pleasent day. We bound up some oats. Charles finished cuting his oats today. Mandy Wite staid here all night.

Tuesday, August 9   This has been quite a day for looking so wet in the morning. It looked like rain all day. Rained a little two or three times this afternoon. Charles bound up all his oats today. I got them all up for him. Mrs. Hall was her[e] this afternoon. Charles Harmon took dinner here today.

Wednesday, August 10   This has been a butiful cool day. We was binding & cuting oats today. Ja [Jo] broke the cradle. Charles helped us bind this afternoon.   Baker was here to Charles today to diner.

Thursday, August 11   This has been a butiful harvest day. Not any too warm. We ware[were] binding & seting up oats. Put up twenty four hundred.   Charles Harmon worked for Alvah today.

Friday, August 12   It was not a very good harvest day today. We ware cuting wheat today. James Harmon & Charles Harmon was helping to bind wheat. Charles drew in his oats today. Frank Beech helped him. Thare was quite a thunder shour this afternoon. Ful heavy thunder.

Saturday, August 13   This has been a nice day. Looked some like rain but did not come but a few drops. We finished cuting our wheat today. Alvah is over to James Harmon cuting his oats for him.

Sunday, August 14   This has been a lowery day. It has been cloudy all day and has rained a little two or three times. Our folks all went to meeting.

Monday, August 15   This has been a pleasent day. Alvah & I comensed to draw in our oats. Charles Went to Gouverneur. A lawer [lawyer] about a Deed.

Tuesday, August 16   This has been another pleasent day not very warm. Alvah & I finished drawing in our oats.

Wednesday, August 17   This has been a pleasent day. We finished binding and drawing in our oats. Got a letter from A. P. Johnson tonight. He told about having an aful hail storm thare [Pine Valley, NY] on the 29 day of July. It destroyed every thing that was on the ground. He said thare was hail stones as larg as a goose egg.

Thursday, August 18   This has been a butiful day. We drew in the Wheat today. That finished our harvesting for this year. Mr. Cole helped us to draw in the wheat.

Friday, August 19   This has been a butiful day. We all Went and helped to cut the brush out of the Graveyard this forenoon. This afternoon I racked the Wheet ground.

Saturday, August 20   This has been a warm day. Alvah and I drew in the wheet scaterins. Then Nancy and I went out to John Alsalom's.

Sunday, August 21   This has been cloudy most of the day. Came a little shour this afternoon. We came home from John Absalom's today. Stoped at Gove Johnsons. Got 23 lbs of butter at 22 cents per pound.

Monday, August 22   This has been a kind of a wet day. It

241

rained a little most of the day. I made a screne door today. I went to the vilage to night.

Tuesday, August 23   This has been a pleasant day. I was fixing fens to keep the cowes out of the [not legible] and hanging screne door. John Absalom came out here today.

Wednesday, August 24   This has been a butiful day. The vilage Sunday school had a picknick in Wilson Grove. They had a nice time. The Band went with them. John Absalom went down to Jason Woodcock to dinner to day.

Thursday, August 25   This has been a butiful day. Not very Warm. I was making Wheelbarow and Alvah was wheeling in Wood into the shed. Charles Went to Hermon and Nancy and Sarah Went up to Charles V. Harmon's. Isaac Brown came to town today from Michegon.

Friday, August 26   This has been a butiful day. I was to work on the wheelbarrow today. Alvah went to Hearmon [Hermon] brot a bedstid up from Greens for us. Charles got home tonight from Hearmon.

Saturday, August 27   This has been a Warm day. It comensed to rain a little about four o'clock. I went to the blacksmith shop to get some irons fixed for Wheelbarow. Paid two shilings. Isaac Brown made a call here this morning.

Sunday, August 28   This has been a warm day. We all staid to home but Charles folks went to Meeting.

Monday, August 29   This has been another Warm day. It is geting aful dry. Isaac Brown was here today. We drew down to the plaining mill two loads of lumber. One load 761 feet; one 520 feet to make caping & 100 feet to plain smoos [smooth] surfis.[surface]

Tuesday, August 30   This has been a aful Warm day.   It is afful dry.   Was working on the Barn.   Thare was a special school meeting tonight to settle about the school house site. The district gave John McGill ten Dollars to give up the land that the district claimed.

Wednesday, August 31   This has been another hot dry day. The wind blew hard from the West.   I was to work on the barn. Alvah was drawing manure from Goodanough.   I had the headach[e] today.

Thursday, September 1   This has been a hot day.   Murcuary Ninety in the shade this afternoon.   Alvah gon to Gouverneur to the fair.   Charles and Martha gon to the fair.   Isaac helped to Milk tonight.   Nelly Thurston went up in a beloon [balloon] at Gouverneur today.   She came down at Little York [NY].

Friday, September 2   Another hot dry day.   This was the last day of the Gouverneur fair.   I am to work at the barn.

Saturday, September 3   This has been another hot dry day. Wind blowes hard from the West.   William Grant was at Alvah's this afternoon.

Sunday, September 4   This has been another hot dry day. Wind south West.   Some sines of rain.   Charles and family went to Meeting.   Nancy went with them.   Alvah started to go out to Grants but went to Cyras Cleland.

Monday, September 5   This has been aful warm day.   It came a few drops of rain this forenoon.   Nancy and I went to Hermon to the shoes today.

Tuesday, September 6   This has been another very warm dry day.   It has been afful hot today.   We had another school meeting this afternoon to consider the repairing the old school house or build a new one. Concludid to build a new school house. I went up to Mr. Carter's with Mrs. Rickanous. [possibly Richmyer].

Wednesday, September 7 This has been a aful hot day. Wind West blowes a perfic gail. Every thing is drying up. Mr. Rickanous [Rickmyer] came up after the funeral of Robert Brown. Erwin Green Was here today to Dinner.

Thursday, September 8 This has been another Warm dry day. The fire are raging in the woods all round about. I worked on the barn today. Elen Cleland was here visiting today.

Friday, August 9 This has been a pleasent day. It came a few drops of rain at noon. John McKee was at Alvah to dinner today. I went down to the vilage with Carter to make out a Deed for Richtmyer for the vilage lot.

Saturday, August 10 This has been a warm day. No rain yet. The wind blowes from the South tonight. Isaac Brown was here to dinner today. I was to work on the barn. Charles Went to the ponds for two cowes today.

Sunday, September 11 Thare was a nice little shour this Morning. Cleared off dry in the afternoon. Phila Webb was buried today.

Monday, September 12 This has been a Warm dry day. We are still to work on the barn. The upper Spring in the pasture has dried up. The first time it ever dried up.

Tuesday, September 13 It rained a very little today. Murcuary 50 this Morning. Wind blew quite hard from the West till three o'clock then turned into the North. Conynes little boy was buried today. Nancy went to the funeral then went over to Stillman Brown.

Wednesday, September 14   This has been Warm Dry day and no signs of rain.   Murcuary at 50 above zero this morning. Loisa Spalding Died today about noon. Live in Russell vilage. I went to the Vilage with Mr. Richtmyer today.

Thursday, September 15   This has been a Warm windy day. Wind blowes from the south.   Blowes hard tonight.   The fires are raging in the Woods all round here.   It looks a little like rain tonight.   I went down to the vilage this forenoon.   Served a notice on Robert Allen to leave the house.

Friday, September 16   This has been another Warm dry day. No sines [signs] of rain yet.   I served a Notice on Robert Allen to leave the house tonight in three days.

Saturday, September 17   This has been another Warm dry day. Worked on the barn this forenoon.   Went to the corcus [caucus] this afternoon.   Murcuary was 80 in the shade this forenoon.

Sunday, September 18   This has bee another Warm Dry day. The Murcuary was 80 in the shade this morning.   Nancy went to Meeting today.   Charles & family Went up to Bengamon Noble's.   Old Mr. Brown died today.

Monday, September 19   This has been another Warm dry day. It fell a few drops of rain this Morning.   Charles Harmon worked for Alvah today.   I went to the vilage this morning. Got 67 cents worth of lumber of H. Rushton.   Paget, 20 cents for planing.   Got 8 lbs of rought nails of Conyne.   President died today.

Tuesday, September 20   This has been quite cool today but afful dry Wind blowed quite hard from the North.   Alvah went with a load of chees to DeKalb Junction today.   Charles Harmon comensed to dig Alvah potatoes today.   Old Mr. Brown was buried today.

Wednesday, September 21   This has been a pleasent cool day. First frost this Morning of the season.   We ware [were] diging potatoes today.

Thursday, September 22   We had a nice thunder shower today at noon.   The first we have had since the seventh of August.   I was to work on the road today.   Charles and Alvah was diging potatoes.   Thomas Grant came home from the West with his little girl Marg.

Friday, September 23   This has been quite a wet day.   A heavy thunder shower this morning.   Another heavy thunder shower at noon.   The lightning struck one of Jason Gates' boys and killed him this morning.   Nancy fell and hurt herself this afternoon. Dr cald up to see her.

Saturday, September 24   This has been a Warm day with showers in the forenoon.   Emma Webb is working here for Nancy.   Comensed today at noon.   Kit Rushton was married at Sedar [Cedar] Springs, Mich. September 15th 1881 to John Hitchcock of Kansas.

Sunday, September 25   This has been a warm day.   Wind blew hard from the West.   I sent $150.00 Dollars to A. O. Brodie & 150.00 to Elizabeth Bignell.   Mrs. Hall made a call this afternoon.

Monday, September 26   This has been a butiful day.   It was quite warm.   Wind south West.   I was working on the barn. Went over to James Harmon this evening for botle of linament.

Tuesday, September 27   This has bee rather wet today.   Bee showers all day.   Alvah was drawing sand.   I was working on the Barn.   Alis Noble is staying at Charles this afternoon and tonight.

Wednesday, September 28   This has been quite wet today. It rained most all forenoon. Old Bloss gave up his job on the school house wall.   Alvah went to mill today.   Charles Harmon came back to work today at noon.

Thursday, September 29   This has been a warm day. The Wind blew hard from the south West. I was hanging stable doors.

Friday, September 30   This has been a Warm Windy day. Wind blew hard from the South. I went to Fine [NY] for a load of lime and to see Irvin to get him to work for me.

Saturday, October 1   This has been a wet day all day. We was proping up at the hophouse and making morter to build the wall under hophouse.

Sunday, October 2   This has been quite a dul day.   Been cloudy all day. Rains a little this evening. Mrs. Hall and her daughter made us a call today.

Monday, October 3   This has been a wet day.   Rained all forenoon.   We ware to work on diging stone and drawing stone.

Tuesday, October 4   This has been a cold day. Wind blew har[d] from the North all day and afful cold.   Mr. Irvin comensed to work on the wal[l] under the hophouse today at noon. Burt Allen don[e] Nancy Washing this forenoon. Elen Cleland called here today.

Wednesday, October 5   This has been a very cold day. Wind blew hard from the north. It frose all day in the shad[e] and whare the wind hit, it frose the ground quite hard last night. It is freesing hard tonight. J. J. drew sand all day. Alvah drew stone. Irvin and his boy laid stone in the wal[l].

247

Thursday, October 6   This has been a nice dry day.   Wind blew hard from the West.   Thare was a hard frost last night. Frose the ground quite hard.   Dora Beech and Ugelia Beech made us a visit this afternoon.   We are to work on the wall under the hop house.

Friday, October 7   This has been another pleasent day.   We are still to work on the Wall.   Irvin and his boy.   Thare is a ball at Mr. Shawes this evening.   Some of the boys got into a fight.   Frank Barens liked [licked] them out.

Saturday, October 8   This has been a wet day.   It rained from ten o'clock to noon and rained hard in the evening.   We finished building the stone wall under the hop house.

Sunday, October 9   This has been a butiful day after the rain yesterday.   I killed a ruster [rooster] today for diner.

Monday, October 10   This has been a cold raw day.   Rained and snowed some this forenoon.   Cleard off this afternoon. Ervin is building the wall for the school house today.   I dug thirteen bushels of potatoes this forenoon.   Wheeled in Wood this afternoon.

Tuesday, October 11   This has been a butiful [day].   I wheeled in wood into the woodshed today.   Alvah drawed wood in the sugarbush today.   Thare was a school meeting at Mrs. Storan's this evening.

Wednesday, October 12   This has been a Windy day.   Wind blew hard from the South all day.   Rained a little all afternoon. Ervin finished the school house wall today at noon.   I was piling wood in the shed today.

Thursday, October 13   This has been a cloudy day.   Looked like rain all day.   Martha and Alis Noble went out to John

Noble today. Alvah comensed plowing today. I finished covering up my wood. Comensed building a henhouse today.

Friday, October 14   This has been a butiful day. The sun shone all day. Quite a hard frost last night. Alvah is plowing and I was building a henhouse today. Charles was drawing lumber from Shawville for the school house today. Alvah baby is sick today.

Saturday, October 15   This has been a wet day. It rained and blowed all day. I plastered a little for James Brown today. Caled on Mr. White and Mr. Richtmyre & Stillman Brown.

Sunday, October 16   This has been a pleasent day. It has been cloudy part of the day. Charles and family and Nancy & Sherman all went to meeting today. Syras Cleland & wife was down to Alvah today. Alvah baby has been [sick] a few days. The Docter was up to see it yesterday. It is sick yet.

Monday, October 17   This has been quite pleasent. Looked like rain all day but did not rain any till after five O'clock then it came quite a thunder shouer. It is thundering and raining this evening. I took some lumber and got it plained. Charles was drawing lumber from Shawville [NY].

Tuesday, October 18   This has been a nasty cold wet day. The sun has not been seen today. It is almost snowing tonight. I paid my school tax tonight. It was four dollars & forty nine cents. I also paid Robert Brown Estate $2.68 cents.

Wednesday, October 19   This has been a butiful day. The sun shone bright all day.

Thursday, October 20   This has been another pleasent day. I had the sick headache this morning. I was working on the barn coping my stagen [staging or ladder platform] broke and let me fall about nine feet amonst the planks and rubbish. James Foster and his wife [Susan Viall] came to Russell today from Michigan to spend the Winter here.

Friday, October 21   This has been a pleasent day for the season.   Wind West.   I comensed to paint the barn this afternoon. Agness Brown was here to dinner today.

Saturday, October 22   It has looked like rain all day. Comensed to rain a little after dark. I was painting on the barn.

Sunday, October 23   This has been a wet day. It has rained all day and s[t]ill rains this evening. I went down to James Webb's today.

Monday, October 24   This has been a cloudy day. Wind North. Did not blow much. I was cleaning up round the hophouse. William McFerren got ten thousand shingles of me for the school house.

Tuesday, October 25   This has been a wet day. It rained all forenoon. Been squally all afternoon. It came a ragler Jamey [of a storm] came just a night blowing the fenses down. Blowed a pile of lumber down. Blowed the stagon down of the school house. They have sold the cheese for 12 cents a pound.   [Not legible] goes tomorrow. Alvah is going with a load.

Wednesday, October 26   This has been a cold day. The Wind blew hard from the north and afful cold. It frose all day whare the sun did not shine. Alvah Brown went to DeKalb with a load of chees today.   I pa[i]nted this forenoon.   Made a manger for the cowes.

Thursday, October 27   This has been a pleasent day. Frose hard last night. Sun shone bright all day. Alvah plowed this afternoon. I was working in the barn. James Foster & Wife came to town yesterday.

Friday, October 28   This has been a butiful day. Warm and pleasent. I built a chimney for James Rushton today.

Saturday, October 29   It rained most all forenoon. Cleared of[f] at noon. Pleasent all afternoon. I plastered for James Rushton today. Dr. Goodnough is very sick.

Sunday, October 30   This has been a butiful day. Warm and pleasent. Nancy & I went up to Charles Harmon's to see Foster and his wife and Phila and all the rest of the family. Warren [William Warren Johnson] & his wife came round to Charles Harmon today.

Monday, October 31   This has been a warm pleasent day. I was fixing Alvah platform to the well. Went to the vilage tonight for a parlor stove & five gallons oil.

Tuesday, November 1   This has been another pleasent warm day. James Foster & Wife been here today. Staying here tonight. Alfred Hall & Wife ware here this evening. Mr. Clark paid me a Note that I took of Robert Brown of two hundred Dollars.

Wednesday, November 2   This has bee a cloudy day but warm. Cleared off at night. I was to work building chimney on the school house all day. Dr. Foster & Wife [Susan Viall] & Nancy are visiting at A. Hall's [Alfred and Emmorancy Johnson Hall] today.

Thursday, November 3   This has been a wet day. Wind blowed hard from the south almost blowed me of[f] the school house. I finished building the chimney on the school house at noon. It has raind some today.

Friday, November 4   This Was a butiful Morning but turned out to be a course afternoon. Snowed and blowed like fury at times. Then clear off and blow.

Saturday, November 5   This has been quite a squally day. Snowed, rained, and blowed. I worked on the Barn. Went to the vilage this morning and then again this evening.

Sunday, November 6   This has been a warm day.   Been cloudy all day. Noe wind today. [Crossed out: I comensed to lay the floor in the hop house.   I went down to Roberts Brown's after the hay knife.]

Monday, November 7   This has been a warm pleasent day. I comensed to lay the flore in the hophouse for the hog pen. Went down to Robert Brown's for the hay knife.

Tuesday, November 8   This has been a warm pleasent day. It rained a little this afternoon.   This was lection [election] day. I went down and voted in the Morning.   Went up to Porter Harmon's to Herretts [Harriet] Harmon's Birthday party.

Wednesday, November 9   This has been a wet forenoon. Cleared of[f] pleasent this afternoon.   I was to work in the hophouse.

Thursday,   November 10   Been quite pleasent but a cold raw North West Wind. Alvah and I dug up a slusway back of the Barn and put in a new one. Stillman was here and paid up for the farm.

Friday, November 11   This has been a pleasent day but quite cold.   It frose all day in the shade.   I worked on the hay pen today.   I went to the vilage tonight.   The Russell Brass Band had a party at the Rushton house this evening.

Saturday, November 12   This has been a wet day. It snowed about one inch last night.   Comensed to rain this morning rained all day.   The snow is all gon this evening.   We finished the hog pen today & put the hogs in it.

Sunday, November 13   This has been quite a raw day. Rained a little by spells most of the day. Mrs. Mary Jane Wight was buried here today. Charles Brown and family went to Pitcairn [NY] today.   James Rushton's house was burned up this morning.

Monday, November 14   This has been a pleasent [day] for the season. I was fixing the thrashing machene today.

Tuesday, November 15   It has been quite pleasent for the season. I have been to work at the machene geting ready to set it up to thrash. It has been some squaly this afternoon. Snow a little then rain a little.

Wednesday, November 16   This has been quite pleasent for the Season. Wind West. Not very cold. Been cloudy all day. Got the machene sat up.

Thursday, November 17   This has been a butiful day. Warm and   sun shone most of the day.   It is raining a little this evening. Alvah gon down to Robert Brown to see if he can get some help to thrash. I done all the chores tonight. Wind blowes hard from the South this afternoon and tonight.

Friday, November 18   This was a wet morning. Faired of[f] about noon. Been very Warm today. Wind blowed hard from the South. I was thrashing today. We thrashed 82 bushels of Wheat today.

Saturday, November 19   This has been a stormy day.   It snowed a little all day. Wind blowed from the North. I was plastering the school house today. Charles was helping Alvah thrash. We had 131 bushels of Wheat. Thrashed 110 bushels of oats this afternoon.

Sunday, November 20   This was a pleasent morning. Been pleasent all day but not very warm. Alvah & Sarah & Burt was here to diner today.

Monday, November 21   This has been a pleasent day. Wind blew from the South. I helped to thrash this forenoon & plastered the school house the afternoon. We thrashed 224 bushels of oats today.

Tuesday, November 22   This has been a cold pleasent day. Wind blowed from the North. We finished thrashing this forenoon. Mrs. Albert White Died today. Alvah went for the young cattle this afternoon.

Wednesday, November 23   This has been a pleasent day but quite cold. Murcuary 5 above zero this morning. Wind blowed from the south. Mrs. Albert White was buried today. I churned for Alvah today. Charles got back with his clapbords this afternoon.

Thursday, November 24   This has been a cold day. Wind blowed hard from the north. I was building a chimney for Conyne today. Alvah went to the mill today. Got a letter from Joseph Brown with receipt for $500 Dollars.

Friday, November 25   This was pleasent but quite cold. Murcuary five above Zero this morning. I was to work in the Barn today. Wind South West.

Saturday, November 26   This has been a cloudy dull raw cold [day]. South West Wind. Snowed a little by squalls. I have been sick most of the day.

Sunday, November 27   This has been a stormy day. Snowed all day. Blowed quite hard. Wind South West. Turns into the North this evening and turns colder. It thawed a little most of the day.

Monday, November 28   This has been a clear pleasent day. Murcuary was twenty blow [below] zero this morning. I was working in the stable today.

Tuesday, November 29   It has been thawing all day. The snow is most all gon. The Wind blowed hard from the South all day. I plastered the chimney in the school house today and finished building Conyne chimney.

Wednesday, November 30   This has been a Warm pleasent day. It was very warm this afternoon. I was to work in the barn & Alvah was drawing out manure. James Foster & Mrs. Foster came here this afternoon to stay awhile. C. V. Harmon brought them here. Mrs. Foster don't feel very well.

Thursday, December 1   This has been a wet day. Rained all forenoon and it has been a warm day. Foster and his Wife are here. I was to work on the barn today.

Friday, December 2   This has been a pleasent day but a little colder. It frose a little last night. I took Foster & Mrs. Foster up to Allen Payne today. Thare was a turkey shute at the vilage today. Stillman Brown was here this evening. I paid him two hundred Dollars.

Saturday, December 3   This has been quite Warm for the season. Snowed a little all day but melted as fast as it came. I finished the Barn for this Fall. Alvah & Sarah has gon to Russell this afternoon. Left Burt Allen to stay alone but she got Iona Cleland to stay with her.

Sunday, December 4   This has been a pleasent day. Alvah has gon to Russell and I am doing the chores alone. I am not feeling very well. Charles went over and helped me do the chores at night. Mrs. Woodcock and Adaline made us a visit yesterday.

Monday, December 5   This has been a cloudy dul day. Snowed a little by spells. I have been sick today. I have not done anything today.

Tuesday, December 6   This has been a Warm pleasent day. I went to the vilag this afternoon.   Stayed till Nine O'clock. Settled with James Rushton for sawing in the years of 1880 and year 1881. It all amounted to Seventy five Dollars & ten cents.

Wednesday, December 7   This has been a wet day. It rained and snowed all day. Turned colder this afternoon. Sid Brown was here today to dinner. Staid most all afternoon.

Thursday, December 8   This has been a pleasent day after the snow storm last night. It snowed about three inches last night. Wind blowes from the South tonight. We killed all of our hogs. Charles had two & we had two big ones. Hiram Hall was moving his house today. They got it to the meeting house.

Friday, December 9   This has been a pleasent day. Murcuary was 30 above Zero this morning.   It thawed some this forenoon. I cut up the hog today.

Saturday, December 10   This has been a cold pleasent day. Murcuary stood at zero this morning.   I went down after sacage grinder and broke it.   Thomas Grant was at Alvah today.

Sunday, December 11   This has been a pleasent day but quite cool. Murcuary at two below zero this Morning. Charles and famley went down to Perces' today. Elder Dick [Dyke] preached today.

Monday, December 12   This has been a windy day. Blowed hard from the South West. Thawed a very little & snowed a very little. Rained a very little. I was helping Charly to thrash today. Thrashed 116 bushels this afternoon.

Tuesday, December 13   This has been a wet day. Rained all day and little raining this evening.   We finished Charles thrashing this afternoon. Thrashed 148 bushels today.

Wednesday, December 14   It has rained and snowed most all day.   Murcuary 54 above Zero this morning and 34 this evening.   I hant [haven't] been very well today.   The snow melted as fast as it fell.

Thursday, December 15   It frose up last night quite hard. Been quite cold all day. Snowed a very little. Wind north. I went down to the Vilag to James McKee's.

Friday, December 16   This has been a pleasent day. Wind South. Sun shone all day. Quite Warm. Thawed a little in the road.   I panted [painted] one of the bobsleds today. Alvah took a load of straw down to Goodanough.

Saturday, December 17   This has been a pleasent day. Quite warm. Sun shone all day and thawed all day. Alvah & I drew wood in the Sugarbush this forenoon. Alvah went back alone to draw wood this afternoon.

Sunday, December 18   This has been a butiful day. Quite Warm. Thawed all day. No snow yet. This winter the roads are afful rought [rough]. Docter Foster and Wife [Susan Viall] came here today. Charles Johnson & Wife, Wm Webb &

Wife, John Hewes, Agness Brown & Ida Brown all came to Alvah today.

Monday, December 19   This has been a pleesent warm day. Thawed all day. Docker Foster & I went down to the talc beds today. The school comensed today. Alvah was to work in the sugarbush today. We had a cow come in last night.

Tuesday, December 20   This has been a warm pleasent day. Thawed all day. Cloudy most of the day. I was fixing Alvah sistern. Foster & Wife are here yet. Emma Hall took supper here tonight. Agness Brown took dinner here today.

Wednesday, December 21   This has been another Warm pleesent day. Sun shone all day. Dr. Foster & Wife & Nancy Brown went over to Alvah Brown's this afternoon. I finished the sistern today.

Thursday, December 22   This has been a wet day. Rained all day but not very hard. Still raining tonight. A. P. Johnson & J. P. Brown and Susa Brown all came here tonight in the stage. Mrs. Foster hant been very well today.

Friday, December 23   This been quite a cold day. Wind blowed hard from the North. Took Foster and his Wife up to Charles Harmon's.

Saturday, December 24   This has been a butiful day. Frose hard last night. Murcuary two degrees above Zero this morning. James Rushton & wife was here today and Alfred Hall & famley. Alvah & Sarah went out to Thomas Grant's to a Crismas party.

Sunday, December 25   This has been another pleesent day. Thawed a little. Lill Gordin is staying here with Susa Brown. Charles & Joseph Brown went out to Wilson's today.   Dr.

Westly Harmon Died this evening buried Monday 17 Edwards, NY

January 23th, 1881 A Boy born to Mr. & Mrs. John Cleland, second

February 9th 1881 John Cleland's [son]Andrew Cleland [and] John ['s] Wife died this morning about four o'clock

Mrs. Wear Died today at Gouverneur February 12th 1881 She is to be brought to Edwards tomorrow to be buried by her husband the 13 February

February 22th, 1881 A Girl baby born to Mr. & Mrs. Alvah Brown early this Morning

February 23 Allen Payn maried to Miss Price

March 2th 1881 Mrs. Burny Downs died this forenoon. Leaves four small children

March 6 Mr. Storen maried the widow of Harvey McGill

March 6 Mr. John C. Boscoe of Hailsborough to Louisa E McGill of Edwards, Maried

March 7th 1881 Miss Emma Nobel died this forenoon. She was going to be maried in a little while

March 15th 1881 Liza Whitehead the widow of John Whitehead Died this forenoon

Mrs. Dolittle Died this afternoon March 17th 1881

March 30th 1881 Mr. George Davis formely of Edwards was married to Miss Mary Martin of Michagan

January 23th, 1881   A Boy worn to Mr. & Mrs. John Cleland, second

February 9th 1881   John Cleland's Andrew Cleland John Wife died this morning about four o'clock

Mrs. Wear Died today at Gouverneur February 12th 1881   She is to be brought to Edwards tomorrow to be buried by her husband the 13 February

February 22th, 1881 A Girl baby born to Mr. & Mrs. Alvah Brown early this Morning
February 23   Allen Payn maried to Miss Price

March 2th 1881   Mrs. Burny Downs died this forenoon. Leaves four small children

March 6   Mr. Storen maried the widow of Harvey McGill

March 6   Mr. John C. Boscoe of Hailsborough to Louisa E McGill of Edwards, Maried

March 7th 1881   Miss Emma Nobel died this forenoon. She was going to be maried in a little while

March 15th 1881   Liza Whitehead the widow of John Whitehead Died this forenoon

Mrs. Dolittle Died this afternoon March 17th 1881

March 30th 1881 Mr. George Davis formely of Edwards was married to Miss Mary Martin of Michagan

Reverent Silas Pratt of Nicholville, St. [Lawrence] County, NY died April the 11 th 1881 aged 78 years

April 26, 1881   Mr. Charles McGill maried to Miss Watson formely of Pitcairn

May 6 th 1881   The Cole Boy died last night.   He lived at James Wilson

May 6 th 1881 Mrs. Ida Ivers Died today about eleven

May 8, 1881   Mr. Wm Whitford maried to Miss May Havens all of South Edwards

May 15 th 1881 Mrs. John Maybee Wife died today.   Leaves a large family of children

May 25, 1881 Mr. Albert Cousins maried to Miss Netie Payn all of Edwards

June 8th, 1881 Aaron Jonison Wife died today.

June 8 th 1881   President Garefield was shot today (crossed off "and killed")

July 19th 1881 Mrs. Nancy Bencraft died this morning

July 24 th 1881   Charles Beech little Girl died this morning. Little Annah Beech is gon

July 28th, 1881 A baby born to Mr. & Mrs. Thomas Cousins

August 2, 1881 A Girl baby born to Charles & Selia Johnson

August 6th 1881 George Baraford died today

August 8th, 1881   A Girl baby born to Mr. & Mrs. Robert Webb

August 9 th 1881 Ai Wooliver baby died this morning

Sept 9th 1881 Miss Phila Webb died today

September 10th, 1881   A little Girl born to Mr. & Mrs. Benjaman Noble

Sept 11 th 1881 Mr. Conynes little boy died today

Sept 14 th 1881 Mrs. Louisa Spalding Died at noon today

Sept 14, 1881   Mr. Milo Woodcock maried to Miss Cora Johnson

Sept 18 th 1881   Old Mr. Robert Brown died today.   James Brown's father

September 19 the 1881   President Garfield died this evening about ten o'clock.

Sept 23 th 1881 the lightening struck and killed one of Jason Gates' little boys

Oct 8, 1881 Mr. Earl Barans maried to Miss Nellie Thurstin

November 4, 1881, Russele [born in Russell, NY] A girl born to Mr. & Mrs. William Grant

November 11 th 1881 Mrs. Mary Jane wife of Edwin Wight Died.

November 22 th 1881 Mrs. Albert White died this afternoon.

1881 William Brown

April 15 th 1881 By cash for butter 10.12
May 27 By cash for chees in sail [sale]
 nomber [number] 1 and 2 11.15
June 6 by cash for chees in sail nomber 3 & 4 18.16
June 21 by cash for cheese in sail nomber 5 26.40
June 24 th 1881 by cash for cheese in sail nomber 6

15.84
July 1 th 1881 by cash for cheese in sail nomber 7 15.00
July 20 th 1881 by cash for ches in sail nomber 8 30.00
August 8 th 1881 by cash for cheese in sail nomber 9 35.00
August 19 th 1881 by cash for cheese in sail No. 10 36.49
Sept 27th 1881 by cash for cheese in sail No. 11 67.00
Oct 24 1881 by cash for cheese in sail Noumber 12 71.02

[The remainder of the Memoranda pages are monthly listing of cash accounts (in this case, money expended). Rather than list each month, the editor has listed the month of January 1881 as an example of William Brown's expenditures.]

Sample Monthly Cash Account

January 6 by cash of James W. Harmon interest on Bond 45.00

January 8   paid the shoemaker for mending Nancy shoes   15 cents

Paid Robert Allen for mending bridle   5 cents

January 10 paid H. Gardner for ink, postage stamps   44 cents

Paid Conyne for file   10 cents

January 14   paid H. Gardner for mustard broom   25 cents

263

January 15	paid Conyne for a bite of glass	25 cents
	Paid the Shumaker for mending boots	10 cents
January 25	paid James Rushton for sled beem	10 cents
January 28	paid Van Burin for horse to hay	30 cents
	Paid Doct Leston for medison	15 dollars
	Paid Wilson for mending rings	50 cents
	Paid Goodnough the balance on Waggon	4 dollars
January 29	Paid H. Gardner for candy for the children	5 cents
January 1881	Received $45.00	Paid $21.29

1883

[On front overleaf of diary]:

Nancy A. Brown   Edwards NY

Eddia Webb died July 31, age 14
Brother Dr. James Foster died Aug 12, 1883, age 83
Ebin Bancroft & Sophronia Laidlaw was maried September 19, 1883, Edwards, NY
Mrs. E. Hitchcock died Oct the first
A girl baby to Charley Johnson, September 1883

Monday, January the first 1883 [To the left is the way Nancy Johnson Brown wrote the day and date. However, the editor has changed the remaining dates to the format used in the entire book in order to have the dates consistent.]   This is the first day of the New Year. One more year is past and gone

264

never more to return. How many of our friends and neighbours have gone to their long home never to return. Charley [Brown] and Martha has gone to Harisville to spend their New Year. A dance thare tonight. This has been quite a windy day. Sister Hall [Emmorancy Johnson Hall] & family made me a visit today. Alvah and family made a visit to her father Grant's today. Albert Eliot came to town last fryday night from Michigan. He is a cousin of Mrs. S. Rushton. The New year dance for Edwards came of last fryday night. A.P. Brown bought a colt of Mr. Grant January 25. Wm Brown payed 100 dollars for the colt.

Tuesday, January 2   This has been a cold day. Snowd this forenoon but Pleasant this afternoon. Sarah Payn [e] and Mrs. Hugh Pratt made me a visit today. This is Mabel Brown's birthday. She is seven years old.

Wednesday, January 3   This has been a stormy day. Snowd nearly all day & the wind has blown terible all day. Frank O'neal and wife from Hermon was visiting to Alvah's this afternoon & evening & also Billy Webb & family & Celia Clealand.

Thursday, January 4   A cold but Pleasant day. Mercury 20 below zero. Wm has been sick all day.

Friday, January 5   A cold morning. Snowing a little. Wm is better today.

Saturday, January 6   A cold morning. Mercury 20 below zero. We just got the news that John Laidlaw died on Christmas. He was formaly [formerly] from Edwards but has resided in Indianah [Indiana] a number of years. His father came here from Scotland 65 years ago.

Sunday, January 7   This is a nice winter day. The wind has

blown hard all day but is pleasant tonight.

Monday, January 8   I received a letter from brother A. P. Johnson [Abel Pratt Johnson, Pine Valley, NY] tonight. His daughter Stellah [Stella] was maried the 27 of December [1882]

Tuesday, January 9   This is A pleasant day. Mercury 10 below zero.

Wednesday, January 10   This has been a cold day. Mercury 25 below. I mad a call to A. P. Brown's [her son] today. Wm has stayed in the house all day.

Thursday, January 11   A cold day. Mercury 25 below zero in the morning.

Friday, January 12   A cold, pleasant day. No wind nor storm. A donation at the Hotell this evening for the benefit of the Rev. Doctor Lee of Canton. He received 60 dollars.

Saturday, January 13   This has been a terible stormy day & the wind is just howlling this evening. Wm has been quite buisy all day fixing ours & Charley's clock.

Sunday, January 14   The wind is blowing hard today but nothing like yesterday. I have written a letter to send to A. P. Johnson if the stage goes out tomorow. It did not get through last night. Has not come yet today at two o'clock. Thare [There]   has teemes [teams] gone out to break the rhodes [roads]. Charley has not any teem now. He sold his horses fryday [Friday] for 300 dollars.

Monday, January 15   This has been A lovely winter day after the storm. The stage did not get through untill tonight.

Tuesday, January 16   This has been A pleasant day. Mercury at zero. Wm & I went to John Absalam's in the town of Fowler [NY] this afternoon.

Wednesday, January 17   This has been A stormy day. Snowd hard all day. We came home this afternoon. This evening the wind blew hard & raind a litle in the night.

Thursday, January 18   The thaw is froze up this morning & this has been a pleasant day. Not very cold. Charley Johnson & Celia made us a visit today.

Friday, January 19   It has been a stormy afternoon.   The snow came down bountifuly. I made A visit to Sister Hall's this afternoon.

Saturday, January 20   This has been A mild day but this evening the wind is blowing from the south and is raining and thawing fast. A. P. Brown & family have gone to Russell [NY] today for a visit.   Addia Fellows came to C. H. Brown's tonight for a visit. Ben Clark & wife from Gouverneur was visiting to C.H. Brown's today & also Sarah & Clarah Payn[e]. They made me a call this afternoon.

Sunday, January 21   The wind is blowing fearfully & is snowing this forenoon. The thaw froze up this morning. We are all at home today.   Amos Newton has just come after Addia. She is teaching the Creek School this winter.

Monday, January 22   This has been a cold windy day. No storm. I have not done my washing today. Done some baking & some ironing. Had a long chat with Charley & Martha. They are thinking of leaving this farm in the Spring. We are sorry to have them go away. We fear they will not do as well but they will do as they think best.

Tuesday, January 23   This has been a cold day. Mercury 10 below zero. We received A letter from Mary McKinney last night. Wm has written one tonight to send to Will Brown in Canada.

Wednesday, Janaury 24   One more cold windy day but not quite as cold as the first of the week. Wm & the boys went to the village this afternoon. I wrote a letter today to Hannah Brown in Canada. Isaac Brown of Michigan was maried [married] to a lady in Canada on Christmas day. There was 60 of the friends attended his weding. [wedding]

Thursday, January 25   This has been A pleasant day. The sone has shone all day. Mercury went 20 degrees above zero at noon today.

Friday, January 26   This morning the mercury was down to 30 below zero but it has been A lovely day. Wm & I went to Brother [William] Warren Johnson's for a visit. He is no better than he was 6 weeks ago.

Saturday, January 27   This has been A stormy day. Snowd some and raind & thawd quite a good deal. Mr. Grant & his wife has been visiting to Alvah's today.

Sunday, January 28   This has been A lovely day. The thaw was froze this morning but the mercury was up to 30 above zero today. Wm has the sick headache today. Sarah Brown & the teacher, Miss Winslow, made us a call this evening & Ida Brown made me a call today. Thare was a party to Robert Webb's last night.

Monday, January 29   This has been a beautiful day, most like spring. Mercury 20 above zero this evening. Alvah & Wm has been geting the wood saw in rediness today to commence sawing wood tomorrow.

Tuesday, January 30   This has been A lovely day. Mild & sone shining all day but this evening A storm is threatning. The south wind is howlling, blinds is slaming. Alvah's folks had company today.   Charley Johnson & wife & Celia Clealand & Nelly Day.   Charley Brown went to Gouverneur today with P. H. Brown.

Wednesday, January 31   This has been A very stormy day. Raind hard this morning then snowd & blowd all the rest of the day. Wm lay in bed all the forenoon & went to the village [Edwards]. Stayed the afternoon. Charley has been to the village nearly all day, has not got home yet at 8 in the evening.

Thursday, February 1   Stormy this forenoon but pleasant this afternoon.   Sister Hall & Emmah made me A visit this afternoon. Charley [son, Charles Hiram Brown] has bought A house in town today.

Fryday [Nancy Brown generally spelled Friday "*Fryday.*" All entries for Fryday have been changed to Friday.] February 2

This has been A good winter day. No storm.   Wm & Alvah has been sawing wood all day. The colts work on the treads very good.   Charley has been helping P. H. Brown draw the school wood today.

Saturday, February 3   This has been quite A stormy day. The snow fell about 5 inches in the night & this morning. Ebin Keer & his wife & litle boy is visiting in Charley's this afternoon & evening.

Sunday, February 4   It has been quite cold today. The limbs of the trees & every thing was covered with ice that fell in the night. A terible crust all over the snow. The wind has blown cold from the west all day.

Monday, February 5   The west wind has blown hard all day. I have done my washing today. Wm & A.P. [Brown] has been sawing wood today. C. H. [Charles Hiram Brown] is away at Fine & Pitcarn to day with Eb Bancroft.

Tuesday, February 6   This has been quite A cold day but not as cold as yesterday. Wm & Alvah has been sawing wood today.

Wednesday, February 7   It has snowd & been Pleasant part of the time today. Not very cold. Mercury 20 above zero. The men have been sawing today. Mrs. Albert Wight has been visiting in Charley's this afternoon & evening.

Thursday, February 8   This has been a stormy day. The wind has blown hard all day & evening. Wm, Clealand & family made us a visit today. Eb[en] Bancroft & Mrs. Laidlaw's family was visiting in Charley's this afternoon & evening.

Friday, February 9   One more terible stormy day of wind & snow. The stage did not go out untill noon today. This is Martha's birthday. She is 35 years old. This is my sister Susan's [Susan Viall Foster] birthday. She is 75.

Saturday, February 10   This has been A very Pleasant day. No wind. Sun shone all day. Mercury 20 below zero this morning. Wm and Alvah finished sawing the wood here today.

Sunday, February 11   Snowed some today. Not so cold as the 10th.

Monday, February 12   This has been A lovely lay. Thawd whare the sun shone but it snowd & blew in the night. Track all filled up this morning. Charley and John McFerren went to Gouverneur today.

Tuesday, February 13   This has been a lovely day. The men all went to town meting today & a number of ladies made visits in town.

Wednesday, February 14   One more Pleasant day. Wm & Alvah has been sawing wood today. C. H. Brown went to Canton [NY] today.

Thursday, February 15   This has been A nice mild day. Wind strong in the south tonight. Thawing quite fast. John Absalan & his wife made us a short visit today. We had the bad luck to loose one of our cows today. She fell dead when they let her out of the barn today. Overflow of the gaul [gall] was the cause of her death.

Friday, February 16   This has been a warm day. Thawd all day.

Saturday, February 17   It rained & thawd fast all night & this morning the stage could not go through today. Pleasant this afternoon. Is freezing tonight. Wind blowing hard and cold. Thaw is froze up.

Sunday, February 18   I received A letter from brother H.A. Johnson of Oregon fryday [Friday] night. It was 16 days coming. This has been A pleasant day but a cold north wind has blown cold all day. I have written a letter to H.A. Johnson today.

Monday, February 19   It snowd 6 inches in the night. Snowd most of this forenoon. Pleasant this afternoon & this is A lovely evening. C. H. Brown has been drawing his stove wood to the village today. Geting ready to moove to the village.

Tuesday, February 20   Pleasant this forenoon but high wind

and snow this afternoon & evening. Wm & Alvah finished sawing their wood today. Jim Comings [Cummings] finished splitting <u>our</u> wood tonight. He worked four days for 6 shillings a day.

Wednesday, February 21   This has been a cold windy day. Wm went to mill & to the blacksmith shop & to Graham Stevenson's this afternoon. I made a Call to Albert Wights & Horace Beech's. Jane Brown is visiting in Charley's tonight.

Thursday, February 22   I received A letter from Sarah Brown of Canada the 21 of this month. This has been A stormy day. The snow came down bountifly. I made A visit to Mr. Payn's [Payne's] this afternoon and evening. Wm & Sherman came over in the evening.

Friday, February 23   This has been A very pleasant day. Charley has been drawing Hay & grain and wood to the village today. P.H. Brown has been helping him. Wm got a letter and one hundred dollars in money from his Brother John Brown this morning of Deer River.

Saturday, February 24   This has been A lovely day. Quite cold in the morning. Mercury 30 below zero at 7 o'clock but it was 45 above at 2 o'clock this afternoon. This evening it is clowdy [cloudy] & the south wind is blowing & looks like A storm.

Sunday, February 25   This has been A stormy day. The wind blew A terible gale all night last and all day today. It has raind most of the day.

Monday, February 26   The thaw took cold froze up this morning. Snowd hard most all day. The wind has blown hard all the forenoon. Thare was an Agent here today to take Photographs to Potsdam to coppy. I let him take one of

Clarah's [daughter of Wm and Nancy Brown who died at the age of 9] to copy.

Tuesday, February 27 This has been A pleasant day but it has snowd some this evening & the wind is blowing some. Agness Brown made me a visit today. John Hughs [Hughes] came this evening.

Wednesday, February 28   This has been A nice winter day. Mercury 10 above zero. Charley's folks are packing up to moove. This is the last day of this month. Eddy Webb is very sick.

Thursday, March 1   This has been a lovely day and a very buisy day with all of us here. Charles's family mooved to the village today. They went bag and bagadge [baggage]. Four large loads of goods from the House & then lots of grain and wood. The wind is just howling tonight.

Friday, March 2   This has been A mild lovely day. Thawd most all day but is freezing hard tonight. We got a letter from Wm E Brown of Canada today. They have a litle boy one month old. Sister Hall made me a visit today.

Saturday, March 3   This has been a cold day. Wm & I took a ride to Charley Harmon's this afternoon.

Sunday, March 4   This has been a Pleasant day but very cold. I attended church today. The young Mr. Dyke spoke to the People in church today here in Edwards.

Monday, March 5   I made a call in Charley Brown's a few minutes yesterday before meting [meeting] at their home in the village.

Tuesday, March 6   This has been A cold stormy day. The

wind is just howlling this evening. Alvah & I attended Mr. Ward's funeral today. The church was well filld. Mr. Wheeler Preached the sermon. Mr. Wm Green of Hermon [NY] was undertaker. I took dinner with Charley Brown's family today after the funeral.

Wednesday, March 7   This has been A cold windy day. Snowed & blew in the night & has been A bad day entirely. I have been making A coat for Sherman today. Wm went to the hardware store to get our pump fixt & to J. Brown's store. Bought cloth for himself, A Pair of Pants & cloth for Sherman coat.

Thursday, March 8   This has been A cold day but no storm. Clarence Brown came to make us a visit today.

Friday, March 9   This has been a pleasant day but quite cold. Alvah and family made a visit to Mr. Grant's today. Brought Mary Grant home with them for a visit.

Saturday, March 10   A stormy day. Raind in the forenoon and snowed all the afternoon & evening. Wm & Alvah was fixing the sugar arch today.

Sunday, March 11   This has been A stormy day all day. Snowed hard all day but not very cold. I commenced to set milk from one cow tonight for the first this spring.

Monday, March 12   This has been a stormy cold day. Snowd all day and quite a strong west wind. I have done a large washing this forenoon.

Tuesday, March 13   This has been a nice pleasant day. Wm took 56 lbs of sugar to J. Brown's store today.

Wednesday, March 14   This has been a pleasant day but the

wind is howling this evening & looks like a storm. I have made a pair of thick pants today for Wm Brown. A. P. [Alvah Percival Brown] has sold two tubs of Butter that they have made this winter. One 60 lbs, one 30 lbs. Got 25 cents a lb.

Thursday, March 15   This has been quite a pleasant day. Thawd some this afternoon.   A call from Mr. John Wesgate[Westgate] & son & Mr. Luke Van Norman [Ornum] & Mr. Gideon Freman [Freeman] today.   Mr. Wesgate of Herman [NY] came and Payed Wm   100.50 dollars of hired money. Mr. Freeman was wanting to buy this farm. Luke was wishing to hire money [meaning wishing to borrow money].

Friday, March 16   This has been a very cold windy day but no storm.   C. H. Brown made us a call & took supper with us today.   I traded 55 cents with him today by the way of Sherman Brown.   I have not cald in their store yet.   A. P. Brown made a Purchase of them today.

Saturday, March 17   This has been a very stormy day with wind & snow. The wind is in the south tonight. Blowing a perfect gale. Mercury 30 above zero.

Sunday, March 18   This has been a very stormy day. It commenced to rain this morning.   Raind hard untill nearly three o'clock. Since then the snow has been coming down at a terible rate.   We received a letter from Hannah Brown of Canada today. She intends to be maried the 21 of this month. She sent an invitation to all of her relitives [relatives] here in Edwards to come to her wedding.

Monday, March 19   This has been A stormy day. Snowed all day. A fearful snow storm in the night. I made a visit to sister Hall's this afternoon. Clarance came home with Sherman & I tonight to stay all night with us.

Tuesday, March 20   This has been A pleasant cold day. I made a visit to Wm Clealand's today. Sherman has gone to stay with Clarance tonight.

Wednesday, March 21   This has been a lovely day. Mercury at zero this morning. Mettie Robertson is making me a visit today & staying all night with us. Intends to make a visit to A. P. Brown's tomorrow.

Thursday, March 22   A very pleasant day but a very cold morning.   The mercury was 24 below zero this morning. Went up to 20 above at noon. A cold west wind. Charley sent a load of potatoes to Gouverneur today from here.   Gets 60 cents a bushel. Hires Ed Wight to draw them. Wm is sick all day today. Alvah has the choures to do at both barns today.

Friday, March 23   This has been a pleasant day. Not near as cold as yesterday. Wm & Sherman & I made a visit to brother Robert Brown's today. Agness & Sidney had gone to Canton [NY]. I received a letter from Vinson [Vincent] Brown of Mich today. He is one of brother Isaac Brown's Boys.

Saturday, March 24   This has been a very pleasant day. Thawd some n the midle of the day. Mercury 12 below zero this morning, 20 above at noon. The stars are shining bright tonight. Bower Brown is staying with us today & tonight & tomorrow. Bower was nine years old the fourth of this month.

Sunday, March 25   This has been a lovely day. Mercury at zero this morning. Thawd some in the midle of the day. Clarence and Bower Brown stayed with us today while Charley's folks went to Russell [NY] to Henry Clark's. Aunt Mary Clark is very sick. Alvah and family went away for a visit today.

Monday, March 26   This has been quite a mild Pleasant day.

The most like spring of any day. The mercury in the morning at zero but at noon 40 above zero. We sent a letter to Jo Brown and one to A. P. Johnson today to Pine Valley, NY.

Tuesday, March 27   A nice mild forenoon but snowed some this afternoon. Some colder tonight. Wm & I took A cutter ride this afternoon to Warren Johnson's. He is no better. He did not sit up any while we was thare.

Wednesday, March 28   This has been a nice pleasant day, not warm enough for sap yet. [maple]

Thursday, March 29   This has been a lovely day. I made a call to Sister Hall's this afternoon. I made a visit to Milo Woodcock's yesterday afternoon & evening. Wm came in the evening. I received a letter from brother Charley [Charles Victor] Johnson [Pittsfield, IL] tonight. Cora Woodcock is quite sick, has been for four weeks. Dr. Kellow is doctoring her.

Friday, March 30   This has been A lovely day. Wm taped 100 & 50 sugar trees this afternoon. The sap run quite well. This is the first day the sap has started in our trees.

Saturday, March 31   A. P. Brown went to Gouverneur yesterday. Took 2 tubs of Butter. Sold for 23 cents a pound. Brought some Butter tubs for Charley. Got home at one o'clock. One more lovely Pleasant day. Wm and Alvah has nearly finished taping [tapping] their trees today. Mable Brown is staying with us today and night.

Sunday, April 1   This has been a cold but pleasant day. The sap has run a litle. Charley's family has made us A call today. Alvah went to Fine [NY] today and brought home Lottia Johnson with him. She intends to work for them this summer.

277

Monday, April 2   One more pleasant day. Not quite warm enough for sap but our men has been taping trees today. Sherman has been quite sick today. He is threatend of a fever. A few families from Fine & Pitcarn [Pitcairn] started their goods for Dakota today. Their families start next week.

Tuesday, April 3   One more Pleasant day. The sleighing is nearly spoilt. Sherman & I made A visit to granpa Clealand's today & A call to Charley Brown's & also in his store. Bought 3 dollars worth of groceries such as tea, crackers, soda, baking powder, etc.

Wednesday, April 4   One more nice day. It has clowded over this afternoon & looks like a storm. Mercury was 15 above zero this morning & 50 this afternoon. Wm received A letter from A. O. Broadia last night. He wants money to hire [wants to borrow money].

Thursday, April 5   This has been a rainy day. Wm & Alvah gathered the sap this morning and boild [boiled] it down to three pails full of sweete but not sirup [syrup]. I received a letter from Susan M. Brown from Pine Valley [NY] last night. Wm sent a box of sugar to Gouverneur today by Leveret Raymond to ship to Millport, Chemung Co, NY. 85 lbs sugar

Friday, April 6   It has not stormed any today nor the sap did not run any. We boild [boiled] down our sweete into sugar today. Was 50 lbs. It was very nice. The Stage went with a wagon yesterday for the first time since last November or the first day of December.

Saturday, April 7   This has been a stormy day. Snowed nearly all night & today. A terible storm for this time of year. A factory meeting tonight.

Sunday, April 8   This has been a nice pleasant day. The sap has run well. A few tubs was over run with sap tonight.

Monday, April 9 This has been a pleasant day but a high wind all day. The sap did not run much today. We did down into sugar 67 lbs this afternoon & have four pails of sirup [syrup].

Tuesday, April 10 This has been a warm lovely day but not much sap. Sister Hall and Alfred made us a visit today. We had warm sugar. It is 17 years today since we came to this farm to reside.

Wednesday, April 11 This has been a terible windy day.

Thursday, April 12 Quite a good day. Boiled in the sap and done it down to sugar. Charley and his boys was here to eat warm sugar. Wm is marking a box of sugar tonight to send to Saginaw City. [Michigan]

Friday, April 13 This has been A lovely day. The sap has run some. Hugh Pratt & Cara mooved into a room in George Padget's house yesterday to commence Housekeeping. Caria attended the funeral of her Brother the day before yesterday in Russell [NY] O. Kelsey's little boy is nine years old.

Saturday, April 14 This has been a lovely day. The sap has run but not very much. They boiled in 7 pails of sirup. Martha Brown & the children was here today to eat warm sugar. A Party to Mrs. Miles Beaches [Beech's] last evening for the benifit of her family. A donation. A surprise donation Party to John Nobles [Noble's] the third of April.

Sunday, April 15 This has been a nice day but the wind is howling tonight.

Monday, April 16 It has been a little cooler today. Clowdy all day. Wm boiled in the sap & sugared it down into tub sugar. We sugared down 100 lbs yesterday. Very nice.

Tuesday, April 17   Just a lovely day. Wm plowd all day. The sugaring is about done. Uncle Sandy Noble died last night.

Wednesday, April 18   One more lovely day but quite a cool wind. We Attended the funeral of Uncle Sandy Noble today. J. Gardener of Canton Preached the sermon. Wm M Green of Hermon officiated as Sexton.

Thursday, April 19   It has been a rainy day & cooller. The grass looks quite green.

Friday, April 20   This has been quite a cool day. We have gathered all of the sap buckets & washed them today. Sarah & Lottie & Cassie Treglown helped me all day.

Saturday, April 21   This has been a pleasant but cold day. A hard frost this morning. The sap run some. Perce brought A load of Harrows from Gouverneur tonight for C. H. Brown.

Sunday, April 22   This has been a cold pleasant day. The sap has run well. I started to go to church today. Cald to sister Hall's [and] found her sick & did not go any further. Stayed thare until four o'clock, and then got a ride home with Alvah. Wm boxt [boxed] 100 lbs of sugar to send to Milport, Chemung co. [NY] Milo caries it to Gouverneur tomorrow. The new Methodist Minister Preached today at Edwards for the first time. His name is Howerd [Howard], a yong [young] 21 years of age.

Monday, April 23   One more cold Pleasant day. A very cold north wind. Wm has been Plowing all day.

Tuesday, April 24   A cold clowdy day. Snowd this evening. Charley Salsbery [Salsbury] from Fine [NY] came here tonight. Stayed with us. He wanted work.

Wednesday, April 25   This has been a very cold day. Cold north wind all day. Mercury stood at freezing mark all day.

Thursday, April 26   This has been A cold windy day. Raining some tonight. Wm has plowd the orched [orchard] & the garden today. Alvah & the hired man has been drawing manure from this barn onto the wheete ground. I have made a shirt for Sherman today & churnd 10 lbs of butter & done lots of work today. Charley Salsbery is working for Alvah.

Friday, April 27   This has been a clowdy day. Not quite as cold as usual. Alvah's hired man left this morning. He was a poor excuse. Mrs. Hellen & Albert Eliot made me a call & took dinner with us today. They intend to start for Detroit, Mich next Tuesday to make that place their future home.

Saturday, April 28   This has been a cold day. Pleasant this afternoon. Agnes & Ira Brown made me a visit today. Sherman made a visit to his grandpa Clealand's today.

Sunday, April 29   This has been a nice pleasant day. I went to church today. The young man Dyke preached today.

Monday, April 30   This has been a nice day, rather cold. I have done A large washing & Baking. Wm has been working for his Brother Robert making A land rooller [roller].

Tuesday, May 1   No frost this morning. Has been a nice warm day.

Wednesday, May 2   It is raining this afternoon & evening. I have had company all day. Sister Hall & Emma made me a visit this forenoon & Mrs. Wm McKee & Addia McKee made me a visit this afternoon.

281

Thursday, May 3   This has been A rainy day & quite cool. I have done a large ironing today.

Friday, May 4   I received a letter from V. Brown yesterday of Mich. Albert Eliot & Hellen [Helen] started for Detroit, Mich the first day of May whare they intend to make their Home. This has been quite a nice day. Wm & Alvah drove the young cattle to Pasture to Albert Noble's. Forest McKee & Addia made us a call tonight. They intend to moove [move] in to the part of our house that Charley occupied. Mrs. Cynthia Payn [Payne] Died today noon.

Saturday, May 5   This has been a rainy day. A hard thunder storm before day light this morning. The first thunder of this year.

Sunday, May 6   This has been a lovely day. The grass is looking green and beautiful. I went to Mrs. Payn's funeral today with Alvah. Cald on Brother Warren. He is no better.

Monday, May 7   This has not been a very pleasant day. It has raind bart [part] of the time. I have commenced cleaning House today.

Tuesday, May 8   This has been A cold day but no storm. I have cleand my kitchen today. Clarance is staying with us tonight. Sherman stayed to Charley's last night.

Wednesday, May 9   This has been A nice day. Hiram Hall worked for Alvah today. We received A letter from Mrs. Stanton of Canada today & James Stanton's Photograph.

Thursday, May 10   This has been the warmest day of this spring. It has thundered & raind terible.
Friday, May 11   This has been quite a cool day. No storm. Forest McKee & Addia moved into a Part of our House

yesterday, the 10th of May.

Saturday, May 12   Quite a cold day. A frost this morning.
Mrs. King Payn & Clarah & Mabel & Bower Brown made me
a visit today. Forest & Addia has gone to Gouverneur [NY]
today from here. We have just started our soap making today.

Sunday, May 13   This has been a pleasant day [to] day but
cold. We did not go to church today. Mabel stayed with us
today. Charley Brown made us a call this afternoon.

Monday, May 14   Pleasant this forenoon. Clowdy this
afternoon. Looks like a storm. A hard frost this morning. I
have done a large washing today & Baking. I received a letter
from A. P. Johnson the 12 of May.

Tuesday, May 15   Lowery [gloomy] in the morning, pleasant
in the afternoon. Sister Haried [Harriet] [Viall] Harmon made
me a visit this afternoon. Intends to stay until tomorow noon.

Wednesday, May 16   This has been a cold pleasant day. A
frost this morning. I made a visit to Sister Hall's today.

Thursday, May 17   A nice day. I finished making up my soap
today.

Friday, May 18   Quite a warm day. I done some cleaning
house & A large Ironing.

Saturday, May 19   The warmest day of this Spring. Addia &
I had company from the village today.

Sunday, May 20   This has been A good day. It looks like rain.
Wm went to George Smith's today. Pasco Whitford's house
& barn was burnt yesterday.

Monday, May 21   It has raind all day & is quite cold. A great fire in Pitcarn [Pitcairn]   the 19th in Lou Graham's sugar woods and Warren Allen's.

Tuesday, May 22   This has been a cold clowdy day & has raind some. Sister Hall [Emmorancy Johnson Hall] made me A visit today. It is her Birthday. She is 56 years old.

Wednesday, May 23   It has raind all day. The ground is well soaked with watter [water]. I have cut & made A pair of Pants for Sherman today & done my work & Baked Bread.

Thursday, May 24   The rain is held and is clearing up. Is quite Pleasant this afternoon. I received A letter from Vincent Brown today from Mich, & one from C. Kirkbride, Granville, Mich.

Friday, May 25   This has been A Pleasant day. Our folks has Planted their potatoes today.

Saturday, May 26   This has been a pleasant day untill near night. It has commenced to rain. I have spent the day in the village. Made one visit & A number of calls.

Sunday, May 27   This has [been] A pleasant day after the rain of last night. Sherman & I went to church today. Elder Dyke Preached today. I took dinner to Charley's today after meting.[meeting] Alvah & family made a visit to Thom Grant's today Lottia had a beau today, Myron Allen. Addia had a lot of company today.

Monday, May 28   It was raining hard this morning. Was pleasant this afternoon. I done A large washing this morning. Alvah went with A load of cheese today to DeKalb [Junction]. Finished Planting the corn & the garden today.

Tuesday, May 29   It raind all this forenoon. Pleasant this afternoon. Quite cool tonight.

Wednesday, May 30   A nice day untill most night. It is raining this evening. Mr. Conine [Conyne] brought Addie's furniture from Gouverneur tonight.   Frank Burdock mooved to Gouverneur Monday, 28.

Thursday, May 31   It was raining hard this morning.

Friday, June 1   This has been quite a good day. Wm finished Planting Potatoes today. I made A call to Sister Hall's this afternoon. I received A letter from Vincent Brown to night.

Saturday, June 2   This has been A lovely day. Wm & A. P. finished their seedeing [seeding] today.

Sunday, June 3   This has been A pleasant day. Now at night it look like rain. Wm & I went to Warren Johnson's today. He is failling [failing] every day. Then we cald to Charley's this afternoon noon & took dinner. John Absalan & wife came here today from West Fowler [NY]. They stayed to Alvah's until we got home.

Monday, June 4   It raind in the night & a litle [little] this morning. Pleasant this afternoon.   Brother Warren [William Warren Johnson] Died at eight this evening.

Tuesday, June 5   This has been a nice Pleasant day. I have been up to Mariah Johnson's all day helping prepare for the funeral which is to be tomorrow. A. P. Johnson came tonight.

Wednesday, June 6   A very warm day. The rhodes [roads] are very dusty. We all attended the funeral of Brother Warren Johnson today. Elder Dyke Preached the funeral Sermon.

Thursday, June 7   Clowdy today. Looks like rain. Mr. Clark brought me Clarah's [Clara Brown] Picture today. I paid him four dollars for it & the frame. It is copied in India Ink.

Friday, June 8   A nice shower this morning but it has been A lovely day. Wm has been shooting black birds all day.

Saturday, June 9   This has been A lovely day. Quite warm. A nice shower at five this afternoon.   John Roach's Brother cald here to dinner. Clarence & Bower Brown has made us a visit today. Will Gardner made us a call today. He wants to buy this farm.   Mrs. Maltby took the train yesterday for Mexico [NY] to make her home with Almeron Thomas. Her brother, C. V. Harmon, caried her & her goods to the Station yesterday.

Sunday, June 10   A Splendid rain in the night. Clowdy & misty this forenoon. Pleasant in afternoon. Charley & Martha & the children & Mark Rushton came here today to dinner.

Monday, June 11   This has been A rainy & windy day. I done a large washing this forenoon & Baked this afternoon. Brother Abel [Johnson] cald this morning. S. P. Rice made us a call this afternoon.

Tuesday, June 12   This has been a clowdy day & raind Part of the time.

Wednesday, June 13   This has been A pleasant day. Nice & cool. The wind is blowing hard tonight. I received A letter from Vincent Brown today.   Brother A. P. Johnson left here this morning in the stage for his home in Pine Valley [NY] The men commenced working on the rhode [road] today on this beat. Wm is P.master [Path master].

Thursday, June 14   This has been A lovely day. Clear & pleasant. Sherman & I went to the shows today.   We took dinner to Charley Brown's.

Friday, June 15   This has been A lovely June day. Wm has been working on the rhode. I have done my baking & ironing today. Bower Brown has come to stay with us tonight.

Saturday, June 16   The wind has blown hard from the south all day.   It looks like rain tonight.   The men has been to a Barn-raising for H. Bancroft this afternoon.   The Barn is 80 x 40.   Forest & Addia went to Russell [NY] to attend a funeral of Harry Palmer's litle Boy. 5 years old.   The Mother Died a few weeks since.

Sunday, June 17   This has been a very warm day.   Lottie & Addie & Forest & Sherman & I went to church today. Alvah & family went to Harry Winslow's for a visit.

Monday, June 18   This is A rainy day.   I have done my washing this forenoon.   Mrs. Gideon Freeman made me a call this afternoon.   We received a letter from Matilda Stanton of Canada tonight.

Tuesday, June 19   Raind in the night & this forenoon.

Wednesday, June 20   Been quite showery today. The men finished working on the rhode tonight.   Sarah Brown made me a call this afternoon.   We had a friendly chat long to be remembered.

Thursday, June 21   This has been A pleasant day. No rain. A. P. Brown cultivated the corn.   Wm has been preparing for his suit with Frank Barnes that comes of tomorow.

Friday, June 22   A very lovely day.   Judge Neary & Mr. Pooller [Pooler] of Gouverneur [NY] took dinner & supper with me today.

Saturday, June 23   A very warm day.

Sunday, June 24   A warm pleasant day. We all stayed at home.

Monday, June 25   A nice cool wind & looks like rain. Wm has been hoing in the garden all day & Alvah in the corn field & the cheese has been sold 6 times.

Tuesday, June 26   This has been a rainy day. Wm finished hoing in the garden this forenoon.

Wednesday, June 27   This has been A warm clowdy day but no rain. Thare has been A large Party to Trout Lake today. Wm has gone to Gouverneur today on law business. He got a letter from lawyer Kellog [g] of Ogdensburg [NY] last night.

Thursday, June 28   This has been A warm day. Showery in the morning. Sister Hall made me a visit today.

Friday, June 29   This has been A pleasant day. Not so very warm but there is a thunder shower this evening.   Mr. Andrews of Gouverneur [NY] made us a call yesterday afternoon.

Saturday, June 30   One more lovely day after the rain of last night.

Sunday, July 1   A nice cool morning. Henry Brown's folks beries [buries] one of their litle Boys today. Rawley [Brown].

Monday, July 2 The wind has blown hard all day. It has raind some today.   Wm went to help raise A barn at Charley Freeman this afternoon. I have done A large washing today & baked bread this afternoon. I send out two letters today, one to Vincent Brown.

Tuesday, July 3   This has been A very pleasant day but it is thundering tonight & looks like rain. Wm & Alvah has been hoing Potatoes today. Sherman has got a very sore foote.

Wednesday, July 4   This has been very showry. A terible thunder shower all night.   The lightning struck A large hemlock tree near our barn. Shivered [Severed] it nearly all to peases [pieces]. Mabel is with us tonight.

Thursday, July 5   This has been A pleasant day. A dance at the Rushton House last night. A letter from Vincent Brown today.   A.P. Brown helped in the cheese factory yesterday, while Sydney went to the fourth.

Friday, July 6   A very warm day. Horis [Horace] Webb hoed Potatoes for Wm today. A letter from Aswald O. Broadia with a note of one hundred dollars.

Saturday, July 7   A pleasant forenoon. A thunder shower this afternoon. Grants [Sarah's] folks are visiting to Alvah's today. I have been caning [canning] curents & baking this afternoon. Clarence & Bower has been with us today.   Cora Main has been staying with Addia & Forest A week. She is A cousin.

Sunday, July 8   This has been A lovely day. Nice & cool. Wm & Sherman & Lottie & I went to Fine today to Mr. Johnson's.

Monday, July 9   A very pleasant day. Alvah has gone with A load of cheese to DeKalb [NY] today. C.H. B [rown] took dinner with us today. Luke Vannornum [Van Ornum] took supper with us tonight. Wm bought A box of nice Honey in Fine [NY].

Tuesday, July10   Some person went in to Mr. Woolever's the other night & stole 30 dollars from his desk. No clew to the thief yet. This has been A nice day but it is clowdy tonight looks like rain. Alvah commended cutting hay today.

289

Wednesday, July 11   This has been a cool Pleasant day. The men took in one load of hay. It was not dry enough to draw in. Forest McKee has been sick all day. Martha Brown made me a short call today. Eddy Webb is very low. Is not expected to live through the night.

Thursday, July 12   A very nice forenoon but A thunder Shower this afternoon. The men drew in three load of hay. Forest & Addie took supper with us tonight. Some person took the gate off last night & let the Horses out into the rhode. Alvah had a long tramp after them. Wm Clealand [Cleland] sent them home. They was in his meadow.

Friday, July 13   This has been A wet day. I made A visit to Alfred Hall's today. Thare is to be a tin wedding party to Albert Wite's this evening. They have been maried 10 years.

Saturday, July 14   It has been A dull clowdy day but has cleard of [off] pleasant this evening. It is just lovely out tonight. The moon & stars are shining so brite. I received A letter from Vincent Brown of Mich [igan] tonight.

Sunday, July 15   This forenoon was very pleasant & warm but it raind hard this afternoon. Charley's folks came this afternoon & made us a call. John Roach & his wife came to Alvah's tonight. He intendes to work here through haying & Harvest.

Monday, July 16   Clowdy this morning but very pleasant this afternoon. The men worked in the Hay field today. I done A large washing this forenoon & Baked bread this afternoon. Had a call from John Roach and his wife tonight. Received A Paper from E. Stanton of Canada.

Tuesday, July 17   A thunder shower this afternoon.

Wednesday, July 18   No rain today. I have done a large ironing this afternoon.

Thursday, July 19   Pleasant in the forenoon. Raind in the afternoon.
Friday, July 20   This has been a pleasant day. No rain. Brother Edward Brown & wife came to our place tonight from Canada.

Saturday, July 21   This has been A very warm day. No rain today. Brother Brown's folks with us today.

Sunday, July 22   One more dry day. We all went to church today. Elder Dyke and wife stayed with us last night. He Preached today. We took dinner to Charley's today after meting [meeting]. 8 years today since Mania [Manie]died.

Monday, July 23   One more pleasant day. The men drew in A lot of Hay. Brother Brown's folks are here today. I bought a Pail of beries tonight & one last Saturday night & one of Hucle Beries [Huckleberries].

Tuesday, July 24   This has been A good day. Brother Edward & Sarah went to brother Robert's today for a visit.

Wednesday, July 25   One more good Hay day. Wm lent Charley Brown five hundred dollars yesterday. I received A letter from Vincent Brown tonight from Mich [igan].

Thursday, July 26   One more lovely pleasant day. The men are taking in hay every day this week.

Friday, July 27   A good hay day untill night. Now it is raining. Some hay out to get wet. Brother Ed [ward] & Sarah is at brother Robert's yet.

Saturday, July 28   A terible rain this forenoon. Pleasant this afternoon. Brother & Sarah & Agnes & Ira Brown came this afternoon to stay with us A few days.

Sunday, July 29   A nice cool day. A shower in the afternoon. Agnes went home today.

Monday, July 30   A pleasant forenoon, rainy afternoon. Brother Ed & Sarah is at A.P. Brown's this afternoon. Alvah went with A load of cheese today. I received a letter from John McBride & Hannah today of Canada.

Tuesday, July 31   A lovely morning. Pleasant this afternoon. Edward Brown & Sarah went to C. H. Brown's today.

Wednesday, August 1   This has not been A very pleasant day. No haying.   Alvah & Roach & their wives all went after Beries. Got A lot of them. Wm Bought A Pailful for me. Brother Ed & Sarah came back here tonight. Eddie Webb Died tonight at 6 o'clock.

Thursday, August 2   Clowdy in the forenoon. We all went to Charley's in the afternoon.   Tom Noble had a large Barn Raised.

Friday, August 3   No hay weather this week.   Brother & Sister Brown Stayed to Charley's last night & today & attended the funeral of Eddia Webb.

Saturday, August 4 This has been A stormy day. No hay day. We all made a visit to Write Robertson's today. I made A call to Charley Johnson's brother. Edward & Sarah Brown are staying to A. P. Brown's tonight.

Sunday, August 5   I payed Charley 5 dollars to turn on the store acount [account]. One more rainy day. We did not go to church today. Charley's folks came here this afternoon. Edward & wife are with us today. Alvah & Sarah Brown made us a call.

Monday, August 6 This has been A pleasant day. The men are working among the Hay quite lively. Sarah & Ed are staying to P. H. Brown's tonight.

Tuesday, August 7 One more Pleasant day. Brother Ed & Sarah are staying to P. H. Brown's tonight. Edward stayed with us today.

Wednesday, August 8 One more good Hay day. Brother Ed stayed here all day.

Thursday, August 9 A lovely day. Mercury up to 90. Our folks finished haying this morning.

Friday, August 10 A very warm day. A shower in the afternoon. Wm & brother Ed & Sister Sarah Brown & I made a visit to Wm Robertson's today.

Saturday, August 11 One more very warm day. Wm & brother Ed took A ride out to Mr. Cambells near Trout Lake today. Charley & family have gone to Pitcarn today. Took our Horses & Buggy. Intend to stay untill tomorow night.

Sunday, August 12 This has been A very warm day. No rain. Ed & Sarah Brown has gone to P. H. Brown's today. Lottie Johnson came back to Alvah's today. Been home for a visit.

Monday, August 13 This has been A rainy day. Brother Ed & wife went to Robert Brown's this afternoon. They are staying to C. H. Brown's tonight. They stayed with us last night & this forenoon.

Tuesday, August 14   A pleasant day. We all made A visit to Alvah's this afternoon.

Wednesday, August 15   This has been A lovely day. Wm has gone to Gouverneur to cary [carry] his brother Edward to take the train for home. They reside in Canada.

Thursday, August 16   This has been A nice cool pleasant day. The Sunday School held a Picnic today in Rob Wilson's grove, the other side of the town.

Friday, August 17   This has been A lovely day. Wm & I have made a visit to John W. Laidlaw's in Pitcarn [Pitcairn] [NY] today.

Saturday, August 18   A rainy day. I have baked Aand Irond. Wm received a letter from Lizzie Bignell.

Sunday, August 19   A rainy morning but pleasant in the afternoon.   The Methodists held their quartily meting at Pitcarn [NY]. Alvah & Sarah was to Russell on a visit today.

Monday, August 20   A lovely day. A terible rain at noon today.

Tuesday, August 21   This has been A nice pleasant day. Our men has commenced their harvesting. Wm sold our Home lot today for four thousand dollars to Gideon Freeman. They were here to supper.

Wednesday, August 22   A lovely day but very warm. Mercury up to 90.

Thursday, August 23   A thunder shower this morning before daylight. One more shower near noon. The men are binding oats.

Friday, August 24 This has been a lovely day. I made a visit to Charley Harmon's today. Their school help A picnic thare again today.

Saturday, August 25 This has been a very pleasant day. Mrs. Gordin made me a call today & also Alma Richmyer & Mrs. Sam Rushton.

Sunday, August 26 This has been A pleasant day. Wm & Alvah has been working among the oats.

Monday, August 27 This has been A lovely day. Our folks been harvesting the wheete today. Six men to work. David Noble bought the Edwards Hotell today.

Tuesday, August 28 A clowdy day, raining hard tonight. Our men finished binding & seting up the wheete. David Noble took posesion of the Hotell today.

Wednesday, August 29 This has been a rainy day. Wm went to town. I have done A large ironing this forenoon.

Thursday, August 30 Clowdy this morning but pleasant this afternoon. Wm went to Sifver [Silver] Hill after beries. Milo Woodcock's wife is very sick today.

Friday, August 31 This has been A nice day. Our folks draw in some grain. Alvah cut grain for Payn[e] & Charley Harmon. Wm & Freeman made out their contract today.

Saturday, September 1 This has been A lovely day. Our men has been drawing in oats today.   Alvah has been cutting wheete [wheat] for Alfred Hall.

Sunday, September 2   This has been A pleasant day untill four o'clock. It is raining hard tonight. Our men drew in 6 loads of oats today. Charley Brown & Forest McKee worked for them today.

Monday, September 3   This has been a dull, cold day. The men cut the remainder of their oats today. Sister Hall made me a visit this afternoon.

Tuesday, September 4   A good harvest day but raining hard tonight. The men has been drawing in grain all day. This is the first day of the Gouverneur [NY] fair.

Wednesday, September 5   This has been a cool pleasant day after the rain. Lots of folks went to the fair today. C.H. Brown is staying evry day.

Thursday, September 6   This has been A pleasant day. The men has been drawing in wheete this afternoon. A Boy [was] born to Mrs. M. Woodcock last night.

Friday, September 7   A clowdy day. Raind a litle tonight. The men finished drawing in their wheete today.

Saturday, September 8   This has been A rainy day. Wm & I went to Mr. Campell's near Trout Lake today.

Sunday, September 9   A cold clowdy day. We all stayed at home.

Monday, September 10   This has been A very pleasant day. A very hard frost this morning. I have done a large washing today. Sarah caried her carpet rugs to the weaver tonight.

Tuesday, September 11   This has been a lovely day. A hard frost this morning. This is the first day of the Canton [NY] fair. I sent out 2 letters, one toE.B., one [to] A.P..

Wednesday, September 12   This has been A nice pleasant day. No frost this morning. Quite warm today. I took up my carpet in the Parlor bedroom today. Vincent Brown from Michigan came in the stage to our house tonight to visit his friends in Edwards.

Thursday, September 13   A very warm day, this. Our men began diging their Potatoes today. Charley & Martha went to Canton [NY] Fair today. Mabel is staying with me tonight. Mrs. Earl Burns & Mrs. Will Alen [Allen] was here today. Vint Brown took breakfast & supper with us today.

Friday, September 14   A rainy day.

Saturday, September 15   A pleasant day.   Our men dug potatoes all day.   Alvah drew a load down & put them in Bogart's cellar.

Sunday, September 16 A nice warm day & pleasant. John & Agnes Hughs made me a call today.

Monday, September 17   A very Pleasant day. A. P. Brown went with a load of cheese today.

Tuesday, September 18   We all attended A party to Wright Robertson's tonight.

Wednesday, September 19 This has been A very pleasant day. I have been spinning stocking yarn. I have got nine lbs of roals [rolls] to spin.

Thursday, September 20   This has been A lovely day. Quite warm. Our men has dug Potatoes all day. Vint Brown is working for them. Mr. Wm Andrews took supper with us tonight. He is from Gouverneur [NY].

Friday, September 21   This has been a Pleasant day. Our men has been diging Potatoes. Gid Freeman made A call.

Saturday, September 22   One more pleasant day. Very warm. Forest & Addia has gone to Herman to the Shows today. Vint Brown went from here last night to Robert Brown.

Sunday, September 23   One more pleasant day. A funeral at the church today. A grand child of B. Hall's died at S.[Silas] P. Rice's.

Monday, September 24   Pleasant this forenoon but raining this afternoon. Gid Freeman brought a load of stove wood here this forenoon & a load of Potatoes this afternoon.
Tuesday, September 25   A terible rainy & windy day. Vint Brown came back here this afternoon.

Wednesday, September 26   This has been a pleasant day but quite cold. Wm Cleland's folks were all here today. The[y] was working on the rhode [road].

Thursday, September 27   This has been a nice day, quite a high wind. Our folks finished taking in their potatoes. Alvah has been drawing stove wood from our Wood House to the village for his own use. Freeman is bringing wood here.

Friday, September 28   This has been a pleasant day. Wm & Vintcut up corn today. I made a visit to Sister Hall's. Thare is A dance to the Rushton house tonight. I bought 6 lbs of sugar the 24th of September of C. H. Brown & McFeran.

Saturday, September 29   This has been A good day. Wm finished cutting & seting up the corn. Gid Freeman was he[re] today.

Sunday, September 30   It was clowdy this forenoon and quite cold all day but did not rain. Wm went to Gouverneur today. His suit [lawsuit] is put over for next week. I wrote a letter to Susa [Brown].

Monday, October 1   This has been A pleasant day. A hard frost this morning. I have been washing windows & cleaning house today. William has bought A pair of fine boots & A suit of cloths for Sherman last week.

Tuesday, October 2   This has been A rainy day. Sherman went to his grandpa Clealand's today for a visit.

Wednesday, October 3   This has been a cold day. Snowd a litle this afternoon. We atended the funeral of Mrs. Hitchcock today.

Thursday, October 4   This has been A Pleasant day. I have been spinning stocking yarn today. I had a call from Emmah Webb and Mrs. Wm Clealand.   John Hughs and Agness mooved into their house today.

Friday, October 5   This has been a pleasant day. Our men have been threshing oats with the mashine today. Wm got a letter from Wm Andrews tonight. I have been spining today.

Saturday, October 6   A pleasant day. An old couple Maried today. Old Mother dummy Allen to old Desmonds, 80 years old.

Sunday, October 7   This has been a lovely day. Sherman & I went down to go to church but the minister did not come. So we stayed to Charley's all day. Wm made a call out.

Monday, October 8   A pleasant day. Looks like rain tonight. I have done A large washing today. Charley Brown sent me 15 lbs of pork & Rob Webb brot me one bushel of onions today. Wm is terible of the books [or hooks] nowadays. Ed Wight mooved [moved] into the bourding [boarding] house the 6th at the talc mines.

Tuesday, October 9   This has been a warm day, high wind. Sister Hall made me a visit today. A call from Mrs. Wm McKee, Vint Brown helped Agness Hughs put down her carpets today.

Wednesday, October 10   This has been a very warm day. Forest and Addia McKee caried their furniture all up in the high stairs & they have gone to John McKee's to stay until spring. We are left alone again.

Thursday, October 11   One more pleasant day. Looks like rain tonight. Brother A. P. Johnson & a Mr. Ketcham from Chemung Co., [NY] came here tonight.

Friday, October 12   It had raind part of the day. Wm B caried A. P. [Johnson] and the other man to Fine [NY] today.

Saturday, October 13   This has been a rainy day. No news today only the new Methodist Preacher has come to town from Oswego [NY]. His name is Smith.

Sunday, October 14   Not a very pleasant day. Raind part of the day. No preaching in town today. C. H. Brown made us a call today.

Monday, October 15   This has been A pleasant day after the rain. Our men have been threshing today in this barn.   Horis [Horace] Webb & Vint Brown & Charley Hall worked for them.

Tuesday, October 16   A hard frost this morning & a very pleasant day but cold. I washed the Parlor windows today &

put a quilt on the frame. Gid Freeman is plowing on this farm now.

Wednesday, October 17   This is a lovely morning but a terible hard frost. I churnd 20 lbs of butter last night. Sid Brown drove a litle colt up here last night. Wm intendes to winter it. A. P. Johnson came here tonight. He has sold his Pine lot in Fine [NY] for 25.00 dollars.

Thursday, October 18   This is a pleasant morning but the wind is blowing hard. No frost. A. P. Johnson started for Home this morning in [the] stage.

Friday, October 19   It raind this morning. Clowdy all day. Moriah Johnson and Sister Hall made me a visit yesterday.

Saturday, October 20   A stormy day & snowda litle this evening. I have made 3 bed quilts this week.

Sunday, October 21   This has been a lovely day. Mr. John Absalam and his son Seymore made us a call today. Payed Wm some money to & took dinner.

Monday, October 22   This has been a pleasant day. Our men are thrashing. I have done a large washing this forenoon & Baking this afternoon. Lottia Johnson came back to Alvah's today to work for them.

Tuesday, October 23   One more Pleasant day today. The men finish the Wheete [wheat] today noon. Thare is 7 men at the threshing.

Wednesday, October 24   Clowdy today. No storm. The Steim [steam] Thresher is to Payns today. At Milo Woodcock's yesterday. Gid Freeman brot a load of furniture here yesterday. They will moove here soon.

Thursday, October 25   This has been A lovely day. Our men are threshing yet. Think they will finish tomorow. I have done a large ironing today & A pair of mittens for Sherman. Finished them.

Friday, October 26   Clowdy all day. Raind some this afternoon. Our men finished threshing today noon. They had nearly nine hundred bushels of grain. I had a call from Wm Green & wife from Hermon on Wednesday of this week.

Saturday, October 27   A good day. I took up my Hall carpet today.

Sunday, October 28   A lovely day. A visit from Charley's folks & Emry Pratt. He is home on A visit from Kansas.

Monday, October 29   This has been A terible windy day & thunder showers this evening. Wm took four bushels of wheete to mill today. Got 30 lbs to bushel of flour. Alvah has been painting in the factory today. They have sold all of the cheese for 12 cents a pound.

Tuesday, October 30   This has been A terible squally day. At 8 o'clock last night thare was a terible thunder storm & wind & at 3 this afternoon it thundered terible & Haild [hailed] & then raind. The wind blew A terible ale. I have been cleaning House.

Wednesday,   October 31   A terible stormy day by spels [spells]. Haild one spell. Freeman was here to plow today. Mrs. Newton & Will's wife was visiting to Alvah's today.

Thursday, November 1   The forenoon was just lovely but stormed this afternoon. Snowd some tonight. I have took up 2 carpets & cleand the rooms this afternoon. Done my Ironing this forenoon. Carpets are all up now.

Friday, November 2   The ground was all covered with snow this morning and snowd some all the forenoon. Mr. Thomas Brayton of our town was beried today. He was sick one week. Dr. Mery [Murray] attended him through his sicness. Wm went as a bearor.   Sarah took up her parlor carpet today. Sidney and Vint Brown took dinner here today.

Saturday, November 3   It has not stormed any today but the wind is blowing hard tonight and looks like a storm. Vint Brown is here tonight. We got a letter from Susan Brown of Pine Valley [NY].

Sunday, November 4   This has been A Pleasant day. Sherman & Lottia [Lottie] & I attended church today. Mr. Watson, the Presiding Elder, Preached today. Vint & Perce & Will Brown & Lottie took dinner with us today. A party of all the Pratts to A. B. Hall's today.

Monday, November 5   A Pleasant day but the wind has blown hard all day.

Tuesday, November 6   This has been A windy & rainy day. This has been Election day. I have stayed alone.

Wednesday, November 7   This has been A pleasant day. This is my birthday. I am 58 years old. I made a visit to Sister Hall's and a call in Charley's store. Traded 5 dollars and Payed Mrs. McFeran one dollar 25 cents for a plume for my bonnet.

Thursday, November 8   This has been A good day. Wm has been sick all day. Sid Brown is staying to Alvah's A few days & Vincent Brown has left town yesterday. His cousin Perce took him to Gouverneur [NY] yesterday.   This is Sister Hariet's [Harriet Viall Harmon] birthday. 78 years old. Emry Pratt and Had took the train on Monday for Allan Cataraugus

303

Co. then Emery starts for Kansas. He is [an] Enjineer on the Railrhode [Railroad].

Friday, November 9   Clowdy this forenoon & raind this afternoon & near night A terible thunder storm.   One more baby to Tom Grant's.   Sarah went out today to visit her stepmother & the young babe.   Wm drew wood for Charley today.

Saturday, November 10   A nice day.   Wm has been drawing wood to Charley's for two days.

Sunday, November 11   This is A lovely day.   No meting [meeting] in town.   We received A letter from Vint Brown this morning.   He is at John Brown's at Deer River [NY...near Malone, NY].

Monday, November 12   A cold windy day.   I have done a large washing.   Wm has been fixing the stall for Nellia [Nellie] & the colt.   The North wind is just howling tonight.

Tuesday, November 13   This has been A stormy afternoon.   It has snowd quite steddy [steadily] & is snowing & the wind is blowing this evening.   Wm drawed a load of wood for Charley Brown today.   Bought A cap & a lot of paper & envelops [envelopes] for writing.   Alvah got a letter & some money from Stilman E Brown of Dacota [Dakota].

Wednesday, November 14   This has been a pleasant day after the snow storm of last night.   It is quite good sleighing today. Wm and Sherman went after the young catle today.   They was to Pasture on Albert Noble's on the Amos Fowler lot.

Thursday, November 15   This has been quite a cold windy day.   It is pleasant this evening.   I sent out two letters today. One to Brother Abel [in Pine Valley, NY] one to Susan Brown to Pine Valley, Chemung Co. [NY] Wm has drawn 3 loads of stove wood for Charley Brown today. I sent my butter crock over today to be filed [filled].

Friday, November 16 It has snowed some today. Wm has been drawing wood on the sleds today for Charley.

Saturday, November 17 It has not stormed any today but a cold wind all day. Wm has done the chours [chores] & drew 4 load of wood for Charley to the village [Edwards, NY]. Alvah & Sarah has gone to Tom Cousins to a Party. It is 15 years tonight at eleven o'clock since our darling Clara left us. Her litle spirit took its flight to the unknown world. Never will I forget that night when the angel of death came into our House and took our loved one away. We trust she has gone to be an Angel now near the throne of God in heaven whare thousands of children are whose sins are all forgiven. Her funeral was attended by the Reverend Mr. Dewy [Dewey] of the M.E. Church [Methodist Episcopal] of Hermon, NY. His text was God does not willingly afflict his People.

Sunday, November 18 This has been A nice mild day. The snow is nearly all gone & Sherman & I took a ride to Sister Johnson's today [probably Moriah Merrill Johnson, wife of William Warren Johnson]. John Hughs and Agnes made us a call this evening. I have written a letter to Eliza Moncreaf tonight.

Monday, November 19 This has been a nice warm day. The rhodes are quite muddy. Wm went to Gouverneur today. Took 3 tubs of butter. He sold it for 24 cents A pound.

Tuesday, November 20 This has been A warm day but the wind is blowing hard tonight. I made a visit to Rob [ert] Webb's today. He is quite sick. Has been for four weeks.

Wednesday, November 21   This has been a clowdy lonely day.   Wm has been sick with the Headache all day.   King Payn's [Payne] family has just got mooved to the Village today.

Thursday, November 22   This has been A warm windy day. The wind blew A terible gale all night & this forenoon and the roof blew of[f] from Tom Grant's barn this morning. Alvah has gone out to help him Put on A new roof.

Friday, November 23   This has been a nice warm day. Wm & Sherman took a ride to town today. They hitcht the colt in the shed & she broke the line & ran away & broke the buggy. Perce & Will Brown came & took home the Barel [barrel] of apples tonight.   Wm bought a Peace [piece] of fresh pork of Charley today.

Saturday, November 24   This has been a lovely day. The sky is terible red in the west tonight.   C. V. Harmon went to Gouverneur today after his son Erwin.   He has been attending school thare [there] the last term.

Sunday, November 25   What A lovely day this has been. Sherman & I went to church today.   Clarance [Clarence] and Bower came home with us.   The New Methodist Preacher Mr. Smith spoke to the People today.

Monday, November 26   A terible windy day.   I done my washing & began to pick up things to get ready to moove. [move].

Tuesday, November 27   This has been A lovely day.   We have mooved over to our new home today and Alvah has come in to our house to stay untill spring.

Wednesday, November 28   A stormy day.   Snow & wind.

We have been very buisy [busy] trying to put things to their place. Got the bedroom carpet down & a bed up & one for Sherman. Clarance [Clarence] Brown is with us a day or two.

Thursday, November 29   Not a very nice day. Quite cold, snowd this afternoon. I got a letter from Eliza Moncreaf [Moncref] tonight. This was Thanksgiving day. Thare was Preaching to the church today.

Friday, November 30   Cold & snowd some today.

Saturday, December 1   This has been a cold pleasant day but it is raining tonight at 8 o'clock. Vint Brown has come to our House tonight from Dear River [NY]. He intends to work for Wm this winter.

Sunday, December 2   A nice day but quite cold.

Monday, December 3   Quite cold this forenoon. Our men have Butchered their pork today.

Tuesday, December 4   This has been a lovely day. John and Altha Laidlaw made us a visit today.

Wednesday, December 5   A lovely day. Wm finished mooving our furniture to our new home. Gid Freeman brout a load of goods today to their new home.

Thursday, December 6   This is a very pleasant day. It froze some last night. Wm McKee made us a call today. Wm B is choping the saucage this afternoon. I made my mince meat for pies last evening.

Friday, December 7   Thawd all day.

Saturday, December 8 A very warm day. Done lots of work.

Sunday, December 9   This has been A nice day.   A litle cooler.   No preaching in town today.   It was the Baptist day. Charley Brown made me a call & took dinner.   Edward Brown is staying with us tonight.

Monday, December 10   This has been A stormy day.   Snowd & the wind has blown hard all day.   I have done a large washing & done my baking.   Worked hard all day.   Gideon Freeman's family finished mooving [moving] today on to the farm they bought of Wm Brown, in the Broadia Mansion whare we have lived 16 years.

Tuesday, December 11   It froze last night.   Quite cold today. Snowing this evening.   Charley V Harmon & Maryette made us A visit today.   I received a letter from Emma Leach tonight.

Wednesday, December 12   Pleasant today, quite cold.   Snowd some in the night but not enough for sleiging.   It is rough wheelling.

Thursday, December 13   A nice pleasant day.   Thawd all day. Sister Hall made me a visit yesterday.   I made a call over to Gid Freeman's tonight.   Wm done own Plastering in our Parlor today.

Friday, December 14   It was raining this forenoon.   Snowing this evening.   Wm went to town today. Brot me some Wall Paper & a Pair of under shirts for himself.

Saturday, December 15   This has been a very cold day.   The coldest we have had.   Sid Brown made us a call this afternoon & Mr. and Mrs. Freeman tonight.

Sunday, December 16   It has snowd some today.   Not quite as cold as yesterday.   A donation for Mr. Leelast Friday night at the Hotell in Edwards.   He received 50 dollars.   It was his day to preach today.

Monday, December 17   This has been a very pleasant day.
Mercury 10 below zero tonight. Jason Woodcock made us A
call this evening. We sold 30 lbs of Butter in the rool [roll] to
H. Gardner today for 20 cents a lb. Bought Paper for the
Parlor.

Tuesday, December 18   This has been a stormy day. It has
snowd fast for A while this afternoon.   Alvah has been
drawing wood to our door two days. Vint Brown is chopping
in the woods & helping load.

Wednesday, December 19   Not so very cold today. Snowd a
litle but no sleighing yet.   Alvah & Vint is drawing wood.
Wm is doing choors [chores].   He churnd [churned] today.
We Have made 80 lbs of Butter since we came here in three
weeks.

Thursday, December 20   Quite a good day. A few flakes of
snow. The boys drawing wood. Wm white washed the Parlor
overhead today. The Book agent cald here today. Sold Alvah
the History of the World for five dollars.

Friday, December 21   This has been quite A good winter day,
but the storm is rageing [raging] tonight. Snowing & blowing.
Wm has Painted the woodwork in the Parlor today & done the
chours. Alvah & Vint has been drawing wood, sled length, to
the house.

Saturday, December 22   This has been a cold pleasant day.
Mercury 10 below zero all day. Wm took the box stove house
to Charley's in the morning. He put the varnish on the
woodwork in our Parlor in the afternoon.

Sunday, December 23   One more cold day.   Mercury 40

below zero this morning. The coldest for two years. I made a call over to Alvah's & to Gid Freeman's this afternoon.

Monday, December 24   Warmer this morning. Raind a litle then snowd a litle. Froze some this afternoon & evening. Gid Freeman payed four thousand dollars to Wm today for the Broadia farm. I have done a large washing today. Wm payed Vint Brown 7 dollars today. I gave Martha Brown 5 dollars in money the 25th of December. [added at top of page]

Tuesday, December 25   This is Christmas day. A nice mild day. Mercury 30 above zero. Charley Brown and family made us a visit today. They made me a nice preasant [present] & silver caster.

Wednesday, December 26   This has been a lovely day, clear & pleasant. Signs of a thaw.   South wind strong tonight. Stilman Brown is staying with us tonight. He is home on a visit from Dakota. A.P. Brown has been drawing goods to town today.

Thursday, December 27   This has been A very pleasant day. It is thawing fast tonight.   Alvah & family has finished mooving to the village [Edwards] today.

Friday, December 28   Our thaw took a very hard cold in the night. It snowd & the wind blew Hard & it has been a very cold day. Snow enough for quite good sleighing. We churnd 20 lbs of Butter today.   Have made some more than one Hundred lbs since we came here. It is four weeks.

Saturday, December 29   This has been A cold Pleasant day. Mercury 20 below zero this morning. We have been Papering the Parlor today. A. P. & family has gone to Tom Grant's today. Clarance Brown is staying with us tonight. Sherman got his boots mended today.

Sunday, December 30   This has been A good day.   Snowd a litle.   Sherman & I went to church today.   We took dinner to Charley's.

Monday, December 31   The last day of the year.   One more year is past and gone never to return.   The reverend Mr. Smith spoke to the People the last Sabath of this year.   The foundation of his sermon was faith, Hope, & charity & the greatest of these is charity.   Percival Brown stayed with us last night.

1884

Tuesday, January 1   This has been a good winter day.   Snowd a litle.   It is good sleighing now.   We have just got our Parlor carpet down & the Pictures Hung in Place this evening.   A dance at the Rushton House tonight.   Laura A. Johnson of Fowler is visiting to Charley's this week.   Stilman E. Brown is in town visiting friends & relatives. He intends to return to Dakota soon.

Wednesday, January 2   This has been a stormy day.   Snowd hard this afternoon.   Wm has been sick all day.   Vint drew wood in for Charley this forenoon from here to the village.

Thursday, January 3   This has been a terible stormy day.   It has snowd & blowd at a fearful rate all of the day & through last night & is blowing yet at nine tonight.   The stage did not get through tonight.   Erwin Harmon, our school teacher, is staying here tonight.

Friday, January 4   The storm of two days has quieted down today but is colder.   Mercury at zero.   The stage did not go out yesterday.   Went today at 10 o'clock.   Wm went to town today.   Took dinner to Charley's.

Saturday, January 5   This has been a cold pleasant day. Mercury 25 below zero at 10 this morning. 30 this evening at nine o'clock. Wm took a load of wood to Charley today.

Sunday, January 6   This has been A very cold day. Mercury was 43 below zero this morning. 22 this evening. No meting today in town.   Charley Brown made us a call today. Wm let him have 373 dollars in money.   Their new organ has just come to Gouverneur [NY] from Detroit Michigan.   C. Kirkbride shiped it to them.   Will Brown stayed with us last night.

Monday, January 7   This has been a nice pleasant day. Mercury 40 below zero this morning. I done a large washing this forenoon. Wm & I went to town this afternoon to sign a deede to Gid Freeman. We traded 5 dollars to C. H. Brown & McFeren's [McFerans's] store. I made a call to A.P. Brown's & C. H. Brown's.

Tuesday, January 8   It has not been quite so cold today. It has been snowing this afternoon. I have writen a letter to brother Charley Johnson [Charles Victor Johnson, Pittsfield, IL] tonight in answer to the one I got last night.

Wednesday, January 9   This has been a stormy day. It raind last night after the snow & thawd some so that the water ran into the cistern in the night then froze this morning.   Then raind hard nearly noon then soon began to snow and blow & we are having a fearful storm.

Thursday, January 10   This has been A nice winter day. Wm and Vint has been cutting ice all day & Alvah has been drawing to the factory. Vint fell into the river.

Friday, January 11 A very nice day. No storm.

Saturday, January 12   A nice pleasant day. Wm & I made a visit to Charley's today.

Sunday, January 13   Sherman E. Brown stayed with us last night. This has been a stormy day. The wind is blowing hard tonight. Alvah's family was here today. Clarence Brown has stayed with us two days.

Monday, January 14   This has [been] quite a good day. Snowd a litle. Stilman Brown & Laura Johnson made us a visit today. Vint drew a load of wood for Charley H. Brown today.

Tuesday, January 15   This has been a cold day. Mercury was 30 below zero this morning & it is 30 this evening at 9 o'clock. I made a visit to A. B. Hall's today. Vint went to mill & drew one load of wood today to town.

Wednesday, January 16   A cold day. Wm went to Fine [NY] today. A donation to the Hotell tonight.

Thursday, January 17   Vint & Sherman Brown went to the Donation last night. It was for the benifit of the Rev. Mr. Smith, the Methodist Preacher. This has been a stormy day. The wind & snow is blowing hard tonight. The Preacher got one hundred dollars of the donation last night. Vint brout me a new wash tub today from C. H. Brown's & McFerin's store. 75 cents.

Friday, January 18   Not so very cold today. Mercury 30 above zero. All day snowd some. A. P. brot the Horses home today. Took one back with him to town. Frank Beache's [Beech's] litle girl died this morning.

Saturday, January 19   A very cold windy & stormy day. Mrs. McCucheon & children cald here to stay untill after dinner.

They moved into the house on the corners today without a shred of wood to build a fire. They cut up their boxes.

Sunday, January 20   A pleasant day. Quite cold. Frank Beache's [Beech's] litle girl was beried today.

Monday, January 21   This has been a pleasant day but the wind is blowing quite hard tonight & looks like a storm. Mercury was 18 below zero this morning.

Tuesday, January 22   A terible windy day. The rhodes all full. Wm and Charley went to Gouverneur [NY] today. Wm got home a litle after dark. I made me a gingham Apron today.

Wednesday, January 23   This has been a nice mild day. Mercury 20 above zero all day.   24 above in the morning. Charley came home tonight in the stage. I made me a new blue apron today & lined a Hose [horse] blankit [blanket] & done lots of work. The dog bit Sherman's arm today.

Thursday, January 24   This has been a cold stormy day. A. P. made us a call [and] took dinner. Wm caried him back home & Bought me 5 lbs of tea at C. H. Brown's. Vint sawd wood in the wood house all day. He went down town tonight.

Friday, January 25   A cold but pleasant day. Mercury 30 below zero this morning. A. P. drew us a load of cedar stakes today. Dora Pratt was Maried last evening to Mr. Spalding of Fine [NY].

Saturday, January 26   This has been a cold day. Snowd some. A.P. drew us a load of stakes today, took dinner here. Mrs. Wooliver [Woolever] died this morning. Bower & Mabel Brown is staying with us today & tonight.

[Nancy Brown writes: my next writing is in another book of

314

1884]
[Next page continues]

Oh Clara dear my Precious one
I have been to walk in the garden green
Whare I have held your hand in mine
Whare we so often have been.

Yes darling often we have walked alone
But none but God does know
The bitter tears that I have wept
Since you to heaven did go.

Will I ever forget that Tuesday night
When thou did take thy fairwell [farewell]
leave. The spotless dove had plumed her wings
Ere darkness chased the night.

And when I knew that you was gone
My spirits sank away
And I have been alone
Since that eventful day.

And as I walk and view the flowers
I often put down my hand
To clasp thy Precious one in mine
While I alone doeth stand.

We trust her feet are walking
Now the shining streets of heaven
And to that dear ones brow
A goldeen [golden]Crown is given.

I missed her when the flowers came
In the garden where she played
But I miss her more by the fireside

315

Now the flowers have all decayed.
How sad to think of this our darling Child
That for only nine short years
Upon our home she smild [smiled]
Her pure, bright unselfish life
Her winning words and ways
This sweet memory we will keep
Through all our future days.

Her mother

[The following entries appear to be on the last pages and overleaf sheets in the 1883/4 book that Nancy Johnson Brown was using.] GGJ

Mr. Charles Johnson born in Brookfield, Massachusetts, February 26, 1785. Died April 20, 1847.

Rachel Johnson Born in Wilsborough [Willsboro] NY May 15, 1787. Died June the 20, 1860

Samson Vial [Viall] died Feb 19, 1813, age 36.

Charles V. Johnson born May the 11, 1815 in Russell, NY
Hiram A. Johnson [born] Feb. 9, 1819
Eliza B. Johnson, born Feb. 22, 1817
Abel P Johnson, born June 7, 1821
William W. Johnson born December 1, 1823
Nancy A Johnson, born November 7, 1825
Emma [Emmorancy] Johnson born May 22, 1827 Edwards, NY

Mr. George W. Freeman died October 4, 1884, age 68, in Gouverneur, NY
Mr. Andrew Clark of Edwards died October the 15, 1884. Found dead in bed at 5 in the morning.

Charley Sullivan & Emmy Leach was maried the 9th of May, 1884 but he did not stay one night with her. He left town in a few days never to return.

Mrs. Cyntha [Cynthia] Payne died May 4, 1883, age 72.

Miss Sarah Welch of Fine, NY died May the 5th, 1883, age 28

Mr. Buscert Died May the 4th, 1883, Russell, NY

Mr. Warren W. Johnson died June the 4th, 1883 Edwards, NY age 59 years of cancers

Rawley Brown Died June the 29th, 1883 age 3 years., son of Henry Brown, Edwards, NY

A girl babe to Mr. & Mrs. Alax [Alex] Herr August the 20th, 1883, Edwards, NY

A boy baby to Milo Woodcock, Edwards, NY September the 5th, 1883

John Hughs and Agnes Brown was maried the 12th of September, 1883

A girl baby to Albert and Celia Cozens [Cousins], September 15, 1883

Charles Freeman and Ella Rushton was Maried today, October, 1883.

A boy babe to Write & Mettia Robertson, January the 17th, 1884.

Mrs. Wesley [Harriet Viall] Harmon died February 10, 1884, age 80 years olde.

Mr. Wesley Harmon died January [25] 1881, Age 86, Edwards, NY

Mrs. Samuel McFeran, died the 28th of February 1884. Age 83.

Mr. James Clealand died March 26, 1884. Age 94. Edwards, N.Y.

Mr. William [Cozens] Cousins died June 21, 1884, age 65. He came to Edwards from Ireland when a young man. Been 40 years maried.

Mrs. William Cousins died Jan 18, 1908

Mr. Robert Webb died April 20, 1884, age

Mrs. Wm Beach [Beech] died March the 6th, 1885. Edwards, N.Y.

Mr. Charles Johnson and Mrs. Rachel P. Vial [Viall] was maried December 16, 1813, Russell, NY

Eliza B. Johnson died May the 22nd, 1818

Mr. C. V. Johnson [Charles Victor Johnson] and Miss Emily Span [Spann] was maried in Pike Co, Ill, July 1, 1837.

Mr. Hiram A. Johnson and Miss Jane Whitny [Whitley] was maried July 25, 1841, Pike Co., Ill.

William Brown & Nancy A. Johnson was maried September the 19th , 1844, Edwards, NY

Alfred B. Hall and Emma Johnson was maried January the first, 1845.
Abel P. Johnson & Lucy Haile was maried Sept the 15th 1846,

Edwards, NY

Mr. Warren W. Johnson and Mariah [Moriah] Merils [Merrill] was maried September 15th , 1846, Russell, NY

Mr. Charles Johnson died, April the 20, 1847, Age 62

Mrs. Rachel P. Johnson died June the 20th, 1860
Clara E. Brown died November 17, 1868

Mr. Leonard Ward of Edwards, NY died March the fourth, 1883, age 54.

Mr. John Crfferd [Clifford] and Caria Towns was maried April the 14th, 1883 at the house of Milo Woodcock's, Edwards, NY

Mr. Alexander Noble died, age 74, April 17, 1883, Edwards, NY

Charles Fenton was beried today in [Pitcarn] Pitcairn, NY. He was drownded in the creek running logs. April the 21st, 1883. age 23 years.

Mrs. Austin Clark of Russell, NY died April the 28th 1883. Her maiden name was Mary Laidlaw. Was maried in this town. Came from Scotland with her Parents when a young lady. Her Parents both died here in Edwards whare they spent their days after they came from Scotland.

[The following recipes were included in the 1883 Diary] GGJ
Ginger Snaps

Put into a tin dish, 2 cups of molasses, 2 teaspoonfuls of ginger, 2 teaspoons of salt. Let this boil untill it reaches the top of the dish. Take it off, add a teaspoonful of soda. Beat quickly then add A cup of Butter or lard & flour enough to roll. Roll thin & bake in a quick oven.

Chalklet Cake

One cup of Butter, three cups of brown sugar, one cup of sweete milk, four cups of flour, 7 eggs, 9 table spoons of grated chocolate, 3 table spoons of Baking Powder. This may a layer cake. Make a white cake of the whites of the eggs. Baking in layers & putting them together with frosting.

Pork Cake

2 cups of pork after being chopped fine, 1 cup of raisins, 3 cups of flour, 1 teaspoon of saleratus [baking soda, used as a leavening agent], 1 of ground cloves, 1 of cinnamon, 2 cups sweet milk. This will make two cakes. Chop the raisins and Pork together. 1 teaspoon cream of tarter.

Coconut Cake

One cup of fine sugar
Four eggs
½ cup of Butter
One cup of sweete milke
21/2 cups of flour
one teaspoon of soda
2 teaspoonfuls of cream of tarter

Bake in three layers, take the whites of 3 eggs, beat to a stiff froth with 1 cup of fine sugar and 1 ½ cups grated coconut. When the cake is done, spread this between the layers. Frost the top & sprinkle with coconut.

Mr. S.E. Brown & Miss Laura Johnson was maried the 30th day of December 1884 of Edwards and Fouler [Fowler]NY

Mrs. Wooliver died January the 25th, 1884, Age 68, Edwards, NY

Mr. Samuel McFeren and Mary Moncrief was Maried Dec the 26th, 1883

Frank Beaches baby died January the 18, 1884. Mabel Beach, age 18 months

[Recipes continued]:

Cookies

2 cups of sugar
1 of Butter
2 Table Spoonfull of Cream
3 eggs
1 teaspoon of Saleratus [BakingSoda]
4 cups of flour

Jell Cake

3 eggs
1 cup of sugar
1 of flour
2 teaspoonful of Saleratus [baking soda] sifted into the flour
A little water or milk
2 large spoons of shortning

Fried Cakes
1 cup of sugar
1 egg
2 Table spoons of Butter
1 cup of sour milk

1 teaspoon of Baking Powder; 1 of Saleratus [Baking Soda]

Custard Cake

1 cup sugar
3ggs
1 cup of flour
2 tablespoons of shortening
2 of water
2 teaspoons of Baking Powder

A Lemon Pie

The juice & rinde [rind] of one lemon
1 cup of Water
1 cup of sugar
1 egg
butter the size of an egg
1 tablespoon of corn starch
boil before putting in the crust. Frost with whites of eggs.

Orange Cake

2 cups of sugar beaten with the yolks of 5 eggs.
1 cup of cold watter. Add whites of four eggs, beaten lightl[y]
2 cups of flour
1 ½ teaspoon baking powder. A little salt. Bake in four
shallow tins. Beat the White of one egg with fine sugar a litle
thicker than frosting. Add to it, the juice of 1 large orange.
Spread between the cakes and frost the top very nice.

Steam Apple Dumplings

1 egg
1 cup sweete milk
2 cups flour
1 teaspoon cream of tarter
salt
Butter the dish. Pour in part of the Batter, then put in the Apple. Cover with more Batter then steam 20 minutes.

Cup Cake

2 cups sugar
3 eggs
1 cup sour milk
4 cups of flour
1 teaspoon Saleratus [baking Soda]
some nut meg
A cup of Butter

Mr. David Noble and Miss Hattie Padgette [Padget] was maried February the 23, 1882

Mr. C. H. Brown and Martha Noble was maried December the 26, 1869

Mr. A. P. Brown & Mania [Manie] Clealand [Cleland] was maried March the 23 1870

Charley Johnson & Celia Laidlaw maried November 10, 1880
Mr. Carlos Kirkbride [Kirkbridge] and Mariah Noble was maried November 23, 1880 all of Edwards, NY

Mr. George Davis and Miss Mary Martin was maried in Michigan 1881

Mr. Forest McKee and Miss Addie Fellows was maried today February the 28ᵗʰ 1883. All of Edwards, NY

Mr. McBride and Hannah Brown was maried Tilsonburg, Ontario March 1883.
Mr. Simeon Richmire & Alma Pratt was maried the 21 of May, 1882

Warren Glasby died the 23 of May, 1882

Mrs. Andrew Clark died the 21ˢᵗ of January, 1882.

Nettia McGill died January the 12ᵗʰ 1882.

Wm Barfords litle boy died the 24ᵗʰ of April, 1882.

George Barford died 1881.

George Ivers died the 12 of March, 1882.

Mrs. Charley L. Harmon died Nov. the 7ᵗʰ, 1880.

Robert Brown died July the 18, 1878.

Mother Brown died October the 8ᵗʰ, 1879.

Sister Margaret Brodia (Brodie) died July the 17ᵗʰ, 1878.

Mrs. Rhoda Bancroft died October 14, 1882.

Mrs. Mania (Manie) Brown died July the 22ⁿᵈ, 1875.

Write [Wright] Robinson & Mettie Brown was maried September 18, 1878.
William Pratt & Jane Raymond was married January the first, 1879

Moris [Morris] Pratt and Venira Hall was maried December the 21st 1881.

Alvah P. Brown & Sarah Grant was maried June the 20th, 1877.

Cyrus Cleland & Celia Gant was maried October, 1877

Mr. Isaac Brown and a widow lady of Canada was maried December 25, 1882.

Mr. John Clealand [Cleland] and Maryette Merchant was maried November, 1882

Miss Hattie Moonia was maried January 24th, 1883.

Mr. Will Allen and Stellah Barns [Stella Barnes] was maried the 27th of December 1882 and also Herbert Jacobs & Miss Alice Holmes, and Mr. Hugh Pratt & Miss Carah Kelsey all of Edwards [NY]

To Mrs. H. Jac a pair of twins, July 27, 1883

William Newton & Kate Stevens was maried January the first, 1883.

Mr. Chadwic [Chadwick] to Miss Clara Wells of Pitcairn, NY maried the same day & one more couple all by Mr. Wheeler of South Edwards, 1883.

Mattia Hall was maried the 16th of November 1882. [Edwards, NY]

Amsi Wels [Wells] maried the last day of November, 1882. All of Edwards, NY

Mr. James [not legible] and Julia Moonia was maried the 11th of February 1882.

June 23, A girl baby to Mrs. Amsie Wells, 1883.

[On leaf]:

5 dollars to C.H. Brown to turn on our store acount, August 5, 1883.

[The Diary entries for 1885, 1886, 1888, 1889, 1890, 1892, and 1894 appear to be genealogical excerpts taken from longer diaries. It was the practice of Nancy Johnson Brown to record much more information such as expressed in the 1879 and 1883 diary information within this book. It was also her practice to write daily. Nonetheless, the excerpts are interesting as well as valuable.] GGJ

1885

Wednesday, 25 July   Mr. David M. Cotton died, age 63 years of Edwards, NY. He died in Bridgeport, Connecticut. His remains was brought to Antwerp, NY to be beried.

1886

Wednesday 8 December   Harison Pratt and Ida Brown of Edwards, NY was maried. They went to Hermon for a ride. Settled for the present in Kansas City. [Ida Brown, a niece of William Brown and an adopted daughter of Percival Brown]

1887

[On inside front cover of 1887 diary of Nancy A. Brown]:

S. W. Brown, born 1873 July 31. Bower [born] March 4, 1874

My next diary will be found in a sort of a note Book Dated January 1888. *[written by Nancy Brown]*

Sister Hariet [Harriet Viall] Harmon Died Feb 10th 1884. She was 80 years old.

[The overleaf pages included information about (1887) Domestic Postage, Foreign Postage, Daily Interest Rates at various per cents, and a Table of Wages by the Week. GGJ]

Saturday, January 1   This is the first day of January, 1887. One more year is past & gone never to return. This has been a stormy day.   Snowd in the night & all day today.   The Sleighing is good now. Quite cold today. Will Woodcock helped Wm Brown to dress a beef Cow today. Wm sold one quarter to Will Woodcock & let Alvah Brown have one quarter & Charly Brown a quarter.   A hind quarter for ourselves. Wm took the beef to town this afternoon. He took 16 lbs of sugar to John Hughs.   Thare was a dance to the Rushton house, Edwards last night.   Sherman went down & stayed all night. Got home at 7 this morning. Thare was lots so drunk they had to be laid away.

Sunday, January 2   This has been a very cold day. Flying frost all day. The windows fairly curtand [curtained] all day. Mercury at 10 below zero all day & this evening. Wm & I have been at home all day.   John & Agness Hughs was here most all day. Clarence Brown came here this afternoon from Dell Freeman's. Sherman Brown made a call to his uncle Wm Clealand's this afternoon. The men have just got the last Coat of Plaster put on the walls of the new Church & 2 men from

327

NY, York are doing the Painting at 4 dollars a day. Have just got the windows. Have not got them put in yet. They have got the seats for the church. The men are fixing them ready to set in when the carpets is down.

Monday, January 3   This has been a cold day. Mercury was 30 below zero here & 10 below in the village. It is 10 below tonight at 8 o'clock. Wm has done the chours today & cut up parte of the beef. I done a large washing this forenoon. John McKee cald here today. He is looking for a chance to hire or buy a horse. Wm said he would sell him Topsy for 50 dollars. Wm payed one hundred & 15 for her four years ago. She was two coming three at that time. He bought her of Tom Grant. She was a nice colt then but she is lame & Will don't like her & he has no yuse for her now. He has got four horses now left if he sels her.

Tuesday, January 4   This has been a pleasant day. Not so cold as yesterday. Mercury was 10 above zero this morning. The wind is blowing some this evening from the south west. Sherman went to town tonight with Clint McGill. He bringth us a letter from Stilman E. Brown of Dakota. He wants to hire 5000 dollars to pay on a steem plowering mill. Alvah cald here today & took the colt & cutter & took his folks to Wm Grant's for a visit. He got back here litle after 6 tonight. John McKee came here today & bought our Topsy Horse. Thare was two men kild at the Jayville mines today while loading oar on to the cars. Have not heard the Particulars about how it hapend.

Wednesday, January 5   Mercury was up to 25 above zero. A nice day but quite a hard wind. Wm has done the chours & he & I have looked over one bushel of wheete. Sherman went home with Robbie Brown from school tonight. Perce & Rob came over tonight & got a pair of sleds of Wm. He intends to haul logs to the mill with two teemes. Rob does not intend to come to school any more this term. I have finished a double mitten this evening for Wm B. James Harmon has been very sick about one week.

Thursday, January 6   This has been a nice mild winter day. Mercury has been up to 25 nearly all day above zero. It is 20 this evening above zero at 8 o'clock. Wm & Sherman done the chours. Sherman stayed out of school this forenoon to help his granpa. Wm went to town & over to his brother Rob's this afternoon with the colts & cutter. I rode as far as A. P. Brown's. Stayed while he was gone to town. Will Clark & Em has been to her father's Alfred Hall's the past week on a visit. We got the sad news today that a girl of Losson Gardener's died of Dypthera on Tuesday of this week. They live in Gouverneur formaly of Edwards. I have been sewing on my new mashine today.

Friday, January 7   This has been a pleasant day. Mercury was 20 above zero today. It is 10 below tonight at 8. Wm has done the chours & drew a load of wood. He went to town this forenoon. Got a horse shod & a paper of tacks. Wm Noys beried 2 children that died with Dypthera in Fine [NY]. The son inlaw of Simeon Wels [Wells] of East Pitcarn Pitcairn] was beried the fourth of January. He died in Gouverneur. His name was Cochrane. Sherman went to town tonight. He found Bower Brown sick of a cold. He was taking a sweate.

Saturday, January 8   This has been a cold day. Mercury was 30 below zero this morning. 10 below all day. Is the same tonight. Mr. Harmon is no better. A man was kild with a load of lumber fell over on him on the rhode between here & Hermon [NY]. Wm went to town tonight. He says Bower is better today. Urban Keer & his wife was visiting to Charley Brown's tonight. Porter Harmon cald here today. He was beging for money to send to NY City to a Mr. Judson, a Baptist minister. He is intending to build a Church in memory of his father Adanirum [Adoniram] Judson a Baptist Misionary [Missionary] that went to Burmah [Burma]100 years ago. He wants every Baptist member to give 10 cents.

Sunday, January 9   One more cold day. Mercury down to 25 this morning. It is 10 above tonight at 5. Clarence Brown & Othnel Clealand came here today. Had a ride with Sherman. He hitched his litle oxen before the cutter & they had a nice ride. They was here to dinner. Wm & I have stayed at home all day & evening. Arba Kerr cald here tonight & Sherman Brown went home with him to stay all night. Abner Rice is on the sick list. Myron Clark's litle girl is sick with scarlat fever.

Monday, January 10   This has been quite a cold day. The air was full of frost. The mercury was 5 below this morning. Just at zero tonight at 9 o'clock. Wm has done the chours today & looked over one bushel of wheete. Sherman stayed with Arba Kerr last night. He did not come home until tonight after school. Alvah came this afternoon & took the horses & sled & drew some wood for himself from Charley's. Hiram McGill mooved his family in to a part of his mother's House last Saturday. He has sold his farm to Charley Noble & he is mooving today whare he mooved out. Thare is four families in Mrs. Storen's House now. I have made a shirt & a bed tie today on the mashine.

Tuesday, January 11   This has been one of the old fashion days. The wind just howling today & this evening the snow pilling up nicely. A good day to stay in the House & keep a good fire. Alvah came up this morning to help his father draw hay from the back barn but they gave up the job & Wm stayed in & looked over wheete for seede. Mercury has been at zero today. Sherman came from school this afternoon & hitched his steers before the cutter & caried Alvah's litle girls home from school.

Wednesday, January 12   One more stormy day but not so cold. Mercury was 10 above this morning. It is 20 above tonight at 8 o'clock. Wm had lots of shovelin snow this morning. He done the chours & cut up the beef & went to bed & slep[t] the afternoon untill 4 o'clock. When he went to the barn he found one of the cows loose & she had hooked one cow so bad. He thinks she will die. We have not heard any news today. No one been here or any of us been to town so I have no news to write. I have filed [filled] my new bed tick with the feathers out of an old tick & put it on my bed & put mine on for Sherman to sleep on this winter.

Thursday, January 13   This has been a nice day. Mercury was 10 below zero this morning. 10 above this afternoon. Wm & Alvah Brown has drawn 3 load of Hay today from the Back barn. I heard of the Death of old Mrs. Gardener today. She died yesterday at Harisville [Harrisville] at her Daughter Mrs. George Miller's. She was 81 years old. She will be brought to Edwards tomorow to be beried. Sherman went to town tonight after the maile & a bottle of medicine for Wm for his cold. The school teacher made us a call today. A larg peace of plaster fell of[f] from overhead in the dining room this afternoon. Plaster fell all over the carpet.

Friday,   January 14   Not so very cold today. Mercury 20 above zero. It has been a stormy day. It Snowd & blew the snow in piles in the night & snowd a lot today. Wm has done the chours & read the paper & then he went to bed & took a good sleepe untill chours time tonight. I broke the needle in my new sewing mashine today. Bower Brown came here tonight after school to stay tonight & tomorow. He says the new church is nearly completed. Mrs. Gardener was brought from Harrisville today & berid in the Cemetery in Edwards by the side of her husband that died 7 years ago last October.

Saturday, January 15   One more stormy day but not very cold.

Mercury 10 above zero all day & tonight. Wm has done the barn chours with Sherman's help. Clarence Brown & Bower & Henry Webb has been here today to visit with Sherman & they had a good time training their stears. They drove over to Alex Kerr's & had a jolly time thare with Arba playing in the barn. They all took dinner here & then went home at 3 o'clock. I have done a lot of Baking Pies & making fried cakes & doing lots of work. Alvah cald today & took a horse & cutter & took his family to Tom Grant's to stay untill tomorow night.

Sunday, January 16   This has been a nice pleasant day. Mercury 10 above zero.   We have all stayed home today. Clarence & Leslie cald here today.   Alvah cald here tonight with the horse that he had away to Russell [NY].   Horis [Horace] Webb & our school teacher rode out this afternoon.

Monday, January 17   This has been a stormy day. The wind has just howld all day & this evening.   It was mild this morning.   Mercury went up to 35.   Thawd a litle bit this afternoon.   How it did snow & blow & turnd colder. I done my washing this forenoon & hung my cloths on lines in the Piasa but they are in a teribel plight tonight.   Wm went to town this afternoon.   Bought him a botle of medicine.   Paid one dollar for it to C. H. Brown's.   I rode as far as Alvah's. We got home at four.   Sarah Brown is making a rag carpet. Her sister Nora is thare to stay a few days.

Tuesday, January 18   This has been a cold day. Mercury 10 below zero all day.   It is 14 below tonight.   The windows in the room with the stove has been curtaind with frost all day. Wm has done the chours & stayd in the house the rest of the time. He took a good sleep in the afternoon from one till four. He wrote a letter to send to Stilman E. Brown of Dakota this evening. I wrote part of it.

Wednesday, January 19   A cold morning. Mercury at zero. It has stormed most all day. The wind has blown hard & has snowd some. Wm has been sick all day with cold & sick headache. Sherman stayed out of school & done the chours. He went to town & mald [mailed] a letter to S. E. Brown. I have been writing all this evening.   James Brown lost a horse this morning. It was sick. He lost one last summer. He is having bad luck.

Thursday, January 20   Not very cold today. Mercury 10 above this morning & 40 above tonight. It has been a teribel wind & storm of snow all day but since dark it has been raining. It is thawing fast now. Wm is feelling a good deal better today. He has done the most of the chours. Sherman went to school & he went to town tonight & got the mail.

Friday, January 21   This has been a lovely day. The thaw was all over this morning. It has been freezing all day. Mercury is 5 above zero tonight at 8 o'clock. The sleighing is splendid. Snow was four feete deep in Fine last week & 3 & a half in Russell. 20 inches here on the level & lots of high drifts. This was the last day of our school. The term has been 8 weeks. We have not had a very good school this term. It commenced with 23 schollars & finished with 13.   Wm has done the chours today & we have picked over one bushel of wheete this afternoon & evening. He has got 10 bushels looked over now for seed.

Saturday, January 22   This has been a windy day. It has raind nearly all of the afternoon & the wind is howling tonight. The mercury is 44 tonight above zero. Wm & Sherman went to town today. Alvah was up today & got a bag of Potatoes & a pail of milk. Clarence Brown came here this evening near 10 o'clock to stay over Sunday. He brought us a letter from Mrs. Stanton of Michigan. They are on a farm of 100 & 40 acres & they raised 2200 bushels of grain the last season.

Sunday, January 23   This has been a rainy day. The snow is nearly gone acept the drifts. The wind is howlling tonight. Mercury 45 above zero all day. We have all stayed at home all day. Robby Brown & Clarence has been here all day. Clarence is here tonight. The men has got the new Church nearly completed. Henry Rushton gave them 25 dollars in adition to what he had paid before.

Monday, January 24   It was raining this morning & evry time we awoke in the night. The snow in the fields was nearly gone & the sleighing very bad. Mercury was up to 45 this morn but about noon it began to turn colder. Then it began to snow. So the ground is all white again & colder tonight. Mercury 15 above zero. Wm & Sherman has done the chours today & run some wheete through the mill. Clarence went home from here this morning.

Tuesday, January 25   This has been quite a good day. Mercury was 10 above zero this morning & 35 near night but the wind has blown hard all day & it snowd a very litle but the sleighing is very poor. Wm & Sherman has done the Chours & drew two load of Hay from the back Barn to the Cow barn. Thare was a tramp cald here this evening. He wanted to stay all night but Wm was gone to town & I did not wish to keep him. He said he had not got any money. He was looking for work. Wm met him on the rhode & he begged [begged] for tobacco. She smelt strong of smoke & whiskey. I told him to go to the Hotell.

Wednesday, January 26   Quite a cold day but no storm. It snowd some in the night & turnd cold. Mercury was 35 last night above zero & this morning it was at zero. It has been up to 10 above [to] day but it is at zero this evening. Wm & Sherman has done the Chours & all the time they had after Chours & before night Chours they run 20 bushels of wheete through the mill. They are geting it ready to sell to Mr. Miles, the miller here in Edwards. I have been knitting on a double mitten for Wm between doing my house work. I had Baking to do today. Thare has not any one clad here today nor any of us been away. So we have no news to write this evening. We have all been adding up figures this evening.

Thursday, January 27   This was quite a cold morning. Mercury was at zero. It is 5 above zero tonight at 8. Thare is some wind tonight. It has been a beautiful day for winter. The sleighing is good but not much snow. Wm & Sherman has done the Chours & drew hay. Sherman went to town tonight. Bought a botle of medicine. Bower Brown came home with him to stay all night. He says the new Church has been full of ladies today making the carpet for the Church. They intend to dedicate it the 15 of Febuary.

Friday, January 28   A cold morning, this. A cold wind all day. Mercury was 10 above zero this morning but it went up to 30 this afternoon but the wind is howlling so tonight that I can't go out with a lite to look at the mercury. Thare has been regular blizards this afternoon with snow and wind. Wm & Sherman has done the chours & run wheete through the mill what time they got between Chours. I have done my house work & been sewing & writing some & mending some this evening. Wm & Sherman went to bed at 7 o'clock.

Saturday, January 29   This has been a lovely day. Just like Spring. It raind nearly all night. The snow was nearly gone this morning. The sleighing done. The Wheeler has been runing plenty today. Wm took forty bushels of wheete to the mill today. He sold it to Mr. Miles for one dollar a bushel. James Nobels [Noble] is begging money to pay up the expences of the new Church. They are asking for one hundred & 70 dollars. They have paid out on the Church now four thousand dollars. The men was nailling down the Carpet today. Sherman Brown has gone to his uncle Wm Clealand's to stay all night & tomorow. Wm & I are here alone tonight.

Sunday, January 30   Tomorrow will be the last day of this month & a stormy month it has been. It has been nice today but the wind is howlling this evening. Sherman got home today about 3 o'clock. Robbie & Clarence & Bower Brown was here today. Wm is writing a letter this evening. We have been at home all day. I looked for Charley & Martha & Mabel up today but they did not come. They have not been here since in the fall. I was thare for a visit in November on Election day. It is snowing & blowing like fury tonight.

Monday, January 31   it was a very good day & quiet. Mercury is 8 above zero. I done a large washing this forenoon. Alvah was here today. Got a pail of milk & a pail of cream. Sarah is bad with salt rheum. [reheumatism] Wm has been fanning wheete this afternoon. This is the last day of January. Young Jim McKee was here Saturday night & borowed 20 dollars in money. It was the 29 of January. Wm took a note against Graham Stevenson for the amount.

Tuesday, February 1   This has been a nice pleasant day with the exception of a cool wind. It was a lovely morning. Wm has done the chours today. Sherman did not come home untill 3 o'clock this afternoon. Robbie & Clarence & Bower Brown was here all day. We have been at home all day as usual. I have not been in the village for nearly two months. Wm is writing a letter this evening. Alvah went to Hermen [Hermon] today after medicine for Sarah. Mercury was at zero all day. Write & Mettie Robbinson [Robinson] was here today for a visit.   Wm fand [fanned] wheete this forenoon and done chours & visited with Write & Mettia this afternoon. Alvah got home at 3 this afternoon.

Wednesday, February 2   This has been a stormy day but not very cold. Mercury 8 above zero all day. It is the same this evening. Wm & Sherman has done the chours this forenoon & this afternoon they have run wheete through the mill. I have done my housework & done some baking today. I made bread & made mince Pies & apple & beries Pies & Cookies. It is snowing hard this evening. The sleighing is quite good again & getting better all the time now. Wm sent a letter to his brother Ed Brown in Canada the 31 of Jan. It was the first letter he has sent to him since he came from thare last Fall.

Thursday, February 3   This has been a mild misty day. Raind & froze on so the sleighing is splendid. Mercury has been up to 35 today. It is 20 above zero tonight at 9 o'clock. Wm has been sick all day with sick headache. Sherman hone the chours & went to town twice today & has gone tonight. He brought me a pail of Siscoes [Ciscoes, a type of white fish] this afternoon. I have done my ironing today. I finished reading the story in the free press tonight. It has been in 4 paper. James McKee cald here today to hire a hundred dollars but Wm had not got that amount so he could not get it.

Friday, February 4   Thare has been a cold wind but pleasant. Mercury 5 above zero. It was 10 above this morning. Wm & Sherman has done the chours & took a load of wheete to Mr. Miles the Miller to sell. Wm went to town this forenoon & got his sled mendid [mended]. Arba Keer stayed here with Sherman last night & to breakfast this morning. Bower Brown is here tonight to stay with Sherman.

Saturday, February 5   This has been quite a cold day. Mercury was 5 below zero this morning. It is 10 above tonight. It is very pleasant. Our men have all been to town tonight to attend the Caucus. Othnel Clealand & Bower Brown is staying here tonight. I have been at home alone this evening. Now Wm & the boys have got home at 10.

Sunday, February 6   It has been quite a stormy day. It has

337

snowd some all day. It is just sifting down nicely. This evening we have all been at home all day. Charley & Martha & Mabel & Clarence & Bower Brown has been here today. Clarence & Bower is staying with us tonight. Arba Keer made us a call this evening while his folks went to town to practice some peaces [pieces] to sing on Dedication day which is to held on the 15 of this month. Martha says the inside of the Church looks lovely. They have not got the seats all fastened in yet but intend to have them all finished nicely the present week. Mercury was 10 above zero this morning. Has been up to 30 today.

Monday, February 7   This has been quite a cold day. Mercury was 10 above zero this morning. Wm has & Sherman has done the chours & run wheete through the mill. They have run one hundred & 20 bushels through to sell. I done my week's washing this forenoon. Got it done at 9 then I washed a bedquilt & a pair of woollen pants, & I done salt bags & had the dinner all on the tabel before noon. Then I done up my work & cleand Sherman's bedroom & done lots of work this afternoon.

Tuesday, February 8   This has been one of the days we read of perfectly awful. The wind has just howld & the rain just pourd down all day & is raining & the wind is awful tonight. This has been town meting day. Wm & Sherman went down with the horse & cutter. Came home at half past three. Then Sherman went back this evening with Robbie Brown & Rob will stay with Sherman tonight. Wm stayed at home tonight. I have been at home all day as usual. Mercury was 40 above zero all day. The boys got home at 10 o'clock. The votes was just counted but they did not stay to learn who got the office.

Wednesday, February 9   The thaw was froze up this morning. The wind has been cold all day. Mercury was 20 above zero this morning. Wm took a load of wheete to Mr. Miles the

Miller. Took his note for 100 & 23 dollars for the wheete at one dollar a bushel. Robbie Brown stayed with Sherman last night untill 10 this morning. Then Sherman went home with him & had a nice time sliding & came home about 3 this afternoon. Dikeman Pratt came to town yesterday to visit his father & mother & friends. He resides in Olean, Catarangus [Cattaraugus] County, NY. He is a merchant in company with his cousin John Pratt. They both went from Edwards [NY].

Thursday, February 10   This has been a nice mild day. Mercury at 20 all day. Wm & Sherman done the Chours then Sherman made a call over to Arba Keer's this afternoon & Wm went to bed & took a sleep. He had the headache. Then in the evening we all attended the union entertainment at the Hall of David Nobel. The Hall was quite well filed. The play was quite good only rather sentimental some part of it. We went with the buggy tonight. It is splendid wheeling. Wm bought me a pair of rubbers in Charley's store tonight. We cald in John Hughs before the entertainment.

Friday, February 11   This has been a stormy day. It has snowd & the wind from the north has blown hard all day & is snowing this evening. Mercury is 10 above zero. Wm & Sherman has done the Chours & run through some wheete & read the paper the acount of a Railrhode disaster on the Vermont Central by a broken rail. Four coaches all went over a bridge 60 feete [feet] & set them botum [bottom] up & they all took fire & the passengers nearly all burnd up. It hapend the 6 of February. We have not got the acount [account] of the number of kild & wounded yet but the pasenger [passenger] trains was full. A great many going to the Mortreall [Montreal] Carnival but they went to their long home never to return.

Saturday, February 12   This has been a pleasant day but rather cold all day. Mercury was 5 below zero this morning. It is just a zero tonight at 8 o'clock. Wm & Sherm has done the

Chours & run quite a lot of wheete through the mill. Finished the job [and] got 50 bushels left to eat & 10 for seed after selling 1.23 bushels. The union brigade that held the entertainment Fryday night at Edwards went to Fine [NY] last night to hold the same at the Town Hall in Fine. They had a stormy day & night. They had not got back today noon.

Sunday, February 13   This has been a lovely day but cold. Mercury was 10 below zero this morning but it went up to 10 above at noon. Sherman took a ride up to his granpa Clealand's today. Wm & I have been at home all day. Charley & family have been to P. H. Brown's today for a visit.

Monday, February 14   This has been a very pleasant day. It was cold this morning. Mercury was 10 below zero but the south wind is blowing quite hard tonight. We fear thare will be another thaw soon. I did not do my washing today. I done a lot of baking. I made bread & mince pies & custard & jelle [jelly]cake & 2 pans of fried cakes & washed my oil cloth carpet in the dineing room & lots of work. Wm done the Chours & he & Sherman took a ride to town & then over to James Harmon's. Mr. Harmon is a quite poorley. He has been sick a long time. Arba Keer & Leslie McGill made us a call this evening.

Tuesday, February 15   This has been a stormy day for the Dedication of the new Church but we all attended in the day time & in the evening. The Church was full to the utmost & it is a beautiful church in the inside. Evry part is lovely. Mercury was 30 above zero all day & the sidewalks was quite sloppy but the people got thare all the same & had a good time. We had an oportuny to meete with our many friends. That was very pleasant indeed.

Wednesday, February 16   It was froze this morning but very nice. Mercury was 20 above zero. Wm & I took a ride to the town of Fowler [NY] & mad a visit to John B. Absalan's. Got home at six tonight. Sherman stayed & done the Chours & made a call to Alex Keer's & Arba came home with him & helped do the Chours & is staying with us all night. We had a good visit. Mr. James Harmon is very sick yet & has been since the forepart of Jan.

Thursday, February 17   Oh what a lovely day this has been. Mercury was 20 above zero this morning & forty at 3 o'clock. We have all been at home all day. Only Sherman hiched his stears before the cutter & drove to town for a ride. Alvah Brown cald this afternoon & took the colt & cutter & drove to Hi Bancraft's to get some money. Cald here when he came back & took home a pail of milk. Wm has had the headache today but he helped some with the chours & then went to bed & took a good sleep. I finished the double mittens for Wm & washed them & I am glad they are done.

Friday, February 18   Thare has been all kinds of weather today. Snow & rain & sonshine & wind a plenty. Mercury was 25 above zero this morning. I think it is 40 tonight. It is thawing fast. Wm & Sherman & I went to town this afternoon. Wm took 6 bushels of wheete to mill today, 3 for Alvah & 3 for ourselfs [ourselves]. I traded some in Charley Brown's store abut fourteen dollars. We took down 2 bushel of Potatoes to Alvah's folks today. I took 5 dozen of new eggs to the store. Charley Brown is talking of selling his House & lot to Frank Raymond for 1200 dollars. He payed 900 for it four years ago this month, mooved in the first of March.

Saturday, February 19   This has been a rough windy day. Snowd a litle. Been very tedious going west. Wm went to town this afternoon. He got my shoes taped. I have been at home all day. I wrote a 2 sheete letter to my nephew Charley Johnson this afternoon of Oregon. Mercury was 25 above zero this morn. It is much colder this afternoon & evening.

Charley Brown has sold his House & lot in town today to Frank Raymond of Edwards.

Sunday, February 20   This has been a nice day. No storm. Quite cool. Mercury was 10 above zero this morning. We all attended Church today & this evening. Clarence & Mabel Brown came home with us this afternoon & went back with us tonight. Dr. Lill of Canton Preached today & this evening the Union reorganized a Sundy School today to comence next Sunday.   They voted Mr. Miles the Miller in for Superintendent of the Union Sunday School & Thomas Todd for asistent.

Monday, February 21   This morning Mercury was 10 above zero. Oh What a lovely day this has been. Not a bit of wind nor a cloud to obscure the beautiful sun. I done two weeks washing this forenoon & cooked dinner. Had it ready before 12. I done lots of work this afternoon. Wm & Sherman done the Chours & Wm went to town this forenoon & got a horse shod. He drew wood out of the woods to the sugar House this afternoon & then he & Sherman drove to P. H. Brown's. Took Sherman's gold watch for Perce to take to Gouverneur tomorow & get a mainspring put in. Then Wm went to town again tonight. Took Ida Pratt to Charley's. She cald here a minute & said good by. She starts for Kansas tomorow. 20 tonite above zero.

Tuesday, February 22   This has been a stormy day but not very cold or any wind. Mercury was 20 above zero all day & is this evening. I have had company all day. Moris Roach & his wife came here this morning before I got my morning work done & Alvah & Sarah & the children came in a litle time after. They was here to diner & supper. Litle Mary was sick this afternoon. Sherman took them home tonight with the Horse & cutter. Alvah has rented out his cheese factory at York to the same man that hired it last year. Perce Brown caried Ida to Gouverneur. She took the afternoon train for Kansas City.

Wednesday, February 23   Oh What a lovely day this has been. Mercury was 5 above zero this morning. It is 25 above tonight. Wm & Sherman has done the Chours & drew wood from the woods out to their sugar house. Alvah Brown was here today. Took the colt & cutter. Drove over to Perce Brown's to see them saw wood with their engine. Perce has just bought him one. Sherman went to town last night. Did not get home untill near 12. Thare was a dance to the Hotell. Bower & Henry Webb was here this afternoon a short time. Wm sent a box of sugar & wheete to a cousin of his in Saginaw City, Michigan. 25 lbs. Alfred & Cary Treglown mooved to Gouverneur today.

Thursday, February 24   This has been a stormy day. The wind commenced to blow in the night & it was raining when we got up this morning & tonight its is snowing & wind is blowing fearfully. One of Sherman's steers has been very sick all day. Wm went to town to get medicine then he went back & got uncle Tom Nobel [Noble] to come & tap the steer. He was bloated fearfully. Jim Webb cald here & brought the Shipping bill of the Box of sugar & wheete that Wm sent to Saginaw to his cousin. Wm paid the Express charge on it. He payed $1.25 cents. He has lots of money to give to his relatives. When I asked for 16 cents to give to a benevolent purpose, he would not give it to me. He says I have no rite today to give away money.

Friday, February 25   This has been a very pleasant day but quite cold. Mercury was 5 below zero this morning. It is at zero tonight. Well we have had a streak of bad luck. The 2 year old steer that was sick yesterday was dead this morning. They took his hide to town & sold it for 3 cents a pound. It weight forty nine lbs. We have a sick cow. Do not think she will live but a few days. Wm & Sherman went to mill today. Took 30 bushels of oats for feed for cows. Alvah cald here today & took dinner & rode home with Wm when he went to mill. Took home a pail of milk. Bower Brown is staying with us tonight. I sent 5 dozen of eggs to C. H. Brown's store today. 20 cents a dozen.

Saturday, February 26   This has been a very unpleasant day. High wind all day & some snow. This evening the wind is howlling fearfully. Mercury was 10 above zero. Sherman went after the oatmeal today & brought Mr. Todd & James Brown to se[e] our sick cow. Wm went to town & got medicine for her. Clarence & Robbie Brown came here today. Clarence & Bower has gone home tonight. Next Monday is the day set for Mrs. Druce to be hung in Hermon. She kild her husband & then boild his remains. I think she should be kild in some way if not hung. It is a fearful thing to hang a human boddy & it is also a terible crime to murder any person. Oh what examples of wickedness thare is set before the young & coming genaration.

Sunday, February 27   What a fearful wind & storm this morning & all night last. The snow is just blinding. Wm & Sherman are doing the barn Chours but they are having a tough time. We did not to Sunday School today on acount of the storm. Mr. Richman from Hermon [NY] was intending to preach in the new Church in Edwards this evening but we have not any of us gone out this evening. We have all been at home all day. Got no news today. Mercury was 10 above zero today. The wind is blowing hard tonight.

Monday, February 28   This has been a very cold day. Mercury was 4 above zero. Quite a lot of wind from the North. I done my washing this forenoon. Wm & Sherm has done the Chours & fused [fussed] lots with the sick cow. Sherman sold a rooster to Hiram McGill for 30 cents. He sold his stear hide for 1.50. Mr. J. Harmon is very poorly yet he has a lot of watter drawn from his lungs every now & then. They do not think he will get well.

Tuesday, March 1   This has been a nice pleasant day. Mercury was 10 above zero this morning. This is a lovely evening. The moon is shining bright. Sherman went to town tonight with Clarence. Thare was an Excurtion train left Gouverneur this afternoon to go to Wasshington City. Will cary Pasengers thare & back to Gouverneur for 10 dollars each. 10 for the found trip & can stop of[f] to NY City on return. Thare has 9 gone from Edwards. Myron Clark & Bill Boys & wife, Charley Haile & Celia & Nin Gardener & Jim Nobel's & Warren Payne & John Cousins. Wm & Sherman has done the Chours & drew wood from the woods to the new sugar house. I sent a paper to A. P. Johnson [Pine Valley, NY].

Wednesday, March 2   This has been a lovely day. Mercury was 25 above zero this morning & 40 above at noon. It has thawd quite a lot today. Wm & Sherman has done the Chours & drew wood to the sugar House. Mrs. Jennia [Jennie] Kerr made me a visit this afternoon & her litle girl. Alex cald for her when he came from town.

We have just finished eating our beef that we kild the first day of January. We kept 1 hind quarter. Gave Alvah 1 quarter & Charley one & sold one quarter.

Thursday, March 3   One more pleasant day. Mercury was 15 above zero this morning & 10 above this evening. Wm has been to town twice today. He bought more medicine for the sick cow. Agness Hughs made me a visit today. I sold her 2 dozen of eggs for 40 cents. Wm caried her home tonight & got the mail. I sent by Nelson Vanorman to get Sherman's gold watch to Gouverneur. Sherman went to town tonight with Clarence Brown.

345

Friday, March 4   This has been a cool pleasant day. Mercury was 12 above zero this morning. Quite a cold wind all day. Wm & Sherman done the Chours & then went to the woods & cut down & sawed with the big saw 3 big logs & took them to the mill.   He went once in the forenoon & once in the afternoon. Sherman has gone to town tonight with Rob Brown. No news today. Bower Brown is 13 years old today. Martha Brown is talking of taking a trip to Cooperville, Michigan & take Bower & Mabel with her.

Saturday, March 5   Quite a cold day this. Mercury was just a zero today. Alvah came up this morning & helped his father saw some logs & draw them to the mill this forenoon & then went home.   Wm & Sherman drew 2 loads of logs this afternoon. Manie Brown & Minnie Hoopper [Hooper] made me a call this forenoon. It is Snowing this evening. Sherman went to town today. We got the news of the execution of Mrs. Druce in our last paper. It was awful to read. She was hung the 28 of febuary, 1887 in Herkimier [Herkimer] Co Jail yard.

Sunday, March 6   The wind commenced to blow in the night & it was Snowing this morning & the snow is drifted in piles as bad or worse than any time this winter. Sherman & I went to Sunday School today noon.   Charley & Martha & the children came up & stayed untill night. Clarence is staying all night with Sherman.   John Laidlaw & Altha cald here to dinner today on their way home from Gouverneur. It has been a rainy day. I commenced to use the new flour of 3 bushels of wheete that was ground the other day & made bread of it yesterday. Fryday was Bower Brown's birthday.

Monday, March 7   The thaw has continued all day today. The rhodes are quite sloppy.   Wm & Sherman went to town this afternoon & got the sap heater fixt. Mercury at 40 above. I went as far as Alvah's & cald in Sister Hall's a few moments. Got home at four. Nelson Vanorman brought Sherman's gold watch from Gouverneur today. Sherman payed him one dollar for what he paid out to Fred Hall for getting it mended. He put in a new mainspring. I brought home my half of the cheese from Alvah's today. I sent 5 dozen of eggs to Charley Brown's Store today & bought a looking glass with them. It was one dollar.

Tuesday, March 8   This has been a lovely day. Mercury was 20 above zero this morning. It is 22 above to night. Alvah came up this morning & he & Sherman & Wm went to the woods & cut 3 load of logs & took them to the sawmill. Alvah got his leg hurt quite bad. A log rooled [rolled] on it. It was swollen very had when he got to the house. Sherman has gone to town tonight to change his new rubber boots & get a larger Pair. Our sick cow does not get much better yet she found a litle calf yesterday the 7 of March. I lent Sherman one dollar tonight to help pay for his boots. They are 2 & a half.

Wednesday, March 9   The mercury was 20 above zero this morning. It froze quite hard in the night but it has thawd a lot today. It raind this afternoon. The wind is howlling tonight. Mercury went up to 45 this afternoon. Wm taped some over one hundred trees today. The sap run a litle but not much. Wm is writing a letter this evening to his cousin in Saginaw City, a Mrs. Denison. He sent a box of sugar & seed wheete 2 weeks ago & paid the express charge on it. 2.25, & I sent a letter the same time & he has not heard a word from it since. Sherman is away to town tonight with Rob &Arther [Arthur]. I have done a lot of baking today.

Thursday, March 10   This has been quite a cold day. Wind north all day. The sap did not run any today. Wm got a letter from his cousin Mrs. Denison from Saginaw City. Her father Mr. Blower died the 11th of January, the one that Wm sent the Box of sugar & wheete to the other day whare Wm made a visit last fall. Clarence Brown is staying here tonight. Bower

347

has been here all day. Sherman went to town tonight & got the mail. Clint McGill was here this evening. The most of the party that went from Edwards to the City of Washington last week has got home. I have been making a shirt for Sherman today. Wm gathered up what litle sap was in the buckets today.

Friday, March 11   This has been a cold day. Wind north all day. Mercury 10 above zero. Wm & Sherman done the chours & boild the sap. Had one pailful of Syrup. Sherman went to Perce Brown's this forenoon to se[e] them run the engine & saw wood. Then he made a call over to se[e] Arba Kerr this evening. Clarence Brown stayed here last night. Went home this morning. Took a pail of milk. Erwin Harmon Preached in the Baptist Church in Gouverneur last Sunday. He is a student in the Seminary at Gouverneur. The term is out today & the next term will commence the 22 of March.

Saturday, March 12   One more pleasant day but quite cold. The mercury was 10 above zero this morning. Wind north but not very much of it. I boild down the litle dab of Syrup into sugar today. Thare was 12 lbs. It was very nice. Sherman took it to C. H. Brown's store tonight. Alvah Brown cald here this afternoon. He brought me a letter from my nephew Charley Johnson of Oregon. I gave him a pail of milk & a cake of new sugar. He is quite lame yet of his hurt he got on Monday. Wm & Sherman has done the Chours & fixed their Arch a litle & kild a calf that was nearly one week old.

Sunday, March 13   What a lovely day this has been. The sap run well. Wm taped a few trees. Sherman & I went to Church & Sundy School. Clarence & Bower came home with us. A young man from Canton preached today. I did not learn his name. I should think thare was nearly one hundred attended the Sundy School today & Bible Class. We went to Church with the buggy today. The sleighing is done.

Monday, March 14   This has been a cold day. Not much like yesterday. It was clowdy & cold & the north wind has blown all day. Wm & the boys gathered up what litle sap thare was in the buckets & boild it. Thare is one pailful of Sirup. I done a two weeks washing this forenoon. I am very tired tonight. Clarence & Bower Brown are here today & tonight. Clarence went home this morning & helped his mother do her washing. We have 3 new milk cows & 2 farow cows. Mercury was 20 above zero today.

Tuesday, March 15   This has been a cold day. Mercury was at zero this morning & a cold north wind all day. We boild down the sirup in to sugar today. Had 25 lbs very nice sugar. Alvah & Sarah & the girls was here to eat warm sugar & Mabel Brown & Mabel Haile & Bower Brown & Clarence took home some sirup to make warm sugar at home. Wm went to town today & got a wheel to make a wheel barow. Wm has finished reading my Sunday School Book through tonight. Mr. Richmyr cald here today to get one 100 sap buckets.

Wednesday, March 16   One more cold day. Mercury was 10 above zero this morning. It is 20 above tonight. It has snowd a very litle. Wm & Sherman has done the Chours & Wm shot a scunk [skunk] that was caut [caught] in a trap & he has commenced to make a wheelbarow. I commenced to make a shirt for Sherman this afternoon & have been reading in my Sunday School Book this evening. Wm has been sleeping in the rocking chair & has now gone to bed. Beat Sherman before 8 o'clock. We have had no company today & no news. Thare was 10 diferent persons here yesterday besides our own family.

Thursday, March 17   Quite a cold day. It snowd some in the night & has snowd some today. We all went to town today on the big sled. I made a visit to John Hughs & a call in C. H.

349

Brown's Store & in the House. Martha is intending to start for Michigan on Saturday next & go as far as Syracuse & stay over Sunday at her brother's that reside in or near that city, B. F. Nobel [Noble] who is working on the Railrhode near that place. I bought a nice covered glass fruit dish & a can of Baking powdr & a glass Butter dish with a cover & 8 yards of towelling. Mercury was 10 above zero this morning.

Friday, March 18 It has snowd some all day & not very cold. Mercury was 20 above zero. Wm & Sherman done the Chours then he worked at making his wheelbarow & Sherm went over to Perce Brown's. Clarence & Bower Brown & Henry Webb came here today & got our five pail ketle to boil sap in. Sister Moriah Johnson & her granddaughter Mirtle Alen [Allen] made me a visit today. Moriah paid me 3 dollars in money. Interest on a note. I done my Ironing after she went home this afternoon. Thare is a sugar party at the Church tonight for the benefit of the Union Aide Society to be held in the basement. Sherman has gone with Robbie Brown.

Saturday, March 19 This has been a mild day. Mercury was up to 35 above 0 but it has snowd a litle all day. A Sugar Snow perhaps. Martha & Bower & Mabel Brown Started today to go to Michigan. Bower and the trunk rode in the Stage & Charley caried Martha & Mabel, went with one Horse & buggy. Sherman went to the mill & over to the village today with the bay teem & sled. Robby Brown Stayed here with Sherman last night when they came home from the party. The Aid Society took in 10 dollars from their sugar party. Wm has been working on his Wheelbarow today betwen Chours. I have baked bread & buiscuit & made a panful of fried cakes.

Sunday, March 20 This has been a lovely day. Wm & I attended Church today. Went with the single Buggy & one horse. It is splendid wheeling. The sap run well today.

Erwin C. Harmon preached in the new Church today. The house was nearly filed with people, nearly one hundred attended the Sundy School this afternoon in the basement. Clarence Brown came here last night. Stayed here today & is staying tonight. Sherman has a very bad cold. James W. Harmon & his litle boy cald here this afternoon. Mercury was 40 above 0.

Monday, March 21   The sap has run some today. Alvah came up this morning to get some Potatoes & a pail of milk. He stayed this forenoon & helped Sherman gather the sap that ran yesterday & Wm boild it down. Had a large pailful of good sirup. Then Wm took the teem & sled & caried Alvah & his potatoes down home & Wm went to the blacksmith shop & got a tire set on his wheelbarow. We got a dispatch from Ed Brown of Watertown tonight saying his litle boy is dead. Will be beried next Thursday. He wants us to come to the funeral but we can't go no how. Mercury was 30 above O. I have done my washing this forenoon. Mr. Richmire & Eb Bancraft got 100 buckets.

Tuesday, March 22   This has been a stormy day. Snowd all day. The wind is blowing hard tonight & quite cold. Wm has had the sick headache all day but he has helped do the chours. We sugared of [off] 26 lbs of sugar today. Alvah's girls & Minnie Hooper was here to eat warm sugar & have a good time. Sherman went to town today & got a horse collar mended. Mr. Fleming mooved out from Mrs. Storen's parlor yesterday in to a part of the Brick house in the Village & Hiram McGill mooved in to Mrs. Storen's parlor today. Mercury was 12 above zero today.

Wednesday, March 23   Mercury 12 above zero. This has been a cold day but pleasant. The sun has shone all day but the water has not run of[f] from the House any it thawd some in the rhode. The Snow was quite deep this morning. The

Sleighs has run nicely today. Wm & Sherman went to town with the horses & sled this forenoon & then Sherman took the teem back this afternoon for Alvah to haul some logs to the mill. Wm took what sugar we made to town & sold it. Dr. Murry bought 8 lbs & C. H. Brown took 12 lbs & John Hughs took 4 lbs & they gave Mrs. Goodnough 2 lbs. I have finished making Sherman's other shirt & cut & made a pair of overalls for him today & done my housework. Have 5 cows to milk now.

Thursday, March 24   One more nice pleasant day. Quite a hard wind this afternoon from the South west. The sap run some this afternoon. Alvah came up this morning & took the teem & drew his sawd timber from the mill. Brought it here. Clarence stayed here last night & he and Sherman took the teem & sled after Alvah got back. They went to town & drew 5 cord of wood from Charley Brown's Store to Jim Shays. He got home at 3 o'clock & then he & Wm gathered the sap & done all the Chours before dark. Ate supper by lamp light. Delbert Freeman & Stellah Vanornum was maried yesterday. It was 17 years yesterday that Alvah & Manie [Cleland] Brown was maried.

Friday, March 25   What a cold windy day this has been & it has snowd some this afternoon. A regular squall. Alvah came up this forenoon. Helped some with Chours & taking of the sirup. Wm boild down the sap & I sugared it of[f] in the house. Had 13 cakes 26 lbs. I have mad[e] a white cotton shirt for Sherman today. I done all my housework & baked 3 pies. A Mr. Fenton cald here today. Sherman made a call to Arb Keer's & to Mr. Storen's. Mercury was 10 above zero this morning & 20 above at noon.

Saturday, March 26   This has been a cold pleasant day. A very cold wind. No sap today. Wm & Sherman hiched up the colts & drove to town & back home & then to Wm Clealand's

& back home before Chour time. They took the new sugar to C. H. Brown's Store & sold it for 10 cents a pound. Thare was a family mooved in to a part of Mrs. Storen's House today. The name was Will Wels [Wells]. I have done lots of work today. My milk work is gaining evry day. Mercury was 10 above zero. Clarence came here tonight to stay all night & tomorow.

Sunday, March 27   This has been a nice pleasant day. The sap has run a very litle. We all stayed at home today. Only Clarence & Sherman went over to stay with Arba Kerr a litle time in the midle of the day. Mercury was 10 above Zero this morning. It is clowding up tonight & looks like a storm.

Monday, March 28   It has stormed all day. Some of the time. it has raind & part of the time it has snowd & the wind is blowing hard tonight. I done my washing this forenoon & lots of work this afternoon. Wm & Sherman done the Chours. Sherman went home with Clarence & helped him cary a basket of bread & pies & a pail of milk. Mercury was 30 above zero.

Tuesday, March 29   It was a cold morning. Mercury was 10 above zero. It has been very cold all day. Alvah came up this morning & took the horses & sled & drew a load of timber to litle York to fix this factory. Got back before three o'clock. We got a letter from Stilman & Laura Brown today & I answerd it. Sent one to the ofice tonight by Alvah. Alex Kerr went after his hired girl today & she comenced work thare today.

Wednesday, March 30   Oh what a cold windy day this has been. Mercury was 10 above zero this morn. It is 20 above this evening. Sherman has been sick with a cold today. Alvah took the teem & sled & took the remainder of his timber to York factory. I have done lots of work today. Baked bread &

pies & done my Ironing & made two pair of pillow caces & done all my housework. I have quite a lot of pans to scim [skim] & wash now days & warm the milk for 6 calvs. Wm has done the Chours today & read the papers what time he gets but that is not much. He has a sick cow to bother with every day for four weeks past.

Thursday, March 31   This has been a lovely day. Cold this morning. Mercury was 5 above zero this morning. Got up to 40 this afternoon. The sap run a litle. Wm & Sherman done the Chours & took the water & ice out of the buckets & then went to mill with a load of oats for feed for the cows & then Wm done a churnning for the first time this Spring. I filed [filled] one tub of butter & had 5 lbs left. Wm broke a needle out of the sewing mashine today. Clint & Leslie McGill cald here a while this evening. Played a few games with Sherm. Sherman took a basket of bread & custerd pie to Charley today. Clarence was not at home.

Friday, April 1   This was the first day of April & a nice pleasant day it has been, but not warm enough for sap. Wm & Sherman went to town this morning & got home at half past 12. They had to wait for the grist. I done a lot of slicking up in the chamber. I emtied two feather beds in to one clean tick & swep & moped Sherm's room & done a lot of cleaning in the other Chamber. Wm sent a tub of Butter to Gouverneur by Nelson Vanorman. Wm brought home 3 butter tubs from Charley Brown's yesterday. Mercury was 10 above Zero this morning. Alvah & family went to Grant's in Russell [NY] yesterday. Came home today.

Saturday, April 2   One more pleasant day but cool. Mercury 12 above Zero this morn. No sap today. Wm gathered what litle thare was. It was not worth boilling. John Roach & his wife & a lady friend of theirs from Colton made us a visit today from Fine, NY. Wm gave me 50 cents in money tonight

out of the butter that he sold today & gave Sherman 25 cents.
He got 20 cents a pound for the Butter. John Cousins &
Theodore Stevenson had a fight this afternoon. Stevenson
pounded John fearfuly. Evryone that was looking on said it
was just what he deserved. He did not come out on the Streets
on Sunday.

Sunday, April 3   It was pleasant this forenoon but clouded up
this afternoon & raind a litle this evening. The sap run a very
litle to some of the trees. It is just no sugar run at all.
Clarence stayed here last night & today & tonight. Martha has
been gone two weeks. We all stayed at home today. It was Dr.
Lee's day to Preach in the Union Church today. Alax Keer
cald here & took dinner with us this afternoon. I scum
[skimmed] & washed 30 pans today & washed nine milk Pails.
Mercury was 20 above 0 this morning at 7. Forty this
afternoon. I got a letter from brother Hiram Johnson last night
from Oregon Salem [Salem, Oregon].

Monday, April 4   Well this has been a rainy day & it raind in
the night some. Wm & Sherman done the Chours & gathered
what sap thare was & boild it down to a litle mess of sweete.
Then Wm took the inside of the reservoy [water reservoir] out
of the big range & took it to town & got it mendid. He had a
hard time of getting it out of the Iron case. I have done a lot of
Hard work today. I did not get my washing all done untill one
o'clock. I had so much milk work to do before I comenced
my washing. Then I washed two bed ticks & a spread extre
[extra] of my week's washing. Then I had the Back kitchen to
mop twice. Then the reservoy leeked [leaked] the water all
out.

Tuesday, April 5   Oh what a cold windy stormy day this has
been. Complete blizards all day. It has cleard of[f] some to
nite but is cold. But thare is a lovely moon sailling through
the sky that makes the evening look lovely. We sugared of[f]

today 35 lbs. Alvah came up this forenoon & done the sugar & cooled & diped it in to the tins. Was here to dinner. He borowed 20 dollars of his father & 10 of me for a few days. I got a letter from Susan Clair of Pine Valley, NY. She is Jo Brown's Daughter. Mr. Powers was beried today. He was taken to Fine [NY] to be beried. He was living on the Cousins farm. He was not sick but four days. Leaves a wife & a few children. I sent two dozen of eggs to Agnes Hughs.

Wednesday, April 6   This has been a cold pleasant day. Some wind. Sap run a very litle. Wm & Sherman done the Chours & done a churning. I packed a tub of butter this afternoon. I done my Baking this forenoon. I have done lots of work today. Clarence Brown came up to nite to stay with Sherman.

Thursday, April 7   A lovely day. Clear & pleasant but not very warm. Sap run a litle. Wm kild his sick cow today. He got tired of waiting for her to die or get well. She has been sick nearly two months. He took the hide to town tonight & sold it for $1.80. I wrote a letter to Susan M. Clair today & sent it to the Post by Sherman tonight. We sent a tub of Butter to Gouverneur tonight by Nelson Vanornum. Clarence went home this morning after Breakfast. He took Home a basket of bread & a mince Pie & a pail of milk. I done my Ironing this forenoon. Wm took two dozen of eggs to John Hughs.

Friday, April 8   One more lovely day. Clear & pleasant. The sap run quite well. Wm & Sherman done the Chours in the forenoon & gathered the sap this afternoon & boild it. I have made three custerd pies this afternoon. It takes me untill nine o'clock evry morning to get my dary [dairy] work done & breakfast dishes. So I do my baking in the afternoon. Wm brout in sirup enough for 32 pounds of sugar. Clarence came up to supper to nite & took home a custerd pie & some bread.

Saturday, April 9   What a love day this has been. The sap has run well. Wm & Sherman & Alvah done the Chours & gathered the sap. They had enough for 35 lbs of Sugar. I sugared of[f] twice today. Alvah took the teem & buggy & he & Sarah attended the funeral of Mrs. Ed Shefnel. He got back here at four o'clock. They took dinner at Wm Grant's, Sarah's Brother. Mercury went up to 60 above zero this afternoon. It has been the warmest day since last fall. It looks like rain tonight. The south wind is blowing hard this evening. Wm & Sherman is sleeping soundly. Nelson Vanornum paid me 7 dollars & 35 cents for butter he sold.

Sunday, April 10   One more lovely pleasant day. Nice & warm so we could keep the outside doors open all day. It did not freeze any so the sap did not run. Alvah came up this morning & helped with the Chours & they went out & gathered up what litle thare was in the buckets but did not boil it. John Hughs & Agness came up this afternoon. We went to Church this evening. The Rev Mr. Richman from Hermon Preached in the new Church to a full house. We got home at nine. It was very dark & the roads very bad. Amos Newton went around among the men before Church time & got up five dollars & gave it to the minister that was good in Amos.

Monday, April 11   Some colder today. It thundered quite hard this morning at 8 o'clock & we looked for a hard shower but it went around to the south. Wm boild the sap & brought home 3 pails of sirup. I done a large washing this forenoon & packed a tub of Butter this afternoon. Wm & Sherman done the Churning. Wm was so tired & nearly sick, he ate no supper. Went to bed at 7. My feat [feet] are so sore on the botoms I can scarcely walk.

Tuesday, April 12   Quite a cold day. The ground was frozen this morning. The sap run today. Wm has been sick all day & last night. Sherman done the Chours this forenoon & Clarence came up this afternoon & helped & is staying all night. Alvah cald here this morning. He went to York in the Stage, he & Truman Thompson. They have gone to fix the factory. Wm sent a Box of sugar to Gouverneur today by Nelson Vanornum to go to Dakota for Stilman Brown. 55 lbs of sugar & we sent a tub of butter to sell to Gouverneur. Let Alvah have two & a half pounds of Butter.

Wednesday, April 13 Not very warm today. A cold wind all day. Wm & the boys gathered the sap & boild it. Brout the sirup home in a milk can. Wm is feelling better today. Clarence went home this morning & took home a loaf of Bread & a tin of cake & a dish of custerd for Charley. Then he came back to help his granpa. Mrs. Gorden & Willie Allen came here for a visit today. Was here to dinner & supper. I have done lots of work today.

Thursday, April 14 Quite a good day but no sap. We sugared of[f] 60 lbs today in the house. We have made nearly 100 pounds. I have done a lot of work today. We got the money for our last tub of Butter today. Wm gave me 50 cents out of it. Sister Hall got home from Gouverneur last nite in the Stage. Her Daughter Emmy Clark was very sick in Gouverneur. She cald her mother out thare last week by telephone.

Friday, April 15 Clowdy all day & raind a litle this afternoon. The wind is blowing to nite quite hard. Wm & Sherman went to mill this forenoon with the colt. Took 3 bushels of wheete. Clarence went home from here this afternoon. He took home a basket with Custerd Pie & cake & a pail of milk. Sarah Brown & the two girls, Manie & Mary, came here this afternoon to stay all night. Alvah is to York all the week to work on his factory. C. H. Brown sent me a Pair of gaters today by his father.

Saturday, April 16 Raind & it has been a nasty wet day all day & raind in the nite. Wm boild in a litle dap of sap. Had one Pailful of thin sirup.   Sarah & the children went home this afternoon.   Sherman took the Horses & wagon & caried them home.   The mud is fearful deep today.   Sherman brought home from Charley's Store a box of medicine for the colts.   It cost one Dollar.   They think the colt has got the Pink eye dissease. Alvah Brown came home in the stage to night.   Clarence was here today.   Went home tonight.   Took a tin of cake & a loaf of bread & a pie from [Sarah] [*Sarah is crossed out*].

Sunday, April 17   A cold morning.   Froze Hard & Clowdy & Snowd a few flakes but before noon cleard of[f] pleasant.   No preaching today.   Wm & Sherman has gone out to the woods to take the water out of the Buckets.   Sherman then took a trip over to Arba Keer's.   Alvah came up & took the bay teem & drove out as far as Rant Loops to see Ed Sheffner about working for him in the factory.   James Cambell cald here this afternoon awhile.   He had stayed to Wm Clealand's all night last & part of today.

Monday, April 18   It was a cold morning.   Froze hard but no sap nor it did not run any yesterday.   I done my washing this forenoon.   I had a lot of Pans & Pails to wash before I commenced my washing.   It was 9 o'clock when I began my washing.   Wm took a walk over to uncle Jim Webb's this forenoon & he & Sherman has gone to town with the teem & big waggon this afternoon.   Took the calf hides with them. Mrs. Maryann Webb has served a sumons on Jim Webb for a note that he claims is paid.   So they are in for trouble.

Tuesday, April 19   A lovely day.   The sap run nicely.   Wm boild & siruped down & left it in the sugar house intending to sugar it off tomorrow.   Clarence came here this afternoon. Intends to stay all night.   He got a letter from his mother.   He thinks she will be home next week.   He is anxious for her to come & so am I.   Charley has not been here since Martha went away.   Wm & Sherman & I done a Churning today-- noon in a few minutes. I have worked & packed a tub of butter so soon as I did today. Nelson was waiting to take it with him to Gouverneur. This is four tubs he has caried . He got 18 cents for the last one.

Wednesday, April 20   One more pleasant day. Some wind. The sap runs well. Wm & Alvah done the sugar in the woods this forenoon. Alvah helped Sherman to gather the sap this forenoon & this afternoon. Sherm brought home 71 pounds of Sugar this afternoon that they boild yesterday. Will have more today. I got a letter from Brother Abel Johnson today. Alvah brought it from the office & I have writen one to send to him. I have had baking to do today. Bread & Pudding & Custerd. I sent a dish of Baked beans & a mess of fried cakes to Charley this morning by Clarence. He stayed here all night last with Sherman.

Thursday, April 21   A very nice pleasant day. To[o] warm for sap. Wm & Sherman gathered & boild all the sap thare was & sugared it of[f] at 3 batches. They do not think they will make any more sugar this Spring. We have made 600 lbs from 200 &45 trees. Clarence Came up to night to stay all night with Sherman. I commenced to yuse the flour of 3 bushels of wheete.

Friday, April 22   One more pleasant day it was. Froze some this morning. Our men did not go to the woods today. Sherman took the teem & went with Clarence & Henry Webb to the village & drew home the sap buckets they have been using of ours. Eb Bancroft gathered his buckets yesterday. Wm went to town today & as far out as Andrew Clealand's to hire some money. Jim Harmon cald here today to see Wm on buisness. [business]

Saturday, April 23   Clowdy this forenoon & commenced to rain before noon. Turnd cold & was a nasty wet day. Fearful muddy. Alvah came over & boild the sap & Clarence & Sherman gathered the sap & part of the buckets. Wm went to town this evening & got some money of Wooliver & H. Rushton & John Newton. Lizie Webb cald here awhile this afternoon. Nelson Vanornum paid Wm 5.94 cents for Butter this afternoon.

Sunday, April 24   This has been a cold windy day but pleasant. Clarence & Sherman, Robby Brown attended Sundy School today. It was Dr. Lee's day to Preach. He sent a young man in his place. The new Methodist Minister preached to day for the first time. Wm had an Introduction to him last evening to John Newton's. James W. Harmon cald here this afternoon & got some money to take to Gouverneur tomorow.

Monday, April 25   A clowdy day. Looks like rain. I done my washing this forenoon & washed sap buckets this afternoon. Alvah came up home & helped wash buckets all day.   Eb Bancroft brout the buckets that Ricmire hired of Wm. Alvah took a grist of wheete to mill from here today. 3 bushels. The factory opend today April 25.

Tuesday, April 26   A frost this morning. Alvah Brown & Jimmy Webb worked for Wm today haulling out manure. I done my baking this forenoon & dary work & this afternoon I finished washing the sap Buckets & spouts & cleand the kitchen. The botoms of my feete are so sore with corns I can hardly walk. Wm & Sherm does the Chours & then puts up fence.

Wednesday, April 27   This has been a cool pleasant day. Alvah & Jim W[ebb] worked here today. Wm fixt fence this forenoon & done the churning this afternoon. I done some Baking today & took care of the Butter & done lots of work. Martha & Mabel & Bower Brown came home tonight from

Michigan. Been gone most six weeks. I fild a crock of Butter for Alvah today & Wm went to town with the colt & Buggy & took the Butter to Alvah's. I sent a loaf of bread & a pie & two dozen of eggs to Charley today.

Thursday, April 28   A cool clowdy day. Looks like rain. Alvah & Jim Webb worked for Wm today. Wm & Sherman fixt fence all day between doing Chours. Old Mr. Frank Allen made us a call this afternoon. He is staying to Gid Freeman's now for a few weeks. He is nearly 80 years old. He is very lame. Walks with a crutch & a cane. He told me he knew that Gid was not wiling to make a home for him & his son Osker's wife is not willing. He should have a home with them. So he is hard up for an old Criple.

Friday, April 29   This has been a rainy day all day. No working today. Wm & I went up to see Sister Johnson today. She has had a shock of palsey. Is very bad. Not able to help herself any. It hapend last Sunday. Dr. Tabor is attending her. Her Daughter Emmy Herington is taking care of her at present.

Saturday, April 30   This has been a rainy forenoon. The mud is fearful again. Very litle travel on the rhodes today. This afternoon it is pleasant but a high wind. Wm sold some Hay to Warren Harmon today.   Mabel Brown came here this afternoon for a visit intending to stay all night but she got in a teribel stew to go home tonite. So she got a ride with Will Newton. Wm has writen a letter to send to S. E. Brown of Dakota today. Elza Webb brought home our spade today.

Sunday, May 1   What a lovely day this has been for the first day of May. But it is clowdy this evening & looks like rain but we hope & wish for a few good dry days to prepare the ground for seede. Sherman & Robby went to Sundy School today. Thare is now about 50 schollars in Sundy School. We put our milk in the factory today for the first time this spring. Wm went to Jim Harmon's today. Took dinner thare. Clarence came up tonite & helped milk & stay all night. I have been home all day.

Monday, May 2   This has been a very warm pleasant day for this time of year. Mercury went up to 84 above zero. Alvah took our teem & Plowd his garden this morning & then he plowd both of our gardens then he went home & Planted some Potatoes for himself. Wm & Sherman drew out manure with the colts. I done my washing this forenoon before nine o'clock then I done lots of sciming [skiming] milke & washing pans & other hard work.

Tuesday, May 3   A high wind all day but pleasant, Mercury up to 80 today. Alvah & Sherm has been haulling manure from the barn to the back end of the farm all day. Wm done two churnings this forenoon. I scim [skimmed] the last milk this forenoon & packed the last butter. I have got 75 lbs of butter for our own yuse. I have made about 300. We are milking 16 cows. It is just one month since I made the first butter.

Wednesday, May 4   A nice pleasant day. Mercury went up to 70.   Alvah Brown & Jim Webb worked for Wm today spreadding manure.   Wm commenced to Harow his wheete ground today. Two wedings in town today. Will Woodcock & Miss Hosmer & Miss Minnie Raymond & a Mr. Tayler from Massachusetts.

Thursday, May 5   One more pleasant day. Some wind. Jim & Alvah worked here today spreading manure. Wm has been Harowing today with three Horses. He is working the big colt. John Newton & James Webb & Wm Beach has gone to Gouverneur today after the Methodist Minister family & goods.   Preacher Smith has gone to Russell to Preach the coming year from Edwards. Charley Beech has got a stroke of

363

num[b] Palsey. Alvah went home at 3 o'clock this afternoon.
Jim Webb worked 5 days. Wm paid him five dollars.

Friday, May 6   It has been clowdy all day & raind a litle now
& then.   A slite shower but not enough to prevent the men
from work.   Alvah has worked here all day Harowing the
wheete ground. Wm & Sherman has done their Chours & fixt
fence. It is raining quite hard this evening. Sherman has gone
to town. I have been cleaning house a litle for two or 3 days.

Saturday, May 7   It was raining this morning when we got up
& was showery this forenoon. Is pleasant this afternoon. Wm
has been harowing this afternoon.   Alvah came up this
morning & got a back load of straw to put under his carpet.
He is putting it down today. I have done some cleaning in the
kitchen today besides my housework & baking. Nathan Shaw
came here this afternoon & bought four bushels of Wheete.
Said he would pay for it in about six weeks.

Sunday, May 8   Oh what a lovely day this has been. Mercury
went up to 80. Sherman & I went to Sunday School today. I
got the news of the Death of my Sister Susan [Viall] Foster.
She died the 16 of April at her Daughter's in Illinois at the
same place whare brother [Dr. James Foster] Foster died. She
was 79 years old last February. Martha & the boys came here
for a ride this afternoon. Wm stayed at home today & took a
good sleep while we was gone to Church.   Then he took a
tramp back to the woods to look for a cow. He found her but
could not find the litle calf.

Monday, May 9   A lovely day. Quite warm. Mercury up to
82. I done a large washing this forenoon & all my house work
& washing pails & 2 milk cans. Wm & Alvah getting the
ground ready to sow wheete. Wm kild a litle calf in the woods
today. Sherman draws the milk evry day. A Pack Pedler cald
here today. I did not trade any with him. He was vext.

Robbie Brown cald here to night to get our wagon.

Tuesday, May 10   One more pleasant day. Some wind but warm. Mercury up to 80. Alvah has been sewing [sowing] the wheete today with the cedar [seeder] & Horses & Wm has been rolling [rolling] the wheete ground with the colts. Wm Clealand cald here this morning & brought four bushels of wheete for seed. Paid five dollars. Berney Vanornum was here to dinner & stayed & set out a lot of maple trees for Wm along the side of the rhode. Wm pays him 10 cents a tree. He payed him 2 dollars & 90 cents tonight & he takes Pork & Sugar for the remainder. It will take 40 lbs of Pork & 10 lbs of Sugar.

Wednesday, May 11   A litle cooler today. Wind north but very pleasant. Wm & Alvah worked all day harowing & putting in grain oats. I think they are getting in now. They finished the wheete. I have been doing my housework & between Chours & Cooking & Baking, I have been cleaning the front room upstairs. Brout down all my feather Beds & quilts & flanel sheetes & buffalow robe & hung them all out to take a good airing. It is a hard task for me to go up & down stairs so much but I have no one to help me do a Chour or give a lift with any of my work. I can't even get a bit of help from Sherman. His grandpa wants all of his help.

Thursday, May 12   Quite a lot of wind today & cool but pleasant. Getting quite dry but the grass is growing finely & the trees are looking nice & green. Plum trees in blosom last week. Wm & Sherman has been diging the holes to plant their potatoes & Alvah has been harowing & sowing oats. Wm is rooling the oat field with the colts this afternoon. Alvah drives the bay teem. I have done lots of hard work today in the line of house cleaning & Baking. I made some pie plant Pies [Rhubarb pies] today for the first time this spring. Lesley Beach is very sick with pneumonia on his lungs. 5 lbs of tea

today.

Friday, May 13   Quite a cool day.   Frost this morning but very pleasant. Alvah worked here today. He finished getting in the grain & Wm finished the rolling & Wm & Sherman & Bower Planted the Potatoes. P. H. Brown cald here tonight to get our seeder to put in his grain. Abner Rice made me a short call today. He has been sick all winter. He is just getting around a litle. He looks very feeble. I have done some cleaning & puting away things today but thare is lots to do yet. It will take one more week if I hold out & am able to work.

Saturday, May 14   A pleasant day but cool. Some frost this morning. Mabel Brown made us a visit today. Wm went to town tonight & I rode as far as Forest McKee's & mad[e] a call. It was the first time I saw her boy. He is 6 months old. He has got 6 teeth cut through good. He is a nice baby. I have not cleand house much today. I had baking & lots of work to do. Alvah took our teem & seeder & worked for Alax Keer today. P. H. Brown & wife went to Russell today after our School teacher, Miss Jessie Blount of Canton to commence school on Monday 16th.

Sunday, May 15   What a lovely pleasant day this has been. We all attended Church & Sunday School. Dr. Lee preached today in the new Church. The rhodes are very dusty. We kneede rain very much at presant. John Hughs & Agness made us a visit today after meting. Wm & Sherman has all the milking to do evryday. They milk 17 cows now. P. H. Brown got five Bushels of Wheete of Wm tonight & took home our seeder with him.

Monday, May 16   As dry as ever. No signs of rain. Wm worked for P. H. Brown today sowing grain with his seeder. Alvah took our teem & big wagon & went to South Edwards & got a large tub from the old Starch factory & brout it here.

Stayed & helped with the milking. I done my washing this forenoon & a lot of work in the Chamber this afternoon. Luke Vanornum cald here today & sold 2 baskets to Wm. I payed him one dollar. Berney Vanornum came today & got 40 lbs of Pork & 10 lbs of Sugar to pay for the trees he sat out on the rhode side. Sherman commenced to go to School today. The teacher made me a call today noon.

Tuesday, May 17   Quite warm & dry today. The rhodes are very dusty. Wm made some mortar [mortar] this forenoon & worked for P. H. Brown this afternoon. Alvah took his big tub to York today to his Cheese Factory to hold whay [whey]. They make nine cheese a day at his factory. Sarah Brown made me a visit today. Rode home in the Stage. She & Alvah. It is clowding over tonight & looks like rain. We hope it will come soon. We got a letter from Stilman Brown today saying the sugar we sent them got thare safe on the 5th of May. He sent 5 dollars & forty cents in money.

Wednesday, May 18   Well it was raining this morning when we got up but did not rain much. But it did lots of good. The grass & trees look lovely. All nature is decked in her robe of green. Our wheete is up nicely. Wm worked for P. H. Brown this forenoon & finished his seeding. Robbie took home our rooller to rool their ground. Wm done a job of plastering over head in our dineing room this afternoon. I got the mess cleand up once more. It has been pleasant this afternoon.

Thursday, May 19   A pleasant day. Just lovely after the shower of yesterday. Wm & I made a visit to John Laidlaw's today. Did not get home untill dark. Alvah came & helped Sherman do the milking tonite. We had a good visit with John's folks & made a call on Sister Phila [Viall] Harmon. A fresh scandal has started out again about Mrs. Wooliver. They say she was caut this time. It is awful to know that such trash is going the rounds & in the mouth of evry litle boy & girl in

367

the village. Bower was just shouting over it this morning out to our barn.

Friday, May 20   It has been very pleasant & warm to day & is getting so very dry. The fires are raging in the woods in evry direction. We hope for a heavy rain soon. Alvah went to Gouverneur today with one of our horses & Charleys & our double Buggy. Caried out an agent & brought back a box of goods. Mrs. Wels made me a call today. Wm done a Job of plastering a cistern for Alax Keer & finished our room over head. I have cleand the mess once more & done my baking & Ironing today & other work & read the paper lots. I got a letter from Oregon today from a niece of mine, Rachel Earl, Daughter of H. A. Johnson.

Saturday, May 21   How dry the dust on the rhodes. Is like a cloud. The sun & moon is very red & dry looking. No signs of rain & the fires in the woods raging. Fifty men in a place in Pitcarn [Pitcairn] fiting [fighting] the fire. Wm went to town twice today. Alvah took our colts & buggy & took his family to Tom Grant's for a visit in Russell. Porter Harmon & Aneliza cald here today on their way home from Gouverneur. Sherman went boat riding today with Clint & Arthur Freeman.

Sunday, May 22   Dry weather continues & warm today. Mercury 90. We have all stayed at home today. I wrote a letter to my niece in Oregon, Mrs. Rachel Earl, a daughter of my brother Hiram Johnson. Wm has finished reading through the Sunday School book today. We had a hen come of with 10 chicks today. The first ones this spring. This is Sister Emmy Hall's birthday. She is 60 years old today. I was 61 last November the 7th. Alvah got home with the colts tonight litle before dark.

Monday, May 23   One more dry hot day. Wm went to town & got 10 bushels of ashes of Dr. Goodnough & some of

Charley Brown. He fild the leach & put ashes on his potatoes. I done my washing this forenoon. Sherman goes to school. Thare is a lot of men fixing the bridge at the mines. Alvah is working thare today. JutGordin is commisioner of the highway of the town of Edwards. He has bought a new fangled thing to scrape the rhodes & it helps scrape the farmers Pockets as well.

Tuesday, May 24   Lots of wind today & looks liked rain. A big shower away in the west today noon. Raind some here near two o'clock. Just a scud [slight sudden shower] but we hope for more. Wm is white washing the dinning room overhead today & we are getting our lye to make soap. Have lots of work to do just now. Clarence is over to P. H. Brown's today to help wash sheep. Alvah is helping on that bridge today. Well we have had a lovely shower since four o'clock. Since Wm finished the whitewash, I have cleand all the woodwork in the dineing room & washed the carpet & the pantry floor & got supper & done up the work.

Wednesday, May 25   This has been a nice pleasant cool day after the rain of last night. We think it raind nearly all night. Our cistern is nearly full of water. Wm has been making the soap today. I have been cleaning house as usual & Baking & Cooking & eating & washing dishes, & patching up the wall paper. Sherman bought me a box of crackers & some lemon Buiskit & a pair of Pants for himself of C. H. Brown's today.

Thursday, May 26   A pleasant forenoon but a thunder shower this afternoon. Wm drew 2 load of manure from the Dr. Goodnough's this forenoon & one load this afternoon. Got caut out in the Shower. I have nearly finished cleaning house. Have got the Parlor to do yet. Wm drew a box of lime to Charley today for to build his Cistern. He commenced it today.

Friday, May 27   This has been a rainy day. Wm & Sherman both went to the factory this morning then Wm & I made a visit to Write Robbinson's. Got home at five then I done my Ironing before dark. Wm went to Maybees Mill to buy some lumber to fix his stabel floor. Robbie Brown came home with Sherman at noon & shot a cat here in the yard.

Saturday, May 28   it raind some this morning & been cool & clowdy all day. I have done a lot of baking & morning made 3 tins of Bread & 7 pies, 5 pieplant & 2 custerd, I painted the wood box & made a shelf behind the stove & made a platform at the woodhouse door. Have work hard all day. Charley Boals from Pitcairn cald here awhile today. Wm & Sherman went to town & got a load of manure & Boals rhode away with them. He is some crazy has been a number of years but not very bad.

Sunday, May 29   This has been a very pleasant day but cool. We attended Church today in the new Union Church.   A Baptist minister from Hamilton College Preached today & this evening. We intend to go tonight. The Methodist held meting in their house today. Both houses was well filled. Clarence came up here this afternoon. Charley Beach is gaining his health quite fast. He walked over to the village the other day & Lillie Beach is improving fast under the treatment of Dr. Goodnough.

Monday, May 30   What a lovely day this has been. Clear & pleasant all day. The people feard a frost this morning but thare was none here. We all attended the meting last evening. I have done my washing this forenoon & white washed my pantry & washed the shelves & moped floor & put clean papers on the shelves & my dary work & cooking three meals. Wm & Sherman went to Maybee's Mills & got a load of lumber this forenoon & one load this afternoon.

Tuesday, May 31   This has been a lovely day.   Clear & pleasant. Mercury is 70 above zero at 7 o'clock tonight. Wm went after a load of lumber today out to Maybee's Mill. Sherman went to School. I have cleaned the Parlor today & have evry thing back in its place.

Wednesday, June 1   It was raining this morning when I got up before five. It raind all the forenoon & a litle this afternoon. I cleand the front Piasa today. Washed all the caping & Posts & casins [casings] & floor. Wm went after a load of lumber to Maybee's Mills this afternoon. Took out one hundred lbs of salt pork. They payed him 10 dollars in lumber for it & he gave them nine dollars in money. This was the first day of June.

Thursday, June 2   This day was pleasant & very warm untill 3 o'clock then clowded up & looked like a shower & the shower came at five or litle before. A hard one it was. The men worked on the rhode today & they was just geting home when the shower over took them. I made a visit to Alvah Brown's today & a call to Sister Hall's. I rode home with the Dr. & got here before the rain. C.V. Harmon cald here this morning. I payed him 50 cents to help pay for a fence around the crick graveyard whare my father & mother [Charles Alvah and Rachel Pratt Viall Johnson] are beried.

Friday, June 3   It was raining this morning. Wet all the forenoon. Pleasant this afternoon. Wm took a barel of soap to Charley this forenoon & worked on the rhode this afternoon. Alex Keer [Kerr] cald here today noon.   Sherman went to school today. I done my work & my ironing. I got two letters today from Pine Valley. One from brother A. P. Johnson & one from Susan Clair.

Saturday, June 4   This has been a good day. Our men worked on the rhode all day. Bower was up & worked with them.

371

The men done a good job with the new scraper on wheels in front of our house. They yuse two span of Horses on it. Well, I hardley know what I have done today. It has been so many kinds of work. Baking pies & Cake & Slicking out in Sherman's room & mopping & cooking, washing pails & cans & dishes & a lot of mending at all events. I am very tired.

Sunday, June 5   It has been clowdy part of the time today & a sprinkle [sprinkle] of rain. Wm & I went to Church this forenoon. It was Dr. Lee's day to preach. This was the Children's Day. His sermon was to the children. The Church was decorated with flors& four Bird Cages of signing [singing] birds. They made music. It was just lovely in the Church. Dr. Lee came home with us to dinner & then he drove to Hailsborouh to preach a funeral sermon at 3 o'clock. He intends to stay with us tonight. We all intend to go to the children's concert this evening.

Monday, June 6   It has been clowdy most all day & just a sprinkle [sprinkle] of rain. Wm & Sherman worked on the rhode all day besides doing chours. I have done my washing & other work. The entertainment of last evening was splendid. Mr. Lee staid with us last night. Left here a little past 8 o'clock for his home in Canton village. The Methodist intend to celebrate the Children's Day next Sunday. Ed Hughs & Jennie Schilar was maried. He works for John McKee & has took his wife thare for a home at [not legible].

Tuesday, June 7   This has been a very warm day. No rain. Wm finished his rhode work today. Sherman went to school. Sister Phila Harmon made me an all day visit today. Maryette came with her but did not stay but went to town & got her silk dress cut & fitted. Charles Luther Harmon sent us 10 lbs of veal today. Porter Harmon & his wife has gone to Madrid [NY] to attend the asociation. They started today. Thare was a couple of men cald to Charley Harmon's yesterday & stole

Ed Cumbers watch. He got a warent for them & folowed as far as Russell.

Wednesday, June 8   This has been a good day. Quite a hard wind this afternoon & some clowdy but no rain. Wm has been hoing in the garden today. Sherman to school. No visitors today. Great excitement in town today about the thieves that stole Cumbers watch. They drove through Edwards today & Dumas caut their Horse by the bridel & one man shot his revolver & hit Dumas through one thum[b]. The men got away & left their Horse & Buggy & trunk but the men in town are after them. We hope they will overhaul them & give them what the deserve & that will be State Prison.

Thursday, June 9   it was raining this morning untill 9. Since then it has been pleasant. Wm & I made a visit to Charley Johnson's today. Got home at 5. We cald over to Wilson's a few moments. I bought one & a half yds of Cashmer to Charley Stevenson's today to fix my dress. Payed 75 cents. Alfred Hall has been on the sick list since last Saturday night. The men are on the look yet for the men that stole Cumbers watch. They was seen to cross the river near Russell village. Cellia Johnson's girl left last Saturday so she is doing her work alone.

Friday, June 10   What a lovely day this has been. Clear & pleasant. Considerabel wind north east all day. Wm has been hoeing in the garden all day. I have done some ironing & made a cotton sheete & read the weekly paper nearly through. Sherman went to school. Maryette Harmon is getting a new black silk dress made to Mrs. Alma Kicmyres [*probably Richmyer*] this week. It will cost her about 40 dollars. Mrs. Wels [Wells] cald here today. She works to Hellen Elliot's helping take the care of old Mr. Clealand. She thinks he can't live through another night. He had not took any food this week. He has got a cancer on his face & it is eating through into his throat.

Saturday, June 11   This has ben a lovely day.   Warm & pleasant. Wm drew two loads of lumber from Maybee's Mill today. I painted the pantry floor & front shelf & mop boards & done a lot of Baking such as pieplant Pies & custerd pies & four loves of Bread & mopped the dineing room carpet & the kitchen floor & all my work. I am tired tonight. Old Mr. Clealand died last night at eleven. Will be Beried tomorrow afternoon. Bower was here today. He & Sherman went in swiming & fishing.

Sunday, June 12   One more warm dry pleasant day. We nead rain very much & it looks a litle like rain tonight. We have all attended the funeral of granpa Clealand today. What a lot of people folowed him to the grave. The funeral was at his house. Mr. Smith Preached the same one that Preached. The same one that Preached granma Clealand's funeral sermon one year ago last Sunday. Mrs. Henry Rushton had quite a hard sick spell in the time of the servis. Mr. Clealand was 93 years old. We intend to go to the Methodist concert this evening. We caried a load to the funeral today. There was 10 of us. Wm Green from Hermon beried Mr. Clealand.

Monday, June 13   Oh what a lovely day. Warm & sonshine all day. Mercury at 80 this afternoon. I done my washing this forenoon & Painted my pantry floor. Done my Chamber work this afternoon & took a good sleap [sleep]. Wm went to town. Stayed all the forenoon then took a sleep in the afternoon. He got his cheese money today. It was 38 dollars. We all had a good time tothe concert last evening. The church was adorned with lovely flowers & signing [singing] birds in their cages hung about. The Church was filld to its utmost. The children did Splendid. Sherman & I took a ride to town tonite.

Tuesday, June 14   One more dry warm pleasant day. We are

wishing for rain. Not much dew this morning. Wm drew in his logs this forenoon to the sawmill & this afternoon he drew home his saed [sawed]scanthings. Sherman went to School this forenoon & had the headache this afternoon & stayed at home & took a good sleep. A German Pack Pedler cald here this afternoon. I bought a pair of socks for Sherm. He caried lots of nice goods. I have been Painting Some today. I made a green paint & painted the window blindes on the Piassa. Mrs. Emmy Clark is home on a visit this week to her father's, A. B. Hall's. She resides in Gouverneur, NY.

Wednesday, June 15   Warm & dry. No rain yet. The dust goes along the rhode like a cloud. I have done a part of my Ironing this forenoon & my other work this afternoon. I painted over the front Blinds & made a Cotton Sheete & partly made a pair of overalls for Wm. Sherman went to school today. Wm hoed some in the garden & slept the rest of the forenoon then after dinner he went to the woods & dug roots & peeld bark to make him a syrup. He is nearly sick with another cold. We have all got colds now. Steven Ward's house was burnt last night. He lives in Fine. The house was rented to George Morows. Their stuff in the House was all burnt.

Thursday, June 16   It commenced to rain this morning at 7. Had a nice shower. Then near night a hard shower. Wm & I went to town. Stayed untill four in the afternoon. He got his Horses shod to John Hughes & I made a visit thare. We both took dinner to John's then he went over in the woods past brother Rob's & dug a lot of roots to make him a syrup. I went as far as his brother Robberts [Robert's]. Stayed until he came back. Sherman went to School. Clarence came up to supper. Helped do the milking. Sarah Brown made a visit to Myron Hall's today.

Friday, June 17   A cool pleasant day after the rain of last nite.

Wm & Sherman has been to the village all day to listen to a lawsuit between Jim Webb & Maryann Webb. It commenced yesterday forenoon. Judge Neary & Vasco Abbot of Gouverneur is the lawyers. Sarah Brown & Edith Scowton has gone to West Edwards for a visit today to Henry Brown's. They drove our Kit Horse. I am to home alone today accept Manie & Mary Brown came & took dinner with me & brout me a cup of strawberies. The first I have had.

Saturday, June 18   This has been a nice cool day. It is clowdy this evening. Looks some like rain. Wm & I made a visit to Wilson's today. We went with the colts. Had a good visit with the old folks & with Maggie. Mary was not at home. She is keeping house for her brother Rob. We had strawbery short cake for supper & buiskit & beries. Sherman went after strawberies this forenoon. Did not get many. Bower & Jene [Gene] Shay was here today noon to dinner. They had been after beries. John Dane has run away to Oregon. Got in debt 1400 dollars to diferent parties.

Sunday, June 19   This has been quite a wet day. We was glad to se[e] the rain today. We did not go to Church. Charley & family came here after Sundy School. Stayed untill night. Clarence stayed all night to take the teem & wagon to Alvah in the morning. He goes with a load of cheese for Wm to DeKalb tomorow. It has been quite cool this afternoon.

Monday, June 20   it was nasty this morning but has cleared of[f] nicely. Just a lovely afternoon. I done my washing this morning. All done at eight o'clock when they got home with the milk cans. Alvah went with a load of cheese today to DeKalb. I wrote a letter to Mr. Phillips today & sent it to the post office by Hiram Hall. He drives the stage from Gouverneur to Fine. C. V. Harmon & Maryette & Allie & Addie Bemas went to Gouverneur today to attend the Commencements today & tomorow. Erwin Harmon, their son,

376

graduates from the high school in Gouverneur. He intends to go to the Hamilton College the first of September.

Tuesday, June 21   A hard thunder shower this morning while the men was gone to the factory but pleasant this afternoon & quite warm. Wm has been making frames for screendowers today. A man by the name of Bicnell from Potsdam cald here this afternoon. He was canvasing for fruit trees & curents & gooseberies & grapes & strawberies & cheries & etc. I have made a frock for Sherman this afternoon. I done my work & Baking this forenoon. Washed windows & put in screens. Wm bought a package of envellopes today when he went to town. He agreed to buy some gooseberry bushes of the agent today. He is to send them in the Spring.

Wednesday, June 22   It has raind nicely though the night. A few slite showers today. It is a nice growing time. Evry thing looks lovely. Sherman sold his od [old] stear to Will Woodcock today for beef. He kild it this afternoon. He sold it for 6 cents & a quarter a pound when dressed. It weight 3.40 without the Hide. Wm has finished one screen door & got it Hung & all in good working order. I cut a coat for Sherman today. Sherman went to school this forenoon & stayed to Travers this afternoon. Alex Kerr brout home the rollers today for mooving the barn.

Thursday, June 23   It raind in the night but it has been pleasant today untill near nite. It clowded over & looks very much like rain. Some hard showers gone around to the South. Wm finished both of the new screen Doors today & hoed in the garden this afternoon. Clarence came up this morning on the milk wagon & took our Nelly Horse & Alvah's Buggy & drove her to his father's & drew lumber from the plaining mill all day. Came home with her at five. He is staying all nite. I have been making a coat for Sherman today but did not finish it. Sherman took a colt of[f] from the road & put it in the barn.

Will Woodcock came & took it away.

Friday, June 24   it has raind some today & pleasant part of the time.   Wm hoed in the garden this forenoon & took a good sleap this afternoon.   John Laidlaw cald here today on his way home from Gouverneur.   He stayed to dinner & near 3 o'clock. I done my Ironing this forenoon & other work & this afternoon I finished Sherman's coat.   Jessie Blount, our teacher, cald here today noon.

Saturday, June 25   it has been quite showery today.   I have been painting today the screens & quite a lot of other things. Thare is a strawbery festival in the Union Church to night. Alvah came today & took 3 bushels of wheete to mill.   He was here to super.   He helped Wm & Sherman look over potatoes. Will Woodcock payed Sherman 10 dollars on the Stear this morning.   Wm got 25 dollars Cheese money today.   I sold 2 dozen of eggs to Jene Shay for 20 cents today.

Sunday, June 26   This has been a lovely day.   We had a lovely Shower last nite at 6.   We attended Church today.   Dr. Lee of Canton Preached this forenoon.   Then we attended the funeral of Dan Noble's litle girl.   She was 7 years old.   The funeral was held in the Methodist Church.   Mr. Haris [Harris] Preached.   A goodly number of the Union People atended the funeral & also Dr. Lee but they did not ask him to a seat in the pulpit.   Thare was a large party at the Union Festival last evening.   They sold ice cream & strawberies.   Sat 3 tabels 3 times over.   They took in about 15 dollars.   It is pay on the new organ.   Lee will preach this evening in the new Church.   I cald in to Charley Brown's today.

Monday,   June 27   This has been a beautiful day.   Wm & Sherman cultivated the field Potatoes this forenoon.   Then Wm hoed them in the afternoon.   12 roose [rows].   Sherm went to School.   I done my washing this forenoon & cleand

378

the oil cloth carpet in the dineing room & the pantry floor & the kitchen this afternoon. Will Woodcock payed Sherman the other 10 dollars for his stear today. Bower made us a call today noon & took dinner & then went to our school this afternoon. Urban Webb & Rhoda Grant was maried the 22 of June. He brout her home to his mother's today.

Tuesday, June 28 One more lovely pleasant day. Quite warm. Wm hoed Potatoes this forenoon & visited with Mr. Absalans [Absolom's] folks this afternoon. They came here at 10 o'clock this forenoon. They Payed Wm $26 that he was owing to Wm. They live 12 miles from here in the town of Fowler. I made Pies & Puding this forenoon before they came. I had my dinner started so I had quite a while to visit with them. Sherman quit the school this forenoon. Thinks he will not go anymore this term. I wrote a letter to John Roach this morning to Fine [NY].

Wednesday, June 29 One more pleasant day. Begins to need rain. Roads quite dusty. Wm & Sherman finished Hoing the Potatoes & sprinkled them with Parish Green this afternoon. I have done lots of Baking today. Bread, pies, & Cookies this forenoon after doing my morning work. Then this afternoon I painted the kitchen floor & got supper. I am tired enough to go to bed. Maggy Worthington & a Mr. Kilbern of Fine was maried today. Both of Fine, NY.

Thursday, June 30 One more hot dry day. Mercury up to 90 this afternoon. This is the last day of June. How swift the year has gone past. One year ago today it was about as warm & dry as it is today. John & Altha Laidlaw made me a visit that day but I have had no company today but my litle grand children Mabel & Manie & Mary Brown & Minnie Hooper. A nice lot of girls as thare is in this town. Wm went to town this morning. He paid a note of $100 to H. Rushton that he hired of him last April. He fixt fence this forenoon & puld yelow weeds out of the grass this afternoon. Sherman took a good sleep this afternoon. He had the headache.

Friday, July 1   One more warm dry day. No rain yet. Wm & I took a ride out this morning up to Mr. Reaford's on the S. Rice farm. Stayed about 2 hours & then came to Abner Rice's & made a visit. Took dinner thare. Got home at four o'clock all tired out & nearly melted. They gave me a pail of goosberies all looked over. I cand them tonight. Will Brown cald here tonight & got the money on a town order of Wm. Old Mr. Steven Eastman was beried last nite in the ground at Edwards by the side of his wife & daughter.

Saturday, July 2   One more warm dry day. No rain. Some wind. Mercury 90. Wm & Sherman has puld cale & diszes [kale and daisies] part of the time [out of the kale] & slept the most of the time between Chours. I have not done much today. Clarence stayed here last nite. The paper gives acount of great fires in the western Cities & in Virginia.

Sunday, July 3   Oh what a hot dry day this has been. Mercury went up to 94 this afternoon. We went to Church today & Sunday School. A Baptist studant from Hamilton College preached today. He intends to preach in the Union Church untill September. The Methodist had preaching in their Church today. We could hear him preach in our Church. The window was open. They have got one of the wide awake preachers this time. He is a big fat man & has a very strong voice.

Monday, July 4   One more dry Hot day. Celebrations in every town around but not any in Edwards only a dance & plenty of drunken men & plenty of fighting among the rowdies. Wm & I went to town & stayed nearly all day. I helped do the milking tonight for the first time this season. Sherman & Clarence went to Fine with P. H. Brown & family to the celebration. Wm & Sherman went to town this evening to look on & see the Catle show. I stayed at Home alone. The Methodists had a picnic in the grove. They ask everyone to come & bring a lot of provisions & pay 25 cents for their dinner. They was getting money to pay on their Church that was one of the ways.

Tuesday, July 5   Very warm this forenoon. Has been looking like Showers this afternoon & did come a litle shower at five o'clock. We are very thankful for it & hope for more rain tonight. I done my washing this forenoon & painted over my kitchen floor this afternoon. Wm commenced to cut his hay on the road side & in the yard today. The School teacher cald here today noon.

Wednesday, July 6   A pleasant day. No rain. Wm finished cutting the grass in the front yard today. Willy Newton is sick with quinsy [quinsy]. Wilber Dumas is crazy from the hurt he got on his head whare Rob McFeran struck him with a stone the fourth. The doctor says he is likely to die anytime. McFeran has gone to Canada. That was a part of the performance on the fourth of July. That is what whiskey does & Tom & Albert Cousins was in the row. They was drunk.

Thursday, July 7   This has been a nice day but very warm but lots of wind, no rain. Fearful dusty on the roads. Wm drew in 2 load of Hay this afternoon. Bower Brown worked here today helping with the Hay. Sarah Brown made us a visit today. I got a letter from Pedler Phillips today with samples of black silk. I answered the letter tonight & sent a sample to him to Watertown. It will go out tomorow.

Friday, July 8   Oh what a hot day this has been. Mercury up to 96 & no rain. Wm & the boys have cut & drew in 2 load of Hay. It is so hot they can't work mutch. I have not done anything but to get the meals & wash my dishes & cans &

pails & done some mending. We got the sad news this morning that Mary Allen Woodcock is dead. Bill Noys has gone to Gouverneur with his herse [hearse] to bring her remains here to be beried by the side of her first Husband, Alax [Alex] Morisson.[Morrison] She maried Asa Woodcock for her 2nd Husband & went to Michigan. Died thare with consumption. She was a daughter of George Allen the land agent of Edwards.

Saturday, July 9   A teribel wind all day and very Hot. Mercury up to 90 at noon in the shade but looked very much like Showers & the rain came at 3 'clock. The mercury went down to 80 in a very short time & it is just lovely now at 6 after the shower. It thundered some & a teribel gale of wind when the rain first came. Wm & Robbie Brown & Sherman took in 2 load of hay before the Shower. Then the boys drew in a lot of wood in to the woodhouse to the School house. I have done lots of work today up stairs & down. Calvin Beach died this morning at 2 o'clock. He took a botle of opium & went to sleep & died.

Sunday, July 10   This has been a nice cool day & raind this afternoon. We all attended Church all day. The funeral of Mrs. Mary Woodcock whose remains was brout here from Wisconsin yesterday was largely attended in the Methodist Church this forenoon & the funeral of Calvin Beach was attended in the Union Church this afternoon. The house was crowded.   Mr. Haris [Harris], the Methodist Minister, Preached both sermons. Mr. Liman the young Baptist Student was present & asisted. This afternoon we had Sundy School at noon. Mr. Liman will preach this evening in the Union Church.

Monday, July 11   A lovely day after the rain of last nite. Wm did not do much with the hay today. He fixt his rake to be drawn with two Horses. I done my washing this forenoon &

baked bread & bery Pies & Custerd Pies. Ida Thompson came here today to work for me through the Haying. She is not 14 years old yet but she can help me some. Gid Freeman is cutting the grass in front of here today. Ida has gone to Hi McGill's to make a call to nite since supper.

Tuesday, July 12   This has been a very hot dry day.   A splendid hay day. Our men took in four load this afternoon & put up a lot. Alvah worked here today. Wm has the headache to nite. He has worked too hard. Ida & I have done the work in the House today but no extra work. Wm got his cheese money today. 29 dollars & 64 cents.

Wednesday, July 13   One more hot dry day. Our men has been Haying today. Wm & Alvah & Sherman Brown. Alvah took the big wagon wheels to the shop tonight to get them fixt. Ida Thompson went to town tonite to stay & came up with Sherm in the morning. She is geting homesick. The Masons are having a Court Marshel with Chauncy [Chauncey] Raymond for his bad character. They intend to clean him out of the lodge. It will be setled the next lodge meting so I just heard since I commenced writing. I sent a letter to Newark Nursemen this morning.

Thursday, July 14   This has been a cool nice hay day. Our men took in six load of Hay this afternoon. Alvah & Clarence Brown worked here today. I milked four cows to nite. I made a shirt for Wm today. I done my Baking this forenoon. Wm got the tires set on his double wagon this forenoon. Did not get home with the cans untill eleven o'clock. Sherman kild the calf that got into the mud hole. He thought it would die. It was 3 months old.

Friday, July 15   A nice cool day. Looks like rain. Our men cut a lot of Hay & put it up. Did not draw it in. Alvah & Clarence worked here today.   Mrs. Paulina   Heminway

[Hemingway] cald here to dinner from Gouverneur. Sarah Brown & the children was here all day. I done a lot of Baking today & Ironing.

Saturday, July 16   It raind some in the nite & this morning our men did not do anything with the Haying today but it was a good day after 8 o'clock but at four this afternoon it thundered hard & was hard Showers went all around & sprinkled a litle. Sherman went after beries with Rob & Arther [Arthur] but did not get many. He bought 2 quarts of Leslie McGill. Alvah took our Horses & double Buggy & took his family to Mr. Grant's this afternoon to stay untill tomorow. Charley Brown has his house all plastered & whitewashed over his store.

Sunday, July 17   We had a lovely Shower this morning. We did not go to Church today. Dr. Lee of Canton Preached today in the Union house. His Daughter late from Germany was with him today. She has been learning music. She is a beautiful singer. I had a call from Mr. & Mrs. Albert Eliot & Miss Adiline [Adaline] Woodcock this afternoon. Alvah came home from Grant's about 5 o'clock. He is helping do the milking tonight.

Monday, July 18   A lovely day after the rain. It raind hard last nite. A hard thunder Shower just nite & it raind in the nite & this morning. Our men cut down some hay but did not get any in. Thare is shows to town to nite, Cald Uncle Tom's Cabin. I have done my washing this forenoon & Baking bread & lots of other work.

Tuesday, July 19   This has been a hot pleasant day. A splendid hay day. Our men took in 7 load of Hay but they are nearly melted & all tired out & so am I & I am just the next thing to being sick & have been for a week past. I have no one to do a Chour for me. I have done my work & some mending today. Wm & I did not go to the Show last evening.

Sherman went. He said it was a good entertainment & the Hall was full. Mabel is over to P. H. Brown's today. Bower cald here today. Alvah worked here today.

Wednesday, July 20   One more Hot dry day. Mercury up above 90. 95 yesterday. Our men cut & drew in four load of hay today. I bout 10 lbs of beef of Milo today. Alvah worked here today. Jessie Blount made me a call today. Mr. Hoappers [Hooper's] family got home from New Jersey today. They have been gone over 2 weeks.

Thursday, July 21   A very poor hay day. Clowdy all the forenoon & rainy this afternoon. Alvah cut down a litle hay & they put it up but did not draw any in today. Alvah went home after dinner & Wm went over to Alax Keer's & Sherman helped me put down a carpet in his bedroom. Silas Rice was here today. He said he would send me some beries. I hope he will. P.H. Brown came here today & bought 3 bushels of Potatoes. Payed the money for them. 40 cents a bushel.

Friday, July 22   Our men Wm & Sherman cut hay this forenoon but it raind all of the afternoon or at least a hard & long thunder shower & thare is another one coming now at six o'clock. Erwin Harmon just cald. He's on his way to Gouverneur to bring the Baptist minister from thare to Preach in the Union Church in Edwards next Sunday evening. He gave me a report of the association of 1867 held at Madrid, NY. Next year it will be held at Richville, NY.

Saturday, July 23   This has been a lovely day. Alvah worked this afternoon. They took in four load of Hay this afternoon. I have done my comon work & done some Baking. Cake & Pies. Wm went with the milk this morning. I have read the papers this afternoon & took a good rest. I am feelling so much better than in the forepart of the week. Work is no dread when I feel well. Clarence came up & got some Pine lumber to make shelves in the store.

Sunday, July 24   This has been a lovely day but very warm.
Mercury 90.   We did not go to Church untill evening.   A
Baptist Minister from Gouverneur preached in the Union
House tonight.   Him & Erwin Harmon cald here on their way
from Gouverneur to Edwards & took supper & rested their
Horse a while.   Then we all went to the evening meting.   The
Church was well filed.   We got home at ten.   The Methodist
minister & E. Harmon took a part in the servis.

Monday, July 25   This has been a rainy day all day.   I done
my washing this forenoon & got dinner & done my work &
have not done much of anything this afternoon.   Wm has gone
to town & Sherman has gone to Arba Kerr's.   The girl that
works for Jennie Kerr was maried thare yesterday to a young
Fairbanks, 91 years old.   She is 22.

Tuesday, July 26   What a lovely day this has been. Mercury
up to 90 at [9] 6 to nite.   Alvah worked here today & Clarence
this afternoon.   They cut & took in 5 load of Hay.   Got done
before 5.   Clarence is mowing since Supper & the others are
milking.   I have done my Baking this forenoon & other work.
Caried watter to the barn for the men this afternoon, & I dug
new Potatoes for supper.   The first we have had.   They are not
very large.

Wednesday, July 27   One more hot day.   A good hay day.
Wm & Alvah finished their Haying today at four o'clock.
Alvah worked here today.   Clarence did not come back.   He
stayed here last nite but went home on the milk wagon this
morning.   Sherman says Charley's folks are moving today in
their new rooms over the store & Frank Raymond will
mooved in whare Charley is moving out.   He has bought that
place of Charley Brown. Alvah has worked here 9 days in
Haying.

386

Thursday, July 28   A very hot day but litle wind. Thare was a lite shower about 2 this afternoon & it looks very much like a shower now at 6. This was the last day of our school for this term of 10 weeks. Our teacher was Miss Jessie Blount of South Canton. She cald here today noon & took dinner with us. She has made her Home at P. H. Brown's through her term of teaching. She goes home next Saturday with Perce & Jane Brown. Wm has been puting his reaper in order to reap his oats. He cut around the outside of the field today with the hand cradle & Sherm bound them & set them up.

Friday, July 29   It was misty & clowdy this morning but very hot & pleasant this afternoon. Wm & I made a visit to John McKee's to day. Cald to Charley Brown's on our way home. They are just strahtning [straightening] things after moving. Martha is nearly tired out & sick. Sherman stayed to the village while we went to John McKee's. He would not go with us.

Saturday, July 30   This has been a very warm day. No rain. Wm has cut a few oats this forenoon. Went to town this afternoon horseback. Had a shoe put on Kit. Sherman has been Binding oats this afternoon. I have done a lot of work today. I done my Baking this forenoon. Pies & Cake & Custerd & Bread & all my other work. Mopped my pantry & Dining room & Kitchen this afternoon & knit a nice lot on Sherm's sock.

Sunday, July 31   One more dry Hot day. Mercury up to 100. Mr. Liman, the Baptist student, Preached in the new Church today & this evening. Sherman & I went to Church today. Wm stayed at home. He had the headache. Alvah has come up & took the teem & gone to load up Cheese to take to DeKalb tomorow. Bower is going with him.

Monday, August 1   Oh what a hot day this has been & no

signs of rain. Alvah went to DeKalb with a load of cheese today. Bower went with him. They got home at 6 tonight. I done my washing this forenoon. Wm went to town & got some lumber plaind to make a sink for Martha Brown. 14 litle Pigs today. Mercury up to 90. We have new Potatoes & cucumbers & onions & beets & Beans all new.

Tuesday, August 2   One more Hot dry day. Wm & Alvah & Sherman has been Harvesting oats today.   They cut them down with the reaper & binder. Will Newton is reaping today with his self binder. Mercury 90 & not much wind.

Wednesday, August 3   one more dry Hot day. Mercury at 92. Wm & Alvah & Sherm finished cutting & binding & seting up their oats today. Mr. Frank Allen Died this afternoon. He has been living with Gid Freeman's family for a few years. He was Mrs. Freeman's father. He was not sick, only one day & night. He has been very lame for a number of years. Had to walk with a crutch & cane. They sent for me & Wm to come over when he was diing. He was just gone when I got thare.

Thursday, August 4   Oh what a hot dry day this has been. Quite a lot of wind, but the wind is so dry the dust is deep in the road. We all attended the funeral of Mr. Frank Allen this afternoon at the House of Gid Freeman. Mr. Haris [Harris] the ME [Methodist] minister Preached the funeral sermon. Bill Noys beried him. Thare was 5 sons & 2 daughters attended his funeral & 4 granddaughters & 3 grandsons.

Friday, August 5   A teribel wind all day & very dry. It has looked like rain evry litle while all day & does tonight. Mercury got up to 80 today. Our men cut & put up their wheete today. Their grain is all cut now & some of it is ready to draw in to the Barn. Will Newton cut his grain today & has just gone past with his binder to work for some of the neighbours. He has been away to work cuting grain all of the week out today But today he has worked for himself. A boy to Mr. & Mrs. Harvy [Harvey] Clealand, Edwards, NY.

Saturday, August 6   The beautiful rain came to us last night at eleven o'clock.   A nice thunder shower & it has been just lovely today.   Mercury stood at 70.   Wm has been making a sink for Martha Brown today.   Sherman went to town this forenoon & took a good sleep this afternoon.   I have done lots of work today.   Wm Clealand & wife cald here this afternoon.

Sunday, August 7   A very cool morning.   Mercury down to 50. Just a lovely day for the first Sunday in August.   We did not go to Church today.   Wm & Sherman & Othnal Clealand took in four load of oats.   John & Agness Hughs came up here this afternoon.   Stayed untill near dark.   Dr. Lee of Canton Preached today in the new Church.   Mr. Fairbanks took his wife from Alex Keer's [Kerr's] today.   She has been thare all summer to work.   They are left with out a girl to help.   Keer [Kerr] was looking for a girl today but did not get one.

Monday, August 8   One more nice cool day & very pleasant. Wm is reaping the grain for Wm Clealand & Alvah & Sherman & Arba & Clarence Brown are drawing oats in for Wm.   I have done my washing this forenoon.   Wm did not get done to Clealand's tonight.   Clarence is staying with us to nite.

Tuesday, August 9   A lovely morning.   Cool & pleasant.   Wm B. has gone to Clealand's to finish his grain cutting.   He got home at 2 this afternoon.   Alvah was here to help draw in our wheete.   It looks some like rain.   Mabel Brown made us a visit this forenoon while Charley went to the mines.   Alvah & Sherman took 6 bushels of wheete to mill this forenoon.

Wednesday, August 10   A good harvest day.   No rain.   Wm & Alvah & Sherman finished drawing in the wheete so our harvest in hay & grain is done for this year.   Alvah went home at 3 o'clock. Took our colts & Buggy & drove to Harvy [Harvey] Winslow's after Mania [Manie] Brown. She was up thare for a visit. I have been Baking for the Picnic which is to come of[f] tomorow if it don't rain.

Thursday, August 11   Well, it did rain this forenoon so thare was no picnic. Wm & Sherman & I went to town. We took dinner to Charley's, then Wm came home & I went with Maryette Harmon & made a[n] afternoon visit to Al & Rhoda Wooliver's. Wm came after me at night. Wm payed C. V. Harmon 5 dollars for Mr. Liman, the preacher.

Friday, August 12   A cool pleasant day. Very dry. Wm & Sherman has been mowing the corners of the fences today whare the grain was cut. Alvah took Nell & his Buggy & went to York today. I made a call to Gid Freeman's this afternoon. Bower & Clarence came up & took our Kit horse & took our double Buggy to Jim Shay's for them to go to Gouverneur tonight. Their brother is very sick.

Saturday, August 13   A very cool morning. Mercury at 40. Been very pleasant all day but cool. Wm & Alvah took in one load of hay this forenoon. Sherman has been binding wheete for his uncle Pearce Brown all day. Wm has been working on Martha's sink but did not get if finished. How we do want rain. The dust in the road is like a cloud. Alvah payed me 10 dollars today that he borowed in the 5 of April.

Sunday, August 14   One more dry pleasant day. Not so very warm. Quite cool this morning. Mercury at 45. We attended Church this forenoon & this evening. Mr. Lyman, the Baptist student Preached. He came home with us after meting to dinner. Went home with C. V. Harmon's folks in the evening. Martha Brown stayed with Mrs. Perce Brown all day. She has been sick most of the past week. We did not stay to Sundy School.

Monday, August 15   Hot & dry as usual.   Wm finished Martha's sink today & took it down & set it in place & fixt the pump in, all ready for work. They have their well pump in now so they have both hard & soft water. I done my washing this forenoon. We commenced to eat our new corn the 13 of this month. Sherman has been working for Perce & Newton today.

Tuesday, August 16   A very nice pleasant day but so dry. No signs of rain tonight. Sherman worked for Alax Keer today helping get in grain.   Wm drew a load of wood from the pasture this morning & then went to town with the bay teem & big wagon. This afternoon wokd [worked] over his papers & took a sleep. He got a postal card from Ogdensburg today. The water is nearly dried up in the cow pasture. Storen's folks drives their Catle to the river for drink 3 times a day. Wm went to town to nite.

Wednesday, August 17   one more pleasant day. Quite warm. We all attended the Union picnic today in Todd's grove just back of Hooper's house. All had a good time & lots of good things. A splendid dinner.   Set 3 long tables. Had plenty left. The Methodist preacher & a few of the Methodist Sundy School Schollars met with us. The Baptist students was thare also. We got home about four o'clock. I payed Maryette one dollar for aples.

Thursday, August 18   Well for sure it was raining this morning before daylight & raind some all of the forenoon & we are truly very thankful for the lovely shower & hope we shall get another such soon.   Clarence & Bower was here & Henry Webb today & Robbie Brown. They drew wood with Sherman this afternoon & Wm pild it in the woodhouse. C. V. Harmon sent me a half bushel of aples today by Sherman.

Friday, August 19 What a lovely day this has been after the rain. We got up this morning at 3 o'clock & got our chours done & milk to the factory & got our selves ready at 7 to start for a long ride of 20 miles & back at 7 at night. We all went to a picnic to a place in Diana cald Bony's lake. John Laidlaw & Altho went in company from Pitcairn with us & some from Pitcairn Forks. It was the good tmplers [?] party. Thare was a steam boat on the lake. We all took a ride out on the lake 9 miles. Thare was 30 persons on the boat. When we rode out they could cary 50. We had a splendid time. All took dinner in the Hall of Lake & Bload, the hotell proprietors. Sherman went with us..

Saturday, August 20   This has been a pleasant day. Sherman has been drawing wood & Wm piling it in the woodhouse. Arba Keer helped him this afternoon. Wm had the Headache today. His trip yesterday was a litle hard for him. I never took such a nice ride in the water. The lake was just lovely. A fun day. & before thare was 6 car load of people from Carthage at the same place for a excurtion [excursion] on the lake. Thare is a nice Hotell on the lake shore. Dining hall out over the lake. It is lovely thare. I would like to go again.

Sunday, August 21 A lovely day. Clowdy near nite & looks like rain. We have been to Church today. A Baptist Minister from Richville preached this forenoon & this evening. Mr. Lyman was thare & took a part in the servis. It is his last day to preach here. He startes for his home tomorow then to College the first of September with Erwin Harmon. They go to Madison University. Mercury 70 this afternoon.

Monday, August 22   It was clowdy this forenoon & looked like rain but did not. Only a litle mist. I done my washing this forenoon & made a lot of pickels this afternoon. Wm & Sherman drew wood & piled it in the woodhouse. The beautiful moon is shining over my head while I am writing.

Our cheese was took to the station today.

Tuesday, August 23   A cool clowdy day. Pleasant part of the time. Wm & Sherman finished drawing their wood & packing in the wood house.   Then Sherman went to town hoseback [horseback] & bought him self a pair of Boots. Payed 2.50. I have done my Baking today. Bread & aple & custerd pies & Jell Cake & 2 tins of plain cake.   A picnic tomorrow if pleasant. In Todd's grove for the Methodist Sundy School.

Wednesday, August 24   We have had a nice lot of rain today. A few bountiful showers.   The Methodist Sundy School had just got nicely in to the grove when the rain began. They went to the Hotell & set their tabels [tables] & had as good a time as as they could in the Hall.   Sherm went to the picnic.   We bought a peace of beef of the Pitcairn meat man.

Thursday, August 25   A nice cool pleasant day. Wm thinks thare will be a frost tonight. I have made a shirt for Sherman today. Wm has been sick with the headache today. Sherman has been drawing manure from the Barn into the lot. Celia Haile & Dora Beach cald here today beging [begging] money to buy a present for Smith Chase.   He is the leader to the singers in the Union Church. C. H. Brown & Frank Raymond went to Syracuse today on the excurtion [excursion] train.

Friday, August 26   A pleasant cool day.   No frost this morning. Mercury at 40 above 0.   Sherman drew out manure all day alone. Wm fixt the stairs that goes into the uper part of grainery [grainary]. I done a large Ironing.   Manie & Mary Brown made me a call today.   They said Henry Grant was out for a visit from Black Lake whare he is making cheese this summer. Alvah is working for John McFeren.

Saturday, August 27   [*see Nancy Brown's comments for Sunday, August 28: she made a mistake in her recording*]

393

What a lovely day this has been. Dr. Lee Preached in the new Church today. Sherman went in the morning & evening. Wm & I took a ride out to John B. Absolom's, Fowler [NY] near Sylvia Lake. We brout home a lot of plumbs. We found Rachel much better than we expected to. Clarence & Robbie helped Sherman do the milking. It was all done when we got Home. We met Nathan Shaw going to visit his girl.

Sunday, August 28   Well, I have made a mistake over the other side of this leaf so I will call this Saturday as I have wrote for Sunday. Saturday was a cool pleasant day. I made a visit to Alvah Brown's in the afternoon & a call in Sister Hall's. I walked down thare & home. The first time I have taken such a walk this summer. Wm & Sherman went to town to attend a Caucus & Sherman went back in the evening.

Monday, August 29   Pleasant this forenoon. A litle frost. It raind a short shower this afternoon. I did not do my washing today. I cand [canned] 40 pounds of plumb sauce & done lots of work. Wm went to town this afternoon. Bought a pound of mustert [mustard] & some camphor. Alvah & Sherman took a load of straw to Dr. Goodnough this forenoon. John & Agness Hughs got home from Deer River tonight. They came from Carthage to Harisville [Harrisville] on the cars. Will Brown went thare and brout them home.

Tuesday, August 30   Oh what a lovely day this has been. Cool this morning but quite warm this afternoon.   I done my washing & Baking this forenoon & got dinner ready at eleven & then at 12 started to go to Mr. Winslow's funeral. Bower drove the Horse for me.   Mr. Haris, the Methodist Preacher, preached the funeral sermon in the Union Church. Wm Green from Hermon was out to Edwards with his Herse & beried him. Wm has been fixing his stable floor today so he could not attend the funeral. Alvah was up this morning & took Nelly & went to York to his Cheese factory. Got back at five to night.

Wm gave Sherm 10 shillings in money to take to the [fair].

Wednesday, August 31   This has been a very pleasant day but it is very dry.   This is the first day of the Gouverneur fair. Thare has been a large number gone out today but tomorow will be the crowde.   Charley & Erwin Harmon cald here this morning on their way to Gouverneur.   Erwin startes for college, a five years term in the town of Hamilton in Madison Co.   Robbie [Brown] cald here to night.   Clarence came up to stay all night to start early to go to the fair.   Sherman is going with him.   Arther Freeman & Rob Brown is going together & Arba Kerr & Othnal [Othnel] Clealand.   Alvah has worked here today helping fix the stable [stable] floor.   We have set our milk tonight to make some Butter.

Thursday, September 1   A pleasant day but to night it looks like rain.   Lots of folks gone to the fair today.   Clarence & Sherm got home at nine this evening.   Sherman brout us a very large nice watermelon.   I payed 3 shillings for it.   Sarah Brown & the girls & Mrs. John Kerr made me a visit today. Wm went with after [not legible] today.   We set the milk 2 days.

Friday, September 2   It was raining hard this morning when we got up & has raind nearly all day & is raining this evening. Wm & I made a visit to Sister Johnson's today.   We had a long ride of 10 miles.   Soon after we drove over the Bridge by the sawmill it all fell in so we had to come around home by South Edwards on this side of the river.

Saturday, September 3   A cool day.   Well Wm took the milk today to the factory.   He drove through the river.   It is a very rough rhode.   Wm & Sherman has not done much of anything today but the Chours.   Frank Barnes & Ida Woodcock was maried in Gouverneur today by Rev. H Schwartz.

Sunday, September 4   This has been a cool pleasant day. We attended the funeral of Ellis Hall this afternoon. We drove through the river with the Buggy & I rode over [*on a boat perhaps*]. It was a Horid place to go through. I have wrote a letter to send to A. P. Johnson today. I scum 20 pans of milk this morning & washed the pans.

Monday, September 5   A lovely day. No rain since last week, a Fryday. Wm & Sherm has been diging the Potatoes in the garden today. They had 20 bushels in one of the gardens. Thare will be about 10 in the other garden. Wm done a churning this forenoon. I scum 35 pans of milk this morning & washed the pans & worked the Butter. I did not wash today. Wm bought a half Bushel of Pears today of a Pedler. Gave one dollar for them.

Tuesday, September 6   Quite a warm day. It has looked like rain today. I done my washing this forenoon. I peared [pared] & cut up Pears ready to can this afternoon. Wm & Sherman took the corn & onions & Pumpkins & evry thing out of the garden ready to turn the cows into the meadow. Oscar Allen cald here this afternoon. He & his family was visiting to Gid Freeman's. His sister Mary is Gid's wife. The men in town are working on the new Bridge now evry day. I bought 3 scains of yarn of the wool pedler today. Paid 35 cents for it. Thare was 15 nots.

Wednesday, September 7   It raind before daylite this morning. Quite a thunder shower. No rain through the day but a teribel wind all day. Just a perfect gale. I have cand my Pears & made pumkin pies & apple pies & done lots of other work. Perce Brown came here this afternoon to get Wm to make a Bolster for his waggon. Wm & Sherman made fence on the side of the rhode this forenoon.

Thursday, September 8   Cloudy this forenoon & quite cool

but pleasant this afternoon. I made a visit to Alax Keer's this afternoon. I found Emmy Webb & Addie Payne thare for a visit. Wm has been making a bolster for P. H. Brown today. Sherman has been drawing away the rubbish & dry boards from the Barn to the Sugar House for kindle wood. They have got the stable [stable] all done for this fall. Jennie Keer [Kerr] & Sarah Brown made a visit to King Payne's yesterday. Crossed the river in a boat. I got a letter from Abel [Johnson] today from Pine Valley.

Friday, September 9   A hard wind all day & cold. Wm & Sherm was working in the stabel fixing it whare the colt fell through. I done lots of work around the House. Had Baking & Ironing. It began to rain at 5 o'clock tonight. The men finished the Bridge today, near the sawmill. They have been done week at work on it & do not know how many men has been at work. We turnd our cows in to this meadow today for the first time this fall. A baby to Frank & Jennia [Jennie] Johnson today.

Saturday, September 10   This has been a nice cool pleasant day after the rain. It raind all night. Wm & Sherman has been working in the stable all day again.

Sunday, September 11   This has been a lovely day. Very pleasant. We did not go to Church today. Charley & Martha & the children came here after the Sundy School. Stayed untill nearly dark. Bower is staying all nite. George Allen & his family came to Gid Freeman's today to make a 2 day's visit. He resides in Pitcarn [Pitcairn]. He is Mrs. Freeman's Brother.

Monday, September 12   This has been a rainy day but not very much rain. Just misty. Wm & Sherman fixt the line fence here between him & Alex Keer [Kerr]. I done my washing this forenoon. Our school commenced today. Carie

Stevens is the teacher. She boards to Will Newton's. Only 7 schollars today. Clarence & Bower commenced to go to school today to the village. Mr. Haris his daughter is teaching a Select School in Had Gardener's Hall over his store. The steem threshers are to Mrs. Rob Webb's today & Shefners.

Tuesday, September 13   It raind some this forenoon but is pleasant this afternoon & lots of wind. Wm commenced to Plow today. The ground is to[o] dry yet for plowing. Sherman helped with the threshing to Wm Clealand's today. The thresher has gone to Jim Webb's this afternoon. Wm went to town this morning with the milk. He brought my watch chain from Charley's. They got it mended. Very nice. Thare is a watch tinker doing such work in a part of the store. I have done a lot of baking pies today, six pumpkins & 2 apple Pies.

Wednesday, September 14   Rainy this morning but after 10 o'clock it was pleasant all the rest of the day. This is the first day of the Canton fair. Wm dug 10 bushels of Potatoes this afternoon & picked them up. Got home at four o'clock. Sherman went to school today for the first day. He & Arthar[Arthur] Freeman. I done my Ironing & other work & made a pair of under pants for Wm. Bower came up to stay all night & get some potatoes.

Thursday, September 15   This was a lovely pleasant day untill 3 o'clock then it began to rain a little. At half past four it raind hard so our men came home to supper. Thare was five of them diging Potatoes. Wm & Sherman & Alvah & Perce & Robbie Brown. All Browns. Alvah got word from Davis of York yesterday that he did not trade so Alvah cannot get Davis to sell to him now. Alvah was intending to buy Davis' house & lot in York & so work his factory next year himself.

Friday, September 16   This has been a very pleasant cool day.

398

We think there will be frost tonight. Our men finished diging their Potatoes this afternoon at 3 o'clock. Alvah & Robbie Brown worked here today. Sherman sold a pair of boots to Rob for his day[s] work and Sherman will work for Perce tomorow to pay for Rob's work yesterday. I made some crab apple sauce today. Arther [Arthur] Freeman brought me a sack full of apples. Bower was here tonight to supper & he picked up the small potatoes for the boys. The ladies cleand the Union Church today. I did not help. I could not get away. This is Alvah's birthday. He is 41.

Saturday, September 17   This has been a lovely day. Not very warm but pleasant. Wm has had the sick headache all day so he did not plow any, but he had a job to look after the cows. He turnd them in to the rhode to feed & he had to keep them from going away. Sherman worked for Perce Brown today. Alvah took the colts & double Buggy & he & Sarah & the children made a visit to Charley Freeman's. They cald here a few minutes when they came home & walked from hear [here] down home. A hard frost this morning.

Sunday, September 18   Oh what a lovely day this has been. Not a clowd to be seen today. Sherman & I attended Church today. Wm Stayed at home. Dr. Lee of Canton Preached today in the new church & Mr. Haris [Harris] in the Methodist Church. Thare will be preaching this evening by the same. I made a call in Charley Brown's before meting this morning. Martha has her new carpet all made ready to put down in her Parlor. Cora Jennie fell from of[f] a lader [ladder] up in the barn today & hurt her very bad. She is to Eb Bancrafts [Bancroft's].

Monday, September 19   Not so nice a day as yesterday. Clowdy this forenoon but no rain. Quite cool & this afternoon awful smoky wind north. I done my washing this forenoon & cleaned. Done my Baking this afternoon. I Cleand my dining room carpet & Mopped my Kitchen floor & this evening I have set up & worked untill nine o'clock fixing blankets to keep the flies of[f] the Horses. Wm has been plowing all day. Sherm went to school.

Tuesday, September 20   No rain today.   Quite pleasant. Sherman went to school. Wm was Plowing all day. I done litle of most evrything & not much of anything. I am stewing away because Charley do not send me word about my silk. I sent 16 lbs of sugar to Ira Miles today to pay on the Church organ. 8 cents a pound.

Wednesday, September 21   A very windy day & clowdy this afternoon. Commenced to rain at five o'clock tonight. Wm has been plowing all day. Sherman has been diging Potatoes for P. H. Brown today with Clarence & Robbie. I have done a lot of Baking Pies today beside my other work. Alvah & Sarah has gone to Fowler to John Absalan's for a visit to stay untill tomorow. I bought 3 brooms of a pedler. Gave him 35 eggs for them.

Thursday, September 22   It is clowdy & smoky this forenoon. We had a lovely shower last night at 6. I helped some with the milking before Sherman came from P. H. Brown's. Sherman has gone to help thresh to P. H. Brown's today. The Steem Threshers came thare last night. Jane has got Sarah Payne to help her do the cooking for the rafle. Wm is away to the factory this morning with milk. Charley Noble just cald here to buy our calves. I done my Ironing today & lots of work fixing for the threshers. Alvah & Sarah cald here when they came home this afternoon from Mr. Absalan's. Wm has drawn watter.

Friday, September 23   A very good day. No rain. Cool morning.   The threshers came here at one o'clock this afternoon. I done lots of Baking today. Wm & Sherman drew some water this forenoon & cleand out the barn ready for work. They got our grain all through at dark. Ate Supper at 7. Thare was 15 of all.

Saturday, September 24   A clowdy Cool day but no storm. The threshers went to Gid Freeman's this morning from here & then to Traver's & tonight they mooved to Alex Keer's. We attended at meting tonight. The Universalists are having a asosiation [association] of 3 day meting in the new Church. Thare is a number of Gentlemen & ladies from out of town. I payed to Charley Brown 20 dollars.

Sunday, September 25   A pleasant day but cool. We all attended Church today. A man from Potsdam preached. We intend to go this evening. Mabel came home with us today. I met Mrs. Celia Earl today, a sister of Charley Haile. She has been gone from here 10 years. She lives in Minasota [Minnesota]. She has come on a visit with Willard Earl, her Brother-in-law from California.

Monday, September 26 This has been a pleasant day. A hard frost this morning. I done my washing this forenoon. Sherman went to school. Wm went out to Write Robbinson's & bought 2 pigs & plowd some this afternoon. Charley Harmon & Maryette went to Harisville today to cary her Brother Clark Maltby to take the train for his home in Philadelphia. He Preached to South Edwards last Sundy & Baptised 3 young ladies in the pond near P. Harmon's.

Tuesday, September 27   One more cool pleasant day. Wm dug the Potatoes in the garden. Sherman went to school. I made a visit to Sister Phila Harmon's. Maryette was gone to Harisville. I drove my own Horse to day. Got home at 3 o'clock. Mrs. Hi Bancraft & Mrs. Alex Keer [Kerr] cald here this afternoon. I got a letter from Charley Johnson of Ill.

Wednesday, September 28   Clowdy this morning.   A litle Sprinkle of rain but cleard away & no rain.   Wm has been plowing all day.   Alvah came up with Sherman this morning & brought up his Potatoes & put them in our cellar & then he took Kit & his buggy & took 3 bushels of wheete to mill from here.   Sherm went to school today.   I done some Baking of Pies.   I got a letter from A. P. Johnson today.   He sent 30 dollars interest to Wm.   Sherm has gone to town to the shows.

Thursday, September 29   One more dry smoky day.   The grass is nearly dried up.   No fall feed at all.   Wm has been drawing manure from Dr. Goodnough today.   Sherm went to school.   I wrote a letter to send to A. P. Johnson.   I have done my work & a large Ironing.   Sherman has gone to town tonight.

Friday, September 30   A very warm pleasant day.   Very dry. Wm Plowd all the afternoon.   Cleand out the well in forenoon. Willber Dumas helped him for 50 cents.   Sherman went to school.   I took a horse & Buggy & went to town.   Cald to Mr. Richmir's & to Sam Rushton's & to Charley Stevenson's store & to Charley Brown's store.   I traded seven dollars & 32 cents & turned 10 dollars on the check that Wm let him have.

Saturday, October 1   This has been quite a rainy day.   A few litle Showers.   We are so very thankful for a litle rain & would be glad if it would rain 2 or 3 days.   It has been so nice & warm.   It is raining this evening.   Wm received 30 dollars of A. P. Johnson.   Interest on a note & 18 dollars of Thomas Todd one day this week.   Interest money.   Mrs. Cornelia Rushton is very sick.   The neighbours in the village does not think she will live more than two months.   She is failling with Consumption.   Alvah Brown & Tom Grant went to Rensalear Falls today.   Alvah cald on my cousin Nor Brown.

Sunday, October 2   What a lovely day this has been.   It raind a very litle in the morning & it is so nice & warm.   The grass is looking quite green. Sherman & Wm has gone over to Chub Lake with a horse & Buggy for a ride & to dig some roots to make a sirup. They got home some past one. Bower Brown came up after Sundy School. Stayd untill near night. He & Sherman took a ramble over on the Hills with granpa's shotgun. Sherman shot one chic mnk [chipmunck] the first animal he ever shot. Wm shot a cat this morning in the Barn. I have been at home all day. Dr. Taylor had the misfortune to loose his best Horse last week. Had a nice Shower this afternoon.

Monday, October 3   It was nice & pleasant this morning but was raining before ten o'clock & has been showers quite often since. It is raining hard now at 5 o'clock. Wm & I was envited to A. P. Brown's to dinner today. We went at eleven & stayed untill nearly four. We viseted with Mr. Grant & W McBrier from Michigan. He is out on a visit. I done my washing this forenoon before I went away. Wm Plowed awhile this morning before the rain. Sherman drew the milk & went to school. Alvah Brown went to DeKalb today with Grant's Horse & Buggy. Had not got home when we came away.

Tuesday, October 4   One more rainy day. Not hard rain. Wm plowd the most of the day. Sherm drew the milk & went to School. I done my Housework & cut a pair of Pants. for Sherm & got them most made. Alvah has ofered H. Johnson 1200 dollars for his House & lot in York near Alvah's cheese factory. Johnson wants 1500 for it. Noris Davenport is badly Hurt. I got a letter from Susia [Susie] Clair of Pine Valley [NY] today.

Wednesday, October 5   It was quite pleasant this forenoon but it raind this afternoon. The rhodes are quite muddy. Wm finished plowing his stuble ground this afternoon. I finished Sherm's Pants this afternoon & made 5 pumkin pies. Sherman went to school & helps with the Chours every day. Clarence sold his yoke of steers today to Jim Alverson.

Thursday, October 6   It was pleasant this forenoon but rainy this afternoon. Sherman went to the factory & then took Fred ['] Colt & Buggy & took me to Sim Richmire's [Simeon Richmyer] to get my silk dress cut & made. Alma is making it. I stayed thare to Dinner & then I came over to Jim Rushton's to see Cornell. She is very sick. Not expected to live but a few days. Dr. Wilson of Gouverneur says thare is no help for her. Wm came after me at 3 o'clock with the colt. He had been making a rhode to the back lot.

Friday, October 7   This has been a good pleasant day. No rain. Clarence got forty-two dollars for his stears. His granpa Brown gave the stears to him when they was calves & kept them for him untill now. They was 2 years old last Spring. Wm has been making a rhode to his back lot. Sherman has gone with Arther[Arthur]Freeman to town tonight. Thare is a Harvest Dance to the Hotell tonight. The Fullerville Band came out to play for them.

Saturday, October 8   This has been a nice pleasant day. Just a sprinkle of rain at noon & then all pleasant again. Wm & Sherman has been working on their rhode through the back lot. Wm fell of[f] the load of logs he was drawing. Hurt his side. Sherman took four Bushels of Wheete to mill this morning on the milk wagon. He & Wm went after the flower [flour] tonight. I have done lots of work today. Had Baking Pies & mopping & Ironing & mending & numerous other things. Wm got a letter from Stilman E. Brown of Dakota today. Pedler Phillips cald here today & a Pack Pedler. I did not trade any.

Sunday, October 9   This has been a lovely day. Quite warm. No preaching in the Union House today. Wm & I went to Jim

Rushton's to day at 10 & stayed untill 3 o'clock. We found Corneell very low. She had a very bad spell in the morning. They thought she was dead but she came to & was alive when we came home. We found the room full of friends, George & Mary Phelps, her Brother was thare with others & the Dr. & H Rushton & wife. Thare was 20 diferent callers in thare today. That was to [o] many for one day. Wm took dinner to Bartlet's. I wrote a letter to send to Susia [Susie] Brown to Pine Valley to since I came home.

Monday, October 10   This is Wm's birthday, 63 years old. This has been a rainy day. It raind in the night. Wm went to town with Sherman when he took the milk to the factory & cald at the blacksmith shop & got his Plow colter fixt then he done a litle Plowing between showers. I done my washing this forenoon. Spread my cloths on the grass. Sherman went to school. Litle Mary Brown came here from school this afternoon sick. We got a ride for her Home with a couple of agents. It was raining hard. Nathan Shaw cald here this morning & Payed me 5 dollars in money for some seede wheete he bought here last Spring. I have dressed two chickens this evening. I am very tired. Corneel Rushton was a litle better this morning.

Tuesday,   This has been a nice pleasant cool day. Wm has been plowing all day. Sherman went to School. Bower Brown came up this afternoon. He is staying all night. The teacher went to Alex Keer's tonight to stay. Arther Freeman & Othnal Clealand cald tonight for Sherman to go Hunting but he did not go. Bower & his granpa played four games of chequers [checkers] tonight.

Wednesday, October 12   A cool pleasant day. It was clowdy this morning & had been snowing in the night. The bridge & every board of the fences was white with snow, the beautiful snow on the morning of the 12th of October. That is giving us

405

a broad hint that winter is not far distant. Wm has commended to feed his catle hay & will feed regular twice a day from now untill the midle of next May. It will be seven long months. Wm has been plowing all day. Sherm to school. I have been fixing over a dress but did not get it done. Clarence came up tonight to supper & to stay all night. He & his granpa had a big time at playing chequers [checkers]. Mrs. Jim Rushton is some better.

Thursday, October 13 It raind in the night again but was cold this morning & all day. Wm plowd all the forenoon but it has raind nearly all the afternoon. A hard thunder Shower at 2 o'clock & at half past 3. Wm went to town this afternoon to get one of the Horses Shod. I have done my Ironing & mopping & other work this forenoon & this afternoon I made 5 pumkin Pies & cleand the Pantry. Mooved a lot of Sugar to get ready for the milk. Will soon be left at home to make butter. Nathan Shaw brout us 3 Bushels of apples tonight. Wm payed him 15 s for them. Wm got his Cheese money today. $22.90 cents payed for 43 lbs of cheese out of it.

Friday, October 14 This has been a cool but a good day. Clowdy but no Storm. The sun shone part of the time. Wm has been plowing all day. Sherm went to school this forenoon. Went with me this afternoon to town. I went to Simeon Richmires [Richmyer's] to try on my dress that Alma is making for me. I cald in Jim Rushton's to see Corneel. She is no better. Then I cald in Charley's Store. I bought 2 lbs of Butter. Payed him 60 cents in money, 5 cents of it for a spool of thread. Sarah Brown rhode home with me as far as her House. Martha & Jane Brown made a visit to Charley Haile's this afternoon. I paid Alma 5 dollars today for making my dress.

Saturday, October 15 This has been a pleasant day but cool. A heavy frost this morning. The hardest thare has been this fall. Wm has been plowing all day or since nine in the morning. Sherm worked in the forenoon & went a hunting in the afternoon but did not shoote any dead thing. Bower was here when Sherman got home & Bower shot of[f] the gun. I have done lots of work today making cake & apple pies & a pan of cookies & washing windows & cleaning the floors & pearing [paring] apples to stew for sauce & all the other work. Wm & Bower has been playing chequers checkers all the evening.

Sunday, October 16   This has been a lovely day. I have been at home all day.   Sherman took a ride to his uncle Wm Clealand's with his colt & Alvah's Buggy.   Martha & Clarence & Bower & Mabel Brown came here after Sundy School. Stayed until night. Charley did not Come today. He was out with Jim & Shay down to the mines. Rwley [Rawley] Todd & Charley Webb was here for a ride this afternoon with Todd's horse & Buggy.   Had scind [skinned]out when his father was milking so that he would not see him. Wm wrote 3 letters today. I wrote one to Laura Brown & S.E. Brown of Dakota. Wm sent one to Wm Green & one to Wm Andrews of Gouverneur & S.E. Brown.

Monday, October 17   This has been a nice lovely day untill Just night. It has clowded up some & the wind is Just howling & looks like rain. I done my washing this forenoon & pealed apples this afternoon & read the paper & done my work. Wm has been plowing all day. Sherm went to school. Clarence came up tonight to stay all night & got a straw tick filed. Alvah went to York today with Charley's Horse & Buggy. Tom Cousins & Albert was arested before daylite & took to Canton to answer to an asault on the Constabel last Fourth of July in a fight between Dumas & Jack McFeran. Jack is at large yet but they are on the lookout for him.

Tuesday, October 18   It raind in the night. Has not raind any today. Been clowdy most of the time. A litle cooller than yesterday but is very pleasant this evening. A new moon. It looks warm. Clarence came up to stay all night & brout his new gun. He & Sherman & a lot of boys are out hunting this evening. Wm has been Plowing all day. I have been working about the house all the forenoon & worked on my dress this afternoon & wrote a letter to send to Fine. We had chicken & dumplings for dinner. Mary & Manie Brown came up from School & ate dinner with us. John Cousins went Bail for his brothers. So they all came Home untill the next Court.

Wednesday, October 19   What a lovely day this has [been]. Alvah helped Wm blast some big stones from the ground whare he was Plowing. Sarah & the children was here today. Bower is here tonight. Sherman went to school.   Lester Clealand went in to the schoolhouse through whare a lite [lot] of glass was broken out & put wood in the stove & left part of it out & the doors wide open & Sherman went & shut the stove doors & made all rite.   Wm got a letter from Enos Stanton & Matilda today. They sent him 12 dollars in money to pay the Interest on a note. They have had the money most two years & he wants to kep [keep] it one more year.   It is $150.

Thursday, October 20   What a lovely day this has been. Quite a lot of wind but warm.   The wind is blowing quite Hard tonight. Wm finished his fall Plowing today. Alvah came up this afternoon & took the colt & his Buggy & drove down to Henry Brown's Cheese Factory. Bower & Mabel was here to Supper tonight. Clint and Leslie McGill was here this evening to play chequers [checkers] with Wm & Sherman.   I have done lots of Hard work today. There has been a gang of men surveying for the Railrhode from Gouverneur to Edwards today. They are all staying to the Hotell tonight.

Friday, October 21   This has been a clowdy & showery day.

Raind hard in the night. The rhodes was very muddy today. Wm & I made a visit to Andrew Clealand's today. Got home at four. It rained a hard shower while we was thare. Mrs. Jim Rushton Died this morning about nine o'clock. Sherman drew the milk & went to School. Albert Farrell cald here this afternoon to get a Job of Chopping Cord wood of Wm. He Hired him to chop 40 cord at 50 cents a Cord & we board him.

Saturday, October 22   A cold windy & clowdy day. Snowed a litle this morning. Sherman took the milk to the factory today for the last day this year. Wm & Sherman went to town this afternoon. Sherman brought home the whay [whey] for the last time this fall. Wm stayed in town untill four o'clock. He got 12 dollars in money of John McFeran that John was owing him. He lent Tomy [Tommy] Todd 100 dollars today & hired of Bartlet & 20 dollars. Mrs. Rushton will be beried tomorow. Funeral at one at the House.

Sunday, October 23   Quite a cold day. Rather pleasant this morning. It is raining tonight. We attended the funeral of Mrs. Jim Rushton this afternoon. The Methodist Church was crowded. Mr. Haris Preached the funeral Sermon & Dr. Lee was envited to the pulpit & took a part. He Preached in the Union Church this forenoon. Wm Green of Hermon was out with his Herse to bry [bury] Mrs. Rushton. A lot of cheese from our factory goes to DeKalb tomorrow.

Monday, October 24   What a teribel wind all last night & today. A very litle Sprinkle of Snow but it is quite pleasant this evening. I done my washing this forenoon. Wm & Sherman done the Chours. Alvah made a call this afternoon. Took home a bag of Potatoes. Clarence is Staying here tonight. Lesley McGill was here this evening. They run two chequer checker Boards. Had lots of fun. I done my work & paird Potatoes & apples & hung out my white cloths. That was my fun & I sponged [spunged] bread. I am fearful tired.

409

Tuesday, October 25   This has been a cool pleasant day. Some wind. Very nice this evening. A lovely moon shining brite.   Have done lots of work today such as Baking & mopping & washing windows & dressing & Cooking chickens & washing dishes & pails & etc. Miss Lizia [Lizie] Webb made me a call this afternoon. Wm went to mill & to the Blacksmith's Shop this forenoon. Got home at 2 o'clock. He took dinner to John Hughs. Cald in Charley's Store. Bought 2 oz of Camphor gum. Brout home 2 bushels of apples that Nathan Shaw left at Charley's Store for us at 50 cents a bushel.

Wednesday, October 26   A nice pleasant day & evening. Wm has been drawing sand all day from Jim Harmon's & one load from near C. V. Harmon's to put at the side of the Hog pen & around the well. I cleand my chamber today & done my Ironing. We all went to town tonight & attended a Republican lecture in D. Nobel's Hall. Two men from Canton, Keeler & Swift spoke. I made a call in Mrs. John McFeren's & in Charley Brown's & in the store. I bouht a ruch [ruche] for the neck of my silk dress [at] 12 cents. Wm has done Chours & tinkered around today. Went to the mill & got a eave spout for the Barn. I scum milk for the first yesterday & today.

Thursday, October 27   A lovely day this has been. Quite warm to what it has been for 2 weeks. I made a false entry at the botom of the page on the other side of this leaf. It was today that Wm went after the eave spouts for the Barn & fixt them on the Barn. I have not done much only my House work today. The men in town has had a squirel hunt today. 2 parties, 15 on each side. Plat Buscart shot two Deer & Henry Grant shot one Deer today. Have not got the news of the number of Squirels yet. Sherman has gone to town tonight. He will learn all about the Hunt. They are all to take supper to the Hotell.

Friday, October 28   This has been just a lovely day & this evening how pleasant & such a beautiful shining moon. Wm has been working for Mr. Bartlet the Cheese maker down town. He got home at 5 o'clock to help milk. Mrs. Alax Keer made me a visit this afternoon & evening. Alax [Alex] & Arba came over in the evening. We all had a good visit. I done a lot of Baking Apple Pies this forenoon & Cleand my Carpet in the dining room & the floor in the kitchen & scum milk & washed pans & pails. Done a lot of work. Just heard they had a girl baby to Had Gardeners. The men in town has not setled the Count on their Squeril Hunt yet. They are having a rough time over it.

Saturday, October 29   Clowdy this morning. Commenced to rain at ten o'clock. Wm went back to town this morning to finish the Chimney. Sherman has gone with Arther Freeman Hunting. Henry Webb & Bower Brown came to go with them. I have scum & washed 25 pans this morning. Jim Rushton got a letter from his daughter from Kansas yesterday. She Intends to come to Edwards in a few days. She had not heard of her mother's death when she wrote. Arba Keer brought me a nice roast of fresh Pork this forenoon & Lesley McGill brot me a peace of fresh Pork this afternoon. It raind untill 3 o'clock & then it began to snow & it came down nicely for a while.

Sunday, October 30   Quite cold this morning & all day. Clowdy but no storm. The ground was white with Snow today. We fear that winter is near at hand. How we dread the cold winter weather. We hear of fearful snow storms in Mich [igan] on the Lakes the 24th of this month. Last year the snow & cold weather set in the 7th of November. That was plenty soon enough. We all stayed at home today & had no Company but Lesley McGill. He came up in the morning & brought me a nice sparerib & he stayed all day. He & Sherman took a trip out in to the sugar woods but did not stay long. I had forty pans of milk to skim & to wash. It took me all of the forenoon.

411

Monday, October 31   Milder today. The snow is all gone & it looks like rain this afternoon. Wm done the Chours this forenoon & has gone to town this afternoon. Sherman went to School & helpt with the Chours. I done my washing this forenoon & lots of other work. I had bread to make this forenoon & milk to scim, pans & pails to wash & dinner to get. I had all done at 10 o'clock but the dinner. Wm made a call to James Harmon's this afternoon after going to town.

Tuesday, November 1   This has been a cool pleasant day. Wind north. Wm went to Fine to day. Got home at 2 o'clock. I have been cleaning the woodwork in my dining room today. Alvah Brown made us a call this afternoon. He is preparing to moove out of Mrs. Barnes' House. He has been thare nearly two years. Albert Farell came here today to commence his job of chopping. Clarence is staying here tonight. The boys in town had a big time last night playing Halloween. They done some dirty tricks. John & Agness Hughs went to Gouverneur today. Wm sent a note by them.

Wednesday, November 2   What a lovely day this has been. Quite warm & very pleasant. Alvah came up today & helped Wm dress a beef cow. She was nice & fat. He intends to take it to Fine tomorow. Sherm did not go to school today. He helped his granpa. A Mr. Wm Andrews of Gouverneur called here today & paid Wm Brown 48 dollars in money that he had been owing for 3 years. Albert Farell has been chopping here today. I done my Ironing today & Baking & lots of work. Wm gave me three dollars in money today out of what he got of Bill Andrews.

Thursday, November 3   One more lovely day. Quite mild. I made a visit to Mr. Henry Travers today with Mrs. Jenia Keer. Had a good visit. Took diner with them. Came Home at four. Wm went to Fine today. Took up his Beef & sold it to Richerd

412

Conboy. It brought him 22 dollars. Hiram McGill & family mooved out of Mrs. Storen's House today on to the farm of Had Gardener formely ownd by Robbert Brown, Seigh Clark, the former ocupent [occupant] mooved to Russell today. Albert Farell has been chopping here today.

Friday, November 4   This has been a variety day. All kinds of weather. Raind hard in the forenoon & then pleasany a while, then it snowd a litle but it is very pleasant this evening. Wm done the Churning this forenoon. Albert worked at the chopping this forenoon untill the rain, then he came home to dinner & went back to the woods this afternoon. Wm went to town this afternoon & bought a buttertub & got his Cheese money. 47 dollars. I packed a tub of Butter this afternoon & done lots of work today. Alvah came up today & took the teem & drew up a load of furniture & thing[s] & left them here. He intends to moove next Monday in a part of Mrs. Storen's House.

Saturday, November 5   A very pleasant day but quite cold. Wind north. Very dark this evening. No moon untill near morning. Sherman is away to the village tonight. Wm has done the most of the Chours today. Sherman helped Albert saw wood today in the woods. Clarence & Bower Brown has been here all day hunting part of the time. Alvah drew 2 load of wood & put it in to Mrs. Storen's Wood house & a load of duffel & left it here to remain untill he moves to York. I have tried out the tallow today & mad[e] apple Pies & done lots of work. Albert has gone to town tonight. Wm paid him one dollar on his work tonight. He has cut 5 cord of wood this week.

Sunday, November 6   What a lovely day this has been. A cool wind. The rhodes ar[e] nice & dry. Just splendid wheeling now. We have been at Home all day but Sherman has gone to Church this evening. Dr. Lee Preached today &

this evening in the new Church. Mr. Haris [Harris] Preached in the Methodist Church. Charley & Martha & Bower Brown made us a call this afternoon. Charley went as far as Henry Brown's factory & brought home a cheese. He left it here for a few days. I expect Alvah & family will come here tomorow to stay a few day[s] untill Storen can get the House fixt for them so they can moove in thare.

Monday, November 7   One more beautiful day. Very warm for this time of the year. I do not remember when thare was so warm a day the 7th of November. This was my birthday. I am 62 years old. Wm was 63 the 10th of October last month. Tomorow is Election day. Alvah & family is with us tonight. They have vacated Mrs. Barnes' House today whare they have been living Just 2 years. They have moovd some of their goods into a part of Mrs. Storen's House to stay untill they go to York. Wm & Sherman has been sawing & chopping in the woods today. Albert did not come today to chop. I have done a large washing the forenoon & done a lot of work besides.

Tuesday, November 8   One more lovely pleasant day. A litle cooller than yesterday. Wm drew wood from the woods that he cut yesterday & went to town this afternoon to attend the Election. Sarah & the Children & Alvah & I all went to town. I took my velvet Bonnet to Mrs. McFeran to get it fixt over & we all cald in Charley's Store & in the House. I bought 5 lbs of white sugar & a botle of pepermint extract & Charley Brown made me a nice present of a large Photograph album, price 5 dollars. Wm went to town again tonight & Sherman went Hunting this afternoon & went to town tonight.

Wednesday, November 9   Quite a cold morning but pleasant all day. Wm & Alvah kild one Hog today noon then Wm & Sherman drove 6 calves & 2 cow to town & sold them to a Mr. Millon for 22 dollars. Old Cows. Alvah worked for Storen on the ceilling of their front room overhead. I have had Baking &

414

lots of work today. Wm went to town tonight & got the Horses Shod. Sherm done the milking alone & has gone to town tonight to attend a temperance lecture in the Methodist Church. A man from Wattertown. I had 2 dollars in money today out of the calves & Cow money & I gave Sherman one doller of it.

Thursday, November 10   This has been a rainy day. Wm went to Fine [NY] today & took up the fat Hog that he dressed yesterday & sold it to Conboy, the meat man, for six cents a pound. It [It's] weight was two Hundred & fifty. Alvah painted the Ceilling & woodwork for Mrs. Storen in the room whare he intends to moove in to next week. Alvah & Sherman & Wm done a Churning this afternoon of 30 pounds of Butter. I packed it in Jars for our own yuse. I have made 80 pounds.

Friday, November 11   It was cold & cloudy this morning & before noon it began to snow a litle & this afternoon it has snowd & the wind is blowing hard tonight. Been a cold stormy afternoon & evening. Wm & Sherman went to the woods after getting the Chours done in the morning. Split wood. Got home at 3 o'clock this afternoon then had the night Chours all to do. We had chicking & dumpling for supper. Alvah's family is with us this week. Alvah went to town this afternoon. Worked painting for Mrs. Storen this forenoon. Thare is a hunter's Supper & a dance at the Hotell this evening in town but we are all at Home tonight.

Saturday, November 12   Not a very bad day this [day] but did not thaw any nor Storm. Wm & Sherman went to P. H. Brown's today & drove home the yearlings. Alvah went to town with the Horses & Sled today & brought away his Cook Stove & set it up in Storen's. He went to town this afternoon with the Colt & Buggy to get a rod for his stove. Henry Grant made a call here this afternoon. Bower came up this morning & got a pail of milk. He & Sherman went to town tonight

415

horse back. Bower is Staying here tonight. Sarah & I have done the work about the House. We have made Bread & Pies & cake.

Sunday, November 13 A nice day for the time of year. No storm nor very warm. The fields are white with snow but none in the rhodes today. Nice wheelling. Sherman went home with Bower today with the Colt & Buggy but did not stay any. Then Alvah drove down town this afternoon & got the lining to his Stove tank. He put down his carpet in the front room to Storen's. This was quarterly meting to the Methodist Church today. We did not any of us go.

Monday, November 14 A good mild day. The snow is nearly gone. Good wheeling. I did not do my washing today. Alvah & his family mooved in to their new quarters today whare they expect to stay untill the first of April. Wm drove out to Urbe Keer's today & bought 25 bushels of oats. Paid 40 cents a Bushel & cald in Charley Brown's Store & bought himself a fine overcoat. Payed 15 dollars & a fine suit of Black Cloths & paid 20 dollars for them. I just heard that Mrs. Altha Laidlaw had a shock of Paralasys last Fryday the 11th of November. They sent to Gouverneur for a doctor.

Tuesday, November 15 This has been a nasty rainy day. It is all mud now. Such a suden change this afternoon. It began to snow about 3 o'clock & it is snowing & the wind is blowing quite Hard this evening at 8. I done a large washing this forenoon. Wm & Alvah took a ride to town near noon. Alvah to buy a tank of lamp oil & a can of Coffie & Wm to order a lot of windows of John McFeran in order to double our windows in the lower rooms in our House. Clarance came home with them. He is Staying here tonight. He & Sherman is out for a call this evening. Litle Manie & Mary Brown came up near night & got a litle pail of milk. Wm is reading in the History of the World this evening.

Wednesday, November 16   A hard wind all night last & quite a lot of Snow but not enough for Sleighing but it has been quite mild & nice to day. No Storm. Not much wind. Wm done a Job of plastering for Mrs. Storen today & Alvah Came up & done our Churning this forenoon. I packed the butter in Alvah's crock for his family yuse.   Sherman had a Job of drawing out manure today. Clarence stayed all night. Took home a pail of milk & a hen to cook for their dinner. We had one for our supper tonight. Bower was here to dinner & Alvah, Clint & Leslie was here this evening. Wm & Les had a big time playing Chequers [Checkers].

Thursday, November 17   A high wind all day & this evening. No Storm today. I made a call in Alvah's down to Storen's. Took dinner with Sarah & the Children. Alvah went to the woods today & cut wood for himself & Wm & Sherman done their Chours & then went to the woods & cut wood. The news came in the paper of the hanging of four men in Chicago, Ill & the death of Wm Chadwick of Dakota. He went from Pitcairn 5 years ago.

Friday, November 18   What a Stormy day this has been. The Snow has come down at a fearful rate. Alvah & Sherman went to the woods in the morning but they came home [this] forenoon. Wm went to town in the storm with the horses & Sled. It is quite Cold tonight. Wm brought home my new Bonnet from the Shop today. It is velvet & very nice & he brought the trimings for Sherman's coat. He brought home the trimings for Sherman's Coat, 1 dollar & 5 cents.

Saturday, November 19   The wind blew very hard this forenoon & blew the snow like clowds through the fields & it snowd some this afternoon. Quite a number of sleighs have gone past today but it is very bad traveling any way. Alvah & Sherman went to the woods with the teem & Sled this forenoon & brought out a load of Stove wood for Alvah. Then Alvah & Sarah & the Children went to the village this afternoon to get their bonnets & caps. I have done some Baking pies today & cleaning the pantry & carpet in the Dining room & some mending & reading the paper. Sherman is away to the village tonight with Clint & Lesslie McGill. He brout me a letter.

Sunday, November 20   This has been a very Stormy day but not very cold. The snow Just come down bountiful but it is very pleasant this evening. Wm went to the Cheese factory & brought home a load of Cheese this afternoon for Alvah to take to DeKalb to morow. He went with the Sled. Mercury is 24 above zero tonight. Mrs. Barnes has got mooved back in to her old home from Robert Brown's whare they have been the past year. She is very low with Consumption. Wm wrote a letter today to send to Stilman Brown of Dakota & one to Wm Green of Hermon.

Monday, November 21   It has been Clowdy all day & snowd part of the time. Quite a number of sleighs on the rhode today & some wagons. The last of the Cheese from our factory went to DeKalb today. Alvah went with a load for Wm.   Ed Shefner & Ellia [Ellie] Woolia [Wooley] was maried last week. His wife Died last April. Bower was here today. I cut a Coat for Sherman today & partely made it. I had the patern to Cut from a overcoat out of Charley's Store. It was a hard task.   Clint & Lesslie McGill was here this evening to Play Checkers.

Tuesday, November 22   This has been a lovely pleasant day. Wm & Sherman done the Chours then Sherm went to the woods & helped Alvah Saw some few logs for Stove wood & Wm went to the village. Payed Mrs. McFeren for my Bonnet 1.75 then in the afternoon he & Sherman drew Stove wood to the house from the woods. Alvah took one load to his house

418

at nite. I have been working on Sherman's new over Coat between Chours. Sarah made me a call. Mania [Manie] & Mary Brown & Minnie Hoopper [Hooper] made me a call. Jenia [Jennie] Keer [Keer] made a call to Alvah's this afternoon.

Wednesday, November 23   This has been quite a good day. No storm. Thawd all day. No snow in the rhodes. Some in the fields yet. Wm has been helping Alvah saw wood today part of the time in the woods. Sherman has been drawing Stove wood to the House. I have been working on Sherman's Coat besides doing my work. I baked bread this morning & made seven Pies this afternoon & evening. Sherman has gone to town tonight with Arba Keer [Kerr] & Clint & Leslie McGill. Thare is a band Show from Fine at Dav's [David Noble] Hotell tonight.

Thursday, November 24   Quite a cold wind today. Cloudy & has looked like rain or snow & it is snowing this evening. Wm & Sherman has been doing the Chours & drawing wood. Alvah & family has gone to Tom Grant's today for a visit & to stay all night. I drest 3 chickens this forenoon & cooked 2 for dinner. Worked on Sherman's over coat a litle this afternoon. Robbie & Clarence Brown Cald here this evening & Fred Freeman cald this evening.   Will Brown has commenced housekeeping. He bought 53 dollars worth of Hardware of Frank Raymond & a lot of nice furniture of John McFeran.

Friday, November 25   This has been a mild day. It was Snowing last night when we went to bed & when we got up this morning it was raining. It has thawd all day. It is quite good wheelling this afternoon. Wm drove to town this afternoon & got the papers. Alvah & family got home tonight from Russell whare they have been on a visit since yesterday morning. They made 2 visits. One to Wm Grant's & one to Tom Grant's. Manie did not come home with them. I have worked very hard today. I did not get my Butter worked & packed & Churn washed & kitchen floor mopped untill near eight. Wm done a Churning this afternoon after he got home from town. I intend the butter for Martha.

Saturday, November 26   This has been a nice warm day but Clowdy & foggy but I mad[e] out to finish Sherman's coat this afternoon. I have been all of the week making it besides doing my house work. Wm & Alvah & Sherman & Bower went to the woods & took their dinner & cut & sawd wood. Sherman has gone to town tonight with Clint & Leslie McGill. It is Just lovely out this evening but the mud is deep on the rhodes.

Sunday, November 27   This has been a lovely day. Warm & pleasant just like a May morning. Sherman & Alvah & Mary went to Sundy School & Clarence stayed here last night & he rode down home with them. It was Dr. Lee's day to Preach & he preaches this evening. Charley & Martha & the children came here after Church & Sundy School. Stayed untill night. I gave them a crock of butter 25 lbs to take home with them. Wm & I have stayed at home all day. Tom Grant brought Manie home today & mad[e] a short call to Alvah's. We cut our cheese this morning. It is very good. It weighs 40 pounds.

Monday, November 28   It was snowing when we got up this morning & it has snowd most all day. It is pleasant this evening & has froze some but the rhodes are fearful sloppy & muddy. Alvah went to mill today. Took 6 bushels of wheete, 3 for himself & 3 for me. Wm & Sherman done the Chours & Sherman went to School. This is the first day of our winter term. A Mr. Loux from Hermon is the teacher. Thare was 16 Schollers today. I done my washing this forenoon & cut out a vest & commenced to make it for Sherman. Bower came up today & is staying here tonight.

Tuesday, November 29   Quite a cold morning. Mercury was

10 above zero. It was nice & pleasant this forenoon. Snowd a litle this afternoon. Wm & Alvah kild our other Hog this forenoon. Bower helped some. He helped his granpa pick the fat of the inwards so I did not do anything about it but to put the fat a soak & clean up the muss. I payed Bower 15 cents for his work for me & gave him a 2 pound Cake of Sugar then he took a pail of milk & got a ride home at 2 o'clock. I done a lot of Baking Bread & Pies. 5 Pumkin & 2 Apple Pies. 3 loaves of Bread & nearly finished Sherman's vest. I broke a needle in the mashine so I was run of[f] the track. Sherm has been to School today. He has gone to town this evening with a lot of boys.

Wednesday, November 30   A very cold day. Mercury 10 above Zero today. It has been clear & pleasant. Wm got a letter from Wm Green of Hermon last night. Wm has cut & salted the Pork this afternoon & evening. Sherman has gone to a donation party for the Methodist Preacher, Mr. Harris. Alvah & Sarah went to town this afternoon with the Horses & Sled. The rhodes are fearful rough. It is neither Sleighing nor decent wheelling. Henry Webb & Had Gardener Started to go to Dakota yesterday.

Thursday, December 1   It was a cold morning & all day but pleasant. Mercury was 10 below Zero this morning for the first time this fall. Sherman went to School. Bower was up today & is staying tonight. The minister got 46 dollars in money & quite a lot of produce at the donation last night. Thare was quite a number of the Union people attended the party. John Newton & his wife did not attend. They have got up on their ear about something. Sherman gave 50 cents. Alvah went to town to day & bought a new copper linen[lining] for his reservoy. [water tank in the stove]. I have tried my lard today. I had 5 pans full & boiled the meat for mince pies. It is choped & the apples.

Friday, December 2   A high wind all day. Mercury at Zero this morning.   Alvah went to the woods today & cut stovewood. Sherman went to School. He has gone to town tonight to atend a Good Templers [Templars] entertainment Cald a Division meting. Wm went to town today with the Colt & Buggy. Got the maile & his Cheese money & 2 dollars of Bartlet. Bower Stayed here last night. He went home with his granpa. Took home a pail of milk & a pail of Pickels & a pail of Cream. I have done my Housework. Our Cheese come to 500 dollars the past Season from the first of May to the 22 of October. I have made one Hundred & 30 pounds of Butter since.

Saturday, December 3   A mild nice day. Mercury was up to 30 this morning. It snowd some in the night but has thawd some all day. Wm has been to the village twice today. Mabel came home with him.   Once rode back home with Will Gardener. Wm Brown took one hundred & 15 pounds of Sugar to Charley Brown today. Clint & Leslie McGill spent this evening here. Leslie & Wm had a game of Chequers [Checkers]. Wm got fearfully beat. Mr. Loux, our teacher, cald here today. Sarah Brown made a call this afternoon. Litle Manie & Mary made a visit to Mr. Hoapers [Hooper's] today. Alvah & Sherman went to the woods to day & cut stove wood. Wm got 23 dollars in money today from Wm Green.

Sunday, December 4   This has been a mild day. Mercury up to 50. It is raining hard this evening. I have been at home all day. Alvah's folks & Sherman went to Church & Sunday School. Mr. Haris [Harris] Preached in the Union Church this evening but it was so dark & rainy we did not go. Wm has been gone all day gading. We don't know whare.

Monday, December 5   It has been a clowdy day but not much storm. It turnd colder & froze some this afternoon & snowd a very litle. The stars are shining some this evening. Clarence stayed here last night. Went home this morning. I sent 2 letters with him to the Post Office. Wm has been sick in bed all day today. He gadded around all day yesterday. Took a tramp over to Harmon's & then from thare to the village to Charley's. Viola Harmon cald here after School. This was her first day to school. She would like to come here & bourd this term of the school. Bower is staying here tonight. Mercury was 30 above Zero today.

Tuesday, December 6   This has been a lovely day. Mercury at 30 above. Wm helped some with the Chours & lay in bed the most of the time. Mr. James Harmon made us a call this afternoon. He payed Wm 51 dollars in money. I done my Baking to day. Bread & mince pies. I made a call to Alvah's this evening. Sherman is away to town tonight. Bower went home today. Wm wrote a letter to send to Wm Green of Hermon today. Sherman took it to the office tonight.

Wednesday, December 7   A white frost this morning. Mercury 25 above Zero. It has been a very nice day. Alvah took Sarah up to Cy Clealand's this forenoon with Kit & the Buggy. Got home since dark. The girls came here to dinner & supper. Stayed untill they came home. Wm & I went to town this afternoon. I made a call in John Hughs. Agnes made me a Chrismas Present of a nice tidy for a chair back. Sherman went to School & made a call in Storen's tonight. A pack Pedler is staying thare tonight. A number of teems went to Gouverneur today after apples for Miron Clark. Sister Hall had a new Cook Stove set up in her Dining room today.

Thursday, December 8   Thare was a very litle snow on the ground this morning. Been clowdy all day. Mercury 25 above. It is fearful dark out tonight. Sherman is away to the village. Othnel Clealand & Arthur Freeman cald here tonight for Sherman to go to town with them. Wm Clealand was here today after the scalding Box.

Friday, December 9 What a lovely day this has been. The sun has shone all day. Wm done the Chours & done the Churning. I have took care of the Butter this evening & washed the Churn & mopped the floor & I am ready to go to bed. Henry Grant came here this morning to chop Stove wood with Alvah for Wm Brown. Sarah Brown made me a call today. Urban Webb cald here today & bought a bushel of wheete. Sherman has gone to town tonight with Clint & Leslie McGill.

Saturday, December 10 It was clowdy this morning. At 10 it began to rain & raind the remainder of the day. William & I made a visit to John Laidlaw's in Pitcairn today. Started to go up a[t] half past 8 got thare at 10. We started for home at half past 3, got home at 5. The rain just come down rite smart all the way home. The mud Just everlastingly flew but we got home before dark & nice & dry but the Horses was dripping with water & mud. We found Altha better. Sherman had the Chours all done good. Bower came up & Stayed part of the day with him. Alvah & Henry Grant chopped in the forenoon for Wm.

Sunday, December 11 A nice warm day like September. Mercury 60. Alvah & Sarah & the Children & Sherman went to Sunday School. Wm & I stayed at home. No rain today but the mud it is fearful. John & Agnes Hughs came up here with Sherman & Stayed untill night then Sherman took them home with his colt & Buggy. I sent a pail of Butter to C. H. Brown to the Store. 27 lbs. He brought me a pair of Shoes.

Monday, December 12 It raind near morning & clowdy all day. Lots of wind. Snowed a litle. Turnd colder. Froze the wet clothes. I done 2 weeks washing this forenoon. Wm & Sherman done the Chours. Alvah & Henry Grant went to the woods to chop at nine this morning. Clarence came up tonight to stay all night. Clint & Leslie McGill cald here after going to town. They brout a letter for Wm from Wm Green of Hermon. Sherman went to school. The winter term of school began the 8 of December.

Tuesday, December 13   Froze a litle this morning. Clowdy all day but no storm. A nice day. Mercury 30 above Zero. Wm went to town & paid his taxes & took some money to lend to Almon Perkins. One hundred dollars. Sherman went to School. He is away some place this evening. Wm brought home a box of medicine, August flowers, from C. H. Brown's. He payed 3 dollars & 50 cents for it. He bought 2 lamp Chimnies, 15 cents. I sent for 5 lbs of raisins but he forgot them. I have done some Baking today. 3 loaves of Bread & a crock of Cookies 75 & cleand my Carpet & done lots of work. Alvah & Henry Grant has been chopping all day for Wm.

Wednesday, December 14   This has been a nice mild day. No storm but dark & clowdy all day but the sky is clear this evening & the stares are shinening through the fog but it is very dark out. Clarence is up here to stay tonight. Alvah & Henry Grant cut wood today. Henry & Sarah & the girls has gone to town tonight to practice for Chrismas. Sarah made me a call this afternoon. Got a peace of meat. Tom & Albert Cousins went to Court this week but they have got out of their trouble by paying $2.80 fine. They say they are glad to get of[f] as well & think they will try & keep out of such trouble the next time.

Thursday, December 15   A lovely forenoon but snowd all of the afternoon. Melted as it fell untill near night. It began to show on the ground & this evening at nine it is snowing & the wind is blowing hard & colder. The mercury was 35 this afternoon but the wind blows so hard I can't go out with a lite [light] to look at the thermomiter this evening. Wm & I went to town this forenoon. We took dinner in Charley's. I traded

$2.25 cents. Bought blue callico for aprons & black velvit & raisins & Pepper & a pair of mittens for Sherman & a pair of Slippers for Sherman. Alvah & Henry Grant cut wood today in the woods for Wm. Sherman went to town tonight & got the mail, rode on Horse Back.

Friday, December 16   Some colder this morning. Mercury 10 above Zero & 15 at night. Alvah & Henry Grant choped wood all day in the woods. Wm went after them at noon with the teem & sled & brought them here to dinner & caried them back to the woods. Sherman went to school. A Mr. Winslow from Russell cald here today. He was selling silver plated ware, knives, forks, & spoons & evry thing in that line.

Saturday, December 17   Milder this morning. Mercury up to 30. Been a nice day. The boys went to the woods as usual. Sherman went after them at noon & brout them here to dinner & took them back. Wm took a trip to Hermon Village today with the colt & Buggy. He took dinner to Wm Green's. He brought me a nice Chrismas present & one for Martha $4 each. Alvah's folks have all gone to town tonight for the Children to practice for the Christmas. [program]

Sunday, December 18   This has been a stormy day. It is snowing tonight & has been snowing all day. We all went to Sundy School today accept Wm. He had the headache & stayed at home. Alex Kerr made us a call this evening. The Sundy School Schollers practiced their pieces after Sundy School. We did not get home untill 3 o'clock. Mercury was 25 above this morning. It is the same tonight at 7 o'clock. Wm brought home from Hermon 2 stands cost eight dollars & a picture frame 60 cents.

Monday, December 19   Quite a winter day this. Mercury 25 above Zero all day. It snowd some in the night so it has been quite good sleighing today. I did a small washing this forenoon & done my Baking Bread & mince Pies & Cake. Wm went to town this afternoon to get a horse Shod. Henry Grant has been cutting wood for Wm B all day. Alvah helped part of the day & drew some wood to his house from the woods & drew a can of water from our cistern for Sarah to do her washing. Clint & Leslie cald here this evening to play chequers [checkers] with Wm & Sherman.

Tuesday, December 20   A nice Winter day. No Storm or wind. Mercury 20 above Zero. Wm has been drawing wood & doing Chours. Sherman has helped with the Chours & went to School. Alvah & Henry Grant has been in the woods all day choping stove wood for Wm Brown. Viola Harmon cald here today noon from school. I finished a pair of socks for Sherman today & handed & mended 2 pair of mittens for Wm. Hank Johnson has sold out the Stage Buisness to Milo Woodcock. He took his first trip yesterday with a Sleigh. Alvah P & Henry Grant finished their chopping for Wm today. 27 cord.

Wednesday, December 21   A Stormy day. Snowd nearly all day. The Sleighing is quite good. The Stage has run on Sleighing all of this week. Wm & Alvah & Henry Grant kild & drest a Beef cow this forenoon. Wm went to town this afternoon & took down the hide to sell & took a quarter of the Beef to Charly Brown. Made him a present of the same for Christmas. He bought a tank of Cerosene [Kerosene] oil 5 gallons and a pair of rubbers for himself. Sherman went to town this evening. He bought a pair of overshoes & a wallet for himself. Alvah & Sarah & the girls all went to the Church to practice for the Sundy School entertainment to come of next Sunday evening. Alvah has a quarter of beef.

Thursday, December 22   This has been a Stormy day. Snowd most of the time. Alvah took the Colt & Cutter & caried Henry Grant out home in Russell. Wm done the Chours & cut

427

up the Beef & packed it in snow in a Barrel. Sherman went to School & he went to town tonight & got the maile. Only. one paper, the freepress, the Herold did not come. Mercury is 12 above Zero. The Methodist intends to have a Christmas tree & a entertainment on Saturday evening. I finished reading through my Sundy School Book today. 348 pages.

Friday, December 23   This has been a very nice pleasant day but quite cold. Mercury was 6 below Zero today. Sherman has gone to town this evening with Alvah & Sarah & the children to practice for Christmas. Alvah & Sarah & her sister Nora went to town this afternoon. Wm has done the Chours & fitted & put in 3 outside windows so now we have double windows in the dining room & our Bedroom. They cost eight dollars. That is one way the money goes. It is necesary to get so many fixings for the house. Thare was a man cald here today Selling lovely Pichures Oil painting but we did not buy any. Had no money to spare. Wm is reading the Sunday School Book tonight.

Saturday, December 24   This has been quite a cold day but no storm. Mercury was four above Zero. Wm went to town this afternoon & caried a nice toilet [toilet] stand to Martha for a Crismas present. They all intend to come here tomorow to dinner & Alvah's family & P. H. Brown's family. Alvah & Sherman drew a few load of wood for Wm today. Wm done the Chours & mended 2 old harness & went to town. I done quite a lot of Baking Bread & Buiscuit & fried cakes & frosted Jell Cake. Sherman is away to town tonight. The Methodist has a Crismas tree tonight. Tomorow is Dr. Lee's day to preach in the Union Church.

Sunday, December 25   Quite a cold pleasant day. We had a houseful of company today. Charley & family & Alvah & family, & P.H. Brown's family & Write Robinson's family. 20 of us to dinner. Then we went to the Sunday School entertainment in the evening. The Church was well filled & had a good time. The children played their part Splendid. Wm stayed at home & left a good fire. Mercury was 10 above Zero. Manie Brown made me a present of a chair tidy that she worked the pattern of two litle girls in the center with red thread & Agness Hughs made me a present of a nice tidy of her own make for my best chair.

Monday, December 26   Quite cold today. Mercury 10 above Zero all day. I commenced to do my washing but before I was half done I had company from Fowler. Mr. & Mrs. John Absolom. I sent for Alvah & Sarah & the Children to come to dinner. We had a good visit. I put my washing aside untill they had all gone then I finished it this evening. Wm & John drove to town. Cald in Charley's Store & in John McFeran's store. Wm bought a nice chair & made a Present to Rachel Absolom for Christmas. Mabel sent me a present today. Miss Cora Jennie made us a call this afternoon.

Tuesday, December 27   This has been quite a cool day. Mercury 10 above Zero. No wind today. Wm & Alvah has been drawing wood out of the woods into the field & pileing it up. Sherman has been to School & helped do the Chours. He has gone to town tonight with a lot of School Boys. Bower was here twice today. I have been quite busy today. The Methodist holds a Mite Society meting at Nelson Freeman's tonight. The Methodist from the village has gone down thare by the sleigh load.

Wednesday, December 28   This has been a stormy day. Snowd & the wind has blown all day & is blowing at a fearful gale this evening. Our Stove Pipe & Chimney burnt out this evening. The pipe was red hot & the room upstairs whare the pipe went through was blue with smoke. We put watter on the pipe & on the floor around the safe. Sherman had gone to bed. Alvah & Sarah & the girls have gone to A. K. Payns' to attend a wedding this evening. Henry Grant & Leona Payne is to be maried this evening at 7 o'clock. Mercury 20 above Zero all day.

Thursday, December 29   One more Stormy day. The wind has blown hard all day & snowd the most of the time. Been a blue day entirely. Wm has helped do the Chours & then stayed in the house & read books & papers. Alvah's folks had company, Cy Clealand & family was thare for a visit. Sherman went to School. He went to town tonight with a horse & cutter & got the papers. Wm paired a lot of apples today for me to put in my mince meat. I made a lot today, enough to fill a large Jar & some in a pan. Henry Grant & Leony [Payne] went to Canton today to visit their friends. They intend to be gone 3 days.

Friday, December 30   This has been a very pleasant but a cold day. Mercury 8 below Zero this morning. 10 below tonight. The moon is Just lovely. The stars are shining brite & the windows are Coating over with frost. Thare is the new year Dance at the Rushton house tonight. Sherman is away to town. Alvah has been drawing Stove wood today to his house from our woods with the Bay teem. Wm has helped do the Chours & red the paper. We have both got bad colds. Gid Freeman's family are visitng to Wm Clealand's this afternoon & evening. Elmer Grant & Mary Grant took Supper to Alvah's tonight & then went to the dance.

Saturday, December 31   It was quite cold this morning. Mercury 10 below Zero. It is 20 above tonight at 8 o'clock. Snowd a very litle. Wm & Sherman drew 3 load of wood & done the Chours. Sherman Stayed all night to the village. Got home at 5 this morning. Clarence came up today. He went home tonight. I made a call to Alvah's today. I wrote a line & sent to the Post for Sister Johnson this afternoon. This is the last day of this year & this is my last leaf & last page. So good by old year of 1887. We hope to begin the new year with a good resolution to reform in many diferent ways & try & start with the new year rite side up with care.

[note: *The next few pages in the diary book were for addresses but instead Nancy Brown kept track of who took how many bushels of wheet to the mill on a monthly basis. She also kept track of butter sold and the amount, and on the "cash account page" Nancy Brown kept track of cheese sale transactions. Interspersed between the various entries were marriages, deaths, births and I have listed them below for the genealogical value. GGJ]*

December 21, 1887   Roseo Todd & Miss Nettie Lumbey was maried of Edwards, NY.

December 28, 1887   Henry Grant of Russell was maried to Miss Leona Payne of Edwards, NY   The weding was held at her father, Mr. A K. [Allen King] Payne in the village of Edwards. About 20 relatives was present & took supper.

October 15, 1887   A baby to Mr. & Mrs. Chester Vanornum

October 24, 1887 A girl born to Mr. & Mrs. Had Gardener

March 23, 1887   Mr. Adelbert Freemen & Miss Stellah Vanornum was maried. The weding at her father's at Silver Hill, Russell, NY

May 4, 1887   Mr. Will Woodcock & Miss Carie Hosmer was maried in Gouverneur [NY] by the Rev Mr. Chace.

Graham Watson Died the 8th of March, 1888 in Michigan, Coopersville, formally of Edwards, NY.

Albert Wight Died the 18th of October, 1888 with Brain fever

431

of Edwards, NY.

Bower Freeman & Lidia Hall was maried March 7, 1888, both of Edwards, NY.

Nathan Shaw & Josaphene [Josephine] Brayton was maried the 28th of February, 1888, both of Edwards, NY.

Noris Rushton & Miss Carie Stevens was maried the 22 of February 1888. Both of Edwards, NY.

Mary Rushton of Canton [NY] was maried the 22 of February, 1888. Daughter of Peter Rushton.

Urban Webb & Miss Rhoda Grant was maried June 23, 1887.

Mr. Kilbarn [Kilbran] & Maggie Worthington was maried the 29th of June, 1887.

Frank Johnson & Miss Jennie Winslow was maried the 4th of July, 1887. Edwards.

William Clealand Died the 10th of June, 1887. Age 93 years. Came from Scotland to Edwards [NY] in the year 1819.

Mrs. Cornelia Phelps, wife of James Ruston, died October 23, 1887, age 53.

Will Brown & Olive Wels [Wells] was maried the 11 of November, 1887.

A boy to Mr. & Mrs. Walter Flemings on Feb. 6, 1888.

1888

Friday, April 20   Mr. Guy Noble died.   Leaves a young wife and a litle boy and a mother and brother and one sister to mourn for him.   He was young and been maried about 3 years.

Friday, November 16   Mrs. Thomas Laidlaw died in Gouverneur on Thursday November 15, whare she has made her home with her son Charley for the last 20 years.   Her former home was in South Edwards and they will bring her there to be beried tomorow Saturday November 17.

Wednesday, November 28   Emeline Fordham died November 27 1888.   She was the daughter of Horris Barnes of Edwards.   About 45 years old.   Leaves no children, no father or mother to mourn her loss.   Funeral, Friday, November 30th.

Friday November 30   I got a letter from Illinois bring the sad news of the death of my Brother Charles [Victor] Johnson.   He died the 12 of this month.   Had been as well as usual, went to feed his pigs and fell dead against the rail of the pen.   His grandson found him dead.   He had not been out of the house more than 10 minutes when they found him dead.   [inserted] My brother, Charles Johnson, died Nov. 12, 1888 of Pittsfield, Pike Co., Ill.   His native town was Edwards, NY.   His age at the time of his death was 73 years.   He left his native town 53 years ago last May and settled in the place where he died.   He had been maried about 50 years.   He left a wife [Emily Spann Johnson] and four daughters and 10 grandchildren to mourn his sudden death.   His only son [Abel] was kild in the war of the rebellion [Civil War] in 1863.

Tuesday, January 1   Mrs. Peter Cook [Nancy Jane McFerran] from the mines was beried today.

Thursday, January 10   Miss Rachel Absolom and Mr. Levi Burnum, both of Fowler, NY was maried at the home of the bride's father, Mr. John B. Absolom.

Saturday, February 9   Mr. Willie Robinson and Miss Manie Watson was maried at the home of the bride, Mr. R. Watson's, Edwards, NY

Saturday March 2   I heard of the death of Betsy Watson of Coopersville, Mich.   She died last Monday, Feb 25, 1889 and was beried today.   Cornelia Winslow, her sister, has gone from Edwards to attend her funeral.   She was a sister of Henry and James Rushton of this place.   [Betsy Watson was the wife of Graham Watson].

Saturday, March 2   Mr. Fleming died this morning at the house of Jim Shay's [Shea's] here in town.   He was sick only 2 days.   He is a brother of Mr. Shay [Shea] and his wife is a sister of Jim Shay [Shea] and there is 3 children left.

Monday, March 4   Bill Noys [Noyes] and Jim Shay [Shea] family has gone to Russell to bery Mr. Fleming today.

Thursday, March 28   Mrs. Eveline Clealand [actually Grant] died. Age 60 years.

Saturday, March 30 Mrs. Clealand [Grant] buried today.

Wednesday, April 3   Mr. Clinton Goodnough of Fowler and

Miss Cora Bancroft was maried at the bride's parents, Hiram Bancroft's of Edwards, NY. It was a fearful stormy day. Complete snow blizard [blizzard] all day.

Sunday, March 31   Henry Webb and family are expected back to Edwards in a few days from Dakota.

Saturday, April 6   Mrs. Henry Webb and four of her children came to Edwards today from Dakota. It will be one year in May since they left here to go to Dakota.

Monday, April 8   Henry Webb and Ossie Noys [Noyes] was up to eat warm sugar today. Henry came home with his mother last Saturday from Dakota.

Old Mr. Thrall died last Saturday at the house of Earl Bancroft in Edwards. He was the father of Mrs. Earl Bancroft. Had been living with them the past winter. He was from Gouverneur. Bill Noys took him to Gouverneur today to bery him there. His wife died in Gouverneur about one year ago. He was an old man some more than 80 years old.

Monday, April 22   Mr. James Bryant and Miss Lizzie Webb was maried. All of Edwards, NY. He is an engineer at one of the mines.

Thursday, April 25   A boy baby born to Mr. and Mrs. Will Newton.

Monday, April 29   Will Newton's litle boy was beried. Died April 28, 1889.

Tuesday, May 7   Mrs. James Nobels [Noble] died in Michigan at the house of her daughter, Mrs. Orrin Sprague. Her husband died 22 years before in Edwards.

Father and mother are both at rest
In heaven, their happy home
Four sons and four daughters left to
Mourn the loss of their dear parents.

Mother is gone but yet she speaks
And she is gone, death claimed her for his own
And on her, lord, his unrelenting hand rested
From earth her quiet spirits flown
To rest in heaven her happy home.
My children dear grieve not for me
For I shall arise when Christ apears [appears].

Mrs. Noble [Isabelle Laidlaw] was mother of Martha [Mrs. Charles Brown]. Had lived in Michigan six years with her children. She is past 79 years. They expect her remains to get to Edwards Fryday [Friday] of this week to beried at Pond Settlement by the side of her husband, Mr. Noble and her daughter Susan.

Saturday, June 1   Mr. Noah Shaw of Edwards, NY died.
Sunday, Mrs. Percival H. Brown of Edwards, NY died, age 50 years.

Wednesday, June 12   Mrs. Abel [Eliza] Pratt died. She was 63 years old. Her husband, Mr. Abel Pratt, died 29 years ago this spring. She died at her son's, William Pratt, in Norwood, NY. Her daughters are Mrs. Sam Rushton and Mrs. Simeon Richmyre of Edwards.

Wednesday, June 19   John Sullivan's beried their boy today. He had a cancer on his face. He was 5 years old.

Monday, June 24   Mr. George Brayton and Miss Viola Ray was maried.

Sunday, June 30   Mr. John Forney and Miss Mure [Nellie M. Muir] was maried in Me. Union Church at Edwards by Dr. Lee of Canton. The couple was from Fine, NY.

Thursday, July 4   Mr. Albert Allen and Miss Maud Wels [Wells] was maried. Albert Allen died May 1890. Run over by the cars [railroad] at DeKalb.

Sunday July 7   Made a short call on Mrs. Henry Webb. Her sick boy, Charley, is failing fast. They expect Henry Webb home in a day or two from Dakota.

Sunday, July 21   The funeral of Charley Webb, son of Henry Webb. He was ten years old. William Green of Hermon beried him. He was beried in a beautiful white casket. The services was held at Henry Webb's house.

Tuesday, August 6   We had company all day. Mr. Guild and wife from Dakota was here and a niece of Mrs. Guild, a young lady, Miss Allis [Alice] Glazier, from Albany, NY and daughter of Willard Glazier. They moved from Edwards 23 years since.

Wednesday August 7   Mr. and Mrs. Guild stayed with us last night. He took our horse and carriage and took his wife to Mrs. David Laidlaw's to spend the day and he took a walk to town. They have been visiting her sister at York, the past two weeks. They intend to visit old friends in Edwards a week or two and then they intend to go to Massachusetts, their old home from where they came from 35 years ago.

Sunday, August 11   John McGill came home to visit his mother and friends last Fryday, from Wisconsin. He has a little boy with him.

Tuesday, August 13   A Mr. Glazier from York called here last night for Mr. and Mrs. Guild to take them to his father's. His mother has just had a shock of paralisis. Mrs. Guild is a sister of Mrs. Glazier on a visit from Dakota. Have been here in Edwards a week. He found them at Alex Kerr's.

Saturday, August 17   Old Mr. Miller of Fine died.

Sunday, August 18   Mr. Levi Phippens died with typhoid fever, age 27. Leaves a wife and 2 children.

Friday, August 23   Mrs. Levi Phippens died with typhoid fever. Leaves two little orphans. She attended funeral of her husband on Tuesday and died on Friday.

Saturday, August 24   William Hall died of cancer, age 73. Edwards, NY. Charley Noble's boy Rawley eleven years old today. Had a party.

Sunday, August 25   Mr. William Hall died last night. Will be beried tomorrow in the creek bering ground.

Thursday, August 29   John McGill formerly of Edwards left to go back to Iowa with his little boy. Had been visiting his mother, Mrs. Storen. His brother Lesly went with him. They met their sister Laura in Syracuse on her way to Edwards to visit their mother.

Wednesday, September 25   James McFerin and Miss [Nora] Madison was maried.

Thursday, September 26   David Nap's [Knapp] house burned last night. Mr. and Mrs. Nap away from home. One man burned to death and the boarder jumped out the chamber window. The burnt man was beried today in the graveyard in Edwards. The town paid the expenses. He was a young man only 18 years old. He was intending to start for England in a few days. They found a few dollars in silver whare he lay. He had no relatives about here.

Monday, September 30   Alex Kerr and his men took up the bridge down here on the cross rhode [road] today to repair or build it new.

Tuesday, October 1   Lellan Bancroft and Miss Nettie Hazelton was maried.

Tuesday, October 8   A boy [born to] Bower Freeman's. [the boy born was Roy Grover Freeman]

Thursday, October 10   This was William Brown's birthday. He is 65 years old today.

Wednesday, October 16   Henry Rushton's family is moving to Gouverneur this week.   They commenced to take their goods last Sunday, so I think they will have good luck.

Thursday, October 17   A girl baby to John and Mrs. Cousins

Monday, October 21   Clementine Noble's little boy was beried this afternoon. He was four years old. He was sick only 2 days. [Merchant Noble]

Monday, October 28   Mrs. Rachel Wels [Wells] of Pitcairn died today. Her maiden name was Rachel Higens [Higgins] of Russell. The first girl born in that town, or the first white girl, and she was nearly black.

Friday, November 1   Henry Webb bought the goods in the hardware store today of C. Stevenson and Billy Webb.

Saturday, November 2   The Pitcairn factory [Cheese] was burnt all up and the cheese last night and one in Fowler and one in Gouverneur all in the last 2 days.

Thursday, November 7   This was my birthday. I was 64 years old.

Thursday, November 21   It was 21 years since our little girl, Clarah [Clara] died the 17th of this month.

Tuesday, November 26   Mr. James Wilson died last Sunday night. Will be beried tomorrow afternoon. He died with the dread disease cancer. He is an old resident of this town. He was from Scotland fifty years ago. He leaves a large family.

Monday, December 9   Got the news of a boy baby to Mr. and Mrs. Cy Cleland born last Saturday night. [boy: Grant Cleland]

Thursday, December 12   Mr. William May of Edwards, NY died today near Freeman's mine. He had been working in the mines. He lived near Nelson Freeman's. [Congestion of the lungs, pleurisy with effusion]

1890

Wednesday, January 1   Mr. T [Theodore] Stevenson and Miss Sarah Stevens was maried in Edwards, NY.

Thursday, January 2   Theodore Stevenson and Miss Sarah Stevens was maried yesterday at her father's in South Edwards. This was Mabel Brown's birthday. She is fourteen years old.

Sunday, January 12   Mr. John Brown died. He was Brown Canada. He was a talc miner here in Edwards. He was beried here in Edwards village cemetery. A young man. Been living to Tom Johnson's and died there.

Monday, February 10   Mrs. Sabrina Hall, wife of John Boid [Boyd] died. Her age was 55

Tuesday, February 11   Warren Earl and Sabrina Boyd died yesterday.

Wednesday, February 12   Mrs. Alfred Hall died. She was 62 years old the 22 of last May. Her maiden name was Emmy [Emmorancy] Johnson. Born in Edwards, NY. She was the youngest child of Charles and Rachel Johnson and the 12th in number and family of six girls [Emmy was the sister of Nancy Johnson Brown who had four half-sisters, Viall.   See Introduction]

Wednesday, February 12   Miss Dora Johnson and a Mr. Stevens was maried.   She is the daughter of A[bel] P[ratt] Johnson of Pine Valley, Chemung County, NY.

Friday, February 28   Mr. John McKee and Lucy Shey [Shea] was maried.

Saturday, March 15   Mrs. May has a baby girl [Flossie].

Tuesday, March 11   Mr. Charley Hall and Miss Lois Wels [Wells] was maried in Gouverneur, NY. [Charles Hall was the son of Alfred B. Hall and Emmorancy Johnson Hall]

Monday, April 14   Mrs. Thomas Freeman died today, age 82 in Edwards, NY [Phoebe Maria Carr Freeman]

Thursday, April 17   A little girl of John McFeran's [McFeran in the 1870 Census] died. [Daisy McFerran]

Thursday, April 24   Thomas Grant died in Edwards

Tuesday, May 6   Mrs. King Payn [Payne] died on the evening of May 6th, 1890, age 60 years.   Her maiden name was Ann Arnold of Fowler, NY.   Has been maried 43 years.   Leaves a kind husband and one son and 5 daughters to mourn for a kind and loving mother.

Friday, May 16   A Mr. McCarty [George] died yesterday.   He has been boss in the Brayton mines.   His mother resides in Richville [NY].

Thursday, May 22   Sister Moriah [Moriah Merrill] Johnson died May 22, 1890, age 65 years.   She was the widow of Brother Warren [William Warren] Johnson.   He died June 4, 1883.   They leave two daughters, Mrs. Eugene Herrington, [Emma] Mrs. Warren Allen [Alvaretta] both of Pitcairn, NY. And four sons, Charley and George and Fred and Frank Johnson.   Beried in the Payne Cemetery beside her husband. Lived around South Edwards, NY. [She] Was a emigrant from Ireland.

Saturday, May 24   Jim Fordham just came to town with his bride from Canada.   Been married about two weeks.   Has brought his new wife home to his father's, Ira Fordham.   Jim's first wife was Emaline Barnes of Edwards.

Tuesday, June 3   Mrs. Fleming and Mr. Stafford was maried June 2nd.

Friday, June 20   It is 13 years since Alvah and Sarah [Brown] was maried.

Monday, June 23   Mrs. Hattie Berley of South Edwards was beried last Saturday.   She left a little babe [George Javall] 2 weeks old.   She gave it to its grandmother.

Tuesday, June 24   Mrs. Dr. Goodnough dying.

Thursday, June 26   Mrs. Dr. Goodnough was beried today in Gouverneur.

Saturday, July 5   Dan Noble and Nelson VanOrnum and Fred Brown started today to Dakota on an excurtion [excursion] train, round ticket $30. Time 2 months.

Thursday, July 24   Rob Casida [Cassidy] died this morning. He had a stroke of apoplexy. He worked in the mines yesterday. Was a well as usual.

Friday, July 25   Harry Treglown died, age 5 years.

Saturday, December 20   Mr. Thomas Freeman died today, age 86 of Edwards NY. Father and mother are both gone to rest and left a large family of grown up children, five boys and four girls, all maried but one. Leaves grandchildren and great grandchildren.

1892

Saturday, April 30   Cassy Treglown, mother to little Harry Treglown, died. Daughter of Harry and Mary McGill of Edwards.

1894

Thursday, March 22   Maried at Parsonage at Prescott, Canada, George Cole of this town and Mrs. Maud [Wells] Allen of Harewood. The bride formerly lived in this town and has many old as well as young friends who hope that her future life may be strewn with happiness. Although young, she has seen her share of the world's troubles. Her husband, Mr. Allen, was killed on the railroad at DeKalb Junction shortly after they married some three years ago.

1898-1899

[the major portion of this diary begins on April 6, 1998 but the editor has added other dates for 1898 found on the back overleaf pages]

On the front overleaf, the following obituaries were pasted in the front pages. No dates are given for any of the obituaries but one can assume that the deaths occurred in 1898:

A newspaper obituary regarding Arda Kerr of Edwards, son of U. O. Kerr, who died of a gunshot wound while hunting. He was eighteen years old.

A newspaper obituary for Ellsworth Carter of Edwards. He was the son of Cornelius Carter of South Edwards. No death date but reference is made that he had gone to Canton to study law with L. P. Hale.

A newspaper obituary for Mrs. Leon A. Freeman, age 21 years. She was Miss Effie C. Allen of West Fowler, NY, daughter of Oscar Allen. She died on April 17 of bronchial pneumonia one month and one day from the time of her marriage.

A newspaper obituary for Ella Clark, wife of William G. Clark. She is buried in the Riverside Cemetery in Edwards. Survived by her husband, a young daughter, and an infant daughter aged three weeks.

A newspaper obituary for the death of Mrs. Caroline M. Haile who died on Nov 17, at the age of 76 years. She was the wife of Charles H. Haile of Edwards, who died 7 years earlier. She is survived by her only daughter, Celia Haile, and brother, The Hon. E.W. Abbott. She is buried in Gouverneur, NY.

March 22, 1998 [Added from Overleaf pages]:   We was milking 8 cows. Done the first churning the 2nd day of April & fild a tub of 30 lbs from the 22 of March to the 27th of April. I made 200 lbs of butter. The last week, I have been milking 13 cows. Took our milk to the factory the 25th of April. Had 100 & 4 lbs of milk.

Beginning of the 1898 diary:

Wednesday, April 6   I now commenced to write in my new Book. This has been a cold day. Wm took a ride over beyond Trout Lake today with a man from Lisbon [NY], a cousin of our neighbor Flack.   Wm sold our Fanny mare to this man from Lisbon for 70 dollars. Bower is helping his grandfather do the Barn chours this week. Clarence has gone to town today. He attendes the store while his father draws the Freight. He had his lame arm undone today. The first since he had it set. It is doing as well as he can expect. He is very anxious for it to get well.

Thursday, April 7   This has been a nice pleasant day.   The mercury at 20 above zero this morning & 50 this afternoon. Wm & Clarence went to town this forenoon. They got the horses shod & brout home 2 butter tubs from Charley Brown's store. Bower Brown has gone to town this evening. A letter from Mabel Brown tonight from Syracuse. [*Mabel Brown attended the School of Music at Syracuse University, 1896-1899. She studied voice and piano.*]

Friday, April 8   A pleasant day. Wm & Bower made fence today.   Clarence went to town. Carrie made a visit to her father, John Clealand's.   Bower went to town tonight and attended a dance at the hotell in Edwards village. Alvah & Sarah & litle Clarah Brown made us a call near night.

Saturday, April 9   A very nice pleasant day. Wm done a churning this morning while Bower was doing Barn chours. Then they both fixt fence all day. Clarence & Carrie & Bower B. has gone to town this evening. Wm has gone to bed early. He is very tired. Harold Brown has got the measels. Broke out today.

Sunday, April 10   Just a lovely Easter Sunday. Warm & pleasant. We all stayed at home today. This was the day for Miss Morgan to preach in the Union Church & Mr. Gale in the Methodist Church & they had Easter Sermons.

Monday, April 11   One more pleasant day. No signs of rain & our cistern is dry & this is washing day & the boys went to the river & drew water for us to do our washing. Frank Harmon commenced to work here today. Will work this week. Then he intends to work on the Railrhode. Wm has been working the colts today for the first time drawing the land rooller. Clarence cannot yuse his lame arm any yet & it Pains him all of the day. But he chours around & does quite a lot of work with his well arm. He has oild his best Harness this afternoon. It looks as good as new.

Tuesday, April 12   One more dry pleasant day & quite warm. Wm finished the roolling the land. He commenced on yesterday and then he drew away the Banking from the house. Then he drove to town & got the colts shod. Clarence & Frank Harmon has gone to town tonight. Mr. Storen, our neighbor, came home today after an Absence of nearly one year.

Wednesday, April 13   One more nice pleasant day. Wm done some Plowing today in the garden with the colts. They done nicely. Mrs. Effie Freeman is very sick with measels. A man cald here tonight from DeKalb & bought one of our colts. Payed 65 dollars.

Thursday, April 14   One more pleasant day but clowdy near night & looks like rain. We hope it will come before morning. The men cleand the cistern today noon so it is ready for rain. Clarence & Frank has gone to town tonight. Wm took a long round about trip today to get to the village. The Bridge is up & the new one is not finished. So he had to go around through the woods bark of Newton's & come out to the village the other side of the river with the colt he sold last night. Wm sold to Alex Kerr six litle Pigs last Saturday. They was four weeks old.

Friday, April 15   Just a lovely day. Quite cool this morning. Wm went to Hermon today. Took 3 tubs of Butter. Sold for 15 cents a pound. Was 90 lbs. He bought a lot of grass seede & four tin poles for milk pails. I made an all day visit in the village to Ch B's & A.P. B's & Altha's.

Saturday, April 16   A very litle rain in the past night but pleasant today. Clarence & Carrie has gone to town tonight. Wm has gone to some of the neighbors for an evening call. I do not know what place & I am at home alone. Jene Laidlaw & another man cald here near night. Mrs. Vint Brown & her mother cald here today. They was selling hard soap & washing Powder. I bout one package. Payed 10 cents in sugar.

Sunday, April 17   A pleasant day. Frank Harmon our hired man went to Fine today. We look for him back here this evening. Clarence & Carrie took a ride this afternoon out to John Clealand's. We heard from Effie Freeman this afternoon. The Doctor thinks she cannot live untill tomorow morning. It will be just one week tomorow since she took a hard cold with the measels.

Mr. Edwin Harmon & Miss   [?]   both of Edwards. November 23, 1898. [presume, marriage]

Monday, April 18   Just a nice pleasant day but lots of wind. We done our washing this forenoon. We got the sad news this morning that Effie Freeman Died last night at 8 o'clock. Will be berried tomorow in the Cemetery at Hailsbourough.[NY] The funeral will be held at the house of Charles Freeman's at ten o'clock tomorrow morning. Clarence has been driving 3 horses before the Spring tooth Harrow. He went to town tonight.

Tuesday, April 19   A cold day & clowdy. Commenced to rain about four o'clock this afternoon. Is raining this evening at nine. Wm & Carrie & I attended the funeral of Mrs. Leon Freeman. A Baptist Minister from Gouverneur, the Rev. Mr. Rogers, preached the funeral sermon. Interment at Hailsburgh. Wm Noys of Edwards Beried her.

Wednesday,   April 20   A splendid rain in the night & this morning & misty most of the time today. The men mooved our cook stove today noon after dinner. Clarence & Frank Harmon has gone to town this evening.

Thursday, April 21   One more rainy day & quite cool. Wm sold 60 bushels of oats today to a Mr. Blonse that workes the Jim Campel farm for 50 cents a bushel. Clarence & Carrie has gone to town this evening. Wm & Frank Harmon is playing backgamon. Frank has worked here 10 days.

Friday, April 22   Raind part of the time today. The mud on the rhod is quite deep but the grass is quite green & the cows are gaining milk. We are milking 12. We are all at home this evening. Clarence & Carrie is in the Parlor singing & playing on the organ.   Frank is reading his new catalog & Wm is looking over his old acount book. I have been reading a story but fell asleep & could not finish it. So I am writing in my diary & will soon retire for the night & sweetely sleepe untill morning light.

Saturday, April 23   A very nice day after the rain. Quite a lot of rain fell in the night of last.   Our men could not do any Harowing today.   The ground was so wet.   Frank Harmon went home this morning.   He has worked for Clarence eleven days.   Clarence thinks he can do the work without any hired man but he has done to much with his lame arm today. Cleaning all of the stabels & shoveling the ashes out of the leach Box & filling it with new ashes & puting on lots of water ready to make the soap.   Wm done a churning this morn & he has been spliting rails this afternoon.   Mrs. Gid Freeman & her daughter Ellie made us a call this afternoon. Clarence & Carrie has gone to town this evening.

[Sunday was crossed out]

Monday, April 25   A pleasant day but cold & a hard wind all day.   We done our washing this forenoon.   Clarence drove 3 Horses all day before the Spring tooth Harrow.   Then after chours he and Carrie made flower beds & set out a nice lot of Pansies.   She picked a boca [bouquet] of Pansies today.   Have been in blosom one week.   Yesterday was a rainy day & cold. I wrote a letter to send to Brother A. P. Johnson to Pine Valley yesterday.   Clarence & Carrie went to Church last evening.   A young student from college spoke to the people in place of Miss Morgan.   Wm finished spliting his rails today.   Manie Brown visited in Fowler & Gouverneur last week.   The trial of Bert for the murder of his father-in-law is in Progress last week & this.   We took our milk to the factory today for the first time this spring.   Only had 100 & 4 lbs.

Tuesday, April 26   A pleasant day but lots of wind.   Clarence scatered the wheet & grass seede today.   Clarence has gone to town tonight.   I finished skiming all of the milk today & washed the Pans.   Got one more churning to do.   Take the milk of eleven cows to the factory today.   Had 200.4 lbs. Carrie commenced to clean a bedroom upstairs today.   Took

449

up the carpet & got the old paper nearly of[f].

Wednesday, April 27   Just a nice pleasant day. A cool wind from the north east.   Clarence was Harowing today with 3 horses preparing the ground for oats. Wm takes the milk to the factory. 200 & 6 lbs. Then he went to town & bought Paper to paper a room upstairs. Martha Brown came home with him & Charley B came up to super and took her home. Clarence & Carrie has gone to town this evening. Lots of war news evry day. The United States & Spain are having hot batles on the ocean evry day. Our ships has captured a large number of Spanish ves[s]els the past week.

Thursday, April 28   One more pleasant day.   Cold this afternoon & clowdy near night. Wm & Clarence was sowing oats today. Carrie & I have been papering a bedroom today upstairs.   Clarence & Carrie is figuring the milk bills this evening.

Friday, April 29   A cold clowdy day. A litle mist of rain. Our men finished their seeding of wheete & oats. We finished papering the room. We was working in for 2 days & Clarence & Carrie put down the carpet this evening.   Wm done a churning this forenoon. The last one for this Spring. Have 100 lbs of Butter put down for our summer yuse.

Saturday, April 30   A pleasant day. Wm Plowed a garden for A. P. Brown near the factory & Sherman Plowed the one near the house for Alvah.   Clarence went to town this evening. Brout the mail. Lots of war news. We received a letter from A. O. Broadia [Broadie] to give us the news that they have a litle boy baby born the 20th of this month April 1898, Prescot[t], Arizona.

Sunday, May 1   Clarence & Carrie attended Church this forenoon. Manie & Rose Brown came here today & Mettie

Clealand came with Carrie.

Monday, May 2   A pleasant day it has been. The warmest day since in March. We done a larg[e] washing this forenoon & Carrie has been cleaning 2 rooms in the chamber this afternoon & helped do the milking morning & night. Wm has been puting water on the leach today & running of lye to make the soap. Clarence has gone to town this evening to take the Butter bills to A. P. Brown. Wm has gone to bed near 8 o'clock to night. I shall soon follow suit. Cy Watson has lately returnd from Vermont whare he has bought a farm & his son Ord intendes to go thare soon & run the farm.

Tuesday, May 3   A rainy day & evening. We finished cleaning our chamber today. Wm has made the soap. Clarence fixt fence today. He & Carrie has gone to town tonight.

Wednesday, May 4   One more rainy day & quite cool. Rhodes quite muddy. Clarence & Carrie has gone to town tonight to attend the Concert in the Church from our village tallent. Smith Chase & a number of others. Wm went to mill today. Took a load of oats. He sold 60 bushels of oats the other day to a man on the Jim Campel farm for 50 cents a Bushel. We have cleand our Pantry today & our Ironing is all done for this week.

Thursday, May 5   Clowdy all day but no rain only misty. Wm drove to town & brout home his feede & then he drove down to Taylor's store & bought 5 gallons of Paint oil & turpentine. Then he mixt some Paint & Clarence Painted the ceiling over head in the kitchen.

Friday, May 6   The moon is full. It looks just lovely this evening but quite cool. Been pleasant all day. A frost this morning. We have been cleaning house today in the kitchen

451

& pantry. Wm & Clarence has been fixing fence all day. Clarence has gone to town tonight. Carrie made a call in Gid Freeman's near night.

Saturday, May 7 A very pleasant day. Mercury 60. Clarence has painted the woodwork in the kitchen today between chours. Wm drove the colt all of this afternoon befor[e] the Buggy to learn her to drive alone. Clarence led Alvah's Horse home last night. He had been working it with one of his to do the Spring work. Clarence & Carrie has gone to town this evening.

Sunday, May 8 A nice pleasant day. Clarence & Carrie went to Church & then drove to J. W. Clealand's to dinner. I rode with them to Alvah's. I had a sick spell when I got home. Alvah commenced making cheese today.

Monday, May 9 One more pleasant day. Clarence & Carrie finished the painting in the kitchen today. I have not done any work today. Alax [Alex] & Jennie & Lena Kerr made us a call this evening.

Tuesday, May 10 A pleasant day. We did not wash. Our boiler leaked. Our men Planted Potatoes today. Rob Brown worked for Clarence & Carrie nearly Papered the kitchen today & done the house & dairy work. She & Clarence took a ride to town this evening.

Wednesday, May 11 Raining this morning & this forenoon. Nice & warm. The grain is up & looks nice. The grass is growing splendid. The cows are giving a nice lot of milk. 22 lbs of milk the average to each cow. Four 2 year old Heifers in the lot.

Thursday, May 12 Some rain today. Carrie & I done our housework & some cleaning & painting & our Ironing.

Clarence went to town this evening.

Friday, May 13   A pleasant day after the rains.   Wm & Clarence mooved our Big Stove out of the Dining room today whare it has been Stationary for the last 13 years.   I was happy to see it go into the grainery [granary].   Then we had a fine time cleaning up the muss & taking of[f] the paper.

Saturday, May 14   A shower this morning but pleasant this afternoon.   We took up our Dining room carpet yesterday & Carrie took the old paper of[f] the walls ready to put on new paper & today she has washed the woodwork & cleand the floor & done lots of work.   Wm & Clarence fixt fence today. Clarence & Carrie has gone to town this evening.   I read in the paper tonight that Wm Moncrief is Pardoned out of prison whare he has been for the past 8 years for the murder of John Farney, a neighbor of his.   Moncrief's sentence was 18 years in Danamara.   The governor Black has Pardond him out last Tuesday.

Sunday, May 15   A nice pleasant day.   We all stayed at home today.   Bower & Martha Brown came up to dinner today.   Wm made a call to Jim Harmon's today.   Frank Harmon is sick with measels.

Monday, May 16   Just a nice warm day.   We done our washing this forenoon.   Wm & I drove to town this afternoon & done some trading.   We bought Paper to paper the Dining room & I traded some to Padget's store & I made a call in A. P. Brown's & in Charley Brown's.   Came home to supper & chours.   Clarence Planted the corn today.   Wm made a call in Mr. Flack's tonight & procured a Pailful of corn to plant.

Tuesday, May 17   Some rain today.   A very litle sunshine & quite cold weather for the time of the year.   Wm planted the cucumber seede today.   Clarence drew lumber from the mill this afternoon. Jimmy McFerin Papered our dining room this forenoon. Carrie spred the paste for him. Shirley Flack cald here near dark to bid us all good by. She intendes to go to Ogdensburg tomorow to work in the Asylum for nine months. Carrie Papered the stairway this afternoon. It looks very nice.

Wednesday, May 18   A very pleasant day. Our men harowed corn ground & planted some corn & beets & pumkin seede & citron. Carrie & I done our house work & cleand the Parlor today.   Clarence & Carrie has gone to town this evening. Clarence sold a calf today to Rob Watson for 75 cents. The men are feeding 15 calves at present. Get 385 lbs of milk a day from 15 cows.

Thursday, May 19   Quite showery today.   A very litle sunshine but quite warm. The Aple trees are in bloom & grass & grain looks well. We have been in a mess all day with one thing & another. Wm & Clarence set up a stove in the Dining room & that made a big muss. Then we had all the things taken out of my Bedroom & took up the carpet & cleand the windows & woodwork. Carpet down & evrything in place tonight. Had callers. Mr. Wm Whitney from Gouverneur made a call & Henry Brown came & took some Potatoes & 25 lbs of sugar to Warren Harmon. Sarah Brown & litle Clarah was here to supper while Alvah was gone to Pleasant Valley.

Friday, May 20   Clowdy nearly all day but no rain. Clarence & Carrie put the carpet down in the Dining room today & we put evrything to its place. So we claim that we are through cleaning house for this time.

Saturday, May 21   A very warm day. Mercury up to 80. No storm today. I done some Baking this forenoon of Bread & Piplant [Rhubarb] Pies & Fried cakes. Carrie made a custerd cake. I made a call in Mrs. Storens since supper. Clarence went to town this evening.

Sunday, May 22   A rainy forenoon. Pleasant this afternoon. We all stayed at home untill evening then Clarence & Carrie went to Church. Arba Kerr made us a call this evening.

Monday, May 23   A thunder shower this forenoon. We done our washing this forenoon. Wm & Clarence was busy taking things out of the woodhouse chamber & taking them into the grainery [granary] making ready to finish the Chamber. Thare is a new moon.

Tuesday, May 24   A wet shower this morning. Pleasant this afternoon. I can't think of anything to write. Wm & Clarence went to town this evening.   Clarence & Carrie figured the cheese bills today.

Wednesday, May 25   Misty this morning & clowdy all day. Murban Webb worked here today helping Wm fix the woodhouse chamber.   Viola Harmon made us a call after school. The pedler that sels Hailes ointment from Adams cald here today. I bought one box of ointment. Payed 25 cents.

Thursday, May 26   Showery pleasant part of the day. Webb worked here today. They have got the chamber all Borded in the inside & commenced to frame the cils [sills] on the cilss [sills] for the piasa.

Friday, May 27   A lovely pleasant day & warm. Webb worked here today. They are puting on the cilss [sills] for the Piasa this afternoon. We read the sad news of the death of Mr. Libby of Watertown.   He hung himself in the asylem in Odgensburg. Carrie & I made a call in the school today.

Saturday, May 28   A pleasant day. No storm. Webb worked here today on the roof of the Piasa. Sarah & Manie Brown went to Gouverneur today. Drove their horse. They cald here. They done some trading & made a visit to Nelson Freeman's.

Clarence & Carrie went to town this evening. Attended the ice cream social in the Union church. Procedes for the benifit of the Sundy school. Martha & Bower Brown cald here today. Mrs. Alex Kerr cald here on her way to town. She was beg[g]ing for eggs to make the ice cream. Eddie Brayton cald here today asking for money to Pay the expenses of Mrs. Ed Leach to go to Montreal to be treated for her Rheumatism. The expense will be $50. Dr. Merkley recomendes he[r] to go to that Institution.

Sunday, May 29   Pleasant this forenoon but a hard shower this afternoon. Wm took a trip to Fairbanks today. Drove the colt before the buggy. Clarence & Carrie attended Church in the Methodist Church today.

The presents we have made some of the grandchildren: [Actually, Martha Brown and Sarah Brown are daughter-in-law's who appear on the following listing]:

Rose Brown

One bedroom set	$20.00
One lop	15.00
One Spring Rocker	7.00
One Stand	1.00
Two chairs	2.00
One organ [crossed out]	
One gold watch & chain	15.50
One pair of pillows	2.25
	62.75

Martha Brown

One table	6.50
One set of chairs	6.00
Two Bedsteads	6.00
One mattress	15.00
One set of chairs	3.00
One comode with glass	7.00
One pair of pillows	2.00
	$36.00

Sarah Brown

One rocker	3.00
One Matrass	5.00
One Comode with glass	7.00
	$15.00

for Clarence & Carrie Brown

One lop $10 on Bedstead 3 one Matrass	5.00
One Rocker 4 cu glass in commode	7.00
In bedroom set, 2 chairs	12.00
	$ 42.00

The amount of furniture that we have given to Mania [Manie] Brown Johnson, our granddaughter:

One bedroom set	$25.00
One lop & stand	12.00
One Spring Rocker	9.00
One willow Rocker	3.50
One tabel	6.50

One set of chairs	4.00
Two cane seat chairs	2.00
Two pairs of Pillows	4.00
One feather Bed	8.00
One bed spread	1.90
One gold watch & chain	15.50
	76.90

to Mabe Brown:

One bedroom set	$24.00
One Lop & Willow Rocker	13.50
One Spring Rocker	9.00
One Matrass	5.00
One pair of Pillows	2.50
One desk & stand	6.00
2 Cane seat chairs	2.61
1 Organ	60.00
One Piano	150.00
One Piano	200.00
A note of 100	100.00
Money	50.00
Money	14.00
Money	12.00
Money	5.00
One Gold Watch	16.00
One Book case	14.00
Dresser & comode	18.00
	$700.00

[On side: One feather bed, 10 dollars]

Monday, May 30   A rainy day. This was Decoration day. Some doings to the village. The Band Played & marched & the People placed flowers on the graves of the soldiers. A minister from Gouverneur made a speach in the Town hall.

458

Clarence drew four load of cheese to the Depo[t] this morning. Then he went to town & attended the store while his father & Bower played in the Band. Carrie & I done our washing this forenoon. Webb worked here today. Alvah & Sarah and litle Clarah made us a call near night. They took home a tabel from here to sit in their dining room.

Tuesday, May 31 A nice pleasant day. Mercury up to 80. Webb worked here today lathing in the woodhouse chamber.

Wednesday, June 1 The first day, a very warm pleasant day. Mercury up to 80. This was Webb's last day to work here. Clarence & Carrie figured the Cheese Bills. They took a ride to town tonight. A deaf & dum[b] man cald here to supper tonight.

Thursday, June 2 One more lovely day & warm. Our last new milk cow today makes 19 in number. 439 lbs of milk today from 18 cows. Min. McGill made us a call this afternoon & Frandy & Hattie Dulack drove here for a ride near night. Carrie strung her sweet peas up in good shape since milking.

Friday, June 3 A nice pleasant day & quite warm. Fred Donelson came here today & fixt the Eave spouts on our House & Clarence planted over some corn & planted some Beans. Wm helped put up the eave spouts & hoed some in the garden. Rob Watson's Boy came here near night and bout the young calf. Payed 1.50 cents for it. 2 days old.

Saturday, June 4 Just a lovely day. Carrie & I made a visit to Alex Kerr's this afternoon. Clarence & Carrie has gone to town this evening. Wm cald on the neighbours on this rhode. Beat & warned them out to work on the rhode next Monday.

Sunday, June 5 One more pleasant & warm day. Clarence &

Carrie & I attended Church this forenoon. I stayed to Charley Brown's to dinner & Clarence & Carrie took dinner to Alvah Brown's. Jim Webb & his litle girl & Cy Webb made a call here near night.

Monday, June 6   Clowdy all day & looks like rain tonight. Our men worked on the rhode today. Carrie & I done our washing this forenoon. We have the cloths all in & folded ready for ironing tomorow morning. Warren Bancroft was beried last Saturday. His home was in Fullerville. He was 25 years old. He Died with consumption.

Tuesday, June 7   A very warm pleasant day. Our men worked on the rhode today. Carrie & I done our ironing today. I cut out my silk cape today and partely made it. Mabel Brown came home today from Syracuse whare she had been attending a music school the past two years. Clarence & Carrie took a ride to town this evening.

Wednesday, June 8   Clowdy all day & a litle rain this afternoon and evening. Mabel Brown came up this afternoon & made us a visit. Clarence took her home this evening & Mrs. Hattie Dulack made is a call near night.

Thursday, June 9   Our men worked on the rhode today. A splendid shower last evening & misty this morning. Pleasant in the midle of the day & a nice shower tonight near dark. Clarence & Carrie made out the cheese bills this evening. Thare was one hundred and nineteen thousand, nine hundred and ninety-eight lbs of milk in the 7 days. 119.9.98. Cash for the same $748.29 cts. Salesman Clealand Nobels [Noble]. A. P. Brown, cheese maker.

Friday, June 10   A cool day. No storm. Had company today to dinner Martha & Mabel Brown & Mrs. Barker, a lady from Syracuse that came with Mabel to visit friends in Edwards &

Fine. Our men worked on the rhode today. Wm sold his black Devil today to Will. Cousins for 17 dollars. This was Manie Brown's birthday. 19 years of age.

Saturday, June 11   Our men finished their rhode work yesterday. Then sprouted pottatoes today. I made a call in Mrs. Storen's & Minny McGills. Leslie McGill was quite sick last night & today. This has been a rainy afternoon. Wm Cleand wheete this afternoon making it ready to take it to Gouverneur to exchange it for Flour. Clarence & Carrie went to town this evening. We had 500 lbs of milk the last 2 days each day.

Sunday, June 12   Misty this morning. No rain this afternoon. Wm has gone for a ride today with the colt. He would not tell me whare he was intending to go. He went in the direction of Fullerville. Mrs. Mary Harmon broke her wrist Friday. She was visiting to Jim Webb's at the time. Dr. Merkley set the limb. The same day he was cald to Russell to set 2 broken bones for a Miss Rolston. She was driving her Horse down the Hamilton hill this side of Russell village. Her Horse became frightond & she fell out & broke both arms & the horse broke his leg & had to be shot. So they had a serious time all around. Dr. Merkley was cald to visit Lesley McGill yesterday morning. Sold George Padget 2.4 lbs of sugar. Took goods from his store. 6 cents a pound. Old sugar.

Monday, June 13   Pleasant forenoon. A thunder shower near night. Clarence went to Gouverneur today with 13 bushels of wheete & brout home 9 sacks of Flour, 50 lbs each. We done our washing this forenoon.

Tuesday, June 14   Misty this forenoon but pleasant this afternoon. I went to town this afternoon. Made a call in A. P. Brown's & in Padget's store & took supper in Charley Brown's. Mrs. Winslow & Mrs. Barker was thare to supper.

Clarence went to Fullerville today with Will Cousins.

Wednesday, June 15   Just a lovely pleasant day & cool. Our men has cultivated their Potatoes today. Clarence & Carrie has gone to John Clealand's this evening for a ride. Mania [Manie] Brown was married today to Earl Johnson of York [Fowler].

Thursday, June 16   One more pleasant day. Not so very warm. Wm & Clarence has been Hoing corn today. I have made my silk cape today. Carrie has been adding up the cheese bills this afternoon. Leon Freeman and Ella Freeman cald here near night. He gave me a peace of his wife's wedding dress & a beautiful memorial card of Effie his wife.

Friday, June 17   A pleasant day. Wm & Clarence hoed corn all day. I finished triming my silk cape this forenoon. Carrie has been figuring the cheese bills today & this evening. I received a letter from Brother A.P. Johnson written the 13 of this month. It was just one year the 12 of June since Sister Lucy [Lucy Haile Johnson] Died, Abel's wife.

Saturday, June 18   Pleasant this forenoon & rainy all of this afternoon. Wm & Clarence hoed Potatoes this forenoon & took sprouts of the Potatoes in the cellar this afternoon. Clarence & Carrie went to town this evening. They brout me a letter from a niece [Rachel Johnson Harritt] in Oregon & a Photograph of my Brother Hiram and his wife's cemetery & their monuments & a sile of lovely flowers in the yard & around their graves. I prise them highly.

Sunday, June 19   A rainy forenoon, pleasant afternoon. Charley & Martha & Mabel Brown came up after Church & took Dinner with us. Clarence & Carrie went to Church this evening.

Monday, June 20 Just a lovely forenoon but a hard thunder shower this afternoon. We done our washing this forenoon & took our clothes all in & folded them ready for ironing tomorow morning. Wm took a ride out to the Jim Campell place this afternoon. A Mr. Brouse cald here today.

Tuesday, June 21 Pleasant today untill near night then a thunder shower. Mabel Brown & Mertle Webb made us a visit this afternoon. Wm took a walk to town near night. Took a pail of goosberies to Sherman's. Clarence went with Will Cousins to Dexter Gear's tonight. He was out in the shower.

Wednesday, June 22 A lovely forenoon. A shower at noon then pleasant this afternoon. Clarence & Carrie have gone to town tonight.

Thursday, June 23 Just a lovely day. No rain. Wm & Clarence has been nailing on lath in the woodhouse chamber. Clarence has drove to town 3 times today. I rode with him to town once & Bower came home with me & stayed to supper. I took dinner in A. P. Brown's & made a call in Padget's store & also in Charley Brown's. Martha was out making calls with Mrs. James Rushton but Mabel was at home making a Buiscit cushion of silk.

Friday, June 24 A very nice plesant day. Wm & Clarence has been Hoing Potatoes all day. Carrie & I have Picked quite a lot of goosberies today between chours. I filed 7 cans of goosberies & six can of Pieplant. Thair is all I have put today.

Saturday, June 25 No storm today but a teribel wind. Wm & Clarence finished hoing their Potatoes this forenoon. Then Wm Picked 13 quarts of goosberies this afternoon & Clarence went bathing in the river then he done some lathing in the chamber & and now after chours are all done, he & Carrie has

gone to town. I done my baking this forenoon of Bread &
Pies & fried cakes & Biscuit. Carrie done lots of work & then
picked a large pailful of Beries.

Sunday, June 26   A pleasant day. Only a fearful wind all day.
A shower in the past night. Clarence & Carrie & I attended
Church this forenoon. The new minister Mr. Carter spoke to
the People in the Union Church today.   I took dinner to
Charley Brown's & Clarence & Carrie made a call out to John
Clealand's. Took dinner. We all got home near five.   Mr.
Balcom was married last Thursday in Canton to a young lady
of that town. They have taken their home in Edwards Village.
Balcom is in company with Dr. Taylor in the drug store. I
payed 25 cents to the minister.

Monday, June 27   A clowdy day. Very litle rain. We done
our washing this forenoon & looked over strawberies &
goosberies this afternoon.   I cand eleven cans of tame
strawberies.   Clarence bought them of Wats[son?] the man
that groos [grows] his beries on a lot of John Clealand. Manie
& Earl Johnson cald here near night. She came home from her
weding visit last night. It will be 2 weekes next Wednesday
since they was maried & they intend to commence
housekeeping on Wednesday.

Tuesday, June 28   A warm pleasant day but a shower in the
night & early this morning. Wm & Clarence naild on lath in
the woodhouse chamber. Mabel Brown came up to dinner
today with grandpa. He took down 20 quarts of goosberies
yesterday. Sold them to Mrs. Traves [or, Traver] and Mrs.
Milo Woodcock & 8 quarts to Dr. Merkley & today he sold 20
quarts to Mrs. John Hughes. Took 5 quarts to Mrs. A. P.
Brown & 5 [quarts] to Mrs. C. H. Brown & we have cand 20
quarts 7 we have 20 quarts of strawberies cand.

Wednesday, June 29   A very warm pleasant day. We done

our Ironing this forenoon. Wm & Clarence been hoing corn today. We had strawbery short cake for super tonight & one for dinner Monday. We have had new Peas twice. Feandy sent me 5 quarts of Strawberies today. He took 5 quarts of goosberies.

Thursday, June 30　A warm pleasant day. Lots of wind. Mercury up to 80. Wm & Clarence finished hoing their Potatoes today. Sarah & Martha Brown came up this afternoon & Picked goosberies & Peas. Went home soon after supper. I received a letter from Ed Brown today from Conneticut.

Friday, July 1　A warm pleasant day it has been. Wm went to Hermon today & brut [brought] some furniture for Manie Brown or Manie Johnson now. I rode to town with Wm this morning. Made a visit to A. P. Brown's & a call in Jim Rushton's a call in Mrs. John Laidlaw's. She had just returnd from a trip on the St. Lawrence with her Brother Porter Harmon & his Daughter Annah Eliza. Clarence & Carrie is down to Clint McGill's to make a call this evening.

Saturday, July 2　A very warm day. Mercury up to 90. Clarence & Wm put wires in the Pigs nose today. Clarence went to town tonight. Mrs. A. Kerr made us a call this evening. Earl Johnson cald here this afternoon with his load of furniture to commence house keeping. We gave him a tabel & a willow Rocker & a Bedroom Set & a Set of Dining Chairs & a Matrass & a number of other articals.

Sunday, July 3　Just fearful Hot all day. Mercury up to 90 this afternoon at 2 & a fearful west wind all day just now at 6. The clowdes in the west look very dark. Very much like a storm. I have been at home all day. Clarence & Carrie attended church this forenoon & Clarence drove to Talcville [NY] this afternoon. Took 2 bushels of Potatoes to a Mr.

465

Wilcox. I wrote a letter to send to Edwin Brown to New Haven, Conn. this afternoon. Wm has been making a railling around the head of the stairs today in the woodhouse chamber.

Monday, July 4   This is Independence Day. A great Cellabration in Gouverneur today. The train went from Edwards to Gouverneur this morning with four coaches to take People to the Cellabration. A Dance to the Thomas House in our village tonight. A horse race this afternoon. Wm & Clarence & Carrie went down to see the race & they have all gone this evening. We done our washing this forenoon & I done a lot of cleaning in the woodhouse chamber this afternoon. A tasal of corn today. A shower last nite. Clowdy today.

Tuesday, July 5   Mabel Brown went to Ogdensburg yesterday on the morning train & from their she intendes to go to Depeyster [NY] to visit Mr. & Mrs. Wildes. A pleasant day today. Our men cut some grass in the front yard today. Wm drove the colt before the Buggy to the village near night. Clarence went to town tonight to hire a man to help with the Haying. The train came to town last night with 6 coaches & 400 passengers.

Wednesday, July 6   Quite a warm day. Mercury 80. Wm & Clarence worked in the hay field & yardes & side of the rhode. Bower came this forenoon & helped them. But he is near faged out after the Cellabration all day to Gouverneur & the dance all night to Edwards. We got the word yesterday that Mr. Johnson one of our village Blacksmiths has left his wife & litle child without any cause accept a ficle [fickle] mind & a desire to secure a nother man's wife. It is hopeful the Devil will take them before he gets into Canada.

Memoranda:

October the 23   Mrs. Ann Boutwell an old friend of our was beried today.

October the 30th Roxana Brayton was beried today.

A girl baby to Mr. and Mrs. Horis [Horace] Webb born Oct 31.

A girl baby to Mr. & Mrs. Leveret Nobels [Noble] Oct the 30th, 1898

A boy baby to Mr. & Mrs. Rastns Whitmarsh the first day of October 1898.

Arde E. Kerr died November the 7 1898 age 18 years.   Was shot in one of his armes.   Died with the influence of either. Was shot on Saturday the 5th by his school teacher accidently. Died Monday night.

Mr. Edwin Harmon and Miss Myrtle Peterson was maried the 23 of November 1898.

Thursday, July 7   Hot, hot.   Say nothing about being warm. Mercury near 90 at 6 o'clock this afternoon.   Wm & Clarence & Bower has been taking in a few load of Hay this afternoon. Has been a splendid day for haying.

Friday, July 8   A warm day.   A shower this afternoon near 3 o'clock.   The men was taking in hay but no more hay went in to the Barn today.   Bower came up & helped them this afternoon untill the rain came.   They have only 7 load in the barn.

Saturday, July 9   A good hay day but looked like showers. But did not come here but went around.   The men took in four load of hay.   Bower helped this afternoon.   Carrie & I had quite a lot of work to do this forenoon of Baking of Bread &

Cakes & Pies & house cleaning & cooking. Earl Johnson & Mania came out today to A. P. Brown's & took the remainder of her furniture home with them. Had a lop & stand & 17 chairs & a lot of quilts. We sold 5 dozen of eggs to C. H. Browns.

Sunday, July 10   A cool day. No storm. Wind north all day. Quite clowdy this afternoon. Clarence & Carrie went to Church this forenoon & we all took a good sleepe this afternoon. No company today. I made a call in Mrs. Storens & Minnie McGills last night. Wm was sick all day of Fryday & yesterday. She was Raking hay with the Horse Rake. I received a letter from a daughter of my Brother Charley Johnson from Pitsfield, [Pittsfield] Ill. Her mother died 2 years since & one years ago their house burnd & nearly all that was in it. Her husband was sick & she was full of trouble. I was very glad to hear from the children of my dear Brother.

Monday, July 11   Just a lovely hay day. A man from Fine [NY] worked here today. I bought a pail full of Red Rasberies [raspberries] today of Charley Brayton. Payed 8 cents a quart. We did our washing the forenoon.

Tuesday, July 12   One more pleasant day. Cool mornings. A litle frost yesterday & this morning. The men all worked in the hay field today. Bower helped this afternoon so thare was four men. They took in six load of hay. Wm & Carrie done all the milking last night & tonight.

Wednesday, July 13   A warm pleasant day. Our men cut & took in 7 load of hay. Had a hen come of[f] with 10 chickens & one with 10 Turkeys yesterday the 12 of July. This was the last day of our school for this term. The Teacher was Viola Harmon. She & her schollars had a Picnic today in the grove near Mr. Freeman's. I bought 2 quarts of red rasberies today of Charley Brayton. Payed 15 cents for them.

Thursday, July 14   A warm pleasant day. Good hay day. Clowdy near night & looks like rain. Lots of wind. Our 3 men worked in the hay field all day. Wm had such a headache, he could not help milk. I received a letter from Ill [Illinois] today.

Friday, July 15   One more dry warm pleasant day. Just a litle sprinkle of rain this morning. Not half as much as a Dew. Our men worked in the hay field all day. Bower came up & helped them get in 2 load of hay this afternoon. Mabel Brown & Eva Clark came here & made us a pleasant call & gave us some very good music. Carrie & Clarence has figured the milk bills yesterday & today & this evening. They have 2 sales to make out this week. I have just finished writing a letter of 7 pages to send to a niece of mine in Pike co. Ill. Mrs. Rebecka [Rebecca] Miller, my Brother Charley's [Charles Victor Johnson] Daughter.

Saturday, July 16   One more warm pleasant day. No signs of rain. The ground is very dry. Our men took in nine large loads of Hay today. John, the hired man, has gone home to Fine to night. Clarence has gone to town this evening. Wm has gone to bed at 8. Clarah is playing on the organ. I am writing in my Book.

Sunday, July 17   One more dry day. Clowdy part of the time & some signs of rain. We have all stayed at home today & had no company. A long lonesome day. Since I wrote the above few lines, I had 2 callers. Charley & Martha Brown & Clarence & Carrie has gone to John W. Clealand's this evening.

Monday, July 18   A very warm day. A litle shower at noon. Clowdy this afternoon & looks some like rain. Our hired man did not come today to work. He came near night to let us know that his mother is very sick & he will stay with her if he cannot get a girl or woman to care for her. So Clarence & Carrie has gone to town tonight to try & find a man to help in haying. I have just bought 2 quarts of Rasberies of Manda McGill, 7 cents a quart. We done our washing this forenoon. Clarence cut hay this forenoon & drew load of stove wood this afternoon.

Tuesday, July 19   Pleasant here today but good showers went around to Pitcairn & Harrisville. We had a lovely thunder shower in the past night from 12 to one O'clock. It has done a great good to the grain & Potatoes. We had quite a lot of hay out that got wet but that will soon be dry.

Wednesday, July 20   A good Hay day. Thare was four men worked in the hay.

Thursday, July 21   One more dry day. Bower came up & helped this afternoon with the hay. Carrie bought 10 quarts of Red Rasberies today of Mrs. Babcock. Payed 6 cents a quart. I put them in to cans since super while they was milking. Clarence took a ride over to Jim Webb's & hired John to come & work in the hay field.

Friday, July 22   A hot day. Mercury up to 90. The men took in nine load of hay today. The 3 men. John Webb worked here today. Wm went to town today & had shoes put on Bess colt. I bout 10 quarts of Beries today. Sold 12 lbs of sugar. 72 cents to Manda for beries.

Saturday, July 23   A change in the weather today. Big signes of rain all of this forenoon but did not come untill one o'clock. Been heavy thunder all of the afternoon. Lots of rain all around us but not much here. We are very thankful for what has fell & clowds look like thare will be a heavy shower soon. No haying today. Clarence ad[d]ed the milk today for the factory. He & Carrie took a ride to town this evening. Mabel

Brown came here this forenoon & took dinner. Went home just before the shower came. I bought 12 quarts of Beries last night. Payed in sugar.

Sunday, July 24 A fearful hot day. Mercury up to 100 at four o'clock this afternoon. Had a hard thunder shower last evening from 8 to 12. The rain came down just nicely. Was 25 lbs of water in the can covers this morning. The lightning struck & burnd a Barn in Hermon yesterday afternoon. Burnd all of the hay. Thare is 40 cows on the farm left without feede for winter.

Monday, July 25 No good hay day this. Clarence cut hay this forenoon. They started to take in some but the rain came so they did not take in any. John Webb worked here today. It was 3 o'clock when the thunder shower came. We done our washing the forenoon. Ninah Gear, a friend of Carrie, cald here this forenoon. She came on her wheel from John W. Clealand's this morning. She stayed with us untill two o'clock this afternoon. Her father lives four miles from here near Fullerville.[NY] Dexter Gear. Mr. David Jones of South Edwards was beried today. He died last Saturday with conjestion of the Brain. Only sick a few hours. Leaves a wife & 6 children. Clarence has gone to town tonight.

Tuesday, July 26 A very warm day. Mercury 90 this afternoon. We got the sad news that Frank Johnson's wife was Beried yesterday of Little York. No Haying today. Clarence & Wm dug out a large stone not far from the Barn. It was in their rhode. Hiram Hall came here near night & bout a bag of Potatoes. Payed 50 cents.

Wednesday, July 27 A nice hay day. Our men finished their haying today before super. They had John Webb & Mr. Barnette to work for them today. They drew in 13 load today. Wm done the Raking. Carrie took watter to the men this afternoon. I think she will remember the last day of the haying of this year. Minna McGill made a call here near night. Mrs. Milo Woodcock cald here today. I payed her 3 dollars for the minister.

Thursday, July 28   One more good day for those that are not through haying. Gid Freeman commenced his Harvest of oats yesterday. He cuts them with the mowing mashine he has. Took them into the Barn today. Carrie went after Beries today with Mina & Laura McGill. The Beries are nearly gone. Clarence has gone to town tonight. Thare has a party of young People from our village gone to Trout Lake to spend a weeke of fun. Martha Brown & Milo & John Woodcock families & Sherm Brown's wife has gone to the lake today for a 2 weekes outing.

Friday, July 29   One more very warm pleasant day. Mercury up to 90. Wm & Clarence put the reaper in shape this forenoon & they cut a few oats this afternoon. We had string beans today for the first time. Will Cousins came here today & took away a yearling calf. Rose Brown is making a visit to her sister Mania [Manie] in Little York this week.

Saturday, July 30   A little cooler today. Clowdy & smoky but no rain. Our men did not harvest any today. Wm drove out to Mag Wilson's & bought a bag of salt. I rode as far as A. P. Brown's & stayed untill he came Back. Got home before supper. Cald to Charley's store & bought 6 fruit cans. Payed 35 cents in money for them. I saw Laura McGill in the village on her wheele. Rose Brown was visiting her sister Mania Johnson in Fowler. S. W. Brown went over to Trout Lake on his wheele [bicycle] last night. We had chicken & dumplin for dinner. The chicken was one year old. A large white Rooster. Carrie's father gave it to her. I was sorry to have it kild but she thout best to have a good dinner of him. He was very nice indeed.

Sunday, July 31   Nice & cool this forenoon but quite warm this afternoon. Wm & I have been at home all day. Clarence & Carrie took a ride over to Trout Lake to visit the young People that is camping over thare from Edwards Village. I had new Potatoes for dinner today for the first time this summer. They was very good. This was Mr. Carter's day to preach in the Union Church. Carrie & I made a call in Mrs. Storen's last evening.

Monday, August 1   A thunder shower commenced today noon. Lasted nearly all the afternoon. Just a regular soaker. We done our washing this forenoon. The men cut oats this forenoon & gave the colt an awful whiping.

Tuesday, August 2   Just a lovely warm pleasant day. Our men cut oats this afternoon. Gave the colt one more warming. She helped draw the Reaper untill supper time. They draw the reaper with 3 horses. I have made yeast today & it is good. This is the evening for the School meting. Mr. & Mrs. James W. Harmon made us an evening call.

Wednesday, August 3   The men cut oats today. It was a good harvest day but a Hard thunder shower in the evening. Wm worked untill dark to get the oates set up before the rain. Clarence & Carrie done all of the milking. Carrie & I had a big time with our sugar in the Pantry. Took the most of it down. It was dreaning teribel on to our best dishes. We done our Baking today of Bread & Buiscit & Pies, Chocklet Cake & Cookies.

Thursday, August 4   A lowry rainy day. No harvest today. We had company today to dinner. Mrs. Ed Barry from Gouverneur, an Aunt of Carrie's & Mrs. Feandy Dulack from Edwards. We had new Potatoes & Beef Steak & Boild onions new & Bread & Butter & Cheese & Cucumbers & Cookies & Chocklete, no it was coconut cake. Mr. Earl Bancroft cald

473

here yesterday & payed us 75 dollars on a note. Clarence walked to town tonight with Harold Brown. He said thare is a lot of Jipsies camping by the side of the rhode over to the Corners near Frank Young. They have 8 Horses.

Friday, August 5   Pleasant this forenoon & our men finished reaping their oates then came a hard thunder shower near 2 o'clock. Then an hour of pleasant & sunshine. Near four a fearful thunder shower & now at five just lovely & pleasant. The sun shining lovely. No callers today but a pedler & Clint McGill & A Mr. Cole buying calves.

Saturday, August 6   A very nice pleasant day. Our men cut wheete this forenoon & set it up this afternoon but did not quite finish cuting their wheete. A cog broke in a wheele or they would of had their grain all cut & set up. Clarence & Carrie drove to town this evening. The jypsies mooved past here this morning. We was glad to see them go. They stayed 2 nights. They was beging milk this morning of the boyes that was going to the factory but they did not get any. I sent 4 dozen of Eggs to Charley's Store this morning & took 6 lbs of white sugar for them.

Sunday, August 7   No storm today but clowdy most of the time. We all stayed at home today. Our men finished reaping their wheete this forenoon, hitched our teem on to Clint McGill's mashine. Took the litle bit of wheete down in a half hour. Rose & Harold & Mabel Brown came up this afternoon. Made us an afternoon visit. Clarence took them home near night.

Monday, August 8   A litle misty & clowdy all day. Some rain in the night about one o'clock. We done our washing this forenoon & a large one it was. 3 long lines full & all the towels & rags on the grass. Clarence has added up the milk from the factory this afternoon & Cleand out the carage

474

[carriage] Barn. Wm has hoed in the garden. They put away all their farming machinery into the Back Barn this forenoon. August 6 payed 90 cents to a man for a map [possibly, mop]. An accident hapend [happened] to one of the miners today at Talcville. The man was drilling & the stone burst & blew the man nearly all to peaces but he was alive this evening.

Tuesday, August 9   Quite a good harvest day. Clowdy this afternoon & evening. No grain dry enough to take into the Barn. Mrs. Gid Freeman & her daughter, Ella, made us a friendly call this afternoon. Wm had a sick turn while milking. He came in & took Pepermint Sling & has gone to Bed.

Wednesday, August 10   A good harvest day but our grain is not dry. The men took in 2 loads of oats. Said it was not fit to go in the Barn. Bower came up & helped them. We had callers this afternoon. Mrs. Flack & Mrs. Alex Kerr. Laura & Minna McGill made a call over to Dan Webb's this afternoon. Found old Mrs. Webb very sick with a cancer in her stomach & one on her face. Miss Lizie Harmon is visiting to Mrs. A. Kerr's this afternoon.

Thursday, August 11   Just a splendid Harvest day. Our men took in the wheete this afternoon. 5 load & one large load of oates. Bower Brown worked for Clarence this afternoon. A pedler cald here today. I bout some tinware. Payed in sugar.

Friday, August 12   The clowds threatned rain all day but the rain did not come untill near 3 o'clock then it came with a downpour & plenty of thunder & lightning. Continued untill dark. The men took in 5 load of oats before the rain. Bower was here to help. Thare is 7 load out now. I think them are quite damp. Alex Kerr & Clint McGill & Horis Webb & Erbin Webb took theirs all in. Mrs. Storen is having her House Painted this week. Jimmy McFerin & Hugh Pratt is doing the work. Our cistern is brim full of water & running over. Wm is out watching this evening. I hope his patient will get along all rite. Carrie took a walk to town yesterday. Made a call in Frandy Dulack's & a short call on Mabel Brown. Ella Freeman was visiting Mabel.

[Memoranda] Wednesday May the 31 day 1899 A. P. Brown payed me 26 dollars & 25 cents today. I payed Charley Brown one dollar for a pair of shirts for Wm Brown.

Saturday, August 13 A good harvest day after the rain. Quite cool all day & A cold wind. Had quite an addition to our swine family this morning. Eleven litle spoted Pigs in the pen. Had a canvas tent over their house through the storm of last night. They are all doing nicely today. I had quite a sick spell the later part of the night or the early part of this morning. Mr. & Mrs. John Clealand cald here this morning on their way to Gouverneur. They left their 2 litle girls here with their sister Carrie. We all had a jolly time with them. They are 2 nice litle girls. Ethia [Ettie] the oldest is nearly ten years old & Venah is nearly five years. Clarence has took a walk to town tonight.

Sunday, August 14 Just a lovely day. Clarence & Carrie & I attended Church this forenoon. Mr. Carter, the Baptist minister, spoke to the People in the Union Church today. I met Erwin Harmon & his wife today. They are home from Kansas on a visit to his friends. He is a teacher in a high school in Kansas. His pay is one thousand a year.

Monday, August 15 Just a splendid harvest day but the rain is coming down this evening at 8 o'clock. A thunder shower is the program for this evening. Our men took in their last load of grain this afternoon at four o'clock. Mr. Barnet & Bower Brown worked here today. We have all done a lot of work today. Clarah done the washing. I done the housework & cand some Black beries. Mrs. Heth brout us eleven quarts this afternoon.   A Mr. Galsteen from Syracuse cald here this afternoon & sold Wm a pair of glases. Wm Payed $2 for them. Clarence has gone to town this evening.

Tuesday, August 16   A hard thunder shower in the night. Hard rain today but lots of wind & signs of a shower this evening. Distant thunder. Hard thunder & sharp lighting this forenoon. Wm & Clarence laid a part of the Back Piasa floor this afternoon. Last Sunday was Carrie's birthday. She was 21 years old.

Wednesday, August 17   No rain this forenoon. A thunder shower from 5 to 7 this afternoon. Pleasant this evening at 8. The stars are shining. Wm & Clarence nearly finished laying the floor on the Back Piasa. Wm took a ride up to John McKee's & got medicine for the colts sore neck. Clarence & Carrie has gone to town this evening. Thare was a quiet weding to Gideon Freeman's this afternoon. Their daughter Ella was maried to Arther Bulloc [Bullock] of Russell. They took this evening train for their weding tour. Have not learnd whare they intend to go.

Thursday, August 18   This has been a nice pleasant day. Not so very warm. Wm went to the mill & bought some lumber for the floor on the piasa & naild down the most of it. Carrie & I made a call in Minna McGill's this afternoon. Soon after we came home, Mr. & Mrs. Erwin Harmon made a friendly call here & Mabel Brown came up on her wheele & stayed to supper with us. Clarence has gone to town tonight. Wm has gone to A. Kerr's to make a call.

Friday, August 19   A cool pleasant day. We all went to town today. Attended fields day. It was made up of Ball playing & Horseracing & Ketching a greast Pig & the gathering of a large number of People from all partes of this town & from Hermon & Fine & Fowler & Gouverneur & Russell.   One

477

would think it was equal to a cellabration on the fourth of July. One of the horses while running stumbled & fell on 3 boys that was near the track & hurt them quite bad. But it is hoped not searious. Wm & I took dinner to Alvah Brown's. Thare was 18 thare to dinner. Clarence & Carrie took dinner to Charley Brown's. Clarence & Carrie has gone to town this evening. Thare is a Dance to the Hotell tonight.

Saturday, August 20   Just a nice pleasant day.   Wm & Clarence finished the Piasa floor & Painted it. Miss Fern Gear & Mrs. Hattia Dulack made us a call this afternoon. Clarence has gone to town to night. Wm has gone to bed at 8 & Carrie is a sleepe on the tabel.

Sunday, August 21   A nice pleasant day. Clowdy & looked like a storm near dark. Quite hard thunder but the shower went around so thare was no rain here this evening. Clarence & Carrie took a trip out to John Absalam's in West Fowler. Drove 2 horses before the new Buggy.   They said they enjoyed the ride. They drove over to Sylva Lake did not make any stop so they got home before dark.   Grant & Sarah Freeman cald here today on their way home from Church asking Wm to sign his name on her Paper to help fix the Cemetery. He signed 2 dollars.

Monday, August 22 Clowdy most of the day but no storm & quite warm. We done our washing this forenoon. Clarence has been drawing stove wood & filling in to the woodhouse. They fixt the chain on the well pump this forenoon. Arther & Ella Bullock came home today from their weding trip. She went home with Arther & his father to her new home in South Russell woods to setle down in an old log house. Not a neighbour in site among the Rocks & hills but we wish her great Joy.

Tuesday, August 23   A misty & clowdy day.   Very litle

sunshine. Clarence drew wood part of this forenoon untill the rain came. Then he figured the cheese bills. He & Carrie are working on them this evening. Mr. Jacob Green of Hermon, an old neighbour & friend of ours, cald here this afternoon & took supper with us. Then he went over to Alex Kerr's to stay overnight. He is calling on old friends. Wm has made the stepws for the Back Piasa today. I sent out a letter to Eddie Brown to New Haven, Conn. yesterday. The 22 of August.

Wednesday, August 24   A damp misty day.   A thunder shower at four this morning & we have had a   regular downpour this evening from 7 to 8. Wm has been painting overhead in the Back piasa. Clarence drew some wood this forenoon.   Minna McGill made us an afternoon call today. The Methodist Sunday School held a picnic near Gid Freeman's. On acount the rain, they ate their dinner on Gid's Piasa. Clarence is finishing making out stationery.

Thursday, August 25   One more rainy day or showery pleasant part of the time. Is nice & pleasant this evening. The harvest moon is shining lovely. Wm & Clarence has been painting overhead in the Back Piasa. I have been spining mitten yarn today. I spun 17 nots & doubled & twisted it. I had not spun any yarn for more than 8 years. Clarence has gone to town to night. He said Bower was very sick last night & this morning. They cald in the Dr. Merkly last evening to attend him. The large Pulp mill at Newton Falls was burnd down last week in the town of Canton, 5 miles from Russell village.

Friday, August 26   A cool pleasant day. Clarence Painted the Back Piasa floor & the steps today. Wm went to Hermon today & bought me a tabel & a pair of Pillows. I done a litle job of spining stocking yarn this afternoon. 8 knots. Clarence & Carrie has gone to Clint McGill's to spend the evening.

Saturday, August 27   A cold north wind all day but pleasant. Clarence drew stove wood & piled it in the woodhouse. We had company today to dinner. Mrs. Emmy Clark & her litle girl Mildred from Gouverneur & Miss Mabel Brown from Edwards Village. We had chicking [chicken] and dumplin & Potatoes & Bread & Butter & Buiscit, Cookies & Cockanut Cake white frosting & Aple Pie & Pickles & tea & sugar. Clarence & Carrie has gone to town this evening. Mabel Brown has gone to Jay Deweys to make a visit untill tomorrow night & Mrs. Emmy Clark will visit to A. P. Brown's tonight.

Sunday, August 28   A nice pleasant day. A cold morning. I attended Church this forenoon. I cald in to A. P. Brown's before church time. I gave Rose a glass this morning. Mr. Carter Preached today & this evening. His last Sunday in this place. The train came to Edwards this morning. Took a number of Passengers to Gouverneur to go to the Thousand Islands today & back this evening. They came at half past eight. Charley Brown & Mr. Holbroock [Holbrook] & I do not know all that went out. They came up with 3 coaches.

Monday, August 29   A clowdy & misty & rainy day. We done our washing this forenoon. This afternoon we looked over Black beries & made sauce of them & wound yarn for mitens & Carrie started to knit a sock for Clarence of Black yarn. Clarence has been hauling stove wood & grandpa has piled it in the wood house. They have it nearly full.

Tuesday, August 30   A very nice warm pleasant day. Our men finished filling the woodhouse with stove wood. I made a call over to Gideon Freeman's but Mr. & Mrs. Freeman was away from home. They have taken a trip up the St. Lawrence to visit their Brother Nelson & family that are staying in their cotage. Elle & Arther Bullock is at home this week doing the chours & work for her father. Clarence & Carrie went to town

480

tonight. Wednesday August 21 the last day of summer. A nice day but in the evening a smart thunder shower. Clarence & Carrie went to town. Got home just before the shower. I done some spining of miten yarn today. 18 knots & twisted 6.

Thursday, September 1   A hot day it has been. Clarence worked for Alvah Brown today in the cheese factory. Alvah attended the Gouverneur fair today. Went on the train. Rose Brown went on the train to Litle York last evening to visit her sister, Mania [Manie Brown Johnson]. I done my baking of bread & biscuit & aple pies this forenoon. Carrie & I have been knitting each a double mitten. Hers for Clarence & mine for Wm Brown. I done some colering [coloring] of Red yarn today for mittins for Bower & S.W. & Harold Brown, my grandsons. Clarence is away to town tonight. Clarah is out making an evening call on some of the neighbours. Clint & Minna & Laura & Lesley McGill all attended the fair today. Thare was 3 coaches on the train yesterday & they was all full & the same today & quite a number drove their teemes. Mr. Carter, the Baptist Preacher, cald here this afternoon on his way to town. He made a visit to Alex Kerrs yesterday & this forenoon. This is his last week in town. He returns to Hamilton College to renew his studies. He is a student of that school.

Friday, September 2   One more warm pleasant day. Some clowdy this evening. We are all at home this evening. We had company today to diner. Martha & Bower & Mabel Brown came up this forenoon & we had a rooster for dinner and dumpling and Bread & Butter & Aple Pie, tea & crackers. Sam Rushton cald here today. He was selling Peaches & Pears. Clarence bought a bascet of Pears & Wm bought a crate of peaches. We cand them this afternoon. Had 6 cans of each. I put in 20 lbs of sugar in the 12 cans.

Saturday, September 3   A fearful hot day. Just awful.

Clarence & Wm was cutting corn. They nearly melted. I went to town this forenoon. Took dinner to Charley Brown's. Attended Church meeting in the afternoon. Then made a call in Alvah Brown's then attended the Ice Cream social in the evening. Thare was quite a number took supper. I cald in Raymond's store & bought four yards of bed tic.

Sunday, September 4   Not quite as warm today. Lots of wind this afternoon   and evening.   We heard today that Mrs. Maryann Web[b] died this morning.   Her daughter Manda from Michigan came to visit her a few days since. Clarence & Carrie has gone out for a ride this evening.

Monday, September 5   A warm pleasant day. Very warm. We done our washing this forenoon. Wm & Clarence cut corn. Wm went with the milk to the factory today. Drove the colt. Mrs. Maryann Webb was Beried today.   She has been sick quite a long time with cancer in the stomach.   She has been living at her old home with her son Dannie the past year. Clarence took a walk to town this evening.   Thare was a sad afair took place at the high falls in the town of Canton a few days since.   A man by the name of Taylor in that place had just got home from the Gouverneur fair last week when he met his wife & her father.   They both pounded him with clubs so that he died in a few days after.   The wife is in Canton jail at present.

Tuesday, September 6   This has been a very warm day but not quite as warm as the past few days.   No rain untill near night. A thunder shower from five to 8.   Our men finished cutting their corn today.   Mr. Shefner the Insurance agent cald here near night. He took supper here.   Mabel Brown came here this afternoon to supper.   Rode home with Mr. Shefner as far as her home.   We had chicken & dumplin & Pumkin Pie & Bread & Butter & frosted cake. Clarence & Carrie is adding the milk this evening.   They sold cheese last Saturday.   They sell every week.

Wednesday, September 7   A rainy day.

Thursday, September 8   A pleasant day after the rain. Clarence & Carrie went to John Clealand's this evening & brout home 2 pails full of Crab Apls [apples] for jelle[jelly]. They dug 5 bushels Potatoes.

Friday, September 9   A pleasant day. Wm & Clarence Dug Potatoes today.   They dug 25 bushels.   They was white Potatoes & very nice. Rose Brown & Ethel Johnson made us a visit today.

Saturday, September 10   A very nice pleasant day. Clowdy this morning. Been a cool day. Good day to dig potatoes. Wm & Clarence put 24 Bushels into the cellar today. Thare is shoes [shows] in the town hall this evening. Clarence & Carrie has gone to town this evening. Wm & I Played four games of India this evening then I finished kniting a mitten for Wm. I finished filling my Pillows today. I have made 2 new pairs & fixt up one more pair of smaller ones. I have six pair of good Pillows. Have just given Mania [Manie Johnson] 2 pair. I done some Baking today of Bread & Pumkin Pies.

Sunday, September 11   A hard frost this morning. Pleasant today but cool. Glad to make a fire in the setting room. Charley & Martha & Mabel came up today to dinner. Clarence & Carrie took Mabel out for a ride to Rob Wilson's. Was home near eight o'clock. We had 2 roosters cooked for dinner & pumkin pie & cream cake & as much of other things as we cared to eat.

Monday, September 12   No frost this morning. Our men finished diging their Potatoes.   Had 75 bushels of good Potatoes. Mr. Barnet worked here today. Clarence payed him

483

one dollar. We done our washing this forenoon. Clarence went to town tonight. Wm made a short call to Mr. Flack's. Carrie made a call in Clint McGills. Mabel B took supper here tonight.

Tuesday, September 13   A nice pleasant day. Some frost this morning. Daniel Sullivan cald here today & bought 2 litle pigs, one dollar each. Four weeks old. Clarence went to town this afternoon to get molly a shod. I rode as far as Sherm Brown's, made a visit thare. This afternoon Martha & Mabel was thare to supper.

Wednesday, September 14   A nice pleasant day. This is the week for the Canton fair. Clarence & Carrie has gone to Canton today to attend the fair. Intend to stay 2 days. Lester Clealand helps do the milkin when they are gone.

Thursday, September 15   One more nice day. Mabel Brown started for Syracuse this morning on the train. Wm drove the colt to town today & got his buggy mended & bought 5 lbs of Battin at 50 cents. Mr. & Mrs. Gideon Freeman made us a call this evening. A Mr. Fuller from Fowler cald to hire money of Wm but he did not get any.

Friday, September 16   A very litle rain today. Our men sold their calves last night for 55 dollars. Wm & Clarence. Wm took a ride to Dan Sullivan's this afternoon. Bought a 2 year old calf. Clarence & Carrie came home from the Canton fair last evening near ten o'clock. Had a pleasant time. Our men put wood in the shugar house this forenoon. Clarence went to town tonight.

Saturday, September 17   One more pleasant day. Quite warm. Wm drew gravel from the Perkin's hill near Harry Clealand's. Mr. & Mrs. Mills from Hermon cald here today. Mrs. Frank Barnes cald here. She was selling hard soap. Clarence has gone to town.

Sunday, September 18   We will set this down as a rainy day. Hard showers this morning & a hard thunder shower near night. But the stars are shining this evening. We all stayed at home today & this evening. A nice young gentleman cald here this afternoon. Came on his wheele [bicycle]. A stranger but we think he was the young man that intendes to teach our school this fall term.

Monday, September 19   Clowdy most of the day. A shower near one o'clock. We done our washing this forenoon. Our school commenced today. A Mr. Obrine from Rossee [Rossie] is the teacher. Wm has been haulling manure today. Clarence & Carrie went to town.

Tuesday, September 20   Quite a good day. No storm but quite cold. Clarence has been haulling out manure today. Wm has been looking over Potatoes today. Picking out the roten [rotten] ones. I finished my last mitten for Wm this evening. Mrs. Rob Webb cald here today & borrowed 21 dollars of Wm. Gave her note to be payed in one year from today. Clarence has gone to town tonight.

Wednesday, September 21   Just a lovely pleasant day but a hard frost this morning. Wm gathered the cucumbers last night for the sweete Pickels. Clarence drew 2 load of manure from the village today. Clarence & Carrie has gone to town to attend the showes. Clarence took them in last evening. Showes are a sort of concert & selling medicine pulling teeth & most anything to pick up a litle money. Wm & I have been playing backgammon. We foold away the evening but did not spend any money on the games.

Thursday, September 22   No storm today untill dark. It is raining some this evening. Clarence drew manure from the village this forenoon & he figured cheese bills this afternoon & this evening. Wm drew a load of manure from Glasby's this afternoon. Alex Kerr attended the Potsdam Fair this week. The train has just come in to Edwards at eight o'clock. They wait for the pasengers from the fair. Mr. & Mrs. John W. Clealand cald here this evening on their way home from Gouverneur.

Friday, September 23 A rainy day it has been & is raining hard this evening. A thunder shower near six o'clock & a steady downpour untill nine. I do not know how much longer it will last. Clarence & Carrie has gone to town in the rain & mud to attend the showes again this evening. I did think I would go tonight but when the thunder & rain commenced, I gave up the pleasure that I had anticipated. Wm & I played 4 games of India & I have set my bread & will soon go to Bed. Clarence took 8 Pigs to Meade Thomas this forenoon & sold them for $8 in money. Wm has got just one left. He intends to keep that & the old mother Pig & we have 3 nice ones of last March. Pigs to dress for ourselves this fall.

Saturday, September 24 No storm today or since morning. An awful rainy night last. Quite cool today & clowdy all day & this evening. Clarence has gone to town this evening. Will attend the showes. Wm & Carrie & I are at home. Wm went to town this forenoon. Took dinner in Charley's. He bought a pair of fulcloth pants for $2.50.

Sunday, September 25 Clowdy all day but no storm. Pleasant this evening. Thare is a lovely moon sailing through the sky this evening. It will give a nice light to the people that attendes the Lecture & Show this evening in the town hall in our litle village of Edwards. Wm & I have been at home today. Had no company. Clarence & Carrie made a visit to her father's, J. W. Clealand's & they have gone to town tonight to attend the shows & lecture. Sherman Brown has

been sick today. Not able to work in the Cheese factory.
Young Jim Harmon worked in his place.

Monday, September 26 Clowdy part of the time. No storm
but now near nine o'clock the rain has commenced to come
down moderate. We done our washing this forenoon.
Mended old Bags this afternoon. Clarence commended his
fall plowing today. He has gone to town tonight. Vint Brown
made us a call this afternoon. Took supper. He had just come
back from Ogdensburg whare he had taken his boy to the
Children's home.

Tuesday, September 27 A nice cool day. A good day to
Plow. Clarence was plowing all day. We do not eat supper
until after milking. Commenced doing this way last Saturday
night. Carrie made tomato Pickels today. Martha Brown
came up to dinner today. She rhode home with Wm & I to
town. I made a call in Alvah's & Wm drove out to Mr.
Beavre [Beaver] on the Jim Campell farm.

Wednesday, September 28 Just a lovely day. Wm & I made
a visit to Earl & Manie Johnson's today to York. We got
home at half past four in time for chours & supper. Clint &
Minna McGill made us an evening call tonight. Frank Ingram
came home from the south on a month ferlow from the
Hospital whare he has been sick since the first of August. He
came last Monday. Wm lent me 3 lbs of Rools today of Dan
Sullivan. Payed 40 cents a pound.

Thursday, September 29 Just a lovely pleasant day. Wm has
done some plowing today. Clarence has not been feling very
well today. He has gone to town this evening to call on Dr.
Merkley. We had roast chicken for dinner today. It was very
good. I made four Pumkin Pies this afternoon.

Friday, September 30 This was the last day of this month & a very warm day it has been. Wm has been working on the Rhode today. The weather has been to[o] warm to do much Plowing today. Mr. Andrews the teacher in the Talcville School Boardes to Mrs. Alex Kerr's this term in this district & our teacher boardes to the hotell in Edwards village. Wm received a letter from Mrs. E. Stanton of Michigan last night with a draft of $30 inclosed.

Saturday, October 1   The first day and a very warm day it has been. Mercury up to 80 this afternoon in the shade. Clarence drew watter to get ready for the thrashers. They will be here next Tuesday. Clarence & Carrie has gone to town tonite.

Sunday, October 2   A very nice day. Not as warm as the past 2 days when the mercury was up to 80 in the shade. It was 60 today. We all spent the day at home. Seymour Absolom & family cald here at short time & Charley & Martha Brown cald a while this afternoon & Mr. & Mrs. John Clealand & 2 litle girls made a short call on their way home from her Sister's, Mrs. Deckgears. [Dexter Gear?]

Monday, October 3   Quite a warm day. Some clowdy & looks like rain. I had company today to dinner. Mrs. Altha Laidlaw. She attended the funeral of Mrs. George Smith yesterday & came down this morn with Charley Laidlaw & family. They was going to Gouverneur with their Son Dean for to take the train to go to Syracuse to enter the medical college. Clarence has gone to town tonight. He done some Plowing this afternoon & Wm done a litle Plowing this forenoon. I sent out a letter to Mabel Brown today. Wrote it last evening. We did not do much of our washing today.

Tuesday, October 4   Clowdy & misty all day. The Thrashers came this forenoon but did not do any work untill after dinner. We had 10 men to dinner & 12 to supper . They just got the wheete threshed today. Thare was 65 bushels of it. Came last evening. We did not do much of our washing today.

Tuesday, October 4   Clowdy & misty all day.   The Thrashers came this forenoon but did not do any work untill after dinner. We had 10 men to dinner & 12 to supper . They just got the wheete threshed today.   Thare was 65 bushels of it.   Came quite a shower so they could not work any more.   Four men stayed with us overnight.

Wednesday, October 5   Misty & some rain but the men got through with the threshing at half past 3 & drove over to Alex Kerr's.   We had 13 men to dinner to day.   2 Barnet Brothers & Lealond [Leland] Cousins & John & Cy Webb, Lester Clealand, Bower Brown, Bruce Ward, Blane [Blaine] Harmon, Warren Harmon, Jap [Jasper] Ward, Wm & Clarence Brown.

Thursday, October 6   A lovely day.   Rather cool this evening. I made a call over to Mrs. Freeman's early this morning.   Mrs. Freeman was very sick today.   Clarence went after Dr. Merkley for her.   I stayed with her untill 3 o'clock.   Their Sister Mrs. Watson came to spend a few days with her.

Friday, October 7   A nice cool day.   Rather clowdy all day.   I had company last night. Mr. and Mrs. Evins [Evans] from Fine village.   They stayed overnight & a part of this forenoon.   We had a splendid visit with them.   Clarence & Carrie went to John Clealand's [this] evening.   She stayed until this evening to help her mother do the house work today while the threshers was thare.   I received a letter from my Brother A. P. Johnson of Pine Valley this evening.   Writen yesterday. Clarence has been Plowing today.   Wm has been Husking corn today.   I have done the housework & some washing today.

Saturday, October 8   A cool pleasant day.   Wm & Clarence husked corn in the Barn this forenoon.   Clarence went to town.

489

Sunday, October 9 Just a lovely cool day. We all stayed at home today. Clarence & Carrie has been adding the milk today. Had no company today.

Monday, October 10 A pleasant day. A very hard frost this morning. The ground was frosen & the watter in the Pail had quite thick ice on it. Carrie done a large washing this

[text continues on page 491]

Sap buckets on a maple tree and a sugar shack

forenoon. Clarence went to town this forenoon. He done some Plowing this afternoon. Clarence & Carrie are making out the statements [cheese statements] this evening. Wm has been shelling corn this morning. This was Wm Brown's Birthday. He is 74 years old.

Tuesday, October 11   A rainy windy day. Wm & Clarence husked corn today.   Clarence done some plowing this afternoon. Carrie & I done a lot of ironing today. I made Bread this morning. I bought a clothe Basket today of a lady Pedler. Payed her 8 lbs of sugar, 60 cents.

Wednesday, October 12   A cold day. No storm. Clowdy this evening. Wm husked corn all day. Clarence plowed this forenoon & husked corn this afternoon. He & Carrie has gone to town this evening. I made a call in Mr. Gid Freeman's today.

Thursday, October 13   A very hard frost this morning. Quite cool & pleasant. Wm & Clarence husked corn in the Barn all day. Carrie & I done quite a job of cleaning in the chamber today. Clarence has gone to town this evening. Wm went to bed at 7 o'clock tonight with a plaster on his lungs. He has a hard cold the past week.

Friday, October 14   It has raind all day since in the night. Wm & Clarence finished husking their corn today. Wm went to bed at seven o'clock.

Saturday, October 15   A rainy day & raining this evening. No work for the men today, only the chours. Sarah & Harold & Clarah Brown made us a visit this afternoon. Clarence went home with them this evening. Wm sent a letter to the offis this evening to go to Enos Stanton in Michigan. Wm & I played 2 games of India this evening. We was even on the games.

491

Sunday, October 16   No storm today but clowdy & cold day. I attended Church today, both forenoon & afternoon. The Universalist held an association in the Union Church yesterday & last evening & today & this evening. Thare was 5 ministers in attendance.   I cald in Charley Brown's after Church time & took dinner thare. Clarence & Carrie has gone to Church this evening.

Monday, October 17   A lovely pleasant day. A very hard frost this morning. Quite cool this evening. We done our washing this forenoon & Carrie cleand her Bedroom this afternoon before chourtime & she has drest a Rooster this evening ready for dinner tomorow.   Clarence has been Plowing all day. He has gone to town tonight. Wm went to town this afternoon. Got some iron fixt for the Plow. Alvah commenced to make Butter today in the Factory.

Tuesday, October 18   A nice pleasant day. Clarence Plowed all day.   Carrie cleand the Parlor today & I cleand my Bedroom & Carrie made a pan of white cookies.

Wednesday, October 19   A rainy day this has been & is raining this evening. It is mud evry place & mudy rhodes a plenty. Clarah done a large ironing today. I have been trying to make a rade [raid?] in the Pantry today. I have lifted & mooved 500 lbs of sugar & washed the shelves & Clarence took four or five Buckets full of cake sugar up in to the woodhouse chamber. I made 4 Pumkin Pies this morning. Wm has been puting glass into the Barn windows today.

Thursday, October 20   Just a lovely day. Clarence has been Plowing all day. He & Carrie has gone to town this evening. Wm went to town this afternoon. He bought himself a fine shirt & drawes & socks & brout him a satchel. He says he intends to go to Syracuse next Saturday & stay thare over Sunday & then go to Pine Valley, Chemung Co. & then to

Canada West.

Friday, October 21   A pleasant day untill near dark.   It commenced to rain & is raining moderate this evening. Clarence has been plowing all day. He has gone to town this evening to do some errands for Wm.   Wm has put in a part of the storm windows today & dug the Beats[beets] & took them in to the cellar & put in the windows in the cellar.   Clarah has cleand the cubbord this afternoon & put on the dishes all in very nicely & clean papers & the Pantry & shelves all look lovely.

Saturday, October 22   one more rainy day after 2 pleasant days.   No plowing today.   Wm Brown started this morning for Syracuse & Pine Valley & Tilsonburg Ontario [Canada].   I made Bread & Pumkin Pies today.   Carrie done the slicking up of the dining room & other work.   She drest a rooster this evening ready for tomorow for dinner.   She & I played four or 5 games of India this evening to pass of the time while Clarence was gone to town.   He took down 26 lbs of sugar to Charley Brown's store.

Sunday, October 23   Raind this forenoon.   Pleasant this afternoon.   Charley & Martha Brown made us a call today. We had chicken for dinner & a few other articals. I just had a call from a young man all drest in a nice Black Suit & Black Hat. His dress was rather loose but he or she was quite a good looking chap. He made rather a short call.

Monday, October 24   A pleasant day.   We done our washing this forenoon.   Arda Kerr made us a call this afternoon.   I brout the school collecter papers to Clarence.   A Miss Carter cald here.   She was selling hard soap.

Tuesday, October 25   One more nice warm pleasant day. Clarence did not take the milk to the factory today.   He done a

493

lot of Plowing all day. He has gone to town this evening to attend a Political lecture. Carrie & I are here at home. Just ourselves. We are a litle bit lonely. We have not heard from Wm since he went away last Saturday. Mrs. Ann Boutwell was beried last Sunday. A friend of mine.

Wednesday, October 26   One more rainy day & this evening. We got a letter from Mabel Brown last night & one from B. F. Nobels [Noble] from Syracuse, NY.   They said that Wm Brown arived thare Saturday evening & left thare Monday to go to Pine Valley. Benny wrote to Clarence to send him 400 lbs of sugar. Clarence took it to the station today. Carrie & I cleand the woodwork in the kitchen today.

Thursday, October 27   We have had our first snow storm today. Been a nasty wet cold day. It is mud everyplace even in the house. We did not try to clean house today. Thought we would wait & perhaps the storm would blow over after a week or two. Clarence has finished the figuring of the milk this afternoon and evening.

Friday, October 28   A pleasant day after the 2 days rain. We cleand our Dining room today.   Clarence plowed all day between doing chours around the Barn. Clarence went to town this evening. Mrs. Roxana Brayton died this morning. She is nearly 80 years old. Will be Beried next Sunday.

Saturday, October 29   Just a lovely pleasant day. Clarence finished his plowing in the Back lot today. He has gone to town tonight. Carrie & I are at home. We had a caller this evening but she did not get into the house. I met her outside & told her to go on. She apeared to be a tramp & wanted to stay overnight & perhaps longer. We do not like such company.

Sunday, October 30   One more pleasant day. A hard frost this morning.   Mrs. Brayton was Beried today in Edwards.

William Green from Hermon made us a call today & took dinner with us. Clarence & Carrie took a ride to John W. Clealand's tonight. I made an Evening call in Charley Brown's tonite.

Monday, October 31   A nasty rainy drisling day. We done our washing this forenoon. Clarence Plowed most of the day if it did rain. Clint McGill cald here today & Paid his school tax. I wrote a letter yesterday to send to Wm Brown in Tilsonburg Canada West. This was the last day of October of 1898.

Tuesday, November 1   No storm today. Clarence has been plowing all day accept chours & thare is a lot of them to do with milking & caring for 3 horses & pigs & hens & turkeys to feede, stabels to clean & lots of ods & ends. Clint & Minna [Minne] McGill is making us a call this evening. We have all been playing games. Clarence went to town tonight & got a pair of rubber Boots for himself. A litle girl to Mr. Boscoes was having fits tonight when Clarence came from town. A litle girl baby to Mr. & Mrs. Horis [Horace] Webb last evening. Weight 8 lbs.

Wednesday, November 2   No storm today. Clarence finished the fall Plowing today. He went to town tonight. He took a deede for Charley to take to Canton.

Thursday, November 3   One more nice pleasant day. Clarence cleand out the Ditches in the back lot. He stayed at home with us this evening.

Friday, November 4   Just a lovely pleasant day. I went to town today. Made a visit to Alvah Brown's and a call in Charley Brown's. Bower came home with me at half past three. We had company this evening. Mr. & Mrs. James Harmon. Clarence went to town tonight. He brout me a letter from Wm Brown. He is in Canada having a good visit with his rellatives thare. He thinks he will come home next Monday night.

Saturday, November 5   A fearful wind all day & this evening & some rain this evening. I made a call in Mrs. Storen's & Minne's this afternoon. Clarence went to town tonight. He brout us the sad news that Arda Kerr had accidently been shot in one of his arms by the school teacher of the village school. The two was out hunting when the accident hapened.

Sunday, November 6   An awful storm of wind & rain at 2 o'clock this morning. The house shooke & trembled like thare had been an Earthquake & quite plenty of wind today & squals of rain & a litle sunshine but clowdy this evening & looks like a storm. We did not any of us go to church today. Clarence made a call to Mr. Flacks & Clint McGills & Carrie made a call in Horis Webb's & Clint McGill's. The doctors got together today 3 of them & succeeded in dresing   Kerr's broken arm. Dr. Taylor & Dr. Merckley & Dr. Drnry had the boy under the influence of cloraform nearly 3 hours.

Monday, November 7 No storm today. We done our washing this forenoon. This was my birthday. I was 73 years old today. William B came home this evening from Canada. He has been gone from home 17 days. Made a number of visits among his friends in Chemung County & in Canada. Arda Kerr died this evening near seven o'clock. His age is 18. He is the only child of Mr. & Mrs. Urban O. Kerr of Edwards, NY.

Tuesday, November 8   This was Election day. Wm & Clarence went to town. They took dinner in Charley Brown's. Mr. & Mrs. Charley Laidlaw took dinner in C. H. Brown's today. Carrie Brown & Min H. Webb made a call in Mr. Flack's this afternoon. I made a call in Alex Kerr's this forenoon. I done my Baking today of four Pumkin pies & 3 loves [loaves] of Bread & done my ironing. Carrie said she saw a lot of Turkeys in Mr. Flack's lot. Thare was more than 300. Horace Webb & Mr. Flack is buying a lot of turkeys for market. They intend to sell near Thanksgiving. They pay 8 cents a pound live waite [weight].

Wednesday, November 9   A misty day. Some fine snow & some rain through the day. Snowing some this evening so the ground is covered. We all attended the funeral of Arda E. Kerr this afternoon. Thare was a full house. The funeral ws attended at the house of the deceast. The Rev. Mr. Gale preached a short sermon. Wm Noys was the undertaker. Thare was 70 teems in the procesion to the cemitery.

Thursday, November 10   This has been an awful stormy day of rain & snow & ice. A bad day intirely.

Friday, November 11 The ground was white with snow & ice this morning & cold & stormy this forenoon. Quite pleasant this afternoon & this evening. Clear & cold. Clarence went to Perce Brown's this forenoon & drove home the 3 head of young cattle that had been thare to Pasture the past summer. Clarence & Carrie has gone to Clint McGill's this evening for an evening visit. Clint & Minna [Minne] intendes to moove next Tuesday on to their farm that they have lately bought of Sina Webb. Location near Wilsons. 3 miles beyond Edwards village in Scotland district.

Saturday, November 12   Just a lovely pleasant day. Quite cool this morning. A hard frost this morning. Mercury 10 above zero this morn. 30 above near night. The snow melted of[f] some but the ground is white yet. Clarence & Carrie has gone to town this evening. Wm & I have been playing games of India & Backgamon from 6 to 8 o'clock.

Sunday, November 13   No storm today. Clowdy this

afternoon & looks like a rain storm. The wind is blowing hard this evening. We have all stayed at home today accept that Clarence drove to the factory & brout home the milk Book. He has the milk for the Butter that has been sold to ad [d] & make out the Statements. Clint McGill came here near night & took home our box for scalding pigs. He intendes to Butcher tomorow & be ready to moove on to his farm on Tuesday.

Monday, November 14   This has been a stormy day. We done our washing this forenoon. Wm & Clarence banked the house today. We had company this evening. Arba Kerr & Mr. Andrews, the teacher from Talcville. They had a good time playing the game of Pede. Wm & Clarence played checkers & Carrie & I played the game of India. We had a good visit.

Tuesday, November 15   Not a very nice day. Clowdy & the ground was froze some this morning. Snowed some this afternoon & it has been a fearful dark evening. Clarence went to town tonight. Charley & Bower went to Harrisville today with the Cornet Band to play for A Jubilee gathering. Clarence drove around among some of the people in this school district & collected taxes. Had good luck at every place accept Jim Webb's & he was not at home. Alex Kerr has been afflicted with a fearful lame back not able to get out at all for 2 days. Clint McGill has given up the farm deed that he had made with Sina Webb. I started to knit a pair of mitens for Wm Brown last night. Carrie commenced to knit a sock for Clarence this evening after finishing the first one. Wm & Carrie played 3 games of checkers this evening & he & I played 2 games of India.

Wednesday, November 16   A very good day. Warm for the this time of year. Mud is plenty every place. Plenty in our kitchen. Clarence went to town this afternoon & collected taxes. Home at 3 o'clock. He & Wm dug ditches this forenoon & yesterday. It is pleasant this evening. The stars are shining & thare was a lovely new moon this evening. I finished one of Wm's new mittens this evening & started the mate for it.

Thursday, November 17   Just a lovely day & a very Hard frost this morning. Clarence took a ride to Jim Webb & P. H. Brown's & collected school Tax.   He & Carrie has gone to town this evening.   Wm & I have played checkers & Backgamon, two games of each.   Thare was a man by the name of McBroom in the town of Fine that was accidently shot last Sunday. He died in Monday while out hunting.

Friday, November 18   A nice warm day.   No storm today. Clint & Minny intendes to moove on to their farm tomorrow. I have writen a letter to send to Mabel tomorow.   Wm went near Charley Harmon's today & brout home a load of sand for the Hens to eat.   Wm & Clarence & Carrie played a few games of Peede this evening.

Saturday, November 19   A clowdy but warm day.   Raind some this afternoon.   Fearful dark this evening & the wind is blowing hard.   Wm Brown went to John B. Absolom's today in West Fowler, 12 miles from here.   Will stay untill tomorow. Clarence has gone to town to night.   Carrie & I are here just by ourselves.   No company today or this evening.   I made a call in Mrs. Storen's today.   Clint & Minna [Minne] McGill mooved today on to their farm.   Went with 2 loads.

Sunday, November 20   Quite cool today & clowdy.   Looks like rain.   Wm came home from Fowler near dark.   Brout home a lot of garget [gargett] Root to feede the cows. Clarence & Carrie took a ride to town.   Got home at half past seven.   Thare was no Preaching.

Monday, November 21   Just a lovely day.   Warm & sunshine.

499

Mercury 62 above 0. The men done the chours & Clarence took a load of Butter to the depot this morning. Clarence & Carrie has gone to John Clealand's this evening for a short visit. I sent a letter to Mabel Brown in Syracuse last Saturday. Carrie done her washing this forenoon & I done the Housework.

Tuesday, November 22   Just a lovely pleasant warm day. Wm & I made a visit to Charley Johnson's today. We had company this evening. Mr. & Mrs. Flack & their two girls. Clarence had gone to town before they came. Got home a litle before they went home. We had a good visit. They brout us a pailful of aples & Clarence bought one Bushel of aples today of a Mr. Brown from Russell. Payed 80 cents a Bushel for them. Wm made a call on Clint & Minne today in their new home. He found Amos Newton & wife thare to make them a visit.

Wednesday, November 23   The ground was white with snow this morning. Been clowdy all day & a mist of snow & the ground has frozen some. I done some baking of Bread & Pies. Carrie made a nice cake & drest a rooster & done lots of other work. She & Clarence has gone to town this evening. A. P. Brown made us a call this afternoon. He envited Wm & I to take dinner at his house tomorow.

Thursday, November 24   Clowdy all day & is snowing this evening. We all went to town today. Clarence & Carrie took dinner to Charley Brown's. Wm & I took dinner to A. P. Brown's. Sherm and Gerta [Gertrude] Brown & Earl Johnson & Manie was thare to dinner & they had Roast Turkey & lots of good things for dinner. We all came home in good season for chours & supper. Then Clarence took a trip back to town. Brout home the maile. Thare was Thanksgiving servis in the Me[thodist] today. Litle Clarah Brown has got the whooping cough very bad. Mercury was 20 above zero this morning.

Friday, November 25   A cold pleasant day. 3 inches of snow fell in the night. Mercury was 10 above zero this morning. It is 8 above zero this evening at nine o'clock. Clarence did not go to town tonight. He spent the evening at home. Wm went to bed at 6 o'clock tonight. He was not feelling very well.

Saturday, November 26   A cold stormy day of snow & wind. Mercury 6 above zero this morning. Wind north all day & this evening.   The men done their chours. They have some spare time to reed [read] or make figures count the interest on some old note.   Clarence has gone to town tonight. Will & I have just played a game of backgammon. He got the start of me & he would not play another game for fear he would loose his game.

Sunday, November 27   A cold pleasant day.   Mercury 6 above zero this morning & 20 above this afternoon. This is a lovely evening. The moon is nearly full & is sailling through the sky in all its grandure. It shines all night. Clarence & Carrie has gone to Church this evening. We have set our milk at home tonight for the first time this fall.

Monday, November 28   Oh what a lovely day this has been & just a beautiful evening. The moon is full today. Mercury was at zero this morning. Clarence took 12 bushels of oats to mill today to be ground into meal for pigs & cattle. Wm went to Gouverneur tonight on the train to be ready to take the early train tomorow for Pine Valley, Chemung Co. He is very fond of taking long trips on the train. He took $500 with him. We bought 5 lbs of Butter today from the factory. We have had in all 15 lbs from the factory this fall & 20 lbs of C. Laidlaw. We packed 100 lbs before the milk went to the factory in the Spring for our own yuse. We have bout 14 lbs of tea since last January. We have bought 38 lbs of lard since the in June last. We have bought 58 lbs of white sugar in the Past year & 18

501

lbs of crackers, 3 brooms, 4 lbs of saleratus, 6 lamp chimneys.

Tuesday, November 29   This has been a nice pleasant day.
Mercury 10 above zero this evening. Clarence went to town
today & took the Statements to A. P. Brown. We have all
been at home this evening. Clarence & Carrie played 4 games
of Checkers. Tomorow is the last day of November. It is
Charley Brown's birthday. He will be 50 years old tomorrow
morning at 5 o'clock. We lived in the old house that stood on
the same foundation that this one does now. 50 years ago,
Wm had been working for his brother-in-law Mr. Broadia
[Brodie] for one year. When our litle Charley was 2 weeks
old, we mooved to the village of Edwards. Wm attended the
grist mill for Henry Ruston for seven years then we mooved in
to the old homestead farm in the Creek Settlement that was
formely ownd by my Father Charles Johnson. We lived thare
10 years then sold to my Brother Wm W. Johnson & bought
this farm of Brother Broadia & have lived on this farm & the
one across the rhode 33 years last April.   Now Wm is 74
years old & I am 73 & we have two children & 8 grand
children, the oldest 26 the next 25, the next 24, the next 23, the
next 20, the next 18, the next 8, the last one nearly 3 years.

Wednesday, November 30   This was the last day of
November & a nice day it has been.   Mercury 12 above zero
this forenoon. Clowdy this evening. A litle fine snow. Wind
south. Clarence & Carrie went to town this afternoon. Clarah
bought cloth for herself a dress. Clarence went to town this
evening & got the male[mail].   This was C. H. Brown's
birthday. He is 50 years old.

Thursday, December 1   Not very cold but some snow. Quite
stormy this evening of wind & snow. We had Roast fowl for
supper & other good things to go with it. Clarence went to
town tonight & got the maile. He brout a postal card from
Wm Brown. He said he arived in Pine Valley Tuesday night.

Carrie has been making herself a dress. Commenced it this afternoon. Edwin P. Harmon & Miss Mertle Pertison [Peterson] was maried last Wednesday in Gouverneur. They are from Edwards. They have took up their home on the Miles farm in the west part of this town. He is the son of my nephew, Porter Harmon. He is a very nice young man, 25 years old the past October.

Friday, December 2   A nice pleasant day. Clarence went to town tonight & got the maile.

Saturday, December 3   Just a lovely day. Warm & pleasant. Wm Brown came home this evening on the train from Pine Valley, Chemung County. Clarence went to town tonight. Mabel Brown sent me a Box of hair. A nice wig for me by her granpa B. He cald in Syracuse & spent the night to B. F. Noble's & Mabel was thare. She intendes to come home near Crismas. Thare is an entertainment in the Church this evening in Edwards Village for the children. Morris Pratt made us a call today.

Sunday, December 4   Clowdy all day. Not very cold. Looks some like snow. Clarence & Carrie made a visit to her father's today. We had company to dinner today. Charley & Martha Brown & Sherm & Gerty Brown & Mr. & Mrs. George Backus & their daughter Pearl. They all started for their homes near night. Thare was a Donation in the town hall December the 2nd day for the benifit of the Rev. Mr. Gale, the Methodist Preacher.

Monday, December 5   A stormy day of snow. The sleighs runs on the rhod quite plenty today. Clarence & Carrie has gone to town this evening to attend a Temperance lecture in the Methodist Church. Wm & I has been playing the game of Backgammon. We done our first Churning today of 30 lbs of Butter. Our men got out their sleighs & cutter today. Wm &

Clarence rode out in the old sled this forenoon. Girty Brown was intending to go to Wm Clealand's tonight & do a job of dressmaking that would take 3 or four days.

Tuesday, December 6   Quite a nice lot of snow fell in the night. Quite a good day. A fine snow near night. We done our washing this forenoon. Had company this afternoon & evening. Mr. & Mrs. Earl Johnson & Mrs. Alvah P. Brown & litle Clarah made us a visit. Wm & Clarence went to town this forenoon & got some of the Horses shode, Bess for one. The sleighing is good & snowing some this evening & the wind is Blowing quite Hard.

Wednesday, December 7   Oh what a wild stormy day of snow & wind. Just piled the snow up nicely & is snowing and blowing this evening. We have all stayed near the house & the Barn & we are all at home this evening. Clarence has oild his Harness today & put it together this evening. Clarah has been working on her calico dress today & this evening. Horace Webb took his wife & litle baby girl to town today & left her to her father's for an all day visit. We thout it was an awful day for a litle baby to be caried out. We had fried chicken for supper & as much other stuff to eat as we cared for. Wm wrote a letter to send to his brother Jo in Pine Valley, Chemung Co. It went out yesterday.

Thursday, December 8   Not a very bad day but some wind & a litle snow. The traveling on the Rhodes is quite bad. Clarence drove to town this morning with the Barn Sleds & helped track out the rhodes. He & his granpa has gone this evening with the cutter. Levy B. Ernum from West Fowler was here to dinner today. He payed Wm Brown some money. Wm gave his note to Carrie Brown for $100 the other day.

Friday, December 9   A cold wind all day & this evening but storm. The rhodes are not broke out very good yet. Charley

Harmon drove down here this morning with a large kettle at the back end of his sled to break the rhodes & he was asking for money to help pay the Insurance on the Union Church. 52 dollars is the amount they are asking for. Clarence has gone to town tonight with Molley & the cutter. Bower Brown & Sam Padget made a call here this forenoon. I promised to buy two Bibels & one other nice Book for the boys. 24 lbs of Butter today.

Saturday, December 10   A very stormy day of snow & wind. The drifts are 7 feete deep near one house & Barn but Clarence & Carrie plunged a horse through & went to town. This was Alvah's last day to work for making Butter for this fall.

Sunday, December 11   One more fearful stormy day of snow & wind. Wm & Clarence shoveld a track through the field to draw out the manure from the Barn. They worked untill 3 o'clock this afternoon. Went to work as soon as they could after Breakfast.

Monday, December 12   A cold wind all day. Mercury was below zero at 3 this afternoon & 10 below at 7 this evening. Clarence has gone to town tonight. He & Wm broke rhodes all of this forenoon as far as Jim Webb's. Carrie done the washing this forenoon. Not much have I done in the shape of work the past weeke.

Tuesday, December 13   A very cold day it has been & is very cold this evening. Mercury was 20 below zero this morning. 12 below at noon & 28 below at 8 o'clock this evening. Whare will it be tomorow morning? Mrs. Frandy Dulark made us a visit this afternoon. A. P. Brown made us a call this afternoon. Clarence went to town this evening. Took a jar of Butter to C. H. Brown's store of 33 lbs. Wm done a churning today of 24 lbs. 78 lbs of Butter is all we have made [in] 15 days & 40 pans of milk in the Pantry.

Wednesday, December 14 Mercury went up a litle last night. Was 4 above zero this morning. The snow began to come down & the wind began to blow again near six o'clock & has been a blue day. So Clarence did not go to Gouverneur today. He & Carrie has gone to town tonight. I have writen a letter to send to Mabel Brown & Wm has read in his story Book all of this evening.

Thursday, December 15 Quite a good day but the travling on the rhodes is hard. Clarence & Alvah Brown went to Gouverneur today. Took a load of wheete & got flour for it. Carrie went as far as Mr. Gear's & made a visit.

Friday, December 16 No storm today. Mercury 12 above zero. No company today. A Mr. Parker from Gouverneur cald here yesterday. A lawyer on Business. Clarence went to town today. He has gone, has gone this evening & led one of our Horses to Alvah's for them to drive to York tomorow.

Saturday, December 17 Quite a nice mild day. Mercury 5 above. The snow has melted some today. The sleighing is splendid. The south wind has blown hard this afternoon & this evening. Carrie went to town this afternoon to visit her sister Hatta [Hatte] Dulack. Clarence has gone down this evening to bring her home. Alvah Brown & Sarah & Harold & Clarah Brown has gone to York today to visit their Daughter Manie. They intend to stay untill tomorow. They drove our Dan colt.

Sunday, December 18 Quite a good day. No storm but clowdy all day & a hard west wind. Clarence & Carrie went to Church this forenoon. Alvah & Sarah returnd home near night from York. The sleighing is good. A number of teams on the road today. A general time for sleigh riding.

506

Monday, December 19   A very cold day. Mercury 10 below zero. Alvah came up & helped dress 3 pigs. He bought one half of a pig. Clarence went home with him tonight & took the pork to town. Its weight was 1.21 lbs. his half. One weight was 2.50, one 2.43 & 244. Carrie done the washing this forenoon with the new kind of Soap Borax soap. The mercury is 10 above zero this evening at 8 o'clock.

Tuesday, December 20   The thaw continues. Raind today & this evening. Wm & Clarence cut up the pork today & Clarence took the other half of the 3d pig & sold it to Myron Hall. I tried out the most of the lard today & the men done a churning of 30 lbs of Butter. Clarence & Carrie went to town this evening to attend the Shows of our village tallent for the bennifit of the Univeralist Church. They took in $30.

Wednesday, December 21   Raind some today. The snow is melting fast. Clarence & Carrie cut & made the sausage today. 30 lbs. Clarence went to town to night to carry Dr. Merkley to his home. His horse ran away near night & threw him out & hurt him very bad.

Thursday, December 22   This has been quite a good day. The thaw continues yet raining this evening. But no rain today untill nine this evening. Wm & Alvah Brown went to Hermon today. Found rather poor sleighing. Alex & Jennie Kerr made us an evening call tonight. Clarence took a ride out to Clint McGill's tonight. Took a peace of fresh Pork to Minne. Dean Laidlaw came to Edwards on this evening train to spend the Hollydays with his Parents at South Edwards. He is studying medicine in Syracuse.

Friday, December 23   No storm today. The wind blew fearfully all night last & the snow was nearly all gone. The sleighing is spoild for the present. Wagons commenced to run today. Clarence went to town this evening. They expected

Mabel Brown home on this evening train from Syracuse.

Saturday, December 24   A litle new snow this morning. Quite a help to the sleighing. A lovely evening. We attended the Christmas entertainment in the Union Church. Mabel came home last evening. Saturday evening we all received a present from our friends but not on the tree. Clarence gave to his mother & myself a lovely glass dish & Carrie gave Martha & Mrs. John Clealand & myself a nice doyley [doily] worked by her own hands. Martha gave me a nice silk tydy that she made herself & the same to Carrie. Mabel gave me a lovely tydy & Clarence gave his granpa Black silk nectie [necktie] & a Silk Hankerchief.   Wm & I made Clarence & Carrie a present of a large Bible & one for Sherman & Girty Brown & a History book to Bower Brown, to Charley a pair of Black stockings & to Martha one dollar.   Clarence gave Mabel one dollar & Carrie a lovely fancy Box & Carrie gave Clarence & Bower a nice pair of gloves.   Carrie gave me callico for a dress.   Granpa gave Clarence & Carrie the framing of 3 pictures, price $2.   Wm payed $8.50 for the Books to Padget for presents.

Sunday, December 25   This was Christmas day. No storm. Charley's family was here to dinner. Charley & Martha & Bower & Mabel Brown. We had chicken & dumplin & cream cake & fried cakes & cookies. Potatoes & Bread & Butter & Cream pie & mince pie & cheese for dinner.   Alvah & family took dinner to Mr. Grant's, Sarah's father. They had the most of their children at home & grandchildren. Was 23 in all.

Monday, December 26   Quite a good day. Frose hard last night. Mercury a litle above zero this morning. Carrie done the washing this forenoon. I done the other work. Clarence drew 2 load of straw to town today, one to Bower Brown & one to Glasby. Clarence went to town tonight.

Tuesday, December 27   A stormy day of snow & wind. Regular Blizzards by spels. We done a churning of 30 lbs of Butter. Clarence did not go to town tonight. He made a call in Mrs. Storens.

Wednesday, December 28   A cold morning & all day. Mercury was 2 below zero this morning & 10 below zero this evening. We had company today to dinner. Mr. & Mrs. John W. Clealand & their two girls. We had a good visit.

Thursday, December 29   A stormy morning of snow & wind until about 10 o'clock then just a lovely day the remainder & this evening just nice. Clarence & Carrie went to town this evening. She brout home her flanel dress from the dressmaker. Wm & Mabel Brown made a visit to Clint McGill's today in Scotland [NY].

Friday, December 30   One more regular thaw. The sleighing all gone. The Bugies are on the rode plenty this afternoon & evening rushing for the Dance to the Thomas House in Edwards. We had company today to dinner. A. P. Brown's family. Clarence & Carrie has gone to town tonight to spend the evening.

Saturday, December 31   This is the last day of this year of 1898. It is past & gone never to return. How many of our friends & neighbors have gone to their long home never to return. This has been a cold day. The thaw took a Hard Cold in the night & quite a nice lot of snow fell that helped the sleighing some. So they have slid along on the rode today very well. Clarence went to town tonight. Wm went to town today.

Sunday, January 1   A cold pleasant day. Mercury was 10 below zero this morning & it is 10 below this evening at half past 8. Clarence & Carrie & Wm & myself was envited to C. H. Brown's today for dinner. We had a good time & a splendid dinner. Had oysters that was cooked splendid & then Baked Beef & Potatoes & Buiscit & Butter & lemon Pie & mince & Brown Cake & then cream cake & Cracker & C[heese] while we was thare & tea. Alvah took our team & caried his family to Cy Clealand's for a visit. We all arived home in good time for chours.

Monday, January 2   A cold day. Lots of wind. Mercury 10 above zero. Clarah done our washing today. The most of the cloths are dry & in the house tonight. Wm went to town this afternoon. He took 2 letters to the Post offis, one to Wm Green of Hermon & one to Arlina [Arline] Brown of Tilsonburg, Canada & Wm bought me 6 yardes of cotton flanel. Clarence went to town tonight. Mr. David Graham cald here today & hired [borrowed] $1.75. Gave his note. Charley Johnson cald here this evening & borowed 63 dollars.

Tuesday, January 3   A very nice pleasant day. Mercury up to 30 above zero. Mabel Brown came here today & stayed all day. Clarence & Carrie went home with her tonight. Our school commenced today for the winter term with Miss Minne Andrews for teacher. The Talcville School commenced today with Mr. Anson Andrews for teacher for the winter term. Our teacher gets $8 a week & boards to A. Kerrs. Wm & I have played 3 games of India. I came out ahead every time so he would not play any more.

Wednesday, January 4   A rainy day it has been & is raining this evening & the South wind has been blowing hard for nearly all of last night & today & this evening. Have had company today. Mr. & Mrs. Della [Dell?] Freeman & their Daughter, Luella. We had a good visit & a good dinner. Clarence went to town this evening. Sherm & Gerty Brown came home from Russell from their 2 weeks visit last Monday. I sent them the Bible yesterday by Charley Brown that I bought them for a Christmas present. I have just finished a job of white sewing for myself.

Thursday, January 5   This has been a lovely day. Warm & pleasant. The weather began to turn colder about 3 o'clock this afternoon & a few flakes of snow & is freesing some this evening. Raind all of last night. Wm has been sick today. Did not get up from his bed until 3 this afternoon. He is feelling better this evening. Clarence & Carrie has gone to town tonight. We done a churning today of 28 lbs [of butter].

Friday, January 6   Colder this morning.   Snowing this afternoon & evening. Wm & Clarence took out the long pipe out of the well today & fixt the chain so we can get watter as good as ever. They have been bringing water from the Spring the past week. Alex Kerr made a call here this afternoon. Clarence made a call in Mr. Storen's this evening. Carrie is working on a doyley with green silk. It will look lovely when finished. She worked a nice one for me for Christmas & one for her mother & one for Martha Brown. I have done my Baking of four loves of Bread this forenoon & done quite a lot of mending this afternoon.

Saturday, January 7   And an awful stormy day it has been of snow & wind. Just regular blizerds all day. But could not prevent Clarence from taking a ride to town on his bobsled this evening. He and Wm went to town this forenoon and got the sled mendid. I have writen a letter to send to my Brother A. P. Johnson of Pine Valley, Chemung Co. this evening.

Sunday, January 8   No snow fell today accept when the wind

blew it from one place to another. The high wind today has made the snow fly round quite lively. Clarence says the snow is coming down from the clouds this evening. I have not been out to see but I can hear the wind just howlling. We have all stayed at home all day & had no company. Been rather a dull day. I have read lots of news in the papers.

Monday, January 9   A cold day. Mercury 10 above zero this morning and 8 this afternoon, 2 below this evening at 7 o'clock. Carrie done our washing this forenoon. Wm went to town this forenoon. Took dinner to A. P. Brown's. Got home near 3. Clarence has gone to town this evening. Carrie is working her Doyley. It is very nice.

Tuesday, January 10   This has been a cold day but very pleasant. No wind. Mercury was 20 below zero this forenoon. 11 below this evening near 8 o'clock. Had no company today. Clarence drove to Talcville. Took a tub of Butter to Ryon but did not sell it. Mabel Whitmarsh cald here today & sold me a package of Ink for 10 cents. I started to knit a pair of mitons today for Wm Brown. Carrie finished her Doyley today. It looks nice. Clarence & Carrie played a number of games of Checkers this evening. The sleighing is very poor but good wheelling.

Wednesday, January 11   A very cold morning and all day. Mercury 20 below zero this morning. Been very pleasant all day. Wm & Mabel Brown took a ride to Hermon today. Went with two Horses & the Bobsleighs. Had rather a rough ride. Wm bought a nice Desk for Mabel Brown & a nice Rocking Chair for Sarah Brown & A. P. Brown. Carrie commenced to peace a Crazy quilt today. Clarence went to town tonight. Rosco[e] Todd cald here near nite.

Thursday, January 12   A very nice day. Quite a change in the weather. Mercury 20 above zero. We done a churning of

20 lbs of Butter today. I made it all into table Balls. Sherman Brown made us a call today. Took dinner here. Clarence & Carrie & Wm & myself made an evening call to Alex Kerrs. Wm and I made a call to Charley Brown's this afternoon. C. H. Brown took a trip to Canton today on the train. Thare was no school here today. Will not be any tomorow. Our teacher has gone to Hermon to attend an Examination. Wm bought 10 lbs of white sugar today of Bower Brown.

Friday, January 13   A nice mild day. Mercury 40 above zero. Clowdy all day.   No storm untill dark then rain all of this evening & very dark. Alvah Brown came up to day & helped Clarence kill & dress a beef cow. Wm went home with Alvah with the horse & cutter. Clarence drove Molly before the cutter to town this evening. Now he & his granfather are playing checkers.

Saturday, January 14   A rainy day. Sleighing done but good wheeling. Mercury up to 40 all day but the thaw is over this evening. The wind and snow is blowing nicely. Clarence took the Beef to town today; one quarter to A. P. Brown & one to Myron Hall & one to Alex Kerr. Wm cut up one hind quarter for ourselfs. It is fine. Just a young 3 year old this coming Spring. Clarence & Carrie has gone to town this evening. They will have a stormy time to come home. They took the Buggy. Wm & I have played 3 games of Backgamon this evening before 8 o'clock.

Sunday, January 15   Not a very cold day. Mercury 35 above zero. Freezing a litle this evening. Been clowdy all day. A very litle snow came in the night & a litle today. We have all been at home all day but near night Clarence & Carrie took a ride to John W. Clealand's to spend the evening.   Wm is reading in the beautiful story [book] this evening. Thare is a Mr. Foly from Star lake been arested & is in Watertown jail making a deal to pays counterfit money.

Monday, January 16   Just a lovely pleasant day. Mercury 40 all day. Mud on the rhodes is quite sloppy. Wm & Clarence went to town this forenoon. Wm stayed untill near 3. Took dinner in Charley Brown's. Wm & Carrie & myself made an Evening call in Mr. W. Flack's tonight. Clarence took us thare in the Buggy then he went to town & cald for us when he came home. John & Cy Webb cald in Mr. Flack's & they & Wm & Mr. Flack had a game of Pede. We all had a nice visit. Wm wrote 2 letters this afternoon. Sent them to the offis tonight. One was to go to Enos Stanton of Michigan, the other to Jo Brown of Pine Valley, Chemung co., NY. Clarence brout home a Package of Envelops tonight for his grandfather.

Tuesday, January 17   Clowdy all day. A litle rain in the morning & Snowing some this evening & froze a litle today, but no sleighing yet. Clarence went to town to day. Came home to chours then went to town this evening. He says Arther Gore is sick with fever. Has been teaching school in Fullerville.

Wednesday, January 18 Quite a cold pleasant day. Mercury at zero this morning. 20 above at noon & it is at zero this evening at 10 o'clock. Wm & Clarence went to town today then we all went to Horis [Horace] Webb's this evening.

Thursday, January 19 A cold pleasant day. Mercury up to 20 above zero but a cold wind all day. Wm & Clarence went to town this forenoon. Got the mail. Clarence went this evening & took a crock of Butter to Mr. Thomas & sold it for 18 cents a pound. He bought 5 gallons of caracine [Kerosene] oil today in C. H. Brown's store & 5 lbs of tea. The Doctors are having a very buisy time among the sick the last 2 weeks.

Friday, January 20 Just a lovely day. Mercury 24 above zero today. Clarence took a ride over to Mr. Watson's on the Trout

Lake rhode to mark some wood. I rode with him as far as Alvah Brown's. Took dinner & then made a visit to Altha Laidlaw's then I spent the evening in Charley Brown's. Clarence came after me this evening.

Saturday, January 21   Mercury up to 32 this morning & very pleasant this forenoon but clowdy & lots of wind this afternoon & near dark had quite a Blizerd of snow & wind but it did not last very long & now at 8 & nine o'clock it is very plesant & just lovely. Clarence went to town this forenoon & then in the afternoon he & a number of men & boys from the village took a trip up the river near Harmon's to enjoy the fun of a horse trot on the ice.   Arba Kerr drove his new trotter. Wm & Carrie has been playing a few games of checkers. Then we played 2 games of Backgamon. Clarence has gone to town this evening.

Sunday, January 22   A stormy day of fine snow but does not make much sleighing. Wm took a cutter ride to town today to make a call in Charley Brown's to see how Mabel is today. We heard she was sick last night. She is not feelling very well today. Alvah & Sarah Brown has gone to Litle York today to visit their Daughter Manie Johnson.   They drove one of our Horses & Buggy. Clarence & Carrie has gone to town tonight.

Monday, January 23   A very nice pleasant day. Mercury up to 40. I made a call in Mrs. Storen's this afternoon. Clint & Minne came home while I was thare to get a load of oates. Mrs. Storen was gone to Russell to visit a sick Brother. Wm & Clarence went to town today & bought a new pump for our well. They payed $5.45 cents. Pump, Pipe & all. We have had our chain pump, the one they have taken up today for 20 years. Clarence & Carrie has gone to town this evening. We got the sad news today of the death of Mr. & Mrs. Porter Johnson of Russell. They both died yesterday & also Mrs. Samuel McFerron of Edwards. She is about 80 years of age.

Her Husband died in the Spring of 1885 at the age of 80 years. The remains of Mrs. Edgar Brayton from Richville will be brout to Edwards tomorow to be Beried by the side of her Husband that Died in our village about 3 years ago. Sherman & Gerty Brown had company from Copenhagen [NY] last Saturday. An Aunt & her Husband & Brother. They all went to Russell yesterday & Sherm & Gerty went with them to visit Mr. Backus & family.

Tuesday, January 24   Raind a litle this morning & then some snow fell but not but a very litle. The wheeling is splendid but no sleighing.   Wm & I took a ride to town this afternoon. Made a visit in C. H. Brown's.   Found Mabel quite a good deal Better.   She was playing on her Piano for company, Miss Eva Clark & Miss Edith O'Shay.   She was envited to go the Town Hall this evening to play for the Burns Social to practice. They hold their final entertainment tomorow evening in the Town Hall. Tickets 20 cents a head.   The funeral of Mrs. Sam McFerin was held today in the ME Church.   Mrs. Edgar Brayton of Richville was beried today in the Edwards Cemitery.   Mrs. Dr. Merkley is on the sick list today in our village & also James Rushton & Stacy Flack & Mrs. Milow Woodcock & one of Jim McFerin's litle girls & also Seth Hughes litle girl. I made 4 loves of Bread today before I went to town.   Mrs. Dr. Goodnough & a Mr. George Dewey of Degrass [NY] was lately married in Russell, NY.

Wednesday, January 25   A pleasant day but quite a cold wind all day.   Mercury 6 above zero this morning & 12 above this evening at nine. Clarence went to town this forenoon & got Molly shod & he & Carrie has gone to town this evening to attend the Burns Festival in the Town hall. Mr. Storen cald here this morning & bought 1 Dozen of new eggs. Payed me 20 cents. Thare was 3 funerals in Russell village yesterday, all 3 Herses met in the Cemitery at the same time & 2 here in Edwards Cemetery both at the same time & one had to wait for the other yesterday. Wm & I stayed at home this evening. We played 4 games of Backgamon. I took my men out first every time. Then he would not play another game. He can get the start of me in playing checkers then he is well pleased.

Thursday, January 26   A squall of snow this forenoon then quite pleasant accept an awful wind all day & now this evening snowing & blowing like the dickens.   Wind just Howling.   Mr. & Mrs. Freeman & Osweld made us an Evening call. Clarence has been sick all day with a bad cold.

Friday, January 27   Been sick all day.   Cannot write much tonight. I have a very bad cold coming on.

Saturday, January 28   A cold day. Wm & Clarence attended the Caucas this afternoon. I have been sick all day with a hard cold.   Carrie has done all of the work.   The men did not get home untill dark. Clarence went to town this evening.

Sunday, January 29 A nice pleasant day. Charley & Martha & Mabel Brown came today to dinner today.

Monday, January 30   Quite a cold day. Wm has been sick all day.   Martha has been here all day & helped us very much.   I have been quite poorly today & Carrie has not felt very well. Dr. Merkley cald here this evening & gave Wm medicine. Alex Kerr & Horace Webb & John Hughes & Earl Bancroft made us a call today & Sherman Brown. A. P. Brown made us a call yesterday.

Tuesday, January 31   Carrie done the washing this forenoon. Alvah & Sarah & Martha & Sherman Brown was here today. The Dr. was here to visit Wm today. Mr. Freeman cald here to see Wm today. Bower was here today.

Wednesday, February 1   Stormy all day after 10 o'clock but

517

not very hard. A cold morning, mercury 8 below zero. Wm has been sick in bed all day. Dr. Merkley made us a call. Mrs. Gid Freeman is very sick. C. H. Brown & Martha came up this morning. Martha stayed all day. She was good help & good company. We think Wm is some better this evening. A. P. Brown made us a call this morning. Clarence went to town tonight. He brout us some nice orenges from Charley B. Mabel B is working for Earl Bancroft on the type writer.

Thursday, February 2   Just a lovely day. The bear could see his shadow today if he came out of his den. Mabel Brown came up today made us a call. Alvah Brown came up today & took the team & drew ice. Thare is a feight Sunday tonight. Look for [not legible].

Friday, February 3   This has been a stormy day of snow. Quite an addition to the sleighing. Martha B came up today & stayed untill night. Clarence went home with her. Earl Bancroft made us a call today & Mr. Gid Freeman. Wm is better today. He drest himself today. He has gone to bed at 8 tonight. Alvah took the teem today & finished hauling his ice. Wm & I wrote a letter to Wm Green of Hermon today.

Saturday, February 4   Just a lovely pleasant day this has been & is a lovely evening. Mercury was 20 above zero today. Thare was Horse trotting on the River Grass near Russell Village this afternoon. Arba Kerr & Urban Webb went from here. I expect a number went from Edwards village. Thare was Horses from diferent parts of this county to join the Race today. The sleighing is good. Thare was a nice lot of snow came in the night & this morning. Wm is feeling some better today & I am much Better of my cold. Clarence & Carrie has gone to town this evening. Frandy Dulark has just bought the House & lot formaly [formerly] ownd by the late Dr. Goodnough.

Sunday, February 5   A nice mild quiet day.   Mercury 20 above zero. Charley & Martha & Mabel made us a visit today. Wm has not set up as much as he did yesterday. He has a hard cough.   Clarence went to Mr. Freeman's tonight & bought some Honey & I have made a syrup of Hoarhoun & Honey. We think that will help our colds.   Mabel B has been writing for Earl Bancroft the past week on his typewriter.

Monday, February 6   Just a lovely day it has been. Carrie & Clarence done the washing this forenoon. We had a very large washing today. A few callers, Miss Lena Kerr & Emma Flack & Mr. Enos, the Haile ointment Pedler. Clarence has gone to town this evening to male[mail] a letter. Wm wrote a letter today to send to E. Stanton of Michigan. A Boy Baby to Mr. & Mrs. Fred Dulark, the 3rd of Feb. Wm received 2 letters tonight. One from Mrs. Tauton, one from Herman.

Tuesday, February 7   One more pleasant day. Mercury was below zero this morning & 20 above at noon. Alvah Brown camp up today & helped Clarence draw Hay from the Back Barn to the Corn Barn. Clarence has gone to town tonite.

Wednesday, February 8   We have quite a change in the weather.   The snow was coming down bountifully this morning & in part, all day. Snow a plenty for good sleighing now. Clarence has gone to town tonight. He has all of the chours to do & it keepes him quite busy. His arm that was hurt last Spring pains him most of the time, but he workes all the same. Seymour Absolom cald here yesterday. He had been to Edwards to mill. He is from West Fowler [NY]. We have not had any company today. It has been a lonely stormy day. The train was one hour late tonight on acount of the storm.

Thursday, February 9   A cold wind all day. Mercury to zero. The snow has drifted lots today.   We have not had any company today. Clarence drove to town this afternoon & had a shew [horse shoe] set on Molly. So he did not go down this evening. Wm received a letter from Arlina [Adaline] Brown of Tilsonburg, Canada West on last night's maile.

Friday, February 10 A very cold pleasant day. Mercury 12 below zero. Clarence went to town tonight & got the maile. Train near 2 hours late. A fire at Gouverneur or at the Dam burning up lots of lumber & their mills. It commenced last night & is rageing now. I done my Baking of Bread today. Four loves.[loaves]

Saturday, February 11 A cold day but pleasant. Mercury 17 below zero this morning. Alvah came up this morning & took a Horse & Cutter home & he & Sarah went to Elmer Grant's for a visit for today & tomorow. Clarence went to mill today with a load of oates. He & Carrie has gone to town this evening. Sherman B was here this forenoon & got a ladder to go up on his house to fix the chimney. Clarence brout home quite a suply of medicine from Dr. Merkley today for Wm. His cough does not get much better.

Sunday, February 12 One more cold pleasant day. We have not had any company today. Alvah cald in a few minutes. Wm sat up most all day. He took a walk to the Barn.

Monday, February 13 A cold day. Mercury below zero. Clowdy & a fine snow falling all day. Wind north. Carrie done our washing this forenoon. Wm has lain in bed all day untill this evening but his cold is better. Miss Minnie Andrews, our school teacher, made us a call this afternoon. She envited Clarence & Carrie to attend a Party to Alex Kerr's this evening that is her boarding place for this term of school. Clarence went to mill today & brout home his meal that was ground last Saturday. He brout home a Box of crackers & 2 dozen of cloths pins. He said that John Cousins was taken home drunk this afternoon to try to get him sober by tomorow so he will be able to attend the town meting. He is the nominee for Supervisor of our town for the Republican party. Won't it be nice if he only gets Elected.

Tuesday, February 14   One more cold day. Mercury at zero & a cold north wind. This was town meting day. Wm went down & put in his vote & came directly home. The first time he has been to town for more than two weeks.

Wednesday, February 15   Wind west all day. Mercury 30 above zero. Clowdy this evening. Clarence went over on Trout Lake rhode this afternoon & brout home some balsam limbs for Wm to peal the Bark to chew it for his cough. Then he went to town tonight & got the maile & a new stone churn. Cyrus Watson is Supervisor in place of John Cousins & Abbie Clark town Clerk.

Thursday, February 16   Just a lovely day. Mercury went up to 40 above zero today. Dr. Merkley was here this morning to give Wm more medicine. Clarence went for him before day light. Wm took a ride as far as Mr. Flack's this afternoon & cald in Mrs. Storen's. He sold her a half bushel of onions. Clarence went to town this evening to get the maile. He has just come home before eight o'clock. Thare is one litle calf in the Barn, 3 days old. Wm sent a letter to Wm Green of Hermon yesterday.

Friday, February 17   Just a lovely pleasant day. Mercury 50 above zero. Wm went to the Barn today & fed 2 litle calves. Clarence & Carrie went to town tonight. Mrs. Alex Kerr & Lena made us an evening call. The Heth [Heath] children was took away from their home today to be placed in the children's home. It is the village gossip that Fred Donalson & his wife has parted. She has gone home to her father's. He is trying to get her to come back to his home but she refuses.

Saturday, February 18   A nice warm day. Mercury up to 40. Thawed all night last & all day today. Raind some near night tonight. Clarence & Carrie has gone to town tonight. Thare is 2 litle calves in the Barn. Wm goes out & feedes them. Mr. Gid Freeman cald here today.

Sunday, February 19   The thaw froze up in the night & quite a snow storm this morning. A high wind all day but turned warm & thawed and the sun shone nicely. Charley & Mabel Brown came up to dinner. Martha has a hard cold so she could not come today. Clarence made a call in Mr. Flack's this evening. Carrie poped [popped] a nice lot of corn tonight. Wm ground a lot of the corn in the Pepermill & we ate it in milk. It was splendid.

Monday, February 20   A warm day. A litle rain. Mercury 40 above zero. We done our washing to this forenoon. Thare was a man from Vermont here today selling sugar evaperators. Wm bought one that will cost 38 dollars. Clarence & I went to town this evening. I made a call on Martha's & Mabel. Bower took a trip away on the train this morning. They think he has gone to Adams to visit his best girl, Mertle Webb. We sold 13 lbs of Butter today to Mrs. Andrews for 16 cents a pound.

Tuesday, February 21   Froze a litle this morning. Been warm & thawed all of this afternoon. The sleighing is done. Mercury up to 40. Wm & Clarence went to town this forenoon. Did not get home until 3 o'clock. Wm got a letter from Arlina Brown of Canada. She wrote that she had received the Bedroom Suit [e] that Wm Brown had made her a present of. She was much pleased with it. Clarence & Carrie has gone to John W. Clealand's this evening. Clarah intends to stay a few days to her father's. Wm done a small churning today of nearly 10 lbs of Butter.

Wednesday, February 22   A very hard wind all day from the west. Snowed some this afternoon. Mercury was 40 the most of the day. Went down to 30 near 3 o'clock. Wm melted over 50 lbs of old sugar today but it is not very good. Clarence has gone to town to night. Carrie is making a visit to her father's today [&] tomorrow.   Thare is a Dance to the Thomas house tonight in Edwards village. A Birthday Party to A. P. Brown's last evening for their daughter Rose. She is 18 years old today.

Thursday, February 23   Quite cool today. Did not thaw any. A nice litle snow storm in the night. So the sleighing was quite good today. Mercury at 30 all day. Very clear & pleasant this evening. Wm & Clarence took a ride over to Luther Harmon's today. Clarence went to town this evening. I done my ironing today and the house work all done this forenoon.   Wm & I played 3 games of Backgamon this evening. Wm sent a letter to Wm Green tonight. Wm has just received a letter from Amelia McKinny of Canada West. Clarence has come home before nine tonight from town. He brout the mail.

Friday, February 24   A very pleasant day but cold. Mercury was down to zero this morning. It is 10 above this evening at 8. A. P. Brown came up today and helped Clarence draw Hay from the Back Barn to the cow barn & drew 4 load. Clarence went home with him & took 20 lbs of Butter to Charley's store to sell to Mr. Mure [Muir] of Fine. We got the sad news last night of the death of Miss Kate Grifen of Fine. She died in the hospital in Utica. She had an operation of some kind I have not learned yet. I expect Carrie will come home tonight with Clarence. She has been gone since Tuesday night. Mabel Whitmarsh & a Miss Paterson [Patterson] cald here this afternoon on the way home from school.

Saturday, February 25   Just a lovely day & this evening. Mercury was 10 above zero this morn & 40 above this afternoon. Clarence & I took a ride to town tonight. I made a call in Charley Brown's. I found Mabel quite Happy. Martha has a fearful cough. Frank Ingram started this morning on the train to go to California then his regiment is ordered from thare to Manila. [Spanish-American War reference]

Sunday, February 26 Some rain today. Clowdy all day. We all stayed at home today. Only since chours Clarence has made a call to Lesley McGill's. Will Newton commenced to moove back on to their old farm & Horace Webb will moove from the Newton farm the first day of March in with his mother, Mrs. Webb & Urban Webb will moove to the village the first of March to make room for his Brother, Horis [Horace].

Monday, February 27 A stormy day & this evening the wind has blown hard all day & just Howling this evening. Been squalls of snow through the day & is snowing quite ha[r]d this evening at 8. We did our washing this forenoon & not much of anything this afternoon & evening. Carrie made a nice Maple Sugar Cake with frosting for supper & Baked Potatoes & beef stake & fried cakes & Bread & Butter & Cheese & strawberies. Clarence has gone to town tonight. He took a jar of Butter to the store & some onions & a can of milk to Martha. Horace Webb mooved from the Newton farm today in with his mother & Urban Webb mooved to the village & Will Newton mooved back on to his father's farm.

Tuesday, February 28 No storm today. Some sunshine & lots of wind. Mercury went up to 40 above zero. Clarence went to town this forenoon. He said thare was a fire over on the Back street. The house that Balcom was living in. It was badly damaged but not all Burnd. Clarence & Carrie went to town this evening. It is snowing & the wind is blowing now near nine o'clock. A Stove Pedler cald here today. Had steel Ranges, his price for them was 69 dollars.

Wednesday, March 1   Just a lovely pleasant day. Mercury 32 above zero. A cool wind. Clarence & Wm went to town this forenoon. Wm stayed untill 3 o'clock then Clarence & I took a ride to town this evening. I made a call in Alvah Brown's. Alvah went to Gouverneur today on the train & home on this evening train. He bought a large rool [roll] of rubber hose. Thare was a dwelling house Burnt last evening near Hermon. The people in Edwards village saw the fire quite plain. Wm bought six yards of cloth for himself, 2 pair of overalls.

Thursday, March 2   Clowdy all day & snowed part of the time. Not very cold. Mercury 30 above zero. Clarence & Carrie went to town this forenoon. Carrie stayed to C. H. Brown's. Mabel B was intending to help her cut a dress. Clarence has gone to town this evening to bring Carrie home. Clarence brout home our Smoked Hams today that has been smoking in Alvah Brown's smokehouse. We had four hams & four shoulders.

Friday, March 3   This has been a lovely day. Mercury 40 above zero. Clarence & Carrie went to town this afternoon. Clarence went over to the river to see the horses trott and Carrie & Martha & Mabel Brown made a visit to Sherman Brown's this afternoon. I had company this afternoon. Mrs. John Laidlaw & Charley & Celia Johnson & 3 of their children. Fern & Vonne & the litle boy Johnney. They stayed in the evening.

Saturday, March 4   A lovely day. Thawed all day. Lesley McGill tap[p]ed his sugar trees today. The sap run well. Clarence & Wm went to town today. Clarence has gone this evening. Thare is 5 litle calves to the Barn now.

Sunday, March 5   Raind hard in the last night & this morning. Clowdy all day & stormy by spels & this evening the wind is howling fearfully. Mercury 40 above zero all day. The rhodes are quite muddy & Wm took a trip over to McGills' sugar place today. Lesley was boilling sap & we had company today. Charley & Martha & Mabel Brown came up to dinner.

Monday, March 6   A cool pleasant day. Mercury 20 above & 40 this afternoon. Wm tap[p]ed 5 trees to see if the sap would run. It run a litle. Clarence went to town tonight. He bought 3 lbs of dried Aples for 3 shillings; a 3 quart pail of beans. Mrs. Storen made some new sugar today. Alex Kerr made us a call this evening. We done our washing this forenoon. I made 4 pies this afternoon in the line of Baking & a good Jonney [Johnny Cake] Cake for supper.

Tuesday, March 7   Wind & snow today & a cold north wind. Mercury 20 above zero. Wm took a walk to the Depot today to see if the Evaperator had come but it had not. Clarence has gone to McGill's this evening to make a call. I received a letter from Dr. Rice last night.

Wednesday, March 8   A cold pleasant day. Mercury 10 above zero. Quite a lot of snow fell in the night. Was snowing some this morning. Wm & Clarence drove to town with the sled. Brout home 2 Butter tubs & a tub for Martha to get some sour milk. Clarence drove down town this evening. The Methodist Society holds an entertainment to Gid Freeman's this afternoon & this evening. Carrie is finishing her blue dress this evening. Mrs. James W. Harmon made us a visit today.

Thursday, March 9   A very stormy forenoon of snow. Mercury 30 above zero. Wm made a call to Mr. Storen's this afternoon & Clarence got a ride to town this afternoon with Eddy Brayton. He went to town tonight with Molly [a horse] & the Buggy & brout home the mail. Wm & Carrie played checkers this evening. I made a pair of pants for Wm today.

Friday, March 10   A lovely pleasant day. Mercury 20 above zero this morning & 40 this afternoon. Wm drove to town this forenoon & brout A. P. Brown up. They did intend to tap some trees but did not. So they all went to town.

Saturday, March 11   Clowdy all day & lots of wind. Mercury went up to 50 above zero this afternoon. The rhodes are very muddy. Wm & Clarence went to town this afternoon with Molly & the Buggy to attend the factory meting held in A. P. Brown's factory. Alvah is the Cheese & Butter maker & he is to sell the goods. Wm's sugar Evaperator came on the noon train today. Clarence drove over with the Span of Horses & the big sled & brout it home before dark. That & the fixings that come with it will cost $40. He has had 2 Evaperators that has cost $40 each in the past 20 years & before that he bought 2 9 feete pans & one 8 foot pan to boil sap in & 2 heaters & 600 tin Buckets & any amount of other articals to use making sugar.   Seth Hughes litle girl died today.   Mrs. William Robinson died last night & Ed Hughes is not expected to live but one or two days. Clarence & Carrie has gone to town this evening.

Sunday, March 12   A hard thunder shower this afternoon & rain all of the forenoon. Martha & Mabel Brown drove up & made us a call near night between the showers. Mercury up to 50 above zero today. A litle cooller this evening. Mercury 34. Wm & Clarence drove to the sugaring place today noon. Took the new pan over & set it on the arch. It fited good. Mabel Brown attended an envited party last evening at Wm Noyes. Their son Oswel has just returnd home from the War department. He has been gone since last spring. They made the party for him. Mabel said they all had a splendid time. Had a nice lunch in the evening of aples & oranges & cream candy & cake.

Monday, March 13   A cold day. Quite a flurry of snow fell in the night or near this morning & the ground froze quite hard. Mercury 20 above zero all day. We done our washing this forenoon & Carrie made a panful of fried cakes this afternoon. Wm & Clarence went to town this afternoon. Got a lot of fixing done at the Hardware for their sap works. Clarence went to town this evening.

Tuesday, March 14   A cold pleasant day. Mercury 20 above zero. Wm & Clarence & Alvah Brown & Jim Harmon taped[tapped] 250 maple trees but the sap did not run any. Clarence went to town tonight & carried Alvah home. Clarah made a nice cream cake today. We looked for Mabel Brown to come but she disapointed us. Will make us a call in the morning before she takes the train to go to Syracuse.

Wednesday, March 15   A stormy day of rain & wind & snow. Our men went to the woods to tap trees this forenoon but they did not tap any. Alvah came up this noon but went back home. Did not work. Bower & Mabel Brown came up this forenoon. Made a short call & said goodbye. She took the train at noon to go to Syracuse. Will arive thare at nine this evening. Clarence & Jim Harmon is playing a game of checkers this evening. I got a letter from Dr. Rice of Adams last evening.

Thursday, March 16   A cold pleasant day. No sap. Mercury 20 above zero all day. Clarence & Jimmy went to the woods & cut sugar wood all day. Took their dinner with them. Brother Abel Johnson of Pine Valley Chemung Co NY came here today to spend a few weeks among his old friends. Wm B gave me 7 dollars in money today.

Friday, March 17   One more cold pleasant day. Mercury 10 above zero this morning. Wm & brother A. P. Johnson went to town this afternoon. Abel did not come back with Wm. Clarence & Jimmy has gone to town this evening with Molly & the Buggy. I got the news today of the death of Mrs. Tom

Dane. She died on Wednesday the 15th. She was a sister to Mrs. Wm Robinson who was beried on Monday the 13th of March. I sent a letter to the offis by Clarence tonight to Dr. Rice. Wm done a churning this forenoon of 30 lbs of Butter.

Saturday, March 18   A stormy day of snow but not very cold. Mercury 36 above zero. Wm went to town this afternoon & sent a check to the company in Vermont that he bought his Evaperator of. He sent 37 dollars. Clarence & Jim & Carrie has gone to town this evening. Clarence sold 2 veal calves this morning for 12 dollars. He took a tub of 22 lbs of Butter to A. P. Brown tonight. Mrs. Dane was beried today. Wm Green of Hermon beried her. Brother Abel has gone to Charley Johnson's today.

Sunday, March 19   One more stormy day of snow. The sleighing is good. One more funeral today. Kid Webb's son was beried today in the cemetery in Edwards. He was 23 years old. Was sick but a few days with pneumonia. We have had no callers to day. All stayed at home. Clarence poped [popped] a panful of corn this evening. We all had a feast. Thare was a hard crust on the snow this morning. Raind all of this forenoon & froze on the [snow] this afternoon. The snow has just come down bountifully.

Monday, March 20   An awful day it has been of wind. The snow has blown like the very old nick all day & the weather is quite cold. Clarence went to town this forenoon to get the cross cut saw filed & has gone down tonight to get it. Jimmy went with him. Wm & Carrie is playing checkers this evening. Charley Johnson & Brother Abel came here this forenoon. Charley payed Wm some money that he was owing Wm. Abel put on a clean shirt & collar & went back with Charley.

Tuesday, March 21   A very nice pleasant day. A cold morning. Mercury at zero. Clarence & Jimmy went to the woods & sawed & split wood untill four o'clock. Clarence & Carrie has gone for a ride & to make a call to John W. Cleland's this evening. Wm & Jimmy is playing checkers this evening. Jimmy Clealand cald here this evening to take a look at the veal calf. I must spunge some Bread this evening. I am having a fearful hard time with one of Jobes comforters.

Wednesday, March 22   Wm sold Mrs. Storen a half Bushel of onions today. She has had one bushel of Wm. Payed 75 cents a bushel. No storm today. Our men tapped sugar trees today. They have got one hundred more to tap. Alvah & Sarah Brown & William Grant & wife cald here this morning & hitched on Dan horse with their colt & drove to York & made a visit to Manie Johnson. Clarence went to town tonight. He & Jimmy brout the maile & a package for me from Adams. He brout me one dozen of milk pans from Bancroft's store. I made Bread today & done the milk work & done the ironing mostly & sat in the rocking chair the rest of the time. I have had a lame ankle the most of the time today & this evening.

Thursday, March 23   A stormy day until 2 o'clock. Raind this morning until nine then the snow came down bountifully. No sap today. Wm & Clarence has gone to town this afternoon. They done a churning this forenoon of 35 lbs of Butter. I packed one tub full & one more nearly full. 15 cents is all we can get a pound for Butter now. We have on hand 100 lbs.

Friday, March 24   A cold stormy day of snow but is very pleasant this evening. Mercury was 20 above zero today. Our men does the Barn Chours & not any other work. They are waiting for sugar weather. Clarence & Jimmy has gone to town this evening.

Saturday, March 25   A cold pleasant day. Mercury at zero this morning. 40 above this afternoon. The sap run a litle this afternoon. Wm & Clarence went to the woods & took out the slop from the Buckets. Lena Kerr & Minna [Minne] Andrews came here this afternoon for a visit but Minne's mother came to take her home but Lena stayed this evening. Clarence & Jimmy went to town this evening. Jim [O] Shey's mother was beried today. Was taken to Rossie to be Beried by the side of her Husband. She has made her home with her son James O'Shey since the death of Husband.

Sunday, March 26   A cold pleasant day. Mercury 20 above 0. Clarence & Carrie made a visit to John Clealand's today & went to town this evening. Brother Abel came here today. He has been visiting in Russell & Hermon.

Monday, March 27   One more cold pleasant day. Mercury 10 above. Wm done a churning this morning of 38 lbs of Butter. We have four tubs to sell. Brother Abel stayed with us last night & this forenoon then he got a ride to town. Clarence took a load of straw to Charley Brown's Barn this forenoon. Wm & Clarence & Jimmy went to the woods & tapped the remainder of their sugar trees. Alvah came up & helped them this afternoon. Minne Andrews came here after school & took supper & stayed untill near 8 then she & Lena Kerr went to town with Mr. Andrews. Clarence & Jim went to town this evening.   Mr. Arther Heth & family mooved in to Mrs. Storen's vacant House last week. Shirley Flack is home from Ogdensburg to make her friend in Edwards a 2 weeks visit.

Tuesday, March 28   A cold windy day. Raind this afternoon. We done our washing this forenoon. Our men kild & drest a hog this afternoon. They took it to town tonight & sold it to Miron [Myron] Hall for 5 & a quarter cents a pound & 2 tubs of Butter at 15 cents a pound.

Wednesday, March 29   This has been an awful day of wind & snow. A perfect blizerd all day. Our cloths on the line was in

531

an awful plite [plight] & the line broke. Wm went to town today & got the cream pump mendid & his beetle [wooden hammer or maul] banded Clarence & Jimmy has gone to town this evening. They took 4 dozen of eggs to Charley B's store.

Thursday, March 30   A cold wind all day. Mercury 20 above 0. Clarence went to mill today with a load of oats & corn for the cows & pigs. They went to the sugar woods today & took out all the watter & sap that was in the buckets & threw it on to the ground. Then Wm & Clarence went to Wm Clealand's & bought four litle pigs, payed 2 dollars a peace for them. Clarence & Jimmy went to town tonight. Brother Abel came home with them. He has been visiting to Charley Harmon's a couple of days.

Friday, March 31   This has been a pleasant day. Mercury 20 above zero this morning & near 40 this afternoon. The sap run a litle today. Brother Abel stayed here last night but went to Frank Johnson's today.

Saturday, April 1   A cold day. Mercury 20 above 0. Our men went to the woods & gathered & boild all of the sap thare was in the Buckets. They brout home the syrup at 3 o'clock. Had 2 pails full of very thin syrup. The first we have had. Wm done a churning today of 30 lbs of Butter. Sherman Brown made us a call today & took dinner with us. Clarence & Jimmy Harmon & Carrie went to town this evening. A. P. Brown made us a call this afternoon.

Sunday, April 2 Easter.   A cold wind all day. No sap. We sugared down the syrup that they boild yesterday today. Had 30 lbs of sugar. Very nice. Bower Brown came up to eat warm sugar & Emmy Clark & her litle girl Mildred came here today. Will stay here untill some time tomorow. Brother Abel stayed with us last night & today but he has gone to town tonight. Jimmy our boy attended the Easter entertainment in the Methodist Church this evening.

Monday, April 3   A cold wind all day. Mercury 30 above zero this morning & 40 above this afternoon. Clarence went to town this forenoon & took the sugar to Charley's store. He has gone to town this evening to carry Emmy Clark to Hiram Hall's from here. We did not do our washing today.

Tuesday, April 4   Just a lovely pleasant day. Mercury 20 this morning & 46 this afternoon. The sap run some today. Wm & I took a slow ride to town this afternoon. Made a call in Charley Brown's. Our boys went to the woods & gathered some sap this afternoon. Carrie done our washing this forenoon. I made Bread & done the dary [dairy] work & got the dinner. Wm has gone to bed at 7 o'clock tonight. Carrie has done quite a lot of stitching on the mashine this afternoon & evening. The rhodes are quite muddy.

Wednesday, April 5   Just a nice pleasant day. Mercury 10 above zero this morning & 42 this afternoon. The men all went to the woods today to gather & boil a litle dab of sap. Charley & Maryetta Harmon made us a visit today. Clarence & Jim has gone to town tonight. Brother Abel came home with them to stay here a day or two. He received a letter from his daughter Jessie from NY City. She is very anxious for him to come to NY & spend the summer with her family.

Thursday, April 6   A lovely day it has been. Mercury went up to 50 in the shade this afternoon. The sap run well today. Our men went to the woods today & gathered & boild & they sugared of 88 lbs of nice sugar. They brout it home with them tonight. Brother Abel went to the woods with them for to sugar eat.   Then he made a call on Mrs. Harmon & Lizzie. He has gone to town tonight with Clarence & Jim Harmon. We done our ironing this forenoon. Carrie lets out the cows & puts them in to the Barn every day when the men are in the woods.

Friday, April 7   Clowdy this forenoon.   Mercury 40.
Commenced to rain about noon & has raind hard this evening.
Our men worked in the sugar work all day. Clarence has gone
to town this evening.   He sold a veal calf today to Will
Cousins.

Saturday, April 8   A rainy day it has been all day & the mud
is fearful evry place.   Our men worked in the sugar place all
day. They brout home 164 lbs of sugar & some syrup in the
can to make into sugar tomorow. Clarence & Jim H has gone
to town this evening with Molly & the Buggy.   Carrie & I
have done quite a lot of work today of diferent kinds of
housework & dary work & Baking. I have made 4 loves of
Bread & a tin of Busicit & five Pies, Aple & goosbery &
Pieplant & custard. Carrie made white cookies & fruit cake &
a white frosted cake & a panful of fried cakes in the baking
line & I cooked pork & beans.

Sunday, April 9   Charley & Martha came up today to dinner.
We sugared of[f] 30 lbs & fild 4 cans of syrup.

Monday, April 10   A lovely pleasant day. Mercury 24 this
morning went up to 50 this afternoon. Clarence & Jim went to
the sugar woods & emptied the rainwater & snow out of the
Buckets. Took their dinner. Wm stayed to the house & done
chours & done a churning of 39 lbs of Butter. Carrie done her
washing this forenoon. I done the housework & the dary work
& worked & packed the Butter. Clarence & Carrie & Jim has
gone to town this evening. They took two 20 lb tubs of Bugter
to sell to just any one they could. We had 6 tubs of Butter to
sell. 120 lbs.

Tuesday, April 11   Just a lovely day. Sap run well. Mercury
went up to 52 above zero.   Our men worked in the sugar

woods all day. It was dark when Wm came home. We ate supper by lamp lite. Carrie helped do the milking. I done my washing this forenoon. Cloths all day tonight & in the house & folded ready to iron. No company today only Mrs. Ashley made a call & took home a pail of sour milk.

Wednesday, April 12 A shower in the night about one o'clock & a hard shower near noon today. Lots of wind this evening. Our men worked in the woods today gathering & boilling sap & they sugared of[f] twice 128 lbs & left a can near full of syrup in the woods to sugar tomorow. Martha came up this forenoon & Brother Abel. They took dinner here then he went to the depot & took the train for his home in Chemung Co.

Thursday, April 13   No storm today. Not much sap. The ground froze a litle this morning. Wm sugared of[f] in the woods 4 times today. Clarence helped then he came home at 2 o'clock & went to town & got the horses shod & took 4 dozen of eggs to Charley's store & took 100 lbs of sugar to the store for Charley to sell. Wm came home from the woods near 5 o'clock. We had 2 roosters cooked for supper tonight. Brower Brown sent a letter to Frank Ingram to the Phillipines started it the 10th of this month in answer to the one he received from Frank just as he was starting from San Francisco to go to Manila.

Friday, April 14   Clowdy most of the day. No sap. The weather warm & spring like. Some sunshine & very nice. Did not freeze any last night. The Frogs has been singing for 3 days past. The rhodes are very muddy. Clarence & Carrie has gone to town tonight. Clarah has a very sore foot. The syrup can fell on to her foot when she was helping strain the syrup. We sugared off in the kitchen today. Clarence sold 100 lbs of sugar yesterday & 27 lbs last Sunday.

Saturday, April 15 Not so warm today but no storm. No sap.

We think the sugaring over for this spring. Clarence sold 100 lbs today to Mr. Dulack for 8 cents a pound. He sent 2- 30 lbs tubs of Butter to NY yesterday. Wm done a churning of Butter today of 40 lbs. Clarence has gone to town tonight alone. Lesley McGill through some accident had a naile run into his leg yesterday. Dr. Merkley was sent for & drest the wound. Clarence cald on Lesley today. He was hurt very bad. Carrie's foot does not get any better today. She suffers very much & cannot step on it.

Sunday, April 16   A cool pleasant day accept a litle flurry of snow this afternoon. Bower Brown came up & made us a call this afternoon. He has been working on the creek the past week running logs for Mr. Stammer & he intendes to work thare this week. He gets 2 dollars a day. Wm took a walk over to the sugar woods. He said the sap was runing quite well today. Clarence made a call to Arba Kerr's today & a call to Mr. Flack's this evening. They have lost their litle colt. It was 3 days old when it died.

Monday, April 17   just a lovely day.   Mercury 24 this morning & 60 above zero this afternoon. Wm & Clarence worked in the sugar woods all day. Clarence gathered 200 pails of sap before 3 o'clock then had the stables all to clean & he & Carrie done the milking. They fed 98 head of beasts & birds of one sort and another of Domestic animals. Wm boild sap untill near dark. Clarence took our milk to the factory this morning for the first time.   Had 300 & 7 lbs.   Milking 15 cows.

Tuesday, April 18   Just a lovely pleasant day. Mercury went up to 70 this afternoon in the shade. Our men worked in the sugar woods all day. They are making lots of poor sugar. The sap was very sour. We done our washing this forenoon & Baking of Bread.   James Harmon came over here this afternoon & took home his cloths. He does not intend to work

536

here any more this spring. He has hired to work in a chair factory in Jefferson County.

Wednesday, April 19   A warm day. Mercury up to 60. A litle rain near night. The grass looks quite green. The frogs make lots of music both day & night. Wm has been doing down the sugar all day in the woods. Clarence has been gathering the Buckets. Sugaring is done for this year. I done my ironing this forenoon & washed the cans & pails & made 3 pies this afternoon. I scum 27 cans of milk with a spoon. Wm took my skimmer to the woods. I washed 30 pans. Put them all away in good shape. Carrie done her ironing & made dounots [doughnuts] & lots of other work.

Thursday, April 20   A litle rain in the night last but a lovely day. We washed buckets today. Wm & Carrie done the scouring of them & Malissa [Melissa] Ashley done the washing of them & I dried them with a towel. We washed 500 Buckets today. We are all very tired tonight.

Friday, April 21   Not so warm today. Quite a cold wind all day. We finished washing our sap Buckets today. We payed Melissa 75 cents for her work helping wash the Buckets. Wm done a churning this afternoon of 45 lbs of Butter. I packed it in jars. I have saved 100 lbs of Butter for our yuse.

Saturday, April 22   A nice warm day. Mercury 70. Clarence sold 100 lbs of sugar to Mr. Dulack yesterday for 8 dollars in money. He has sold Dulack 200 lbs. Wm & Clarence brout home the Evaperator & sugar & all of the sugar tools from the woods today. Clarence & Carrie has gone to town tonight. The rhodes are quite good in most of the way to town.

Sunday, April 23   A pleasant day. Not so very warm. Mercury up to 60. We have all been at home all day & had no company.

Monday, April 24   A warm nice day. Mercury up to 70 near 6 o'clock. We done our washing this forenoon. Then Carrie commenced cleaning in the chamber this afternoon. Clarence drew out manure all day in the filed. Wm took off the most of the storm windows this forenoon. Then he was setting fires in the old dry graps in the back lots. Clarence made Bonfires in the front yard this evening with dry grass. The fires looked nice but they made a great smoke.

Tuesday, April 25   A lovely day. Warm but clowdy part of the day. A sprinkle of rain this afternoon. The grass is looking quite green. Clarence drew manure in the field. A Mr. Charley Smith cald here & bought 2 bushels of seed wheete. Did not pay for it. Edwin Harmon cald & bought some wheete. Did not take it home today.

Wednesday, April 26   A warm pleasant day. Mercury 74. Carrie took up the carpet in the midle room upstairs & cleand the room & she & I cleand the pantry this afternoon. Clarence has gone to town tonight. Wm has been runing wheete through the fanning mill today ready for seede.

Thursday, April 27   Near 80. We took everything out of the parlor today accept the organ & cleand & put things all to their place.   Edwin Harmon came tonight & bought 3 bags of wheete. Payed the money for it. Barnet worked here today. Lesley McGill had a nail run into his leg last week. He has took cold in it & is hard up. Cald the Dr. and had the bone scraped. He will have a hard time.

[*Nancy, on a separate page, had the following additional information*]:

A nice pleasant day. Mercury went up to 80. Benn Barnet worked for Clarence today. They have gone to town tonight. April the 27, 21 eggs today. We have sold 40 dozen of eggs since the last of January up to this date, April 27.

Friday, April 28   A pleasant day & warm.   Mercury 84.   I cleand the front chamber today & put things all to their place. Clarence has a bad boil on his face today.   It pains him very bad this evening.   He has had a hard chore after the Heifers to get them to pasture to P. H. Brown's.

[Nancy had the following information on an overleaf page for April 28];

One more warm pleasant day.   Mercury up to 84.   Ben Barnet worked here today.   Clarence & Cland Rushton drove our yearling calves to P. H. Brown's tonight for him to pasture. Wm planted some potatoes in the garden today & a few peas.

Saturday, April 29   Mercury 86 above zero.   One more warm day.   No hired man today.   Clarence worked alone.   Has a very sore boil on his face.   He lanced it today with a needle. He & Carrie went to town this evening.   Wm planted onions today & peas & radishes.   Carrie & I done quite a lot of work. She made fried cakes & orange cake & lemon Pie & tartes [tarts].   We had white cookies & ginger cookies & cup cakes & fruit cake ready made so I think we will have plenty to last over Monday.   Miss Mary A Freeman is very sick the past week with pneumonia.

[Additionally, Nancy wrote in the overleaf: 15 eggs today.]

Sunday, April 30   One more warm day after the thunder this morning but not much rain.   Mercury up to 84.   Company today, Charley & Martha Brown came up to dinner.   Rose Brown & Della & Arther Dulack made us a call near night. Clarence & Carrie took a ride out to Clint McGill's after chours.   Maine & Earl Johnson was to Alvah's today for a visit.   This is the last day of April.

539

[Nancy Brown added in the overleaf for this date: 15 eggs today.]

<u>Memoranda</u>

[Note: The following pages were in the ending overleaf pages and appear to be an accounting of payments made, purchases made, and produce grown and animals raised on the farm. These entries were not in date order, but I have put them in the correct order by date. GGJ]

January 17, 1899	sold 4 dozen eggs
January 19	sold 1 dozen eggs
January 22	sold 1 dozen eggs
January 25	sold 1 dozen eggs
January 26	
January 27	1 dozen eggs
January 28	
January 30	
January 31	1 dozen

[It appears that in the following month, she listed the number of eggs laid and the number of eggs sold. GGJ]

February 1	4 eggs	
February 2	4 eggs	
February 3	4 eggs	1 dozen eggs sold
February 4		1 dozen eggs sold
February 5	3 eggs	
February 6	4 eggs	2 dozen eggs sold
February 7	3 eggs	
February 8	2 eggs	1 dozen eggs sold
February 9	6 eggs	
February 10	2 eggs	
February 11	3 eggs	

February 12	1 egg	1 dozen eggs sold
February 13	6 eggs	
February 14	4 eggs	
February 15	3 eggs	1 dozen eggs sold
February 15		sold 3 dozen eggs
February 16	4 eggs	
February 17	4 eggs	
February 18	5 eggs	1 dozen eggs sold
February 19	5 eggs	
February 20	6 eggs	1 dozen eggs sold
February 21	3 eggs	
February 22	6 eggs	2 dozen eggs sold
February 23	5 eggs	
February 24	6 eggs	
February 25	5 eggs	
February 26	8 eggs	2 dozen eggs sold
February 27	10 eggs	
February 28	7 eggs	3 dozen eggs sold
March 1	10 eggs	
March 2	10 eggs	
March 3	10 eggs	2 dozen eggs dold
March 4	9 eggs	
March 5	17 eggs	
March 6	12 eggs	3 dozen eggs sold
March 7	12 eggs	
March 8	18 eggs	
March 9	15 eggs	
March 10	12 eggs	
March 11	16 eggs	
March 12	15 eggs	
March 13	16 eggs	
March 14	18 eggs	
March 15	20 eggs	11 dozen eggs sold
March 16	17 eggs	
March 17	13 eggs	

March 18	15 eggs	4 dozen eggs sold
March 19	22 eggs	
March 20	17 eggs	
March 21	17 eggs	
March 22	15 eggs	
March 23	16 eggs	
March 24	19 eggs	
March 25	20 eggs	
March 26	17 eggs	
March 27	18 eggs	
March 28	17 eggs	
March 29	17 eggs	4 dozen eggs sold
March 30	13 eggs	
March 31	15 eggs	
April 1	15 eggs	1 dozen eggs sold
April 2	17 eggs	
April 3	17 eggs	
April 4	17 eggs	
April 5	14 eggs	
April 6	20 eggs	
April 7	15 eggs	
April 8	18 eggs	
April 9	16 eggs	
April 10	19 eggs	
April 11	16 eggs	
April 12	19 eggs	
April 13	14 eggs	
April 14	19 eggs	4 dozen eggs sold
April 15	17 eggs	
April 16	19 eggs	
April 17	15 eggs	
April 18	17 eggs	3 dozen eggs sold
April 19	16 eggs	
April 20	14 eggs	
April 21	14 eggs	
April 22	19 eggs	

April 23	16 eggs	
April 24	14 eggs	
April 25	16 eggs	
April 26	17 eggs	3 dozen eggs sold

May 1, 1899	20 eggs today
May 2	15 eggs
May 3	12 eggs
May 4	15 eggs
May 5	17 eggs
May 6	15 eggs
May 7	16 eggs
May 8	15 eggs
May 9	17 eggs

Sold 4 dozen eggs today

May 10	21 eggs
May 11	18 eggs
May 12	16 eggs
May 13	15 eggs
May 14	16 eggs
May 15	17 eggs
May 16	14 eggs
May 17	13 eggs
May 18	13 eggs
May 19	13 eggs
May 20	15 eggs
May 21	16 eggs
May 22	14 eggs
May 23	15 eggs
May 24	16 eggs
May 25	15 eggs
May 26	16 eggs

Sold 2 dozen

May 27	15 eggs
May 28	16 eggs
May 29	nothing listed

543

May 30	20 eggs
May 31	22 eggs

[Additionally on the overleaf pages at the back of the 1898-1899 diary were numerous account pages of expenses paid for items bought at various stores, from peddlers, donations to the church, as well as income from products sold other than eggs.]

[Nancy Johnson Brown also listed the following births on the back overleaf pages, GGJ]:

BORN

February 4, 1883	Wm Angus Ferguson Brown
April 14, 1884	Margaret Jane Brown
November 7, 1885	Colin Edward Brown
January 28, 1887	Annie Belle Brown
March 25, 1889	Beatrice Blanche Brown
August 16, 1890	Helen Victoria Brown

EPILOGUE

Nancy A. Johnson Brown died in Edwards, New York on March 23, 1909 of cancer. Her husband, William H. Brown died in Edwards, New York on March 3, 1914. They were preceded in death in Edwards, New York by two of their three children: Clara E. Brown November 17, 1868 of scarlet fever complicated by measles, whooping cough, and pneumonia, and by Alvah Percival Brown on March 3, 1906 of complications of Diabetes at age 60.

INDEX

A

A. P. *See* Alvah Percival
Brown and Abel Pratt
Johnson
Abbot, Naslo, 376
Abbot, V. P., 122
Absalom [Abaslom, Abaslon,
Absalam, Absalan,
Absolam, Alsalom] John.
B., 96, 122, 166-167, 224,
241-243, 266, 270, 284,
301, 341, 378, 394, 400,
429, 478, 499
Absalom, Mrs. John, 96, 270,
284, 429
Absalom [Absalon], Rachel,
394, 434
Absalom, Seymour, 301, 488,
519
Adams, NY, 455, 522, 528,
530
Agness, Agnys. *See* Agnes
Brown Hughes
Albany, NY, 437
Allen, A. C., 157
Allen, Albert, 437
Allen, Alvaretta Johnson, 442
Allen, Bob, 29, 77-78
Allen, Burt, 247, 255
Allen, Emma [Emmy], 52, 55
Allen, Frank, 388
Allen, George, 382, 400
Allen, John, 12, 48, 50, 54,
58, 148, 163

Allen, Laura, 53, 75, 86
Allen, Laureta, 94
Allen, Maud Wells, 437
Allen, Mirtle, granddaughter
of Moriah Merrill Johnson,
350
Allen, Mr., first husband of
Maud Wells Allen, 444
Allen, Mrs. Byron, 48
Allen, Mrs. Robert, 98, 205
Allen, Mrs. Will [Wil], 296
Allen, Myron, 284
Allen, Old Mr. Frank, 362
Allen, Oscar, 396
Allen, Rob, 31, 56, 59, 156,
160-161
Allen, Robert, 105, 111, 115-
116, 205, 215, 244, 263
Allen, Stella Barnes, 29, 32,
325
Allen, Warren, 283
Allen, Wilber, 81, 89
Allen, Will, 325
Allen, Willie, 358
Alvay. *See* Alvah Percival
Brown
Alverson, Jim, 404
Ama. *See* Amos C. Newton
Anders, [Andrews], William,
407
Anderson, Joseph, 235
Andrews, Anson, 510
Andrews, Minnie [Minne],
510, 522, 531

Andrews, Mr., 287, 488, 498, 531
Andrews, William, 297, 299, 407, 412
Antwerp, NY, 326
Ashley, Melissa, 537
Austin, Frank, 71, 75, 101
Austin, Fred, 323

B

Backus, George, 503
Backus, Mrs. George, 503
Backus, Pearl, 506
Baker, 42, 46, 108, 110, 129, 152,168, 184,206, 215, 230, 240
Balcom, Mr., 464, 524
Bancroft, Sophronia Laidlaw, 264
Bancroft, Earl, 435, 474, 517-519
Bancroft [Bencraft], Eben [Eb], 264, 269, 351, 360-61, 399
Bancroft [Bencraft], Hiram [H, Hi], 121, 286, 341, 402, 435
Bancroft, John, 50
Bancroft, Lellan, 439
Bancroft, Mrs. Earl, 435
Bancroft [Bancroaft], Mrs. Hiram [Hi], 402
Bancroft, Nettie Hazelton, 439
Bancroft, store owner, 530

Bancroft, Warren, 460
Baraford, George, 239-240, 261
Barans, Earl, 262
Barans, Nellie Thurstin, 262
Barens, Frank, 247
Barford, William [Wm], 192
Son of, 324
Barnes, Emaline, 442
Barnes, Frank, 287, 396
Barnes, Horris, 433
Barnes, Ida Woodcock (Mrs. Frank Barnes), 396, 412, 485
Barnet Brothers, 489
Barnet, Ben, 538
Barnet [Barnette], Mr., 475, 480, 487
Barraford, Agnes, 100
Barkey, Mrs. Ed, 474
Bartlet, Mr., 405, 409, 411, 422
Beavins, Charley,500
Beech, Amy, 237
Beech [Beach], Anna [Annah], 193, 261
Beech [Beach], Calvin, 382
Beech, Charles [Charley], 212, 238, 261, 364, 370
Beech, Dora, 225, 247, 393
Beech, Frank, 74, 146, 240, 313, 320
Beech, Frank, daughter of, 313
Beech [Beach], George, 97

Beech, Horace [Horis], 128, 131, 174, 177, 271
Beech, Lesley, 366
Beech [Beach], Lillie, 370
Beech, Mabel, 320
Beech, Mrs. Charles [Charley], 75, 212
Beech, Mrs. Charley, 75
Beech, Mrs. Miles, 279
Beech [Beach], Nila, 127
Beech, Rhoda, 173
Beech, Ugelia, 247
Beech, William, 92, 317, 364
Belleville, NY, 173
Bemas, Addie, 377
Bencraft family, 167
Bencraft, Nancy, 237, 261
Bennet, Henry, 38
Bennet, Lidia [Lidie], 38, 97
Berley, George Javall, 443
Berley, Hattie, 443
Bevins [Bevin], Martin, 190, 205, 221
Bignal [Bignell], A., 202
Bignal, Clinton, 9
Bignal [Bignel, Bignell], Elizabeth [Lizie, Lizzie] Brodie, 9, 38, 167, 202, 204, 236, 246, 293
Bignal [Bignel], Robby B., 9
Bignal, Wilber, 2
Black Lake, 394
Bloss, Henry, 224
Blount, Jessie, 366, 378, 385, 387
Bogart, 296

Boscoe, John C., 260
Boscoe, Louisa E. McGill, 260
Boulet [Bullock], Arthur, 477, 479, 481
Boulet [Bullock], father of, 479
Boulet [Bullock], Ella Freeman, 462, 475-477, 479, 481
Boutwell, Mrs. Ann, 467, 494
Bower. *See* Oswald Bower Brown
Boyd, John, 441
Boyd, Sabrina Hall, 441
Boys, Bill, 348
Boys, Mrs. Bill, 345
Brayton, 236
Brayton, Charley, 468
Brayton, Eddie [Eddy], 456, 526
Brayton, George, 437
Brayton, Josephine, 432
Brayton, Mrs. Edgar, 516
Brayton, NY, 442
Brayton, Roxanna, 467, 494
Brayton, Thomas, 302
Brayton, Viola Ray, 437
Bridgeport, CT, 326
Brodie family, 4, 38, 200, 307, 309
Brodie [Broadie], A. C., 280
Brodie, A. V., 45
Brodie [Broadia, Broadie,], Alexander Oswald, [A. O.],

9, 39, 45, 164, 176, 219, 246, 288, 451,

Brodie, Aswald O., son of, 451

Brodie [Broadie], Joseph, 2, 9, 502

Brodie, Louise H.[Harriet Louisa], 202

Brodie, Margaret Brown, 2, 192, 324

Brodie, Robert B., 191

Brookfield, MA, 319

Brother Ed. *See* Edward Brown (the elder)

Brother Hawley, 192

Brother Robert. *See* Robert Brown (the younger)

Brouse, Mr., 463

Brown, Adaline [Arlina], 510, 520, 522

Brown, Agnes Gowen [Graney, Mother, Mother Brown], 1, 4, 13, 16-17, 20-24, 26, 28-77, 85-86, 99, 182, 199, 324, 436

Brown, Alvah Percival [A., A. P., Alvay], 2, 4, 12-13, 15-16, 18-67, 69-130, 137-148, 152-164, 166-183, 185, 186-192, 195, 197, 198, 200-202, 203-259, 265-272, 273-277, 280-285, 287-299, 301-306, 308-310, 312-314, 323-324, 327, 329-334, 337-337, 341-344, 345-346,

349, 351-369, 371, 376-378, 383-390, 394-395, 398-400, 402-403, 407-409, 412-430, 442, 444, 451-453, 454-455, 462-460, 462-463, 465, 468, 472, 476, 478, 480-482, 487, 472, 495, 500-501, 505-510, 513-514, 517, 518-520, 525, 527, 528-532, 539, 544

Brown, Annie Belle, 544

Brown, Arline. *See* Adaline Brown

Brown, Beatrice Blanche, 544

Brown, Brother John. *See* John Brown

Brown, Brower. *See* Oswald Bower Brown

Brown, C. *See* Charles Hiram Brown

Brown, Carrie Cleland, 5, 446-457, 459-466, 468-474, 476-539

Brown, Carrie Cleland, brother of, 489

Brown, Charles Hiram, [C., C. H., CHB, Chary], 2-4, 11-19, 25, 28, 29-36, 40-49, 51-52, 54-55, 57-58, 60-62, 64-67, 69-70, 72, 74, 78-83, 84-88, 90-97, 99-102, 104-106, 108-113, 114, 116-119, 123-131, 137, 139-145, 147, 149-159, 161-202, 207, 208,

210-214, 216-217, 218-224, 226-229, 230-231, 234-235, 236-249, 253-254, 256-257, 591-260, 264, 266-267, 269-283, 287, 291-295, 296-297, 299-301, 303-305, 307-308, 310-315, 324, 326-328, 331, 334, 337, 339, 341, 343-345, 347-348, 350-356, 359-361, 362, 369-371, 376, 378, 384, 387, 390, 393, 397-402, 406-407, 416, 418, 420, 422-425, 427-429, 446, 450, 454, 460-462, 463-465, 469-471, 473, 474, 477, 478, 480, 482, 483, 486, 488, 492-493, 495-498, 502- 504, 508, 510, 511-512, 515-521, 524-528, 533-537, 539

Brown, Clara E. [Clarah], 2, 4, 21, 99, 198, 201, 273, 285, 304, 314-15, 318, 443, 544

Brown, Clara Pearl, 2, 121, 282, 446, 455, 459, 469, 477, 481, 491-492, 500, 502-503, 506, 510, 522, 528, 535

Brown, Clarence [Clarance], 2, 5, 10-11, 22, 25, 32, 36-37, 39, 45-46, 48-51, 55, 57-58, 64-65, 69, 77, 83-86, 88, 96, 165, 196, 274-276, 282, 285, 288, 307, 311, 312, 328, 330, 332, 334, 336-338, 342, 344-361, 363, 369-370, 376, 377, 380-381, 383-384, 386-387, 389-390, 392, 394-395, 398, 400, 404, 406-410, 412-416, 417-418, 420-422, 423, 425-426, 441, 445-458, 459-463, 539

Brown, Colin Edward, 544

Brown, cousin Nor, 403

Brown, David, 2, 194

Brown, Ed. *See* Edward Brown (the younger)

Brown, Eddie. *See* Edwin Brown

Brown, Edward (the elder) [Brother Ed], 24, 38, 40, 44, 76, 132-135, 138, 156, 178, 202-203, 209, 218, 228, 290-293, 337

Brown, Edward (the younger) [Ed], 21, 30, 35, 37, 41, 58, 151, 212, 310, 351

Brown, Edward of Watertown, son of, 351

Brown, Edwin [Eddie], 465-466, 479

Brown, Eliza Hitchcock, 3,9

Brown, Elizabeth [Lizzie, Sister Elizabeth], 1, 49, 76-77

Brown, Fred, 443

Brown, Gerty [Girty], 503-4, 508, 511, 516
Brown, Harold, 2, 446, 474-475, 481, 491, 506
Brown, Harriet, 2, 21, 194
Brown, Harry A., 194
Brown, Harvey A., 2
Brown, Helen Victoria, 544
Brown, Henry, 1, 2, 4-5, 34, 288, 316, 376, 408, 414, 454
Brown, Ira, 2, 43, 280
Brown, Isaac, 2, 42, 62-65, 67, 236, 241-244, 267, 276, 325
Brown, J. P., 27
Brown, James [Jim], 20, 34, 40, 48, 76, 86, 103, 163, 179, 185, 194-196, 200, 248, 262, 333, 344
Brown, Jane, 159
Brown, Jane, 162, 271, 387, 406
Brown, John [Brother John], 2, 24, 76-77, 271, 304
Brown, John, talc miner, 441
Brown, Joseph [Jo] P., 1, 8-10, 12-14, 18, 24, 26, 42, 69, 92, 94, 102-103, 106, 147-148, 166, 179, 198, 254, 258, 276, 356, 504, 514
Brown, Julia Wight, 2
Brown, Laura, 2, 407
Brown, Lauren, 353
Brown, Lilia M. Allen, 2

Brown, Lizzie. *See* Elizabeth Brown
Brown, Lona, 70, 77, 101
Brown, Mabel [Mable, [Mabe], 2, 8, 15, 32, 34, 46, 66, 96, 155-156, 158, 161, 164, 176, 180, 199, 264, 277, 282, 288, 296, 314, 338, 340, 342, 346, 350, 362, 367, 385, 389, 401, 407-408, 422, 429, 440, 445, 458, 460-461, 463, 464-466, 469, 471, 474-476, 480, 481-484, 489, 494, 500-503, 505, 506, 508-510, 512-513, 517-518, 522, 523-530
Brown, Mana. *See* Manie Brown Johnson
Brown, Manie Cleland, 2, 150,172, 198, 202,290, 323, 352
Brown, Many. *See* Manie Brown Johnson
Brown, Margaret Jane, 544
Brown, Martha Noble (Mrs. Charles Hiram Brown), 2, 11, 18, 29, 32, 36, 41, 44-45, 46, 48, 51, 53, 62, 64, 65, 69, 74, 83, 87, 89-95, 115, 124, 130-131, 137, 141-145,149-151, 156, 160-162, 164-166, 170, 172-175, 176-177, 182-199, 221, 235, 249, 264, 267, 270, 279, 288, 309,

312, 322, 338, 341, 346,
349, 350-352, 355, 359,
361, 364, 387-390, 391,
397, 399, 406-407, 414,
420, 426, 428, 436, 450,
453, 456-457, 461, 465,
465, 469, 472, 483, 484,
487, 488, 493, 503, 508,
511, 517, 518-519, 522,
524-527, 534-535, 539
Brown, Mary Rose [Rose], 2,
343, 358, 376, 380, 393,
405, 408, 417, 420, 422,
451, 456, 472-473, 480-
481, 483, 523, 539
Brown, Mary, 56
Brown, Matilda, 24, 132
Brown, Mettie E., 13,
101,324
Brown, Mr., from Russell,
500
Brown, Mrs. A. P. *See* Sarah
Grant Brown
Brown, Mrs. Alvah P. *See*
Sarah Grant Brown
Brown, Mrs. C. H. *See*
Martha Noble Brown
Brown, Mrs. Edward. *See*
Sarah Brown.
Brown, Mrs. Henry, 74
Brown, Mrs. Percival H., 391,
436
Brown, Mrs. Vincent, 447
Brown, Nancy A. Johnson
[N,A,B], 1-10, 12, 16, 20,
23, 25, 29, 37, 40, 42, 53,

55, 79, 81, 90, 92, 96, 97,
100, 107, 109-112, 115,
117, 119-122, 124-127,
129-130, 132, 136-142,
144-146, 161, 184, 205,
207-208, 212, 215, 218-
220, 223-229, 231-232,
235-236, 238-244, 248-
249, 251, 253-257, 265-
266, 275, 315, 319, 321,
362
Brown, Nancy Allen, 2
Brown, Old Mr. Robert,
father of James Brown, 264
Brown, Old Mr., 243, 245
Brown, Olive Wells, 435
Brown, Orpah Jane Ferguson,
323
Brown, Oswald Bower
[Brower], 2, 9-10, 18, 22,
32, 36, 39, 54-55, 69, 77,
85, 88, 94-95, 195, 276,
280, 282, 286-287, 291,
306, 314, 327, 329-31,
332, 335-337, 343-344,
346-353, 362, 366, 368,
372, 374, 376, 379, 381,
385, 388, 390, 392, 394,
397-399, 403, 405, 407-
408, 411, 413-414, 416-
418, 420-424, 429, 445-
446, 453, 456, 459, 463,
467-470, 475-477, 479,
481-482, 489, 495, 498,
502, 508-509, 513, 517,
522, 528, 532, 536-537

Brown, P., 461

Brown, Percival H., 2, 12, 36, 47, 62, 65-66, 68, 77, 97, 117, 150, 174, 200, 234, 256, 268, 271, 278, 292-293, 303, 305, 326, 328, 340, 342-343, 348, 350, 366-367, 369, 381, 385, 387, 390-393, 397-400, 415, 428, 501, 539

Brown, Percival, 2, 45, 68, 117, 234, 311

Brown, Pet, 390

Brown, Rawley, 288, 316

Brown, Robbie. *See* Robby B. Brown

Brown, Robby [Robbie] B., 29, 62, 329, 334, 336-337, 339, 344, 346, 347, 350-353, 361, 363, 365, 367, 370, 382, 385, 392, 394-396, 398-400, 419, 452

Brown, Robert (the elder) [Father Brown], 1, 13, 17, 23, 35, 68, 89, 95, 194, 235, 249, 413

Brown, Robert (the younger) [Brother Robert], 1, 13, 26, 29, 32, 40-41, 49, 53, 55-56, 65, 74, 77, 84, 94, 103-104, 106, 117, 123, 131, 141-142, 162, 178, 180, 187, 188, 200, 220, 224, 235, 243, 251-253, 275, 291, 293, 297, 329, 375, 418.

Brown, Robert, deceased, 23

Brown, S. W., 327, 473, 481

Brown, S., 127

Brown, Sarah (Mrs. Edward Brown), 24, 37-38, 40, 44, 218, 273, 291-293

Brown, Sarah Grant (Mrs. Alvah Percival Brown), 2, 15-16, 20, 23, 27, 32, 34, 38-39, 41, 49, 54, 56-58, 61, 64, 66, 71, 73, 77, 83, 87-88, 90-96, 105-106, 111, 114-116, 118-123, 125, 128, 132, 137, 145, 147, 150-151, 155-160, 163, 165-168, 170-171, 174-175, 180-182, 185, 187-189, 190, 205, 206, 207, 215-216, 225-226, 234, 241, 253, 255, 258, 264, 267-268, 279, 287, 292, 294, 296, 302-304, 324, 332, 336-337, 343, 352, 360, 362, 370, 379, 381, 384, 395, 397, 400-402, 406, 408, 414, 417, 418-420, 421-425, 427-429, 442, 446, 456-458, 459, 465, 491, 504, 506, 508, 512, 515, 517, 520, 530

Brown, Sherman, 2, 10, 11, 15, 18, 22-23, 27, 29, 31, 33-36, 38-39, 43-44, 47-51, 54-56, 58-61, 63-64, 67, 71, 73, 75, 79-87, 91-93,

95-96, 112, 115, 117, 124,
143, 148, 155, 160, 162,
164, 166-167, 171-172,
174-177, 180, 182, 185-
187, 188, 191-192, 195-
196, 214, 238, 248, 271,
273-275, 277, 280-281,
283, 286, 288-289, 298-
299, 301, 305-308, 310,
313-314, 327-430, 450,
463, 472, 484, 487, 500,
503, 508, 511, 513, 516,
517, 520, 525, 532
Brown, Sherman E., 313
Brown, Sidney, 2, 35, 41,
219, 256, 275, 288, 302,
302-303, 308
Brown, Stillman [Sillman
Stilman] E., 2, 13, 32, 36,
40-41, 44, 49, 84, 88, 92-
93, 96, 98, 100, 106, 110,
116, 120, 124, 138, 140,
145, 154, 166, 169, 180,
185-186, 200, 207, 224,
244, 248, 252, 255, 304,
310-312, 320, 328, 333,
353, 358, 362, 367, 404,
407, 418
Brown, Storkels, 173
Brown, Susa. *See* Susan M.
Brown Clair
Brown, Theresa, 67
Brown, Vincent [V., Vent,
Vint], 276, 281, 283-284,
286, 288-291, 292, 296-

300, 302-304, 306, 308-
309, 311-314, 487
Brown, Vincent, son of, 487
Brown, William [Will, Willia,
Wm.] E., 22, 131-136, 184,
203, 267, 272, 302, 305,
311, 324, 380, 394, 419,
432
Brown, William Angus
Ferguson, 544
Brown, William H., 1, 2, 4-7,
9-13, 15, 18-98, 100-102,
146-192, 197-198, 200-
204, 263-264, 265-283,
284-290, 291, 293-309,
315-316, 318, 327-384,
385-430, 439, 446-457,
462-471, 472-473, 475-
522, 525-539
Brown, Willie, 63, 84
Broyton, Charles, 238
Bryant, James, 435
Bryant, Lizzie Webb, 435
Buck, Horace, 23
Buck, William, 23
Buffalo, NY, 136
Bullock, Arther. *See* Arthur
Boulet
Bullock, Ella. *See* Ella
Freeman Boulet
Bunnell, Jessie, 193
Bunnell [Bunnel], Mariah, 21,
28-31, 41, 47, 55-56, 68
Bunnell, Susan, 193
Burdick, Ellen, 100
Burdick, Frank, 72

Burdick, Mrs. Frank, 99
Burdock, Frank, 284
Burell, L.W., 213
Burlingame, William, 146
Burns, Mrs. Earl, 296
Burnum, Levi, 434
Burnum, Rachel Absalom, 434
Buscart, Plot, 410

C

Campbell [Cambell, Campel, Campell], James [Jim], 230, 293, 296, 359, 448, 451, 463, 487
Canton, NY, 12-14, 17, 29-30, 62, 70, 72, 96-97, 104, 112-113, 118, 143, 148, 157, 159, 163, 191-192, 193, 202, 206, 266, 270, 275, 279, 296, 342, 349, 366, 372, 378, 384, 389, 398-399, 408, 410, 430, 432, 437, 464, 480, 484, 495, 513
Cara. *See* Carrie McGill Pratt
Carr, J., 231
Carter, 15, 17, 23-25, 72, 84, 103, 112-115, 122-123, 148, 159, 243
Carter, Cornelius, 444
Carter, Ellsworth, 444
Carter, Mr., the Baptist minister, 464, 473-476, 480-1

Carthage [Cartrage], NY, 392
Casada, [Malice] Molie [Mrs. Had Gardner], 100
Casada, Rob, 114, 443
Cedar Springs, MI, 246
Ch B. *See* Charley Hiram Brown
Chadwick, Clara Wells, 325
Chadwick, William, 325, 417
Chary. *See* Charles Hiram Brown
Chase, Smith, 393, 451
CHB. *See* Charles Hiram Brown
Chicago, IL, 15, 417
Chub Lake, NY, 403
City of Washington, 348
Clair, Susan [Susa] M. Brown, 1, 19, 35, 42, 59-60, 64, 72, 79-80, 98, 151, 153, 157, 179, 258-260, 278, 298, 302, 304, 356, 372, 403, 405
Clark, Abbie, 521
Clark, Andrew, 316
Clark, Anna Robertson, 323
Clark, Ben, 267
Clark, Ella, 444
Clark, Emma Hall, 328, 358, 375, 480, 532
Clark, Eva, 469, 516
Clark, Henry, 276
Clark, Mary Laidlaw, 276, 322
Clark, Mildred, 480, 532

Clark, Mr., 78, 129, 139, 251, 285
Clark, Mrs. Austin, 319
Clark, Mrs. Ben, 267
Clark, Myron, 175, 180, 330, 345, 423
Clark, Myron, daughter of, 330
Clark, Robert, 323
Clark, Seigh, 413
Clark, Will, 329
Clark, William G., 444
Cleland [Clealand], Old Mr., 374
Cleland [Clealand], Othnel [Othnal], 338, 389, 395, 405, 424
Cleland, Alex, 82, 86, 190
Cleland [Clealand], Andrew, 360, 408
Cleland, Bell, 22
Cleland, Celia Gant, 32, 38, 83-84, 206, 265, 268, 325
Cleland [Clealand], Cyrus [Cy, Cyras, Syras], 12-13, 37, 49, 54, 58-60, 64, 66, 83, 87, 94, 98, 118, 120, 205-206, 209-210, 231, 233, 243, 249, 325, 423, 430, 440, 510
Cleland, Daniel [Dan], 129, 175, 196
Cleland [Clealand], Ellen [Elin, Elen], 52, 55, 76, 143, 153, 225, 243, 247
Cleland, Ettie, 476

Cleland, Grant, 440
Cleland, H., 122
Cleland, Harley, 222
Cleland, Harry, 168, 485
Cleland, Harvey, son of, 389
Cleland, Harvey, 118-120, 131, 221, 238, 389
Cleland, Helen, 17, 197, 323
Cleland, Iona, 255
Cleland, J. W., 452, 487
Cleland, James, 118
Cleland, Jimmy, 530
Cleland [Clealand], John W., 44, 113, 259, 325, 446, 447, 462, 464, 471-472, 476, 483, 486, 488-489, 495, 500, 509, 513, 522, 530-533
Cleland, Lester, 408, 484, 489
Cleland, Mary, 177, 196
Cleland, Maryette Merchant, 325
Cleland, Mettie, 451
Cleland, Mrs. Cyrus, 98, 440
Cleland, Mrs. Harry, 389
Cleland [Clealand], Mrs. John W., 213, 476, 486, 488, 508, 509
Cleland, Mrs. William, 298, 389
Cleland, Syras. See Cyrus Cleland
Cleland, Thomas, 193
Cleland, Venah, 476
Cleland [Clealand], William [Wm], 51, 100, 102, 105-

107, 117, 128, 150, 173, 175, 231, 269, 275, 289, 298, 328, 336, 353, 359, 365, 389, 430, 432, 504, 532

Clifford, Carie Towns, 318

Clifford, John, 318

Clinton, IA, 194, 202

Cochrane, son in law of Simeon Wiels, 329

Cole, Mr., 474

Cole, George, 447

Cole, lived at James Wilson's, 260

Cole, Mrs. Maud Wells Allen, 443

Cole, Mrs. Nicholas, 74

Cole, Nicholas [Niclious], 21-22, 53, 55, 74, 83, 114, 206, 241

Cole, Perlina Hall Brown, 28

Colton, NY, 30, 355

Commissioner Cole, 214

Conboy, 415

Conboy, Richerd, 413

Conine, Mrs., 76, 98, 169

Conyne, [Conne], C., 44-45, 112, 244-245, 254-257, 261, 263, 284

Cook, Nancy Jane McFerran, 434

Coopersville, MI, 56, 70, 73, 196, 346, 432, 434

Copenhagen, NY, 516

Corbin, 131

Corneel. *See* Cornelia Phelps Rushton

Cotton, David M., 326

Cousins family, 356

Cousins [Cousens], Albert, 203, 229, 260, 319, 323, 381, 407, 425

Cousins, Albert, daughter of, 317

Cousins, Celia, 317

Cousins [Cozen], John, 24, 38, 86, 88, 96, 158, 345, 355, 408, 439, 520

Cousins, John, daughter of, 439

Cousins, Leland, 489

Cousins, Mabel, 74

Cousins, Metta [Nettie?] Payne, 323

Cousins, Mrs. John, 439

Cousins, Mrs. William, 317

Cousins, Nettie Payne [Payn], 229, 260 [see Metta above]

Cousins, Thomas [Tom], 304, 381, 407, 425

Cousins, Will, 462-463, 472, 534

Cousins, William [Will, above] 113, 317,461

Cozen, John. *See* John Cousin

Cross, Ben, 100

Cumber, Ed, 178, 373

Cummings, Jim, 271

D

Danamara, 456

Dane [Dain], John, 204, 379

Dane, Mrs. Tom, 531

Dart, Daniel, 129, 176, 229-30

Dart, Don, 224

Davenport family, 70

Davenport, Norris, 403

Davis, Mary Martin, 326

Davis, George, 58, 65, 72, 73-75, 77, 260, 323

Davis, Mary Martin, 263

Davis, Mr., 398-399

Day, Grace, 144

Day, Nelly, 271

De Kalb Junction, NY, 33, 58, 126, 236, 237, 245, 284, 444 [same as below]

De Kalb, NY, 19, 31, 42, 118, 140, 180, 187, 235, 250, 289, 376-377, 388, 403, 409, 418, 437, 447

De Peyster, NY, 466

Deer River, NY, 76, 272, 303, 306, 394

DeGrass, NY, 516

Desmonds, Old Mr., 299

Detroit, MI, 280-281, 311

Dewey, George, 516

Dewey, Jay, 480

Dewey, Mrs. Dr. Goodnough, 516

Dike. *See* Elder Dyke

Docter Foster. *See* Dr. James Foster

Doctor Jay, 134

Doctor Liston [Leston], 208, 210, 263

Donaldson [Donalson, Donelson], Fred, 459 521

Donaldson, Mrs. Fred, 521

Downs, Mrs. Burny, 259

Dr. Danry, 496

Dr. Dow, 258

Dr. Drury, 100, 151

Dr. Kellow, 276

Dr. Lee, 268, 355, 361, 366, 372, 378, 384, 389, 394, 399, 409, 414, 420, 428, 437

Dr. Lill, 342

Dr. Merkley, 456, 461, 465, 479, 488-489, 496, 506, 517-519, 520-521, 536

Dr. Merkley, Mrs., 516

Dr. Murray [Murry, Mury], 11, 37, 47, 82, 106, 123, 156, 302, 352

Dr. Murray, Mrs., 98

Dr. Rice, 526, 528, 529

Dr. Semore, 156

Dr. Tabor, 362

Dr. Taylor, 403, 464, 496

Dr. Wilson, 404

Dulark, Arther, Della, 539

Dulark, Frandy, 459, 476, 518

Dulark, Fred, 518

Dulark, Fred, son of, 518

Dulark, Hattie, 460-461, 478, 506

Dulark, Mrs. Feandy, 474

Dulark, Mrs. Frandy, 505
Dulark, Mrs. Fred, 518
Dulette, Sherm, 115
Dumas, Abram, 20
Dumas, Henry, 28
Dumas, Jenny, 71
Dumas, Mrs., 27-28
Dumas, Wilber [Willie], 27, 202, 206, 208, 235, 373, 381, 402, 408
Dunn [Dun], Robert, [Rob], 104, 113, 116, 124, 158
Dygart, Mrs. John, 155, 198
Dyke, young Mr., [see also Elder Dyke] 273, 281

E

Earl, Alice [Allise], 51, 173
Earl, Celia Haile, 401
Earl, Guy, 193
Earl, Hat, 115
Earl, Henry, 123
Earl, Otis, 193
Earl, Warren, 441
Earl, Willard, 401
East Pitcairn, NY, 329
Eastman, 229
Eastman, Mrs. Steven, 380
Eastman, Old Mr. Steven, 380
Eastman, Steven, daughter of, 380
Edwards, NY, 1, 4-5, 7, 10, 15, 21, 38, 44, 50, 54, 57, 68, 72, 75, 85, 97, 101,

157, 159, 193-96, 198-203, 222, 259-260, 264-266, 268, 273, 275, 280, 294, 296, 304, 308, 310, 316-320, 323-327, 329, 331-332, 335, 339-340, 342, 345, 348, 364, 373, 376, 380-382, 385-386, 389, 395, 409, 411, 432-449, 461, 464, 466-467, 473-474, 480, 486-488, 494, 497-498, 503-504, 507-508, 516-519, 522, 525, 529, 531
Elder Dyke [Dike], 18, 29, 54, 70, 79, 87, 93, 122, 150, 154, 161, 175, 197, 256, 284, 285, 290
Elder Dyke, Mrs., 290
Elder Hitchcock, 229
Elder Holly, 140, 144, 211
Elder Wood, 152
Eliot, Albert, 264, 280-281, 323, 384
Eliot, Helen Cleland [Mrs. Albert Eliot], 17, 197, 280-281, 323, 374, 384
Ellis, John, 97
Elmira, NY, 15
Ervin [Irvin], Mr., 210, 248-250
Erwin, Mr., 70, 130-131, 173, 177-179, 207

F

Fairbanks, Mr., 386, 389, 456
Fairbanks, Mrs., 389
Farell, Albert, 412-414
Farney, John, 456
Father Brown. *See* Robert
  Brown (the elder)
Fellows [Fellow, Felows],
  Addie [Ada, Adah, Addia,
  Adie, Idda] *See* Addie
  Fellows McKee
Fenton, Charles, 322
Fine, NY, 41, 43, 51, 55, 67,
  71-72, 90, 102-104, 108,
  130, 147-149, 178, 207,
  213, 233, 237, 246, 269,
  277, 280, 289, 300, 312-
  314, 316, 329, 333, 340,
  356-357, 375, 379 381,
  408, 412-413, 415, 419,
  438-439, 447, 461, 468-
  469, 478, 489, 499, 523-
  524
Flack, Emma, 519
Flack, Mr., 445, 454, 484,
  496-497, 500, 514, 521-
  522, 536
Flack, Mrs., 475, 500
Flack, Shirley, 454, 531
Flack, Stacy, 516
Flack, W., 514
Fleming, Mr., 351, 434
Fleming [Flemings], Mrs.
  Walter, 433, 434
Fleming [Flemings], Walter,
  433

Fleming [Flemings], Water,
  son of, 433
Fordham, Emeline [Emaline]
  Barnes, 433, 442
Fordham, Ira, 27, 442
Fordham, Jim, 442
Fordham, Mrs. Jim (second
  wife), 442
Forney, John, 437
Forney, Nellie M. Muir, 437
Foster, Dr. James, 3, 165,
  171, 190, 205, 249-250,
  255, 257, 264, 364
Foster, Susan Viall (Mrs. Dr.
  James Foster), 3, 171, 205,
  249-250, 255, 257, 270,
  364
Foster, Susan Viall, daughter
  of, 364
Fowler, Amos, 304
Fowler, NY, 149, 266, 310,
  323, 341, 394, 400, 429,
  434-436, 440, 442, 449,
  462, 473, 478, 484, 499
Freeman, Arthur, 369, 395,
  399-400, 405-406, 412,
  424
Freeman, Bower, 432, 439
Freeman, Charles, 317, 448
Freeman, Charley, 288, 400
Freeman, Clint, 369
Freeman, Delbert [Dell], 328,
  353, 432, 511
Freeman, Effie (Mrs. Leon A.
  Freeman), 445, 447-448,
  462

Freeman, Ella Rushton, 317

Freeman, Ellie, daughter of Gideon Freeman, 449

Freeman, Fred, 420

Freeman, George, 34, 40, 97, 121

Freeman, George W., 115, 127, 166, 316

Freeman, Gideon, 294-295, 297-298, 300-301, 307-309, 312, 383, 389, 391, 397-398, 401, 431, 452, 472, 477, 479, 481, 484, 491, 517, 522, 526

Freeman, Grant, 478

Freeman, LaVerne, 6

Freeman, Leon, 462

Freeman, Lidia Hall, 432

Freeman, Luella, 511

Freeman, Mary Allen, 397-398, 475, 539

Freeman, Mrs. Dell, 511

Freeman, Mrs. George, 110, 155, 198

Freeman, Mrs. Gideon [Gid], 274, 286, 389, 449, 484, 517

Freeman, Mrs. Leon A. *See* Effie Freeman

Freeman, Nelson, 121, 167, 176, 181, 184, 430, 441, 456

Freeman, Osker, 362

Freeman, Osweld, 517

Freeman, Phoebe Maria Carr, 442

Freeman, Roy Grover, 439

Freeman, Sarah, 478

Freeman [Freemen], Stellah Van Ornum [Vanornum], 353, 432

Freeman, Thomas, 198, 443

Fullerville, NY, 57, 190, 203, 405, 462-464, 472

Furguson [Furgason], 132

G

Gaddis, 103, 112-114, 148, 149, 213, 235

Gardner family, 61

Gardner, Alvin [A.], 227, 230

Gardner, Amelia, 37

Gardner [Gardener, Gardiner], Had [H.], 33, 53, 55, 72, 86, 94, 100, 196, 263-264, 308, 398, 411, 413, 421, 431

Gardner, Had, daughter of, 411

Gardner [Gardener], J., 279

Gardner [Gardener], Losson, daughter of, 329

Gardner, John, 230

Gardner, M., 85

Gardner, Martha, 53, 98

Gardner [Gardener], Mrs. Had, 431

Gardner, Mrs. L. M., 98

Gardner [Gardener], Nan [Nin], 61, 63, 100, 345

Gardner, Old Mr., 81, 101

Gardner [Gardener], Old
Mrs., 331-332
Gardner, Nin, 101
Gardner [Gardener], Will,
285, 422
Gardner, William, 50
Gates, Jason, 245, 262
Gear, Dexter, 463, 471, 506
Gear, Fern, 478
Gear, Ninah, 471
Gear, Mrs., 33
Gibbons, Chauncy, 74
Glasby, Daniel, 38
Glasby, Nick, 108
Glasby, Warren, 83
Glazier, Allis [Alice?], 437
Glazier, Willard, 437
Gleason, Betsy, 98
Goodnough [Goodenough,
Goonanough], Dr. A. B.,
13, 40, 64, 88, 104, 119,
141, 153, 165, 214, 231,
245, 250, 263, 369-370,
394, 402, 528
Goodnough, Clinton, 435
Goodnough, Cora Bancroft,
433
Goodnough, Mrs. A. B., 217,
352, 443
Goodnough, Mrs. Jane, 25
Gorden, Angelia, 79, 81, 84
Gorden, Curtis, 106
Gorden, I., 38, 139
Gorden, Laura, 75, 81, 204
Gorden, Libby, 107, 151

Gorden [Gordin], Lillian
[Leillie, Lilian, Lill, Lily],
34, 53, 59, 72-73, 77, 81,
97, 185, 212, 258
Gorden, Lizzie [Lizie], 107
Gorden [Gordin], Mr. 31-32,
34, 36, 38, 40, 43, 61, 75,
77-78, 80, 84, 89, 92, 151,
232, 369
Gorden [Gordin, Gordon],
Mrs., 12-13, 33, 36, 51,
61, 68, 70, 75-82, 86-87,
103, 148, 158, 222, 294,
358
Gouldston, Joseph, 238
Gouverneur, NY, 10, 12, 14,
24-25, 29, 39, 46, 49, 56-
58, 64-66, 71, 79-81, 94,
100, 126, 130, 136, 140,
164, 166, 173, 177, 180-
182, 184-185, 187, 188-
190, 208, 210-214, 219,
221-225, 229, 233, 235,
240, 242, 259, 267, 268-
272, 275-277, 280, 282,
284, 287, 293, 295, 297-
300, 303, 305-306, 311,
313, 316, 329, 342-343,
345-348, 354-356, 358,
360-361, 364, 368, 375-
378, 382, 384-386, 390,
395-396, 404, 407-408,
412, 416, 423, 431, 433,
435, 439-440, 442-443,
445, 448, 450, 454, 456,
459, 461, 466-467, 474,

476, 478, 480-482, 486,
488, 501-503, 506, 520,
525
Governor Black, 453
Graham, David, 510
Graham, Lou, 283
Graham, Mrs. John, 149
Grandma Cleland, mother of
Manie Cleland, 85, 374
Grandpa Cleland, father of
Manie Cleland, 51, 54, 56,
60, 80, 81, 85, 167, 190,
277, 280, 297, 340, 374
Graney. *See* Agnes Gowen
Brown
Grant, Adelle, 149
Grant, Anne, 7
Grant, Cora, 38
Grant, Elmer, 430, 520
Grant, Eveline [Evaline]
Cleland, 80, 115, 117, 162,
434
Grant, Henry, 110, 393, 411,
416, 424-427, 430-432
Grant, James, 7-8, 12-13, 21-
23, 28-29, 63
Grant, Julia Rushton (Mrs.
Thomas Grant), 38-39, 41,
82, 110-111, 113, 155-156,
156-157, 198-200
Grant, Leona Payne, 430-431
Grant, Marg, 245
Grant, Mary, 159, 273, 430
Grant, Mrs. Thomas [Tomas].
See Julia Rushton Grant

Grant, Mrs. William, 262,
530
Grant, Nora, 213, 332, 428
Grant, Rhoda, 379, 432
Grant, Thomas [Thom], 16,
32, 38, 56, 58, 64, 82, 91,
108-110, 113-114, 118,
153, 155-156, 172, 175,
189, 200-201, 206, 213,
227, 233, 243, 245, 256,
258, 264, 284, 288, 303,
305, 310, 328, 332, 368,
403, 419-420, 442
Grant, William [Bill, Wm.],
76, 94, 115, 121, 161, 172,
230, 243, 262, 328, 357,
420, 530
Granville, MI, 283
Green, Agnes [Agness], 180-
182
Green, Erwin, 243
Green, Frank, 18
Green, Jacob, 479
Green, Libbie [Libby], 18
Green, Mrs. William, 170,
301
Green, William M, 279
Green, William [Wm], 18, 38,
68, 170, 216-217, 273, 301,
374, 395, 407, 409, 418,
421-424, 426, 437, 495,
510, 518, 521, 523, 529
Green, Willie [William Green
(the younger)], 170
Greenwood, MO, 14

Grieves [Grieve], Mrs., 39,
    73, 122
Griffin, Kate, 75, 523
Grifin, Lizie, 197

H

Haile, Caroline M., 445
Haile, Celia, 393, 445
Haile, Charles H. [Charley],
    53, 64, 345, 401, 406, 445
Haile, Fred, 60, 64
Haile, John, 169
Haile, Mabel, 349
Haile, Nin, 53
Hailesboro[Hailsbourough,
    Hailsburg], NY, 100, 260,
    372, 448
Hale, L. P., 444
Hall, A., 168
Hall [Hull], Alfred B. [A. B.],
    4, 8, 10, 12, 26-28, 31, 37,
    42, 43, 51, 60, 67, 91, 214,
    251, 252, 258, 278, 289,
    295, 302, 312, 318, 329,
    373, 375, 441
Hall, B., grandchild of, 297
Hall, Charles [Charley], 219,
    300, 441
Hall, Ellis, 396
Hall, Emma D., 71, 76, 81
Hall, Emmorancy Johnson
    [Emma J., Em, Sister Hall]
    (Mrs. Alfred B. Hall), 3, 7,
    10, 22, 26-28, 31, 33-36,
    39-41, 48, 51, 53-56, 61,
63, 67-68, 71, 73, 76, 80-
    81, 87, 94, 137, 142-143,
    146-147, 156-157, 168,
    174, 179, 181-185, 189,
    191-192, 204-205, 208,
    214, 221, 222, 238, 246-
    247, 251-252, 257, 264,
    266, 268, 273, 275, 276,
    278-280, 281-284, 287,
    295, 298-300, 303, 308,
    318, 347, 358, 362, 368,
    371, 394, 423, 431, 441-
    442
Hall, Fred, 347
Hall, Hiram, 26, 53, 69, 71,
    74, 108, 256, 282, 377,
    471, 533
Hall, Jenny, 31-32, 40, 78
Hall, Lois Wells, 441
Hall, Mattie, 328
Hall, Mrs. Alfred B., *See*
    Emmorancy Johnson Hall
Hall, Mrs. Hiram, 75, 98
Hall, Myron, 376, 507, 513,
    531
Hall, Neary [Meary, Nera].
    See Vanera Hall Pratt
Hall, Vanesa, 49
Hall, Venera, 55
Hall, William, 438
Hamilton, NY, 395
Hamilton, ON, 133
Hanny. *See* Hannah Brown
    McBride
Harewood, 443
Harmon, Alice, 41, 186, 199

565

Harmon, Annah Eliza [Aneliza], 368, 465
Harmon, Bertie, 22
Harmon, Blaine, 489
Harmon, Charles [Charley], 15, 77, 95, 106, 128, 138-139, 155, 167, 170, 173, 185, 186-187, 192, 199, 202, 208, 222, 228-227, 239, 245, 246, 250, 258, 273, 294-295, 373, 401, 499, 504, 532-530
Harmon, Charles H. [C. H.], 227
Harmon, Charles Luther, 199, 373
Harmon, Charles [Charley] V., 22, 41, 73, 138, 241, 255, 285, 305, 309, 371, 377, 390-392, 410
Harmon, Edwin P., 448, 467, 503, 538
Harmon, Erwin C., 306, 311, 348, 351, 377, 386-387, 392, 395, 476-477
Harmon, Frank, 446-449, 453
Harmon, Harriet [Haried, Hariet] Viall (Mrs. Wesley Porter Harmon), 3, 115, 227, 252, 303, 327, 327, 373
Harmon, Jim, 361, 363
Harmon, James (the younger) [Jim, Jimmy], 488, 528-534, 536

Harmon, James Ebenezer [Eben], 3, 137, 195
Harmon, James H., 138, 184-5
Harmon [Hermon], James [J., Jim] W., 94, 100, 104, 121, 127-128, 147, 173, 182-184, 191, 204, 227, 240, 246, 263, 329-330, 340-341, 345, 351, 361, 410, 412, 423, 453, 473, 495
Harmon, James W., son of, 351
Harmon, Lizzie [Lizie], 475, 533
Harmon, Luther, 523
Harmon, Mary, 461
Harmon [Harvmon], Maryette [Maryett, Maryetta], 41, 127, 183, 311, 373-374, 377, 390-391, 401-402, 533
Harmon, Mertle Peterson, 467, 503
Harmon, Mrs. Charles [Charley], 138-139, 174
Harmon, Mrs. Edwin, 448
Harmon, Mrs. Erwin, 476-477
Harmon, Mrs. James W., 100, 473, 495, 526
Harmon, Mrs. James, 128, 174, 323
Harmon, Mrs. Wesley Porter. *See* Harriet Viall Harmon

Harmon, Phila [Philey] Viall (Mrs. James Ebenezer Harmon), 3, 13, 21, 41-42, 54, 70, 73, 77, 95, 106, 110, 137, 145, 150, 168, 183-184, 191, 206, 228, 250, 368, 373, 402

Harmon, Viola, 423, 427, 455, 469

Harmon, Warren, 362, 454, 489

Harmon, Wesley [Westly] Porter, 3, 206, 252, 259, 317, 330, 368, 373, 465, 503

Harrisville [Harisville], NY, 82, 105, 130, 149, 158, 177, 264, 331-332, 394, 401-402, 470, 498

Harris, Mr., 378, 382, 388, 394, 399-400, 409, 414, 421-422

Harris, Mr., daughter of, 398

Harritt, Rachel Earl Johnson, 14, 368, 462

Harvmon, Maryett. *See* Maryette Harmon

Hearmon. *See* Hermon, NY

Heath children, 521

Hemingway, Pauline [Paulina], 384

Henderson, Fanny, 47

Hepenstall [Hapenstall, Hefenstall], Ruby [Reuby], 31, 39, 67-68, 76-77, 80-82, 85-87, 114, 159, 200

Herington [Herrington], Emma Johnson [Emmy] (Mrs. Eugene Herington), 68-69, 362, 442

Herington, Eugene [Jean, Jene], 68-69, 169

Hermon [Hearmon, Herman], NY, 4, 19, 34, 38, 44, 47-50, 58, 91, 95-96, 100, 118, 123, 163, 169-170, 172, 176, 182, 193, 198-199, 208, 232-233, 235, 241-242, 258, 265, 273-274, 279, 297, 301, 304, 328, 330, 336, 344-345, 357, 374, 395, 469, 418, 420-421, 423, 425-426, 437, 447, 465, 471, 478-480, 485, 495, 507, 510, 512-513, 518-519, 521, 525, 529, 531

Herington [Herrington], Mrs. Eugene. *See* Emma Johnson Herington

Herr, Arba. *See* Ardan O. Kerr

Heth, Arther, 531

Heth, Mrs., 477

Heuvelton, NY, 124, 170

Hitchcock, John, 246

Hitchcock, Mrs., 215

Hitchcock, Mrs. E., 264, 298

Hitchcock, Watson, 53

Hoffman, Leona, 78

Homes, [Holms]Peter, 103, 148

567

Hooper [Hoper], Minnie, 346, 351, 380, 419

Hoooper, Mr., 385, 391, 422

Houlan, Thomas, 207

Howerd, Rev., 280

Huffman, Lona Brown, 70, 101

Hughes [Hughs], Agnes [Agness, Agnys] Brown (Mrs. John Hughes), 1, 10, 13, 27, 31, 40, 42, 44, 53, 62-65, 67, 84, 86, 99, 109, 127, 154, 159, 178, 183, 200, 204, 207, 222, 249, 257, 272, 275, 280, 291, 297, 298, 305, 317, 328, 346, 356-357, 366, 389, 394, 412, 423, 424, 429, 465

Hughes, Ed, 372, 527

Hughes, [Hughs] Ella, 29, 33, 35-36, 40-41, 43, 191

Hughes, Jennie Schilar, 372

Hughes, John, 1, 272, 297, 298, 305, 317, 327-328, 339, 350, 352, 356, 366, 378, 392, 397, 413, 415, 423-465, 517

Hughes, Seth, daughter of, 516, 527

Hughs, Emmy, 63

Hunt, Dave, 96

Hulbert, Charles, 121

Hull, A. B., *See* Alfred B. Hall

Hunt, Pet, 19, 34, 47-49, 58, 92, 94-96, 99

I

Ingersoll [Ingersol], 135, 183

Ingraham, 4

Ingram, Frank, 487, 524, 535

Ivers, George, 11, 82, 100, 185, 324

Ivers, Ida [I.], 11, 45, 51, 82, 226, 260

Ivers, Louisa, 11

J

Jacson, JS, 101

Jackson [Jacson], NY [FL], 195

Jacobs, Alice Holmes, 325

Jacobs, Herbert, 325

Jane, aunt of Mary Grant, 159, 198, 200, 399, 400, 429

Jennie, Cora, 399, 429

Jim H. *See* Jim Harmon

Johnson, Abel Pratt [A. P., Brother A. P.], 4, 9-10, 12-15, 18, 28, 123-124, 153, 167-169, 171, 177-178, 184, 201, 207, 231, 240, 258, 265, 276, 282, 286-287, 300, 304, 316, 318, 345, 360, 372, 397-398, 402, 441, 449, 462, 489, 511, 528-535

Johnson, Abel, son of Charles Victor Johnson, 434
Johnson, Alvah, 3, 4, 14
Johnson, Brother A. P. *See* Abel P. Johnson
Johnson, Celia Laidlaw, 38, 192, 197, 266, 268, 323, 373
Johnson, Charles Alvah, 3, 4, 9-10, 195, 201, 318, 371, 441, 502
Johnson, Charles V., 60, 118, 190, 264, 268, 292, 373, 500, 510, 525, 529-531
Johnson, Charles Victor, 3, 9-10, 14, 102, 147, 276, 312, 317, 318, 402, 433, 468
Johnson, Charles [see John Charles Johnson]
Johnson, Charles, [son of William Warren Johnson] 192, 197, 223, 257
Johnson, Earl, 462, 464, 465, 468, 500, 504, 539
Johnson, Elgin, 15
Johnson, Eliza B., 3, 316, 318
Johnson, Elizabeth Jane Whitley [Whitney], 3-4, 10, 14, 318, 462
Johnson, Emily Spann, 3, 10, 14, 318, 433, 468
Johnson, Emma, 14
Johnson, Ethel, 483
Johnson, Fern, 525
Johnson, Frank, 14, 397, 432, 442, 532

Johnson, Frank and Jennie, child of, 397
Johnson, Fred, 442
Johnson, George, 11, 14, 36, 68, 442
Johnson, George John, 23
Johnson, Gove, 241
Johnson, H., 403
Johnson, H. A. *See* Hiram Alvah Johnson
Johnson, Hank, 427
Johnson, Henry, 120, 129, 175, 210
Johnson, Hiram Alvah [H. A.], 3-4, 9-10, 14, 23, 271, 316, 318, 355, 368-369, 466
Johnson, Jennie Winslow, 397, 432
Johnson, Jessie, 15
Johnson, John Charles [Charley], 14-15, 342, 348
Johnson, John, 15
Johnson, Johnney, 525
Johnson, Laura, 238, 312, 320
Johnson, Laura A., 310
Johnson, Lottie [Lottia], 277, 284, 286, 289, 293, 301, 302
Johnson, Lucy Haile, 4, 10, 321, 462
Johnson, Manie [Maine, Mania, Many] Brown (Mrs. Earl Johnson), 2, 122, 150, 198, 202, 209, 346, 358, 376, 380, 390,

393, 408, 417, 419-420,
422, 429, 449-451, 456,
457, 461-462, 465-466,
468, 472-473, 481, 483,
487, 500, 504, 506, 515,
530, 539
Johnson, Moriah [Maria,
Mariah] Merrill [Merill]
(Mrs. William Warren
Johnson), 10, 59, 132, 137,
149, 202, 207, 250, 285,
300, 305, 318, 350, 395,
442
Johnson, Mrs. Charles, 257
Johnson, Mrs. Earl. *See*
Manie Brown Johnson
Johnson, Mrs. Frank, 471
Johnson, Mrs. Porter, 518
Johnson, Porter, 515
Johnson, Rachel Pratt Viall,
3-4, 9-10, 194, 201, 315,
318, 371, 441
Johnson, Selah, 223
Johnson, Thurstin, 14
Johnson, Tom, 441
Johnson, Vonne, 525
Johnson, William Warren
[Waren W., Warren, Wm.
W.], 3, 10, 12, 14, 55, 59,
119, 132, 149, 164, 168,
171, 178, 202, 207, 250,
268, 276, 281, 285-286,
305, 316-318, 442, 502
Jones, David, 471
Jones, Mrs. David, 471
Judson, Ad, 330

Junction, Juncktion. *See* De
Kalb Junction, NY

K

Kansas City, 330, 346
Keer, [Kerr], Arba, [Arda],
337-41 [*see* also Kerr]
Keer, Eben, 269
Keer, Mrs. Eben. 269
Kees, Mrs. Urban, 330
Kees, Urban, 330
Kellogg, [lawyer] 287
Kelsey, O., son of, 279
Kelsey [Kelsay], Carie,
[Carah] 188, 191, 196, 203,
325
Kelsey [Kelsy], Clara [Clary],
128, 141, 144
Kelsey [Kelsay], Cora, 155
Kenville, 227
Kerr A., 478, 510
Kerr, Alex, [Alexander], 12,
140, 176, 316, 332, 341,
345, 355-356, 366, 368,
371, 377, 385, 389, 391,
397-398, 401, 405, 411,
426, 438-439, 447, 452,
460, 476, 479, 481, 486,
489, 496, 498, 507, 511,
513, 517, 520, 526
Kerr [Keer], Alexander,
daughter of, 316
Kerr, Amelia, 202
Kerr [Herr, Keer], Ardan
[Arb, Arba, Arda, Arde] O.

359, 330, 332, 337-339,
341, 348, 353, 386, 389,
392, 395, 411, 419, 455,
493, 496, 498, 515, 518,
536
Kerr, Ardan [Arda, Arde] E.,
444, 467, 497
Kerr, Ilene, 455
Kerr, Jennie [Jenie, Jenia],
386, 397, 413, 419, 452,
507
Kerr, Jennie, daughter of, 345
Kerr, Lena, 519, 452, 524,
531
Kerr [Herr], Mrs. A., 465,
475
Kerr, Mrs. Alex, 11, 176,
316, 402, 414, 459, 475,
488, 521
Kerr, Mrs. Ardan O., 498
Kerr, Mrs. Jennie, 345
Kerr, Mrs. John, 395
Kerr, U. O., 444
Kerr, Urbe, 416
Kilbern, [Kilbran] Maggy
[Maggie]Worthington, 378,
432
King, Henry, 85
Kingsbury [Kingsbery], John,
15, 19, 22, 28, 66, 85, 87-
88, 152, 160, 200
Kingsbury [Kingsbery], Mrs.,
31, 64, 74, 76, 78, 82, 85,
86

Kirkbridge [Kirkbride],
Carlos [C.], 188, 199, 283,
311, 323
Kirkbridge, Mariah Noble,
65, 75, 77, 141, 155, 161,
176, 181-182, 186, 188-
189, 199, 323
Knapp, David, 438
Knapp, Mrs. David, 438
Knox, Mrs. Eri, 74

L

Laidlaw, Altha Harmon (Mrs.
John Laidlaw), 21, 92, 119,
164, 307, 346, 379, 392,
416, 424, 447, 465, 488,
515, 525
Laidlaw, C., 501
Laidlaw, Celia, 38, 192, 197
Laidlaw, Charley, 433, 488,
496
Laidlaw, David, 55
Laidlaw, Dean, 488, 507
Laidlaw, Jane, 159
Laidlaw, Jene, 447
Laidlaw, John W., 21, 92, 95,
119, 126, 164, 173, 214,
265, 293, 307, 346, 367,
378-379, 392, 424
Laidlaw, Mrs. Charley, 496
Laidlaw, Mrs. David, 437
Laidlaw, Mrs. John. *See*
Altha Harmon Laidlaw
Laidlaw, Mrs. Thomas, 433

Laidlaw, William, 192
Leach, Ed, 456
Leach, Emma [Emmy], 307, 316
Leadville, CO, 82
Lee, Dr., daughter of, 383
Lewis, Alice Robinson, 323
Lewis, E., 323
Linden, MI, 236
Lisbon, NY, 445
Little [Litle] York, NY, 45, 102, 104, 115, 118, 141, 146, 181, 243, 353, 471-472, 481, 515
Lizie. See Elizabeth Brown
London, ON, 135
Loap [Loop], Dave, 34
Loop, Rant, 359
Loops, Frank, 20-21, 99
Lowery, Bell, 231
Lowery, Mrs., 231
Lyman [Liman], Mr., 382-383, 387, 390-392

M

Mabe. See Mabel Brown
Madison, Quincy, 48
Madrid, NY, 373, 385
Main, Cora, 288
Maine. See Manie Brown Johnson
Maltby, Clark, 168, 401
Maltby, Mrs., 41, 284
Manchester, Harriet [Herriett], 128, 174

Mania. See Manie Cleland Brown
Manila, the Philippines, 524, 537
Maria, Mariah. See Moriah Merrill Johnson
Martin, 139-141, 144-146, 187, 191, 207-213, 215-221
Mason family, 383
May, Flossie, 441
May, Mrs. William, 441
May, William, 440
Maybee, Manard, 224, 370, 374
Maybee, Mrs. John H., 227, 257
McBride, Hannah [Hanny] Brown, 38, 56, 133, 267, 275, 291, 324
McBride, John, 291
McBrier, Jane, 159
McBrier, Wesley [W., Westely, Westley], 113, 158, 159, 197, 200, 403
McCargin [McCargins], Mrs., 21, 27, 31, 33, 37, 43-44, 56, 59, 65-66, 73, 79-80, 87
McCargin, Robert, 193
McCarty, George, 442
McColum, Old Mr., 132, 200
McFarlen, John, 114, 214, 221
McFarlen, Sarah, 124, 221

McFerran [McFeran,
McFerin] Charley, 63, 94,
298, 303, 313-314, 339
McFerran, Daisy, 442
McFerran [McFeran], Jack,
408
McFerran [McFeran], James
[Jimmy], 438, 454, 476
McFerran, James [Jim],
daughter of, 516
McFerran, John (the elder),
193
McFerran [McFerin,
McFerren], John, 12, 21,
32, 64, 170, 193, 270, 394,
409, 416, 419, 429, 442
McFerran [McFeran], Mary
Monerief, 320
McFerran [McFeran], Mrs.
Charley, 303
McFerran [McFeran], Mrs.
John, 65, 74, 78, 410
McFerran [McFeran], Mrs.
Samuel, 198, 317, 516
McFerran, Nora Madison,
438
McFerran, Rob, 381
McFerran [McFeran],
Samuel, 198, 320
McFerran [McFeran,
McFerans, McFerin], Sarah,
9, 24, 69, 71-72, 170, 198
McFerran [McFeran], W. A.,
141
McFerran [McFeran],
William, 250

McGee, John, 112
McGill, Carrie. See Carrie
McGill Pratt
McGill, Charles, 260
McGill, Clint, 338, 348, 354,
408, 418-422, 422, 424,
427, 465, 474, 480-481,
484, 487, 495-496, 498-
500, 507-508, 515, 539
McGill, Harry, 443
McGill, Harvey, widow of,
260
McGill, Hiram [Hi], 330, 345,
351, 383, 413
McGill, John, 97, 242, 438
McGill, Laura, 51, 55, 58,
101, 441, 472-473, 475,
481
McGill, Lesley [Leslie], 340,
354, 384, 408-409, 411,
418-420, 424, 427, 461,
481, 524, 526, 536, 538
McGill, Manda [Mande], 470
McGill, Marsha, 223
McGill, Mary, 151, 443
McGill [McGil], Minnie
[Mine, Minna, Minny],
459, 461, 468, 472, 475,
477, 479, 481, 487, 495,
499-500, 515
McGill, Netta, 223, 324
McKee, Old Mr. James, 130
McGill, widow of, 215
McKee, Addie [Ada, Adah,
Addia, Adie, Idda, Ida]
Fellows [Fellow, Felows],

573

87, 153, 161, 199, 267,
281-284, 286, 288-289,
297, 299, 324

McKee, Amelia, 55

McKee, Forest, 82, 97, 120,
125, 167, 170, 172, 225,
281-282, 286, 288-289,
295, 297, 299, 324, 366

McKee, Harriet, 64

McKee, James [Jim], 49, 73,
82, 101, 122, 199, 257, 337

McKee, Jane, 17, 225

McKee, Janet, 33

McKee, John, 59, 82, 90, 94,
100, 104, 164, 243, 299,
328-329, 372, 387, 441,
477

McKee, Lucy Shea, 441

McKee, Millie [Melia, Milla,
Millia, Milly], 40, 68, 73,
82, 83

McKee, Mrs. James, 35

McKee, Mrs. William [Bill],
76, 281

McKee, Old Mrs. James, 17-
18

McKee, William [Wm.], 307

McKee, young Jim, 336

McKiney, 203

McKinney [McKinny],
Amelia, 523

McKinney, Mary, 74, 136,
267

McKinney [McKiney],
Thomas, 132, 136

Meril, Mariah. *See* Moriah
Merrill Johnson

Mexico, NY, 285

Mil. *See* Milo Woodcock

Miles, 20, 503

Miles, Ira, 400

Miles, J., 212, 335-336, 339-
343, 342

Millar, Samuel, 14

Miller, Mrs. George, 331

Miller, Old Mr., 438

Miller, Rebecca Johnson, 14,
468-469

Millport, NY, 278, 280

Moncrief, William, 453

Moorie [Morris], Julia, 326

Moors, Mrs. Alfred, 193

Moriah Merils. *See* Moriah
Merrill Johnson

Morrison, Alex, 382

Morrisville [Morsville,
Marshville], NY, 118

Morrows, George, 375

Mother, Mother Brown. *See*
Agnes Gowen Brown

Murry, Mury. *See* Dr.
Murray.

N

N,A,B. *See* Nancy A. Johnson
Brown

Neary [Nery], Judge [Juge,
Lawyer] E. H., 10, 24, 29,
68-69, 74, 208, 287, 376

Nebo, IL, 14

New Haven, CT, 466, 479
New York City, NY, 15, 50, 99, 330, 345, 533
Newton Falls, NY, 479
Newton, Amos [Ama] C., 151-152, 267, 357, 500
Newton, Amos S., 106-9, 201-202
Newton, Anna, 100
Newton, John, 75, 181, 216, 361, 364, 421
Newton, Kate Stevens, 302, 325
Newton, Mrs. Amos C., 149, 500
Newton, Mrs. John, 184, 421
Newton, Mrs. Will, 435
Newton, William [Wiley, Will, Willy], 188, 325, 363, 381, 388-389, 389-91, 398, 435, 524
Nicholson, John, 14
Nicholville, NY, 260
Nobels, James. *See* James Noble
Noble family, 400
Noble, Albert, 281, 304
Noble, Alexander, 318
Noble, Alis, 246-48
Noble, Ann, 55, 76, 77, 153, 177, 200
Noble, Benjamin [Bengaman, Bengamon, Bengman, Benny] F., 47, 77, 90, 95, 137, 141-142, 143-144, 150, 154, 160-161, 170, 173-174, 177-178, 181, 182, 185-191, 210, 227, 245, 261, 350, 494, 503
Noble, Charley, 63, 330, 400, 438
Noble, Clealand, 193, 461
Noble, Clementine [Clemantine] Merchant, 327, 439
Noble, Cora, 59
Noble, D., 410
Noble, Dan, 96, 443
Noble, Dan, daughter of, 337
Noble, David [Dave], 17, 23, 36, 41, 79, 203, 294-295, 322, 339, 419
Noble, Ed, 28, 30, 41, 51, 64, 70, 98
Noble [Nobel], Emma [Emmah, Emmy], 44-45, 54, 57, 66, 94, 97, 106, 126, 150, 156-157, 163-165, 188-189, 197, 216, 260
Noble, Emma, father of, 57
Noble, Guy, 323, 433
Noble, Guy, brother of, 433
Noble, Guy, sister of, 433
Noble, Guy, son of, 433
Noble, Hattie Padget [Pagget], 63, 72, 98, 218, 322
Noble, Isabelle Laidlaw, 436
Noble, Jack, 60
Noble, James (the elder), 436

Noble [Nobels], James [Jim], 8-10, 12-13, 20-23, 25, 29, 34, 77, 99, 101, 337, 345

Noble, Jenny, 161, 168

Noble, John, 139, 186, 248, 279

Noble, Josephine, 54, 74

Noble, Juraine [Jurane], 20, 99, 194

Noble, Leverette [Leveret], 24, 467

Noble, Leverette [Leveret], daughter of, 467

Noble, Mag, 21-23, 25, 57, 60, 65, 82, 99

Noble, Merchant, 439

Noble, Mrs. Charles, 99

Noble, Mrs. Ed, 51

Noble, Mrs. Guy, 433

Noble, Mrs. John, 192

Noble, Mrs. Leverette [Leveret], 467

Noble, Mrs. Tom, 63

Noble, Rawley, 438

Noble, [Uncle] Sandy, 36, 65, 191, 279

Noble, Susan, 436

Noble, Tom, 156, 181, 292, 343

Norris, Hattie, 325

Norwood, NY, 438

Noyes [Noys], Ossie, 435

Noyes, William, son of, 527

Noyes [Noise, Noys, Noyses], William [Bill, W. H., Wm.] H., 12, 13, 20, 66, 73, 76-77, 85, 101, 105, 123, 226, 329, 382, 388, 435, 448, 497, 527

O

Ogdensburg [Odgensburg, Odgensburgh], NY, 57, 67-68, 80, 117, 127, 136, 173, 234, 287, 391, 454, 466, 488, 531

Olean, NY, 342

Oliver, 46

O'Neal [O'Neil], Frank, 265

O'Neal [O'Neil], Mrs. Frank, 265

O'Shay, Edith, 516

O'Shey, James, 531

Osmore, Harvey, 180

P

Padget [Pagett], Alma, 160

Padget [Pagget], George, 33, 42, 43-44, 47, 50, 61, 63, 68, 123, 231, 278, 453-454, 461-462, 505, 508

Padget, Hattie, 74

Padget [Pagget], Mrs. George, 218

Padget, Sam, 45, 505

Palmer, Harry, 286

Palmer, Mrs. Harry, 286

Payne, Addie, 497

Payne [Pain, Payn], Allen King [A. K., Alen, King],

66, 131, 175, 182, 206, 224, 255, 271, 295, 305, 397, 431

Payne, Allen (the younger), 259

Payne, Ann Arnold, 442

Payne [Payn], A. R., 152

Payne [Payn], Clara, 267

Payne, Cynthia, 281, 316

Payne, Eliza, 11

Payne family, 442

Payne, [Payn], Mrs. Allen King, 285, 442

Payne, Sarah, 400

Payne [Payn], Warren, 188, 345

Peat, Hugh. *See* Hugh Pratt

Pedler Phillips, 381, 405

Perkins, Almon, 425

Pery, Adelia Johnson,15

Phelps, Elijuh, 3

Phelps, George, 21, 405

Phelps, Levitia Viall, 3

Phelps, Mary, 405

Philadelphia, NY, 401

Philadelphia, PA, 15

Philey. *See* Phila Viall Harmon.

Phinney [Finney, Phiney], Margaret, 23, 72, 100, 104, 148, 230

Phippens, Levi, 438

Phippens, Mrs. Levi, 438

Pierrepoint, 230

Pine Valley, NY, 12, 14-15, 23, 79, 149, 169-170, 200,

203-204, 231, 240, 265, 276-278, 286, 302, 304, 345, 356, 372, 397, 403, 405, 441, 449, 489, 492-493, 501-504, 511, 514, 528

Pitcairn, NY, 4, 40, 104, 131, 148, 152, 173, 177, 182, 192, 199, 230, 252, 260, 269, 277, 283, 293-294, 318, 325, 368, 370, 392-393, 397, 417, 424, 440, 442, 470

Pittsfield, IL, 14, 147, 276, 312, 433, 468

Pleasant Valley, NY, 454

Pond Settlement [Setlement], NY, 41, 45, 60, 86-87, 95, 124, 436

Porter Hill, 231

Portland, OR, 15

Potsdam, NY, 46, 272, 377, 401, 486

Powers, Mr., 204, 356

Pratt family, 302

Pratt, Aaron, 199

Pratt, Abel, 194, 199, 436

Pratt, Alma, 96-97, 118, 159, 183, 198

Pratt, Carah Kelsey (Mrs. Hugh Pratt), 264, 325

Pratt, Carrie [Carie, Cara] McGill, 176, 181-182, 187-190, 278

Pratt, Dikeman, 339

Pratt, Eliza, 436

Pratt, Emery, 303-304
Pratt, Harriet, 53
Pratt, Harrison, 326
Pratt [Peat, Prat], Hugh
[Hew], 29, 34-35, 47-48,
54, 58, 66, 102, 107, 131,
179, 181, 264, 278, 325,
476
Pratt, Ida Brown, 221, 257,
268, 326, 342
Pratt, Jane Raymond, 324
Pratt, John, 339
Pratt, Maud, 174
Pratt, Morris [Moris], 128,
131, 142, 192, 325, 503
Pratt, Rachel Payne [Payn],
200
Pratt, Vanera [Meary, Neary,
Nera] Hall, 46, 142, 168,
192, 325
Pratt, William, 324, 436
Preacher Hitchcock, 55, 159,
176, 229
Preacher Smith, 364
Prescott, AZ, 451
Prescott, ON, 443
President Lincoln, 25
Professor Lee, 19, 47, 95, 162

R

Ransom, Emma Johnson, 14
Ransom, Monroe [Monral],
14
Raymond, C. H., 123
Raymond, Chauncey, 383

Raymond, Frank, 31, 341,
387, 393, 419, 482
Raymond, Jenny [Jenney],
200
Raymond, Leverette [Lev,
Leveret], 78, 132, 219,
235, 278
Raymond, Mina Hutchins,
146
Raymond, Minnie, 363
Raymond, Mrs., 62, 128
Raymond, Mrs. Leveret, 159
Raymond, William [Willie],
37, 146
Rensselear Falls, NY, 193,
403
Rev. Doctor Lee. *See* Dr. Lee
Rev. H Schwartz, 396
Rev. Mr. Chace, 434
Rev. Mr. Gale, 497, 503
Rev. Mr. Hawley, 164, 170-
171, 178, 191
Rev. Mr. Richman, 357
Rev. Mr. Rogers, 448
Rev. Mr. Smith, 309, 313
Reverend Mr. Dewey, 304
Reverend Silas Pratt, 260
Rice, Abner, 175, 330, 366,
380
Rice, Billy, 55, 56
Rice, Dr., 526
Rice, Lilly, 31
Rice [Rise], Silas [S] P., 116,
131, 175, 177, 197, 226,
286, 297, 380, 385
Rice, Wade, 30

Rice, William, 100
Richmyer [Richmier, Richmir, Richmire, Richtmyer, Rickmire], Simeon, 244-245, 248, 349, 351, 361, 402, 404, 406
Richmyer [Richmyre], Mrs. Simeon, 436
Richville, NY, 130, 176, 385, 392, 442, 516
Rilbown, A., 148
Rite. *See* Wright Robinson
Roach, John, 285, 290-291, 355, 379
Roach, John, brother of, 285
Roach, Morris, 342
Roach, Mrs. John, 290, 355
Roach, Mrs. Morris, 342
Robertson, Millie, 320
Robinson [Robertson], Franky, 201
Robinson, Manie Watson, 434
Robinson [Robertson], Mettie [Mettia] Brown, 98, 176, 190, 199, 275, 324, 336
Robinson [Robertson], Mrs. William [Wm.], 176, 527, 529
Robinson [Robertson], William, 293
Robinson, Willie, 434
Robinson [Robertson, Robison], Wright [Rite, Write], 13, 93, 101, 108, 143, 190, 201, 292, 317, 324, 336, 370, 401, 429
Robinson [Robison], Wright [Write], son of 14, 108, 317
Rochester, NY, 182, 199
Rockaway [Rocaway] Beach [Beech], NY, 114, 172
Rossie, NY, 485, 531
Rushton, Carie Stevens, 432
Rushton, Clend, 539
Rushton, Cornelia [Corneel] Phelps, 24, 26, 40, 58, 67, 69, 402, 405-407, 409, 411, 432
Rushton, Evah, 170
Rushton, H., 44, 245, 361, 380, 405
Rushton, Henry, 69, 334, 434, 439, 502
Rushton, James [J.], 11, 20, 24-25, 30-31, 42, 67, 75, 82, 88, 115, 137, 250, 252, 255, 258, 263, 404-406, 411, 434, 465, 516
Rushton, James [Jim], daughter of, 411
Rushton, Kit, 246
Rushton, L., 124
Rushton, Mark, 285
Rushton, Mary, 432
Rushton, Mr., 43, 252, 298, 310, 430
Rushton, Mrs. H., 405
Rushton, Mrs. Henry, 374

579

Rushton, Mrs. James [Jim], 67, 258, 409, 463
Rushton, Mrs. Sam [S.], 264, 294, 436
Rushton, Nettie [Kettie], 123
Rushton, Norris, 67, 69, 432
Rushton, Sam, 402, 482
Russell, F. W., 117
Russell, L. W., 102, 120
Russell, Mr., 17, 118
Russell, NY, 4, 9-10, 33, 48, 58, 67, 70, 108, 140-141, 154, 156, 169, 177, 181-184, 187-188, 192, 225-226, 230, 244, 249, 255, 267, 276, 279, 286, 316, 318-319, 332-333, 354, 364, 366, 368, 373, 413, 420, 426-427, 431, 439, 461, 477-478, 479, 500, 511, 515-518, 531
Rushton, Hugh [Henry], 502
Rushton, James, 432

S

Saginaw [Saginaw City], MI, 278, 343-344, 348
Sairsburg, 214
Salem, OR, 14, 355
Salsbury, Charley, 280
San Francisco, CA, 535
Sandy Creek, NY, 228
Scaval, James, 228
Scene, Lawrence, 109, 110, 112-114, 157

Scotland, NY, 170, 509
Scott, Eliza, 159
Scott, Mrs., 55, 60
Shaw, Josephine Brayton, 432
Shaw, Nathan, 364, 394, 405-406, 410, 432
Shaw, Noah, 129, 175, 436
Shawville [Shawvile], NY, 50, 123, 129, 131, 168-169, 177, 197, 248
Shea [Shay], Gene [Jene], 376, 378
Shea [Shay, Shays], Jim, 352, 390, 434-435
Shea, Jim, brother of, 390
Shefner, 398
Shefner [Shelfulr], Ed, 359, 418
Shefner, Ellie Wooley, 418
Shefnel [Shefner], Mrs. Ed, 357
Sister Elizabeth. See Elizabeth Brown (Mrs. John Brown)
Sister Hall. See Emmorancy Johnson Hall
Slowton [Scowton], Edith, 376
Smith, 303
Smith, Charley, 538
Smith, George, 283
Smith, Mrs. George, 203, 488
Smith, Rod, 21, 22, 99
South Canton, NY, 387

South Edwards, NY, 260, 325, 367, 395, 401, 433, 440, 442-444, 471, 507
South Russell, NY, 479
Spalding, Dora Pratt, 314
Spalding, Louisa [Loisa], 244, 261
Spaldings, 131, 132, 177
Sprague, Emeline Noble (Mrs. Oren Sprague), 19, 138, 144, 182-183, 188, 190-191, 210, 436
Sprague, Oren [Orin, Orrin], 138, 140-142, 144, 182-183, 187-188, 190-192, 210
Stafford, Mrs. Fleming, 442
Stanton, Enos [E., Eanis, Enis], 133, 135-136, 290, 408, 491, 514, 519
Stanton, James, 285
Stanton, Matilda, 40, 49, 133, 282, 286, 334, 408
Stanton, Mrs. E. of Michigan, 488
Stanton, Sam, 133
Star Lake, NY, 513
Stelly. *See* Stella Johnson Ward
Stevens, Carie, 398
Stevens, Dora Johnson, 15, 444
Stevenson, C., 440
Stevenson, Charley, 373, 402

Stevenson, Graham [Grahm], 105, 139, 149, 186, 271, 336
Stevenson, Sarah Stevens, 440
Stevenson, Theodore, 44, 358, 444
Stevenson, Wilber, 44
Storen [Storan], James, 16, 207, 260, 353, 391, 414-417, 423, 446, 511, 516-518, 528
Storen [Storan, Storens], Mrs., 248, 330, 351-352, 413-415, 417, 438, 455, 461, 468, 473, 476, 496, 499, 509, 515, 521, 526, 530-531
Streeter, Edward, 182
Streeter, Warren, 182
Stuart, Russell, 199
Sturt, Old Mr., 116
Sulivan, 98
Sullivan, Charley, 316
Sullivan, Daniel, 484, 487
Sullivan [Sulivan], John, 225, 233, 436
Sydney. *See* Sidney Brown
Sylvia Lake, NY, 394, 478
Syracuse, NY, 350, 393, 438, 445, 460-461, 477, 484, 488, 492-493, 500, 503, 507, 528

T

Talcville [Talcvile], NY, 466, 475, 488, 498, 510, 512
Taylor, Dr., 403, 464, 496
Taylor, Mr. from Canton, 482
Taylor, Mrs. from Canton, 482
Taylor's Store, 451
Taylorville, IL, 101
Thomas, Almeron, 285
Thomas, Meade, 486
Thompson [Thomson], Ida, 383
Thompson, Mrs. Freeman, 196
Thompson, Truman, 358
Thornton, Phila Johnson, 14
Thornton, Richard, 14
Thurston, Nelly, 242
Tillsonburg [Tilsonburg, Tilsonbury], ON, 132-133, 135-136, 179-180, 203, 324, 493, 495, 510, 520
Todd, Nettie Lumbey, 431
Todd, Roscoe [Roseo], 431, 512
Todd, Rawley, 407
Todd [Tod], Thomas [Tommy], 68, 233, 342, 402, 409
Tompson, Henry, 7, 181
Traver, 401
Travers, 377
Travers, Henry, 413
Travers, Mrs., 463
Treglown, Alfred, 323, 343
Treglown, Cary, 343
Treglown, Casie [Cassie, Cassy] McGill, 279, 323, 443
Treglown, Harry, 443-444
Trout Lake, NY, 36-37, 47, 53, 57, 176, 214, 234, 287, 293, 296, 445, 472-473, 516, 521

U

Utica, NY, 523

V

Van Burin, 263
Van Ornum, Berney, 365, 367
Van Ornum, Chester, 431
Van Ornum [Van Norman, Vannorman], Luke, 45-46, 95, 274, 289, 367
Vanornum, Mrs. Chester, 431
Van Ornum [Vanorman, Vanornum], Nelson, 346-349, 356-359, 361- 362, 443
Vent, Vint. *See* Vincent Brown
Viall, Samson, 3-4, 9, 316
Vialson, Rosa, 167

W

W. W. Johnson. *See* William Warren Johnson

Ward, Bruce, 489

Ward, Jasper [Jap, Jas, Jass], 29-31, 36, 108-109, 153-154, 178, 180, 489

Ward, Lena, 50

Ward, Leonard, 318

Ward, Lydia [Lidia], 71-72, 194

Ward, Mrs. Jasper, 200

Ward, Mrs. Steven, 99

Ward, Rodie, 127

Ward, Stella [Stellah] Johnson, 15, 122, 168-169, 201, 265

Ward, Steven, 375

Ward, Vanila [Nile, Nily] 50, 108, 173

Waren, [Warren W., William Warren] *See* William Warren Johnson

Washington, City of, 548

Washington, D.C., 14

Watertown, NY, 43, 351, 381, 415, 455, 513

Watson, Alexander, 39

Watson, Betsy, 44, 434

Watson, Cyrus, 451, 521

Watson, Graham, 44, 56, 432, 434

Watson, Henry, 119, 122, 167

Watson, Mrs. Graham, 53, 56

Watson, Mrs. Thomas, 181

Watson, Ord, 451

Watson, R., 434

Watson, Rob, 454

Watson, Rob, son of, 459

Watson, William, 53, 115-116, 161-162

Wear, Mrs., 211-212, 263

Webb, Addie, 181

Webb, Billy, 46, 265, 440

Webb, Charley, 407, 437

Webb, Cyrus, 460, 489, 514

Webb, Dan, 475

Webb, Dannie, 482

Webb, Eddia, 264

Webb, Eddie [Eddy], 272, 289, 292

Webb, Eliza, 362

Webb, Emmah [Emmy], 246, 298, 397

Webb, Henry, 22, 210, 332, 343, 350, 360, 392, 411, 421, 435, 437, 440

Webb [Well], Horace [Horis], 288, 300, 332, 467, 476, 497, 504, 514, 517, 524

Webb, Horace, daughter of, 467, 495, 504

Webb, James, 229, 232, 249, 343, 359, 362-363, 376, 398, 460-461, 470, 498-99, 506

Webb, James [Jim], daughter of 460

Webb, Jimmy, 361

Webb, John, 470-472, 489, 514

Webb, Kid, son of, 529
Webb, Lidia, 38
Webb, Lizie, 361, 410, 435
Webb, Lucinda Stevenson, 46
Webb, Manda, 482
Webb, Maryann, 376, 482
Webb, Mertle, 463, 522
Webb, Min H., 496
Webb, Mrs. Henry, 435, 437
Webb, Mrs. Horace, 467, 495, 504
Webb, Mrs. Maryann, 359, 482
Webb, Mrs. Rob, 398, 485
Webb, Mrs. William, 257
Webb, Old Mrs., mother of Dan Webb, 475
Webb, Pet, 44, 121
Webb, Phila, 244, 261
Webb, Rhoda Woolever, 390
Webb, Rob, 74, 189-190, 299, 305
Webb, Robert, 44, 94, 108, 122, 142, 145, 230-232, 268, 317
Webb, Sina, 497, 501
Webb, Urban, 382, 424, 432, 476, 518, 524
Webb, William [Wm.], 257
Webb, young Rob, 189
Welch, 90
Welch, Sarah, 316
Well, Horace. *See* Horace Webb
Wells, Rachel Higgins, 439

Wells, Mr. and Mrs., daughter of, 326
Wells [Wels], Mrs., 368, 374
Wells, Simeon, 329
Wells, Will, 353
West Edwards, NY 376
West Fowler, NY, 284, 444, 478, 499, 504, 519
Westgate [Westgat], John, 274
Wheeler, Mr., 186, 273, 325
Whipple [Whiple], Mr., 30, 33, 53, 58, 71, 75, 76, 81, 85, 90-92, 96, 109, 147, 153-155
Whiple, Nettie, 159
White, Adah, 27, 28
White, Albert (the younger), 72
White [Wight, Wite], Albert, 20, 24, 26, 43, 71, 78, 99, 117, 185, 238, 271, 289, 432
White, Cora, 26, 28, 29
White [Wight], Ed, 163, 275, 299
White [Wight], Edwin, 262
White, Flora, 26, 28-29
White, Fred, 28-29
White, Jenny, 27
White, Josephine, 33, 49, 55
White [Wite], Mandy, 239
White [Wight, Wite], Mrs. Albert, 30, 48, 53, 75-76, 254, 262, 269
White, Sylvia [Silvia], 25-32

Whitehead, John, 260
Whitehead, Liza [Lizzie], 26, 38, 56, 71, 260
Whitehead, Old Mrs., 217
Whitford Brown, Adaline, 1, 9-10, 12-14, 19, 24, 26, 35-37, 42, 49-50, 60, 64, 92, 103, 148-149, 198
Whitford, Charley, 16
Whitford, Joseph [J., Jo] B., 10, 12, 19, 23
Whitford, May Havens, 260
Whitford, Pasco, 50, 283
Whitford, Sidney, 9, 12, 14, 18, 32, 49, 72
Whitford, William, 260
Whitford,Willey, 16
Whitley, Jane. See Elizabeth Jane Whitley Johnson
Whitemarsh, Mr. and Mrs., a boy born to, 467
Whitmarsh, Mabel, 512, 524
Whitney, Mrs. Finney, 23
Whitney, William, 454
Wight, Mary Jane, wife of Edwin, 252, 262
Wilcox, Mr. , 466
Wiles, Al, 16
Wiley, Nemiah, 43, 45
Will [H. Brown]. See William H. Brown
Willsboro, NY, 9, 315
Wilson family, 20, 119, 172, 244, 258, 373, 376, 497
Wilson, B., 113
Wilson, Bob, 95

Wilson, Brother, 164
Wilson, James, 193, 260, 440
Wilson, Janet, 193
Wilson, Maggie [Mag], 376, 472
Wilson, Mary, 376
Wilson, Rob, 95, 151, 156, 163, 188, 293, 376, 483
Wilson, Robert, 106, 120, 126
Winslow, Cornelia, 434
Winslow, Harry, 56, 286, 390
Winslow, Harvey, 115
Winslow, Mary, 57
Winslow, Mr., 394, 426
Wite, Albert. See Albert White
Woodcock, Adaline, 255, 384
Woodcock, Asa, 382
Woodcock, Carie Hosmer, 431
Woodcock, Cora Johnson (Mrs. Milo Woodcock), 261, 276, 295-296, 465, 472, 516
Woodcock, J., 164, 191
Woodcock, Jason, 13, 107, 117, 143-144, 218, 232-242, 308
Woodcock, John, 472
Woodcock, Mary Allen, 382
Woodcock, Milo [Mil], 40, 42-44, 98, 119, 261, 276, 280, 295, 301, 316, 318, 385, 427, 472
Woodcock, Milo, son of, 316

Woodcock, Mr. 20, 40, 42, 117, 144, 191, 193
Woodcock, Philip, 19
Woodcock, Will, 327, 363, 377-379, 431
Woolever [Wooliver], Mr., 24-25, 31, 34, 41, 56, 180, 289, 361
Woolever [Wooliver], Mrs., 314, 320, 368
Woolever, Al, 390
Wright, Allen, 141

Y

York, NY, 4-5, 67, 150, 160, 231, 328, 343, 353, 358-359, 367, 390, 395, 399-400, 403, 408, 413-414, 437-438, 462, 487, 506-507, 530
Young, Frank, 474